]

THE DEVELOPMENT OF PERSISTENT
CRIMINALITY

The Development of Persistent Criminality

Edited by
Joanne Savage

OXFORD
UNIVERSITY PRESS

2009

Oxford University Press, Inc., publishes works that further
Oxford University's objective of excellence
in research, scholarship, and education.

Oxford New York
Auckland Cape Town Dar es Salaam Hong Kong Karachi
Kuala Lumpur Madrid Melbourne Mexico City Nairobi
New Delhi Shanghai Taipei Toronto

With offices in
Argentina Austria Brazil Chile Czech Republic France Greece
Guatemala Hungary Italy Japan Poland Portugal Singapore
South Korea Switzerland Thailand Turkey Ukraine Vietnam

Published by Oxford University Press, Inc.
198 Madison Avenue, New York, New York 10016

www.oup.com

Oxford is a registered trademark of Oxford University Press

Library of Congress Cataloging-in-Publication Data
The development of persistent criminality / edited by Joanne Savage.
    p. cm.
Includes bibliographical references and index.
ISBN 978-0-19-531031-3
1. Recidivists. 2. Criminology. 3. Crime. 4. Criminals.
    I. Savage, Joanne.
HV6049.D48 2009
364.3—dc22   2008015614

9 8 7 6 5 4 3 2 1

Printed in the United States of America
on acid-free paper

This book is dedicated to my grandmother, Betty Savage, who has been an inspiration and a friend to me and to countless others.

PREFACE

This book was inspired by the desire to learn more about the development of persistent criminality. As the editor, I must acknowledge that it would not have been possible to compile this book without the authors, who so willingly shared their work. I wish to express my profound appreciation to them. I would also like to thank, separately, Linda Pagani for her advice throughout the process, and my friends, "Bry and Cyn" (Bryan Vila and Cyn Morris), for their *years* of mentoring on writing and publishing. Finally, I must thank my editors, Lori Handelman and Jennifer Rappaport at Oxford University Press, for their interest in the project, their counsel and wisdom, and their patience. They were both a delight to work with and provided friendly encouragement and support throughout the process.

CONTENTS

CONTRIBUTORS

S. AMANDA ALDEN
Department of Psychology
Emory University

WILLIAM D. BALES
School of Criminology and Criminal
*   Justice*
Florida State University

KEVIN M. BEAVER
College of Criminology and Criminal
*   Justice*
Florida State University

THOMAS G. BLOMBERG
School of Criminology and Criminal
*   Justice*
Florida State University

PATRICIA A. BRENNAN
Department of Psychology
Emory University

LEE BRITTON
Juvenile Research Branch, Office
*   of Research*
California Department of Corrections
*   and Rehabilitation*

LISA M. BROIDY
Department of Sociology
University of New Mexico

DEBORAH M. CAPALDI
Oregon Social Learning Center
Eugene, OR

ELIZABETH CAUFFMAN
Department of Psychology and Social
*   Behavior*
University of California, Irvine

BRANKO COEBERGH
Juvenile Research Branch, Office
*   of Research*
California Department of Corrections
*   and Rehabilitation*

TIM CROISDALE
Juvenile Research Branch, Office
*   of Research*
California Department of Corrections
*   and Rehabilitation*

MARY ANN DAVIS
Department of Sociology
Sam Houston State University

STEPHANIE ELLIS
Department of Sociology
Marymount University

DANIEL J. FLANNERY
Institute for the Prevention of Violence
Kent State University

WALTER FORREST
College of Criminal Justice
Northeastern University

ASHA GOLDWEBER
Department of Psychology and
  Social Behavior
University of California, Irvine

ELIZABETH A. GONCY
Department of Psychology
Kent State University

RUDY HAAPANEN
Juvenile Research Branch, Office
  of Research
California Department of Corrections
  and Rehabilitation

CARTER HAY
College of Criminology and Criminal
  Justice
Florida State University

JOHN P. HOFFMANN
Department of Sociology
Brigham Young University

TIMOTHY O. IRELAND
Department of Criminal Justice
Niagara University

KIDEUK KIM
Office of Justice Research and Performance
NYS Division of Criminal Justice Services

PAUL MILLAR
Department of Community
  Health Sciences
Brock University

LINDA S. PAGANI
École de psychoéducation
Université de Montréal, Canada

ALEX R. PIQUERO
Department of Criminology
  and Criminal Justice
University of Maryland

TRAVIS C. PRATT
School of Criminology and Criminal
  Justice
Arizona State University

CRAIG J. RIVERA
Department of Criminal Justice
Niagara University

STACY R. RYAN
Department of Psychology
Emory University

JOANNE SAVAGE
Department of Justice, Law and Society
American University

PATRICK SYLVERS
Department of Psychology
Emory University

STEPHEN G. TIBBETTS
California State University
San Bernardino

KYLE TREIBER
Institute of Criminology
Cambridge University

MANFRED H. M. VAN DULMEN
Department of Psychology
Kent State University

ANDREA VEST
Department of Psychology
Kent State University

COURTNEY A. WAID
School of Criminology and Criminal
*   Justice*
Florida State University

MARGIT WIESNER
Department of Educational
*   Psychology*
University of Houston

PER-OLOF H. WIKSTRÖM
Institute of Criminology
Cambridge University

JOHN PAUL WRIGHT
Division of Criminal Justice
University of Cincinnati

THE DEVELOPMENT OF PERSISTENT
CRIMINALITY

CHAPTER 1

Understanding Persistent Offending: Linking Developmental Psychology with Research on the Criminal Career

JOANNE SAVAGE

That serious and violent criminal behavior does not arise anew or seren-dipitously is among the core assumptions of most delinquency theories and is primary justification for early identification efforts and related preven-tion activities. Whether the belief is that such behavior is the expression of an unfolding predisposition, training, or the culmination of neurological, psychological, and social damage to the child, there is an assumption that such behavior *develops* in some ordered fashion (Tolan & Gorman-Smith, 1998, p. 68).

Persistent and Chronic Offending

We now know that a small percentage of individuals, whom we refer to as "chronic offenders," are responsible for about half of all the crime that is committed (e.g., Petersilia, 1980; Piper, 1985; Piquero, 2000a; Tracy, Wolfgang, & Figlio, 1990). More than two decades ago, this finding inspired a new approach to the field of criminology: examining "criminal careers." In recent years, research in this area has focused on the "life course" perspective, the criminal trajectories of offenders, and tests of Moffitt's (1993) "adolescence-limited" and "life-course-persistent" typology. The emphasis has been on distinguishing various types of offending trajectories, methodological issues for doing this type of analysis, and debating some foundational issues, such as the nature of the age-crime curve and the necessity of longitudinal research.

Meanwhile, in the world of child development, researchers have produced voluminous documentation on the risk factors for conduct disorders and aggression. There are many longitudinal studies, well-informed about the stages of early life and concepts such as "attachment" which psychologists believe are important for healthy development. In some cases our fields combine and "developmental criminologists" examine the risk factors for delinquency and criminal behavior. Studies such as the Cambridge Study in Delinquent Development (e.g., Farrington, 1995), the Pittsburgh Youth Study (e.g., Loeber et al., 2002), the Danish Longitudinal Study (Kyvsgaard, 2002), the Dunedin Longitudinal Study (e.g., Henry, Caspi, Moffitt, & Silva, 1996), the Montreal Longitudinal-Experimental Study (e.g., Haapasalo & Tremblay, 1994), the National Youth Survey (Elliott, 1994), the Oregon Youth Study (e.g., Capaldi & Patterson, 1996), and the Seattle Social Development Project (Hawkins et al., 1992) among others have generated an enormous amount of empirical data that has revealed dozens of developmental correlates of criminal offending such as maternal age and marital status, parenting styles, school achievement, attachment and attainment, harsh discipline and child abuse, and association with delinquent peers.

Yet, while we have come to understand ways of looking at criminal offending over time, and we know of many risk factors for aggression and delinquency, it is not clear which factors lead specifically to the persistent and serious patterns of criminality that cause so much harm to society. In short, we know there are chronic offenders, and generally agree on many of the risk factors for offending, but we have not yet established which of these risk factors apply to persistent and serious offending in particular. The inspiration for the present book was to bring together scholars from both criminology and developmental psychology to forward our understanding of the development of persistent criminality. In the present chapter, I review some of the related literature to set the context and tone for the rest of the chapters.

Risk Factors for Conduct Disorders, Aggression, and Delinquency

It is beyond the scope of this chapter to review the enormous literature on the risk factors for conduct disorder, aggression, and delinquency in its entirety. I limit my discussion to those that I believe are likely candidates for risk factors for *persistent offending*.

Personal Risk Factors

Stability of Antisocial Behavior: The Aggressive "Trait"

As Patterson (1992) has pointed out, stability of aggression is now "part of the conventional wisdom" (p. 52), though the nature of antisocial behavior changes over time. Reviewers in the field of developmental psychology have been concluding for decades that aggression is a stable behavioral characteristic, though Tolan and Gorman-Smith (1998) point out that high coefficients may reflect the high stability of the nonaggressive majority of subjects included in the computations. Patterson's (1992) findings provide evidence that a childhood trait for antisocial behavior "is highly stable over a five-year interval" (p. 79). Longitudinal studies uniformly report significant correlations between current and past aggressive, conduct-disordered, and delinquent behavior in many forms. Authors of virtually all the major, recent, longitudinal studies on criminality report evidence for continuity.

It is not surprising to find that personality traits demonstrate continuity over time. Morizot and Le Blanc (2003) found evidence for stability in personality characteristics associated with antisocial behavior including authority opposition, mistrust, anxiousness, negative emotionality, tough-mindedness and others. Kim-Cohen et al. (2003) found that most adults with mental disorders in their sample had been diagnosed with a mental disorder by age 18 and about half or more by age 15, suggesting substantial continuity in a variety of mental and behavioral problems.

There is less consensus about the continuity of antisociality among girls. For example, Stattin and Magnusson (1984) found early adolescent aggressiveness was associated with adult delinquency for boys but not girls in their Swedish sample. Broidy, Cauffman et al. (2003) also found no association between childhood physical aggression and adolescent offending among girls. Landsheer and van Dijkum (2005) found that middle (but not early) delinquency predicted late adolescent delinquency for girls.

The explanations for stability can be categorized, broadly, into three groups. Some authors emphasize an aggressive character trait that is likely to be due, in part, to genetic and biological factors (e.g., Botha & Mels, 1990; Walters, 2000). (Some authors emphasize a trait, such as low self-control, but de-emphasize biology and focus on early-childhood socialization; e.g., Gottfredson & Hirschi, 1990; Robins & Ratcliff, 1980.) Many authors have proposed or reported that "trait" characteristics are likely to be associated with the development of persistent conduct problems (e.g., Moffitt, 2003; Nagin & Farrington, 1992a). Farrington (1978) found that personality characteristics such as daring and low intelligence were characteristic of delinquents in his sample. Lahey et al. (1999) propose that a single latent construct of antisocial propensity exists; it has multiple causal sequences that begin with temperamental factors such as oppositional temperament, harm avoidance, and callousness. Farrington (1995) also came to believe, after analyzing the Cambridge data, that a larger syndrome of antisocial tendency exists.

A second reason for stability is consistency in the environment that elicits the antisocial behavior (Patterson, Reid, & Dishion, 1992). Ongoing relationships with delinquent peers, residence in a high-crime neighborhood, exposure to criminal family members are likely to lead to criminal activity, regardless of individual propensity. Because these endure over time, so will antisocial behavior.

Finally, some emphasize reciprocal relationships between past behavior, its consequences, and future behavior. For example, Laub and Sampson (2003) maintain that prior antisocial behavior sets the context for future behavior by, for example, severing social bonds, causing job loss, harming intimate relationships or resulting in criminal justice interventions. Antisocial behavior may also interrupt education or work life. Vila (1994) would argue that the interplay is one step deeper. Not only do situations frame criminal activity, but individuals develop "strategic styles" resulting from the differential reinforcement of past behavior. In individuals faced with stifling situational constraints, habits of using force, fraud, or stealth may evolve. Wright et al. (2001) propose an interaction; based on the "life-course interdependence" view, the authors argue that prosocial ties like education and antisocial ties like association with deviant peers are likely to have a greater influence on those high in criminality.

Of course, many authors have come to believe that stability is due to combinations of these causes. Wiesner et al. (2003) detail three processes that are related to persistent patterns of offending: coercive behavior patterns, developmental failures (often due to these behavior patterns), and ongoing exposure to contexts conducive to offending (such as associating with deviant peers or becoming involved with an antisocial partner).

In spite of significant evidence for stability, it is still the case that most individuals who commit delinquent acts in their youth do not become serious persistent offenders. Werner and Smith (1992) found that while a retrospective analysis showed that 70% of males arrested for a criminal offense as an adult had a delinquent record, a prospective analysis revealed that only 28% of male delinquents were convicted of adult crimes. Similar observations have been made by Robins (1978) who noted that while most antisocial children recover, "…severe adult antisocial behaviour does seem virtually to require a history of antisocial behaviour in childhood" (p. 618). So understanding more about the particular biological predispositions, situations, behaviors, and consequences that contribute to the development of the stable pattern would be useful for our goal (For a discussion of psychopathy, related to the issue of antisocial "traits," see Chapter 7).

Cognitive Abilities. There is significant evidence, going back many decades, that low intelligence is partly due to neurobiology and is associated with delinquent and criminal behavior (for an excellent, detailed discussion, see Nigg & Huang-Pollock, 2003; also see Chapter 7, for discussions of neurobiology, executive functions, and various chronic antisocial behaviors). In recent years, researchers have focused their attention on the association between criminality and deficits in verbal abilities (e.g., Henry & Moffitt, 1997; Moffitt, Caspi, Silva, & Stouthamer-Loeber, 1995) and the discrepancy between verbal and performance IQ (e.g., Cornell & Wilson, 1992; Walsh, Petee, & Beyer, 1987). Studies commonly discover very low IQ scores among incarcerated offenders. For example, Hollander and Turner (1985) found that 47% of consecutively admitted incarcerated male juvenile offenders had IQ scores between 70 and 85.

With regard to longitudinal relationships, in the Cambridge Study in Delinquent Development, one of the most important childhood predictors of adult antisociality was having low intelligence (Farrington, 2000). Hechtman et al. (1984) found that IQ predicted the number of offenses committed over a 10-year follow-up. Data from a Danish longitudinal study indicate a correlation between childhood IQ scores and arrests in young adulthood (Wallander, 1988). Sampson and Laub (1993) found a significant negative relationship between juvenile IQ and adult criminal activity in their analysis of the supplemented Unraveling Juvenile Delinquency dataset (e.g., Glueck & Glueck, 1950).

Attention Deficit and Low Self-Control. One view of the "personality" issue came to the forefront in criminological theory with the publication of *A general theory of crime* by Gottfredson and Hirschi (1990). The authors argue that low self-control constitutes a persistent trait that results when there are deficiencies in socialization in early life (for more on Gottfredson and Hirschi's theory and low self-control, see Chapter 17).

There is significant evidence supporting the hypothesis that low self-control or related characteristics such as attention deficit disorder (ADD) are associated with criminal behavior. Studies of "behavioral activation" (hyperactivity) and behavioral disinhibition suggest that they are longitudinally related to later delinquency (Tremblay & LeMarquand, 2001). Satterfield et al. (1982) compared a group of children diagnosed with ADD to a group of matched controls. At follow-up, significantly more subjects from the ADD group had been arrested. Hyperactivity and emotional stability measured at ages 6 to 12 has been related to offenses measured 10 years later (Hechtman, Weiss, Perlman, & Amsel, 1984).

Lahey and Loeber (1997) point out that, while several prospective longitudinal studies report that children with attention-deficit/hyperactivity disorder (ADHD) exhibit antisocial behavior later in life, the analyses do not control for other conduct disorders. Because attention problems are often found in children with conduct disorder, for example, they concluded, at that time, that studies of the independent effect of ADHD had "failed to provide an unambiguous answer to this question" (p. 56). More recent studies have also provided mixed findings. Wallander (1988) did not find a relationship between attention problems in males ages 10 to 13 and cumulative arrest frequency 8 years later, controlling for IQ and father's alcohol problems. Broidy, Nagin et al. (2003) controlled for other disruptive behaviors and found that hyperactivity did not have an independent effect on criminal outcomes. A meta-analysis of empirical tests of the general theory by Pratt and Cullen (2000) suggests that while low self-control is an important predictor of criminal behavior, its effects are weak in longitudinal studies.

Other Biological Factors. There is a vast literature on the effects of various genetic, neurobiological, and psychophysiological factors on aggression, conduct problems and criminal behavior. Most authors agree that such factors are less likely to have important direct effects than they are to influence antisociality indirectly, through their impact on the development of self-control, executive functions, and verbal abilities, for example, which may in turn affect opposition, attention, hyperactivity, and aggression (Tremblay & LeMarquand, 2001). Pre- and perinatal insults may also impair social skill acquisition and bring about peer rejection. For example, they may cause impairment in the ability to read facial expressions or increase behavioral problems such as impulsivity (Brennan, Grekin, & Mednick, 2003).

Many studies aggregate factors into measures of neurophysiological risk or neuropsychological profiles and these measures are often associated with delinquency. Moffitt et al. (1994), for example, found that age 13 neuropsychological scores predicted later delinquency. Because the realm of factors that can influence these developments is quite large, it would be difficult to list them all. It is reasonable to assume that any genetic, prenatal, perinatal, or early childhood experience that can change brain function, or bodily form or function in such a way that it results in problems with intellectual abilities, response to discipline, academic achievement, or peer acceptance could potentially influence the development of delinquent behavior (see Chapter 7, for a more detailed discussion of this issue). Some studies suggest that differences may be substantial. Yeudall et al. (1982) compared delinquents admitted to a residential treatment center in Canada to a nondelinquent control group and found that 84% compared to only 11% of the control group had abnormal neuropsychological profiles, assessed through a battery of tests. It is worth mentioning that factors such as delivery complications (e.g., Brennan, Mednick, & Mednick, 1993), maternal alcohol use and smoking during pregnancy (e.g., Bagley, 1992; Wakschlag et al., 1997), minor physical anomalies, and low-resting heart rate are common in this literature (see also Tremblay & LeMarquand, 2001; also see Chapter 17, for the association between biological factors and low self-control). Genetic and biological factors are likely to have very complex indirect and reciprocal effects on behavior; see Wright and Beaver (Chapter 8) for more detail on gene by environment interactions.

Empathy. Studies of empathy indicate an association with conduct problems and delinquency (e.g., Broidy, Cauffman et al., 2003). Empathy is thought to require both a cognitive process of understanding the feelings of others and an affective response to those emotions (Broidy, Cauffman et al., 2003; for more, see Preston & de Waal, 2002). It is easy to see how neurobiological impairments or major socialization problems could interrupt the normal development of empathic response. Keenan (2001) emphasizes that early precursors to problem behavior, identifiable in the preschool years, may affect later problem behavior through their effects on empathy development. While the concept of empathy has drawn significant attention in the field of sex offending (e.g., Geer, Estupninan, & Manguno-Mire, 2000), little empirical evidence is available regarding the long-term link between empathy deficits in childhood and later persistent offending.

Situational and Contextual Risk

Family Factors

Family factors associated with conduct problems and delinquency include family structure, parenting factors, parent alcohol and drug use, parent attitudes favorable to crime, parent mental health, parent education, family discord, and age of mother (Morash & Rucker, 1989; for reviews see Farrington, 1978; Hawkins et al., 1998; Lutz & Baughman, 1988; Seydlitz & Jenkins, 1998). Here I discuss the factors most relevant for longitudinal prediction of persistent offending. The relationship is treated as unidirectional (e.g., family factor→child delinquency), though many authors have raised the possibility that childhood factors can elicit poor parenting (also see Chapters 2 and 6).

Attachment. The role of attachment in early child development is of particular interest to developmental psychologists. Sroufe et al. (2005) speculate that attachment might be "the most important developmental construct ever investigated" (p. 51). There are reasons to believe that good attachment relations in early life are critically important to normal human development and are a fundamental part of our nature. It has been suggested that dramatically impaired attachment relationships may influence the development of serious psychiatric problems such as psychopathy and related lack of trust and disturbed social relationships (Nelson & Lewak, 1988).

Belsky (2005) believes that attachment relationships also provide information to the developing child about environmental conditions and the type of world he or she is likely to face. He suggests that the security afforded by strong attachment

> represents an evolved psychological mechanism that "informs" the child, based upon the sensitive care he or she has experienced, that others can be trusted; that close, affectional bonds are enduring; and that the world is a more rather than a less caring place (p. 91).

While insecure attachment might convey "to the child the developing understanding that others cannot be trusted; that close, affectional bonds are unlikely to be enduring; and that it makes more sense to participate in opportunistic, self-serving relationships rather than mutually beneficial ones" (p. 91). Many developmental studies examine attachment, but few look at its association with delinquency and offending. An exception is Allen et al. (2002) who found that "insecure-preoccupied" attachment style was associated with increasing delinquency in the late teenage years.

Attachment theorists and researchers recognize that relationships may not be linear, and that attachment problems are not an inevitable cause of behavior problems. A great deal remains to be understood about the association between attachment disruption and persistent antisociality (Sroufe et al., 2005). For example, Hoeve et al. (2007) looked for long-term effects of "established" family risk factors and found that attachment was not related to delinquency in the long term.

Child Abuse. Like attachment problems, child abuse may represent a disruption in fundamental normative processes of brain and behavior development that evolved in the ancestral environment and are part of human nature. Abuse is thought to increase the probability of a wide range of serious disorders (Cicchetti & Valentino, 2006). Brezina (1998) concludes that there is a general consensus among criminologists, and an abundance of evidence that points "decisively" in the direction of a connection between maltreatment and delinquency. This probably extends to "harsh punishment" as well. Farrington (1978) reviewed extant studies and found consistent evidence that harsh punishment by parents was associated with delinquency. Cohen et al. (2002) found an association between prior exposure to abuse and arrest for violence in adulthood. However, Hoeve et al. (2007) did not find that parental punitiveness was associated with delinquency in the long term (see Chapters 2 and 6).

There are several likely reasons for the connection between abuse and delinquency, though their relative contributions have yet to be established empirically. Some authors have emphasized role modeling of violent behavior and learning of aggressive styles, others argue that abuse acts on delinquency by way of neurological damage due to physical injury or emotional trauma (e.g., Teicher, 2002). In recent years, psychologists emphasize a variety of disruptions in the developmental process including dysregulation of emotions, deficits in social awareness, cognitive impairments and academic problems (Wolfe, 1999). Cicchetti and Valentino (2006) conclude that maltreated children are likely to exhibit atypicalities and deficits in many areas, including neurobiological processes, physiological responsiveness, and affect differentiation and regulation. A line of research by Dodge and colleagues suggests that maltreatment causes children to develop biased patterns of social information processing (such as hostile attribution bias and hypervigilance to threat cues) that make it more likely a child will respond aggressively (e.g., Crick & Dodge, 1996; Dodge, 2003; Dodge & Coie, 1987). Brezina (1998) also explores the inhibition of the formation of close social ties and attachments to others (which can protect against delinquency) (also see Cicchetti & Valentino, 2006) and how abusive treatment generates negative emotions such as anger, frustration, and resentment which create the desire to retaliate. Finally, some conclude that child abuse can affect school factors such as achievement and commitment to school which in turn can affect delinquency.

Research on the association between child abuse and delinquency is less consistent than we might expect (Widom, 1989c). But case studies of very serious offenders almost always reveal experience of significant childhood trauma and abuse (see, e.g., Athens, 1997). Boswell (1996) studied Section 53 offenders (adolescents who commit very serious crimes in England) and noted the "unanticipated byproduct" that many of her subjects had been exposed to very serious abuse and that many of them fulfill the criteria for post-traumatic stress disorder (PTSD). Schumacher and Kurz (2000) note that neglect and abuse are common among chronic juvenile offenders. Because the expectation of a strong effect is common among psychologists and researchers, some authors have turned to examining resilience to find out what factors are at play in protecting children from the ill effects of child abuse.

Maternal Age and Education. Parent characteristics are often associated with delinquency (see Chapter 2 for a more complete treatment of parenting and family factors). Numerous authors have reported negative correlations between mother's age and delinquency (e.g., Brennan, Grekin, & Mednick, 1999; Moffitt, 2003; Piquero, Farrington, & Blumstein, 2007). A few, such as Harachi et al. (2006), have found that low parental education is also associated with aggression.

Parent Mental Health. One potentially important area is parent mental health. We might hypothesize that severely mentally ill parents could potentially cause significant behavior problems in children through problems with attachment and caregiving, parenting styles, neglect or disruption of caregiving (if parent is hospitalized, for example). It may be difficult for a mentally ill parent to meet the demands of caring for infants, and socializing children—particularly under the demands of the complex modern world. Mental illness of family members measured at ages 6 to 12 was found to be related to offenses committed as of a 10-year follow-up in one longitudinal study (Hechtman et al., 1984). Rutter (1985) found that parental mental disorder only had an effect on psychiatric risk when combined with other adversities. Werner and Smith (1992) report that female persisters, in their sample, often had mentally retarded or mentally ill parents.

Concentration of Offending in Families. Parent criminality is a very strong risk factor in studies of the development of delinquency (e.g., Farrington & West, 1993). Farrington et al. (2001) review the literature on the concentration of offenders in families and report that although having a father who has been arrested tends to predict more serious offending (arrest, for example, rather than self-reported delinquency), it is not yet clear if father's arrest is associated with persistent criminality. Farrington et al. (2001) also discuss six possible reasons for intrafamilial correlations in antisocial conduct, but it is not yet known which of these explanations are most apt.

Supervision, Large Family Size, and Siblings. Poor supervision and large family size have been associated with delinquency in the Cambridge Study and other datasets (Farrington, 1978; Johnson, Smailes, Cohen, Kasen, & Brook, 2004; Morrison, Robertson, Laurie, & Kelly, 2002; Patterson, 1992;

Piquero et al., 2007). Hoeve et al. (2007) found that parental supervision was not associated with delinquency in the long term, however. Luthar (2006) reviews the evidence and concludes that parental monitoring is protective against the effects of child maltreatment (see Chapter 2, for more on family structure, supervision, and family size).

Delinquency of siblings is associated with behavior problems (e.g., Piquero et al., 2007). Slomkowski et al. (2001) studied sibling relationships over a 4-year period and found that older sibling delinquency was predictive of change in younger sibling delinquency over time. Farrington et al. (1988) report that not having siblings with serious problems was a protective factor against delinquency in their sample.

Socioeconomic Status

Socioeconomic status (SES) is a very common correlate of conduct-disordered, aggressive and delinquent behavior. SES measured at ages 6 to 12 has been associated with offenses committed as of a 10-year follow-up (Hechtman et al., 1984). Lutz and Baughman (1988) review longitudinal studies and conclude that low SES is a risk factor for later offending (also see Farrington, 1978). Farrington (1993) found that childhood economic deprivation was one of the most important predictors of teenage antisocial behavior and convictions. Hoeve et al. (2007), however, did not find an association between family SES and delinquency in the long term. Harachi et al. (2006) looked at predictors of trajectories in elementary and middle school and found that low-income status predicted higher aggression group membership for girls only.

School

Studies suggest that school attachment, attainment and achievement (including drop-out) are all associated with delinquency (e.g., Seydlitz & Jenkins, 1998). It is common among offenders to have very significant school problems; Mullis et al. (2005) found that more than half of their chronic juvenile offender sample were in special education programs at school—mostly for emotional problems, remedial education, or learning disabilities (see also Uggen & Wakefield, 2005).

Some factors appear to exert their effects on delinquency by affecting the individual's school experience (Chung, Little, & Steinberg, 2005; Laub & Sampson, 1993). For example, Brezina (1998) reported that maltreatment adversely affected commitment to school which in turn affected delinquency.

With regard to longitudinal effects of school factors on later delinquent behavior, Tremblay and LeMarquand (2001) conclude that when children are examined from elementary school to high school, academic failure "clearly predates" (p. 150) delinquency. Jessor et al. (1991) found a significant negative association between both school performance and adolescent value on academic achievement and later, an index of multiple problem behaviors in young adulthood. Using data from a panel of California and Oregon middle and junior high schools, Ellickson and McGuigan (2000) found that doing poorly in school in 7th grade was related to violent behavior by the end of high school, controlling for numerous other factors. Horney et al. (1995) found that being enrolled in school reduced the likelihood of offending in their sample of convicted offenders. Blomberg et al. (Chapter 12) discuss the issue of education for the offending population in detail.

Peers

The most consistent predictor of delinquency in cross-sectional studies is association with deviant peers (Warr, 2002). While it is easy to imagine that association with deviant peers might draw a youth, temporarily, into delinquent behavior, it is more difficult to believe that peers would have a strong effect in the etiology of significant, persistent, and serious criminal behavior. Some authors have reported such a longitudinal relationship. Peer relations measured at ages 6 to 12 were found to be related to subsequent offenses committed through a 10-year follow-up (Hechtman et al., 1984). Jessor et al. (1991) found a highly significant positive correlation between friends' approval and modeling of problem behavior and later, an index of multiple problem behaviors in young adulthood.

Some persistence may be explained by association with peers as the adolescent makes the transition into adulthood. It is possible that association with deviant peers during this important transition period will prevent the desistance in offending that is normative in this age group (e.g., Wiesner et al., 2003).

Dodge (2003) concludes that a major predictor of growth in aggressive behavior is early rejection by the peer group. Guerra et al. (2004) found that rejection by peers is associated with later aggression. This particular factor is little researched. It may be a causative factor on its own (due to negative emotionality from having few friends, or failure to engage in same-age socialization), or it may be indicative of other factors that are associated with delinquency (such as intellectual or social impairments or other physical or neuropsychological problems that may cause other peer rejection).

Neighborhoods and Community

Inner city neighborhoods tend to have the highest crime rates and they endure the most serious forms of crime to a much greater degree than their suburban and rural counterparts. While the literature on neighborhood and community effects provides a strong theoretical basis for understanding contemporaneous effects of neighborhood on current crime patterns, there is very little research that bears upon the question of whether growing up in a significantly disadvantaged, high-crime neighborhood merely sustains behavior for those living there, or has long-term effects on individuals who would be affected even if they moved away. While it is obvious that some communities might have more temptations, provocations, and weaker deterrence that would play a contemporaneous role in criminogenesis, Wikström and Sampson (2003) propose that the community also influences the socialization of self-control and moral values, which might affect criminal behavior over the long term. Wikström and Loeber (2000) found a significant direct effect of neighborhood disadvantage on well-adjusted children "influencing them to become involved in serious offending...." (p. 1133). (See also Chapter 17 for a discussion of the role of communities in the development of self-control.)

Cumulative Risk

Rutter (1979) concluded, some time ago, that particular risk factors do not cause serious behavior problems so much as the accumulation of multiple risk factors. Rochester Longitudinal Study data indicate that some specific factors are associated with risk for delinquency but the effects of single factors are small in comparison to the effects of the accumulation of multiple negative influences that characterize high-risk groups (Sameroff, 1998).

One problem with accepting this conclusion is that some risk factors are not tested in their severest forms. For example, while case studies of serious offenders almost uniformly suggest that they experienced very serious abuse of some kind during childhood (e.g., Athens, 1997), studies of child abuse sometimes find no effect on later criminal involvement. This is probably because the operationalization of child abuse may include nontraumatic abuse, the effects of which are easily overcome by most individuals. Such findings cannot refute the possibility that very serious and traumatic abuse causes behavioral problems later in life. Most risk factors considered in these cumulative disadvantage studies are minor—family size, family support, education, and single-parent, for example. Although it makes sense that cumulative risk would lead to a higher probability of offending, it does not make sense that a mere accumulation of weak risk factors would lead to the serious psychosocial disturbances that we see in many serious persistent offenders. Such disturbances are more likely to come from brain damage, trauma, or severe social adversity that impedes normative development than they are to result simply from living with a single, uneducated mother, and several brothers and sisters in a low-income neighborhood.

Authors in recent years echo the conclusions about cumulative risk first made decades ago. Findings by Appleyard et al. (2005) are consistent with the idea that cumulative risk is associated with adverse child behavioral outcomes more than the individual effects of any particular risk factor (they looked at maltreatment, interparental violence, family disruption, maternal life stress, and socioeconomic status). Lacourse et al. (2006) found that kindergarten boys were at highest risk of an early onset of deviant peer group affiliation if they scored high on dimensions of hyperactivity, fearlessness, and low on prosocial behaviors—but the risk was much less if they scored high on only two of these factors. Family adversity alone had no main effect, but significantly increased risk of early onset of deviant peer affiliation if it was combined with the hyperactive, fearless, low prosocial profile. Juon et al. (2006) suggest that a consensus "that risk factors do not appear to function as independent entities separable from the web of influences in which they occur" (p. 195) has been reached.

Rutter (1985) points out that in come cases certain risk factors may *only* have an effect when they occur in combination with other factors. In his study he found that family discord, parental mental disorder and some other factors did not have an effect on psychiatric risk in isolation, but risk increased sharply when several adversities occurred at once.

The Life Course and Criminal Careers

Several chapters in this book characterize and describe chronic offenders (see Chapters 8 and 16, for example). We turn now to the research on crime and the life course.

The Vocabulary of Looking at Crime over the Life Course

Beginning in the 1980s, Blumstein and colleagues challenged us to embrace a new paradigm for understanding criminal behavior. The language of criminal careers (Blumstein, Cohen, & Farrington, 1988a, 1988b; Blumstein, Cohen,

Roth, & Visher, 1986) included discussions of onset, participation, career length, prevalence, and frequency (lambda). Sampson and Laub (1990) added to this lexicon by introducing us to Elder's "trajectories" and "transitions" (Elder, 1985) and a view of the criminal career in the context of a "life course." Le Blanc (1990) adds the concepts of "activation" and "escalation" to our conceptualization of developmental patterns and Loeber (e.g., Loeber, 1988; Loeber & Hay, 1997) has elucidated some of the different pathways of development to delinquency. In response, rather than simply looking at correlates of crime, many researchers are asking whether criminogenic factors are associated with different aspects of the career such as participation, early onset, or persistence (e.g., Farrington & Hawkins, 1991). Piquero et al. (2003) provide a review of all major aspects of the literature on criminal careers.

Moffitt's Typology

Moffitt (1993) developed a now well-known and widely cited theory for distinguishing the life-course-persistent offender from the adolescence-limited-offender. Although most of us probably recognized that there were people who committed crimes in their teenage years who were not serious "criminals," Moffitt was among the first to systematically lay out some ideas regarding how we could tell the difference. Patterson et al. (1991) are also cited for their "early starter model" of persistent offending.

The timing could not have been better for Moffitt's theory. Also in 1993, Nagin and Land published their seminal article on mixed poisson models. This was followed by a series of published works developing techniques for growth curve trajectory modeling which could be used to investigate longitudinal trajectories of behavior (e.g., Land, McCall, & Nagin, 1996; Land & Nagin, 1996; Nagin, 1999). These allow the analyst to assess whether there really are identifiable groups of life-course-persistent or adolescence-limited offenders, as Moffitt proposed, and to look at correlates of persistent trajectories of offending. An explosion of research has emanated from these papers.

Moffitt's theory identified two types of offenders. Adolescence-limited offenders are marked by no notable history of problem behavior in childhood and, by definition, desist from criminality by the end of their teenage years. By contrast, continuity and consistency of antisocial behavior are the hallmarks of life-course-persistent offenders, who are likely to demonstrate marked aggression in childhood and to persist in criminality into adulthood. (Several chapters in this book describe this theory in some detail—Chapters 4, 7, 9, and 13—so I will abbreviate my treatment here.) According to Moffitt, life-course-persistent offending is likely to be caused by a combination of neuropsychological risks and a criminogenic environment. By contrast, adolescence-limited offenders are more likely to be influenced by factors such as social mimicry, deviant peers, and the desire for maturity and autonomy.

Tests of Moffitt's propositions have supported some but not all of her hypotheses. First, there are usually more groups identified than the two that she offers. Often, there are high-level chronic and low-level chronic groups and sometimes groups such as high-level declining and low-level declining. The number of groups typically varies between three and five and sometimes as many as seven (see Chapter 14 for a detailed discussion of this issue).

Moffitt (2006a) reviews 10 years of research on her typology and concludes that there is strong support for the hypothesis that life-course-persistent antisocial development emerges from early neurodevelopmental and family-adversity risk factors and for the hypothesis that life-course-persistent development is differentially associated in adulthood with serious offending and violence. For example, Raine et al. (1996) found that subjects who had both early neuromotor deficits and unstable family environments incurred more than twice as many adult arrests for violence, theft, and total crime. Many other studies have reported findings on this issue (e.g., Moffitt & Caspi, 2001; Raine, Brennan, & Mednick, 1994).

In some studies, however, the differences between adolescence-limited and life-course-persistent groups are not completely consistent with Moffitt's original characterization. Nagin et al. (1995) found that adolescence-limited offenders were significantly better off than chronics at age 32. However, these subjects still tended to drink heavily and use drugs and commit some crime, contradicting the idea that adolescence-limited offenders have little in common with life-course-persistent offenders. Moffitt and colleagues identified an adolescence-limited group and a life-course-persistent group and found that while the life-course-persisters certainly accounted for more than their share of offenses—especially violent ones (10% of the cohort committed 43% of the violent offenses by age 26)—the adolescence-limited group certainly weren't desisters and they committed more than their share of violent offenses, too (26% of the cohort, 43% of the violent offenses) (Moffitt, Caspi, Harrington, & Milne, 2001).

Early Onset and Chronic Offending

Early onset has been established as a strong predictor of chronic offending. When Pritchard (1979) reviewed the literature, going back to the early 1900s, there were already 77 studies that suggested that age of first arrest was associated with recidivism. In Petersilia's (1980) early review on this topic, she already recognized that "[t]hose who engage in serious crime at an early age are the most likely to continue to commit crimes as adults. By contrast, when juvenile criminality is lacking, sporadic, or unserious, an adult criminal career is exceedingly uncommon" (p. 347). Petersilia also concluded that an overwhelming predictor of seriousness of juvenile criminality was age at first police contact. That conclusion has not changed. Fergusson et al. (2000) concluded that early onset conduct problems and early onset attention problems were associated with chronic offending. Early acting out behavior, conduct disorder, age at first conviction and related problem behavior have all been found to be related to later chronic offending in numerous datasets (Blokland, 2005; Cottle, Lee, & Heilbrun, 2001; Ezell, 2007a; Farrington & West, 1993; Ge, Donnellan, & Wenk, 2001; Le Blanc & Loeber, 1998; Mazerolle, Brame, Paternoster, Piquero, & Dean, 2000; Nagin & Farrington, 1992a; Piquero et al., 2007; Tolan & Thomas, 1995). Earlier onset of conduct problems has also been associated with offense versatility and seriousness (Piquero & Chung, 2001; Le Blanc & Loeber, 1998; Mazerolle et al., 2000; Tolan, 1987) (see a more complete review of the literature on early onset in Chapter 9).

Predictors of Early Onset. Some researchers have turned their attention to the prediction of early onset. Factors found to have an association with early onset of offending include parental discord (Fergusson, Horwood, & Lynskey, 1992; Juby & Farrington, 2001), personality (measured in kindergarten) (Tremblay, Pihl, Vitaro, & Dobkin, 1994), symptoms of attention deficit with hyperactivity (Van Lier, Wanner, & Vitaro, 2007), low SES (Janson & Wikstrom, 1995), life stress, early parent support/involvement, quality of caregiving, internalizing behavior, psychological unavailability of mother, neglect, and physical abuse (Aguilar, Sroufe, Egeland, & Carlson, 2000), and parent death (Juby & Farrington, 2001). Most notably, numerous authors have examined the role of biological factors (e.g., Gibson, Piquero & Tibbetts, 2000; Hill, Lowers, Locke-Wellman, & Shen, 2000; Moffitt, Lynam, & Silva, 1994; Tibbetts & Piquero, 1999). Nonetheless, Tremblay and LeMarquand (2001) conclude, on the basis of longitudinal studies from five countries, that the best predictor of early onset delinquency for boys is antecedent antisocial behavior (see Chapter 9 for more on the causes of early onset problem behavior).

It should not be assumed that all factors that may be associated with onset are also associated with persistence. Nagin and Farrington (1992a) discovered that while many factors were associated with both onset and continuation of offending, separation from a parent, for example, was significantly associated with onset but not persistence.

Life Course Transitions

We have previously emphasized the development of highly criminal people. Some authors emphasize, instead, the role of external factors and social situations in sustaining offending. They argue that the illusion of strong stability of behavior is due, in part, to the fact that criminal behavior *affects* relationships, situations, opportunities and other things that influence offending (Laub & Sampson, 1993). This controversy has come to be known as the debate between the population heterogeneity perspective (stability of antisocial behavior is due to a trait that varies across persons in the population) and the state dependence perspective (criminal behavior appears to be consistent because it weakens social bonds, strengthens affiliations with deviant others, and interferes with work life—which increases the likelihood of criminal activity) (Paternoster, Dean, Piquero, Mazerolle, & Brame, 1997). The former implies that individuals develop antisocial character early in life and little can be done to change them in the future; the latter suggests that criminal behavior can be altered by life events (for more, see Ezell & Cohen, 2005; Nagin, 2000).

Sampson and Laub (1990) have been the strongest proponents of the state-dependence perspective, arguing that social bonds in adulthood explain changes in crime and deviance. Sampson and Laub (1992) believe that stability is exaggerated and point out that most antisocial children do not become antisocial adults. They emphasize change and the problem of imperfect continuity. When we overemphasize antisocial traits, they argue, false positive prediction will result (Laub & Sampson, 1993). For them, that continuity stems from "cumulative disadvantage" (Sampson & Laub, 1997). Previous authors have made similar points (e.g., Cline, 1980; Gove, 1985).

Sampson and Laub (1997) frame the crime problem as one of criminal trajectory. Long-term patterns of behavior are marked by transitions and life events:

> [A] major thesis of our work is that social bonds in adolescence (e.g., to family, peers, and school) and adulthood (e.g., attachment to the labor force, cohesive marriage) explain criminal behavior regardless of prior differences in criminal propensity—that age-graded changes in social bonds explain changes in crime. We also contend that early (and distal) precursors to adult crime (e.g., conduct disorder, low self-control) are mediated in developmental pathways by key age-graded institutions of informal and formal social control, especially in the transition to adulthood (e.g., via employment, military service, marriage, official sanctions) (p. 142).

In their view, turning points can modify life trajectories and redirect pathways. Laub and Sampson (1993) emphasize, in particular, key social bonds of marriage and employment which are linked to criminality. They propose that arrest and incarceration may cause failure in school, or unemployment, or weak community bonds that in turn perpetuate criminal activity. Offenders have fewer options for a conventional life; thus offending changes social circumstances, which in turn sustain offending.

Several authors have attempted to adjudicate the dispute about trait heterogeneity versus state dependence (e.g., Ezell & Cohen, 2005; Paternoster et al., 1997). Paternoster et al. (2001) suggest that offending in adult years is a random process after prior criminal tendencies (adolescent offending) are accounted for. This is not consistent with the life course view. A replication by Piquero et al. (2005) also found evidence that individual differences play a major role in persistent criminal activity. Like Paternoster et al. (2001), they found that a mixed poisson model fitted the data, and that offending was a random process after accounting for criminal tendencies. Piquero et al. acknowledge, though, that "change in life circumstances may occur on very different schedules for different people" (p. 238); their analysis would not therefore be able to detect whether such life changes were associated with desistance from offending.

In the end, most authors conclude that both continuity and change matter (e.g., Simons, Johnson, Conger, & Elder, 1998). Paternoster et al. (1997) analyzed the Cambridge data and state: "One unequivocal conclusion from our analyses is that purely static or purely dynamic models of criminal offending do not appear to fit the facts" (p. 262). Blokland's (2005) recent findings from a large Dutch dataset are also consistent with this conclusion.

The specific turning points that Sampson and Laub emphasize in their work are marriage, employment, and military service. Numerous authors have found a negative effect of marriage on measures of offending (e.g., Laub, Nagin, & Sampson, 1998; Rutter & Quinton, 1984; Sampson & Laub, 1993). Farrington and West (1995) found that enduring marriage was associated with reduced offending (though marriage and separation were associated with increased offending, alcohol and drug use). Horney et al. (1995) found that living with a wife (but not a girlfriend) reduced the odds of offending in a sample of convicted offenders. Werner and Smith (1992) report that their persistent group of offenders had broken marriage rates twice as high as those of delinquents who did not go on to have an adult criminal record. Maume et al. (2005) even found that high marital attachment was associated with desistance from marijuana use. Warr (1998) found that when he controlled for delinquent friends, however, the relationship between marriage and desistance was not significant.

With regard to military service as a turning point, Sampson and Laub (1996) report that overseas duty and participation in programs related to the G.I. Bill were associated with socioeconomic benefits for the Glueck sample and that these benefits were greater for those with a delinquent past. Data reported by Werner and Smith (1992) also suggest that military service was associated with resilience in their sample. Bouffard and Laub (2004) found that serving in the military significantly reduced the likelihood of later offense among subjects who had been serious juvenile delinquents.

It has been known for some time that employment status is associated with recidivism (Pritchard, 1979). Mulvey and Aber (1988) report that the high-rate offenders in their sample were less likely to be working—some indicating that crime was their job. Job stability is associated with reduced recidivism (Kruttschnitt, Uggen, & Shelton, 2000). However, Horney et al. (1995) found that their subjects committed more property crime during times when they were employed versus unemployed, and Maume et al. (2005) found that employment was not related to desistance.

The reciprocal relationships proposed by Sampson and Laub are largely supported by a variety of studies. Huebner (2005) reports that incarceration is negatively associated with life events such as marriage and employment that are associated with persistence. Interestingly, Wright et al. (2001) found an interaction effect supporting the proposition that social bonds exert an effect mainly on individuals who are low in self-control. They found no effect of education, employment, family ties, on partnerships on the criminality of high self-control individuals (see Chapter 18 for more on these effects in the transition to adulthood).

Laub et al. (2006) assessed the empirical status of their theory and concluded that the strongest support exists for the influence of social bonds over the life course. They also acknowledge evidence that suggests that routine activities, changes in patterns of behavior associated with marriage, for example, may account for some of the changes in offending with marriage or work. There are many reasons to believe that associations between marriage and persistence or desistance will be less than we might expect from a pure social control theory. Findings reported by Morizot and Le Blanc (2007) on the effects of informal social control were weaker than expected. Rutter and Rutter (1993) point out that the meaning of marriage may vary a great deal across individuals and cultures. In many Western cultures, it implies a long-term commitment to another person and new financial or family responsibilities, or benefits. The character of many marriages is such that these outcomes may not be as salient, however, as a sudden pregnancy that prompted the marriage, or the fear of terminating a relationship, or the urgency and desire for children.

Where We Stand

At present, we understand the role of many correlates of conduct problems, aggression, and delinquency and we have a basic literature and framework for understanding criminal careers. Now, we combine these to examine the likely risk factors for *persistent* criminality.

Risk Factors for Persistent Offending

The focus here will be on factors that are either associated with chronic or persistent offending compared to other groups of offenders or which predict high-level chronic trajectories compared to adolescence-limited or late teen declining trajectories. For our purposes, studies of recidivism (which indicate persistence) and early onset (which has been associated with persistence) are also of interest. Research that demonstrates links between risk factors and any adult offending, conviction, or imprisonment, for example, will largely be ignored unless it demonstrates that offenders were persistent or chronic. A growing number of studies has begun to report these comparisons and we will examine the emerging set of predictors.

It should be noted that in many cases, researchers have difficulty distinguishing between chronic offenders and less-persistent offending groups. Piquero et al. (2007) found that harsh parental discipline, teen mothers, large family size, low family income, poor supervision, a daring disposition, short stature, low nonverbal IQ, psychomotor impulsivity and "troublesomeness" were common for *both* the high adolescence-peaked offending group and the high-rate chronic group. Wiesner and Capaldi (2003) used Oregon Youth Study data and found "relatively few" factors that discriminated persisters from other groups. None of the childhood factors and adolescent covariates assessed in their study significantly distinguished between membership in a decreasing high-level offender class relative to a chronic high-level offender class. Tabular results presented by Fergusson et al. (2000) show that many factors are most prevalent among the chronic offenders but the authors conclude that a common set of factors act cumulatively to determine trajectories—not that there are differential etiologies for chronic offending and ordinary offending. Sampson and Laub (2003) conclude that crime declines sooner or later for all offender groups (but their tables do suggest many differences between high-rate chronics compared to other groups). Their findings also suggest that high-rate chronics have the same risks as other offenders, and that these risks are more prevalent among chronics than other offenders.

Nevertheless, some studies have reported differences between persistent and nonpersistent offenders. Here I propose a list of "best prospects" as a starting point for a list of risk factors for persistent offending. Clearly, a great many research questions remain to be answered.

Personal Factors

Biology, Intelligence, and Personality

Many authors have tested Moffitt's (1993) proposition that life-course-persistent offenders would be likely to have neurobiological impairments and this should be a starting point for any search for causes. There is an overwhelming number of studies which suggest that a wide range of insults and conditions are, or could be, associated with persistent aggressive behavior and offending. These include lesions to the prefrontal cortex (Ishikawa & Raine, 2003), pregnancy and delivery conditions (e.g., Denno, 1990), lead intoxication (e.g., Denno, 1990), maternal smoking (e.g., Brennan et al., 1999; Burke, Loeber, Mutchka, & Lahey, 2002; Räsänen et al., 1999), and perinatal factors (Yoshikawa, 1994). Moffitt (2006b) reports that persistent serious offenders show the greatest deficits on standard neuropsychological tests. Moffitt's (2006b) review cites a variety of neurodevelopmental and neurocognitive factors that are differentially associated with later membership in life-course-persistent offending groups such as undercontrolled temperament measured at age 3, neurological abnormalities and delayed motor development at age 3, low intellectual ability, reading difficulties, poor scores on neuropsychological test of memory, hyperactivity, and slow heart rate (measured in childhood).

Notably, the effect of childhood attention and hyperactivity problems on later chronic or serious offending remains to be established. Satterfield et al. (1982) found that subjects earlier diagnosed with ADD were much more likely to have multiple arrests for serious offenses than matched controls, but they did not control for other conduct disorders (25% of the ADD group compared to 1% of the control group eventually was institutionalized in juvenile hall, probation camp, prison or jail). Farrington et al. (1990) report that hyperactivity and attention deficit problems were predictive of chronic offending (even in the absence of conduct problems). Harachi et al. (2006) found that attention problems in elementary and middle school were associated with membership in high childhood aggression trajectory groups for both boys and girls, but they controlled for depression and shyness, not other conduct problems. Attention problems did not distinguish between

high- and moderate-aggression groups. Perhaps more relevant, for our purposes, Wallander (1988) did not find a relationship between attention problems
in males aged 10 to 13 and cumulative arrest frequency 8 years later, controlling for IQ and father's alcohol problems.

Moffitt (1993) had emphasized that among chronic offenders, neuropsychological deficits in verbal and executive functions would play a crucial role
in the development of persistent offending. This implies that the related literature on cognitive abilities and intelligence is relevant here. There is substantial
evidence of highly significant intelligence deficits among this offender population. Many have shown an association between intellectual function
and chronic offending (Cottle et al., 2001; Denno, 1990; Farrington, 2000;
Farrington & West, 1993; Ge et al., 2001; Piquero & White, 2003; Sampson &
Laub, 2003). Deficits have been found specifically in verbal and executive
functions (Cottle et al., 2001; Denno, 1990; Piquero, 2001). Fergusson et al.
(2000) report that chronic offenders, compared to all other groups (which were
similar to one another) had almost twice the likelihood of appearing in the
lowest quartile on an IQ test taken when they were 8 years old. Werner and
Smith (1992) found that two-thirds of their persistent offenders had Primary
Mental Abilities (PMA) IQ scores less than 90. But Benda et al. (2001) did not
find that IQ was related to entry into the adult correctional system for a sample
of juvenile delinquents and Donnellan et al. (2000) found that cognitive abilities were lower among their persistent offenders, but only for Caucasian and
Hispanic subjects.

Situational and Contextual Factors

Family

Many family risk factors have been associated with persistent criminality
(e.g., family structure, maternal age and education, parental supervision, large
family size, and sibling delinquency). These are likely to have weak effects,
due to their frequency in the general population, and to operate in combination, if at all, in their effect on persistent or serious offending. In some cases,
their effects may be exaggerated due to collinearity with other factors (e.g.,
large family size may be associated with neglect, which is often unmeasured
in these studies). Nevertheless, there is sufficient empirical evidence associating factors with persistent offending to warrant their discussion here. Other
family factors hold more promise in our search for causes of persistent offending. These include, for example, severe attachment problems, child abuse and

neglect, parent alcohol and drug abuse, parent mental illness, and parent criminality.

Severe Attachment Problems. Although attachment and social support are good candidates for predictors of chronic offending, I was unable to identify any published studies that examined their long-term effects on persistent offending. As described earlier, attachment to caregivers is believed to be a fundamental element in the healthy socialization of infants and interruptions in these relationships are thought to cause severe psychosocial disturbances of many kinds. Because, by definition, antisociality requires aggressive, confrontational, or detached interactions with others, unsound attachment relationships are likely to play a key role in the etiology of serious and persistent offending.

Abuse and Neglect. Severe abuse is a likely contender in the etiology of persistent criminality. Not only does it play a role in the learning of deviant behavior, it also causes emotional and sometimes neurological trauma that may affect cognitive, emotional, and social development. Yoshikawa's (1994) seminal review concludes that chronic offending is associated with child abuse victimization. Farrington and West (1993) report that harsh erratic discipline was associated with chronic offending in the Cambridge sample. Moffitt (2003) reports that experiences of harsh and inconsistent discipline were associated with the persistent path of offending in the Dunedin Study. A meta-analysis conducted by Cottle et al. (2001) indicated that a history of physical or sexual abuse is associated with juvenile recidivism. Klevens et al. (2000) found that experience of severe punishment was associated with early onset of offending in their sample of Colombian offenders. Werner and Smith (1992) found that chronic offenders had a greater history of family abuse than juvenile delinquents who did not persist in offending into adulthood. Aguilar et al. (2000) found that childhood neglect and physical abuse were significantly worse for early onset persistent delinquent adolescents compared to other trajectory groups.

Maternal Age and Education: Supervision, Large Family Size, and Siblings. Parent education is negatively associated with persistent and chronic offending (Fergusson et al., 2000; Lutz & Baughman, 1988; Piquero et al., 2007; Wiesner & Windle, 2004) and persistent offenders are more likely to have very young mothers (Conseur, Rivara, Barnoski, & Emanuel, 1997; Denno, 1990; Farrington, 2000). Wiesner and Windle (2004) found that high-level chronics had the highest prevalence of low parent education and low support from family. Nagin and Tremblay (2001b) found that the only characteristics they examined that distinguished between boys in the high but declining physical aggression group from the persistent high aggression group were maternal factors. Those with Moms who were teen mothers and had low educational attainment had nine times the risk of persisting in physical aggression, though they still have low predictive ability because most of the boys with both these risks were not in the high persistent group.

Chronic offenders come from larger families than one-time offenders (Denno, 1990). In the Cambridge study, family size was one of the most important childhood predictors of adult antisociality (Farrington, 2000; Piquero et al., 2007). The study also found having a delinquent sibling to be a significant predictor of chronic offending (Farrington & West, 1993). Mullis et al. (2005) found that 33% of their chronic offenders had siblings involved with the juvenile justice system. Longitudinal effects of supervision on persistent antisocial behavior have not been reported.

Parent Mental Illness. Although there is little specific research on this issue, one would expect that problems related to parent mental illness might be ongoing. Moffitt (2003) reports that having a mother with poor mental health differentially predicted the persistent path of offending in the Dunedin Study. Sampson and Laub's (2003) table shows that high-rate chronic offenders had the highest likelihood of having parents characterized as unstable. However, having a neurotic father was *lowest* for this group in the Cambridge data (Piquero et al., 2007).

Parent Drug and Alcohol Abuse. Parental alcohol and drug use has been tied to chronic offending (Fergusson et al., 2000). Not only do alcoholic or drug-addicted parents influence offending through role modeling, their substance use may affect the neurobiology of their children (if substances are ingested during pregnancy, for example) and their parenting may be poor. Sampson and Laub (2003) found that high-rate chronic offenders had the highest likelihood of having parents characterized as having alcohol problems. Benda et al. (2001) did not find that maternal drug abuse was related to entry into the adult correctional system for a sample of juvenile delinquents, however.

Parent Criminality. One of the most important childhood predictors of adult antisociality was having a convicted parent in the Cambridge Study (Farrington, 2000; Farrington & West, 1993). But their later analysis found that when controls are applied to some models, the effect disappears in some analyses, suggesting that perhaps other factors associated with having a father who has been arrested are more important (e.g., neighborhood, mother's age) (Farrington et al., 2001). Farrington et al. (2001) concluded that it is not yet clear whether having a father who has been arrested predicts persistent offending but because of the many ways that parent criminality can influence youth offending, this factor remains a strong contender in our search for causes of persistent offending. Sampson and Laub (2003) found that subjects in the high-rate chronic offending group were most likely to have criminal parents.

Fergusson et al. (2000) also report that parent criminality distinguishes between chronic compared to other minor offending groups. Parent antisociality also contributes to long-term development of aggression through its association with problematic parenting behaviors such as using guilt to control the child, inconsistent enforcement of rules, loud arguments between parents, cigarette smoking, reduced educational aspirations for child, possessiveness, problems controlling anger toward child, and inadequate supervision of child (Johnson et al., 2004).

Poverty

Poverty can play a direct role in the etiology of offending, by preventing access to the fundamental requirements of life (food, decent shelter, etc.) and thus creating severe stress. It can play an indirect role by increasing the stress of caregivers, reducing the amount or quality of supervision of children (if parents work many hours or cannot afford babysitting), or removing children from school prematurely (so that they can find paid employment). Families in poverty are often plagued by other problems associated with delinquency such as low parental education and residence in disadvantaged neighborhoods. It is likely that severe poverty will be among our risk factors for persistent offending (see Chapter 3, for a full chapter on poverty in the etiology of persistence).

With regard to the empirical evidence, Yoshikawa (1994) concluded that family and community SES were associated with chronic offending. Fergusson et al. (2000) found that family SES and family living standard were associated with chronic offending. Low family income was among the best predictors of chronic offenders in the Cambridge Study (Farrington & West, 1993) and the Dunedin Study (Moffitt, 2003). High-rate chronic offenders were more likely to come from low-income families than high adolescence-peaked offenders or other groups (Piquero et al., 2007). Low SES is associated with recidivism as well (Cottle et al., 2001). Others have also reported lower income, on some measures, for chronic versus one-time offenders (e.g., Denno, 1990).

School

School factors are likely to be protective against the development of persistence in offending. Ayers et al. (1999) looked at correlates of onset, escalation and desistance and found that factors such as academic skills, attachment.

and commitment to school did differ between desisters and comparison groups. They found that deescalating males, compared to stable low-, moderate-, and high-rate offenders had higher quality schoolwork when assessed in 7th grade, performed better on the California Achievement Test, and reported more school rewards. Male desisters in their study had higher grades, and greater attachment and commitment to school. Harachi et al. (2006) looked at predictors of trajectories in elementary and middle school and found that low school commitment and attachment were associated with membership in higher aggression groups for both boys and girls. Wiesner and Windle (2004) found that high-level chronics had the highest prevalence of poor academic achievement. Low junior school attainment was among the best predictors of chronic offenders in the Cambridge Study as well (Farrington & West, 1993). Chung, Hill et al. (2002) found that less school bonding distinguished "escalators" from "desisters" in their analysis. A meta-analysis suggests that having been in a special education program is associated with juvenile recidivism (Cottle et al., 2001); so is having a low achievement test score. Academic achievement and attendance were not found to be relevant.

Association with Deviant Peers and Peer Rejection

We might expect prolonged exposure to deviant peers, or association with them at key points in time to affect persistence in criminality. A meta-analysis suggests that delinquency of peers is associated with juvenile recidivism (Cottle et al., 2001; see also Reiss, 1986). Maume et al. (2005) found that reducing association with deviant friends was associated with desistance from marijuana use in the National Youth Survey sample. Chung et al. (2002) used Seattle Social Development Project data and found that having more antisocial peers distinguished "escalators" from "desisters" in an analysis which looked at five offense trajectories. Ayers et al. (1999) found that deescalating males, compared to stable low-, moderate-, and high-offenders had been perceived by teachers to have more association with antisocial peers when assessed in seventh grade. Desisters in their study had more conventional peer involvement and activities and more bonding to conventional peers.

Little is known about the effect of peer rejection on later involvement in chronic offending. Moffitt (2003) reports that rejection by school peers was a differential predictor of the life-course-persistent path of offending. Piquero et al. (2007) report that unpopularity was highest among their high-rate, chronic offenders.

Neighborhood

Living in the inner city is also associated with criminal behavior and is likely to be associated with recidivism and persistent offending. This is due to exposure to temptations, provocations, weak deterrence and possibly poor socialization, and cultural features associated with criminality, weak social controls, or the extreme stress of modern life in a disadvantaged neighborhood (Bernard, 1990; Sampson & Wilson, 1995; Wikström & Sampson, 2003). Lutz and Baughman (1988) reviewed several longitudinal studies and conclude that those serious delinquents who persist to adult offending are more likely to be from urban areas. Others have found associations between neighborhood and recidivism and escalation in offending (Chiricos, Barrick, Bales, & Bontrager, 2007; Chung et al., 2002). Stouthamer-Loeber et al. (2002) found that while some promotive effects were helpful in low-SES neighborhoods, those in low-SES neighborhoods were more likely to become serious persistent delinquents given the same combination of other risks and promotive effects.

Behavior and Its Consequences

Drug and Alcohol Abuse. Decades ago Pritchard (1979) reviewed the literature and concluded that histories of opiate use or alcohol abuse were associated with recidivism. A review almost a decade later found the findings to be inconclusive, regarding a causative association between substance abuse and criminal careers (Collins, 1986; Wish & Johnson, 1986). The most likely associations are between alcohol abuse and violence and drug addiction and theft (Parker & Auerhahn, 1998).

The evidence appears to be nearing consensus that alcohol and drug abuse are associated with persistent offending (e.g., Benda et al., 2001; Farrington, 1997; Morizot & Le Blanc, 2007; Stouthamer-Loeber et al., 2004; Wiesner & Capaldi, 2003). Wiesner and Windle (2004) report that hard drug use was associated with persistence in their sample. Jessor et al. (1991) found very consistent positive associations between indicators of substance problems (for males) such as "times drunk in the past year," marijuana involvement, psychadelic drug use and later, an index of multiple problem behaviors in young adulthood. Horney et al. (1995) look at monthly offending and find sizable coefficients linking heavy drinking to the commission of crime although these are not statistically significant. Blokland (2005) found that among his sample of adult offenders, those with a drug offense were significantly likely to reoffend (p. 59), and persistence was strongly associated with drug dependence;

the authors conclude "...we feel confident to conclude that the average persistent offender was an addict committing crimes to provide for his drug-habit" (p. 80).

A meta-analysis suggests that substance abuse (as distinct from use) is associated with juvenile recidivism (Cottle et al., 2001). Schumacher and Kurz (2000) also emphasize abuse: "We are not talking about kids who drink an occasional beer or try smoking a marijuana joint at a party..." (p. 8). Desisters in a study by Ayers et al. (1999) had better substance use refusal skills, and fewer opportunities to get marijuana.

Adolescent Delinquency and Criminal Justice Intervention: Cumulative Disadvantage. One of the best predictors of adult persistent offending is frequent adolescent offending (e.g., Denno, 1990; Hodgins, 1994; Lutz & Baughman, 1988; Robins, 1993; Scholte, 1999). There are several reasons we should attend to this "marker." First, adolescent offending may indicate an antisocial trait. Second, humans develop habits and are likely to repeat behaviors in the absence of adverse consequences. Third, adolescent offending brings on criminal justice interventions and while these interventions are designed to reduce the likelihood of subsequent misbehavior, they may serve the opposite function.

Many studies in our field report that criminal justice interventions increase rather than diminish the chances that a young person will reoffend. Such findings are the rule, not the exception. For example, Shannon et al. (1988) reported that "severity of sanctions was related to more contacts and more serious reasons for contacts in subsequent years" (p. 168). Farrington and West (1993) report that offending gets "worse rather than better" after first conviction in their sample (p. 504). Having prior incarcerations was one of the best predictors of entry into the adult correctional system for a sample of serious adolescent offenders (Benda et al., 2001). Chiricos et al. (2007) found that felons who were "adjudicated" versus those who were allowed to plead guilty without a formal label were more likely to recidivate. McAra and McVie (2007) also find that deeper "penetration" into the formal youth justice system makes it less likely a child will desist from offending. Winner et al. (1997) compared juveniles transferred to the adult system to other juvenile offenders (matched for offense seriousness and offense history among other things) and found that there was an increased chance for rearrest among transfers for almost all offense categories (including personal offenses and felonies). In a meta-analysis by Cottle et al. (2001), length of previous incarcerations was positively associated with juvenile recidivism.

Theories of cumulative disadvantage suggest that criminal justice intervention may affect reoffending indirectly, by disrupting normative transitions that most people make as they approach adulthood. Sampson and Laub (1993) report that incarceration as a juvenile reduced the chances of later job stability, increasing the likelihood of crime in adulthood (see also Laub & Sampson, 1995). They emphasize the adverse effects of delinquency on life chances (Sampson & Laub, 1997). Bernbrg and Krohn (2003) report that "official intervention in adolescence increases involvement in crime in early adulthood due to the negative effect of intervention on educational attainment and employment" (p. 1287). Lanctôt et al. (2007) compared a sample of individuals who had been institutionalized for juvenile delinquency as adolescents to a comparison group. They conclude that institutionalization "seriously compromises multiple life domains in adulthood" (p. 131); these include income and work, transition to adulthood, intimate relationships, and emotional well-being.

An emphasis on adolescent offending and cumulative disadvantage begs the question: "where did it start?" If it were merely the case that the fact of having committed numerous offenses during adolescence changed behavior, neurochemistry, and social circumstances making reoffense more likely, we could end our discussion here. But it is unlikely that the earliest antisocial acts are wholly random. Why do some individuals commit serious antisocial acts at 12 years of age while most do not? Why are some 5-year-olds seemingly unaffected by punishment or informal social control in school, while most of their classmates are conforming to social norms? In many cases, individuals have already established a pattern of chronic problem behavior before or during their teenage years. Discovering the causes of this pattern remains an important task.

Race and Gender

African Americans and males are disproportionately represented in arrest statistics and disproportionately represented among those thought to be serious, persistent offenders. Lutz and Baughman (1988) review longitudinal studies and find that being nonwhite is a risk factor for persistent offending into adulthood. Studies routinely find that high-level chronic offending is more common among males (e.g., Piquero, 2001; Wiesner & Windle, 2004). Being male is also a risk factor for recidivism among juvenile offenders (Cottle, et al., 2001). Many authors have suggested that race is likely to be a proxy for social conditions such as concentrated disadvantage (e.g., Sampson & Wilson, 1995). Cottle et al. (2001) conclude that minority status is not associated with recidivism if SES is controlled. Others have even called into question the use of "race" as a concept because of the unlikelihood that there are inherent properties of racial groups that cause crime (e.g., Savage, 2006). We suggest that race continue to be used as a control factor until we have better measures of the factors for which race is likely serving as a proxy. In future research, understanding why males and minorities are overrepresented among serious offenders should be a key goal.

Conclusions

While we are beginning to understand factors that distinguish between chronic and other offenders, we have a great deal of work to do before a consensus can be reached on most of them. This disjuncture is problematic because so much crime is thought to be committed by "chronic offenders" and the advantages of understanding them have been widely acknowledged by criminologists and policymakers alike. While the commission of infrequent, minor offenses is known to be normative in American society, especially among boys, serious and chronic offending is unusual and is more worthy of our considered attention. A variety of cost-benefit analyses place losses per victim as quite high (e.g., Macmillan, 2000; Miller, Cohen, & Wiersema, 1996). Estimated monetary losses due to the average homicide may be $2.2 million, the average robbery $8000 to $19,200 (Cohen, 2001; Cohen, Miller & Rossman, 1994) and the average rape $87,000 (Cohen, 2001). The ability to prevent chronic offending could clearly have a massive impact in economic terms. Welsh and Farrington (2001) reviewed the cost-benefit research and note that five of six cost-benefit studies of developmental crime prevention programs found an overall benefit. Greenwood et al. (2001) estimated that the net savings to government for the average participant in a nurse home visit program was $18,611 ($4828 in criminal justice costs alone) and this did not include any victim costs. Beyond the monetary appeal, the benefits of preventing chronic and serious criminality for human well-being and quality of life would certainly be enormous. Serious crimes can have deep and long-term impacts on victims and their families. In addition to any physical injury, there is work loss, and emotional problems such as fear and anxiety; in some cases, there may be medical costs and relocation costs. There are few topics in the field of criminology as important or of as broad interest as this one.

Part I

The Family, Poverty, and Stressful
Life Events

CHAPTER 2

The Influence of Family Context on the Development and Persistence of Antisocial Behavior

LINDA S. PAGANI

The pertinence of civil behavior and how we learn it is not a recent topic.[1] In the philosophical era of *free will* in Ancient Greece, Plato (b. 428 BCE) declares that how we conduct ourselves is no trifling matter. Later, in *Ethics*, Aristotle (b. 384 BCE) tells us that to live well, one needs to properly appreciate the way friendship, pleasure, virtue, honor, and wealth operate together as a whole in the person-environment interaction. Appreciation, in this context, represents the ability to evaluate which course of action is correct.

More than two millennia later, proper conduct remains no trifling matter. Antisocial behavior, of the persistent kind since childhood (Moffitt, 1993), exacts extensive costs to society (Foster, Jones, & the Conduct Problems Prevention Research Group, 2005; Hamermesh, 1999; Lynch & Rasmussen, 2001). These costs are multiplied toward unimaginable lengths when intergenerational effects are considered.

Much like his philosophical ancestors before him, Aristotle asserted that reasoning, which leads to knowing proper conduct, is acquired from a proper upbringing. As such, motivating the responsible use of free will and,

---

[1] *Reviewed by* White (2002).

consequently, a life course of adjustment, was very much a child-rearing outcome. Further along, Saint Augustine (b. 354) was convinced that the deviant nature of the human spirit required learning self-restraint. Today, we call this self-regulation, which is achieved through effortful control (Ruff & Rothbart, 1996). In his scholarly *Confessions*, he pondered about the relative benefits and consequences of rearing quality in childhood. Children should not be indulged, for if they are, their inherent deviance would not be mastered. As a result, they would not be properly socialized. Much later, Saint Thomas Aquinas (b. 1225) reintroduced thoughts of free will from classical antiquity in his *Summa theologica*, but retained the idea that supervision and discipline were required to learn self-regulation and social responsibility. It is not surprising that, in more recent times, Darwin (b. 1809), the biologist, remarked in his *Voyage of the Beagle*, how an untamed human savage awesomely resembled a wild animal in need of domestication. Hence, time and time again, our scholarly ancestry concludes that proper socialization represents an essential element for optimal human development and survival, both as individuals and as a species.

This chapter examines the influence of family context upon the development and persistence of antisocial behavior. There are two problems in the established social science literature with respect to this link. First, persistent antisocial behavior is not typically addressed using longitudinal data in the literature. Development and persistence imply follow-up designs because they bring correlational studies one step closer to causality. As such, there is a strong preference in this paper toward citing longitudinal designs. The advent of trajectory modeling with longitudinal data promises studies that are more causally suggestive in the future. Second, given that so much of the research in the last 30 years has clumped the criminal deviance and aggression research together, some of this chapter relies upon the general literature on antisocial behavior. Specifically, we synthesize literature addressing both structural and process factors in the home environment that are associated with aggression, theft, vandalism, problematic substance use, and the violation of societal rules. We view these associations using a number of conceptual backdrops, including theories emanating from social learning and behavioral genetics approaches. We conclude with concrete implications for effective family approaches in prevention.

Conceptual Backdrop

The *attachment and social learning* literatures have contributed explanations of the link between parenting and later antisocial behavior in children (see

Shaw & Bell, 1993 for a critical review). The common thread among these two conceptualizations is how care-giving interactions influence the child's representation of the world, and how such representations shape behavior, motivation, and relationships in general. The best of these treat childhood as a life-course process, consider reciprocal relations, and appreciate the transactional nature of family relationships. This is not surprising, given that both these literatures have contributed to the field of developmental psychopathology.

Guiding Principles

Developmental psychopathology concerns itself with continuities and discontinuities in mental health throughout development (Cicchetti, 1993; Sroufe & Rutter, 1984). Its life-span approach, which focuses upon the nature, origins, and sequelae of individual patterns of development, encourages relatively large samples and quantitative methods. These characteristics help explicate the interindividual differences in developmental pathways of antisocial behavior (Richters, 1997; Sullivan, 1998). Because this chapter addresses family influence and its influence upon individual development, it would be necessary to underscore how family systems theory contributes to the field of developmental psychopathology.

Family systems theory, guided by the principle of holism, asserts that pathways linking parent and child dynamics must be fully understood within the collective family experience (Minuchin, 1985) above and beyond dyadic relations (Byng-Hall, 1999; Cox & Paley, 1997; Hayden et al., 1998). This collective experience represents a rich characterization of the relationships between family members, providing specific attention to the structures and boundaries that modulate autonomy and self-expression, power distributions, and patterns of communication (Cox & Paley, 1997; Minuchin, 1985). This theoretical orientation suggests looking at interaction patterns within the entire unit of analysis—the family—to better grasp the psychosocial outcomes of its individual members. Noteworthy is that family systems scholars have been typically concerned with concurrent family processes, often limiting their sample sizes to qualitatively analyze more complex family dynamics (Byng-Hall, 1999; Rothbaum, Rosen, Ujiie, & Uchida, 2002). On one hand, this thorough methodological feature captures the intricacies of family dynamics. On the other hand, the snapshot-in-time and small sample characteristics may sacrifice the actual process aspect that is highly regarded by those concerned with family studies in child development and the generalizability of their findings.

These two frameworks do more than complement each other. Developmental psychopathology benefits from the modeling of contextual inputs espoused by family systems. Family systems theorists need the prospective longitudinal approach to fully realize the impact of transactions among family members. That is, developmental outcomes that we observe represent the continuous and iterative exchanges between individual and environmental characteristics (Cicchetti & Cohen, 1995).

Concepts of Risk

A classic paper on family predictors of conduct disorder, produced by Loeber and Stouthamer-Loeber (1986), represents a productive starting point for this topic. They identified the best predictors as: poor parental supervision, harsh punishment, large family size, low parent-child involvement, interparental conflict, and antisocial parents. Of course, such papers, even as exhaustive as theirs, remain limited by the nature of the research strategies and controls implemented in the material reviewed. Although more recent work offers better controls to build upon their initial conclusions, this early work sets the stage for generating a useful model of families at risk.

A commonsense cumulative risk perspective (Rutter, Champion, Quinton, Maughan, & Pickles, 1995; Sameroff, Bartko, Baldwin, Baldwin, & Seifer, 1998) tells us that as more predictors associated with negative outcomes come into play, estimated developmental risk goes up. In their extensive review of the literature on family adversity, Repetti et al. (2002) offer the concept of risky families in predicting consequences for healthy development. For them, risky family contexts feature low warmth and support, and are neglectful. Recurrent social adversity disrupts basic homeostatic functioning that is central to development. This disequilibrium is linked with disturbances in emotion and social cognition processing. In turn, such regulatory systems influence stress responses and maladaptation across the life span. Exposure to conflict and aggression—which are frequent concomitants of prolonged dysfunctional family relations—encourages deficits in control and expression of emotion and social competence (attributable to faulty cognitive processing of emotion and social situations), disturbances in physiologic and neuroendocrine system regulation (especially sympathetic-adrenomedullary reactivity, hypothalamic-pituitary-adrenocortical reactivity, and serotonergic functioning), and high-risk (health threatening) addictions. Therefore, children growing in risky environments face a compounded "cascade of risk" for mental and physical health disorders across the life span.

In early development, such outcomes manifest themselves most often as behavior problems (Tremblay, Vitaro, Nagin, Pagani, & Séguin, 2003). The more specific literature documents an increased risk of behavioral difficulty in association with parental conflict (Emery, 1999, 2001; Fincham, Grych, & Osborne, 1994; Grych, Fincham, Jouriles, & McDonald, 2001; Wagner, 1997), control (Barber, 1996), and coercion and countercoercion (O'Connor, Deater-Deckard, Fulker, Rutter, & Plomin, 1998; Patterson, 2002; Rothbaum & Weisz, 1994). Other research, using a broader scope of methods and measures, reliably links family dysfunction with aggression, oppositional-defiant, and conduct-disordered behaviors (Steinberg, Lamborn, Darling, Mounts, & Dornbush, 1994) and depression, anxiety, and even suicidal behavior (Chorpita & Barlow, 1998; Kaslow, Deering, & Racusia, 1994).

Rutter (1994, 2002) critically summarizes the methodological issues regarding links between family functioning and children's behavioral development. To better understand directionality of influence (and even in some cases causality), he underscores the need to demonstrate a consistent tendency for the risks of an adverse response to increase with greater doses (in frequency or severity) of the postulated environmental risk factor. He also calls for longitudinal designs that offer the possibility to test the presence of a consistent dose-response relationship under varying conditions.

The family context-antisocial behavior nexus has not traditionally been investigated from a life-course perspective (Loeber & LeBlanc, 1990). Developmental conceptualizations represent a relatively recent innovation. The advent of developmental psychopathology has facilitated this theoretical advancement in this literature. In this chapter, we refer to the developmental continuity of antisocial behavior by subscribing to the life-course analytical framework (Elder, 1995, 1996).

Extrafamilial Predictors of Antisocial Behavior

Neighborhoods that have a high density of risk factors generally show more important prevalence rates of crime and violence, especially among youth (Ludwig, Duncan, & Hirschfield, 2001). This established effect is explained by collective risk and socialization processes, namely parenting and peer characteristics (Brody et al., 2001; Chung & Steinberg, 2006). This relationship not only appeals to common sense but also offers more intervention options at the microsystem levels within such sectors.

Peer group affiliation predicts onset, persistence, and exacerbation of youthful antisocial behavior (Vitaro, Tremblay, Kerr, Pagani, & Bukowski,

1997). This appears straightforward enough. However, does the peer group really have a negative influence on the individual or is the deviant individual attracted to deviant peers? Like other natural variables, it seems that assortative selection, in large part, drives the influence behind this variable. Children that are rated as hyperactive, fearless, and not very prosocial at school entry tend to select themselves on a deviant life course characterized by later deviant peer group affiliations (Lacourse et al., 2006). Family socioeconomic factors seem to moderate this propensity. Sameroff et al. (2004) found a similar moderator effect of parenting.

Family Predictors of Antisocial Behavior

Family factors can be classified discretely or dynamically, as these reflect the flip side of the same coin. For the purposes of this chapter, discrete factors refer to the presence (or not) of a given characteristic, whereas process factors refer to the dynamic, transactional nature of family relationships (Cicchetti & Cohen, 1995). The links between these two kinds of propensity indicators are vigorous, often helping researchers and clinicians compute estimates of risk for a given family or individual.

Discrete Factors

Family Size. Coming from a family with a large number of siblings represents a reliable structural factor in the prediction of antisocial behavior (Farrington & Loeber, 1999). Several explanations have been put forth, including but not being limited to lower levels of individual attention per child, frustration and conflict related to space constraints, greater chances of ineffective parenting given the adult-child ratio, birth order, economic deprivation, family stress, increased chances of having an older sibling as a delinquent role model, and financial hardship as a consequence of an insufficient proportion of family income to needs. Like most discrete variables, it is likely that all of the above contribute, in part, to the robustness of this factor.

Nevertheless, with data from the National Study of Children and Youth, we found that the effects of family size were moderated by sex. Boys from larger families tend to be characterized by more chronic middle childhood dysfunction than girls (Pagani et al., 2006). In that same study, girls from larger families showed better conduct and a more prosocial predisposition than boys, confirming previous research (Eisenberg et al., 1999). Such characteristics might help stabilize the home environment and needs of larger families (Grusec, Davidov, & Lundell, 2002). Parents of larger families are probably very receptive and likely to reward their daughters' inclination to contribute to family functioning (Grusec, 2002).

Family Adversity and Poverty. Financial hardship predicts cognitive outcomes, even after controlling for its developmental timing and duration and family transitions (Duncan & Brooks-Gunn, 1997; Pagani, Boulerice, & Tremblay, 1997; Pagani, Boulerice, Tremblay, & Vitaro, 1999). Antisocial behavior and academic outcomes are strongly linked in light of shared environmental variables (Trzesniewski, Moffitt, Caspi, Taylor, & Maughan, 2006), offering an explanation of why poverty represents an effective distal predictor of antisocial behavior. The broader term *family adversity* refers to these shared environmental variables that are also considered classic propensity indicators for aversive socialization processes and psychosocial risk. These typically include, but should not be limited to, the three sociodemographic measures discussed next.

Maternal Education. Among the most ardent measures of access and control over wealth, having a mother with limited human capital seems to be reliably associated with negative child outcomes. In an extensive review of the literature on the relationship between parental education and children's developmental outcomes, Davis-Keane (2006) concludes that parental education generates cognitive resources that, in turn, are likely to influence the family environment. Higher educational levels are associated with more adaptive cognitive and analytical competencies in parents. Such characteristics, in turn, benefit children's development. Two other papers (Davis-Keane, 2005; Davis-Keane, Sexton, & Magnuson, 2006) support this conclusion, showing how parental education is mediated by parental beliefs and behaviors. Interestingly, several studies have examined the beneficial effect of changes in maternal education upon children's development (Japel, Pagani, McDuff, Mousseau, & Tremblay, in press; Magnuson, 2006). Such evidence contributes to its robust nature in family influence equations.

Early Parenthood. Children of younger mothers are more prone to antisocial behaviors (Jaffee, Caspi, Moffitt, Taylor, & Dickson, 2001; Smith et al., 2000). Premature parenthood remains symptomatic of female delinquency, resulting in disrupted educational and employment opportunities (Shaw, 2003). Antisocial females assortatively mate (Krueger, Moffitt, Caspi, Bleske, & Silva, 1998) with individuals living in similar circumstances (Rowe & Farrington, 1997). As such, one has to ask about the young fathers and their own life-course characteristics to properly decipher the confluence of factors that make this variable so powerful, both as a direct and indirect (i.e., proxy) predictor of parent and child characteristics.

Family Structure. Longitudinal studies on children navigating from intact families to other family forms estimate a nontrivial effect of divorce and remarriage upon children (Pagani, Tremblay, Vitaro, Kerr, & McDuff, 1998). Family transition is a time when both parents and children are challenged by the emotional disequilibrium associated with changes in life style and family relationships, making them at risk for psychosocial maladjustment. Early childhood divorce is associated with both internalizing and externalizing in later childhood, regardless of sex (Pagani et al., 1997). For boys, a middle childhood divorce (between ages 6 and 11), compounded by a remarriage in later childhood (between ages 12 to 15) is associated with more theft and fighting than their same-neighborhood peers from always-intact families. They also engage in such behaviors at comparatively earlier ages than do their peers (Pagani et al., 1998). These estimations are above and beyond the competing effects of financial hardship (Pagani et al., 1999).

It would be too simple to assert that all children in intact families will be free of such developmental challenges. We have known for quite some time that children living in intact families characterized by high conflict do not fare as well as their peers experiencing a low-conflict divorce process (Grych et al., 2001; Grych, Harold, & Miles, 2003). Second, findings from a genetically sensitive design with a national UK sample suggest that living in an intact family is beneficial only if the father has no history of antisocial behavior (Jaffee, Moffitt, Caspi, & Taylor, 2003). Children living in a risky intact family context with antisocial fathers were more likely to have conduct problems. Children's behavior problems were directly related to the amount of time they lived with their antisocial fathers. Hence, given the genetic risk compounded by the environmental risk, living in an intact family with an antisocial parent can create a double jeopardy situation for children,

Antisocial Parents and Siblings. The biological and environmental influence of an antisocial parent is detrimental to behavioral development (Jaffee et al., 2003). Not only is there an undeniable genetic influence of between 40% and 80% (Rhee & Waldman, 2002), parents remain the primary vehicle of socialization. The role of siblings in the development of deviance has received attention more recently. Their influence is thought to operate through two developmentally sequenced social learning processes (Bank, Patterson, & Reid, 1996): (1) imitation of coercive interactions with parents, and (2) collusion and participation in antisocial acts. Aversive social exchanges between siblings, perhaps the result of parent–child conflict, represents a third synergistic factor (Bank, Burraston, & Snyder, 2004), depending on the gender combination and age difference (Snyder, Bank, & Burraston, 2005).

Maternal Depression. Maternal depression predicts youthful antisocial behavior and its persistence as well as it does youthful depression (Goodman &

Gotlib, 1999). Representing an important inherent parental characteristic, maternal depression plays an important role in adding to the directionality of family influences upon children's outcomes through both its undeniable transmission of biological risk and its impact on the family process (via maternal negativity, irritability, and unresponsiveness, Jaffee & Poulton, 2006; Nolen-Hoeksema, Wolfson, Mumme, & Guskin, 1995). Some suggest that parental stress triggers depression, influencing coercive parental practices, which in turn, influence antisocial outcomes in children (Conger, Patterson, & Ge, 1995). In a recent study using a national longitudinal sample, early childhood maternal depression predicted a 13-fold risk of later belonging to the most severe trajectories of family dysfunction during middle childhood (Pagani et al., 2006). It is worth noting that a recent monozygotic twin differences study conducted by Asbury et al. (2003) found that nonshared environmental influences (that are independent of genetic predisposition) upon internalizing, externalizing, and prosocial behavior are stronger in higher risk environments featuring low socioeconomic status (SES), greater family chaos, and greater maternal depression. This is likely because the individual factors that comprise risky settings often act in confluence, as predicted by a cumulative effects model discussed earlier in the text.

Parental Substance Use. The influence of parental smoking and drinking during pregnancy is well documented (Brennan, Hall, Bor, Najman, & Williams, 2003; Kandel, Wu, & Davies, 1994; Räsänen et al., 1999). A child rearing environment influenced by parental substance use also predicts dire consequences for behavioral development (Newcomb & Loeb, 1999). Problematic alcohol and drug use is associated with extremely ineffective parenting skills (Vaillant & Milofsky, 1982; Kandel, 1990, 1996).

Process Factors

Process factors are essential matter in any equation that looks at transactional processes. Dynamic constructs remain more difficult to operationalize and measure than variables that are either structural or static (family size, presence of a specific parental characteristic, poverty status). A review by Rothbaum and Weisz (1994) tells us that the strength of the association varies according to data source, with more direct means (e.g., observations and face-to-face interviews) showing stronger associations than less direct means (e.g., self report). Nevertheless, the associations remain robust across sources.

Family Dysfunction. Using the Canadian *National* Longitudinal Survey of Children and Youth (NLSCY) data set, we charted the nature and course of family dysfunction through middle childhood (Pagani et al., 2006). We observed four distinct life-course patterns of family dysfunction (based upon a global assessment of family dynamics such as problem solving, communication, roles, affective involvement, affective responsiveness, and self-regulation): two extreme patterns (under one-tenth of the sample) showing persistence at high and low levels and two others rated as medium-high (one-fifth) and medium-low (almost two-thirds), respectively. We then examined the link between family dysfunction and children's middle childhood behavioral trajectories. Girls from the highest physical aggression and depression trajectory groups were respectively five and twenty times more likely to belong to the most dysfunctional families than their peers from the lowest behavioral trajectory groups; whereas, for boys, the same relationship was associated with a three- and six-fold risk. The intensity of the risk relationship suggests a greater vulnerability for girls, above and beyond the influence afforded by SES, family size and configuration, and maternal depression.

Much in line with these findings, poor communication and family cohesiveness predict antisocial behavior (Farrington & Welsh, 2007). Throughout development, communication remains an important cultivator of good parent–child relations and this might be harder for families characterized high on risk indicators. It becomes harder for parents with adolescents, given their growing need for autonomy and independence. Many adolescents become increasingly sensitive to judgmental "you" messages conveyed by parents as they attempt to impose their views, values, and instructions. Such messages, even in the best of situations, generate stronger antagonistic response inclinations than "I" statements motivated by intent/distress/concern, which typically accompany goal-directed parental behavior. Kubany et al. (1992) conclude that a majority of "you" statements are cases of verbal aggression, since they are often perceived, upon impact, as accusatory and punitive. When children deviate from what is expected, parents often use a repertoire of negative communication habits: accusing, blaming, lecturing, shaming, commanding, ordering, and others (Robin & Foster, 2002). In their experimental analyses of verbal aggression, Kubany and colleagues observed that "you" messages are likely result in verbal counterattacks and conflict escalation. It might be that a child with a predisposition toward aggression could find parental limit-setting, supervision, and expression of negative feelings atypically frustrating as an adolescent. This leads to what social psychologists (e.g., Vuchinich, 1986) call familiar conflict routines between parent and child. Shown next, these variables play an important role in dissecting family dysfunction and its relationship to antisocial behavior.

Parenting: Supervision, Corporal Punishment, and Parent–Child Relations

Younger children can be directly supervised. The motivation behind such supervision is more about safety and basic socialization issues. When supervision is achieved through indirect observations, as is often the case with older children (especially during adolescence), then it becomes monitoring. Lack of parental monitoring of whereabouts, activities, and associations represents the most steadfast predictor of persistent youthful conduct problems (Farrington & Welsh, 2007; Kerr, 2000). Basically, this variable refers to parental knowledge of children's whereabouts, peer associations, and activities when not within sight and sound. This variable serves as an excellent proxy for parental involvement (Farrington & Hawkins, 1991). In our own studies with French-Canadian boys from impoverished neighborhoods of Montreal, low supervision during later childhood predicted 40% greater chances of self-reported theft, fighting, vandalism, and extreme delinquency during adolescence compared to normative supervision levels (Pagani et al., 1999). McCord (1979) found poor childhood supervision highly predictive of violence and property crimes up to age 45.

When we found theft and fighting associated with family transition in impoverished neighborhoods (Pagani et al., 1998), sons of parents that divorced during middle childhood and remarried during later childhood reported increasingly less effective parental supervision (monitoring) and parent–child relations (expression and acceptance of feelings, rewards for good behavior, explanations when implementing a punishment) throughout the time periods observed. It seems that the life changes associated with remarriage impeded effective supervision.

How parents implement control in limit-setting interactions seems important for the development of antisocial behavior. In an illustration of this idea with a large American sample, developmentally inappropriate and ineffective parental control (autonomy, rule enforcement, and monitoring) and discipline harshness (self-centeredness, rule-enforcement style, and use of physical punishment) predicted a worsening of conduct problems from middle school through to 1 year after graduating from high school (Sameroff, et al., 2004). Although they are associated with immediate compliance, high intensity discipline strategies by parents during middle childhood such as yelling, threatening, and hitting are indeed predictive of teacher- and peer-reported aggression over the short term (6 months later, Dodge, Coie, Pettit, & Price, 1990) and, over the long term, violent and criminal offenses (at age 32, Farrington & Hawkins, 1991) and lower levels of moral internalization and overall mental health (MacMillan et al., 1999; Thompson, 2002). Moreover, harsh punishment at age 8 not only predicts officially documented violence as an adult, but more importantly, it predicts the use of harsh punishment and violence with spouses and children (Eron & Huesmann, 1990).

Parental responses to overwhelming child behavior could reinforce a coercive sequence of inconsistent and inappropriately aggressive rearing responses. The cycle of coercion between parent and child, where punishment and reward are not administered contingently, comprises a four-step process that predicts later aggressive and disruptive behaviors in children (Patterson, 2002): (1) child perceives the parental request/demand/limit setting as an intrusion or an attack on the current activities; (2) child counterattacks with aggressive behavior; (3) parent is yielded into submission, relinquishing authority and initiating a negative reinforcement contingency cycle; and (4) child and parent maintain the contingency cycle. This coercive conceptual framework is compatible with clinical portraits of tyrannical children (e.g., Harbin & Madden, 1979) and their habitual socially aggressive transaction patterns (Snyder & Patterson, 1995). In fact, the relative utility of aggressive counterattacking in response to parental limit-setting is associated with later, more general, childhood and adolescent aggression (Patterson, 1995).

Interestingly, the idea that "violence begets violence" (Dodge, Bates, & Pettit, 1990; Widom, 1989b) gathers support along these lines of research. Survey research has suggested links between use of verbal and corporal punishment and adolescent aggression toward parents (see Agnew, & Huguley, 1989; Straus, 1991; Ulman & Straus, 2003 for reviews). Corporal punishment refers to the use of physical force with the intention of causing pain (but not injury), for purposes of management (control) and/or education (correction) of problem child behavior or attitude. In one study using a populational sample of French-Canadian children, 10% of parents used such strategies to control or correct their almost, if not, "adult-sized" 15/16-year-old adolescent children (Pagani et al., 2006). Although persistent teacher-rated aggression during middle childhood predicted verbal and physical aggression toward mothers during adolescence, harsh punishment of the adolescent further increased the odds of such adolescent aggression, regardless of sex.

Does the influence of parenting prevail when competing explanatory variables are included in the model? In a reanalysis of the Gluecks' classic data set, Laub and Sampson (2003) found that ineffective parental practices (inconsistent and coercive parenting, harsh discipline, and low supervision) and weak relations between parent and child mediated the link between poverty and its cofactors and delinquency. This mediational effect remained even after conditioning out the effects of antisocial predispositions in both parents and children. The influence of parenting also prevails in Sameroff et al. (2004).

Behavioral Genetics Issues in Continuity and Genetically-Mediated Environmental Issues

Behavioral geneticists tell us that, much like depression, the genetic theory behind conduct disorder remains multifactorial and polygenic (Plomin & Asbury, 2002). The conceptual interface between heredity and environment holds that a complex trait culminates from a large number of participant genes, each exerting a minute influence in conjunction with contextual factors. This interaction generates a continuous phenotypic distribution, within which, beyond a certain threshold, we find greater odds for developmental psychopathology.

Some children inherit traits that may be directly involved in the development of persistent and antisocial behavior, while others may receive an indirect transmission of heredity. In the case of indirect influence, inherited predispositions toward a specific associated characteristic (temperament, substance use, sensations-seeking) influence eventual life experiences (that are associated with the development of conduct disorder), which in turn, impact upon later antisocial outcomes. Specifically, genetic factors might influence the emergence of environmental risk conditions that are associated with criminality and violence. The genetic predisposition is not toward criminality but toward some other risk factor. For example, having a genetic predisposition toward a difficult or irritable temperament increases the probability of parental aggression via harsh child-rearing practices (a risk factor). Child irritability might also eventually elicit harsh treatment from peers (another risk factor). This is the case where one might not necessarily have a gene for antisocial behavior, but some other factor which elicits contextual risk factors that could culminate in an antisocial developmental pathway. There is also the indirect case of having the gene for criminality that is not activated unless environment risk is high. For example, Caspi et al. (2002) identified a specific gene that confers greater receptivity to the negative effects of early maltreatment. Although it is likely that this gene is one among many genes that act in confluence, a similar model could operate for antisocial behavior (see Chapter 8, for more on gene x environment interactions).

Genetic influence can also operate through negative family functioning and parenting (Kaslow, Deering, & Racusia, 1994; Suomi, 1997). In other words, family adversity could be an intermediate factor in the expression of genetic risk. Let us imagine that the child born with the difficult temperament discussed earlier has grown up, assortatively mated, reproduced, and has become a parent with a difficult adult temperament. This would result in what Repetti et al. (2002) refer to as a risky family. Children of this parent are born with their inherent predispositions, transact with their parents in such an environment, culminating in factors that predict some sort of developmental psychopathology. This genuine genetic mediation of family life makes discussions about gene-environment transactions, directionality influences, and children's outcomes even more complex.

Although the behavioral genetics literature underscores an important effect of inherent predispositions in the gene-environment interchange, there is also evidence indicating a direct and indirect influence of family dysfunction that goes beyond genes (Rutter, 2002). For illustrative purposes we will cite two genetically informed investigations followed by a nongenetically informed yet prospective study of parenting to make our point. First, O'Connor et al. (1998) observed the influence of negative parenting upon children's externalizing behavior in adoptive families. These results are independent of inherent predispositions that the child brought to the adoptive family. Similar results regarding risky family environments have been noted in a recent twin study (Asbury, Dunn, Pike, & Plomin, 2003). Johnson et al. (2001) found prospective associations between maladaptive parental practices and later risk of child psychopathology during late adolescence and early adulthood, above and beyond the influence of inherent parent and child mental health characteristics.

Indeed, behavioral genetics research has underscored the contribution of nature to the development of deviance, either through the individual or through the environment. Its technology has also allowed us to correct for genetic-environmental mediation and estimate the actual impact of the environmental risk. The conclusion is that a risky family environment does forecast negative outcomes for both internalizing and externalizing.

Developmental Continuity of Inherent Predispositions of Poor Parenting as a Form of Adult Deviance

Inherent predispositions toward childhood deviance have a pervasive influence upon developmental continuity, which later manifests itself as poor parenting. This line of research ties in very well with the aforementioned findings that tell us about the nature of nurture. A millennium paper by Avshalom Caspi (2000) vividly depicts this prediction in its title, "The Child That Becomes the Father of the Man." With the Dunedin, New Zealand data set he found that early dysfunctional behavior predicted behavior along the same lines in adulthood. Other prospective analyses with longitudinal data sets support the developmental continuity hypothesis (Capaldi, Pears, Patterson, & Owen, 2003; Dishion, Owen, & Bullock, 2004; Johnson, Smailes, Cohen, Kasen, & Brook, 2004; Shaw, 2003; Smith & Farrington, 2004; Thornberry, Freeman-Gallant, Lizotte, Krohn, & Smith, 2003). Hence, ineffective parenting begets ineffective parenting by virtue of genetic and environmental predispositions and their transactional influences on developmental continuity of antisocial behavior, likely explaining intergenerational effects of both family adversity and deviance.

Conclusion

Childhood is about learning to self-regulate and honing this skill as we face the challenges of effortful control across each developmental period. Parenting too, is about self-regulation, given that it involves planning before execution to evaluate and reevaluate the correct course of action. Given the preceding discussion about family factors, processes, and the inevitable gene-environment correlations, we can conclude that there are as many at-risk parents as there are at-risk children in the population. Persistent antisocial behavior has its developmental course, which begins with early temperament and undesirable social conduct risks in childhood and adolescence. Individuals then assortatively select mates, reproduce, and become parents. As adults, there are risks for developmental continuity that involve greater chances of marital strife and impatient child rearing. Many overlook this form of persistent antisocial behavior, with the exception of researchers and clinicians who are acquainted with a social ecology perspective of human development (i.e., Bronfenbrenner, 1979).

What are the most critical factors associated with persistent antisocial behavior problems? The answer lies in the developmental psychopathology and family systems literature (Davies & Cicchetti, 2004). The ideal child-rearing equation involves an optimal dosage of warmth and control, developmentally appropriate and effective child supervision, consistent avoidance of coercion, habitual choice of privilege loss as a punishment or consequence, and regular use of social and nonsocial reinforcement. Although many of us treat these factors as though they operate independently and directly, much of what goes on is indirect and relational in a chain of events model (see Rutter, 2002), as risk levels of such factors can trigger the presence or propensity toward other risk factors (e.g., deviant peers, substance use, etc.).

Parental supervision is determined by parental knowledge (Kerr, 2000). This has two caveats. First, such knowledge often requires the children themselves as a data source. Second, many parents of at-risk children did not experience effective care and supervision themselves as children. Intrinsic motivation and insight on how to be an effective parent would have to be very high to overcome such a personal life history. Parents with an at-risk life-course history many not be inclined, by nature, to engage in effective, patient, and developmentally appropriate parenting. This is especially applicable if parents are confronted with a difficult or aggressive child and if they have natural inclinations toward aggression to relieve tension.

Self-regulation skills are essential for proper socialization for parents and children alike. It is clear that parental feelings are ubiquitous influences upon child rearing (Dix, 1991). That is, the emotional nature of parenting represents an important predictor of how parents approach interactions with their children (Zahn-Waxler, Kochanska, Krupnick, & McKnew, 1990). Influenced by both parent and child characteristics, parenting actions can be classified proactive or reactive, just as they are in children's relations with their peers (Crick & Dodge, 1996). Proactive parenting anticipates the child's actions and point of view, modulates warmth and control, and provides structure and organization for positive interactions. Reactive parenting responds as behavior comes along and is associated with excessive prohibitions, verbal aggression, and corporal punishment. Anger and other negative emotions represent key elements in stimulating such at-risk parenting. Thus, intervention approaches that encourage positive self-regulation skills in parents may foster proactive parenting.

The eminent behavioral geneticist, Sandra Scarr (1992), concludes that children who experience "good enough" parenting, defined as average expected environments, are likely to grow up socially adjusted. As a behavioral geneticist, she makes the case that, much like other species, nature has not left child development that susceptible to variations in their environments. Going beyond normative does not promise any greater benefits than "good enough" parenting. After decades of studying socialization processes associated with childrearing, Baumrind (1993), on the other hand, counters by saying that the average normative environment is not good enough and that we, as a species, should strive for better.

Using cluster analysis in a recent study, Davies et al. (2004) derived a normative cluster of families characterized by elevated psychological control by parents, low conflict, and high warmth as an "average" collective family experience. They called these adequate families, which corresponds to Scarr's (1992) "good enough" concept. Davies et al. (2004) also derived a less frequent, but highly functioning cluster characterized by high warmth and affection, and flexible, well-defined rules in family relationships. Remarkably, it was this cluster that was found significantly associated with less psychopathology, suggesting that families which they call cohesive, foster emotional security and positively influence mental health. This kind of study supports Baumrind's (1993) idea that we ought to strive beyond the normative, especially given the prevalence of developmental psychopathology in today's youthful populations. While they need to be replicated with larger samples, studies like this give us an idea of what might be the most common kind of parenting encountered in large populations. They also give us a sense of what could be done better.

Effective parenting, representing an appropriate equilibrium of the classic dimensions of warmth (care-giving, affection, involvement) and control (discipline, supervision, limit-setting), becomes bona fide by clear boundary rules about emotional and behavioral conduct in specific dyadic family relationships (e.g., parent–child, intermarital, interparental, fraternal). With respect to control, if parents misinterpret the recurring concept of *Free Will* in human nature, they might assume that their children will eventually do whatever they want regardless of how they rear them. This is completely untrue, given that a proper dose of these three components in parenting children of any age will teach them the responsibilities associated with their actions and decisions (Baumrind, 1993). With respect to warmth, parents who undervalue their own importance during childhood and adolescence tend to supervise less at a time when children need that expression of parental concern. As children get older, effective parents normally change their rearing and supervision patterns, giving children more freedom to make decisions about their actions, good or bad. Nevertheless, parents need to transmit the ideas that they remain involved and available for advice, and that freedom has its responsibilities when loosening the reins of supervision (Kerr, 2000).

Warmth, control, and relationship rules remain the most critical features of effective nurturing. Without these, the risks of antisocial behavior and its developmental continuity become important. Thus, we need to teach at-risk parents how to proactively apply strategies of warmth, control, and rules to support healthy child development.

CHAPTER 3

The Implications of Family Poverty for a Pattern of Persistent Offending

CARTER HAY AND WALTER FORREST

Up through the 1960s, poverty was widely seen as having a strong effect on criminal involvement, largely on the basis of research that measured crime in terms of official data. Such data may, of course, reflect legal system biases that make poor individuals more vulnerable to being caught and punished for their criminal acts (Tittle, Villemez, & Smith, 1978). Early self-report research—which should be free of such biases—seemed to support this possibility, with several studies indicating only a weak or nonexistent effect of poverty on crime (Hirschi, 1969; Nye, 1958; Tittle et al., 1978; Williams & Gold, 1972).

And yet, these self-report studies also would attract criticism, with many scholars pointing to sampling and measurement problems that prevented this research from adequately assessing serious crime among the truly poor (Braithwaite, 1981; Elliott & Ageton, 1980; Hagan, 1992; Hindelang, Hirschi, & Weis, 1979). The dialogue on this issue ultimately would represent one of the more significant criminological debates of recent decades, as highly respected scholars engaged in sometimes-heated exchanges over their conflicting views (see Braithwaite, 1981; Elliott & Ageton, 1980; Hagan, 1992; Hindelang et al., 1979; Kleck, 1982; Tittle et al., 1978).

In more recent years, the disagreements in this area have diminished, in part because of recognition that recent self-report studies of the poverty-crime relationship address many of the limitations of earlier research, and these studies find consistent support for an effect of poverty on delinquency (Bjerk, 2007; Brown, 1984; Brownfield, 1986; Elliott & Ageton 1980; Farnworth, Thornberry, Krohn, & Lizotte, 1994; Hay, Fortson, Hollist, Altheimer, & Schaible, 2007; Hindelang et al., 1979; Jarjoura, Triplett, & Brinker, 2002; Wright, Caspi, Moffitt, Miech, & Silva, 1999). Thus, any suggestion that the link between poverty and individual-level crime is purely mythical appears to be incorrect. A point to emphasize, however, is that even these more recent studies are limited in a key respect—with few exceptions, they largely ignore the link between poverty and *persistent* involvement in crime. Most studies do not consider this issue, because they are purely cross-sectional in nature—they analyze the link between poverty and crime at a single point in the life course (often adolescence). There is good reason to expect, however, that poverty is especially important for the etiology of long-term patterns of offending in which individuals show an early onset of criminal behavior and then persist with crime well into adulthood. This may be especially the case when poverty is experienced at extreme levels over a long duration.

Supporting this possibility are the broad socioeconomic differences between the general U.S. population and the population of offenders in the criminal justice system. The latter group are likely to be frequent, serious, and persistent offenders (Dunford & Elliott, 1984), and they are also marked by significant socioeconomic disadvantage. For example, those in the correctional system are disproportionately likely to come from poor families of origin—roughly half of state prison inmates have lived in public housing or had parents who received welfare (Harlow, 2003). In addition, while less than 20% of the general population of U.S. adults have not graduated from high school, this is true for more than 60% of jail and prison inmates (Harlow, 2003). Also, in terms of employment, Harlow (1998) found that nearly 40% of jail inmates were unemployed at the time of their arrest; this compares to an unemployment rate of 5% for the general population (Bureau of Labor Statistics, 2007).

These patterns point to a possible link between poverty and persistent offending, but the evidence is far from conclusive, given that entry into the criminal justice system may be a poor proxy for persistent offending—perhaps poor individuals are not more likely to become persistent offenders, but are just more likely to be caught and severely sanctioned. The uncertainty over this issue can only be resolved with analyses that are explicitly focused on assessing the link between poverty and direct involvement in persistent offending. Notably, such research is rare. The purpose of this study is to address this limitation of prior research, and therefore offer insight into the implications of poverty for a pattern of long-term offending.

In approaching this issue, we focus on the link between poverty and the early onset of criminal offending, which we define as repeated involvement in crime during a 5-year stretch that includes ages 10 to 14. By itself, this amounts to involvement in persistent offending. In addition, however, because the age of criminal onset is a strong predictor of a pattern of life-course-persistent (LCP) offending (Fergusson, Horwood, & Nagin, 2000; Moffitt, 1993; Tibbetts & Piquero, 1999), persistent offending from ages 10 to 14 may also foreshadow a pattern of persistent crime that will extend into adulthood. Our central question in this study is this: are individuals who fit this pattern significantly different from others with respect to their exposure to poverty?

This research question will be examined with long-term, longitudinal data collected from a sample of U.S. children and their families. Before describing our own analysis, we first review prior research on the effects of poverty on crime, highlighting how this work has evolved over time. Next, we consider the disjuncture between, on the one hand, prominent theories that argue that the poverty-crime relationship should be approached with a longitudinal focus on persistent crime and, on the other hand, the empirical research that has been largely cross-sectional in nature. We discuss the limited empirical exceptions to this pattern, noting that these few studies suggest the potential knowledge that can be gained by examining the poverty-crime relationship in a longitudinal manner.

Prior Research on the Poverty-Crime Relationship

Classic criminological theories like social disorganization theory (Shaw & McKay, 1942), strain theory (Cloward & Ohlin, 1960; Cohen, 1955), and theories of lower class culture conflict (Miller, 1958; Sellin, 1938; Wolfgang & Ferracuti, 1967) predict a positive relationship between poverty and delinquency. Indeed, these theories appear to have been developed in large part to explain the overrepresentation of the American poor in official crime statistics. They therefore were dealt a significant blow in the 1960s and 1970s when studies using the newly-developed self-report methodology concluded that family poverty and individual-level delinquency were only weakly correlated (Hirschi, 1969; Nye, 1958; Williams & Gold, 1972). Indeed, in their meta-analysis that summarized the results of 35 studies, Tittle et al. (1978) concluded that a poverty-delinquency relationship was more a matter of myth than reality.

That conclusion would be significantly challenged, however, by those arguing that the early self-report studies were themselves flawed in key respects. First, they often examined behaviors that were trivial crimes or not crimes at all (Braithwaite, 1981; Elliott & Ageton, 1980). Second, they often used samples of rural or suburban school students who were at low risk for delinquency (Braithwaite, 1981; Elliott & Ageton, 1980; Hindelang et al., 1979). Thus, both the most serious offenders and those from the extremely poor underclass—two groups perhaps most relevant to the poverty-crime association—were likely excluded from these studies. Third, these studies were often modeled to detect direct effects of poverty on crime, when in fact, the effects of poverty almost certainly operate through various intervening mechanisms, including peer associations and commitments to conventional goals (Hagan, 1992).

Many studies address some or all of these problems, and they often reveal significant effects of poverty. Most notably, effects of poverty on delinquency are especially evident in studies that measure crime in terms of involvement in serious rather than trivial offending (Elliott & Ageton, 1980; Farnworth et al., 1994; Hay et al., 2007), that use samples with a high representation of those at risk for crime (Farnworth et al., 1994; Jarjoura et al., 2002), and that examine the indirect effects of poverty through various intervening mechanisms (Jarjoura et al., 2002; Larzelere & Patterson, 1990; Wright et al., 1999). In addition, both Bjerk (2007) and Hay and his colleagues (2007) found that the effects of poverty were most pronounced when the magnitude of a child's exposure to poverty was more precisely considered. For example, Bjerk (2007) found significant effects when using a measure that identified respondents living in families not just with low income in the most recent year, but with more enduring patterns of poverty, while Hay and his colleagues (2007) found that children from poor families were involved in significantly more delinquency if they lived in a community that was marked by significant levels of poverty as well.

The Link between Poverty and Persistent Offending

Much of the recent research that supports a causal link between poverty and crime is itself limited in one key respect: those studies overwhelmingly relied on cross-sectional analyses of the relationship between family poverty at a single point in time and adolescent involvement in crime reported at that same single point in time. With this cross-sectional focus, it is impossible to discern whether poverty has implications for *persistent* patterns of offending. Relatedly, with this cross-sectional focus, it is impossible to know whether any effects of poverty on crime depend upon whether exposure to poverty is itself temporary or persistent. The inability to consider these issues amounts to much more than just a minor methodological drawback. From a policy standpoint, ignoring the etiology of persistent offending is problematic in light of the clear importance of persistent offenders—a relatively small group of frequent, chronic offenders (perhaps 5% of the population) may be responsible for as much as 50% of the serious crimes that are committed each year (Wolfgang, Figlio, & Sellin, 1972). In addition, once apprehended, these offenders will spend significant amounts of time in jail or prison, therefore placing a significant financial burden on federal, state, and local governments. Thus, understanding the etiology of this pattern of offending therefore is of central policy importance.

In addition, examining the effects of poverty on persistent offending makes good theoretical sense. Indeed, *not* doing so leads research to stray from the arguments made by the key theories that emphasize the criminogenic effects of poverty. Those theories are largely unconcerned with temporary spells of poverty and crime, but instead, are primarily focused on persistent patterns of poverty and crime. Although considering the arguments of all of these theories is not possible, the emphasis on a long-term approach to this issue can be illustrated by considering three examples: Cohen's (1955) strain theory (a classic poverty-oriented theory of crime), Wilson's (1987) theory of urban poverty (a dominant perspective in the broader social scientific study of poverty), and Moffitt's (1993) theory of life-course-persistent-offending (one of the more influential theories in life-course criminology).

Cohen (1955) argued that poverty increases crime because of problems with parental socialization that are more common in lower-class households. Specifically, lower-class parents are less likely to emphasize qualities such as self-restraint, punctuality, and motivation to work for distant goals—qualities that are essential for success in school, which is an inherently middle-class institution. Children from lower-class households therefore enter school at a disadvantage and their lack of success produces feelings of frustration and inadequacy. Cohen (1955) saw involvement in crime as a common adaptation to this strain. A criminal way of life— characterized by involvement in subcultures that emphasize "nonutilitarian, malicious, and negativistic" acts of aggression (p. 25)—provides poor adolescents a set of status criteria for which they *can* succeed. Moreover, pursuing a criminal way of life is a means by which they make an "explicit and wholesale repudiation of [the] middle-class standards" (p. 129) that created such strain for them in the first place.

Cohen's work clearly is characterized by an emphasis on the *persistent* nature of both poverty and crime. In discussing socialization problems in lower-class households, Cohen (1955, pp. 97–102) clearly is speaking not of families that have experienced a temporary drop in income, but instead, about families whose poverty endures to the point that it shapes parents' values, frames of reference, and views of what qualities should be instilled in children. Cohen's interest in crime was similarly long term in nature— crime is part of an enduring "delinquent system of values and way of life" (p. 134), in which those who are denied status by respectable society reject that society's norms and values, and replace them with the values of the criminal subculture.

A similar long-term perspective was presented by Wilson (1987), whose seminal works significantly guide recent research on the consequences of poverty. Wilson (1987) has argued that persistent family poverty is harmful because it increases the chances that the family will reside in a community in which a large percentage of residents are themselves persistently poor. This intense exposure to persistent poverty—at both the family and community level—places a child at risk for a range of problems, including delinquency, premarital pregnancy, and school dropout, because children living in these communities will be isolated from the social institutions and norms needed to achieve conventional success in the United States. Precisely because of this social isolation from mainstream society, the problems experienced by these most disadvantaged members of the population will be persistent in nature. These individuals will carry out their lives in social environments in which "crime, disorder, and drug use are…expected as part of everyday life" (Sampson & Wilson, 1995, p. 47), and therefore develop subcultural affiliations and values that give rise to persisting patterns of problem behavior, including involvement in crime.

A final theory that directs attention to a long-term link between poverty and crime is Moffitt's (1993) theory of life-course-persistent offending. Moffitt argued that a small portion of the population (about 5% of males) follow a trajectory of LCP offending—they begin crime early in life, persist with it well into adulthood, and their criminal involvement is marked by both high frequency and seriousness. Moffitt argued that the etiology of LCP offending can be traced to an interaction between neuropsychological deficits developed in early childhood and a criminogenic social environment that gives these deficits behavioral implications. Neuropsychological deficits result from such things as maternal drug and alcohol abuse during pregnancy, poor prenatal nutrition, pre- or postnatal exposure to toxic agents, child abuse and neglect, and a neonatal deprivation of stimulation and affection. A criminogenic social environment, on the other hand, will involve a family context in which warm relationships with parents are lacking, supervision is inconsistent, and discipline is harsh and erratic.

A key point that Moffitt (1993, pp. 680–683) makes is that both of these sources of difficulty—neuropsychological deficits and criminogenic family environments—are likely to be rooted in the experience of severe poverty. Poverty places a family at greater risk of having children with key cognitive deficits; moreover, criminogenic patterns of family social interaction may arise from both the stresses of poverty and the parents' own characteristics (including cognitive deficits) that may have contributed to the family's poverty in the first place. Thus, children from poor families will often have not just one of these risk factors for crime, but instead will experience both, therefore producing a situation in which "the children who are most in need of [help] ... will have parents who may be least able to provide it" (Moffitt, 1993, p. 681). The end result will involve a heightened level of persistent offending among children from poor families.

Taken together, these theories call for a longitudinal approach to studying the link between poverty and persistent involvement in crime. Few empirical studies have adopted this focus, but the studies that have suggest the promise of this approach. For example, Farnworth and her colleagues (1994) examined data from the Rochester Youth Development Study to examine the link between poverty and delinquency across four data collection periods that spanned 2 years. Although their cross-sectional analyses revealed scattered support for a poverty-crime relationship, much stronger evidence of such a relationship emerged in analyses that examined the effects of persistent poverty on persistent crime over the full 2-year period. Two additional studies (Fergusson et al., 2000; Nagin, Farrington, & Moffitt, 1995) were devoted explicitly to identifying individuals that followed a pattern of persistent offending that emerged as early as age 12. Both studies found that a small percentage of individuals fit this pattern and that these individuals were significantly more likely to come from poor families than individuals who were uninvolved in crime or whose involvement was more moderate and short term.

A final study is notable for its examination of persistent poverty. Jarjoura et al. (2002) analyzed the effects of poverty experienced in the child's first 15 years of life. Their descriptive results offer some insight into the problem with examining poverty in a cross-sectional analysis that focuses on a single year of time. They observed, for example, that 56% of the study families who were poor in a select year did *not* fit a pattern of persistent poverty when the other years were taken into account. On the other hand, 28% of families that *did* fit a pattern of persistent poverty were not poor in that one selected year. Their analysis, went on to consider the implications of long-term poverty for delinquency during a single year when respondents were between the ages 10 to 15. They found that the greatest effects of poverty were for those who had experienced it on a persistent basis.

These studies suggest the value in considering the poverty-crime relationship from a longitudinal standpoint. Importantly, however, evidence from just a handful of studies is insufficient for reaching a conclusion on this issue. Moreover, these studies are limited in some respects. The study by Farnworth and her colleagues (1994), for example, examined respondents over just a 2-year period. Jarjoura et al. (2002), on the other hand, were able to examine poverty over a much longer period (up to 15 years), but their analysis examined the effects of persistent poverty on delinquency at just a single point in time. Fergusson et al. (2000) examined crime over a longer stretch (from age 12 to 18), but as Moffitt (1993) pointed out, persistent crime that is centered during the period of adolescence may fit an adolescence-limited pattern of offending rather than a life-course-persistent one. Thus, in large part, the relationship between persistent poverty and persistent offending remains underexplored.

The Present Study

The purpose of this study is to examine the effect of poverty on the development of a pattern of persistent crime. Ideally, this would be done with data that provide information on criminal involvement from age 10 (the first age at which crime becomes legally possible) well into adulthood. Such long-term data rarely are available, however, and this obviously may explain the lack of attention to this issue in prior research. Thus, in approaching this issue, we focus on the link between poverty and the early onset of persistent criminal offending, which we define as repeated involvement in crime during a 5-year stretch that includes ages 10 to 14. As others have shown (see Moffitt, 1993; Nagin & Land, 1993; Tibbetts & Piquero, 1999) persistent offending during this period of early onset is a strong predictor of long-term offending that will extend into adulthood.[1]

In examining the association between poverty and persistent crime from ages 10 to 14, researchers face a key analytical question: should the

---

[1] We emphasize here that while crime during this period places one at heightened risk for persistent offending in adulthood, it clearly does not guarantee that such a pattern would emerge. Not all antisocial children develop into antisocial adults even if most antisocial adults were antisocial as children (Laub & Sampson, 2003; Sampson & Laub, 1993).

analysis focus on recent poverty exposure (poverty experienced at the end of the first decade of life) or earlier exposure to poverty (poverty that begins as early as the first year of life)? On the one hand, much social science research indicates that individual behavior is most affected by recent rather than temporally distal experiences and circumstances. On the other hand, poverty in the early years of life may have special implications for biological development, and therefore may have enduring consequences. With these two possibilities in mind, our approach is to consider the effects of both recent poverty and poverty that is experienced over the course of the first decade in life.

Data

We analyzed data from the Child Supplement of the National Longitudinal Survey of Youth (NLSY79). The NLSY79 is a national longitudinal study of more than 12,000 men and women who were aged between 14 and 21 when the study commenced in 1979. The project was supported by the United States Department of Labor and was administered by the National Opinion Research Center. Its purpose was to assess the period of life in which youths completed high school and enter the labor force. The study was designed to over-sample Blacks, Hispanics, and economically disadvantaged non-Hispanic Whites, who were expected to be at greater risk for experiencing problems in the transition from adolescence to adulthood. The NLSY79 Child Supplement is a longitudinal study of the children of mothers from the principal NLSY79 sample (see Chase-Landsdale, Mott, Brooks-Gunn, & Phillips, 1991 for a more detailed discussion of the Child Supplement). Interviews with mothers and their children have been conducted approximately every 2 years since 1986 to the point that the study now includes information on more than 11,000 children. The sample analyzed for the study is restricted to those individuals who were age 10 when interviewed between 1988 and 2002 (thus providing poverty data for the first decade of life) and who then answered questions about their involvement in crime and delinquency on two or more occasions when between ages 10 and 14.

One of the principal advantages of the NLSY79 over many other surveys used in criminological research is that it combines detailed longitudinal information about the household dynamics of respondents and their families beginning well before the children were born and continuing throughout childhood and into adolescence. This, combined with the inclusion of longitudinal information about their involvement in crime and delinquency, makes the NLSY79 an ideal source of data with which to assess the effects of living in persistent poverty on the chances of becoming a serious and persistent offender.

Measures

Since 1988, children aged 10 and above have been asked about their involvement in the past year in a range of offenses, including assault ("hurt someone badly enough to need a doctor"), theft ("stole something from a store"), and vandalism ("damaged property at school"). In most cases, these questions were asked in interviews conducted every 2 years until the children turned 15. Of the 10-year-olds who were asked about their involvement in the aforementioned offenses, therefore, most were reinterviewed at least two more times when they were ages 12 and 14. These items, covering a 5-year period, provide an opportunity to measure persistent involvement in crime and delinquency at a time in the life course when only a small minority of children are likely to report having committed such acts. To that end, we developed a dichotomous indicator of persistent offending (coded 1 if the respondent reported committing one or more of the above offenses in two or more survey years while she or he was between 10 and 14 years old, 0 otherwise). Given the emphasis on repeated offenses committed throughout the period of late childhood and early adolescence, we believe that this indicator can satisfactorily distinguish those offenders who are more likely to develop into serious persistent offenders than those who may have engaged only in minor, low-level offending over the short term. In fact, there is considerable empirical evidence that most serious adult offenders were engaged in crime at high levels in childhood (Laub & Sampson, 2003).

To measure poverty in childhood, we used a dichotomous indicator based on the relationship between total household income in the year before the child turned 10 and the official poverty level for that year (coded 1 if total household income failed to exceed the official poverty level, 0 otherwise). The indicator, developed by the principal investigators of the NLSY79, takes account of all household income sources as reported by the mother of the child, including receipt of welfare benefits.

This measure is available for all children in the sample for all years of their lives, but we initially restricted our attention to poverty in the year before the child turned 10 to determine the extent to which poverty at a critical period in development of the child was associated with his or her involvement in crime in later years. Although useful for evaluating the impact of living in poverty at a given point in time on the probability of engaging in crime at subsequent periods, the above indicator says little about the effects of being in poverty over a prolonged period of time. To assess more directly the effects of persistent poverty on the chances of becoming a persistent offender, we created an additional indicator based on the amount of time each respondent had spent living in a household below the poverty line. We began by recording whether each respondent had lived in poverty in each year of his or her life, and then calculated the mean across the first 10 years of life. This measure corresponds to the proportion of time the respondent has lived in poverty during his or her life, and therefore ranges between 0.00 and 1.00. As a result, it provides a useful basis for assessing the links between persistent poverty in childhood and involvement in criminal and delinquent behavior in later years.

All analyses also will include a number of controls to protect against concerns about spuriousness—poverty could be correlated with persistent crime in early adolescence only because it is correlated with other background variables that are key predictors of crime. Each analysis therefore will include controls for sex (coded 1 if male, 0 if female), the mother's age, race and ethnicity (with dummy variables for Hispanic and African-American), and household size (the number of people living in the house).

Results

Analyses were conducted using logistic regression. The dependent variable in all equations is the dichotomous measure of persistent offending between ages 10 and 14. Given our interest in the links between childhood deprivation and subsequent patterns of offending, we used measures of recent and long-term poverty to predict offending in later years. Two models were initially estimated. The independent variable in Model 1 is the measure of recent poverty—poverty at or around age 9. Then, in Model 2, we used an indicator of long-term poverty—the proportion of time in the first decade of life that was spent in poverty.[2]

Table 3.1 reports the results for these two equations and shows that living in poverty as a child increases persistent offending from ages 10 to 14. As shown in Model 1, children living in poverty at the end of their first decade of life were significantly more likely to engage in repeated criminal offending in early adolescence than those not living in poverty at that time. The

---

[2] Results, including significance tests, are based on robust standard errors intended to take account of the presence of multiple children in the sample from the each household.

TABLE 3.1   Results for Logistic Regression of Persistent Offending between Ages 10 and 14

	Model 1			Model 2		
	B	SE	p	B	SE	p
Male	0.82***	0.13	0.00	0.81***	0.13	0.00
Hispanic	0.37**	0.17	0.03	0.32*	0.17	0.06
Black	0.45***	0.16	0.00	0.36**	0.17	0.03
Age of mother	−0.02	0.02	0.32	−0.01	0.02	0.47
Household size	0.15***	0.04	0.00	0.14***	0.04	0.00
Recent poverty (Age 9)	0.37**	0.14	0.01	—	—	—
Long-term poverty (Age 0–9)	—	—	—	0.58***	0.20	0.00
Constant	−2.58***	0.48	0.00	−2.66***	0.48	0.00
Log pseudolikelihood	−779.70			−778.45		
N	1714			1714		
Households	1351			1351		

* $p \leq .05$; ** $p \leq .01$; *** $p \leq .001$.

logistic regression coefficient of 0.37 translates into an odds ratio of 1.44, therefore indicating a roughly 45% greater likelihood of persistent offending among those in poverty at age 9. The results of Model 2 provide even further support for the notion that childhood deprivation is associated with the development of ongoing patterns of criminal behavior. Those who lived in poverty throughout the first decade of their lives were 79% more likely (B = 0.58, odds ratio = 1.79) to show signs of persistent crime than children who had never lived in poverty during that time.

Figure 3.1 provides an additional view of these patterns by showing, for the measures of both recent and long-term poverty, the estimated change in the predicted probability of being classified as a persistent offender.[3] For the measure of recent poverty, the predicted probability of being a persistent offender increases from 0.16 to 0.21 when comparing those from poor and nonpoor families. For the measure of long-term poverty, the increase is slightly greater—the probability of being a persistent offender increases from 0.15 to 0.24 when comparing those who experienced no poverty in the first decade of life to those who spent the entire first decade of their lives in

[3] Predicted probabilities were estimated using CLARIFY with the values of the remaining independent variables set to their means (Tomz, Wittenberg, & King, 2001).

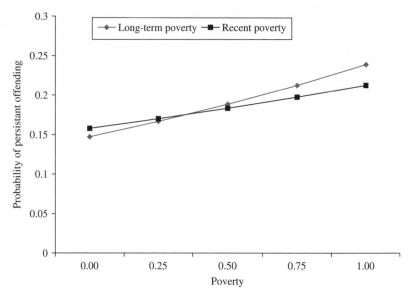

FIGURE 3.1   Changes in the predicted probabilities of being a persistent offender.

poverty. Thus, while neither recent nor long-term poverty is sufficient to propel an individual into a pattern of persistent offending (as indicated by the maximum predicted probability of 0.24), both of these forms of poverty nevertheless increase the chances of persistent offending.

These results suggest that long-term poverty is more consequential for persistent offending than living in poverty at a single point in time, given the greater effects of long-term poverty on the estimated change in the odds of being classified as a persistent offender. Because of two caveats, however, our conclusions on this issue must be tentative. First, we cannot conclude that the difference in effects of these variables is statistically significant, because standard approaches for comparing models (e.g., comparing log-likelihoods) are not appropriate, given that these are independent rather than nested models (Tabachnick & Fidell, 2007, p. 447). Indeed, contradicting the view that there is a statistically significant difference in the two effects, we found that confidence intervals surrounding the two lines shown in Figure 3.1 overlapped one another.

A second caveat, however, raises the possibility that our analysis underestimates the difference in effects for recent and long-term poverty. In contrast to other studies that have found that families tend to move in and out of poverty (e.g., Duncan & Rodgers, 1988), we found a very high correlation ($r = 0.72$) between recent and long-term poverty. This makes it difficult to identify differential effects of the two variables, because most of the families experiencing recent poverty also experienced long-term poverty. All else being equal, this covariation between recent and long-term poverty should work to minimize the difference in effects for these two measures. Thus, the apparently greater effects of long-term poverty revealed in this analysis may therefore be quite telling.

Overall, the most defensible conclusion to be drawn from these analyses is that both types of childhood poverty—long-term and recent—increase involvement in persistent offending during early adolescence, and that long-term poverty may be the more important of the two. The effects of both poverty variables, however, are notable, given that persistent offending during this period of early onset places one at heightened risk for a pattern of persistent offending into adulthood (Moffitt, 1993; Nagin & Land, 1993; Tibbetts & Piquero, 1999). Thus, poverty is associated not just with sporadic or intermittent offending, but perhaps that form of offending that is most likely to ultimately attract significant attention from the criminal justice system.

Discussion and Conclusion

The effects of poverty on individual involvement in crime has been the focus of extensive research in criminology for decades. With few exceptions, however, this research has been cross-sectional in nature—it has examined the link between poverty and crime at a single point in the life course (often adolescence), and then used this analysis to make inferences about the overall causal link between poverty and crime. Thus, very little is known about the implications of poverty for long-term patterns of persistent offending. In this study, we have attempted to address this void both theoretically and empirically. With respect to theory, we have reviewed a number of prominent theories (Cohen, 1955; Moffitt, 1993; Wilson, 1987), highlighting the fact that their arguments about the poverty-crime association are in large part longitudinal in nature—they pertain much more to the link between persistent poverty and persistent offending than they do to temporary or episodic spells of poverty and crime.

Empirically, we examined this issue with an analysis that considered whether poverty had implications for persistent offending from ages 10 to 14—an outcome that reflects an early onset pattern of offending. We found that persistent offending during this stretch was significantly affected by both the recent experience of poverty and by long-term patterns of poverty experienced during the first decade of life. Specifically, the chances of being a persistent offender were increased by roughly 45% for those experiencing poverty at age 9 and by roughly 80% for those experiencing poverty during one's entire first decade of life. Given the link between early onset and involvement in later patterns of persistent, serious offending, the clear conclusion of this study is that poverty during childhood may have much more lasting implications for crime than what most studies in this area have considered.

This is an informative conclusion, but our analysis leaves a number of key issues unaddressed. These issues could help guide future research on the link between poverty and persistent offending. Most notably, future research should try to examine persistent offending over a longer period of time than we were able to. Because of data limitations, our analysis was limited to persistent offending during early adolescence. For all of its strengths, one limitation of the NLSY79 is that it does not contain a uniform battery of self-reported offending items that appear in each survey and for all age groups. In short, as subjects age and participate in additional interviews, they often are asked about a different set of crimes, therefore precluding a long-term analysis of specific offenses. Thus, we were limited to examining three offenses (assault, theft, and vandalism) for which data existed across three surveys (spanning 5 years). Fortunately, this 5-year period pertained to a time in the life course (age 10 to 14) that has been shown in prior research to have lasting implications—crime during this period often (but obviously not always) foreshadows persistent involvement in crime at later points, including crime in adulthood (Sampson & Laub, 1993).

Importantly, though, a better approach would use data that contain repeated, identical measures of crime for a long span of time—at least through the end of adolescence, and ideally into adulthood. Moreover, in light of our finding that persistent poverty from age 0 to 9 was causally significant, data collection likely should begin at or near birth. There obviously are significant obstacles to collecting data over a span of at least two and perhaps three decades. A point to emphasize, however, is that if the causes of persistent offending are to be truly understood, such data are necessary.

A second key issue to consider in future research involves the identification of key tipping points in which differences in income become consequential. Our analysis used a dichotomous measure of poverty that focused on whether a family's income was above or below the official poverty level. Although this particular threshold is commonly used in poverty research and likely has some significance, it is subject to the criticism that families just above the poverty line are themselves still quite poor and, thus, are inaccurately coded as fitting into the "non-poor" group. An important approach to dealing with this issue will be to use ratio-level measures of income to empirically identify the key thresholds at which poverty becomes consequential for crime (see Bjerk, 2007).

A third key issue to be addressed involves the theoretical mechanisms that explain the effects of poverty on persistent offending. We should emphasize that, with few exceptions (Larzelere & Patterson, 1990; Wright et al., 1999), virtually no research in this area—either of the cross-sectional or longitudinal variety—has considered intervening mechanisms. Thus, while much attention has been devoted to considering whether poverty affects crime, the question of why it may do so has been largely ignored in empirical research. This obviously is true of our own analysis as well.

A number of poverty-oriented theories specify key intervening mechanisms that should be considered. For example, Cohen (1955) emphasized the effects of poverty on such things as a juvenile's ability to succeed in school, their attachment to school, and their proximity to other juveniles who experience similar frustrations at school. In addition, Wilson (1987) emphasized the implications that poverty has for one's neighborhood context—those who are persistently poor in urban areas are likely to live in neighborhoods with other similarly poor individuals. Over time, these neighborhoods become socially and economically isolated from mainstream, conventional institutions, therefore allowing deviant subcultures and values to develop. Thus, from Wilson's (1987) perspective, the relationship between poverty and crime should be mediated by the quality of the neighborhood environment and the implications it has for a child's subcultural affiliations and values.[4]

It also should be emphasized that a long-term, longitudinal approach to studying the poverty-crime association should lead researchers to focus on some intervening mechanisms that have been largely ignored in theoretical discussions of the poverty-crime association. Specifically, persistent poverty in the first decade of life could have major implications not just for "sociological" variables of importance (e.g., commitment to education), but also for variables that relate to biological development. In short, persistent poverty during this period may lead to such things as poor nutrition, exposure to lead (from living in dilapidated housing), and lack of access to health care, all of which could indirectly affect later crime by producing cognitive deficits, problems with impulsivity, or other neuropsychological deficits

---

[4] Many prominent theories of crime that largely ignore the effects of poverty may also identify variables that can explain why poverty affects crime. For example, Akers's (1998) social learning theory would emphasize the relationship between poverty and access to delinquent reinforcements (especially those in peer groups), while social control theory (Hirschi, 1969) would emphasize the effect of poverty on one's attachment and commitment to conventional individuals and goals.

(Moffitt, 1993). The point therefore to emphasize is that knowing that poverty affects persistent offending is of limited value if research does not also discern *why* such an effect occurs.

A final key issue that was not considered in this study but that merits attention in future research involves the nexus between family poverty, community poverty, and crime. Our study did what many have done in this area—we conceptualized poverty entirely in terms of the poverty experienced by the child's family. This approach neglects an empirical fact in the United States: among poor U.S. families, there is significant variation in the level of poverty found in their surrounding communities, with some poor families living in communities with high concentrations of poverty and others living in communities in which most households have incomes above the poverty level (Jargowsky, 1997; Lynn & McGeary, 1990). This variation among the U.S. poor raises the logical possibility that the effects of family poverty on crime depend in part on the extent of community poverty (Hay et al., 2007). In short, family poverty may have its greatest effects on crime among children whose families live in extremely poor communities that have weak community social control and an established presence of criminal subcultures—factors that themselves can encourage crime (Bursik & Grasmick, 1993; Sampson, Raudenbush, & Earls, 1997).

This possibility may be especially relevant to explaining persistent offending, given that this pattern of offending is associated with such a high frequency and seriousness of offending. In short, such a serious brand of offending may emerge not just in response to a single risk factor for crime (like family poverty), but instead, in response to multiple, co-occurring risk factors, which would be most expected to exist for those poor children whose families also live in extremely poor communities.

In conclusion, it simply can be noted that while research on the poverty-crime association advances each year, much remains unknown. The effects of poverty on persistent offending in particular remains largely unaddressed, despite the possibility that this is precisely the pattern of offending for which poverty may be most important.

CHAPTER 4

Strain, Social Support, and Persistent Criminality

STEPHANIE ELLIS AND JOANNE SAVAGE

There is general agreement among criminologists about the relationship between age and crime. Rates of crime tend to rise and peak during the adolescent years and then taper off as the individual ages (e.g., Ezell & Cohen, 2005; Farrington, 1986; Hirschi & Gottfredson, 1983; Sampson & Laub, 1992). However, while many offenders transition into adult roles and out of delinquent behaviors, some problematic offenders will continue to offend into young adulthood and throughout the life course.

While a multitude of articles that examine offending trajectories has been published in recent years, most of these focus on whether there *are* distinctive criminal trajectories (as Moffitt [1993] proposed, for example). Less attention has been devoted to the differential causes of persistent versus adolescence-limited offending, for example. There are exceptions, of course, such as the literature on "early onset" (e.g., Tibbetts & Piquero, 1999; Tolan & Thomas, 1995), numerous articles out of several prominent longitudinal studies (e.g., Ayers et al., 1999; Farrington, 2001; Gorman-Smith, Tolan, Loeber, & Henry, 1998; Herrenkohl et al., 2001; Laub & Sampson, 2003; Lay, Ihle, Esser, & Schmidt, 2005; Wiesner & Capaldi, 2003), and relevant work on desistance (e.g., Brame, Bushway, & Paternoster, 2003; Bushway, Thornberry, & Krohn, 2003), but the field's approach to studying this issue has been unsystematic.

We do not know as much as we should about whether the causes of persistent offending are distinct from those of less serious offending.

Two factors that may be important for understanding persistent criminality are strain and social support. Many authors have tested the contemporaneous effects of strain on offending (see Agnew, 1992; Colvin, Cullen, & VanderVen, 2002; Robbers, 2004); however, few have examined the effects of strain on the developmental pathway to persistent offending. Similarly, the long-term effects of social support (both direct and indirect) on persistent criminality remain unknown. Further, it is possible that the effects of strain may vary depending on stages of childhood, adolescent or early adult development or that other factors, most notably social support, may mediate its long-term effects. Accordingly, this chapter will focus on the effects of strain and social support on persistent criminality, and will provide an analysis to test the effects of traumatic strain and social support on persistent offending in young adulthood.

Review of the Literature on Persistent Criminality

Although criminologists generally agree about the shape of the age-crime curve, the interpretation of the nature of this relationship has been a topic of debate in the literature (Ezell & Cohen, 2005; Mazerolle & Piquero 2001). On one side of the debate are those who argue that the age-crime curve is "invariant," regardless of geographic location or historical context; all individuals are expected to commit less crime after they reach adulthood (Gottfredson & Hirschi, 1987, 1988, 1990). In contrast, other researchers emphasize the need to focus on the variation beneath the curve as it is related to both desistance from crime and persistent offending and argue that active offenders will continue to offend regardless of age (Blumstein, Cohen, & Farrington, 1988a; Blumstein, Cohen, Roth, & Visher, 1986; Elder, 1993; Farrington, 1986; Moffitt, 1993).

State dependence theories suggest that an individual's criminal propensity changes over time (depending upon the social context). Sampson and Laub's (1993) age-graded theory of social control is an example of a state dependence theory of persistent offending. On the basis of Hirschi's (1969) social control theory, which proposes that weak bonds to society cause delinquency, Sampson and Laub (1993) emphasize that transitions in social bonds (salient events that represent discrete changes of state) can modify criminal trajectories. A distinguishing characteristic of the age-graded theory of social control is the emphasis not merely on *the presence* of social institutions or bonds at different stages of life, but rather on the quality of the relationships that are fostered through these social institutions. For example, informal social control does not result from simply having a parent, but rather it results from having a good relationship with that parent.

The population heterogeneity view suggests that individuals vary in their propensity to commit crime. From this point of view, persistent offenders are those who are the most criminal in trait or behavioral habits. Gottfredson and Hirschi (1990) propose that low self-control is the critical feature of the criminal personality. They maintain that poor parenting fails to instill self-control, that this failure occurs early in childhood, and that the impulsive character that results adversely affects a broad array behavior throughout life. Moffitt (1993, 1997) proposes that the disposition for "life-course-persistent" offending develops due to an interaction between neuropsychological dysfunction and environment (e.g., poverty and parenting). Moffitt (1993) argues that "the topography of their behavior may change with changing opportunities, but the underlying disposition persists throughout the life course" (p. 669). In life-course-persistent offenders, impaired cognitive development and difficult temperament in childhood are often coupled with suboptimal environments that reinforce antisocial behavior.

We speculate that other factors may be associated with the development of criminal habits or traits. Strain and social support are two good candidates. Hypotheses about the effects of strain could be based on the state dependence perspective, from which we would expect that strain causes delinquency contemporaneously and those with ongoing stressors would be most likely to persist in criminality into adulthood. Most empirical tests of the effects of strain on delinquency are implicitly based on this assumption. But, based on readings in other fields and anecdotal evidence, we also wonder if *traumatic* or *chronic* strain could change an individual's personality in such a way that it would lead to future offending, even in the absence of ongoing stressful experiences. For example, one might expect that extreme stress could undermine a person's sense of security, or ability to calm the nervous system, or cause a "scary" worldview. Findings from studies on child abuse, for example, suggest that victims are vulnerable to many negative long-term effects (e.g., Fagan, 2005; Smith & Thornberry, 1995; Widom & Maxfield, 2001). In this case, the developmental timing, type, and intensity of the stressors may all matter a great deal in the long-term effects of strain.

In addition, we wonder whether social support operates in much the same way. Most authors implicitly emphasize a "state-dependent" role of social support in the etiology of negative outcomes—its presence is thought to prevent them. But one might also consider that ongoing social support could instill coping styles or a physiological calm that could become part of a person's set of "traits" that suppress offending. As with strain, the timing, type, and intensity of social support may matter a great deal. Further, social support may have the capacity to mitigate the adverse effects of other factors, such as strain, on offending. It is possible that the most important role that social support has is to attenuate the effects of other criminogenic factors.

In the following sections we will explore the theoretical and empirical connections between strain, social support, and offending and discuss the implications for the study of persistence. Then we will present a set of analyses that explore the relationships between adolescent strain and social support and young adult offending. Finally, we will discuss some directions for future research.

An Overview of General Strain Theory

Agnew (1992) proposes that strain causes delinquency. He identifies three main sources of strain (1) the disjuncture between expectations and achievements (failure to achieve positively valued goals), (2) the removal or anticipated removal of positively valued stimuli, and (3) the experience of or anticipation of noxious stimuli. Examples of stressors for adolescents include negative relationships with peers, teachers or parents, parent divorce or death, bad grades, and other negative school experiences. Agnew also suggests that responding to strain with delinquency will be more likely when the individual responds to strain with anger, or other negative affective states. These are the basic tenets of *general strain theory* (GST).

Here we are most interested in Agnew's suggestion that strain may result from the experience of or anticipation of noxious stimuli. Agnew focuses on the adolescents' inability to escape from negative experiences because of their status within the social structure. Negative or noxious stimuli may take various forms—physical, sexual, even verbal abuse. Delinquency may be the result of the adolescent's attempt to escape from the painful situation, or may result as an attempt to manage the strain (e.g., through the use of alcohol and/or drugs).

Agnew (1992) also contends that the effect of strain is cumulative. When adolescents can no longer find a way to cope with their problems conventionally, they often resort to deviance or delinquency. Regarding our interest in persistent offending, Agnew's discussion suggests a tipping point wherein a significant amount of stress would trigger offending. However, if the effects of strain accumulate, we might also expect that extreme or chronic strain could cause severe or persistent offending.

Agnew's (1997) discussion of the role of strain in the etiology of persistent criminality, however, emphasizes the dynamics between traits such as impulsivity, insensitivity, hyperactivity, difficult temperament, and low self-control, and experiences of strain. Agnew focuses on trait aggression—which has both direct and indirect effects on persistent criminality. First, aggressive individuals are more likely to experience strain of all types than nonaggressive individuals. These persons are more likely to have problems in several areas of life; they are more difficult to parent, more likely to be rejected by peers, and more likely to have problems at school or work (Agnew, 1997; Moffitt, 1993). Further, aggressive individuals are more likely to blame their problems on others and therefore are more likely to respond to a situation with anger—a key variable in general strain theory. Agnew also notes that aggressive personality traits are partly heritable, therefore, children who are aggressive are more likely to be raised in an aversive environment than other children are. As a result, these individuals are more likely to experience high levels of strain and respond with criminal behaviors. These processes interact not only to increase the likelihood of involvement in crime but also to reinforce the aggressive personality traits. This explanation also parallels Thornberry's theory of social control, social learning, and delinquency as occurring in an amplifying loop.

There is a substantial volume of literature that supports the prediction that adolescents who experience greater strain are more likely to engage in delinquent behavior (e.g., Agnew & White, 1992; Broidy, 2001; Hoffmann & Cerbone, 1999; Mazerolle, 2000; Mazerolle & Piquero, 1998; Paternoster & Mazerolle, 1994). Few studies have examined the detailed questions we have outlined here regarding the timing, type, and intensity of strain and its effects on the severity and chronicity of offending. Hoffmann and colleagues have been looking at some of these issues. Hoffmann and Cerbone (1999), for example, hypothesized that experiencing a high number of stressful life events in early adolescence would lead to an escalation in delinquency in early and midadolescence. They found that stressful life events such as a death in the family, serious accident and divorce were associated with an escalation in delinquency. Their use of major stressors is probably important here; many tests of strain theory use minor stressors that may not have a permanent impact on personality or behavior (for more, see Chapter 5).

Fagan (2005) used data from the National Youth Survey to examine the effects of self-reported physical abuse during adolescence on self-reported offending during adolescence and early adulthood. She included measures of serious violence, nonviolent offending, drug use, and serious and minor incidents of domestic violence. While there have been several reports of the contemporaneous effects of physical abuse on delinquency (Brezina, 1998;

Thornberry, Ireland, & Smith, 2001), few have investigated the long-term effects of physical abuse that occurs during adolescence. Fagan found a moderate positive relationship between the experience of physical abuse during adolescence and continued involvement in a broad array of criminal endeavors both during the transition to adulthood and young adulthood.

Social Support

Another factor that might be related to persistent offending is social support. It is possible that social support may have a direct effect on reducing an individual's involvement in delinquent activities at each stage (state-dependent) or change a person's character by increasing a sense of security, for example, or self-confidence. Social support may also mitigate the effects of factors such as strain and thereby reduce the likelihood of a traumatically strained individual becoming a chronic offender.

Cullen and Wright (1997) point out that the concept of social support has largely been ignored by criminologists. Findings from their work suggest that social support should be included as a key variable, or more specifically an intervening variable, in empirical tests of Agnew's GST. They contend that social support may have the potential to explain whether individuals adapt to strain with delinquent coping or engage in legitimate coping mechanisms. Even Agnew (1992) acknowledges the importance of social support and predicts that "adolescents with conventional supports, then, should be better able to respond to objective strains in a nondelinquent manner" (p. 72). Thus, numerous authors believe that social support can insulate adolescents from delinquency.

The concept of social support has informed sociological, psychological, and even medical research for quite some time. Research on social support suggests that it has many benefits. For example, social support, when provided on a consistent basis, has the potential to strengthen social bonds (Colvin et al., 2002; Cullen, 1994; Hirschi, 1969), to improve adolescents' physical and psychological well-being (Bowen & Chapman, 1996), and to enhance coping skills (Bowen & Chapman, 1996; Cohen, Underwood & Gottlieb, 2000). The data suggest that social support may serve as a buffer to attenuate the effects of strain and thereby reduce crime and delinquency (Agnew, 1992; Colvin et al., 2002; Cullen, 1994; Robbers, 2004).

Social support theory has been especially influential in medical and epidemiological research (Cohen et al., 2000). Medical researchers and epidemiologists have examined the influence of social support on a variety of health conditions. Most of the research looks at the potential of social support to cushion individuals from the psychological consequences of stressful life events. Social support has been said to influence a variety of health conditions, such as arthritis (e.g., Penninx, Van Tilburg, Deeg, & Kriegsman, 1997), cardiovascular disease (see Cohen, Kaplan & Manuck, 1994), HIV/AIDS (see Nott & Power, 1995), and even pregnancy outcomes (see McWilliams, 1994). Likewise, the health risks (cigarette smoking, high blood pressure and obesity) associated with low levels of social support have been examined extensively (see House, 2002).

According to Cohen et al. (2000), social support is often used to refer to any process through which social relationships promote health and well-being. One could argue that the broad definition of social support forwarded by Cohen et al. (2000) could also be used to describe the construct of social control as social bonds may also serve to promote health and well-being. However, while social support and social control overlap (social support can be part of attachment, commitment, involvement, and beliefs), the two constructs are not entirely synonymous. Social support extends beyond being a mere agent of social control. This is clear in Cullen's (1994) conceptualization of social support. Cullen asserts that the distinguishing feature of social support "is that it involves the transferring of resources" (p. 194). Social support in the form of instrumental services may serve to meet physical, social, psychological, and/or emotional needs in a fashion that the bonds of social control do not. From this point of view, attachment may include sharing feelings, and the provision of affection that may fulfill an individual's psychological needs for love, and a reinforced sense of self-worth. From the point of view of Hirschi's social control model, attachment means that a person will be deterred from antisocial behavior out of fear of losing that relationship. Thus, the construct of social support, depending upon the context, has the potential to explain both deviant and nondeviant behavior, while social control theory provides only an explanation of deviant behaviors.

Several authors have examined the role of social support as a safeguard in moderating risk and reducing delinquency (Bowen & Chapman, 1996; Carr & Vandiver, 2001). Bowen and Chapman (1996) sampled 525 at-risk youth involved in a program called *Communities in Schools* (CIS). Their analysis of neighborhood danger and the potential of social support to aid individual adaptation yielded some significant findings. They found that higher physical and psychological well-being were associated with higher levels of neighborhood, teacher, and parent support. Overall, social support was more powerful than neighborhood danger in predicting level of physical and psychological health and adjustment. This is an important finding because it indicates that social support does mitigate risk.

A small number of empirical studies with cross-sectional data suggest that social support mediates the effects of strain on delinquency/criminality (Carr & Vandiver, 2001; Robbers, 2004). Robbers (2004) tested the effects of the interaction between social support and strain on delinquency using data from Wave VI of the National Youth Survey. She found that social support did mediate the effects of some types of strain (failure to achieve goals) on delinquency.

Some authors suggest that protective factors may be the key to understanding desistance (Bowen & Chapman, 1996; Carr & Vandiver, 2001; Cullen & Wright, 1997); however, more information on how these protective factors work in the context of the life course is needed to fully understand why some individuals desist from crime while others become persistent and chronic offenders.

Methodology

Data

In an effort to understand the dynamics of strain and social support in the etiology of persistence, we combined multiple waves of the National Youth Survey (NYS) to address the following three research questions: (1) Does strain in early adolescence contribute to the development of persistent offending? (2) Does the presence of social support protect strained adolescents from this effect? (3) Does the timing of the strain and social support matter?

The NYS has been used in many instances for testing theories of delinquency and is a good source of data for our purposes because it has previously been used to test effects of strain and social support on delinquency and also provides items related to other constructs necessary for our empirical test. For more information on the NYS, see Elliott et al. (1989).

We hypothesized that stressful events experienced earlier in the life course would be more likely to have long-term impacts than later stressful events, so both strain and social support were measured in early adolescence and late adolescence (they were also measured in early adulthood, to be used as control variables to ensure that the effects we were estimating were really lagged). We combined data from Waves I, V, and VII and used only subjects who were between the ages of 11 and 14 in Wave I to represent early adolescents (Wave I of the survey includes subjects aged 11 to 17). In Wave I, data were collected from both the youth subjects and one of their legal guardians. In Wave V these respondents were between the ages of 15 and 18 (which we will refer to as late adolescence), and in Wave VII they were between the ages of 21 and 24. Thus, we could look at the effects of early adolescent strain on young adult offending.

Measures

Violent and Nonviolent Criminality at Ages 21 to 24. Wave VII data were used to compute measures of violent and nonviolent young adult criminality. Respondents were asked about their involvement in a broad array of criminal acts and for each act they were asked "How many times in the last year have you...." For our purposes, raw frequency data were used rather than the ordinal level data (for more detail, see Ellis, 2006; for a more lengthy discussion on the use of open-ended vs. fixed-choice response categories see Converse & Presser, 1986).

Violent offending at ages 21 to 24 was operationalized by summing the responses to seven items such as "How many times in the last year have you attacked someone with the idea of seriously hurting or killing him or her?" and "How many times in the past year have you been involved in gang fights?" See Table 4.1 for a list of items. This measure is a sum of the number of violent acts within the previous year. The range of the scores for the violent behavior scale was 0 to 12 violent acts. The scale had a mean of 0.29 and a standard deviation of 1.14. Similar items have been used to measure violence/delinquency in other studies (e.g., Hoffman & Cerbone, 1999; Mazerolle & Maahs, 2000; Paternoster & Mazerolle, 1994; Peter, LaGrange, & Silverman, 2003).

Nonviolent offending at ages 21 to 24 was operationalized by summing the responses to eight items such as "How many times in the last year have you purposely damaged or destroyed property that did not belong to you?" and "How many times in the last year have you stolen, or tried to steal, a motor vehicle, such as a car or motorcycle?" See Table 4.1 for the complete list of items for this scale. The scores on the index measuring nonviolent offending had a range from 0 to 365 with a mean of 2.97 and a standard deviation of 20.2.

Originally, the multiple regression models were run with the natural log transformations of violent and nonviolent offending; however, this transformation did not appear to increase the explanatory power of the models, and as a result, the original variables were used for the analysis presented here to facilitate interpretation.

Strain. Strain was measured in Wave I (ages 11 to 14), Wave V (ages 15 to 18), and Wave VII (ages 21 to 24). The measure of strain was operationalized by

TABLE 4.1   Items Included in Measures of Violent and Nonviolent Criminal Behavior Scales

Violent Behavior Scale

How many times in the last year have you...

1. Attacked someone with the idea of seriously hurting or killing him/her?

2. Hit (or threatened to hit) one of your parents?

3. Had (or tried to have) sexual relations with someone against their will?

4. Used force to rob a person/business?

5. Used force (strong-arm methods) to get money or things from other people?

6. Used force (strong-arm methods) to get money or things from someone (students, teachers, other people)?

7. Hit someone at work?

Nonviolent Criminal Behavior Scale

How many times in the last year have you...

1. Purposely damaged or destroyed property belonging to your parents or other family members?

2. Purposely damaged or destroyed other property that did not belong to you?

3. Stolen (or tried to steal) a motor vehicle, such as a car or motorcycle?

4. Stolen (or tried to steal) something worth more than $50?

5. Stolen (or tried to steal) things worth between $5 and $50?

6. Sold marijuana?

7. Sold hard drugs such as heroin, cocaine, and LSD?

8. Broken into a building or vehicle (or tried to break in) to steal something or just to look around?

summing seven items that asked whether respondents had experienced stressful events in the past year such as divorce, accident, or death in the family. We intentionally used fairly traumatic items because we expected them to have a long-term impact. See Table 4.2 for a list of items. The items in this scale were recoded as no = 0 and yes = 1. A high score indicates that the respondent experienced a greater number of stressful life events. For respondents between the ages of 11 and 14, the scale ranged from 0 to 5 with a mean of 0.58 and a standard deviation of 0.86. The measure of strain for respondents aged 15 to 18 and 21 to 24 had one fewer question than the measure of strain for individuals between the ages of 11 to 14 (data on a family move was not available in Wave V or Wave VII). The scale for Wave V ranged from 0 to 4 with a mean of 0.31 and a standard deviation of 0.69. The data for the scale in Wave VII had a range of 0 to 3 with a mean of 0.22.

Social Support. Social support at ages 11 to 14 was operationalized by summing together 10 items that measure the respondent's perceived emotional support from both family and friends. Because the social support

TABLE 4.2   Items Included in Measures of Strain at Ages 11–14 (Wave I),
15–18 (Wave V), and 21–24 (Wave VII)

Which of the following events have occurred in your home or to members of your family during the past year?

1. Divorce?
2. Separation?
3. Serious illness/death?
4. Serious accident?
5. Father figure lost job?
6. Mother figure lost job?
7. Family move? (this item only occurs in Wave I)

items were based on differing scales (e.g., some had "Yes" or "No" response categories while others had a rating scale) z-scores were computed before combining them. According to Wilkinson et al. (1996), "standardizing the data changes nothing but the scale on which the data are measured" (p. 696). See Table 4.3 for a complete list of the items used for this scale. A high score indicates greater social support than a low score. The scale for respondents between the age of 11 and 14 (using Wave I data) had a range of 12.2 to 22.7, with a mean of 0.90 and a standard deviation of 4.49.

There was a slight change in the social support measure from Wave I to Wave V. The three questions regarding parent/family involvement in school activities, community activities, and activities with friends were not present in the instrument used for Wave V. Seven items were summed to measure respondents' perceived social support when they were between the ages of 15 and 18. These items were all based upon the same scale so standardization was unnecessary. A high score for this measure indicates greater perceived social support from friends and family. The values ranged from 13 to 31, and had a mean score of 25.3 and a standard deviation of 3.3.

The measure of social support at the ages of 21 to 24 was operationalized by summing three items. We were unable to include items related to perceived support from family and parents because of large amounts of missing data. The scale values ranged from 2 to 12, with a mean of 7.7. Respondents who were not living with their significant other were not asked about the social support they received from their partner; accordingly, their scores were recoded to zero. The limitation in recoding the variable in this way is that a respondent could be involved in and receive support from a partner with whom they do not cohabitate.

Interaction Between Social Support and Strain. Interaction terms were computed by standardizing and multiplying strain and social support

TABLE 4.3   Items Included in Measures of Social Support

A. Social Support in Early Adolescence (Wave I)

1. Do you have a particular group of friends that you run around with?
2. How often have your parents/family taken part or shared in your school activities, for example, games, homework, and assemblies?
3. How often have your parents/family taken part or shared in your community activities, for example, ballgames, plays, and church activities?
4. How often have your parents/family taken part or shared in your activities with your friends, for example, parties, dances, and hikes?
5. Do you have parents that you can talk to about almost anything?
6. Do your parents comfort you when you're unhappy about something?
7. My family is willing to listen to my problems. (agree/disagree)
8. My friends are willing to listen to my problems. (agree/disagree)
9. I feel close to my family. (agree/disagree)
10. I feel close to my friends. (agree/disagree)

B. Social Support in Later Adolescence at Ages 15–18 (Wave V)

1. Do you have a particular group of friends that you run around with?
2. Rate how well you are doing at having parents that you can talk to about almost anything. (very well/not well at all)
3. Rate how well your parents comfort you when you're unhappy about something. (very well/not well at all)
4. My family is willing to listen to my problems. (agree/disagree)
5. My friends are willing to listen to my problems. (agree/disagree)
6. I feel close to my family. (agree/disagree)
7. I feel close to my friends. (agree/disagree)

C. Social Support in Young Adulthood at Ages 21–24 (Wave VII)

1. Do you have a particular group of friends that you run around with?
2. How much support and encouragement have you received from your friends?
3. How much support and encouragement have you received from your partner?
4. How much support have you received from your parents?

variables. To test the hypothesis that early adolescent social support mediates the effects of early adolescent strain on persistent criminality, we multiplied measures of strain and social support from Wave I. To test the hypothesis that social support in late adolescence mediates the effects of early adolescent strain on the development of persistent criminality, we multiplied the measure of strain from Wave I with the measure of social support from Wave V.

Control Variables. To distill the effects of early strain and social support on later criminality, measures of strain and social support during early adulthood years were used as controls. In addition, measures of economic disadvantage, race, gender, and exposure to delinquent peers were used as controls for potential spuriousness. Race and gender were self-reported in Wave I and are coded here as follows: 1 = White; 0 = Non-White; 1 = Male; and 2 = Female. Economic disadvantage was measured using the Hollingshead Index of Social Position (ISP), which combines information on an individual's level of education and occupational rank (Hollingshead & Redlich, 1958; Hollingshead 1975). Overall, the scores range from 11 to 77 with a low score indicating greater social status than a high score; thus there is an anticipated *positive* coefficient for the relationship between this index and criminality.

Exposure to delinquent peers was operationalized by summing eight items. Respondents were asked how many of their friends had engaged in a number of delinquent/criminal endeavors (e.g., "How many of your friends have hit or threatened to hit someone without any reason?" And, "How many of your friends have stolen something worth more than $50?"). They are coded as follows: 1 = none of them; 2 = very few of them; 3 = some of them; 4 = most of them; 5 = all of them. Higher scores reflect greater peer delinquency. The scores for the scale measuring the respondents' exposure to delinquent peers at ages 11 to 14 ranged from 8 to 35 with a mean score of 11.6 and a standard deviation of 4.1 (Cronbach's coefficient α = 0.79). The scores for the scale measuring the respondents' exposure to deviant peers at the ages of 15 to 18 had a range of 8 to 35 with a mean of 13.5 and a standard deviation of 4.8 (Cronbach's coefficient α = 0.85).

Analysis

Various multiple regression models were run to assess the age-graded effects of the various independent variables on violent and nonviolent offending during young adulthood. With respect to model specification, first, both violent and nonviolent offending in Wave VII were regressed onto Wave I strain and social support with controls for exposure to delinquent peers in Wave I, gender, race, and economic disadvantage. Measures of contemporaneous strain and social support were subsequently added to the models.[1]

[1] Originally, social control variables were included in the models; however, collinearity diagnostics run using SYSTAT revealed several multicollinear relationships among the social control variables. Tolerance, Eigenvalues, condition indicies, and auxiliary regression models were run to establish which variables were damaged by collinearity (see Wilkinson et al., 1996 for a complete discussion on collinearity diagnostics using SYSTAT). Considering that the primary focus of this chapter is the dynamics between

In these models, we used a conservative approach to testing these relationships. Some analysts might not control for Wave VII strain and social support because individual factors such as strain and social support are likely to be correlated over time. In other words, by controlling for Wave VII strain and social support we might inadvertently be controlling out some of the effects of Wave I or Wave V strain or social support.

Findings

Multiple regression models of the relationship between Wave VII violent and nonviolent behavior and Wave I strain and social support are displayed in Table 4.4. The analysis suggests that early adolescent strain did not have significant effects on violent offending in early adulthood (see Table 4.4). Early adolescent social support was negatively associated with violence in early adulthood, though the relationship was marginal and became statistically significant when a control for contemporaneous social support was applied. Early strain was positively and significantly associated with early adult nonviolent criminality and this effect was stable across a variety of model specifications.

In testing the question of whether social support mediated the effects of early strain on later violent and nonviolent offending, interaction terms were added to the regression models (see Table 4.5). We found that late adolescent social support mediated the effects of Wave I strain on violent behavior in young adulthood. We also found that early adolescent social support was a significant mediator of the effects of Wave I strain on later nonviolent offending. Because there was no significant interaction between early social support and later strain, we believe that the proper interpretation is likely to be that social support alleviates the effects of strain and not that strain reverses the effects of social support.

To convey the meaning of the interaction coefficients, we divided the sample into subjects who were high (based on the 90th percentile) or low (based on the 10th percentile) in early adolescent strain and social support at Waves I and V (see Table 4.6). While the direct effect of strain on violence was not statistically significant, the table shows that individuals in the high strain group reported, on average, more than twice as many violent acts as

---

strain, social support, and offending in young adulthood, both of the control variables for social control were removed from the models. Further testing indicated that the removal of the social control variables resolved the problem of collinearity. One outlier was removed because of an exceptionally high value for violent offending in Wave VII.

TABLE 4.4   The Relationship between Wave VII Violent Behavior and Nonviolent Behavior and Wave I Strain and Social Support. Partial *t* Values (*p* Values in Parenthesis)

Independent Variables	Violent Offending			Nonviolent Offending		
	Model 1	Model 2	Model 3	Model 1	Model 2	Model 3
Strain Wave I	1.03	1.32	0.27	2.19*	2.21*	2.23*
(Early adolescence)	(.30)	(.19)	(.79)	(.03)	(.03)	(.02)
Social support Wave I	−1.73+	−1.88+	−2.21*	−1.84+	−1.92+	−1.75+
(Early adolescence)	(.08)	(.06)	(.03)	(.07)	(.06)	(.08)
Exposure to delinquent	1.16	0.60	0.29	0.39	−0.37	0.55
Friends Wave I	(.25)	(.55)	(.77)	(.70)	(.71)	(.58)
Gender	−3.77**	−3.54**	−3.50**	−2.41*	−2.62**	−2.11*
	(.00)	(.00)	(.00)	(.02)	(.01)	(.04)
SES Wave VII	1.06	0.68	1.59	−0.10	−0.03	0.03
	(.29)	(.50)	(.11)	(.92)	(.98)	(.98)
Race	0.52	−0.41	0.92	−0.19	−0.08	0.02
	(.88)	(.68)	(.36)	(.85)	(.94)	(.99)
Strain at Wave VII		0.54			−0.62	
		(.59)			(.54)	
Social support Wave VII			1.21			0.02
			(.23)			(.98)
R^2	0.05	0.04	0.05	0.03	0.03	0.03
n	569	542	497	606	576	532

$+ p \leq .10; * p \leq .05; ** p \leq .01.$

those in the low strain group. Individuals who reported high levels of strain in early adolescence and low levels of social support in late adolescence committed more violent offenses (0.99) during young adulthood than individuals who were high in social support and high in strain at those times (0.70; see Table 4.6). In other words, strain in early adolescence had a greater effect on later violence when subjects had low levels of social support in later adolescence. In this table, though, it is clear that social support does not eliminate the effects of strain; high strain, high social support subjects report more violent acts than low strain, high social support individuals do. Overall, it appears that while social support does not eliminate the effects of strain on violence, individuals who are high in strain and high in social support are better off than individuals who are high in strain and low in social support.

As the findings at the bottom of Table 4.6 show, adolescents who had experienced a high number of stressful life events in early adolescence had

TABLE 4.5 The Interaction between Strain and Social Support and Wave VII Violent Behavior and Nonviolent Behavior. Partial t Values (p Values in Parenthesis)

Independent Variables	Violent Offending			Nonviolent Offending		
	Model 1	Model 2	Model 3	Model 4	Model 5	Model 6
Strain Wave I (Early adolescence)	1.72+ (.09)	1.58 (.12)		2.79** (.01)	1.63+ (.10)	
Social support Wave I (Early adolescence)	−1.86+ (.06)		−2.08* (.04)	−1.93* (.05)		−1.82+ (.07)
Strain Wave V (Late adolescence)			1.32 (.19)			1.09 (.28)
Social support Wave V (Late adolescence)		0.30 (.77)			−0.42 (.67)	
Exposure to delinquent Friends Wave I	0.62 (.54)	0.57 (.57)	0.26 (.80)	−0.35 (.73)	0.49 (.62)	−0.04 (.97)
Gender	−3.52** (.00)	−3.85** (.00)	−3.45** (.00)	−2.58** (.01)	−2.26* (.02)	−2.20* (.03)
SES Wave VII	0.62 (.53)	0.77 (.44)	0.69 (.49)	−0.10 (.92)	0.30 (.77)	0.19 (.85)
Race	−0.50 (.62)	−0.12 (.91)	−0.33 (.74)	−0.05 (.96)	0.53 (.59)	0.13 (.90)
Strain at Wave VII	0.66 (.51)	0.92 (.36)	0.33 (.74)	−0.45 (.65)	0.09 (.92)	−0.99 (.32)
Strain Wave I * Social support Wave I	−1.76+ (.08)			−2.50** (.01)		
Strain Wave I * Social support Wave V		−3.32** (.00)			−0.42 (.67)	
Social support Wave I * Strain Wave V			−0.75 (.46)			0.97 (.33)
R^2	0.05	0.06	0.05	0.04	0.02	0.03
n	542	526	516	576	563	548

$+ p \leq .10; * p \leq .05; ** p \leq .01.$

nonviolent criminality scores more than three times that of their low-strain counterparts, if they had low social support in early adolescence. By contrast, early adolescents who had high social support not only had much lower scores on nonviolent criminality when they reached young adulthood, but differences between those who had experienced many stressful life events and those who had experienced few disappear.

With regard to the timing of strain and social support (early adolescent vs. late adolescent), neither strain nor social support in late adolescence

TABLE 4.6   Interaction Effects: Predicted Values for
Violent Criminality in Wave VII

	Strain wave I (Early adolescence)	
Predicted Values for Violent Criminality in Wave VII		
Social support Wave V: (Late adolescence)	Low	High
Low	0.39	0.99
High	0.32	0.70
Predicted Values for Nonviolent Criminality in Wave VII		
Social support wave I: (Early adolescence)	Low	High
Low	2.41	7.94
High	0.73	−0.09

(Wave V) appeared to have any direct effect on offending in young adult-hood. This finding is consistent with the hypothesis that early adolescent strain or trauma is likely to have a more significant long-term effect on behavior than that experienced in late adolescence. But the interaction effects are not conclusive about the optimal timing of social support if it were used to combat the effects of strain. The results for violence suggest that social support experienced in the late teenage years was most helpful (this conclusion is tentative); the results for nonviolence suggest that social support experienced in early adolescence was clearly associated with reductions in the effects of strain.

Conclusions

Our findings support the proposition that early adolescent strain has a direct effect on later nonviolent but not violent conduct. We anticipated that traumatic strain would be most predictive of serious or violent criminality, but it was not. It is possible that limitations of our analyses on this topic disguise the effects. First, it is possible that in the context of a normal sample of youths it requires very significant traumatic strain—either very intense or chronic—to cause persistent criminality. Although our sample did report some fairly significant stressors—such as parent deaths, divorce and the like—the number of subjects with high enough levels of "strain" to cause severe antisociality may have been too few to detect this effect. It is also possible that our sample, which consisted of a nationally representative group of young persons, did not contain enough individuals committing serious violent offenses to detect small effects. Lauritsen (1998, 1999) warns that self-reported involvement in crime declined substantially over time in the NYS regardless of subject's age and that although these measures of delinquency may be reliable for studying between-individual differences in crime, they may lack reliability necessary for studying change over time.

An important finding, we believe, is the consistent negative association between social support and later offending and its interaction with strain in our models. Considering our empirical test was conservative and controlled for contemporaneous effects of social support and strain, this finding suggests great promise for a potential, practical source of intervention. Social support clearly mediated the effects of early adolescent strain on later non-violent offending, reducing the predicted number of offenses substantially. While the comparison of violent offenses was less dramatic, subjects in our sample with high strain and low social support also reported the highest number of these. The fact that social support applied during adolescence might mitigate the effects of strain on future offending, encourages optimism for prevention efforts targeted at persistent offending.

We believe that more attention to the role of traumatic strain in the etiology of serious and persistent criminality is desirable. Case studies of very serious offenders almost uniformly discuss extensive trauma and abuse in the childhood histories of the most serious offenders. Of course, many non-criminal individuals have also experienced significant stressors in their lives. Thus, research attention to the types of trauma or strain that are associated with persistent offending would be very helpful in identifying at-risk individuals. Further, it is important for us to explore the timing of those stressors. It is unlikely that trauma or stressors applied late in adolescence would have the impact on long-term behavior that those endured in early adolescence or childhood would. In our work, we found weak effects for early adolescent strain on property offending in young adulthood, but no effect of late adolescent strain. Using a sample of individuals with a greater number of traumatic experiences and more serious criminal activity might allow researchers to identify the ages at which risk of stress-related effects are highest, if they exist. Thus, more longitudinal research on high-risk samples could be extremely useful for developing targeted interventions and, ultimately, reducing serious crime.

In spite of the fact that violent crime has been declining in the United States, there are still more than 16,000 homicides, 400,000 robberies and 800,000 aggravated assaults reported to police annually. Many of these are perpetrated by the thousands of individuals exhibiting patterns of very serious crime. Current research and theory make it difficult to identify these individuals in adolescence. The general theory, for example, suggests that low self-control is established very early in life–but information documenting "self-control" is not readily available to potential intervenors. Moffitt's proposition that persistent offending results from a combination of neuropsychological deficits and adverse environments is very instructive, but this information, too, may be unavailable to school or social service or criminal justice authorities who might have the ability to step in if they believe that a young person is at risk for serious behavioral problems. Case studies of serious offenders often suggest that they have endured significant abuse and trauma—in some cases barbaric treatment. Certainly, we already know that prevention of child abuse could help us reduce crime. But other indicators of strain and trauma, such as parent death, divorce, multiple moves, and so on, might be easily ascertained markers for future likelihood of persistent criminal behavior. Research that identifies these markers might help agencies justify the targeting of significant resources for high-risk cases. Not only might we ameliorate the very difficult and miserable lives of many of the nation's children, but we might have the added effect of reducing crime and its costs and associated misery as well.

CHAPTER 5

Developmental Trajectories, Stressful Life Events, and Delinquency*

TIMOTHY O. IRELAND, CRAIG J. RIVERA,
AND JOHN P. HOFFMANN

Quite some time ago, Marvin Wolfgang and colleagues (1972) began a discussion regarding chronic offenders. In their 1945 cohort study of Philadelphia-born males, they found that approximately 6% of the birth cohort was responsible for a majority of serious delinquency arrests, and this basic finding has been replicated with other data (e.g., Hamparian, Schuster, Dinitz, & Conrad, 1978; Shannon, 1978). In subsequent research, that followed a random sample of the original 1945 cohort into adulthood, Wolfgang et al. (1987) discovered that "half the chronic juvenile offenders had at least four adult arrests" and the "dominant finding...is that nondelinquent careers were likely to be followed by noncriminal careers, and delinquent careers were likely to be followed by criminal careers" (pp. 33–34). This pattern of continuing criminal involvement into adulthood has been replicated with the 1958 Philadelphia cohort (e.g., Kempf, 1990) as well as other samples. However, much of the research relies upon either official data or retrospective

* An earlier version of this text was presented at the annual meetings of the American Society of Criminology, 2006 in Los Angeles, California.

data among institutionalized samples (Dunford & Elliott, 1984; Piquero, Farrington, & Blumstein, 2003a).

Dunford and Elliott (1984), using self-report data from the National Youth Survey, revealed that in all likelihood serious chronic offending is more pervasive than arrest data indicate. Using a fairly narrow definition of chronic offending that included high-rate, persistent offending, Dunford and Elliott identified approximately 15% of the sample as chronic offenders. Thornberry et al. (1995) also relied on self-reported involvement in crime and identified approximately 15% of the Rochester Youth Development Study (RYDS) sample as chronic violent offenders during adolescence (between 7th/8th grade and 10th/11th grade). These chronic violent offenders were responsible for 75% of all violent delinquency reported in the Rochester sample (the Denver Youth Survey data generally replicated this distribution).

Furthermore, Thornberry et al. (1995) discovered that these chronic violent offenders were far more involved in property crime, public disorder, status offenses, drug sales, and alcohol and marijuana use when compared to nonchronic violent offenders or nonviolent offenders. The chronic violent offenders were also more likely to drop out of school, own a gun for protection, belong to a gang, be sexually active, and experience teenage parenthood (see also Huizinga, Loeber, Thornberry, & Cothern, 2000).

Therefore, the research from the Philadelphia cohort and from the Program of Research on the Causes and Correlates of Delinquency (Rochester, Denver, and Pittsburgh) using different sampling techniques and different measurement strategies, and drawing data from different generations, reached the same conclusion: a small proportion of adolescent offenders are responsible for a majority of the crime committed by the cohort.

Along similar lines, Blumstein and colleagues (1986) focused efforts on understanding and exploring the concept of the criminal career. A recent review of the literature on criminal careers reveals the powerful effect that this conceptualization of offending has had upon the discipline of criminology (Piquero et al., 2003a). Furthermore, the notion of a chronic offender "is one of the key foundations of the criminal career paradigm and its resultant policies" (Piquero et al., 2003a, p. 462). The basic premise of the criminal career paradigm is that a criminal career has a beginning (i.e., onset), a middle (e.g., persistence, escalation in frequency and severity, specialization) and an end (i.e., desistance)—much like any other career trajectory. Much debate has surrounded the notion of a criminal career, but in conjunction with research from the Philadelphia cohort studies as well as self-report studies, the high-rate offender (career criminal) whose behavior persists over time is at the very core of the criminal career paradigm and life-course criminology.

Practically speaking, if one could identify the causes and correlates of high-rate offending then programs and policies could be implemented to reduce crime and to correct or incapacitate the high-rate offenders. In addition, given the findings from the Program of Research on the Causes and Correlates of Delinquency, identification and correction of high-rate violent offenders during adolescence could have desirable consequences for a litany of other social problems including teenage parenthood and premature departure from school. Nevertheless, as Piquero et al. (2003a) point out..."predictive classifications (to identify incipient chronic offenders) have been fraught with problems including a high false positive rate" (p. 470).

As these discussions and debates regarding identification of high rate offenders and the description of offending patterns began to unfold, theoreticians began to develop taxonomies to help explain the different patterns of offending. For example, Moffitt (1993) argued for two distinct developmental trajectories for offending patterns—the life-course persistent and the adolescence limited. Generally, the life-course-persistent offender starts early with antisocial, aggressive tendencies in childhood and his or her antisocial behavior remains stable well into adulthood. The adolescence-limited offender, on the other hand, has later onset of offending, a shorter duration of offending, and desists by early adulthood. Moffitt's two types of offender clusters significantly contributed to the foundation of contemporary developmental criminology and remain central to much of the contemporary research into persistent problem behavior (see also Loeber, Stouthamer-Loeber, Huizinga, & Thornberry, 1999; Patterson, DeBaryshe, & Ramsey, 1989).

Capturing the Unfolding of Delinquent Behavior

In recent years, newly developed methodologies have facilitated elaborations of Moffitt's original classification scheme. For example, Nagin (1999) described a statistical procedure—group-based trajectory modeling—for analyzing developmental trajectories that is "well suited to analyzing questions about developmental trajectories that are inherently categorical—do certain types of people tend to have distinctive developmental trajectories" (p. 140) (see also Land & Nagin, 1996; Nagin, 2005; Nagin & Land, 1993; Nagin & Tremblay, 2005). Estimating developmental trajectories takes full advantage of longitudinal data. The procedure estimates dynamic measures that unfold over the life course, rather than static measures from one point in time or averaged across time.

Ensuing utilization of group-based trajectory modeling has identified at least four and as many as seven different trajectories of adolescent and adult offending patterns, and many recent studies have focused on estimating these behaviorally based developmental trajectories (e.g., Bushway, Thornberry, & Krohn, 2003; Chung, Hill, Hawkins, Gilchrist, & Nagin, 2002; Wiesner & Capaldi, 2003).

Some recent research not only has identified multiple behavioral trajectories, but has also begun to consider predictors and consequences of being, for example, on a chronic delinquency trajectory. This line of research has unfolded in three different ways: dynamic independent variables predicting static dependent variables (e.g., Broidy, Nagin et al., 2003); static independent variables predicting dynamic dependent variables (e.g., Chung et al., 2002; Nagin & Tremblay, 2001a; Tremblay, Nagin, Seguin et al., 2004; Wiesner & Capaldi, 2003; Wiesner & Windle, 2004); and dynamic independent variables predicting dynamic dependent variables (e.g., Brame, Nagin, & Tremblay, 2001; Nagin & Tremblay, 2001a).

Dynamic Independent Constructs

Broidy, Nagin et al. (2003) explored homotypic and heterotypic continuity using six different longitudinal data sets from three different countries. They used Nagin and Tremblay's (2001a) definition of heterotypic continuity: "...the manifestation over time of a latent individual trait in different but analogous behaviors" (p. 18). Homotypic continuity, on the other hand, is a behavioral pattern over time that manifests as behaviors that are more similar than different, for example physical aggression in childhood and violence during adolescence. Broidy, Nagin et al. (2003) identified multiple trajectories for physical aggression during childhood, and found that, at least for boys, being on a chronic trajectory for physical aggression during childhood significantly increased the risk for violent delinquency in adolescence (homotypic continuity) as well as nonviolent delinquency (heterotypic continuity).

Dynamic Dependent Constructs

Most of the literature has considered the relationship between dynamic dependent constructs and fairly static independent constructs in an attempt to ascertain whether "predictor variables have uniform or specific effects on different trajectories of offending" (Chung et al., 2002, p. 62). For example, Tremblay, Nagin, Seguin et al. (2004), using data collected from a sample of 504 children during early childhood, identified three trajectories for physical aggression. The first group was comprised of those displaying little or no physical aggression over time. The second group started at a low level of aggression but slowly escalated in physical aggression during the course of the study. The final group was physically aggressive in early childhood and remained on a high and rising physically aggressive trajectory. Tremblay, Nagin, Seguin et al. (2004) found that having young siblings, having low income, having a young mother who is antisocial and smoked during the pregnancy, as well as having a mother suffering from postpartum depression all increased the risk of being on the high, physically aggressive trajectory in early childhood compared to the other two trajectories. Family dysfunction and maternal coercive parenting also increased the likelihood that a young child would be on the high, increasing physical aggression trajectory.

While Tremblay, Nagin, Seguin et al. (2004) considered childhood physical aggression, Wiesner and Windle (2004), using data from the Middle Adolescent Vulnerability Study, estimated six different delinquent trajectories covering a period from approximately age 15.5 to age 17. They identified the resulting trajectories as (1) rare offenders (50.0% of the sample); (2) moderate late peakers (19.6%); (3) high-level chronics (6.4%); (4) decreasers (5.2%); (5) high late peakers (8.9%); (6) moderate level chronics (10.0%). To consider whether selected covariates discriminated among trajectories, Wiesner and Windle (2004) used multinomial logistic regression and excluded the high-level chronics as the reference category.

In general, those subjects classified as rare offenders or moderate late peakers (approximately 70% of the sample) were significantly less likely than those on the high-level chronic trajectory to be male, to have poor academic achievement, to have low social support from family, to experience stressful life events, and to use alcohol or other substances. However, these covariates did not differentiate the high late peakers, the decreasers, or the moderate level chronics from the high level chronics.

Dynamic Independent and Dependent Constructs

Additional research using the group-based trajectory estimates has considered dual or joint trajectory models. In particular, "The joint trajectory model advances conventional approaches...by providing the capability to examine the linkages between the dynamic unfolding of the two behaviors over the entire period of observation (Nagin & Tremblay, 2001a, p. 20).

For example, Nagin and Tremblay (2001a) used the dual trajectory method to consider the relationship between childhood oppositional behavior and adolescent property offending with longitudinal data from a Montreal based prospective study. First, univariate trajectories were estimated for both time-varying constructs. A four-trajectory solution was arrived at for childhood oppositional behavior. One of the four trajectories of childhood oppositional behavior was labeled as chronic oppositional behavior and consisted of approximately 5% of the sample.

A six-trajectory solution fit the adolescent property offending data best (two chronic trajectories—medium and high, two low but rising trajectories, a low trajectory, and a declining trajectory). Conditional probabilities were than calculated. The majority of the low opposition children were assigned to the low adolescent property delinquency trajectory (53%), compared to approximately 20% of the chronic oppositional children who ended up on the low adolescent property delinquency trajectory. Conversely, approximately 30% of the chronic oppositional children were assigned to a chronic property trajectory during adolescence "whereas for the low-oppositional group this probability was only .03" (Nagin & Tremblay, 2001a, p. 26).

Brame, Nagin et al. (2001) considered the relationship between physical aggression in childhood and adolescent self-reported violent offending also using the dual trajectory method. First, separate trajectories for childhood aggression (a three trajectory model) and adolescent violence (a four trajectory model) were estimated. Approximately 20% of the sample was assigned to the chronic, high aggression group Approximately 5% of the subjects were classified as having high chronic aggression during adolescence. Dual trajectories were then estimated that considered both childhood and adolescent aggression. A seven-group model best fit the data. Based upon the estimated joint trajectories, Brame, Nagin et al., (2001, p. 509) find "a general tendency to transition to less physical aggression" irrespective of the level of childhood aggression. Nevertheless, chronically aggressive children are more likely to be in the adolescent high chronic aggressive group (13%) than are those in the childhood low aggression group (2%). Finally, "the analysis suggests that adolescent initiation of high levels of sustained physical aggression among those without childhood aggression is a rare event" (Brame, Nagin et al., 2001, p. 509).

Summary

Analyses exploring group-based trajectories takes full advantage of longitudinal data to understand how delinquency and its covariates may unfold over the life course. However, much of the work in the arena of chronic offending has remained descriptive in nature—describing onset, how much, how often, what types of offenses, and desistance. As a result, theory building in criminology has spent much time working to understand the dynamics of the dependent variable, yet little focus has been directed at the potential dynamic characteristics of independent variables and what such dynamic measures might mean for understanding delinquent or criminal involvement (for exceptions, see Brame, Nagin et al., 2001; Broidy, Nagin et al., 2003; Nagin & Tremblay, 2001a).

For example, Ireland (2002) considered the importance of timing of substantiated maltreatment and whether the timing of maltreatment in the life course matters in predicting delinquency during adolescence. Rather than relying upon a static measure of maltreatment, Ireland et al. (2002) introduced a modicum of change into the measurement of maltreatment and the result was simultaneously surprising and intriguing. Although a static ever/never measure of maltreatment consistently predicted a variety of adolescent delinquency outcomes, a more dynamic measure that took into consideration when the maltreatment started and when it stopped resulted in findings that suggested that the association between delinquent behavior and maltreatment occurring in adolescence was significantly stronger than that for maltreatment that was restricted to childhood only.

Of particular interest here is to join the ideas surrounding offending trajectories to a theoretical foundation that may facilitate our understanding of why some adolescents remain nonoffenders, whereas others become chronic offenders, and still others experience either reductions or increases in delinquent behavior during adolescence and early adulthood. Integral to our exploration of dynamic measures of the dependent variable is also our exploration of dynamic measures of the independent variable—with a basic question being addressed: does a more dynamic measure of the independent variable of interest better predict a dynamic measure of chronic delinquency than does a static measure of the independent variable?

We assess this general hypothesis using a specific theoretical framework that has consistently maintained the need for more dynamic measures of causal factors when predicting delinquent behavior—general strain theory (GST, Agnew, 1992). However, it is conceivable that any number of alternative theoretical models could utilize the strategy espoused here, as long as the selected theory recognizes the possibility of state dependence rather than an exclusive focus on persistent heterogeneity (Piquero et al., 2003a).

Theoretical Framework

Robert Agnew (1992) made a significant theoretical contribution to criminology that focuses attention on individual-level experiences and how those experiences increase or decrease the risk for criminal involvement. At the core of GST are aversive stimuli or strains, and how such strains increase the risk of delinquent activity. Agnew identified three broad categories of aversive stimuli: (a) blockage of positively valued goals, (b) negative stimuli, (c) loss of positive stimuli. He also provided a strategy to operationalize these constructs in several subsequent articles designed to test several major GST propositions (e.g., Agnew & White, 1992).

Blockage of Positively Valued Goals

Agnew argues that traditional strain (i.e., Cloward & Ohlin, 1960; Cohen, 1955; Merton, 1938) represents one facet of a more general type of strain that he refers to as blockage of positively valued goals. Also placed under the umbrella of blockage of positively valued goals is strain in the form of disjunctions between "expectations and actual achievement" and disjunctions between "just/fair outcomes and actual outcomes." The development of this dimension of strain continues to evolve with the identification of goal blockage in terms of masculinity and autonomy goals as well as economic goals (Agnew, 2001). An example of blockage of positively valued goals is a student who wants to make a lot of money but is currently failing high school (Hoffmann & Ireland, 2004).

Negative Stimuli

Agnew's (1992, 2001) second broad category of strain emphasizes "relationships in which others present the individual with noxious or negative stimuli." Noxious stimuli cover a broad spectrum of aversive events and situations that present an individual with unwanted or deleterious stimuli. Negative stimuli include persistent experiences or situations such as child abuse and neglect, excessively punitive parents, and daily hassles. Noxious stimuli (Agnew, 1992, 2001) include, in addition to aversive situations or environments, specific negative life events. Types of negative life events considered by Agnew as noxious stimuli include divorce, remarriage, relocation, and criminal victimization (Agnew, 1992, 2001; Agnew & White, 1992). Hoffmann and Cerbone (1999), for example, used a scale of stressful life events to tap into noxious stimuli in their test of negative life events and delinquency escalation.

Loss of Positively Valued Stimuli

Agnew (1992) refers to his third category of strain as "the removal or anticipated removal of positively valued stimuli" (p. 49). Agnew implicates research related to stress as the primary support for this type of strain. He suggests that "…numerous examples of such loss can be found in the inventories of stressful life-events" (Agnew, 1992, p. 57). An example of loss of positive stimuli might be the departure of a valued teacher/mentor from a school district (Hoffmann & Ireland, 2004).

Strain and Delinquency

The effect of these different dimensions of strain on delinquency is influenced, in part, by the duration, frequency, and recency of strains, as well as the actual number of strains or stressors that converge upon the individual (Agnew, 1992). Therefore, one broad overarching theoretical argument raised by Agnew (1992) is that the timing and duration of these experienced strains matter in terms of emotional, psychological, and behavioral development. For example, those stresses or strains that are more proximal, contemporary, or ongoing are expected to be more detrimental to development (specifically negative behavioral outcomes like delinquency and drug use) than strains that are more distal, less contemporary, or sporadic in nature (Hoffmann & Cerbone, 1999).

Furthermore, Agnew (1992) argued that in conjunction with recency, the duration of the experienced strain is also important in understanding any negative behavioral consequences. He states, "Much theory and data from the equity and stress literatures suggest that events of long duration (chronic stressors) have a greater impact on a variety of negative psychological outcomes" (p. 65) compared to those of a short duration or a sporadic nature. Therefore, what Agnew proposes in his theoretical model is strain as a dynamic construct rather than a static construct. The simultaneous consideration of recency and duration has remained largely unexplored within the framework of GST, and yet the timing and duration of experienced strain remains a central argument of the entire perspective.

Like much analysis in criminology, we are constrained in our assessment of the dynamic relationship between strain and delinquency by the available data to explore this question. Consequently, our test here of GST cannot be considered a wholesale examination of the perspective. As a result, we are not able to consider all three dimensions of strain in our analysis; however, we do utilize measures of stressful life events that assess both noxious stimuli (as events) as well as loss of positive stimuli.

Generally, research focusing on how stressors are related to antisocial behavior has adopted one of two broad theoretical orientations. One orientation referred to as the developmental perspective "suggests that youths who have experienced *a traumatic event* of sufficient magnitude, such as child physical abuse, may experience long-term, negative consequences—psychological, social, and behavioral—that continue and sometimes worsen in adolescence and adulthood" (Maschi, 2006, p. 59). Research tends to support this position (e.g., Ireland & Widom, 1994). An alternative view is the cumulative risk perspective that argues "that youths who experience an accumulation of negative or stressful life events, such as parental divorce or school suspension, increase their risk of engaging in juvenile delinquency" (Maschi, 2006, p. 59). Therefore, this perspective suggests that a single event may not typically alter the life course, but rather altered trajectories arise from an accumulation of stressors over time. Empirical support exists for this perspective as well and findings are consistent with the GST framework (e.g., Hoffmann & Cerbone, 1999). Therefore, the stress literature in general has considered stressful life events as either static—a traumatic event, or dynamic—accumulation of stressful life events over time. Here our focus is on the dynamic conceptualization of stressful life events and how the dynamic nature of stressful life events has not been fully examined in previous research on the link between stressful life events and delinquency.

Summary of Research

GST Cross-sectional Studies

A series of recent publications utilize cross-sectional data to assess the relationship between various dimensions of experienced strain and self-reported delinquency (e.g., Broidy, 2001; Hoffmann & Su, 1997; Jang & Johnson, 2003). Cross-sectional results generally indicate that delinquency is influenced by aversive events or loss of positively valued stimuli. Although cross-sectional data allows for the consideration of a "recency" effect, the design of cross-sectional studies prohibits the development of dynamic measures of chronic strain.

Longitudinal Studies

Several longitudinal studies have also shown a significant relationship between experiencing negative or stressful life events (negative stimuli and loss of positive stimuli) and self-reported delinquency (e.g., Agnew & White, 1992; Aseltine, Gore, & Gordon, 2000; Eitle, Gunkel, & Van Gundy, 2004; Hoffmann & Cerbone, 1999; Hoffmann & Miller, 1998; Kim, Conger,

Elder, & Lorenz, 2003; Paternoster & Mazerolle, 1994; Wiesner & Windle, 2004). However, only three of these studies consider strain experienced over time—Hoffmann and Cerbone (1999), Kim et al. (2003), and Eitle et al. (2004). Eitle et al. (2004) created a cumulative stressful life events scale that assessed all negative life events that occurred before age 12. The cumulative stressful life events scale was retrospective, and in multivariate models the measure was only marginally related to gang membership ($p < .10$). Kim et al. (2003) argued that it is likely that stressful life events and delinquency are reciprocally related such that stressful life events increases the risk for emotional and behavioral problems (social condition hypothesis), and such problems increase the subsequent risk for stressful life events (social selection hypothesis). They used five waves of data collected on adolescents. At each wave, stressful life events were assessed with 25 questions about negative events in the past year. Behavioral problems were measured with self-reported delinquency scales and each respondent was asked to report on delinquent involvement over the preceding year. Emotional problems were measured with the SCL-90R, and both the depression and the anxiety subscale were used in the analysis. Kim et al., (2003) found that stressful life events and delinquency behaviors were reciprocally related over time and so also were stressful life events and internalizing behaviors. They conclude "stressful life events and adolescent maladjustment can be thought of as both causes and effects over time" (Kim et al., 2003, p. 139). Hoffmann and Cerbone (1999) used a multilevel growth curve model to examine the longitudinal impact of stressful life events on delinquency. Using prospective, longitudinal data they found that an increase in stressful life experiences was accompanied, contemporaneously, by increases in delinquency.

Even so, none of these studies utilize fully dynamic measures of stress. Eitle et al. (2004) measure the total number of stressful life events before age 12, and Kim et al. (2003) have discrete measures at each wave, but neither study considers stress as a time-varying construct. Hoffmann and Cerbone (1999) consider stress as a time-varying covariate of delinquency, but their growth curve analysis considered a single growth curve for delinquency, and did not consider whether there was a chronic stress group, a low stress group, or other various time-varying patterns of stress during adolescence. Furthermore, traditional estimation procedures estimate a relationship between strain at Time 1 and delinquency at Time 2. The lag between the measure of strain and the outcome ranges from 6 months to 3 years, thereby minimizing the likelihood of finding a statistically significant relationship because of the elapsed time between strain and delinquency. Therefore, the accumulation of negative or stressful life events is usually simply an additive measure obtained at one point in time, or is an additive measure obtained cross waves of data collection, and neither of these strategies actually assesses stressful life events as a time-varying covariate.

Here, the proposed analytical strategy draws upon newly evolving statistical strategies, specifically trajectory analysis, that allow for consideration of both the recency and the duration of the independent variable as well as the dependent variable. In other words, instead of having estimates of strain and delinquency at specific points in time, trajectory analysis allows estimation of patterns of experienced strain and involvement in delinquency over a specified time. Therefore, we expect that the more dynamic measure of stressful life events will be a better predictor of the delinquency trajectories than is the more often utilized static measures of stressful life events. More specifically, we predict that when static and dynamic measures of stressful life events are included in the same model, only the dynamic measures will be statistically significant. Further, we predict that individuals on increasing and/or chronic stressful life events trajectories will be more likely to also be on a chronic delinquency trajectory compared to youth following more normative patterns of stressful life events. These two basic hypotheses are consistent with Agnew's (1992) argument that strain is a dynamic process much like delinquency, and that chronic stress or strain may be more behaviorally detrimental (i.e., increased risk for chronic offending) than acute stress or strain.

Data, Measurement, and Methods

Data

The data used in this project come from the Family Health Study (FHS). The FHS uses a longitudinal sample of largely urban youth and their parents. Data were collected in a large upper Midwestern metropolitan area. Data collection began in 1991 and was completed in 1998. The initial design of the study focused on assessing how parental mental health disorders affect adolescent behavior and development. Parents were recruited in a nonrandom fashion from community mental health care facilities and, community centers, neighborhood organizations, and through local advertising. A significant proportion of the final sample included families with parents who were diagnosed with a psychoactive drug disorder (29%) or an affective disorder (23%). The remaining parents in the study did not have a diagnosable mental health disorder (48%). On an annual basis parents and their adolescent children completed a self-administered questionnaire that addressed a number of topics, including stressful life events, psychosocial support systems, health status, drug and alcohol use, and delinquency. A total of 861 adolescents from the sampled families participated in the first year and 814 adolescents participated in each of the annual follow-up data collection efforts (a 95% follow-up rate). These subjects completed self-administered, confidential questionnaires once a year for 7 consecutive years. The sample members were about 51% female and 88% White.

Measurement

Aversive stimuli and loss of positively valued stimuli are operationalized using a stressful life events scale. It is based on 16 possible events reported by the adolescents during each of the 7 years they participated in the study. The life events included incidents of death, illness, or accidents of family or friends, changes in school or residence, and family problems—financial problems, separation, or divorce. The theoretical maximum score for stressful life events at any one wave is therefore 16.

Delinquency is measured by 13 questions that ask about the frequency of involvement over the previous year in each of a variety of offenses ranging from rather minor ones, such as lying about one's age to purchase cigarettes, to rather serious offenses such as gang fights and robbery. Each offense question had a forced choice response set of five categories (0 through 4 where 4 indicates participation in 10 or more item-specific incidents in the past year). The scores for each of the 13 items are summed to yield a total delinquency score for each wave. The theoretical maximum for delinquency in any one wave is therefore 52 (13 $\times$ 4). The alpha reliability coefficients are generally greater than 0.75 for each wave.

Because most previous studies of stressful life events and delinquency have assessed static models, we include one static measure—stressful life events at Wave 1—in the empirical model to compare its predictions of delinquency trajectories to those based on the dynamic measure. We also include as control variables gender (female = 0; male = 1), Caucasian ethnicity (0 = nonwhite, 1 = white), lives with both biological parents (0 = no, 1 = yes), and annual family income (a 12 category measure that ranges from 1 = less than $10,000 to 12 = more than $150,000).

Analysis Strategy

The initial wave of data included adolescents whose ages ranged from 11 to 14, and 7 years later these sampled adolescents were between the ages of 17 and 21. The data were therefore transformed from the sample cohorts to age cohorts. For example, instead of delinquency and stressful life events at Wave 1, Wave 2, and so forth, the analysis involves an assessment of delinquency and stressful life events at age 11, delinquency and stressful life events at age 12, and so forth. This data structure facilitates the use of a nonparametric, group-based technique for estimating developmental trajectories (e.g., Nagin, 1999, 2005; Nagin & Land, 1993). Hence, we estimate separate trajectory models for stressful life events and delinquency, followed by a regression model that assesses the predictive ability of stressful life event trajectories and the other covariates.

The trajectory procedure, which is estimated using the SAS macro developed by Jones and colleagues (2001), models developmental trajectories for variables of interest. Specifically, the procedure identifies distinct groups of subjects demonstrating within-group homogeneity in terms of patterns of offending (or stressful life events) over time, and then models a separate developmental trajectory for each group. The procedure also allows the "direction" of the trajectory to differ for each group, so that some groups may have increasing trajectories, some may be decreasing, and some may even both increase and decrease over the time period under investigation (Nagin, 1999, 2005). Once each respondent in the sample is placed onto a developmental trajectory for both stressful life events and delinquency, we can ascertain the associations between the stress and delinquency trajectories using traditional regression techniques. Since delinquency trajectories may be seen as a categorical response variable, we utilize multinomial logistic regression (Hoffmann, 2004) to estimate the association between delinquency trajectories, stressful life event trajectories, stressful life events at Time 1, and the control variables.

We chose to utilize multinomial logistic regression, as opposed to estimating a joint trajectory model (Nagin, 2005), to examine the links between stress and delinquency trajectories for three primary reasons. First, for each construct this allowed us to "combine" several of the trajectory groups that followed conceptually similar patterns over time before estimating the relationship between stress and delinquency (see below for more detail), thereby simplifying the subsequent modeling. Second, the multinomial regression approach provided more accessible measures of statistical significance for the model parameters and third, this analytical strategy allows for the inclusion of control variables.

Results

Using the PROC TRAJ macro in SAS developed by Jones and colleagues (2001), we estimated the trajectory models for both delinquency and stressful life events. Specifically, the delinquency trajectories were modeled using the zero-inflated Poisson (ZIP) distribution, to account for the larger number of zeroes than would be expected under the regular Poisson distribution. The stressful life events trajectories were modeled using the Poisson distribution.

Model selection involves two decisions—the number of groups and the functional form of each group (e.g., quadratic, linear, etc.). The Bayesian information criterion (BIC) provides an objective criterion to guide model selection, and the model with the smallest absolute BIC value is usually chosen (Nagin, 1999, 2005). However, as has been pointed out (e.g., Nagin, 2005), use of the BIC must be tempered with knowledge of the domain being modeled and practical considerations, such as whether each additional group contains enough subjects and is substantively meaningful. For example, assume we have a general delinquency model with four trajectory groups, one of which is a "flat," low-level trajectory. We then estimate a five group model which winds up simply splitting the one low-level group into two flat, low-level groups, with slightly different intercepts and only a few subjects in the "new" group. Even if the five group model has an improved BIC score, substantive and practical considerations would likely lead to the selection of the four group model.

On the basis of these criteria, a six-group model, with each group having a quadratic functional form, was the best model for general delinquency. A five-group model, with four quadratic and one linear group, was selected as the best model for stressful life events. Figures 5.1 and 5.2 depict the estimated trajectories for delinquency and stressful life events, and Tables 5.1

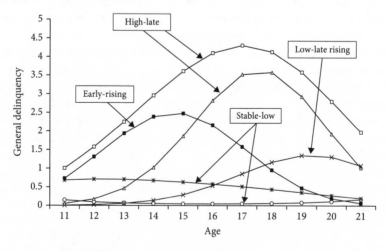

FIGURE 5.1   General delinquency trajectories (estimated).

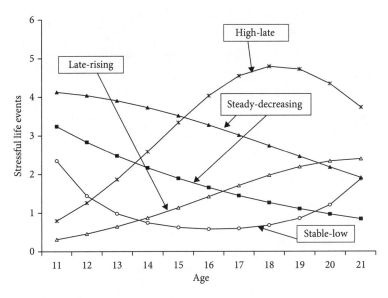

FIGURE 5.2   Stressful life events trajectories (estimated).

and 5.2 provide information on the size and average posterior probability for each trajectory group.[1]

The delinquency trajectories (Figure 5.1) are quite consistent with the groups identified in other data sets (Broidy, Nagin et al., 2003), with stable groups, high increasing groups, and modestly increasing groups. To simplify subsequent modeling, we opted to combine the two "stable-low" groups (a combined 52% of the sample), since each shows stable-low delinquency from ages 11 to 21. This combined group will serve as the reference category in the multivariate analyses to follow, and the dependent variable will be a series of dummy codes comparing each delinquency trajectory—early-rising, low-late rising, high-late—to this stable-low trajectory. Selection of the reference category is somewhat arbitrary as we are primarily concerned with whether time-varying measures of stress improve prediction relative to static

---

[1] Since the trajectory groups identified with this procedure are approximations, and are not actual "preexisting" groups, we cannot be certain to which group an individual truly belongs (Nagin, 1999, 2005). The posterior probability reflects the likelihood that an individual belongs to a particular trajectory group, given his or her actual pattern of behavior or stress over time (Nagin, 1999, 2005), and PROC TRAJ automatically assigns subjects to the group for which they have the highest posterior probability. The average posterior probability reported in Tables 5.1 and 5.2 is simply the average likelihood for all subjects assigned to that group.

TABLE 5.1   Frequencies and Posterior Probabilities for General
Delinquency Trajectory Groups

Trajectory Group	Frequency	Percent	Average Posterior Probability
Stable-low	270	33.1	.77
Stable-low	152	18.6	.66
Low-late rising	179	21.9	.71
Early-rising	70	8.6	.77
High-late	53	6.5	.80
High-late	92	11.3	.79
Total	816	100	

TABLE 5.2   Frequencies and Posterior Probabilities for Stressful Life
Events Trajectory Groups

Trajectory Group	Frequency	Percent	Average Posterior Probability
Stable-low	186	22.8	.76
Late-rising	57	7.0	.76
Steady-decreasing	312	38.2	.74
Steady-decreasing	225	27.6	.74
High-late	36	4.4	.78
Total	816	100	

measures of stress. However, the decision to use the stable-low delinquency trajectory for comparison allows us to examine whether adolescents with more serious delinquency trajectories are more likely to experience higher levels of stress over time compared to stable-low delinquents.

We also combined the two "high-late" groups, resulting in a combined group (18% of the sample) that peaks in late adolescence, and, although decreasing into adulthood, remains at levels above the other trajectories until age 21. This combined trajectory of high-late offending is most closely aligned with the concept of chronic offending. By about age 15 those on the high-late trajectories are the highest rate offenders and their high rate of offending, relative to the other trajectories, persists throughout late adolescence and into early adulthood.

The other groups include a "low-late rising" group (22%) that starts relatively flat and then shows a modest increase in delinquency from approximately age 16 to 19 and by age 21 has one of the highest levels of delinquency; and an "early-rising" group (9%) that displays steady increasing delinquency from age 11 to 15, followed by a steady decrease until age 21, at which point it is at or below the "stable-low" trajectories. This final early-rising group is perhaps the group that best represents Moffitt's (1993) adolescent-limited delinquent.

The stressful life events trajectories (Figure 5.2) show a variety of patterns of stress through the adolescent years indicating that experienced stress is not a static construct, but rather a dynamic process that unfolds over the life course. Again, to simplify the analysis, we opted to combine two groups, labeled "steady-decreasing" in Figure 5.2, since they showed a similar pattern of steady-decreasing exposure to stressful life events from age 11 to 21. Note, however, that each of these groups included adolescents who reported a high number of stressful life events during early adolescence. In fact, among those respondents aged 11 to 13, the adolescents in this combined group were at or above the 75th percentile in the distribution of stressful life events. After combining these two trajectories, we used four life events groups: "stable-low" (23%), which followed a decreasing pattern until age 14 and then remained relatively low and stable through the remainder of adolescence but increased somewhat in early adulthood; "late-rising" (7%), which has among the lowest levels of stressful life events until age 16, but has the second highest stress scores by age 20; "high-late" stress (4%), which achieves a peak at about 18 and then although decreasing remains high relative to the other trajectories into early adulthood; and the combined "steady-decreasing" group (66%) mentioned earlier (see Table 5.2). In the subsequent regression analysis the "stable-low" group is the omitted reference category. This group consistently has among the lowest estimated levels of stressful life events, and actually has the lowest levels of stressful life events during the majority of adolescence (age 14 to 19).

The analysis in Figure 5.2 indicates that, like delinquency, stressful life events unfold over the life course and that static measures at Time 1 would probably misclassify the high stress individuals. For example, those very low on stressful life events at age 11 (the high-late group) turn out to have some of the highest levels of stress by ages 15 and 16, and this persists into early adulthood.

Table 5.3 provides the results of the multinomial logistic regression model designed to predict delinquency trajectories. The model includes controls for gender, ethnicity, whether the individual lives with both biological parents, and family income. Multinomial logistic regression models may be envisioned as a set of binomial logistic regression models that are estimated simultaneously.

First and foremost, our theoretical argument that dynamic measures of stress would be a better predictor of the dynamic measures of delinquency compared to static, more traditional measures of stress, is supported by the results presented in Table 5.3. Across the multinomial models estimated,

TABLE 5.3   Dynamic Versus Static Measures of Stress*

Variables	Coefficient	Standard Error	p-Value
High-Late Delinquency			
Intercept	−2.631	0.460	<0.001
Stress trajectory			
Stress, late-rising	1.589	0.487	0.001
Stress, high-late	1.785	0.553	0.001
Stress, steady-decreasing	1.113	0.335	0.001
Stress, Wave 1	0.025	0.019	0.204
Early Rising			
Intercept	−3.216	0.726	<0.001
Stress trajectory			
Stress, late-rising	1.961	0.707	0.006
Stress, high-late	2.037	0.791	0.010
Stress, steady-decreasing	1.234	0.547	0.024
Stress, Wave 1	0.027	0.023	0.237
Low-Late Rising			
Intercept	−1.228	0.342	<0.001
Stress trajectory			
Stress, late-rising	0.304	0.392	0.438
Stress, high-late	0.223	0.534	0.676
Stress, steady-decreasing	0.124	0.226	0.584
Stress, Wave 1	−0.023	0.022	0.283
BIC	−3418.10		

* Includes controls for gender, ethnicity, family structure, and family income.

the measure of static stress from Wave 1 does not differentiate between the stable-low delinquency trajectory and the early-rising, the low-late rising, or the high-late delinquency trajectories.

In addition, the analysis provides insight into the relationship between high levels of persistent stress (high-late trajectory) and chronic delinquency (high-late trajectory). The top section of Table 5.3 (labeled "High-Late Delinquency") indicates that membership in all three stress groups, relative to the stable-low group (reference group), predicts membership in the high-late delinquency group relative to the stable-low delinquency group. Exponentiating the coefficients suggests that the odds that those in the high-late stress group fall into the combined high-late delinquency group relative to the stable-low delinquency group is six times the odds for those in the reference stress group (OR = 5.96). In other words, individuals whose stress was high and still increasing by age 16 or 17 (high-late) were significantly more likely to be on the high-late delinquency trajectory (chronic) compared to individuals with relatively consistent low levels of stress throughout adolescence.

However, the odds for those in the steady-decreasing stress group are also significantly higher than the excluded group, but their odds ratio is less than that for the high-late stress group (OR = 3.04). Thus, even if they were on a decreasing trajectory, individuals who were still high on stress by age 16 or 17 were also significantly more likely than their low stress counterparts to be on a problematic delinquency trajectory, although the consequences were not as severe as for individuals experiencing high-late levels of stress.

In fact, the stress-delinquency link remains fairly consistent in the comparison between the early-rising delinquents and the stable-low delinquents. Each stress trajectory classification compared to the low-stable stress trajectory indicates increased risk for early-rising delinquency compared to stable-low delinquency. It is interesting to note that being on the high-late stress trajectory as opposed to the low-stable one increases the odds of being on the early-rising as opposed to the stable-low delinquency trajectory by a factor of about 7.5. In other words, individuals whose stress was high and still increasing by age 16 or 17 were not only at increased risk for chronic delinquency, but also for a pattern of delinquent behavior that escalated early in adolescence and decreased by the mid to late teens. Note that these associations persist even after adjusting for the effects of control variables mentioned earlier. Finally, knowing the particular stress trajectory of an individual does not help discriminate between the low-late rising delinquents and the stable-low delinquents.

Therefore, the relationship between stress and delinquency can be captured when both stress and delinquency are measured dynamically rather than statically. Apparently, knowing the level of stress at Time 1 does not help to discriminate among the delinquency trajectories, and in previous research stress at Time 1 likely acted as a proxy (albeit a somewhat inaccurate one) for stress over the developmental time frame under consideration. Additionally, it appears that high-late stress (chronic) increases the risk of being on the most developmentally disruptive delinquency trajectories (i.e., the high-late trajectories and the early-rising trajectory).

Figure 5.3 presents another view of the results by providing a graph with predicted probabilities that are estimated from the model. Note, first, that

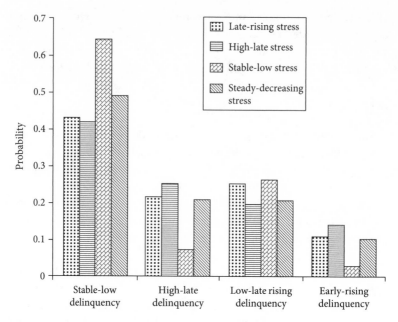

FIGURE 5.3   Probability of delinquency trajectory, by stress trajectory. Family Health Study, 1991–1998.

the stressful life events reference group—low-stable—is most likely found in the stable-low delinquency group: we expect more than 60% of this group to be involved in stable-low delinquency. They are, however, rarely found in the high-late or early-rising delinquency groups. For example, whereas we expect approximately 25% of the high-late stress group to be in the high-late delinquency group, less than 10% of the low-stable stress group is found among the high-late delinquency group. Therefore, as anticipated based on GST, those on chronic stress trajectories during adolescence and early adulthood are also most likely to be on a chronic delinquency trajectory during the same developmental timeframe, and those on a low stable stress trajectory are also most likely to be on a low-stable delinquency trajectory.

Also intriguing is that the group that followed a steady-decreasing pattern of stress over time (the steady-decreasing group) is not infrequently found in the high-late (approximately 21%) and low-late rising (approximately 21%) delinquency groups. As we discuss later, we suspect this reflects the impact of their early exposure to stressful life events. Given their high exposure to various troubling experiences during early adolescence, this likely reflects some residual influence or the persistent effects of early exposure to stressful events.

Discussion

We began this investigation with a straightforward idea. Much effort has been directed at understanding delinquency as a dynamic process—when delinquency starts, how frequent and severe the delinquency is, and when delinquency ends. However, much less attention has been directed at the dynamic nature of possible independent constructs thought to influence the development of delinquency. Thornberry (1987) in his initial statement of interactional theory argued, for example, that "during early adolescent years, the family is the most salient area for social interaction and involvement and, because of this, attachment to parents has a stronger influence on other aspects of the youth's life at this stage then it does at later stages of development" (p. 873). In other words, attachment to parents is not a static structure but rather attachment to parents is likely to ebb and flow over the developmental life course and that ebb and flow may influence the onset, persistence, and desistance of delinquency. Taking the basic idea that independent constructs that influence delinquency may be better operationalized as dynamic rather than static structures, we explore the issue within the context of general strain theory. Agnew (1992) clearly articulated the possibility that experienced strains and stressors are better conceptualized as dynamic constructs that take into consideration when the events occur and how long the events persist, and that those strains that are of longer duration (chronic) and ongoing (recent) are likely to be more influential than strains that are distal and of relatively short duration.

Testing this basic hypothesis, we estimated trajectory models for both delinquency and stressful life events during adolescence from age 11 through age 21. Like previous work on delinquency trajectories we found multiple patterns of delinquency—a total of six trajectories fit the data the best. This finding is quite consistent with other previous work on adolescent delinquency trajectories (e.g., Bushway et al., 2003; Chung et al., 2002; Wiesner & Capaldi, 2003). We next estimated trajectories for stressful life events. Five trajectories fit the data best and indicated that, like delinquency, stressful life events are a time-varying construct that vary not only across individuals, but also over time. In the literature on stressful life events and their impact on antisocial behavior, this represents one of the first attempts at considering stressful life events as a time-varying measure unfolding over time rather than as a static measure.

Next we compared a dynamic to a static measure of stress and concluded that stress as a measure that varies over time better predicts delinquency trajectories than does stress as a static measure assessed at one point in time. In particular, membership in the "high-late" stress group, relative to the "stable-low" group, was a significant predictor of membership in the "high-late" delinquency group (relative to the "stable-low" delinquency group), and the static measure of stress was not statistically significant. Therefore, it seems reasonable in the domain of both theory development and theory testing to begin to consider the relationship between dynamic measures of independent constructs as well as dynamic measures of dependent constructs.

Furthermore, the results have not only general implications for theory development, but also specific implications for GST and chronic offending. As Piquero et al. (2003a) pointed out in their review of the literature on career criminals, it has been exceedingly difficult to identify chronic offenders because the false-positive rate is consistently very high—identifying those who do not meet the criteria of chronic offending as chronic offenders. Yet, as Agnew argued, more dynamic measures of strains and stressors may better capture the relationship between strain and delinquency. We addressed this issue here, and found that a static measure of stress taken at Time 1 could not discriminate between those on relatively malignant delinquency trajectories compared to those on relatively benign delinquency trajectories. However, as indicated in the results, the dynamic measure of stress could discriminate between those on the most severe delinquency trajectories and those in the least severe delinquency trajectories. Furthermore, those exposed to chronic stressful life events (high-late) were also most likely to be on a chronic delinquency trajectory (high-late). Therefore, chronic stress measured dynamically helps discriminate between persistent offenders and low rate offenders.

Nevertheless, there is some indication from the findings that early onset of a high rate of stressful life events may persist in influencing delinquent behavior over time. Our findings indicate that those who experience a high number of stressful life events in early adolescence (age 11) but experience consistently decreasing stressful life events over time are still at increased risk for both early-rising delinquency and high-late adolescent delinquency, compared to those who experienced a relatively low level of stressful life events throughout adolescence. Therefore, it is conceivable that high rates of early stressful life events begin a process of delinquency that is difficult to disrupt even when stressful life events decrease during the adolescent years. However, it should be noted that these groups, although decreasing, still had among the highest levels of stressful life events until approximately age 17.

Also, it is important to note that the "reverse" of this finding is not true—low rates of early stressful life events do not insulate an individual from future delinquency. Youths who had low rates of early stress but whose stress increased throughout adolescence (e.g., the high-late group) were significantly more likely to be on the most problematic delinquency trajectory. Thus, although early levels of stress may have an influence, the dynamic pattern of stress over time is crucial in determining the link with a delinquency career.

Finally, while the stress trajectories help discriminate between high-late delinquency and low-stable delinquency, and early-rising delinquency and low-stable delinquency, the pattern of results indicate (although we did not directly examine this) that there is probably not much difference between the high-late delinquency trajectory and the early-rising delinquency trajectories as they pertain to experienced stress or strain. Yet, it would be valuable to know why, as can be seen in Figure 5.3, a relatively large proportion (compared to the other stress trajectories) of those on the chronic stress trajectory (high-late) experienced early inflated delinquency, but then decreased rapidly to almost no delinquency by early adulthood, while others on the chronic stress trajectory were likely to be classified as chronic offenders (high-late delinquency trajectory). Although this moves beyond the scope of this project, the divergent stress-delinquency trajectories may reflect gender differences in responding to chronic-stress, may reflect variations in social capital, or possibly reflect successful intervention or coping for some who experience chronic (high-late) stress.

There are obviously limitations in the analysis presented here. First, the data used are from a nonprobability sample and as a result it is not clear how generalizable the results are to the population from which the sample was drawn. For example, the majority (52%) of the families sampled have a parent with either a psychoactive drug disorder or a diagnosable mental health disorder. Second, in the delinquency literature there is some indication that delinquency trajectories may unfold differently for males and females. For example, Broidy, Nagin et al. (2003) conducted gender-based analysis when predicting adolescent delinquency from physical aggression trajectories in childhood. While they found a pattern of results suggesting that physical aggression in childhood influenced delinquency among the boys in their samples, they concluded "[t]he prediction results for girls confirmed that girls' involvement in juvenile delinquency is extremely difficult to predict. These null findings are impressive because they were replicated in four distinct samples" (Broidy, Nagin et al., 2003, p. 236). Therefore, although we controlled for gender in the analysis we did not conduct gender-based analysis. It is conceivable that including females in the analysis actually muted some of the effects of stressful life events on delinquency given research that suggests that females are more likely to respond to stressful life events with depressive symptoms rather than delinquency (e.g., Ge, Lorenz, Conger, Elder, & Simons, 1994; Gjerde, Block, & Block, 1988; Hoffmann & Su, 1997; Meadows, Brown, & Elder, 2006) (also see Chapter 10 for a review of the literature on persistent female offending).

Third, although we have found that dynamic measures of stressful life events co-vary with dynamic measures of delinquency we have not untangled the temporal order between the two constructs. GST indicates that stressful life events are the cause and thus we tend to assume that stressful life events increase the risk for high rate offending during adolescence. However, Kim et al. (2003), in considering the reciprocal effects (cross-lagged models instead of contemporaneous models) of stressful life events on externalizing behaviors, found that while stressful life events had a greater impact on externalizing behaviors in early adolescence, in later adolescence externalizing behaviors had a greater impact on stressful life events. We do not address the issue of causation here but instead consider the contemporaneous relationship between stress and delinquency as each unfolds during adolescence. We do recognize that causation—chronic stress causes chronic delinquency, for example—needs to be addressed in future work to provide a more definitive test of the GST hypothesis. However, our failure to explore reciprocal causation does not detract from the observation that stress and delinquency clearly unfold together over time, and that their development is likely intertwined, nor does it detract from the central finding that the dynamic measure of stress is related to delinquency trajectories, but the static measure is not.

Finally, we considered the total number of stressful life events at each age regardless of the actual type of stressor, or the magnitude of the stressor. It is possible to disaggregate the stressors into specific domains and it may be that stressors in one domain (e.g., family) are particularly disruptive while stressors in another domain are relatively benign in terms of their effects on behavior. The same may be argued regarding the perceived magnitude of the stressors. It is quite possible that several of the stressful life events items are objectively stressful, but when the perceptions of stress are taken into account quite the opposite might be true. For example, divorce maybe considered objectively stressful and a negative life event, but the perception may also be that the divorce was a positive event if the departing partner was abusive, and the departure results in the cessation of abuse.

Despite these limitations, we offer an attempt to consider dynamic independent and dynamic dependent constructs simultaneously. We anticipate that this strategy, with improvement by others, should result in several intriguing intellectual and empirical advances for theory building and testing in criminology. In particular, we see important theoretical limitations in the current state of research on developmental trajectories and strongly recommend that the marriage of this research with well established theoretical work in criminology promises to yield fruitful results.

CHAPTER 6

The Effects of Family on Children's Behavioral Difficulties

Paul Millar

An important question in life-course criminology concerns the development of the persistent offender. Since the propensity for the commission of offenses peaks in the late teen years regardless of gender, race, or ethnicity (Gottfredson & Hirschi, 1990), this question is best tackled by looking at children, since the tendencies in question are likely to have formed early in life. Moreover, the importance of family in the production of violent offenders has long been a relatively neglected field of research for criminologists, partly because criminologists focus primarily on criminals, who are, by definition, not young children. It is also possible that there is a reluctance to focus on parents because it is coherent with the organization of criminal justice principles to blame the offender, which would weaken the case for his or her punishment. Yet, this position is hardly defensible since parents and families are responsible for the proper socialization of children into productive citizens in the vast majority of cases. Orphanages or other forms of state care have generally been far less successful in raising healthy productive citizens. It is this fact that can be used to orient research questions in a more positive frame: what is it about families that make them able to successfully socialize most children? Many prominent social theorists argue that parents are the primary socializing agents of society, and it is to this source that we should look for the installation of social policies that have promise to reduce violent crime.

Theoretical Frameworks Addressing the Development of Criminality

An influential theory in the history of criminology is the theory of differential association proposed by Edwin Sutherland (Sutherland & Cressey, 1974). Differential association views the development of criminal tendencies as a cognitive process, whereby criminality is learned through interaction with an intimate reference group. According to Sutherland, the family "plays an exceptionally important role in determining the behaviour patterns which any individual follows" (Sutherland & Cressey, 1974, p. 203). Sutherland assumes no particular predispositions of children and argues that criminal behavior not only requires learning behavior patterns but also attitudes and rationalizations to manage the social moral deficits often involved in criminal behavior. Differential association's proposals—still popular today—argue that the development of criminal tendencies in the individual are a mainly cognitive process. That is, the tendency to use violence, for example, is learned, much in the same way that any other task is learned. In this way the tendency to violence or other forms of criminality is a process of acquisition, similar to the learning of, say, table manners or calculus. Hence differential association stresses the acquisition of certain behaviors as opposed to the suppression of innate or natural tendencies.

A group of social theories, philosophically similar to that of Sutherland, could be characterized as theories of cultural learning through which social class is reproduced through cultural transmission of values that result in children ending up in similar circumstances to their parents, *ceteris paribus*. Perhaps one of the more infamous of these theories is the culture of poverty thesis developed by Oscar Lewis (1961). The *culture of poverty* paradigm suggests that children learn attitudes and values that facilitate the intergenerational transmission of poverty:

> By the time slum children are age six or seven they have usually absorbed the basic values and attitudes of their subculture and are not psychologically geared to take full advantage of changing conditions or increased opportunities which may occur in their lifetime (Lewis, 1968, p. xlv).

According to Lewis, the culture of poverty involves "frequent resort to violence in the settlement of quarrels, frequent use of physical violence in the training of children, wife beating,...relatively little ability to defer gratification and plan for the future" (Lewis, 1961, p. xxvi). Thus, Lewis suggests that characteristics particular to poverty are learned as young children, through the family and that, once instilled, the values and attitudes acquired in this way lead to the child making decisions that result in circumstances of deprivation. Lewis's conception of the socialization process would have the child acquiring greater tendencies to violence and the increasing inability to delay gratification.

Another cultural learning theory is that expressed by Anderson in his "Code of the Streets" (1994). Anderson typologizes cultural values in disadvantaged neighborhoods into either "decent"—consistent with mainstream middle class ideals—or "street" values. Street values authorize violence in a wide range of circumstances so long as a minor provocation (usually characterized as disrespect) is encountered. The code of the street, then, consists of a set of rules that permit the use of violence in a much broader set of circumstances than would otherwise be possible. Since there are many of these rules, violence is more easily employed by those who adhere to these values. Anderson argues that parents with "street" values easily resort to violence when parenting, which then teaches children to resort to violence to solve problems.

Another paradigm that employs ideas similar to Anderson's *code of the street* yet suggests a causal framework limited to the immediate social environment is articulated by Bernard (1990) in his theory of the *subculture of angry aggression*. According to Bernard, angry aggression is a response to psychological arousal, which is in turn a response to a stressful urban environment, low social status and ethnic discrimination, all of which are aggravated by social isolation. These social factors create provocations—irritations and annoyances—that induce arousal that spawns angry aggression, which, as in the *code of the street*, is mediated somewhat by rules in its expression. This theory suggests that there is no effect of parenting, but that angry aggression is the result of a confluence of social factors—an adaptive form of learning where the individual is attempting to reduce arousal responses in the context of a stressful environment.

Another cultural theory explaining behavior is that of Bourdieu (2000). As with Sutherland, Bourdieu assumes no particular predispositions among young children who are taught the social order through the risk of emotion and physical harm in daily practice (Bourdieu, 2000). That is to say, the child's environment is fraught with emotional and physical coercions that affect the child in a way that is not transitory, so that stable dispositions are formed. In this formulation, children bodily (physically and psychologically) incorporate their surroundings and interactions like a kind of memory pad that, over time, forms into a collection of more or less stable dispositions which he calls *habitus*. For Bourdieu, experiences in the family are very important, in particular the experience of violence. Bourdieu proposes a "law of the conservation of violence" whereby "ill-treatment in childhood (in particular, beatings by parents) is linked to increased chances of using violence against others" (Bourdieu, 2000, p. 233). Of course, this idea is not new, numerous authors have proposed a link between child abuse and later aggressive behavior, but Bourdieu's *habitus* includes violence that we would not necessarily categorize as abuse and combines this idea with the development of dispositions, similar in concept to behavioral or psychological traits. This early exposure to violence leads to the development of a series of embodied dispositions—*habitus*—which are stable, although not immutable. The inferred solution to reducing societal violence then, would consequently lie largely in reducing violence against children. This view, like other social and cultural learning theories, suggests that violence is instilled in children rather than a natural propensity that must be socialized away.

Other theorists suggest that human beings are naturally violent and that these tendencies are socialized or "civilized" out of them. For example, Elias (2000) argues that people have natural and functional tendencies to adopt violent strategies for conflict resolution. In this paradigm children develop self-control given a context of a *pacified space*, that is, an environment where the likelihood of violence in daily life is very small. In Elias's formulation, life in premodern society demanded "a constant readiness to fight, and free play of the emotions in defence of one's life or possessions from physical attack" (Elias, 2000, p. 368). Thus, aggression is functional and necessary when violence is a part of everyday life. Life in premodern society depends more on the ability to react instantly with violence at unpredictable moments rather than on capacities of foresight and restraint. Adolescence was a relatively short affair, with adult responsibilities following shortly after puberty. Modern societies, by contrast, require individuals with a high degree of self-control in order to function. Modernization of behavior involves progressively restrained action and feeling, in addition to a transformation from a short- to a long-term perspective in day-to-day thinking, from freely expressed emotions to the repression of emotions in what Elias calls the "civilizing process." The civilizing process is ingrained in childhood, whereby "from earliest youth individuals are trained in the constant restraint and foresight that they need for adult functions" (Elias, 2000, p. 374). This creates a kind of self-supervision of drives and emotions that becomes automatic in most individuals. As society industrializes further, the socialization process becomes more involved, extending adolescence, increasing the suppression of emotion (and therefore also psychological maladjustment) and making self-control more essential for societal functioning. Historical trends in homicide data for European societies appear to bear this out, showing declines in individual lethal violence, which are correlated with modernization (Eisner, 2001). Hence in the framework proposed by Elias, self-control is an essential result of the civilizing process that restrains the natural tendency of humans for emotion and violence; in modern society individuals who lack self-control are those who threaten society the most. While a major orienting concept for Elias was self-control, the application of this concept to the problem of crime was undertaken independently by two American theorists, Michael Gottfredson and Travis Hirschi.

Gottfredson and Hirschi (1990) developed their *general theory of crime* (also referred to as self-control theory) not from the work of Elias or any other social theorist, but from the empirical nature of crime and those who commit it. Gottfredson and Hirschi make the following observations about crime: it provides immediate gratification of desire (criminal acts are—for the most part—easy or simple, exciting, requiring little skill or planning, and result in pain or discomfort for the victim) and most criminal acts are shortsighted in terms of their benefits (even a minimum wage job provides more income than most street crime). Moreover, Gottfredson and Hirschi note that individual differences in the propensity to commit crime are stable over time, that criminals tend to commit a wide variety of offenses instead of specializing, that they are less social than noncriminals, and that criminals commit a variety of other deviant acts apart from those defined as crime. These observations led Gottfredson and Hirschi to conclude that a main underlying cause of individual difference in the commission of crime is a cluster of individual traits which they call *low self-control*.

Low self-control, in this theoretical construction, is the natural state of human beings: socialization is required to instill self-control in people as they develop. Since the main agents of socialization are parents, the underdevelopment of self-control, they hypothesize, derives from ineffective parenting. The salient aspect of parenting, for Gottfredson and Hirschi, is supervision—the ability to recognize deviant acts and provide effective punishment when deviance is observed. Thus Gottfredson and Hirschi, like Elias, suggest that the use of violence is natural and that individuals develop self-control to suppress these natural tendencies. It is variation in the development of self-control, in this latter theoretical framework, which explains individual differences in the propensity to violence.

Building on Gottfredson and Hirschi's work, Sampson and Laub (1993) argue that differences in self-control are accomplished through an indirect model of causation, whereby structural factors such as family size, socioeconomic status, and family disruption have weak or no significant effect on children's delinquency. Instead, these factors affect parenting, which then influences the behavior of the child. Sampson and Laub argue in this way that parenting is the factor affecting children and that structural forces on the family impact children only indirectly through parents.

Research on Parenting and Violence

An important aspect of parental socialization is the use of physical violence against children by parents. In the United States, a fairly large number of studies have been conducted on the use of nonabusive corporal punishment and its effect on children (Straus, 2001a, 2001b). For example, Gershoff (2002) performed a meta-analysis on 88 such studies of corporal punishment. Twenty-eight datasets had aggression as a dependent variable. All of these studies found a positive association between corporal punishment and child aggression; that is, every study examined found that corporal punishment was associated with higher levels of aggression in children. None of the studies examined found that corporal punishment was associated with a reduced aggression in children, and, in my own research, I have not been able to find any study that shows reduced aggression as a response to corporal punishment.

The amount of research on violence by parents against children in Canada is relatively small, especially when compared with similar research on spousal violence and violence against women. For example the most recent report on family violence in Canada includes only assaults of children reported to the police (Statistics Canada, 2005). The same publication reports major social surveys on spousal violence. The report notes the absence of reports on psychological/emotional abuse or witnessing spousal violence without remarking on the lack of research into nonabusive violence inflicted on children. In this way, the very existence of parent-to-child violence does not reach the threshold of awareness.

On the other hand, there are a number of studies documenting the effects of exposure of children to spousal abuse on subsequent violence in children.[1]

---

[1] This situation may be due in part to the Canadian approach of gathering data, which is mainly accomplished by the national, centralized government organization called Statistics Canada. Centralizing data collection removes the burden of data collection and some technical matters such as sample weights from the individual researcher; however, if the design of a survey neglects certain important measures, researchers are in a difficult position since funding for independent data collection is limited.

While research on corporal punishment appears to indicate a universal association with increased aggression, presence of other kinds of violence in the home appear to have similar effects on violence in later life (Herrera & McCloskey, 2001; Widom & Maxfield, 2001). This has led some to call for a legal ban (under civil as opposed to criminal legislation) on corporal punishment, despite popular support for corporal punishment (Straus, 2001b). A much less researched subject is the effect of other punishing parental practices such as yelling on childhood aggression and related outcomes.

Causal Direction

Some authors contend that the relationship between abuse and aggression may be due, at least in part, to the degree that aggressive children *elicit* severe discipline by parents. For example, aggressive children may cause increased corporal punishment and other harsh disciplinary measures by their behavior (Ambert, 2000). Social factors may also diminish parenting effectiveness. For example, single mothers may have a difficult time socializing their children because their children do not respect their lower social status (Ambert, 2000). Some research finds a unidirectional effect from parent to child (Kandel & Wu, 1995), while other research finds a bidirectional effect—a feedback loop whereby difficult child behavior aggravates harsh discipline (Ge, et al., 1996). This study assumes that the behavior of parents affects the behavior of children, for the following reasons. First, as a rule of thumb, the individual with the most power is the most influential in any given social situation, other things being equal. It is hard to imagine a social situation where there is a greater power differential than between parent and child. Second, assuming the child was not adopted, the same parent has been involved with the child since his or her birth, and presumably the parent had an important role in the development of any nonbiological component in the child's aggression. Third, even though a child may have a difficult temperament or may have developed aggression after some time, this by no means indicates that the parent can do nothing to ameliorate the situation. While parents deserve our sympathy with the difficult task before them, we should not lose sight of who has the greater ability to make a situation improve. Fourth, parental traits that dispose them to use certain parenting styles or behaviors are likely to be more stable than the characteristics of newborns since they have had more time to stabilize; the criteria of time order in causal theory is best satisfied by parental traits as opposed to traits of the children because they are formed first. Moreover, public education and other implications of research have a far better opportunity for impacting parental behavior versus child temperament. Even if parental behavior may be difficult to change, it is parents who have the greater ability to marshal the help of external agents who can mediate difficult situations. For these reasons, this analysis assumes that the most important causal direction for behavior changes is from parent to child.

Causal Mechanisms

It is clear from the previous discussion of theory that while there is disagreement as to the process by which problematic behavior develops, virtually all theorists agree that the principal vehicle of socialization for children, especially young children, is through the family. However, there are a variety of causal mechanisms that are involved. Some theorists suggest a model whereby structural factors impact children's development directly. Others, such as Sampson and Laub (1993) suggest that the effect of structural factors on children is weak. Instead, structural factors operate by weakening the ability of parents to foster positive development in their children: the strain model. Still others, for example, the paradigm suggested by cultural learning theorists such as Lewis, suggest that parents of a particular cultural type produce children of a similar culture—a model, which I will call the selectivity model of causation. Here, I will examine the effects of the parents and parenting, the structure of the family and characteristics of the child himself or herself, using three different models of causation.

Data and Method

This analysis uses the National Longitudinal Survey of Children and Youth (NLSCY) (Statistics Canada, 2003) to examine the predictors of violent and destructive behavior in children. The NLSCY is a combined cross-sectional and prospective longitudinal survey of a stratified sample representative of Canadian children, which measures a wide variety of attributes of the children and their environments. The longitudinal portion of the survey is not strictly a prospective panel survey since subjects were added with each successive wave; however, it is possible to construct a prospective panel survey by limiting the sample to those subjects for whom data is available from the beginning of data collection (referred to as Cycle 1). The first wave of data for the NLSCY was collected from December, 1994 to April 1995 and the longitudinal subjects have been resurveyed approximately every 2 years. This analysis uses the first four such surveys: Cycles one through four. The data were analyzed in the Statistics Canada Regional Data Centre, located at the University of Calgary, since much of the data are not released to the public by Statistics Canada because of the need to ensure confidentiality for respondents. The initial survey (Cycle 1) involved 22,831 children of whom 16,903 were earmarked for follow-up until the age of 25. The data used in this analysis were gathered from questions asked to a single person determined by Statistics Canada to be the Person Most Knowledgeable (PMK), most frequently, the mother. Since the behavioral measures that are used as dependent variables in this analysis were only asked of caregivers of children between the ages of 4 and 11 years, the sample was limited to children of these ages, leaving a total of 9789 individual children.

The NLSCY is not a simple probability sample, but a stratified sample with random sampling within the lowest stratum. Statistics Canada provides sample weights for each child to compensate for oversampling in some strata. The weights are given for each child, for each cycle. In this analysis, the cross-sectional weights given for Cycle 4, divided by the average weight, were used for this purpose, since this allowed the greatest number of subjects and data points to be used. Hence, the analysis will be representative of the population of Canadian children aged 4 to 11 years at the time that Cycle 4 was gathered, that is, late in the year 2000 or early 2001. Since Cycle 4 did not include children from previous cycles who were not present in Cycle 4; many cases could not be weighted, resulting in the loss of more than 15,000 data points when running weighted models. After weighting, the total sample size involved 38,517 cases (subject/cycle), roughly 49% of which were of girls. Each variable was measured for each cycle.

Outcome Measures

All behavioral outcome measures are summated rating scales developed from questions asked of the PMK about the child at Cycles 1 through 4. While this person, in theory, could be anyone who has daily contact with the child, this analysis will treat the PMK as a parental or caregiver figure. *Aggression* measures the degree to which the child physically assaults other children. The respondent is asked to rate the frequency of three behaviors, and the measure is a summated rating scale of his or her responses. The items include the following: (1) When another child accidentally hurts [child's name], he/she reacts with anger and fighting? (2) Physically attacks people? (3) Kicks, bites, hits other children? Response options are "never," "sometimes," or "often." The measure of *Property offenses* is a summated rating scale based on the PMK frequency estimates for the following two questions: (1) Destroys his/her own things?

(2) How often would you say that [child's first name] destroys things belonging to his/her family, or other children? The same three response options are used as for aggression. *Anxiety* measures the degree to which the child is unhappy, worried, nervous, or tense. For the purposes of this examination, this outcome is only used in descriptive and bivariate analyses and is a summated rating scale based on the answer to the following three questions: How often would you say that [child's first name]: (1) seems to be unhappy or sad? (2) is worried? (3) is nervous, high strung, or tense? The answers are coded on a three point scale and then summed. Frequencies for the outcome variables are shown in Table 6.1 (note that the frequencies are for the number of measurements, not the number of children, since most children have been measured more than once).

Endogenous Variables

Five measures of parental behavior or characteristics are used in this analysis derived from questions asked of the PMK about interactions with the child. *Positive interaction* is a summated rating scale composed of three questions representing the degree to which the parent praises, laughs, or plays with the child. *Consistency* is a summated rating scale of three questions representing the degree to which the child is unable to get away with behavior that should be punished. *Yell* is a single question measuring the frequency of the PMK yelling, scolding, or raising his or her voice at the child. *Spank* is a single question measuring the degree to which physical punishment is used on the child. *Depression* in the PMK is a summated rating scale of three questions representing the degree to which the PMK feels depressed, that everything is an effort, or could not shake off the blues. While depression is not a behavior as are the other endogenous measures, it is a time-variant characteristic of the parent, as opposed to, say, education which varies to a lesser degree. Hence it is included with the variables which measure time-variant aspects of parenting. Frequencies for the endogenous variables are given in Table 6.2.

Exogenous Variables

Child's age was derived by taking the child's age in months at the time of the interview and dividing by 12, a slightly different and more precise measure than the nominal age in years used to limit the sample. *Child gender* was coded one for male (51% of the sample), zero for female. *PMK education* was measured in years and ranged from zero to twenty. *PMK gender* was coded

TABLE 6.1   Distribution of Outcome Variables

	Frequency	Percent	Cumulative Percent
Aggression			
0	20,588	53.5	53.5
1	9,247	24.0	77.5
2	3,864	10.0	87.5
3	2,422	6.3	93.8
4	870	2.3	96.0
5	180	0.5	96.5
6	138	0.4	96.9
Missing	1208	3.1	100.0
Total	38,517	100.0	
Anxiety			
0	14,846	38.5	38.5
1	9,988	25.9	64.5
2	7423	19.3	83.8
3	3711	9.6	93.4
4	982	2.6	95.9
5	349	0.9	96.8
6	83	0.2	97.1
Missing	1134	2.9	100.0
Total	38,517	100.0	
Property Offenses			
0	25,376	65.9	65.9
1	4713	12.2	78.1
2	2279	5.9	84.0
3	380	1.0	85.0
4	140	0.4	85.4
Missing	5628	14.6	100.0
Total	38,517	100.0	

one for male (7% of the sample) and zero for female. *Intact family* was coded as one if the family included both biological parents who were continuously married (70% of the sample) and zero otherwise. *Supervision* was measured as the child–parent ratio, that is, the number of children in the family per parent. *Household income* was measured in Canadian dollars. This variable was not normally distributed, so several transformation options were examined and the

TABLE 6.2   Descriptive Statistics for Endogenous Variables

	Frequency	Percent	Cumulative Percent
Positive Interaction			
0/1	7	0.0	0.0
2	12	0.0	0.1
3	112	0.3	0.3
4	220	0.6	0.9
5	739	1.9	2.8
6	2710	7.0	9.9
7	3124	8.1	18.0
8	4598	11.9	29.9
9	7364	19.1	49.0
10	6668	17.3	66.3
11	5233	13.6	79.9
12	6396	16.6	96.5
Missing	1335	3.5	100.0
Total	38,517	100.0	
Consistent Boundaries			
0	85	0.2	0.2
1	74	0.2	0.4
2	167	0.4	0.9
3	460	1.2	2.0
4	739	1.9	4.0
5	1291	3.4	7.3
6	1970	5.1	12.4
7	3422	8.9	21.3
8	4148	10.8	32.1
9	7514	19.5	51.6
10	7006	18.2	69.8
11	5513	14.3	84.1
12	4318	11.2	95.3
Missing	1809	4.7	100.0
Total	38,517	100.0	
Spank			
1	23,926	62.1	62.1
2	10,684	27.7	89.9
3	2363	6.1	96.0
4	150	0.4	96.4
5	16	0.0	96.4
Missing	1379	3.6	100.0
Total	38,517	100.0	

(continued)

TABLE 6.2   Continued

	Frequency	Percent	Cumulative Percent
Yell			
1	1,571	4.1	4.1
2	8410	21.8	25.9
3	19,041	49.4	75.4
4	7187	18.7	94.0
5	933	2.4	96.4
Missing	1377	3.6	100.0
Total	38,517	100.0	
PMK Depression			
0	21,368	55.5	55.5
1	6259	16.3	71.7
2	3733	9.7	81.4
3	2388	6.2	87.6
4	1,284	3.3	91.0
5	776	2.0	93.0
6	683	1.8	94.7
7	342	0.9	95.6
8	276	0.7	96.3
9	400	1.0	97.4
Missing	1009	2.6	100.0
Total	38,517	100.0	

base 10 logarithm was chosen to normalize the distribution and because base 10 is easier to interpret. For every 10-fold increase in the base 10 logarithm of income the outcome is expected to increase by one unit. *Income adequacy* was coded as adequate (one) if it was deemed at least lower middle income, according to Statistics Canada, and zero otherwise. *Custody* was derived by examining changes in marital status to see who the caregiver was after the dissolution of the relationship. It is coded as zero for no change, one for a custody change from previous cycles to the mother, and two for a custody change to the father. Since this variable relies on changes from one cycle to the next, all the values for custody are missing for the first cycle. In the tables, the measures of outcomes for the prior cycle (*Previous value*) are explicitly included in the model to ensure all results control for the expected correlations of previous measures of each outcome and to represent the degree to which the behavior is

TABLE 6.3   Descriptive Statistics for Exogenous Variables

Variable	Observation*	Mean	Standard Deviation
Child's age	38,517	8.01	2.278
Child's gender	38,517	0.51	
PMK's gender	38,517	0.08	
PMK's education (years)	38,140	12.68	2.183
Intact family	38,517	0.70	
Supervision	38,517	0.89	0.419
Log_{10}(household income)	30,132	4.70	0.289
Adequate income	38,517	0.14	
No change in custody	28,613	0.88	
Custody to mother	28,613	0.11	
Custody to father	28,613	0.01	

*After the application of sample weights.

persistent. Descriptive statistics for the exogenous variables in this analysis are shown in Table 6.3.

Cluster Analysis

The selectivity causal mechanism is associated with cultural transmission theories such as those of Anderson and Lewis; according to these theories parents can be categorized *a priori* and this categorization is predictive of children's outcomes. In order to test for the existence of the selectivity causal mechanism, the parents were separated (selected) into three groups according to parenting characteristics. This was accomplished using the statistical technique of cluster analysis, which allocates like cases into a specified number of groups according to scores along given variables. The allocation of like cases into groups can be accomplished according to several methods; in this case, the method chosen was the square root of the sum of the squares of the differences between cases for each variable specified so that parents with the smallest differences are grouped together. The groups are arranged to minimize the differences between the cases in each group. This technique was used to group PMKs with respect to their parenting ability in Cycle 1 into three groups: from those with the most favorable parenting characteristics to those with the worst (see Table 6.4 for parental characteristics). This group assignment in the first cycle was then used in the model explaining children's outcomes to test the selectivity causal mechanism. The results obtained

TABLE 6.4   Parental Cluster Properties: Mean Values

Parental Cluster/Category	Yell	Spank	Positive Interaction	Consistency	PMK Depression	PMK Education
0—Best	3.22	4.61	10.81	10.14	0.80	13.10
1—Middle	2.87	4.36	7.35	9.43	1.23	11.73
2—Worst	2.82	4.36	10.08	5.68	1.92	11.28

Note: Higher is better for all measures except PMK depression.
PMK: person most knowledgeable about the child.

from the cluster analysis follow the expected ordinal ranking (parents in the highest group have the highest values for most measures) except for *Positive interaction* (see Table 6.4). PMKs are assigned to one of three clusters: Best (0), Middle (1), or Worst (2) (see Table 6.4).

Analytic Method

The outcome and endogenous variables in this analysis are all summated or singular rating scales and hence although their empirical measures are integers, they are continuous rather than discrete. These scales are all distributed nonnormally in a manner that is best represented by either a negative binomial or gamma distribution. For continuous variables, the gamma distribution is appropriate since it represents a continuous distribution that can take a shape similar to the negative binomial (Evans, Hastings, & Peacock, 2000). The Poisson distribution can also be used for discrete dependent variables; however, this distribution assumes that the mean and variance are the same, making the negative binomial or gamma distributions a more flexible choice. The data are part of a combined prospective panel and sequential cross-sectional time series survey for which four measurements, or cycles, of the respondents have been taken. The models developed for this analysis consequently use panel regression or cross-sectional time series modeling, utilizing the general linear model for correlated data to estimate the effects of the explanatory variables on children's outcomes. This method specifically accommodates the nature of these data—repeated measures over time for the subjects. This was accomplished using Stata's XTGEE command using a gamma distribution with a natural logarithm link function and a one cycle autoregressive correlations structure. The autoregressive correlation structure was applied since most of the variables in these models have autocorrelation from one measure (cycle) to the next.

Results

Propensity for Violence versus Social Learning

Figure 6.1 shows that as children get older, their aggression decreases at about the same rate for boys and girls; however, boys' aggression starts at a higher rate than does girls'aggression. The dispersion for both also decreases at a similar rate, once again, with boys' aggression starting at a more variable rate than that of girls. The more children are socialized the less likely they are to use violence and the more stringently they adhere to social expectations vis-à-vis violence. This would tend to support the view that the propensity to use violence is innate or "natural" as opposed to being acquired over time. Moreover, the effect of socialization for boys and girls is approximately the same, suggesting that gender differences in aggression—a common finding in social science research—is not an artifact of socialization but a consequence of boys starting out more aggressive than girls from an early age. In this way, although there is undoubtedly social learning involved in the socialization process, it appears that learning of self-control or the ability to restrain oneself from violence rather than learning to be violent is driving this process. Thus the main contentions of Elias and Gottfredson and Hirschi are supported.

A similar story arises from an examination of the propensity of children to destroy things (denoted here as property offenses), given in Figure 6.2.

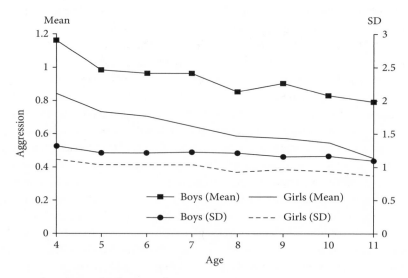

FIGURE 6.1   Aggression by age and sex.

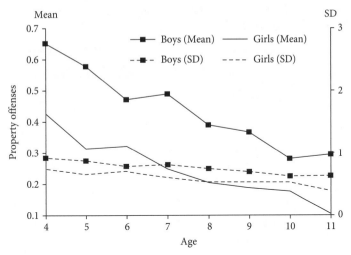

FIGURE 6.2   Property offenses by age and sex.

Again, the effect of socialization on children's propensity for material destruction is similar for boys and girls; however, boys start at a higher level. As with aggression against people, the dispersion decreases as children age, so that the behavior is not only reduced but the variation in the behavior is reduced as well. From a theoretical perspective, this again is consistent with the contentions of Elias and Gottfredson and Hirschi and in particular the latter's argument that the development of self-control can be observed in several behaviors. Children appear to be learning how to restrain themselves from these behaviors, which, later in life, are defined as criminal.

Testing Mechanisms of Socialization

The results for the two direct models testing the effects of the child, the parent, the family, parenting, and custody changes are shown in Table 6.5 (Figure 6.3 and Figure 6.4 provide marginal effects). Whereas the graphs shown illustrate the direction of socialization—that violence is socialized out of children—the models presented in Table 6.5 demonstrate *how* this socialization is accomplished. The models show very similar results for both aggression (physical violence) and property offenses (material destruction), with the exception of the logarithm of income which only had a statistically significant effect on property offenses and the effect of age, which is not significant for aggression. All other variables had effects that were consistent for both outcomes. This first finding suggests a high degree of comorbidity

TABLE 6.5   Models Predicting Aggression and Property Offenses in Children Aged 4 to 11 Years

Entity	Variable	Outcome Variable	
		Aggression	Property Offenses
Child	Previous measure	0.41***	0.90***
	Age	−0.01	−0.16***
	Boy	0.25***	0.44***
Parent	Yell (verbal)	0.28***	0.48***
	Spank (physical)	0.27***	0.34***
	Positive interaction	−0.04***	−0.09**
	Consistency	−0.08***	−0.10***
	PMK depression	0.07***	0.05*
	PMK education	0.00	−0.02
	PMK gender	−0.16	−0.30
	PMK cluster (0) (referent)†		
	PMK cluster (1)	−0.11	0.10
	PMK cluster (2)	−0.02	0.13
Family	Intact family	0.07	−0.16
	Supervision	−0.47***	−0.39**
	Log_{10}(income)	−0.11	−0.57*
	Adequate income	−0.06	−0.21
Custody Change	No change (referent)		
	Custody to mother	0.02	0.05
	Custody to father	0.32	0.19
	No. of children	4,855	4,806
	No. of observations	11,153	11,077

* $p < 0.05$; ** $p < 0.01$; *** $p < 0.001$ (two tailed tests).
Notes:
1. Negative coefficients signify beneficial effects for both outcome variables.
2. Coefficients are unexponentiated (the link function is the natural logarithm).
† Parents were clustered into three categories on preexisting parenting characteristics to test the selectivity model of causation.

among behavioral indicators of delinquency, consistent with self-control theory. The next finding with respect to these two outcomes is that they are both highly persistent, that is, the previous measure of both aggression and property offenses is highly predictive of the next measure, suggesting that behavioral difficulties in children are challenging problems to overcome.

Boys were found to be both more aggressive and more destructive of property than girls. The proposition of most of the theorists reviewed earlier

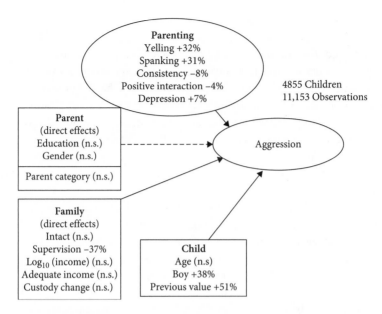

FIGURE 6.3 Marginal direct effects on aggression (n.s. = not statistically significant).

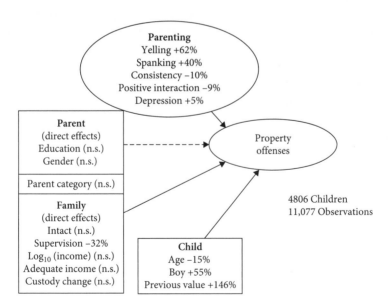

FIGURE 6.4 Marginal direct effects on property offenses (n.s. = not statistically significant).

in the paper—that parenting is the major mechanism for socialization of children in our society—was supported; large effects for parenting were observed, even after controlling for the previous tendencies in the child. In partial agreement with the contentions of Sampson and Laub, except for supervision, the structural considerations of the family do not have significant direct effects on the children's aggressive or destructive behavior. However, the direct effect of supervision—both statistically significant and substantively large—on both behavioral outcomes as well as a strong effect of the log of income on the propensity of children to destroy things[2] belie Sampson and Laub's contention that only weak structural effects are to be expected on children's delinquency. On the other hand, the emphasis placed by Gottfredson and Hirschi on the importance of supervision in the formation of children's behavior appears to be strongly supported and the effects of the variables measuring parenting—corporal punishment, yelling, consistent discipline, and positive interaction—have significant and strong effects on both outcome variables, supporting the model of Gottfredson and Hirschi and other socialization theories. The finding with respect to corporal punishment agrees with work by earlier research by Straus (Straus, 2001a, 2001b; Straus & Donnelly, 1993). While the variable measuring consistency in discipline has a beneficial effect, it is of particular importance to note that two behaviors associated with discipline—yelling and corporal punishment—both have strong detrimental effects on children's behavior. Hence it appears that it is not only discipline that is important, but the manner in which the discipline is applied.

There is persuasive evidence of the persistence of problematic behaviors in children from this analysis. After controlling for parental characteristics, parenting, and family attributes, the highest marginal effect for both aggression and property offenses is the previous tendency for each of these behaviors respectively (see Figures 6.3 and 6.4). While this is a result that would be expected given the theoretical framework of Gottfredson and Hirschi, Bourdieu and Lewis, and others, it is apparent from these models that while these behaviors are persistent, there are other powerful forces at play, which also factor into the production of children's behavior problems. In addition to the direct effects of these variables on children's behavioral outcomes, there are also potentially important effects possible through their effect on parental behavior. For this reason, a causal model for each parental behavior was estimated to understand the production of these endogenous variables, the results of which are presented in Table 6.6. Each of these models was

[2] To ensure that the two measures of income in the models were independent, the models were run first with only log income, then with both measures.

TABLE 6.6   Causal Models for Endogenous Variables

	Yell	Spank	Positive Interaction	Consistency	PMK Depression
Adequate income	−0.03*	−0.05*	0.07	−0.02	−0.01
Custody to father	−0.03	−0.10*	−0.02	0.16*	0.14
Custody to mother	−0.02	−0.02	−0.07	0.04	0.06
Intact family	0.02*	0.06***	0.00	0.10***	−0.21***
Log$_{10}$(income)	−0.02	−0.16***	−0.12*	0.12*	−0.76***
No custody change (ref.)					
No. of children	8281	8280	8301	8174	8518
No. of observations	20,175	20,175	20,226	19,829	20,757
PMK education	0.00	−0.01*	0.02***	0.03***	−0.05***
PMK gender (male)	−0.03*	0.01	−0.07	−0.02	−0.19*
Supervision	−0.05***	−0.07***	0.24***	−0.07**	−0.04

* $p < .05$; ** $p < .01$; *** $p < .001$ (two tailed tests).
Notes:
1. Negative coefficients signify beneficial effects for all outcome variables.
2. Coefficients are unexponentiated (the link function is the natural logarithm).

estimated using the same method as for aggression and property offenses (panel regression with an assumed gamma distribution for the dependent variable, a log link function and an autoregressive correlation structure).

The results for the endogenous variables indicate that where PMK education has an effect on the endogenous variables, it is consistently beneficial although small in magnitude. While fathers reported less depression than mothers and a change in custody to the father also had some beneficial effects, it should be kept in mind that this sample had a relatively small proportion of male caregivers (8%), so it is possible that these parental figures might not be representative of all males, although the finding that men, on average score 17% lower on depression is not unexpected, since it is a common finding that women report more depression than do men (Dowrick et al., 2006; Kessler, 2000; Prior, 1999). There is a large effect in these models of log household income on depression: for each tenfold increase in household income, the depression in the caregiver is reduced by 53% (marginal effect).

Discussion

This research began with a review of theoretical perspectives showing broad agreement on the importance of parenting as the main engine of child socialization. In contrast to this agreement, there is sharp disagreement regarding what this socialization entails: do children learn to be violent or do they learn self-control? This study finds that the tendency to use violence is not a learned attribute. Instead, children learn to restrain themselves from using violence and destructive acts; they learn self-control. Both aggression (the tendency to hit other children) and property offenses (the tendency to destroy property) decrease as children age, suggesting that children do not learn these tendencies (later defined as criminal) as they mature; instead they learn to repress their emotions and violent acts, as suggested by Elias and Gottfredson and Hirschi. Perhaps this explains why teaching children martial arts is an appropriate response to a violent ghetto environment (Canada, 1996); it teaches self-discipline. If violence were learned, police officers would be the most violent people of all since they are highly trained in, and are constantly exposed to, violence or the threat of violence. The people who deal with violence best are those who have mastered it within themselves.

Although the consensus on the importance of parenting was strongly supported by the results presented here, the important factors involved in the development of problem behavior have, according to these results, not previously been fully articulated. While supervision and consistent discipline have been previously highlighted by Gottfredson and Hirschi, the role of corporal punishment and yelling have received relatively little attention from criminologists. A major exception to this rule is the work of family violence expert Murray Straus (Straus, 2001a, 2001b) who has done extensive work on the consequences of corporal punishment. This research, combined with the theoretical insight of Elias, would suggest that a violence-free household—a "pacified space" in his terms—facilitates the civilizing process for children. Children learn to be nonviolent, a task which is made considerably more difficult in a violent environment. Since the internalization of norms of social behavior has an important emotional component in Elias's formulation, it would seem consistent that yelling would have a similar effect as does corporal punishment.

Research on yelling is still in its infancy. However, the findings here suggest that this is a fertile area for research into factors that promote children's well-being. Further, this research confirms the persistence of problem behaviors such as aggression and property destruction, suggesting that behavior problems are challenging to deal with by parents and others interested in fostering good child development. On the other hand, while the tendency to be violent is persistent—as predicted by such theorists as Gottfredson and Hirschi and Bourdieu—it is by no means an entirely hopeless situation since many other factors also have important effects. Arranging for better supervision and the promotion of positive-parenting practices that do not rely on corporal punishment or yelling can open the door to behavior improvement. Given the degree of persistence, the earlier in the child's life this takes place, the better. Like all deeply ingrained cultural values, removing the association of discipline—a crucial aspect of child rearing—with corporal punishment and yelling will take many years and determined social effort to achieve. Yet, the findings of this study suggest benefits of so doing are compelling. The cost of violent and destructive behavior—human, social, and economic—is difficult to overestimate. Prisons and offender programs are very expensive and too rarely effective. Prevention, while also challenging, is far cheaper and easier in the long run.

Another finding from this study is that there are no special benefits of maternal care over the care performed by fathers. Fathers need not be concerned that their parenting is deficient on account of their gender. This confirms much other research on the ability of people of both sexes being able to fill most social roles. It should be kept in mind that this study looked only at children aged 4 to 11 years, and as such did not look into factors more relevant for older children such as peer relationships. Moreover, the use of a structural measurement of supervision, the parent–child ratio, could be improved in further research by having a more direct measure of this concept.

Policy Implications

One might think, given near-unanimous agreement on the importance of parenting in the prevention of problem behavior in children, that governments would be investing heavily in programs that support parents and children at risk. With prevention likely to cost a fraction of the cost of "treatment" (if current practices can be characterized in this way), the payoffs for public education and support programs for children and their parents would seem easy to justify. Yet, there is a dearth of research, population-based research in particular, on parenting practices, especially yelling, and their role in creating antisocial behavior in young people. Many researchers do not even consider violence against children to be in the category of family violence, a premise that is reflected in the datasets and reports available in Canada. Moreover the idea that corporal punishment might have negative consequences for children suffers from a kind of political incorrectness that need not extend to the academy, and which needs to be addressed in the interest of our children. For example, polls show that about two-thirds of Americans believe that children should be spanked (Crandall, 2002; Dewberry, 2007; Stewart, 2007). Public education in this area is relatively inexpensive, and over time can have important effects on parenting practices. It is important that these efforts do not demonize parents, but instead aim to support them in their efforts to raise their children in the best possible way. Government institutions have an abysmal record in the business of child rearing and, in any case, government care for children is far more expensive than enabling care through parents. Because the tendency to use violence and to destroy property is persistent, the earlier the intervention is applied, the better. This finding also explains the difficult challenge that programs for youth at risk face; if these tendencies are persistent in elementary school-aged children, they are likely just as ingrained, or even more so, by the time they attract the attention of the justice system. While many of the opportunities for benefiting children through policy are related to researching best parenting practices and communicating these to the public, there are others. For example, this study finds that parental behavior is far more important than, say, parental gender; knowledge that could improve children's lives through child custody decisions that are less reliant on parental gender. Moreover, the importance of supervision would suggest that upon family break up, policy should make every effort to maintain the child's relationship with both parents as well as with extended family members so that supportive adults may continue to act as resources and guide children in their upbringing. The potential for social benefits through support and education of parents is an important opportunity that should not be ignored.

Part II

Biosocial Influences on Persistent Criminality

CHAPTER 7

Biological Factors and the Development of Persistent Criminality

PATRICK SYLVERS, STACY R. RYAN, S. AMANDA ALDEN, AND PATRICIA A. BRENNAN

Crime is a heterogeneous and culturally defined construct with numerous etiological pathways. To understand these pathways, psychological researchers typically study crime within the context of specific mental disorders, marked by persistent rule breaking, such as early-onset conduct disorder. The preponderance of data suggests that both environmental and biological vulnerabilities likely underpin the development of these disorders. The overall goal of the present chapter is to orient the reader to the current biological models of delinquent psychopathology and provide an overview of the biological literature, including heritability, psychophysiology, neurobiology, and endocrinology related to the development of persistent criminal behavior in children and adolescents. In doing so, this chapter highlights the strengths and limitations of the existing literature, consolidates this literature to identify patterns of convergence and divergence across disorders, and suggests areas for future research. Before discussing the theoretical and empirical literature linking biological factors to criminal behavior, however, it is essential to discuss common misconceptions regarding the relationship between biological factors and crime.

Misconceptions Regarding Biology and Crime

Adrian Raine (1993) outlined 10 misconceptions regarding the genetics of criminal behavior. The overall sentiment of his arguments applies more broadly to the ability of other biological factors to predict crime. As some of these arguments are integral to contextualizing the relationships between biology and crime, a subset of these arguments and their refutations are presented here in modified form.

1. *Biological factors are directly responsible for criminal behavior.* Although individuals may inherit biological predispositions toward crime or incur brain damage, it is likely that the complex interplay of biological and environmental influences is responsible for the majority of persistent criminal behavior.
2. *Biological factors can explain why specific individuals commit crime.* There are no one-to-one relationships between particular biological factors and criminal behavior. Therefore, biological factors can only be viewed as vulnerabilities, not determinants.
3. *Biological factors cannot underpin criminal behavior because crime is culturally constructed.* Criminal behavior, like mental disorder, is culturally constructed as a cluster of behaviors causing distress that lie outside of the normative range of behaviors. As Raine (1993) points out, schizophrenia is a disorder constructed by international psychiatric systems with different systems defining it somewhat differently; however, the preponderance of evidence suggests common biological predispositions for schizophrenia across countries and systems. Similarly, violent or persistent forms of aggression might be defined differently across cultures, but there is consistent evidence that biological predispositions are associated with them, variously defined.

Biological Theories of Crime

Antiquated theories of crime and criminal behavior fueled many of the misconceptions regarding biology and crime. Cesare Lombroso (1836–1909), for example, suggested that criminals were born predisposed to engage in antisocial behaviors. Lombroso used Darwinian Theory to suggest that criminals were inferior, genetic throwbacks to good, honest people (Gibson & Rafter, 2006). Moreover, he insisted that criminals were distinguishable from noncriminals by virtue of physical anomalies, such as large ears and a low narrow forehead.

Although Lombroso's specific theoretical position and diagnostic methodologies were not sound, the idea that persistent criminal behavior is influenced by biology has endured and gained a significant amount of empirical support. For example, researchers have continued the investigation of minor physical anomalies (MPAs; Arseneault, Tremblay, Boulerice, Seguin, & Saucier, 2000; Pine, Schonfeld, Davies, & Shaffer, 1997). This research has established a link between fetal central nervous system development and the development of such phenotypic anomalies as single palmar crease, malformed ears, curved pinky finger, furrowed tongue, and a palate that is highly arched. Additional research has established a link between MPAs, aggression, and violent offenses (Kandel, Brennan, Mednick, & Michelson, 1989).

Although these empirical findings lend some support to Lombroso's proposition that there is a biological basis to criminal behavior, his theory has largely dropped out of favor due to its simplistic and potentially harmful views of individual and group differences. Moffitt, Damasio, and Gray now provide the field with the most widely accepted and prominently researched biologically based theories of criminal behavior.

First, Moffitt's (1993) seminal work on the trajectories of conduct disorder (CD) (see definition below) provided a groundbreaking theoretical explanation for the development of a particularly violent and noxious strain of delinquency. According to the theory, persistent offending is due to prenatal and perinatal disruptions in neural development, which lead to neuropsychological deficits—namely, developmental impairments in executive and verbal functioning. These neurological deficits, which may be too subtle to attract clinical attempts at remediation, cumulatively result in an infant/toddler with a difficult temperament, poor behavioral regulation, and deficient cognitive abilities. Her theory suggested that children with these deficits, manifested as clumsiness, inattention, hyperactivity, impulsivity, and irritability, are at-risk for developing early-onset CD. When these specific deficits interact with an unsupportive environment, they produce persistent delinquent outcomes.

Second, Damasio's (1994) somatic marker hypothesis represented a complementary theory that readily applies to the development of violence. Damasio suggested that damage to the amygdala or orbitomedial prefrontal cortex results in the failure of an individual to "mark" experiences as either positive or negative. According to the theory, somatic markers allow healthy individuals to categorize and learn from negative experiences. Hence, individuals with damage to these brain structures fail to experience the feedback responsible for avoiding future aversive situations. In the context of conflict, these individuals may resort to violence in the absence of appropriate cognitive processing and subsequently fail to "mark" the experience as negative, which in turn may result in further violence in future conflict situations. In the context of crime, these individuals may fail to learn from punishment and therefore recidivate.

Third, at a broader level, Gray (1982) posited two competing motivational systems: the behavioral inhibition system (BIS) and the behavioral activation system (BAS) (Fowles, 1988; Gray, 1982). The BIS functions as a means of withholding behavior in ambiguously threatening situations. Gray identified the septo-hippocampal system as the primary brain structure involved in BIS activation. As the name implies, the BIS represents an inhibitory system. The BAS, on the other hand, functions as an approach system facilitating behavior. Gray (1994) identified the basal ganglia, thalamic nuclei surrounding the basal ganglia, and the ventral tegmental area as the brain structures involved in BAS activation. Whereas the BIS represents the behavioral braking system, the BAS represents the accelerator. Scarpa and Raine (1997) suggest that violent behavior is a function of an underactive BIS, an overactive BAS, or a combination of both. Moreover, several researchers (e.g., Fowles, 1988; Quay, 1993) have suggested that an underactive BIS and overactive BAS underpin psychopathy, a disorder often marked by criminal recidivism.

As the theories of Moffitt, Damasio, and Gray suggest, the developmental processes linking biological factors to persistent criminal outcomes are complex and multifaceted. Empirical research on biological factors, however, is typically presented in a more simplistic fashion with a single biological factor being linked to a particular disorder or criminal outcome. In addition, "criminal" outcomes per se, are not commonly studied in children. Instead, biological factors have been linked to related outcomes such as conduct disorder, juvenile psychopathy, bullying, and sexual aggression. In the following sections, we will examine each of these outcomes in turn, and provide a summary of the findings regarding biological risk factors for each.

Early-Onset Conduct Disorder and Juvenile Delinquency

As stated previously, criminal behavior occurring in childhood is often studied in the context of conduct disorder. Conduct disorder is defined by the *Diagnostic and Statistical Manual for Mental Disorders* (DSM-IV-TR) as a pattern of behavior that violates social rules and the rights of others (American Psychiatric Association, 2000). Although CD is not synonymous with crime, moderate to severe CD is characterized by harm to others and the property of others. The DSM-IV contains two distinct subtypes of CD diagnoses: early onset and late onset. Whereas late onset is considered primarily an adolescence-limited phenomenon, early-onset conduct disorder is characterized by a trajectory of offending that oftentimes persists into adulthood. The violent criteria include bullying or intimidating others, initiating physical fights, using a weapon to physically harm others, being physically cruel to animals, being physically cruel to people, robbing others, and forcing someone into sexual activity. Juvenile delinquency is a legal rather than psychological term and, in the United States, refers to crimes committed by a child younger than 18 years of age (although this slightly varies by state).

Pre- and Perinatal Factors

Moffitt (1993) theorized that prenatal and perinatal disruptions in neural development lead to neuropsychological deficits (e.g., executive and verbal functioning) and that these deficits predict early-onset conduct problems and violent behavior. Additionally, birth and neonatal complications, collectively referred to as obstetric complications, are also implicated in the development of violent behavior (Brennan, Grekin, & Mednick, 2003). A host of factors, such as maternal stress, poor nutrition, viral infection, maternal cigarette smoking, and alcohol and drug use, are related to obstetric complications and thus indirectly related to early-onset CD and violent behavior.

Prenatal Stress. Epidemiological studies suggest that maternal psychological well-being (e.g., stress, anxiety, and depression) and certain behaviors (i.e., alcohol, cigarette, and drug use) may increase the likelihood of obstetric complications. Researchers have found that prenatal stress has adverse effects on the development and gestation of the fetus. Researchers initially studied maternal stress during pregnancy in association with outcomes of serious mental health problems, such as schizophrenia (Huttunen & Niskanen, 1978). More recent animal studies on stress and early brain development suggest that maternal stress might also play a role in increasing risk for youth behavior problems such as aggression and substance abuse (Dawson, Ashman, & Carver, 2000; DeKloet, Korte, Rots, & Kruk, 1996).

Stressful life events, which influence psychological distress, have been theorized to have a specific effect on the developing fetus. Typically, when an individual is under stress a homeostatic response is initiated in which the hypothalamic-pituitary-adrenal (HPA) axis releases adrenocorticotropin (ACTH), and corticotrophin-releasing (CRH) hormones, and these hormones activate the adrenal glands, which activate the release of cortisol. Throughout pregnancy, these hormones steadily increase, reaching a peak in the last trimester (Smith, 1999). It is also understood that the placenta releases CRH as well. Thus, when a mother is under duress, there is an influx in both maternal and placental stress hormones that enter the circulation of the fetus. It has been theorized that this additive effect bombards the developing fetal brain, finally resulting in the dysregulation of the HPA axis. Elevated levels of CRH have been associated with spontaneous labor and preterm birth (Dunkel-Schetter, 1998; Hobel, Dunkel-Schetter, Roesch, Castro, & Arora, 1999; Wadhwa, Porto, Garite, Chicz-DeMet, & Sandman, 1998).

The dysregulation of the HPA axis has also been associated with adverse behavioral outcomes. Specifically, early-onset conduct disorder has been related to lower mean levels of cortisol (the final byproduct of the stress response in humans) in a clinical sample of boys (McBurnett, Lahey, Rathouz, & Loeber, 2000). Similarly, in a sample of boys at high risk for alcohol abuse, aggression was related to a lower cortisol response in anticipation of a stressor (Moss, Mezzich, Yao, Gavaler, & Martin, 1995). These findings are consistent with the notion that aggressive or delinquent children may be underresponsive to stressors or stimuli in their environment, and may act aggressively either because they lack fear, or because they have a physiological need to seek stimulation.

It is important to examine whether these hormonal levels still predict aggression if factors that covary with the alteration of the HPA axis (e.g., pregnancy and delivery complications) are controlled. Recently, research has suggested that hormonal levels may not uniquely predict a large percent of the variance in the association between the dysregulation of the HPA axis and adverse behavioral outcomes. For example, Huizink et al. (2002) found that in an early measure of behavior (i.e., temperament), stress hormones accounted for a very small percentage of the variance when controlling for factors that covary with stress, such as socioeconomic status (SES), biomedical risk factors during pregnancy, and perinatal and postnatal factors.

Maternal Cigarette Smoking. Prenatal cigarette smoking has been associated with early-onset/life-course-persistent offending, impulsivity, CD, and attentional problems (Day, Richardson, Goldschmidt, & Cornelius, 2000; Wakschlag et al., 1997; Weissman, Warner, Wickramaratne, & Kandel, 1999). Prenatal smoking has also been associated with crime in adulthood (Brennan, Grekin, & Mednick, 1999). The effects of maternal prenatal smoking appear to be specific to externalizing or acting out behaviors; there does not appear to be an association between maternal prenatal smoking and increased risk for internalizing problems such as depression (Orlebeke, Knol, & Verhulst, 1999). Case control studies support these findings (O'Callaghan, Williams,

Anderson, Bor, & Najman, 1997; Williams et al., 1998). Additionally, statistical control for a range of potential confounds including maternal antisocial behavior, maternal mental health, parenting behavior, SES, prenatal exposure to drugs and alcohol, and other perinatal complications do not change this general pattern of results (Orlebeke et al., 1999).

One mechanism by which prenatal smoking affects the developing fetus is by depriving the fetus of oxygen (a condition known as hypoxia). Hypoxia is evident in the prenatal complications that are associated with maternal smoking: placental abruption, premature births (Cnattingius & Lambe, 2002), and placenta previa (Ananth, Demissie, Smulian, & Vintzileos, 2001), all of which have also been linked to behavioral problems in offspring.

Maternal Drug Use. Cocaine is another teratogen (which is defined as an agent that is related to, or causes a developmental malformation) that researchers have focused on when examining types of prenatal drug use and detrimental outcomes of the offspring. Researchers examining the effects of cocaine exposure typically focus on infants or the longitudinal effects of cocaine exposure on developmental delays and/or behavioral outcomes. The research literature on the impact of cocaine exposure during infancy is somewhat mixed in its conclusions (Frank, Augustyn, Knight, Pell, & Zuckerman, 2001).

For example, some researchers in the infant literature focus on the noticeable decrease in such growth parameters as birth weight and head circumference (e.g., Richardson, Hamel, Goldschmidt, & Day, 1999; Shankaran et al., 2004; Singer et al., 2002), while others focus on adverse effects on nervous system regulation (e.g., Dennis, Bendersky, Ramsey, & Lewis, 2006; Gingras & O'Donnell, 1998; John et al., 2007). Additionally, some studies find that decreased growth parameters due to maternal cocaine use influences nervous system regulation (Messinger et al., 2004; Scafidi et al., 1996; Schuetze & Eiden, 2006) and developmental delays (Beeghly et al., 2006; Behnke, Eyler, Garvan, Wobie, & Hou, 2002), while others do not (Bandstra et al., 2001; Bandstra et al., 2002; Nulman et al., 2001; Schuetze, Eiden, & Coles, 2007).

Furthermore, some of these studies report noticeable differences between infants born to cocaine-using mothers and those born to nonusing mothers (e.g., John et al., 2007) while others report a dose-response effect several days after birth (Tronick, Frank, Cabral, Mircochnick, & Zuckerman, 1996; Schuetze & Eiden, 2006). Other researchers have consistently reported a dose-response relationship between cocaine exposure and adverse neurological and physiological development (e.g., Bateman & Chiriboga, 2000; Chiriboga, Brust, Bateman, & Hauser, 1999; Frank et al., 1999; Lester et al., 2003; Shankaran et al., 2004; Tronick et al., 1996), though longitudinal research suggests that over time this relationship appears to diminish.

Longitudinal research suggests that at the outset there is a significant difference between cocaine-exposed infants and non–cocaine-exposed infants, but over the span of development this gap closes and differences are no longer significant by 3 years of age (for a review see Chiriboga, 1998; Frank et al., 2001; Mayes, Cicchetti, Acharyya, & Zhang, 2003; Richardson, Conroy, & Day, 1996). Researchers have also reported relatively small effect sizes as early as 15 months after birth (Fetters & Tronick, 1996; Dennis et al., 2006).

In terms of behavioral outcome, Chiriboga (1998) found that problems with inattention are the only consistent negative behavioral outcome of cocaine exposure. A more current review of the literature revealed similar findings (Gaultney, Gingras, Martin, & DeBrule, 2005). Some researchers have failed to find support for the association between cocaine exposure and externalizing and internalizing problems using parental report (Accornero, Anthony, Morrow, Xue, & Bandstra, 2006) but others have found that internalizing and externalizing symptom ratings from nonmaternal caregivers were lower for cocaine-exposed children (Warner et al., 2006). One difference between these two studies is that the former assessed children before they were school age and the latter assessed school-aged children. It is possible that the inconsistencies in these findings are due to the age of the subjects.

One reason for these mixed results is that studies have shown that maternal cocaine users are often polydrug users and that they tend to also use marijuana, cigarettes, and alcohol (Arendt, Angelopoulos, Salvator, & Singer, 1999; Azuma & Chasnoff, 1993; Jacobson, Jacobson, Sokol, Martier, & Chiodo, 1996). During early investigations of the effects of cocaine on fetuses, researchers failed to control for these confounds; with more methodologically sound designs that controlled for polydrug use, the effects of cocaine diminished (Landry & Whitney, 1996). For example, one study demonstrated that when cocaine is independently analyzed from alcohol exposure, cocaine no longer predicts behavior problems in children (Griffith, Chasnoff, & Azuma, 1994). Another reason for the mixed results is that researchers failed to control for such adverse environmental factors as economic disadvantage or poor parent-child relationships. In some studies, when inadequate parenting is considered, researchers find that developmental delays are more highly associated with inadequate parenting than cocaine exposure (Arendt et al., 2004; Hurt, Malmud, Betancourt, Brodsky, & Giannetta, 2001). Yet in other studies, developmental delays are still apparent after considering caregiver environment (Morrow, Vogel, Anthony, Ofir, Dausa, & Bandstra, 2004).

There is a weakness to conducting multivariate statistical analyses that consider control variables. Specifically, if controls are included in a model testing biological factors, any common variance between an environmental factor and a biological factor will not be included in the computation of the partial t statistics. So sometimes, we "lose" effects. For example, if a child has a difficult temperament (in this case due to cocaine exposure), and elicits poor parenting, when cocaine exposure and poor parenting are included in a model together, theoretically only the effect of cocaine exposure above and beyond its effects on this environmental factor will be estimated in the partial t statistic (see Chapter 8, for a more detailed discussion of how biological factors contribute to shaping the environment and Chapter 9 for more on indirect effects).

Addis and colleagues (2001) conducted a meta-analysis of 33 studies and compared several groups: mainly cocaine, cocaine plus polydrug, polydrug but no cocaine, and drug free. These researchers found that decreased growth parameters and labor and delivery complications were higher in the cocaine-exposed group but when compared to children exposed to polydrug but no cocaine, the adverse effects of cocaine exposure disappeared.

Maternal Alcohol Use. There appears to be a clearer picture of the deleterious effects of alcohol on a developing fetus than the effects of cocaine on a developing fetus. Prenatal alcohol use has detrimental effects on a developing fetus, marked by a constellation of significant levels of maladaptive behaviors, poor concentration and attention, dependency, stubbornness, social withdrawal, bullying, and impulsivity, (Steissguth et al., 1991). Researchers have found that even a small amount of alcohol (i.e., alcohol levels associated with social drinking) used in pregnancy is significantly associated with behavioral problems such as antisocial behaviors and laboratory observations of impulsivity and disorganization (Olson et al., 1997).

Research suggests that maternal alcohol consumption can cause structural damage to the frontal lobes. For example, Wass et al. (2001) found a relationship between maternal prenatal alcohol consumption and offspring frontal cortex size. Specifically, 23% of fetuses exposed to maternal alcohol consumption had a cortex size below the 10th percentile, while only 4% of nonexposed fetuses had a cortex size that small. More evidence is needed to determine whether the reduction in size is associated with impaired brain functioning. This finding is certainly consistent with the literature linking frontal lobe functioning and child CD and delinquency.

Genetically sensitive designs are needed to assess and tease out the role of genetic influences in the studies of adverse perinatal factors associated with child aggression and antisocial behavior. As Raz et al. (1996) point out, twin designs can be used to control for genetic and other postnatal environmental influences, so that the effect of the perinatal complication can be separated out and examined. More complex twin designs (e.g., the children of twins design) or adoptee designs could be used to test the genetic and environmental influences reflected in the relationship between a wide variety or perinatal problems and antisocial behavior (Rutter, Pickles, Murray, & Eaves, 2001).

Genetics

Current knowledge concerning gene expression of behavior patterns—such as CD and delinquency—indicates that genes, the network of intermediate traits that they influence, and the environmental context that dampens or enhances their expression interact in complicated ways during the entire lifespan. The expression of genes and the development of the cells of the brain and nervous system depend on the action of hormones, neurotransmitters, and growth factors, which, in turn, are influenced by the environment in which they develop. Genetic research on youth problem behaviors has not revealed any one-to-one correspondence between a particular genetic defect and the occurrence of early-onset conduct problems. Evidence for genetic contribution in the development of problem behaviors comes from studies that focus on behavioral as well as molecular genetics.

First, much of the evidence for genetic contribution in the development of problem behaviors comes from studies of twins and of adoption, which focus on behavioral genetics. Mason and Frick (1994) conducted a meta-analysis of 12 twin studies and 3 adoption studies exploring the genetic influence on antisocial behavior and found that genes accounted for approximately 50% of the variance. Moreover, they found that this estimate increased with the severity of antisocial behavior. In a more recent meta-analysis of behavioral genetics, Rhee and Waldman (2002) found that when studies were aggregated together, the definition of antisocial behavior, reporter, and age moderated the relationship between genetic contribution and problem behavior. More specifically, these researchers found that genetic effects appeared most strongly in studies using criminal conviction as a definition, parental report, and child subjects. Their findings of reporter effects are shown to be consistent in ethnically and economically diverse samples as well (Baker, Jacobson, Raine, Lozano, & Bezdjian, 2007).

Another avenue for the investigation of genetic contribution has been the focus of gene polymorphisms (which is defined as existing in many forms) for neurotransmitters. With the use of DNA tests, some have linked particular gene polymorphisms of the serotonin transporter neurotransmitter to the behavioral symptoms of CD (Sakai et al., 2006). With the use of blood tests, others have found that low levels of monoamine oxidase (MAO) (an enzyme responsible for the breakdown of dopamine, norepinephrine, and epinephrine) have been associated with violent offending (Belfrage, Lidberg, & Oreland, 1992).

Lastly, genetics researchers have attempted to identify genes that are responsible for producing symptoms of CD and aggression. Aside from research that has reported a link between functional polymorphisms of genes that code for neurotransmission (see earlier discussion), much of this research focuses on identifying genes that increase one's susceptibility for conduct disordered behavior through the associative link with alcoholism (e.g., Dick et al., 2004; Stallings et al., 2005; Kendler et al., 2006). Thus, researchers have not identified a single gene of chromosomal loci responsible for the expression of CD or delinquent behavior. Much of the research focuses on susceptibility for CD behavior through the associative link with alcoholism because researchers have consistently found support for a genetic susceptibility for alcoholism, and consistent evidence that alcohol consumption is associated with externalizing behaviors (Hesselbrock, Higuchi, & Soyka, 2005). Given that many children with CD symptoms grow up to abuse alcohol and related drugs, this area of research seems promising.

Neurobiology

Consistently, researchers have found that executive functioning deficits are the most reliable neurocognitive correlate of conduct problems (Morgan & Lilienfeld, 2000; Sergeant, Geurts, & Oosterlaan, 2002). Poor executive functioning is characterized by disorganized planning and limited ability to initiate appropriate activities and to inhibit inappropriate actions. Executive functioning is largely controlled by the frontal lobes and frontal lobe damage has been associated with aggressive behavior. A large body of evidence supports this association (see chapter by Ishikawa and Raine [2002], a meta-analytical review by Morgan and Lilienfeld [2000], and a recent article by Raine, Loeber et al. [2005], which begins to tackle limitations of this association). In addition to frontal lobe deficits and aggression, research has also focused on overall IQ and verbal functioning deficits (e.g., Moffitt, 1990b; Moffitt & Silva, 1988) in children with early-onset CD.

It should be noted that there are several confounds in the frontal lobe-antisocial behavior relationship that these reviews have not resolved. First, many studies rely on neuropsychological tests as indirect measures of brain damage, thus diluting the findings for a frontal lobe–antisocial behavior relationship. Structural damage would be better assessed through the use of brain imaging techniques. Second, measures of frontal lobe structure and function have been taken after conduct problems have been established. Given the fact that early-onset CD is also associated with environmental correlates that are themselves associated with brain abnormalities (e.g., poor nutrition and inadequate stimulation), the causal role of brain damage cannot be established in these correlational or retrospective studies.

Although a large number of studies have linked frontal lobe and executive functioning deficits to child CD and delinquency, there is no agreed upon functional explanation for this connection. For example, impulse control, poor memory functioning, deficits in processing emotional stimuli, and low academic achievement have all been suggested as potential explanations for this association. Future work in this area would benefit from the explicit articulation of the role of relevant neurocognitive functions in a theoretical context.

Psychophysiology

In light of the theories positing a relationship between central nervous system functioning and delinquent behavior, researchers have investigated the autonomic nervous system substrates of delinquency. Lorber (2004) conducted a meta-analysis of studies investigating the association between heart rate, heart rate reactivity, skin conductance (SCR), and antisocial behavior in children and adults. SCR is a gross measure of sympathetic nervous system arousal and is often considered one indicator of BIS activation (see Beauchaine, 2001). Child studies were included if the sample consisted of children exhibiting delinquent behavior or CD. The primary findings from the meta-analysis were as follows:

1. Lower resting heart rate and greater heart rate reactivity were associated with conduct problems in children and adolescents.
2. Lower resting SCR was associated with conduct problems in children but not adolescents.
3. Attenuated task SCR was associated with conduct problems in children and adolescents.

In addition to studies measuring heart rate, some researchers have investigated more specific indices of cardiac functioning. Beauchaine et al. (2001) investigated the associations between preejection period (PEP) and respiratory sinus arrhythmia (RSA) and comorbid CD/attention-deficit/hyperactivity disorder (ADHD) in adolescents. PEP is one indicator of the sympathetic nervous system influence on the heart period (see Sherwood, Allen, Obrist, & Langer, 1986) and is considered an indicator of BAS functioning (see

Beauchaine, 2001). RSA, on the other hand, is one indicator of parasympathetic nervous system influence on the heart period (see Porges, 1995). Beauchaine and colleagues found that children with comorbid CD/ADHD, compared with controls, displayed reduced resting RSA, similar RSA reactivity to threat, less resting PEP activity, and less PEP reactivity to reward. Similarly, Pine et al. (1998) found that attenuated RSA was associated with conduct problems in children aged 7 to 11.

Taken together, these data support an autonomic nervous system underarousal hypothesis (e.g., Hare, 1978) of criminal behavior. Essentially, this hypothesis contends that persistent criminals are chronically physiologically underaroused, which causes sensation seeking and failure to learn from punishment. This hypothesis fits neatly with the broader biological theories outlined earlier in that these physiological deficits are presumably the result of anatomical and/or functional deficits in the prefrontal cortex. Raine et al. (1990) found support for the predictive utility of these indicators, showing that autonomic hypoarousal at age 15 predicted criminal behavior at age 24 in a male sample. Moreover, Raine, Venables, and Mednick et al. (1997) found further support; autonomic hypoarousal at age 3 predicted aggressive behavior at age 11 in a sample of 1795 male and female children.

There are three major limitations to research on psychophysiological correlates of conduct problems: first, assessment measures and the definition of delinquency and/or CD varies greatly across studies; second, the types of threatening and reward stimuli used in these experiments also varies greatly across studies; lastly, the examination of potential cultural and ethnic differences in the relationship between criminal behavior and psychophysiological reactivity in children is lacking. More broadly speaking, much of the research on biological factors and CD and delinquency does not take into account the social context. We will demonstrate the importance of doing so by highlighting one further biological factor that has been examined in association with conduct disorders—testosterone.

Gonadal Hormones

Because of research evidence that boys are more likely to be aggressive than girls, it has repeatedly been suggested that gonadal hormones may be an important cause of aggression. Of particular interest has been the relationship between testosterone and aggression. In a meta-analysis investigating the relationship between testosterone and aggression, investigators found a large range of correlations, ranging from −0.28 to 0.71, with a weak overall weighted mean of 0.14 (Book, Starzyk, & Quinsey, 2001). Such a range in estimates of the link between testosterone and aggression is partly due to measuring aggression that is context specific. For example, positive correlations have been more consistent among studies examining the testosterone and aggression link in competitive situations, or in response to threat (Olweus, 1986).

As suggested earlier, research on testosterone in puberty does not suggest a direct causal connection to violent behavior. Contrary to what they hypothesized, researchers have not found that early-maturing, high testosterone boys are more aggressive. Instead, research on hormonal changes of adolescents suggests that the timing of maturation relates to behavior problems in a more complex manner. Specifically, both early and late maturation have links to increased risk for problems, and these appear to be gender specific (Susman, Nottelmann, Dorn, Inoff-Germain, & Chrousos, 1988). For boys, late pubertal maturation may be associated with aggression. The picture is different for girls. Here, early maturation is a risk factor for conduct problems (Tarter et al., 1999). The link may be due to environmental influences such as increased contact with males involved in risky behavior (Caspi, Lynam, Moffitt, & Silva, 1993). Later maturation appears to be a protective factor for girls in this regard.

Recent research on the interaction between testosterone and social context seems to be a promising avenue for future research. For example, Booth et al. (2003) found that a high quality parent–son relationship diminished the impact of testosterone on risk behaviors, and a poor parent–son relationship strengthened the link. Furthermore, Rowe et al. (2004) found that the relationship between testosterone and level of externalizing behavior was impacted by association with deviant peer groups. Specifically, testosterone was related to delinquent behaviors among boys who had deviant peer groups, whereas it was associated with leadership in boys who did not have deviant peers.

The research on testosterone and aggression highlights several of the problematic issues in research linking biological factors with CD and delinquency. First, researchers do not define their dependent measure consistently across studies. Most pressingly, future research should focus on deriving consistent operationalizations of delinquent and CD behaviors for specific age-groups. Second, biological researchers often do not attend to potentially important environmental moderators in their analyses. Third, females have typically been neglected or understudied in relation to the biological bases of CD. Finally, much of the empirical literature to date has been atheoretical in nature (however, this has been changing for the better in the past two decades).

Juvenile Psychopathy

A subset of child and adolescent delinquents show especially poor long-term prognoses. These children are commonly referred to as fledgling psycho-paths (Lynam, 1998) or juvenile psychopaths, and are described as conduct-disordered children exhibiting a callous and unemotional interpersonal style characteristic of adult psychopathy. In addition to delinquency, these children display lack of guilt, lack of empathy, pathological lying, and shallow affect (Blair, 2001). Although psychopathy is not synonymous with violent behavior, psychopathic offenders are four to six times more likely to engage in repeated violence than nonpsychopathic offenders (e.g., Hemphill, Hare, & Wong, 1998; Wong, 1985). Therefore, the biological substrates of psychopathy are particularly salient when considering the developmental pathways to violent behavior.

Genetics and Psychopathy

Lykken (1995) argued that the etiology of psychopathy is largely biological. Twin studies investigating the heritability of psychopathy support Lykken's contention (e.g., Blonigen, Carlson, Krueger, & Patrick, 2003; Larsson et al., 2007; Taylor, Loney, Bobadilla, Iacono, & McGue, 2003; Viding, Blair, Moffitt, & Plomin, 2005). For example, Viding and colleagues investigated the heritability of psychopathic traits in a sample of 459 male twin pairs at age 7 from the Twins Early Development Study (Trouton, Spinath, & Plomin, 2002). Psychopathic traits were assessed using the Minnesota Temperament Inventory (MTI; Loney, Taylor, Butler, & Iacono, 2002), a 19-item Likert-scaled self-report measure. Overall, the authors found that the heritability of high levels of callous-unemotional traits was 0.67 (95% confidence interval: 0.47 to 0.87). When combining high levels of callous-unemotional traits and antisocial behavior, the authors found that the heritability estimate was 0.81 (95% confidence interval: 0.50 to 1.12).

Taylor and colleagues (2003) investigated the heritability of psychopathic traits in a sample of 270 monozygotic (MZ) and 128 dizygotic (DZ) male twin pairs at ages 16 to 18 from the Minnesota Twin Family Study. Similar to Viding and colleagues, the authors measured psychopathy using the MTI. The results indicated that the heritability of the callous and unemotional traits (referred to as the Detachment scale in this study) was 0.42 (0.32 to 0.51), and that the heritability of antisocial behaviors was 0.39 (0.28 to 0.48). The combined bivariate heritability estimate of callous-unemotional traits and antisocial behavior was 0.53.

Larsson and colleagues (2007) expanded on the findings of Taylor et al. (2003) and Viding et al. (2005) by investigating the heritability of psychopathic traits in a large Swedish sample of adolescent male and female twins from the Twin Study of Child and Adolescent Development. The sample was comprised of 2198 twin pairs, of which 714 were males, 818 were females, and 666 were opposite sex pairs. Psychopathic personality traits were measured using the Youth Psychopathic Traits Inventory (YPI; Andershed, Kerr, Stattin, & Levander, 2002). Similar to previous studies, Larsson and colleagues (2007) found that the heritability estimate for psychopathic traits was 0.63. They also found that this estimate was similar across genders.

Taken together, these studies suggest that more than half of the variance in psychopathic traits is heritable. These findings are robust given the size of the effect, the large sample sizes, and the consistency across measures of psychopathic traits. Moreover, the heritability estimates appear to remain consistent from childhood through adolescence with the possibility of a small decline with age. However, longitudinal investigations indicating intraindividual changes over time are required to explore potential developmental shifts in heritability estimates. Future studies should also investigate potential differences in the heritability of classes of antisocial behaviors (e.g., violent vs. nonviolent), as studies have found that physically aggressive (or violent) children perform worse on measures of executive functioning than their nonviolent peers (e.g., Seguin, Boulerice, Harden, Tremblay, & Pihl, 1999).

Similar to those for CD, there are some methodological limitations to these studies (as pointed out by the authors). First, all three studies used self-report measures of psychopathy. This is a serious limitation, given that deceitfulness and manipulation are characteristics of the disorder. Future studies should incorporate structured interview measures (e.g., Psychopathy Checklist-Revised) that use file information (such as criminal or educational records) to check the accuracy of the participant statements. Second, although twin studies are convenient and useful for testing heritability, it remains unclear whether twins are representative of the population at large. Moreover, it is also unclear whether estimates of the shared environment are comparable across MZ and DZ twins.

Neurobiology and Psychopathy

Although genetic studies suggest that psychopathy is largely heritable, they do not address the specific biological mechanisms through which genetic influences perpetuate violent behavior. Blair et al. (2006) conducted a thorough review of this literature. Their findings suggest that the amygdala and orbitofrontal and ventrolateral frontal cortex are implicated in psychopathy. In short, the same brain areas implicated in the development of early-onset CD are implicated in the development of psychopathy. However, as Blair et al. point out, it is likely that these brain structures are not exclusively responsible for the phenomenon of psychopathy.

Gonadal Hormones and Psychopathy

There is a dearth of research examining the association between hormone functioning and juvenile psychopathy. Loney et al. (2006) found that lower resting salivary cortisol was higher in juvenile psychopaths, compared with controls and nonpsychopathic children with conduct problems, and in males compared to females in a sample of 108 adolescents. They did not find any association between resting testosterone levels and juvenile psychopathy. This study represents a new area of research requiring replication and the inclusion of additional moderators (e.g., ethnicity), however, before any firm conclusions can be drawn about the relationship.

Bullying Behavior and Proactive Aggression

Because instrumental aggression is considered a predictor of persistent offending, we examine bullying behavior in school-aged children. Within the aggression literature, studies have focused either on aggression as a general concept or on distinct subtypes of aggression. One subtype distinction concerns the differences between reactive (or hostile) aggression and proactive (or instrumental) aggression. Reactive aggression is defined as aggressive acts that occur in response to the hostile behavior of another. In contrast, proactive aggression occurs without provocation. Planned aggression and bullying behavior fall into the category of proactive aggression (Dodge, 1991; Dodge & Coie, 1987). Bullying behavior has most frequently been examined in relation to the attitudes and behaviors of bullies (Atlas & Pepler, 1998; Glover, Gough, Johnson, & Cartwright, 2000; Whitney & Smith, 1993). There are very few investigations focusing on the neuropsychological and psychophysiological correlates of proactive aggression. This section focuses on these correlates in general aggression, as a framework for understanding the current literature regarding proactive aggression.

IQ and Proactive Aggression

One neurological factor that is frequently cited in the literature in relationship to aggression is intelligence as measured by IQ. Low IQ is consistently associated with increases in aggressive behavior across childhood and adulthood (DeYoung et al., 2006; Giancola & Zeichner, 1994). One longitudinal study examined IQ and aggression in over 600 subjects, their parents, and their children (Huesmann, Eron, & Yarmel, 1987). Results from the study revealed that early IQ predicted changes in aggression until the age of eight. Furthermore, it was revealed that childhood aggression was related to low intellectual functioning into adulthood. On the basis of these findings, the authors hypothesized that individuals with low intellectual functioning were more likely to learn aggressive behaviors early in life and that these behaviors in turn interfered with the development of intellectual functioning.

Another study investigated gender differences in aggression in a sample of children and adolescents. While rates of aggression were high in both males and females, low verbal IQ was most strongly related to proactive aggression in girls (Connor, Steingard, Anderson, & Melloni, 2003). Low verbal scores may be indicative of skill deficits in such areas as receptive listening and reading, expressive speech and writing, and memory for verbal material (Moffitt, 1990b). Deficits in these areas may frustrate individuals and lead them to act out aggressively when they are unable to communicate effectively verbally. Low verbal IQ scores have been the focus of other studies of delinquency and aggression. Discrepancies between the two components of the full scale IQ, verbal and performance, are well documented in the literature (Sattler, 1992). A performance IQ score that is significantly higher than the verbal IQ score has been associated with delinquency (Cornell & Wilson, 1992; Wong & Cornell, 1999). Some studies have further documented a link between this discrepancy and violence or aggression (DeWolfe & Ryan, 1984; Petee & Walsh, 1987), while others have not found such a relationship (Cornell & Wilson, 1992; Wong & Cornell, 1999). If low verbal IQ scores are indicative of proactive aggression, a discrepancy between the performance and verbal IQ may also be related to proactive aggression. Further investigation into this issue is required to determine the validity of discrepancies between performance and verbal IQ as an indicator of proactive aggression.

Though IQ scores can provide important neuropsychological information, they do not provide enough information regarding the specific neuropsychological deficits that underlie the association between IQ and aggression (Block, 1995; Kandel & Freed, 1989; Moffitt & Silva, 1988). Tests of executive functioning, brain imaging techniques, and psychophysiological measures provide more information regarding these deficits.

Neurobiology and Bullying

On the basis of a theoretical framework for understanding bullying behavior, suggested by Grigsby and Stevens (2000), researchers examined deficits in the functioning of the frontal lobes in a sample of middle school students between the ages of 11 and 15 (Coolidge, DenBoer, & Segal, 2004). Grigsby and Stevens (2000) suggest that appropriate functioning in the frontal lobes is necessary for appropriate social behavior. Bullies may act out inappropriately due to dysfunction in their frontal lobes. Coolidge et al. (2004) found that subjects who were identified as bullies exhibited greater neuropsychological dysfunction than controls. Executive function deficits were detected in the areas of (1) decision making, planning, organizing; (2) learning and integrating information; and (3) making appropriate social judgments (Coolidge et al., 2004). Poor executive functions have also been noted in juvenile delinquents (Coolidge et al., 1992) and adolescents who are aggressive (LeMarquand, et al., 1998; Moffitt, Lynam, & Silva, 1994; Seguin, Nagin, Assaad, & Tremblay, 2004; Seguin, Pihl, Harden, Tremblay, & Boulerice, 1995). The relationship between executive functions and aggression remained after controlling for ADHD, general memory, and IQ (Seguin et al., 1999).

As noted previously, brain imaging studies have also provided evidence supporting a relationship between frontal lobe dysfunction and aggression. There have been few studies examining proactive aggression in particular as related to brain functioning. One study detected lower prefrontal function in individuals who had committed impulsive murders than those who planned their murders. This finding suggests that prefrontal function may be lower in reactive aggression than proactive aggression (Raine, Buchsbaum et al., 1994). Further investigation is warranted in this area.

Psychophysiology and Proactive Aggression

An investigation of children's aggression examined the psychophysiological measures of skin conductance reactivity and heart rate reactivity in relationship to proactive and reactive aggression. Reactive aggression was positively related to skin conductance reactivity. Proactive aggression was not related to any psychophysiological measures (Hubbard et al., 2002). Scarpa and Raine (1997) conducted a review of psychophysiological findings related to proactive and reactive aggression. Measures included skin conductance, heart rate, electro-cardiogram (EEG), and event-related potential. Findings indicated that pro-active aggression may be related to underarousal and that reactive aggression may be related to overarousal.

Sexual Aggression

Sexual violence is a subset of violent behavior that is often examined sepa-rately from other types of aggression and characterized by compulsive and persistent offending. These violent acts include physical assaults that leave long-lasting effects on the victims leading to a variety of internalizing and ext-ernalizing disorders. A variety of neuropsychological characteristics have been investigated in an attempt to better understand and prevent these behaviors.

IQ and Sexual Aggression

IQ is one of the most commonly studied neuropsychological characteristics of sexual offenders. Studies have produced inconsistent results. Cantor et al. (2005) conducted a meta-analysis of the literature. They determined that adult and adolescent sexual offenders exhibited significantly lower IQ scores than nonsexual offenders (offenders who had committed other types of crimes). Among the adult sexual offenders, they further determined that those who targeted child victims exhibited a lower IQ than nonsexual offend-ers. Adult sexual offenders who targeted adult victims did not differ signif-icantly from those who targeted child victims or nonsexual offenders. No significant differences in IQ were found between adult sexual offenders who target individuals outside of their family as compared to incestual offenders. There were also no significant differences between adult offenders who pre-ferred male as compared to female victims (Cantor, Blanchard, Robichaud, & Christensen, 2005). As with studies of general delinquency and aggression, it is important to examine other neuropsychological characteristics of sexual offenders.

Neurobiology and Sexual Aggression

One important neuropsychological characteristic is frontal-executive func-tioning. The findings in literature regarding this area of functioning in sexual offenders are mixed. Kelly et al. (2002) examined response speed, planning and organization, verbal conceptualization, and motor organization in a sample of adolescent sex offenders compared to a control group of nonoffenders matched for age. The sexual offenders exhibited significantly lower scores only on the response speed component. No other differences were detected. Another study examining executive functioning compared functioning in a sample of adolescent sexual offenders with a sample of adolescent nonsexual offenders. The Trail Making Test, the Controlled Oral Word Association test of the Multilingual Aphasia Examination, the Tower of London, and the Wisconsin Card-sorting Test were administered. Results revealed a pattern of frontal-executive dysfunction in both groups (Veneziano, Veneziano, LeGrand, & Richards, 2004). On the basis of this evidence, it appears that frontal-executive dysfunction may be related to delinquency in general, but not adolescent sexual offenses in particular.

Evidence from adult brain imaging studies has allowed researchers to begin to tease apart the functional information regarding violent and sexual offending. Mills and Raine (1994) conducted a meta-analysis of 20 studies that used computerized tomography (CT), magnetic resonance imaging (MRI), and positron emission tomography (PET) techniques to provide structural and functional information about brain dysfunction in violent and sexual offenders. Results indicated that frontal lobe dysfunction may be associated with violent offending and that dysfunction in the temporal lobe may be associated with sexual offending. Fronto-temporal lobe dysfunction may be associated with violent sexual offending (Mills & Raine, 1994). Consistent with these results, a later study using PET scans found decreased glucose metabolism in the temporal and frontal cortices of pedophiles (L. J. Cohen et al., 2002). Further investigation using these techniques is merited in the examination of neuropsychological deficits that may be associated with sexual offending. Brain imaging techniques are now safer for use with children, and it appears that further examination of brain deficits that may be specifically linked to sexual offending might be of value in prevention and intervention in this area.

Conclusion

The preceding summary of biological factors and behavior associated with persistent offending (child conduct disorders and delinquency, juvenile psychopathy, bullying, and sexual aggression) reveals a similarity of findings across the divergent but related outcomes that have been examined. A variety of biological factors, including genetics, perinatal insults, frontal lobe function-ing, hormones, and psychophysiology have been associated with the various child outcomes. Some biological factors appear to be specific to particular developmental outcomes, such as sexual aggression. Empirical support was noted for Moffitt, Gray and Damasio's theories. For example, perinatal factors were related to persistent aggression (as per Moffitt), BIS hypoarousal was related to delinquency (as per Gray), and physiological hyporesponsive-ness to threat cues was related to delinquency (as per Damasio). Nevertheless, the empirical studies of biological factors and delinquent and criminal out-comes in childhood are largely atheoretical, and lack an overarching model that could inform prevention and intervention efforts in this area. At the outset of this chapter, we outlined some common misperceptions about the role of biological factors in crime. One of the most feared notions is that biological risk factors might be equated with a predetermined outcome, from the earliest phases of life. In fact, biological factors are influenced by the envi-ronment throughout development, and may suggest important distinctions for the tailoring of intervention programs to meet individual needs for change. Further theoretical explications and tests of biological risk—criminal out-come relationships that can be tested in the context of developmentally sensi-tive research paradigms are necessary for this area of research to reach its full potential.

CHAPTER 8

A Systematic Approach to Understanding Human Variability in Serious, Persistent Offending

JOHN PAUL WRIGHT AND KEVIN M. BEAVER

> Life can only be understood backwards; but it must be lived
> forwards.
> —*Soren Kierkegaard, Danish Philosopher (1813–1855)*

Human development is subject to myriad influences that occur at varying levels (Wachs, 2000). From conception forward, the development of the human organism relies on the constant interplay between biological, genetic, and social influences. While these interactions are infinitely complex, the modal outcome is the production of an adaptable individual capable of abstract reasoning and behavioral self-regulation. Whether an individual was born into a nomadic tribe in Saudi Arabia, was placed into a Romanian orphanage, or grew up with all the comforts available in Western civilization, the likelihood is high that he/she will mature into an adaptive and capable adult. Indeed, despite the potential adverse influences of a variety of social risk factors, despite tremendous differences across cultures in socialization practices and social resources, and despite exposure to extremely depriving environments, most individuals develop into functional adults capable of socially appropriate ethical behavior.

Serious, persistent offenders (SPOs), however, stand in stark contrast to this general developmental rule. Instead of developing into socially sophisticated adults capable of adapting to multiple social roles, SPOs tend to follow a life-course pathway that departs substantially from normative developmental parameters and that leads to limited adaptability across varying contexts. SPOs, for example, tend to have deficits in executive functions, such as self-control, planning, abstract reasoning, language use, and comprehension and they score, on average, one standard deviation below normal on IQ (DeLisi, 2005). They also tend to score in the clinical range on a variety of criminogenic precursors, such as oppositional defiant disorder and conduct disorder in childhood. Due in part to these limitations and behavioral patterns, SPOs frequently reach adulthood with limited personal and social resources (Moffitt, 1993). They are likely to have dropped out of high school, to have fathered offspring, to have been arrested as a youth, to be unemployed or unemployable, and to have been incarcerated (Moffitt, Caspi, Rutter, & Silva, 2001).

Serious, persistent offenders are not only unique because of their departure from normative developmental pathways but also because of their persistence in criminal conduct, which is a marker for serious social pathology. For adults in the general population, the base-rate for involvement in serious criminal conduct, such as murder, robbery, or rape, is zero; for adolescents, the base-rate for involvement in serious criminal behavior ranges between zero and one (Elliott, 1994). Simply put, the vast majority of individuals never engage in a serious act of criminal behavior. Deviations from these base rates, especially deviations substantively different from zero, thus represent the deep end of the continuum of psychopathological behavior (Caspi & Moffitt, 1995; Caspi & Roberts, 2001; Loeber, 1982).

Serious and persistent offenders represent a distinct subgroup of individuals even within the offender population. Unlike low-rate, temporally limited offenders, persistent offenders are typically highly active in their offending, they commit a diverse array of crimes, and their "criminal careers" can extend into old age (Caspi & Moffitt, 1995; Caspi et al., 2003; DeLisi, 2005; Moffitt, 1993; Trulson, Marquart, Mullings, & Caeti, 2005). They are also more similar to one another in personality and behavioral history compared to the less embedded, less serious offenders. Moreover, compared to temporally limited offenders, persistent offenders are significantly more likely to show an early onset of behavioral dysregulation (Arseneault et al., 2003; Campbell, Shaw, & Gilliom, 2000; Nagin & Farrington, 1992a, 1992b; see also Chapter 9), to show a consistent pattern of hostility in relationships, to show a consistent pattern of low impulse control and limited emotional regulation (Caspi et al., 2003; Pratt & Cullen, 2000), and to show a consistent pattern of failing to attain normative social roles (Sampson & Laub, 1993).

High-rate, persistent offenders represent a somewhat homogenous group of individuals whose antisocial behavioral patterns show remarkable cross-time and cross-situation continuity. From a developmental perspective, however, they also represent a substantial deviation from normative developmental trajectories and associated outcomes. In this chapter, we examine the underlying genetic and biological mechanics of variance in human traits associated with serious and prolonged offending. We are guided by a simple and straightforward insight, namely that variance in certain traits, such as IQ or low self-control, leads to more, or less, interpersonal susceptibility to criminogenic environmental influences. These underlying mechanics thus link biological and genetic sources of variance to deviant behavioral pathways and to deficiencies in social functioning. Our work is rooted in Darwinian evolution, with its focus on the selection of traits across unique environments. However, we also utilize contemporary work in molecular and behavioral genetics to help pinpoint the mechanisms that make some individuals more, or less, vulnerable to social risk factors. We close the chapter with an illustration of the nexus between genes and environmental risk factors—in this case, serious physical abuse.

An Evolutionary Background

Contemporary neuroscience has laid waste to the Lockean notion that individuals are born "blank slates"—that is, that humans have no innate capacities and are highly pliable and receptive to socialization (Harris, 1998; Pinker, 2002). As science has shown, human development relies on a complex mix of evolutionarily influenced genetic traits that unfold in, interact with, and correlate with, environmental conditions (Rowe, 1994). Far from being wholly dependent on socialization influences, modern humans enter the world with some well developed instincts, such as the ability to distinguish their mother's voice from all other voices and their ability to recognize the face of their mother against similar faces (Barrera & Maurer, 1981; Bushnell, Sai, & Mullin, 1989; Cohen, 1974; DeCasper & Fifer, 1980). While this does not deny the importance of socialization, it does force a more complex understanding of the development of serious, persistent offending. Indeed, *tabula rasa* views of any trait or behavior stand contrary to the laws of genetics and to established empirical findings (Pinker, 2002).

Because of evolutionary processes, the majority of individuals in any society are adaptable, are capable of prosocially solving problems, and are *resistant* to environmental risk factors. Human evolution, after all, has been a hard and labor-intensive process guided by the hand of natural selection. With this in mind, we first note that human DNA has been under constant selection pressure. Selection pressures, as well as random mutations and genetic drift, created complex, evolved genotypes that are generally adaptable to a range of environmental conditions. From this standpoint, contemporary genotypes represent the sum total of evolved, and largely adaptive, changes in the structure of genes over millions of years of human evolution. As Darwinian evolution reminds us, genes are retained over time because they have provided the human organism with an adaptive response to prior environmental problems.

This point is often lost when discussing the influence genes have on human behavioral traits, especially behaviors or traits associated with serious negative consequences. For the most part, our genes have evolved and have been successfully passed through generations *because* they aided our survival—that is, most genes exist to protect us from various threats. The human capacity to act violently, especially in males, illustrates this point well. The ability to summon merciless violence was clearly an advantage in prehistoric times when intertribal or clan warfare was waged, when animals had to be hunted and killed by hand, and when the protection of self and kin was necessary (Wade, 2006).

Predatory violence, we also note, has been and remains the domain of males (Ghiglieri, 1999). That the tasks of hunting and warfare have historically fallen to males seems consistent with the fact that males are 40% biochemically stronger—that is, their muscles oxygenate quicker and remove waste byproducts more efficiently than females—have 2.5 times the brain volume dedicated to aggression and sex, and have larger amygdalas, which register fear and anxiety, than do females (Brizendine, 2006; Ghiglieri, 1999). This may be why every culture in recorded history has experienced male dominated warfare and violence (Ghiglieri, 1999). Violence, it appears, is a uniform human capacity that is much more common among males than females because of its evolutionary necessity.

The critic may point out that, given our evolutionary backdrop, violent individuals should be more plentiful. After all, if violence is genetically encoded, it should be more frequent. This criticism overlooks the powerful evolutionary forces that aided in the creation of "social" human beings—that is, humans who extend trust to others, who act altruistically, and who do not use violence as the primary mechanism to achieve goals or status. Even though the capacity for violence may be uniform across individuals and societies, it remains a fact that contemporary human development, more often than not, produces adaptive and prosocial individuals. This is true across virtually every culture. Indeed, anthropologists point out that a reduction in overt aggression and a concomitant increase in social reciprocity may have served as turning points in human evolution (Wade, 2006). The genetic and social changes that allowed the formation of nonkin dominated societies necessarily meant that individuals incapable of regulating their conduct had to be regulated, supervised, banished, or killed. Thus for at least the last 25,000 years, human civilizations have become progressively less violent and more heavily regulated by state power (Richerson & Boyd, 2005).

Evolutionary changes help to explain why persistent offenders are relatively few in number in any society. Where evolution primes the genotype for survival, persistent offenders in modern society have substantially elevated mortality rates, largely because their behaviors and lifestyles place them at an elevated risk of early death. Where evolution should produce individuals capable of adapting in a range of social settings, persistent offenders most frequently fail at common and expected social transitions. Finally, in complex situations where novel behaviors are required, persistent offenders are significantly more likely to employ ineffective and potentially destructive behaviors. Serious and persistent criminals are uncommon, partly because their behavioral orientations are pathologically deviant to the expectations of any society. By modern standards, they also represent the "deep end" of human pathology.

The Mechanics of Individual Variability

Siblings growing up in the same household, being raised by the same parents, residing in the same neighborhoods, and attending the same schools often turn out different from each other. Consider, for example, a hypothetical example of two siblings. One sibling led a relatively prosocial life; he graduated from high school, secured legal employment, and raised a family. His sibling, however, had a very different life. During adolescence he was arrested for physically assaulting an elderly neighbor and was thus remanded to a juvenile detention center. The remainder of his adolescence was punctuated by bouts of violent aggression, which ultimately resulted in even more contact with the criminal justice system. By adulthood, he had a substantial criminal record and continued to engage in acts of serious violence. Eventually, he was killed in a street fight.

The preceding example strongly suggests that nonenvironmental factors are important in the development of persistent criminality. If antisocial phenotypes were due solely to environmental and social factors, then siblings should be very similar to each other in terms of their personalities, their talents, their interests, their values, and especially their behaviors. Empirical evidence does not bear these points out, however. Indeed, behavioral genetic research has revealed that once genetic effects are held constant, two siblings from the same household are no more similar to each other on myriad phenotypes than two unrelated children picked at random (Harris, 1998; Rowe, 1994).

This poses a problem for most environmental theories of crime. Many sociological perspectives forecast that similar environmental influences and socialization efforts produce individuals with similar behavioral repertoires. Various studies, however, have shown just the opposite. Exposure to similar environments or to similar socialization efforts highlights individual differences instead of creating uniform individuals (Rutter, 2006). Studies conducted at the neighborhood level reveal, for instance, substantial individual differences in self-control and other crime-related traits within the same neighborhood. Moreover, numerous studies into family processes reveal tremendous variability between children raised in the same environment (Harris, 1998).

Why do individuals exposed to the same environmental influences vary, sometimes dramatically, in their development? The passive transfer of nuclear material from one generation to the next is an obvious suspect. However, contemporary estimates of the number of genes in the human genotype range between 19,000 and 25,000. This number is significantly smaller than those found in "lower" life forms, such as some plants and bacteria. The limited number of genes in the *Homo sapiens* genotype is far too small for it to code for many single-gene-single-disorder effects, such as Fragile X syndrome or Huntington's disease. Indeed, complex behaviors, such as predatory criminal conduct, are polygenetic, with each gene contributing a small to moderate *bias* toward a specific crime-related trait.

Traditional genetic estimates have found that 99.9% of genes are the same in humans. Traditional genetic estimates found that only 0.1% of all genes varied between humans, largely due to natural selection and chance mutations. This limited range of variance, however, was still associated with a 3,000,000 base-pair difference between individuals (differences across individuals in DNA base pairs are referred to as variable nucleotide tandem repeats [VNTRs]). Recently, three independent international research projects have discovered that at least 10% of all human genes, or roughly 2900 genes, can vary in their number of copies within an individual. Thus, estimates that used to indicate that humans were 99.9% genetically similar have to be revised to approximately 99% genetically similar. This means that instead of a 3 million base-pair difference between humans, there are at least 30 million base-pairs that differ.

Clearly, if these studies are correct, there is sufficient genetic variation across humans to account for the formation of heritable traits that create susceptibility to criminogenic environments. Genetic variation occurs at multiple levels. VNTRs, which we have just discussed, represent only one form of genetic difference. Other molecular differences occur when nucleotide chains are altered by a single base pair difference, known as a single nucleotide polymorphism (SNP). There are literally millions of SNPs that vary across individuals. Unfortunately, little is currently known about the relationship between SNPs and human traits and behaviors.

Variable nucleotide tandem repeats and SNPs vary across individuals, often by race and ethnicity. They create differences across individuals in their response to internal processes. For example, it is well known in the medical community that drugs do not have the same effect on everyone. Researchers have found, for example, that the effectiveness of the breast cancer drug tamoxifen depends on the ratio of activity between an active *HOXB13* gene and an inactive *IL17BR* gene (Michalides et al., 2004). Similarly, people with certain other genotypes appear to be hyporesponsive to opiates (D2) and to alcohol, making addiction significantly more likely.

For the most part, gene-directed development relies on ontogenic processes, but researchers are discovering that genes also operate through sociogenic processes whereby environmental elements influence alterations in gene-directed developmental sequelae. For example, at any point along the developmental cycle, from the moment gametes and their genetic materials are combined and begin the cycle of meiosis, through pre- and perinatal development, insults to the central nervous system that cause the human organism to function at less than its optimal genetic potential can occur. This can be seen, for example, when complications at birth deprive the fetus of sufficient oxygen (anoxia), which can cause minor to major brain damage, or even death (Beaver & Wright, 2005), or when neurotoxins disrupt normative brain development (McGloin, Pratt, & Piquero, 2006; Piquero, Gibson, Tibbetts, Turner, & Katz, 2002; Yolton, Dietrich, Auinger, Lanphear, & Hornung, 2005), or when environments are so absent of stimulation that IQ is suppressed (Rowe, Almeida, & Jacobson, 1999).

Contemporary genotypes thus reflect evolved genetic potentials. We emphasize the term "potentials" because genes direct the creation and maintenance of human organs, primarily the brain and the central nervous system, and they regulate the production of amino acids. Genes do not "cause" behavior in the traditional sense of the word. What they do, however, is create individual response biases to internal and external stimuli. It is these evolved biases and potentials that are heritable—that is, partially transferable from one generation to the next—and it is these genetically influenced biases and potentials that create individual differences in environmental susceptibility.

The Long Road from Gene to Individual Difference

As Gottesman and Hanson (2005) caution, it is a long way on the causal pathway from genes to any specific phenotype. As we have already mentioned, polymorphic genes create the first level of individual differences. These genes create amino acids that are then used to structure proteins. Virtually every cell in the adult body contains an individual's genotype. For this to be accomplished, DNA has to be reliably replicated. DNA replication occurs with a high degree of fidelity, yet errors do happen. Most of these replication errors have no known effect on human development and behavior, yet some do.

Genes monitor internal processes and respond to environmental stressors. Surprisingly, genes are not always active. Instead, they tend to turn "on" and "off" through a complex system that includes environmental input. Transcription factors, or proteins that alter the binding of RNA polymerase to DNA, trigger or silence genetic expression. Most human genes are expressed in the brain and the central nervous system. They lay the groundwork for the structure and functioning of the human brain, which includes neurotransmission, receptor sensitivity, and the number of receptor sites in postsynaptic dendrites. Genes also code for neuroendocrine activity, which attempts to keep internal processes in equilibrium.

Taken together, these processes create endophenotypes. An endophenotype is a biologically influenced trait associated with an outcome of interest, in this case persistent violence. As we have mentioned before, the hallmark of persistent criminals is their lack of self-control. In this sense, self-control, which is highly heritable (Wright & Beaver, 2005), falls midway on the causal chain between the genome and the expression of criminal conduct.

For an endophenotype to exist, it must meet the following guidelines (Gottesman & Hanson, 2005, p. 269):

1. The endophenotype is associated with the trait in the population.
2. The endophenotype is heritable.
3. The endophenotype is present even if the trait is not present.
4. The endophenotype and the trait cosegregate (imperfectly) within families.

5. The endophenotype found in families with the trait is found in nonaffected family members at a higher rate than in the general population.

Various scholars advocate research into endophenotypes for two primary reasons (Gottesman & Hanson, 2005). First, the closer the linkage between a gene and its biological expression the greater the statistical power to detect its influence (Gottesman & Hanson, 2005). Second, and more importantly, the identification of endophenotypes associated with persistent criminal conduct may aid in the broader understanding of the complementary roles of genetic and social influences. As we have mentioned before, the hallmark of persistent criminals is their lack of self-control. In this sense, self-control, which is highly heritable (Wright & Beaver, 2005), falls somewhere midway on the causal chain between the genome and the expression of criminal conduct and is a good candidate for an important endophenotype associated with persistent violence. Identifying the genetic linkage, markers, and processes will likely help to explain why some individuals score in the clinical range on low self-control, attentional deficiencies, and impulsiveness while others in the same families and social settings do not. Endophenotypes essentially bring us closer to understanding the processes that create disturbances or perturbations in brain and central nervous system functioning that lay the groundwork for persistent criminal behavior.

Moving forward along the genetic highway we find the connection between endophenotypes and the immediate environment. Youth low in self-control, for instance, are more likely to get into trouble for violating school rules, and they are more likely to do poorly in their educational pursuits. Perhaps because of these factors, they are more likely to interpret the school environment as onerous and are thus more likely to drop out, an environmental factor associated with criminal behavior.

Through these multiple genetically influenced mechanisms emerges behavior. Of course, the behaviors of persistent criminals tend to bring about consequences that range from minor to severe. These consequences are often interpreted as learning contingencies, but they have the effect of reinforcing the genetic processes that have led up to that point. Chronic misbehavior, for example, can lead to social exclusion in childhood, to gang membership in adolescence, and to entrance into adult criminal networks later in life.

The preceding discussion illustrates that a range of genetic and biologically influenced characteristics condition the expression of heritable behavioral traits (endophenotypes). Because of this, the influence of any single gene on behavior is likely to be small. This situation helps to explain why twin studies may show substantial heritability while molecular studies reveal small influences associated with specific candidate genes (Frazzetto et al., 2007). Moreover, understanding that genetic influences are pervasive in human functioning necessarily draws attention to the gene X environment nexus (Rutter, 2007).

The Connection between Genes and Environmental Susceptibility

A complex arrangement of genetic predispositions and environmental factors contributes to persistent criminality and lifelong violent aggression. Biogenic predispositions may provide the initial nudge needed for an individual to begin to move down an antisocial pathway, but the environment is also responsible for sustaining continuity in offending behaviors over long swaths of the life course. The environment and genes are not insulated from each other. Instead, they are highly interdependent. An emerging line of empirical and theoretical research has begun to unpack the ways in which genes and the environment interlock to bring about phenotypic differences. In general, behavioral geneticists have identified two different types of gene-environment interplay: gene X environment interactions (GxE) and gene X environment correlations (rGE).

Gene X Environment Interactions

One of the more promising explanations for why social factors impinge upon people differently is the concept of gene X environment interactions (GxE). The logic of GxEs holds that the effect that a particular criminogenic environment has on human development is conditioned by each person's unique genotype (and vice versa). The genotype is largely responsible for how people filter information, for how they process social cues, and for how they respond to environmental stimuli. Two people exposed to the same environment may respond to it quite differently because of their different genotypes. The environment can blunt genetic effects, such as when an at-risk youth is raised by nurturing parents, or the environment can exacerbate genetic effects, such as when a troubled youth is being raised by abusive parents. Taken together, GxEs can begin to explain why two people with very similar socialization experiences have very divergent life outcomes.

Twin-based research, adoption studies, and molecular genetic studies have pointed to the importance of GxEs in the creation of violent and persistent offending. For example, Jaffee and her colleagues (2005) analyzed twin pairs from the Environmental Risk Study to examine genetic and environmental effects on childhood conduct problems. The results of their analyses revealed that externalizing problem behaviors were due, in part, to the interaction between genetic risk and maltreatment—that is, individuals at the highest level of genetic risk were most affected by maltreatment. Similar results have been reported by Cadoret et al. (1995) in their study employing a sample of adopted children. They examined whether each adoptee resembled his or her biological parents (genetic factors) and whether the adoptee resembled his or her adoptive parents (environmental factor) in terms of antisocial behaviors. Analysis of the data provided evidence suggesting that children most at-risk for aggression, conduct disorder, and adult antisocial behavior were those whose biological parents and adoptive parents had histories of antisocial conduct. Additional studies, using different samples of twins and adoptees, have arrived at similar conclusions—namely, that genes and the environment interact to predispose people to persistent criminality (Mednick, Gabrielli, & Hutchings, 1984).

Perhaps the most convincing evidence of GxEs in the production of antisocial behavior comes from a study conducted by Caspi and his associates (2002). In this study, Caspi et al. were interested in examining whether a functional polymorphism in the MAOA gene and a history of childhood maltreatment were associated with measures of antisocial behavior. Analysis of data from the Dunedin Multidisciplinary Health and Development Study revealed that MAOA and maltreatment interacted to predict variation in antisocial behavior. The findings were striking: although only 12% of the sample had been maltreated and had the low-functioning MAOA genotype, they accounted for 44% of all violent offenses.

The GxE literature has shed new light on the potential ways that genes and the environment may interface in the development of serious, persistent offending. Clearly, studies that focus only on genetic effects or only on environmental effects present an incomplete picture of reality. In all likelihood, genes and the environment interact to affect phenotypic variation. However, behavioral geneticists have also outlined another type of gene-environment interplay—gene X environment correlations—which are also important to the study of persistent criminality.

Gene X Environment Correlations

One of the reasons that social explanations of antisocial behavior dominate criminology is because of the consistent finding that environmental conditions are correlated with individual behaviors and personality traits. According to standard social science perspectives, the environmental effect predates or is antecedent to the behavior. For example, an association between unemployment and violent offending is often interpreted to mean that unemployment causes criminal behavior. But some of these "environmental effects" may be due to biology. Difficult and taxing children are more likely to be raised by cold and withdrawn parents. Academically gifted students are more likely to be reared in enriched environments. Persistently violent adults are unemployed, live in poverty, and reside in disadvantaged neighborhoods. Therefore, it is just as plausible to argue that criminal behavior causes unemployment. After all, most persistent offenders are not reliable workers, they do not arrive to work on time, and they are not model employees. The important point is that individuals, including criminals, are actively involved in selecting, modifying, and shaping their own environment (Scarr & McCartney, 1983). In the present example, criminal offenders may engage in certain actions and behaviors that make them more likely to be unemployed.

Of course, we are not the first to argue that individuals act on their environments. In 1983, Scarr and McCartney (1983) described a theory of genotype → environment effects, where they underscored "the role of the genotype in determining not only which environments are experienced by individuals but also which environments individuals seek for themselves" (p. 424). The key point of their theory was that the genotype was responsible for how people create their own environments (Scarr, 1992). More recently, this theory has evolved into the concept of a gene X environment correlation (rGE). The logic underlying rGEs is that genotypes and environments are often correlated, and the reason for this correlation is because genotype → environment. There are three different types of rGEs—passive rGE, evocative rGE, and active rGE—and each describe a slightly different way that genotypes and environments become correlated.

Children receive two different elements from their parents: genes and an environment. Given that the child's genes and environment are both passed on from the same source (i.e., their parents), they are likely to be correlated with each other. Since children receive genotype and environment passively, this first type of rGE is referred to as a passive rGE. For example, suppose a child was genetically-predisposed to be a gifted athlete because both of his parents were athletically talented. At the same time, the parents also provide an atmosphere that encourages athleticism, such as running and jumping. In this case, the child received the genetic propensity to be an athlete and an environment conducive to athleticism (i.e., genotype correlated with environment). Passive rGEs are important to persistent offending because children at risk for becoming chronic offenders are often hit with a "double whammy," where they are genetically at risk for engaging in delinquency and they are also reared in a criminogenic environment.

The second type of rGE is referred to as an evocative rGE. Evocative rGEs build upon the fact that people elicit or evoke certain responses from the environment due, at least in part, to their genotype (Caspi & Moffitt, 1995). Persistent criminals, for instance, tend to have problems that cut across virtually every sphere of their life. At work, they might be fired because they insulted their boss. At home, their spouse might leave because of physical abuse. At the bar, they may wind up in a fight because they called someone a derogatory term. All of these problems are self-induced: *they* insulted their boss, *they* abused their spouse, and *they* used a derogatory term.

Of course, genes do not directly insult bosses, abuse spouses, or call names. But genes are partially responsible for personality traits that may predispose someone to act in these ways. Research has found that genetics contributes to low self-control, attention-deficit/hyperactivity disorder (ADHD), explosive temper, novelty seeking, sensation seeking, and almost every other imaginable personality trait. But we argue that these traits, to a large extent, are the main cause of environmental reactions. That is to say, genes → personality traits → environments.

The last type of rGE is called an active rGE and refers to the fact that individuals play an active role in finding environments or choosing niches that are conducive to the behaviors they wish to perform. Athletes play sports. Singers sing. Even spouses are very similar to each other on many measurable traits (assortative mating). And criminals, well, they seek out other criminals to befriend and to victimize.

Active rGEs have a great deal of potential in elucidating the underlying causes of some strong criminogenic risk factors. To illustrate, one of the strongest predictors of adolescent delinquent involvement is associating with antisocial peers (Warr, 2002). There is, however, an ongoing debate about whether the delinquent peers-delinquent involvement relationship is due to self-selection (Gottfredson & Hirschi, 1990) or whether it is due to social causation (Akers, 1998). A third potential explanation is that genetic factors are partially responsible for why certain youths affiliate with delinquent friends. To address this question, Cleveland et al. (2005) analyzed data from the National Longitudinal Study of Adolescent Health. The results of their analyses revealed that genetic factors accounted for 64% of the variance in the delinquent peers scale, while the remaining variance was explained by nonshared environmental factors.

An Example of Genetically Influenced Susceptibility to Environmental Conditions

Numerous studies document the correlation between early abuse, severe trauma, social deprivation and later behavioral problems (e.g., Widom, 1989a). While these studies are important, they have rarely been able to explain why the majority of children who have experienced severe abuse and neglect do not develop into SPOs. Contemporary biosocial research, however, has shed new light onto the processes that differentiate abused youth who become SPOs from those who do not.

Monoamine oxidase A (MAOA) is an enzyme that catabolizes mono-amines, such as serotonin, dopamine, and norepinephrine. Release of these neurotransmitters from the postsynaptic membrane of the dendrite invokes the "reuptake" process where free neurotransmitters are reabsorbed by axons and "cleaned up" by the enzymatic activity of MAOA. MAOA is an X-linked polymorphic gene that consists of a 30 base-pair repeated sequences in 3, 3.5, 4, or 5 copies (Sabol, Hu, & Hamer, 1998). Transcriptional efficiency of this enzyme varies according to the number of repeat copies. High-activity alleles are 2 to 10 times more efficient than low-activity alleles and high-activity alleles, when compared to the low-functioning alleles, are also associated with increased catabolization of neurotransmitters.

As discussed previously, Caspi and his colleagues (2002) were the first to report that individuals who were abused as children and who had the low-activity MAOA alleles were at an elevated risk of adult conduct disorder and adult antisocial personality disorder. Follow-up studies have produced mixed results (Young et al., 2006) but have been generally supportive (Foley et al., 2004; Frazzetto et al., 2007). Continued investigations by Kim-Cohen and her colleagues (2006) have produced further evidence in favor of this gene (MAOA) by environment (maltreatment) interaction.

The causal connection between low-activity MAOA alleles and childhood maltreatment remains unclear, however. MAOA activity has been associated with various personality characteristics, such as hyperactivity, impulsivity, and low self-control (Paaver, Eensoo, Pulver, & Harro, 2006) and it interacts with androgens, such as testosterone, that are also associated with these characteristics (Sjoberg et al., 2008). Youth with MAOA risk alleles may be more susceptible to negative environmental influences and, given their tendency to be hyperactive and impulsive, they may be more likely to experience serious abuse and neglect.

Brain imaging studies of the MAOA genotype have added another layer of evidence. A functional Magnetic Resonance Imaging (fMRI) study of the brains of MAOA genotyped individuals by Meyer-Lindenberg et al. (2006) found substantive structural differences between those with the low and high efficient MAOA alleles. The less efficient alleles were associated with an average 8% reduction in the size of the amygdala and the cingulated gyrus. Their study also found that males, but not females, with the less efficient MAOA alleles had 14% more volume in the orbital frontal cortex (OFC) but that the OFC was less active and less integrated into the amygdala. Male brains also showed less activation in tests of inhibitory control.

These findings are impressive; they emerge from different disciplines and by use of varying methodologies. Survey data, experimental data, animal data, genetic studies, and imaging studies have informed our understanding of why individuals vary in their response to environmental risk factors. Moreover, because of the union of biological, genetic, and social disciplines we have come closer to understanding why abused and neglected children take divergent behavior pathways.

Conclusions

We started this chapter with a straightforward insight—that variance in traits associated with serious and prolonged offending creates susceptibility to criminogenic environmental influences. This insight has at least three logical consequences. First, it forces scholars of criminal behavior to place a greater emphasis on why developmental pathways vary between individuals exposed to the same environmental conditions. Instead of viewing childhood abuse and neglect, for example, as a risk factor for future pathological behavior for all children, greater specificity in the cause-effect relationship may be warranted. Only some children within a home may be abused, and only certain children may go on to show substantive behavioral disturbances because of the abuse.

Second, human traits, such as low self-control, are influenced by genes and by complex gene X environment interactions. Unfortunately, criminologists have long ignored the "gene" in the gene X environment interaction. This has led to overly simplistic causal models of the development of serious, violent conduct and, more importantly, it has led us away from important findings from other disciplines. Understanding how genes create differential susceptibilities to criminogenic environmental forces brings us closer to understanding the core components of criminal behavior. Moreover, the integration of criminological research into SPOs with studies from other sciences can shed new light into the processes of human adaptation and behavioral pathology.

Finally, in terms of practical utility we see progressive avenues for more specific interventions, including pharmacological interventions. The pharmacological treatment of ADHD (which is related to increased involvement in crime) has been successful for a broad range of youth. A variety of early interventions, including enriched preschool experiences, multisystemic therapy (MST), and functional family therapy (FFT) have also been shown to be effective at reducing serious behavioral problems in children and adolescents (Farrington & Welsh, 2007).

CHAPTER 9

Perinatal and Developmental Determinants of Early Onset of Offending: A Biosocial Approach for Explaining the Two Peaks of Early Antisocial Behavior

STEPHEN G. TIBBETTS

A recent, highly comprehensive summary of research on the criminal career paradigm examining the issue of why and when individuals start offending was provided by Piquero et al. (2003a). This thorough review concluded, as have virtually all previous studies on the topic, that chronic, persistent, serious offenders typically exhibit an early onset of antisocial and/or criminal behavior. At this point in time, given the state of research on the subject, such a conclusion is not surprising. After all, a recent meta-analysis of 19 studies of criminal careers (Krohn, Thornberry, Rivera, & Le Blanc, 2001) demonstrated that early-onset offenders committed far more crimes than late onsetters; specifically, early onsetters committed between 40% to 700% more crimes than offenders who onset later. Furthermore, early-onset offenders were more than forty times more likely to become chronic, persistent offenders than those exhibiting late onset (see discussion in DeLisi, 2006).

Thus, most criminologists now recognize the fact that most serious, persistent offenders begin their criminal career well before the age of 18, and this finding is generally true across gender, race, and social class (see review in Piquero, Farrington, & Blumstein, 2003a; also see Blumstein, Cohen, Roth, & Visher, 1986; DeLisi, 2006; Elliott, 1994; Farrington, 2003c; Moffitt, 1993; Taylor, Iacono, & McGue, 2000). Unfortunately, the reasons for this observation, as well as the definition and measure of early onset, are not agreed on by criminologists, nor are the reasons why certain individuals tend to onset in early years of life (Farrington, Loeber, Elliott et al., 1990). The goal of this chapter is to review the current state of scientific knowledge on the role of early onset in the etiology of persistent criminality and to address such issues as the definition of early onset, measurement, prevalence, and causes.

Defining Early Onset

Heretofore, we have been using the term "early onset" without defining it. As it happens, the definition is not straightforward. The first problem is that antisocial behavior starts at a very early age, a much earlier age than the traditional "age-crime" curve reflects. Work by Tremblay and colleagues (Nagin & Tremblay, 1999; Tremblay, 2004; Tremblay, Nagin, & Seguin, 2004; for a summary piece, see Tremblay, 2006) shows that most children engage in violence (pushing, hitting, biting, kicking, etc.) at very early ages of life, with most showing a peak at 27-months of age. Violent behavior falls substantially after this and remains low from age 3 until at least the mid-teenage years. This observation suggests that the best model for examining early onset is one such as a social- or self-control model of criminal offending, which assumes that individuals are born with a propensity toward aggression/offending, and are then socialized or trained to be conforming to fit societal rules and norms.

In light of these findings, Tremblay (2006) recently drew several conclusions. First, the traditional age-crime curve for violent behaviors, which is based almost entirely on official measures like police reports and peaks in the mid- to late-teenage years, is largely a product of what he calls the "chronic physical aggression" (CPA) trajectory. The CPA trajectory has two peaks, with the first and highest one being at the point described above (in the early years of life), but not accounted for by official measures because police virtually never arrest a 2- or 3-year-old for any type of offense, even for murder.

The second peak refers to that occurring in the mid-teenage years, which is the one depicted in nearly all official measures and graphs reported using police and governmental data. It is primarily the latter, official peak that Tremblay is referring to with this conclusion about the CPA trajectory. Tremblay (2006) goes on to conclude that if humans are learning to aggress through imitation, this learning occurs in the first 2 years after birth, so it is unlikely such learning is due to media images, whether they be movies, television, or video games. Tremblay claims that the question that most people (even experts) ask, "how do humans *learn* to aggress?" is wrong. Rather, he concludes that humans do not learn to use aggression. Instead, virtually all individuals become aggressive, most of them physically, once they have sufficient control of their muscles, to obtain what they desire or to express their anger. He goes on to say that the "the important learning which is going on during the early childhood years is <u>learning not to use physical aggression</u> and <u>learning to use alternative strategies to achieve your aims</u>" (emphasis is from the original source, Tremblay, 2006, p. 6).

Furthermore, regarding "property" violations, namely taking things from others, Tremblay (2004) reports that virtually all (more than 90% of) boys and girls had engaged in this type of activity by age 2, with prevalence among boys being slightly higher (also see Tremblay, 2006). The near-universal nature of aggression is thus, not restricted to physical aggression, but also applies to stealing, vandalism, and lying behaviors that are very commonly found in children. Additionally, Tremblay (2006) noted that antisocial behaviors are found in the young throughout the animal kingdom. For a similar theoretical argument, see Tibbetts' (2003) discussion of the innate and often beneficial nature of selfishness and aggression in terms of survival and evolution.

Thus, onset of aggressive behavior is not only nearly universal, but it occurs when humans are only 1 or 2 years of age. However, after peaking at approximately age 27 months, infant aggression declines precipitously and is normally absent from about age 3 through midadolescence when the second peak in aggression occurs. It is the age-crime curve that represents this peak that has been the focus of attention and which has been used to define early onset in criminological studies.

So, for the purposes of this examination, we will focus on studies which define onset as offending, either self-reported or officially recorded, occurring at or after the approximate age of 6. This age of 6 not only seems to be a natural cutoff point given Tremblay's research but it was also the minimum range in a recent study on early onset published in the journal *Archives of General Psychiatry* (Thapar, Langley, & Fowler, 2005). Coincidentally, this is also consistent with most scholarly interpretations of Gottfredson and Hirschi's (1990) theory which state that self-control must be acquired before age 8 to 10.

However, an equally important, and far more controversial issue is the higher-end cutoff age for what constitutes early onset. Most studies have used the age of 14 as the cutoff (see Farrington et al., 1990; Gibson, Piquero, & Tibbetts, 2000; Gibson & Tibbetts, 2000; Gibson & West, 1970; McGloin & Pratt, 2003; Moffitt, Lynam, & Silva, 1994; Patterson, Crosby, & Vuchinich, 1992; Simons,

Wu, Conger, & Lorenz, 1994; Tibbetts & Piquero, 1999). Some of these studies, such as G.L. Patterson et al. (1992), showed that arrest rates for boys not identified as troublemakers in elementary school are nearly zero until the age of 14 or after. Even the earliest study that examined early onset that is archived in *Criminal Justice Abstracts* (Gibson & West, 1970) used age 14 as the cutoff for determining early onset.

In terms of when onset of "criminal" delinquency typically occurs, it is notable that there are some differences between self-report data and official data, with self-report data showing that onset occurs earlier on average. Specifically, most self-report studies put the peak of onset of offending at 13 to 16 (Elliott, 1994; Piquero, Farrington, & Blumstein, 2003b). On the other hand, most studies that use official data find that initiation rates of offending peak at approximately 16, which is the upper limit for the self-report estimate (see review in Piquero et al., 2003b). However, both tend to agree that most males (as well as females) commit their first criminal offense before age 18 (Blumstein et al., 1986; Elliott, 1994; Moffitt, 1993; Piquero, Brame, & Lynam, 2004). However, such observations are somewhat complicated, by the observation that virtually everyone onsets, or commits crime, at some point in his or her life. Specifically, studies such as David Farrington's Cambridge Study in Delinquent Development (2003) found that 96% of males reported committing at least 1 of 10 nontraffic offenses, such as burglary, assault, and other offenses, by the time they were 32 years old (see discussion in Piquero et al., 2003b). This conclusion is consistent with other recent studies and theoretical models (see Moffitt, 1993, for a review of empirical evidence, as well as a theoretical framework for why this occurs). In fact, some experts have claimed that virtually all individuals, who have normal development and social interaction, will commit criminal offenses, typically during their teenage or young-adult years (Moffitt, 1993; Warr & Stafford, 1991). In contrast, the small percentage of individuals who do not commit criminal offenses by this time tend to be somewhat abnormal, in terms of lacking normal social interaction and natural development (Moffitt, 1993).

It should be noted that a number of studies use other ages as the cutoff for early onset. For example, a recent study by Taylor and her colleagues (2000) used a cutoff prior to age 12, but it is notable that this measure was based on nonofficial (i.e., nonpolice) records. Also, it is quite common for studies of drug or alcohol usage onset to use an age prior to 14 (Moffitt, 1993).

But, the age 14 cutoff has stood up to further scrutiny. For example, some of the studies which used an alternate cutoff age to define early onset have done subsequent analyses using other cutoffs or continuous measures for early onset, and most conclude that an arrest/contact or reported offending at or before age 14 is likely the best threshold to determine early onset (Gibson &

Tibbetts, 2000; also see discussion in Tibbetts & Piquero, 1999), from both empirical and theoretical perspectives (Moffitt, 1993). Even some of the studies that are exceptions to the age 14 cutoff, and used another cutoff age for early onset, specifically noted that they also examined the age of 14 as the criteria for subsequent or confirmatory analyses, because it is widely recognized as the general cutoff age when defining early onset (Farrington, Loeber, Elliott et al., 1990; McGloin & Pratt, 2003; G.L. Patterson et al., 1992; Taylor et al., 2000). Furthermore, DeLisi (2006) examined hazard rates for determining which age would likely be the best cutoff for determining early onset, and he concluded that

> The current study concurred with prior investigators who found that age fourteen was useful in differentiating early- and late-starters.... In the regression analyses, age fourteen was significantly predictive of chronicity, dangerousness, offending frequency... career span, and violence specialization (p. 24).

Additionally, several authors have provided theoretical frameworks that provide a rationale for why individuals who are in their midteenage years commit crime that differ from those who offend prior to age 14 (e.g., Moffitt, 1993; Moffitt et al., 1994; G.L. Patterson et al., 1992; Simons et al., 1994) and the age 14 cutoff is also consistent with other discussions about the transition between childhood and adolescence (for a discussion, see Tibbetts & Piquero, 1999; also see, Bartusch, Lynam, Moffitt, & Silva, 1997). Thus, most researchers recommend using age 14 as the cutoff for defining early onset and predicting persistent offending.

Early Onset and Offending

Virtually, all studies that use official and unofficial measures of onset are consistent in concluding that early onset is the most important factor in predicting which individuals are most likely to become chronic, habitual offenders. Such studies support the claim of earlier theoretical propositions, such as Moffitt (1993) who concludes that:

> [E]stimates of individual stability of antisocial behavior are expected to violate the *longitudinal law*, which states that relationships between variables become weaker as the time interval between them grow longer... [studies have] found evidence that the longitudinal law is

violated in this way when antisocial behavior is studied in the same individuals over time...adult crime was predicted more strongly by behavior at [or before] age 10 than by behavior between ages 15 and 17 (p. 698).

It appears that there is a growing consensus, both theoretically and empirically, that early onset is one of, if not the most, predictive variables for determining the most likely candidates for becoming habitual and persistent offenders. Even scholars outside our field have come to agree. For example, a recent study published in the medical literature by Taylor and her colleagues (2000) claims that the "age of onset is the single best predictor of severity and course of antisocial behavior" (p. 634). Thus, it is widely recognized that early onset is generally considered one of, if not the best, predictor of chronic, serious offending that exists in the scientific literature. Here we will review some of the theory and empirical evidence on the relationship between early onset and persistent offending.

Theoretically, most scholars have taken the position that offenders who engage in early-onset offending are categorically different from those who during their mid- to late-teenage years. For example, DiLalla and Gottesman (1989) in their review of the behavioral genetic studies claimed that there were two groups of criminal offenders, namely "continuous antisocials" and "transitory delinquents." DiLalla and Gottesman proposed that the former type of offending was caused by a genetic influence, whereas transitory offenders were largely engaged in crime due to peer influences and other environmental factors (for further discussion, see Taylor et al., 2000). This model suggests that one of the primary causes of chronic, serious offending (namely, the continuous antisocials trajectory) is physiological due to genetic predisposition.

Terrie Moffitt's (1993) Developmental Taxonomy further specifies these two types of offenders, which she labels "life-course-persistent offenders" and "adolescence-limited offenders." Like the DiLalla and Gottesman model, Moffitt claims that the adolescence-limited group of offenders are primarily influenced by peers and other social factors, whereas the life-course-persistent offenders become offenders due to a biosocial interaction that involves neuropsychological disorders/problems that occur in conjunction with disadvantaged or criminogenic environments. Moffitt claims that early offenders tend to experience perinatal complications at birth, such as low birth weight, prolapsed umbilical cord, low Apgar scores, brain trauma, and others, which cause problems in the central nervous system of the child, and manifest in temperament problems, cognitive deficits, and other consequences (see discussion in Tibbetts & Piquero, 1999). Unfortunately, the children most likely to have such perinatal problems are also more likely to inhabit deficient social environments, such as poor or broken families. Such interactions between perinatal disorders and environmental problems give rise to early onset, which is often a precursor of persistent, chronic offending (Moffitt, 1993).

Numerous longitudinal studies have reported that early onset is a significant predictor of future offending. In fact, some of the seminal longitudinal studies report early offending as a major predictor of chronic offending. For example, Wolfgang et al. (1972) found that age of onset and seriousness of offending were highly associated (bivariate correlation was 0.57). Furthermore, in this breakthrough study, it was found that boys who began their offending before the age of 14 committed more offenses through age 17 than those who began at any later time. Further support for the predictive ability of early onset regarding the nature of the persistent or dangerousness of offending is seen in the findings of Thornberry and his colleagues (1995). They compared the Rochester Youth Development Study, the Pittsburgh Youth Study, and the Denver Youth Survey, and they found a consistently strong relationship between early onset (before age 10) and chronic, persistent violent offending; specifically, 37% of youths who experienced early onset became chronic violent offenders, with 62% of early-onset youths in the Denver sample becoming chronic violent offenders. Virtually all of the chronic violent offenders reported that they began their offending between the ages of 9 and 12 (for a discussion, see DeLisi, 2006). DeLisi (2006) reviews the evidence and concludes that there is a significant association between serious criminal offending and early onset. Thus, it is clear that early onset is a consistent, strong predictor of future offending, particularly persistent, violent crime, and this finding holds across various sampling populations, using all forms of measures of criminality (official, self reports, etc.), and across various geographic regions.

Another aspect of offending that has also gained recent attention is the issue of versatility, or generality, of offending. Some have argued that early-onset offenders are more likely to engage in many forms of criminal activity because they have a greater disposition toward impulsive actions, and thus cannot resist opportunities for crime when they come across them. Such propositions are consistent with Gottfredson and Hirschi's (1990) original theoretical model of low self-control being a primary factor in determining why certain individuals are predisposed toward committing crime. This theoretical assumption is largely supported by the extant research.

Studies show that individuals who onset early are more likely to commit a large array of criminal offenses. Such versatility of offending has been reported by numerous studies across a number of samples in various geographic locations, including the Cambridge Study in Delinquent Development (Nagin, Farrington, & Moffitt, 1995), the Pittsburgh Youth Study (van Kammen &

Loeber, 1994), the Rochester Youth Development Study (Thornberry et al., 1995), a Swedish cohort study (Kratzer & Hodgins, 1999), and a New York study (Huesmann, Eron, Lefkowitz, & Walder, 1984). All of these studies showed that early onset was predictive of versatility in criminal offenses committed (for a review, see DeLisi, 2006).

Thus, it is clear from all empirical and theoretical examinations of developmental studies that early onset is an important, if not the most important variable, in terms of an individual's criminal severity, persistence, violence, recidivism, and other factors. Relatedly, a recent study (Piquero, Brame et al., 2004) that examined 377 male offenders paroled from the California Youth Authority showed that those with early onset tended to have significantly longer criminal careers. Additionally, recent evidence suggests that early onset is a predictor of chronic, persistent offending even in rural areas, not just urban cities (Berg & DeLisi, 2005).

Prevalence

Theoretical propositions and empirical research are quite consistent with the estimates provided by longitudinal/cohort studies that show that only 4% to 8% of individuals become chronic offenders (see Wolfgang et al., 1972; Tracy, Wolfgang, & Figlio, 1985, 1990). Further, this small portion of the population is responsible for the vast majority of violent offenses (typically estimated between approximately 60%–80% of offenses). It appears obvious that understanding and/or identifying this small portion of habitual, serious offenders should be a primary goal of criminological research. Studies consistently show that the vast majority (in fact, virtually all) of these chronic offenders show an early onset of offending (for a review, see Piquero et al., 2003a).

Predictors of Early Onset

We will now examine the evidence regarding the predictors of early onset. First, we will discuss direct correlates of early onset and then we will turn our attention interactions between physiological and environmental factors, which virtually all experts agree is the "answer" in explaining not only early onset, but also chronic, habitual offending.

Sheldon and Eleanor Glueck in many ways set the stage for investigation of early onset of offending. Specifically, the Gluecks were adamant about the physiological disposition of some individuals toward both early offending, as well as chronic, violent criminality (Glueck & Glueck, 1940, 1950). The Gluecks noted that individuals who had antisocial personality tendencies, low IQ, and negative family living conditions at approximately age 14 tended to be more likely to become offenders in adulthood than those who did not exhibit such traits. Specifically, early delinquents tend to be defiant and destructive, and this type of temperament (which they referred to as somotonic, which means risk taking and aggressive) appears to persist throughout life. Such findings are consistent with a recent meta-analysis of 59 studies examining antisocial temperaments and criminal behavior (Miller & Lynam, 2001). Miller and Lynam (2001) found evidence that antisocial personality is stable over time, appears early in life, and that the earlier such a pattern appears, the worse the prognosis for the long term. Since the Glueck study, numerous investigators have examined predictors of early onset. We will review the recent literature here.

Nonbiological Environmental Factors

Studies have shown that a variety of environmental factors are important in determining early onset, including absence of father, poverty, weak family structure, stressful environment, inconsistent discipline, and maternal rejection (Caspi et al., 2004; Comings, Muhleman, Johnson, & MacMurray, 2002; Gibson & Tibbetts, 1998; Gottfredson & Hirschi, 1990; Raine, Brennan & Mednick, 1994; Tibbetts & Piquero, 1999). Caspi et al. (2004) examined a sample of identical (monozygotic) twin pairs, with one of the twins in each pair receiving more maternal negativity and less warmth. Within these identical twin pairs, the twin receiving less warmth and more maternal negativity had significantly more antisocial behavior problems than his or her counterpart at age 5. Although genetic makeup was perfectly (100%) shared by these twin pairs, this study showed that the way that mothers responded to them had a significant impact on their future behavior. Maternal rejection has consistently been found to be an important mediating factor in early antisocial behavior (for a review, see Raine, 2002). Thus, it becomes quite clear that genetics, while providing a large piece of the puzzle in determining which individuals will exhibit early-onset/antisocial behavior, is conditioned by environmental factors, in this case the way that mothers nurture them.

A number of behavioral genetic studies, many of which utilize samples of twins, have shown that environmental variables, such as family adversity and peer influence, play a large part in offending, particularly early onset (Doyle, McGue, & Iacono, 1998; Eley, 1997; Harris, 1998; Taylor et al., 2000). Both twin and adoption studies have demonstrated that early antisocial behavior is significantly influenced by "nonshared" environmental factors, meaning influences that are uniquely experienced by an individual (for a review, see Rhee & Waldman, 2002). For example, even children raised in the same household are likely to experience varying discipline or socialization from their parents.

Biological Factors

There is a long list of "miscellaneous" biological factors that are empirically correlated with early onset of offending. These include, for example, slower brain-wave patterns as measured by electroencephalogram (EEG) studies and lower heart-rate levels, with the latter being the most supported physiological factor in predicting violent offending (for a review, see Raine, 1993, 2002). Even prospective studies have found that lower arousal (as measured by EEG, skin conductance activity, or heart-rate levels) at very young ages predict future violent activity, particularly persistent offending (Farrington, 1987; Moffitt, 1993; Raine, Venables, & Williams, 1990). These findings are highly consistent with the mainstream proposition that individuals who are predisposed toward fearlessness and stimulation-seeking activities (i.e., low self-control), which such individuals with low arousal tend to engage in, are far more likely to engage in crime (see Gottfredson & Hirschi, 1990). Such characteristics tend to be found in youths properly diagnosed as having attention-deficit/hyperactivity disorder (ADHD), largely due to their neurological disposition of low arousal/anxiety (which is why stimulants are prescribed to such individuals). Without treatment, these individuals tend to be constantly seeking more stimuli (i.e., sensation), which is often referred to as "stimulus-hunger."

Brain trauma, which often occurs either in the pre- or perinatal stages, or due to abuse during early childhood, is another likely candidate in the etiology of early onset of offending. Brain imaging studies, especially positron emission tomography (PET) and magnetic resonance imaging (MRI) scans, have shown that damage to several brain regions are the most important when it comes to predicting early-onset or persistent offending. The regions of the

brain that have been most linked to chronic offending behavior are the frontal lobe (especially the prefrontal cortex), the temporal lobe, the corpus callosum (which is responsible for communication between the two hemispheres),
and the left angular gyrus (which is located at the junction of the temporal,
parietal, and occipital lobes of the brain) that plays a key role in integrating
information from various lobes of the brain (for a review, see Raine, 1993, 2002).
Further studies have linked structural and/or activity abnormalities of several
limbic/subcortical structures, such as the amygdala (which is responsible for
emotional responses), to violent and persistent offending.

Nutrition and toxicity are also implicated in the area of early-onset and
persistent criminality. Scientific findings reveal that diets high in simple car-
bohydrates (i.e., sugars) or low in protein and zinc tend to exhibit significantly
higher levels of early onset or aggression. Furthermore, there is evidence that
such diets affect the structure and/or activity of notable brain structures, such
as the corpus callosum or amygdala (for a review, see Raine, 2002). Recent
studies have also shown that high levels of lead, especially those acquired at
young ages, are very detrimental in terms of onset and persistence of offending (Pihl & Ervin, 1990; see review in Raine, 1993).

Personality

Recent studies have also shown that individuals who exhibit early onset tend
to have a certain temperament or personality that predicts chronic, habitual antisocial tendencies (Carroll et al., 2006). Consistent with Gottfredson
and Hirschi's (1990) model of low self-control, virtually all studies support
the concept that individuals who show early propensities (ages 8–10) toward
criminality and deviance are the same individuals who show such propensities in adulthood (for a review regarding low self-control, see Pratt & Cullen,
2000; also see Piquero & Tibbetts, 1996). Recent studies have shown that a
propensity toward impulsivity and poor mental inhibitory control predicts
early onset among adolescents (Carroll et al., 2006). Thus, there is a general
consensus among researchers that early onset is largely a result of personality/
attitudinal disposition toward risk-taking or aggressive personality.

Studies have also shown that children, especially boys, who experience
early onset also exhibit autonomic hypoactivity, meaning that they have
an abnormally low level of arousal (see Raine, 1993; Taylor et al., 2000).
The autonomic nervous system (ANS) is responsible for our involuntary
motor actions, which includes our "fight or flight" response, as well as our
anxiety in response to punishment. Thus, if an individual tends to have a

lower level of autonomic arousal, then it is likely that he or she is not highly responsive to discipline because a lack of anxiety leads to a lower fear of punishment.

So, perhaps it is not surprising that individuals with low levels of autonomic arousal, such as low heart rate, slower brain wave patterns, and low anxiety levels, are predisposed toward early onset (Fishbein, 2001; Moffitt, 1993; Raine, 1993, 2002). Notably, propensities toward low autonomic arousal tend to be associated with higher levels of fearlessness, sensation seeking and risk taking because, in order to gain the high level of arousal that it takes to feel excited or aroused, those with low autonomic arousal may need to resort to more extreme behaviors (see Shaw, Gilliom, Ingoldbsy, & Nagin, 2003) such as those which are dangerous and illegal. Findings that early onset is linked to such physiological indicators as low heart rate, slower brainwave patterns, low anxiety/autonomic hypoactivity, and sensation seeking/risk taking, (for a review, see Raine, 1993, 2002) are highly consistent with additional studies that show that although ADHD is not consistently associated directly with either conduct disorder in youth or with antisocial personality disorder (APD) in adulthood (Farrington & Coid, 2003), ADHD *is* directly associated with *early* conduct disorder, which, in turn, is related to later APD as adults (Farrington & Coid, 2003).

Pre- and Perinatal Disorders / Delivery Complications

Studies have found support for the hypothesis that perinatal complications result in damage to the central nervous system (CNS), which would explain high levels of ADHD found in such groups (Brennan, Mednick, & Kandel, 1993). Studies have shown that both male and female infants with perinatal disorders have a higher disposition toward early onset than do persons without such disorders. For example, being born at low birth weight (less than 5 pounds, 8 ounces) has been shown to be related to early onset of offending (for a review, see Tibbetts & Piquero, 1999; for a recent study, see McGloin & Pratt, 2003).

Numerous studies have also found associations between prenatal malnutrition or exposure to toxins and early onset. Specifically, studies have shown that malnutrition among pregnant mothers can have a significant impact on the future antisocial tendencies of their offspring. Neugebauer et al. (1999) found that the offspring of pregnant women in Holland who were starved during World War II had 2.5 times the rate of antisocial disorders by adulthood compared to a control group.

Interactions

Ultimately, it is clear that both genetic and environmental/social factors both play a significant, independent role in predicting early onset of antisocial behavior. However, virtually all experts are now in consensus that the etiology of early onset is a function of *both* genetic *and* environmental factors. This has become known as the *"nature via nurture"* perspective (Tibbetts, 2003), which can be contrasted against the "nature versus nurture" approach that has been common in traditional criminological literature. We will now explore the interactions, specifically the "nature via nurture" perspective, among these factors.

Before we begin, it is important to understand what interaction effects are and how they work. Many readers are familiar with the effects of certain drugs, whether they are illegal substances or over-the-counter medicines. You may have noticed that the effect of a drug when taken alone is very different than when the drug is taken with other drugs and/or alcohol. This is due to the interaction amongst the drugs, and such effects tend to be nonlinear. In other words, this means that a dose of nighttime cough medicine combined with a dose of decongestant, along with two glasses of wine at dinner, may not simply result in the additive effects of each drug; rather, their effects tend to be enhanced due to the way the drugs and alcohol interact with each other. Thus, the person who takes substances simultaneously may "pass out," and in extreme cases may require hospitalization, because the drugs interact and cause an effect that is far beyond what the separate doses would normally cause in the sick person. Thus, when different variables interact, they tend to lead to exaggerated results, in which the whole is far greater than the sum of its parts. This is why interaction effects are considered "nonlinear;" the resulting effect is not simply the sum of its component variables.

Another, perhaps more relevant, example of interaction effects can be seen regarding an individual's height. Although it is well known that the height of a person tends to be a result of one's genotype, the nature of the environment has a major impact on realizing that height (or exceeding it). Specifically, if an individual is deprived of food and/or nutrients, he will not grow to the height determined by his genetic makeup. For example, persons raised in Central America or Asia tend to be shorter in stature. However, the offspring of parents from these regions who are raised in the United States tend to grow to the average height of US citizens. This provides an example of how diets, particularly those low in protein and/or caloric content, can affect the growth and development of a person, regardless of his genetic coding. This example reveals how an environmental factor (diet) can affect a biological variable (genotype coding for height), which provides a true representation of how nature (biology) interacts with nurture (diet). Another example can also be seen in children who have been neglected by having received very limited food; such children are at risk of severe growth interruption, but if they are removed from an abusive/neglectful environment, they will often grow many inches in a matter of months. Ultimately, the interaction between nature and nurture is extremely important, and recent studies have observed such a phenomenon among the etiological factors associated with offending at an early age.

Biosocial Interactions in Determining Early Onset

Research has revealed that it is often through an interaction with the early environment, such as a weak family structure or low socioeconomic status (SES), that physiological predictors, such as perinatal complications in pregnancy/delivery, have the largest effect on early onset (Piquero & Tibbetts, 1999). For example, Tibbetts and Piquero (1999) examined the effects of low birth weight in predicting early onset among both males and females, and found support for Moffitt's model that early neurological disadvantages generally predict early onset. They also found a significant interaction between low birth weight and disadvantaged social environments, such as lower SES and broken family structure. Specifically, individuals who are born at a low birth weight were found only to be at risk when they were raised in a family that had weak family structure or lower SES. On the other hand, for individuals who did not have weak family structure or were relatively higher in terms of SES, low birth weight did not have a significant effect on early onset of offending. However, it is notable that this study found that the interaction between low birth weight and environmental disadvantages was primarily valid for male offenders, not females.

Similarly, Gibson et al. (2001) demonstrated that low verbal IQ, was linked to early onset of offending. Here, the effect was largely due to the interaction between cognitive ability and family adversity. While low verbal IQ was shown to be a significant predictor of early onset, we found that family adversity had less of an impact on early onset among subjects with high verbal ability than it did on subjects with low verbal ability.

Another example of a biosocial interaction can be seen in the findings of McGloin and Pratt (2003). They found that low birth weight and cognitive abilities were highly predictive of delinquent behaviors among a sample of inner city youth. However, these researchers also found that these effects were largely mediated by other factors, for example, findings varied by gender and whether participants had experienced concentrated disadvantage. This finding is highly consistent with previous studies (e.g., Tibbetts & Piquero, 1999), which found that gender and SES mediated the effects of low birth weight on early onset.

Leve and Chamberlain (2004) reported that IQ, biological parent criminality, and parental transitions significantly predicted age of first arrest. Notably, the estimated model in this study accounted for 52% of the variance, and accurately classified up to 90% of early onset girls. The two most important variables were biological parent criminality and parental transitions, which appeared to interact. Specifically, the father being absent and a parent having a criminal history was highly predictive of the girls onsetting early.

Other studies have found an interaction between delivery complications and hyperactivity among youth (Brennan, Mednick, & Kandel, 1993), and an interaction between family instability and minor physical anomalies (MPAs) (see review in Raine, 1993; Mednick & Kandel, 1988). Importantly, these studies (e.g., Mednick & Kandel, 1988; Piquero & Tibbetts, 1999) often find that such interactions between perinatal factors and environmental variables predict violent offending, but not property offending, in early development and adolescence.

Perhaps the most specific examination of perinatal disorders and the link to early onset of offending was provided by Arseneault and colleagues (2002). Their study focused on the interaction of obstetrical complications and early family adversity in predicting violent offending through adolescence in a sample of 849 boys. They conclude that higher levels of obstetrical complications (especially induced labor, preeclampsia, and umbilical cord prolapse) only increase the risk of being violent at ages 6 and 17 among those subjects who experienced high levels of family adversity.

One important criticism of this study and similar ones, is that (for a review, see Raine, 1993) the authors usually measure perinatal complications using dichotomous measures, while others tend to assign cumulative scores based on problems weighted according to medical severity. Both of these types of scoring—dichotomized versus continuous—tend to "cloud" the perinatal complications that are actually problematic in terms of cause and effect. Specifically, many studies that examine the perinatal factors that predict early onset tend to collapse such perinatal factors into a prevalence measure (see Brennan, Hall, Bor, Najman, & Williams, 2003; Denno, 1990; Piquero & Tibbetts, 1999), which distorts the actual independent effect that certain particular factors (such as low birth weight by itself) have on early onset of offending. One recommendation for future research would be to isolate the effects of each of the perinatal factors that have been included in such scales for predicting early onset, as well as examining the interactions among such factors in predicting early onset.

A very important finding among recent studies (Gibson et al., 2000; Gibson & Tibbetts, 2000) is that maternal cigarette smoking, especially when in conjunction with environmental variables (such as father absence or low SES) predicts early-onset offending (for a review, see Wakschlag, Pickett, Cook, Benowitz, & Leventhal, 2002). Although the strength of the estimated interaction effects is not strong, the interactions are more significant and tend to be stronger in magnitude than the individual effects of the physiological or environmental variables alone. Like alcohol, cigarettes/tobacco are a legal, over-the-counter drug that have a significant impact on the likelihood of early onset, and this is alarming because these are the most used types of substances, especially by pregnant women. Because it is largely lower-SES mothers who are most likely to use tobacco during pregnancy (see discussion in Wakschlag et al., 2002), perhaps as a result of poor education and awareness among this population as well as high levels of dependence on alcohol and other substances, the threat that interaction effects between maternal smoking and other adversities poses in this population is significant. Furthermore, these same individuals are least likely to be given adequate maternal care during pregnancy, which may lead to substance use during pregnancy and the failure to address consequent health problems.

Some researchers have begun to disaggregate interaction effects by sex and have found that some interactions operate differently for males and females. A recent study showed that among a high-risk sample of Australian adolescents, the interaction of biological factors (such as perinatal and birth complications) and social risk factors (such as mother's negative attitude toward the infant and inadequate parental monitoring) was significantly related to early-onset persistent aggression, but that gender mediated the relationship (Brennan, Hall et al., 2003). Furthermore, findings showed that it was cumulative social risk factors alone that predicted early onset among females, whereas males fit the biosocial interaction model predicted by Moffitt (1993). Brennan, Hall et al. (2003) claimed,

> Our results suggest that the processes that are related to persistent aggressive behavior patterns in boys and girls may be somewhat different.... Biological risk factors or their interaction did not significantly differentiate these aggressive behavior patterns in girls (p. 320).

Such findings are consistent with previous studies, such as Tibbetts and Piquero (1999), which found that interactions between physiological and environmental deficits were stronger for males than for females, which have not shown the same consistencies regarding interaction effects between perinatal and environmental factors. Thus, much more research must be done regarding the gender differential in biosocial predictors of early onset, specifically why females do not appear to be as vulnerable to biosocial interactions in predicting early onset as are males.

A recent study found an interaction between association with deviant peers and several traits such as hyperactivity and fearlessness in a sample of kindergarten boys (Lacourse et al., 2006). Those who scored low on these traits were less vulnerable to the effects of deviant peers on early onset. In this same study, it was found that family adversity had no main effect, but substantially increased the risk of early-onset trajectory of deviant activity due to peer group affiliation with hyperactivity, fearlessness and low prosocial behavior. Other recent studies have found that parenting influences do not seem to have significant effects on early onset of offending outside of the effects that parenting has on peer group influences (Harris, 1998; Rutter, 2003; Tolan, Gorman-Smith & Henry, 2003). Thus, it appears that parents do have an effect on their children's offending behavior, largely through controlling their children's peer associations.

One of the best recent developmental studies that have examined the causes of early onset is that of Brennan and her colleagues (2003). This study examined the association between social and biological risk factors in predicting aggression patterns among a high-risk sample in Australia. A wide range of measures were taken during pregnancy, immediately after birth, and at 6 months, age 5, age 14, and age 15. Results revealed that the interaction between biological and social risk factors was significantly related to early-onset persistent aggression (as opposed to adolescent-onset aggression or nonaggression). Specifically, the interaction between biological (e.g., perinatal and birth complications, infant temperament, etc.) and social risk factors (e.g., maternal depression, parental substance abuse, etc.), was found to predict early onset of offending among boys.

In addition to father absence and related factors, studies have also examined interactions between maternal aspects and early antisocial propensities. For example, one study (Rubin, Burgess, Dwyer, & Hastings, 2003) found that aggression at age 4 was highest among children who had an antisocial temperament (or propensity toward aggression as measured by aggression at age 2) in conjunction with high levels of maternal negativity. Maternal negativity was also found to play an important causal role in the development of antisocial behavior among a birth cohort of 565 identical (monozygotic) twin pairs (Caspi et al., 2004). Within pairs, the twin receiving more maternal negativity and less warmth had more antisocial behavior problems at age 5.

These researchers were able to make strong conclusions about the influence of social factors (specifically, maternal negativity) because using monozygotic twins controls for genetic similarity. In addition, Raine, Brennan et al. (1994) found that the interaction between birth complications and maternal rejection resulted in antisocial aggression, and consistently Arsenault et al. (2002) found that interactions between specific obstetrical complications (e.g., preeclampsia, prolapsed umbilical cord, and induced labor) with highly adverse familial environments predicted violent behavior in childhood and adolescence. Such findings are consistent with theoretical frameworks presented by Moffitt (1993) and G.L. Patterson and his colleagues (1992) that "early-starters" or children with bad temperaments often produce parent–child conflicts, which would include maternal or parental negativity.

Additional perinatal factors, particularly delivery complications (Brennan, Mednick, & Kandel, 1993; Kandel & Mednick, 1991), have also been found to interact with familial factors, such as weak family structure, to produce early antisocial behavior (Piquero & Tibbetts, 1999). A very recent study from the medical literature (published in *Archives of General Psychiatry*) found evidence that early onset was significantly predicted by an interaction between the *COMT* gene variant and low birth weight (Thapar et al., 2005).

In conclusion, such findings are highly consistent with recent findings that support biosocial interactions in predicting offending patterns, particularly for violent crimes (Brennan & Raine, 1997; Kandel & Mednick, 1991; Piquero & Tibbetts, 1999; Raine, Brennan, & Mednick, 1997). Perhaps most telling is the fact that there are virtually *no* scientific studies have failed to find evidence that support the proposition that perinatal/biological disorders and environmental/familial problems interact to predict persistent criminal offending, and the same can be said for early onset of criminality.

One promising outcome of several studies is that certain interactions were predictive of early-onset offending, but not offending more generally. Because of the need to distinguish between early-onset/chronic offenders, and less serious adolescence-limited offenders, this is seen as progress. Gibson and his colleagues (2001) found that although verbal intelligence, when coupled with family adversity (an environmental trait), did not significantly increase the odds of becoming an offender, the combination did increase the odds of early onset of offending.

This finding is consistent with other studies that show that some predictors do not tend to distinguish offenders from nonoffenders, but do distinguish early onset-offenders from other offenders (for further discussion, see Taylor et al., 2000), and lends further support that there are categorical differences between early-onset offenders, and late-onset offenders or nonoffenders. In addition, findings by Gibson et al. support an interaction model in determining early onset, which the Gluecks also predicted in their seminal studies. Namely, it was the interaction between low verbal IQ with family adversity that predicted early onset, and it is the cumulative impact of both of these problems that distinguish early onsetters from other offenders, as opposed to the independent effects of either low IQ or family adversity alone. Not only did the Gluecks emphasize the importance of family adversity, especially such factors as inconsistent parental discipline, parental rejection/ lack of affection, or weak familial cohesiveness, but they also stressed the importance of the interaction among the personality, intelligence, and family environment factors.

Interventions and Policy

One of the key recommendations from this chapter is that very early intervention may have a long-term impact in reducing the likelihood of early onset of offending and persistence in criminal activity (Farrington & Coid, 2003; Vitaro, Brendgen, & Tremblay, 2001; Vitaro & Tremblay, 1994). Studies are consistent in showing that early prevention programs, especially those for pregnant women, can save a lot of money and future expenses by reducing the number of predisposed criminals in our society.

Some of the most effective and beneficial intervention programs are likely to begin before an individual is even born. Unfortunately, while it is considered a civil right in most developed countries to obtain adequate and effective maternal health care, this does not seem to be as much of a priority in the United States. Given the consistent biosocial interaction effects that have been documented by virtually every study done on this issue, and given that the very populations that are most susceptible to environmental disadvantages (e.g., poverty, single-headed households, etc.) are the most likely to lack adequate maternal health care, this is one of the most important factors in reducing early offending.

Perhaps the greatest impact that policy can have in reducing early onset (and therefore persistent offending) would result by providing excellent maternal care during pregnancy. If our country wants to deal with serious crime, then we should provide far more funding for women during pregnancy, as well as early infancy/childhood programs, particularly for persons in disadvantaged environments. Once a woman becomes pregnant, medical studies support the importance of health care and monitoring the developing infant. In fact, the nutrition of the mother before and during pregnancy may be the single most important intervention that can be used for preventing perinatal and/or developmental disorders. Studies have shown that simply advising pregnant women regarding health, nutrition, and child rearing led to a reduction in delinquency among their offspring at age 15 (Lally, Mangione, Honig & Wittner, 1988). Therefore, if our society ever invests the resources to provide (better yet, require) such advice, this could go a long way toward reducing crime in the long term. Additionally, a lot can be done by simply educating mothers that smoking or drinking during pregnancy can radically affect the child growing in their womb. Studies from various sources (Olds et al., 1998) demonstrate that for every dollar invested into health, family, or school intervention programs, many dollars that would have been spent reacting crimes that would result without such programs would be saved.

As it happens, there is some evidence that other types of early intervention programs can also have a mitigating effect on the trajectory between middle childhood offending and adult criminality (Aber, Brown, & Jones, 2003; Flannery, Singer, & Wester, 2003). For example, one recent study found that children who were exposed to a high number of lessons in a conflict resolution curriculum in early grades demonstrated positive changes in their developmental trajectories and deflections from paths toward aggression (Aber et al., 2003). Another program, called *Peace Builders*, that focuses on children in early grades, was shown by a recent study (Flannery et al., 2003) to be effective in producing gains in social competence and peacebuilding behavior, as well as to produce reductions in aggression, and most of these changes were maintained for a long period of time. Weichold (2004) showed that an antiaggression training program had a positive effect on factors, such as empathy, self-efficacy, attribution style, and other factors in a group of foster home boys who had exhibited early-onset aggression (although it did not directly reduce aggressive behaviors) and Tolan et al. (2003) also report benefits of intervention programs targeting parental supervision and monitoring on early onset. Some studies have not found that intervention programs work, thus, the conclusion regarding school and family programs is that some intervention programs work and others fail, so it is advised that models of the successful programs should be followed. Obviously, success (or failure) of a given program should be determined by an independent evaluation.

Another conclusion of this chapter is that the earlier the intervention starts, the better. The same advice was recently given by Richard Tremblay (2006), who showed evidence that many programs start far too late to do any good. Many experts consider programs that start at age 10 as being ill-timed, largely because the early-onset trajectory is set in motion long before the age of 10. Thus, intervention programs should start far earlier than age 10 in order to maximize their effectiveness. Furthermore, such interventions should address both physiological (e.g., ADHD) and environmental factors (e.g., poverty). Although most programs are not equipped to deal with both physiological and social factors, perhaps such programs should be created.

Another recommendation is the creation of a national agency in the United States, which other nations may want to replicate, with the primary mission of funding, fostering, and evaluating programs for intervention and/or prevention of criminality, particularly the programs that focus on juveniles. This recommendation echoes that of many leading theorists that have called for the same (see discussion in final chapter of Farrington & Coid, 2003). Currently, there is no such agency with this specific function; rather, there are a variety of agencies that engage in many of these activities (e.g., Office of Juvenile Justice and Delinquency Prevention), but always in addition to numerous other functions.

Future Research

A second set of recommendations of this chapter relate to future research on early onset. First, in order to fully understand early onset of aggression we must look outside the criminological/sociological literature. Although only approximately 70 or so studies are cited each by *Criminal Justice Abstracts* and *Sociological Abstracts* since 1968, far more studies are cited in the psychological literature (and many studies of early onset can be found in the medical and biological fields as well). For example, *PubMed* abstracts database, which is the government sponsored database for medical sciences, had 176 studies indexed in a cross-search of "early onset" and "crime." The same can be said regarding *Biological Abstracts*, which lists 72 studies indexed in a cross-search of "early onset" and "aggression" since only 1980.

This recommendation includes studies gathered from nonhuman subjects. Criminologists, as well as other social scientists, tend to be highly averse to including such studies. However, incorporating findings from the animal world, especially primates or other mammals closely related to Homo sapiens would likely provide invaluable information in advancing our understanding of early aggression, as well as other aspects of criminality among humans. For example, there have been a number of studies on mice, rats, squirrels, hamsters, chimps, marine species, and other subjects, that have examined early aggression. Specifically, much of the knowledge we have gained regarding the *COMT* and *MAOA* gene variations we discussed above were gained from experiments with mice (e.g., Cases, Seif, & Grimsby, 1995), which led to testing among humans. It is likely that examining and incorporating the extant literature from zoology and biology would go a long way toward explaining our own antisocial behavior.

Although a great deal is known about correlates of early onset in offending, further research is needed, especially regarding the extent to which the interaction between biological/physiological factors and environmental/social factors explain the early onset of individual offending, particularly across gender. It is up to researchers to search further in identifying various perinatal and early-developmental factors that lead to early onset, and more importantly to examine the way that these various factors interact with each other in causing not only early onset, but lead to persistent criminal behavior into adulthood. As with virtually every other issue in criminology, it seems to be a habit of criminologists to only examine the prior research in the criminological/sociological journals before developing a theoretical framework or initiating a scientific study. Although some of the psychological research and theoretical models, such as those by Moffitt, as well as Patterson, have been incorporated into criminological research, there are many other theoretical frameworks (e.g., DiLalla & Gottesman, 1989) and many scientific studies on early onset that have been reported in the psychological, medical and biological literature that are not frequently cited in our work. The time has come that criminologists begin to explore the scientific evidence provided by other fields, such as psychology, economics, anthropology, medicine, geography, and in this case the psychological and medical sciences for causal factors regarding why certain individuals onset earlier than others.

Some good candidates for factors to look at to learn more about early onset include older siblings or large family size, hormones, toxins, and chromosomal makeup of individuals. Studies have consistently shown that having siblings tends to increase early physical aggression (Tremblay, 2006), whether it be due to having a target or from having a role model, in the case of having older siblings who provide constant models of behavior. Consistent with this finding, a recent study (Gilbert, 2005) found that the amount of offending in adolescence increased 300% for youths from larger families (with five or more members) and that seriousness increased 400% (as measured by the Sellin-Wolfgang seriousness score) in juvenile offenders from larger families, often starting at earlier ages. Another study (Tremblay, Nagin et al., 2004) also found that having siblings increased the odds of showing high levels of physical aggression in early childhood. Thus, although it remains to be empirically established, we might hypothesize that having numerous siblings would be a risk factor for early onset.

Hormones may also play a role. It is likely that male sex hormones may be related, considering that males are far more likely to become early-onset, chronic offenders (see Chapter 7, for a discussion of the role of the endocrine system in the development of persistent criminality). But since most males do not become early-onset, chronic offenders, we cannot infer without empirical evidence that hormones play a role in early onset per se, even if they play a role in criminality more generally. One candidate for a possible hormonal influence on early onset is cortisol (also known as glucocorticoid), which is released when an individual experiences stress or anxiety. Most studies show low base (resting) cortisol levels are linked to aggressive, antisocial behavior, in both young males and incarcerated offenders (McBurnett, Lahey, & Frick., 1991; Raine, 1993, 2002; Tennes & Kreye, 1985; Van Goozen, Matthys, & Cohen-Kettenis, 1998). Notably, cortisol is produced by the hypothalamus, the region of the brain which regulates autonomic functions (such as heart rate and other arousal tasks), and may cause low arousal and fearlessness frequently found among most early onsetters and persistent offenders.

Alcohol consumption is also a primary factor in early onset, whether it be the parents who drink (Brennan, Hall et al., 2003) or the actual individual who drinks alcohol. Studies are clear that early onset of alcohol usage is linked to early onset of criminal behavior (Rudy, 1986). Persistent use of alcohol physiologically reduces the users' inhibition for committing crime, which further predisposes them for criminal activity. The usage of other drugs follows a similar pattern, whereby early onset of use predicts an early onset of criminal behavior. Far more research must be dedicated to substance use/abuse in predicting early onset.

Finally, an additional recommendation is that more research must be dedicated to examining the mode of mediation and/or interaction among genetic and environmental factors. Currently, little is known about how much environmental factors mediate the effects of purely genetic variables (e.g., XYY chromosomal makeup), or how certain genetic variations mediate the effects of certain environmental factors, such as poverty or maternal rejection. Far more research is required to enhance our understanding of mediation effects on both nature and nurture aspects. Relatedly, more research is needed in the area of bidirectional (i.e., transactional) effects among genetic-environment variables (see Dodge & Pettit, 2003; Rutter, 2003). Finally, empirical research in needed that examines the "threshold" of various factors, from physiological to social factors, that determines the highest probabilities for engaging in early offending.

Part III

Special Topics and Populations

CHAPTER 10

Interdisciplinary Perspectives on Persistent Female Offending: A Review of Theory and Research

Asha Goldweber, Lisa M. Broidy,
and Elizabeth Cauffman

Chronic offenders, though rare, commit a disproportionate amount of crime and generate notable public concern. The bulk of this concern, as well as the majority of related policy, practice, theory, and research, is focused on male chronic offenders. This is hardly surprising since evidence supports the existence of a subset of males (albeit a relatively small one) who begin offending early and persist in their criminal activities into young adulthood and beyond (Moffitt, 2006b; Nagin, Farrington, & Moffitt, 1995; Raine, Moffitt et al., 2005; Scott, Knapp, Henderson, & Maughan, 2001; Soothill, Ackerley, & Francis, 2003; Tremblay, Tremblay, & Saucier, 2004). Research on female offenders, however, is lacking, and some question whether a comparable group of persistent female offenders exists. However, as we highlight below, evidence consistently documents a small but observable group of persistent female offenders whose pathways into and out of offending both mirror and diverge from those of their male counterparts in notable ways.

Gender is arguably one of the most important variables in understanding delinquency, and yet has received little attention in theory development

(Krisberg, 1992). As most feminist criminology indicates, female offenders have been overlooked, misrepresented, or stereotyped in the literature. Indeed, many leading theories, (at least at the outset) have had an explicitly or implicitly male focus, leading some to argue against their adequacy for explaining female criminality (Chesney-Lind, 1989). To date, developmental models of delinquency are heavily influenced by Moffitt's (1993) dual trajectory typology: adolescence-limited (AL) offending versus life-course-persistent (LCP) offending. Youth who are of the AL offending type begin their offending during the adolescent years and tend to desist shortly thereafter. According to both theory and research, offending by AL youths is largely confined to the teenage years and results from a desire to access adult roles prematurely (i.e., "the maturity gap") coupled with exposure to and mimicry of antisocial role models. Moffitt hypothesizes that most female antisocial behavior is of the adolescence-limited and not the life-course-persistent type. However, the theory also assumes that labeling effects, or "snares," can result in a continuation of a criminal career that might otherwise decline naturally. Among ALs especially, such snares can include a criminal record, drug or alcohol addiction, and for girls, unwanted pregnancy.

LCP offending, on the other hand, exhibits a childhood onset, emerging from early neurodevelopmental deficits typically coupled with family adversity. While most adolescents (both male and female) follow the AL pathway, a small subset of offenders follow the LCP pathway. Data from the Dunedin Multidisciplinary Health and Development Study (ages 3 to 21) suggest that LCP offenders are almost exclusively male (Moffitt, 2006b; Moffitt, Caspi, Rutter, & Silva, 2001), leaving open the question of whether a LCP offending pathway is relevant to females.

In this chapter, we address four key areas regarding the persistent female offender. We begin with a review of the evidence documenting a persistent female offender group and outlining the characteristics of this group. Next, we identify the sex-specific biological, psychological, and sociological risk and protective factors related to persistent female offending. Third, we examine how persistent female offenders fare in adulthood and compare these outcomes with those of their male counterparts. We end with a discussion of the interpersonal and societal costs of chronic female offending.

The Persistent Female Offender: Assessing the Evidence

Self-report and arrest studies indicate that chronic offenders (traditionally comprised of male samples) make up only 5% of the offending population but are responsible for a majority of serious violent crimes (Tolan & Gorman-Smith, 1998; Tracy & Kempf-Leonard, 1996). Relative to one-time and recidivist offenders (2–4 offenses), research shows that chronic offenders (five or more offenses), are more likely to engage in offending early in the lifespan (age 13 and younger) and to participate in more violent offenses as they age (Piquero, 2000a). Life-course-persistent (or chronic) offending is based on Moffitt's (1993) typologies but has been operationalized differently across studies. Some studies operationalize LCP predominantly by age, severity, and/or duration (e.g., Aguilar, Sroufe, Egeland, & Carlson, 2000; Ayers et al., 1999; Lanctôt, Emond, & Le Blanc, 2004); others operationalize it by the number of offenses (e.g., DeLisi, 2002; Soothill et al., 2003). Regardless of how it is defined, it is extremely difficult to identify a group of LCP females because of their low base rate, even within offender populations. When males and females are held to the same definitional criteria, fewer than 1 in 100 females in a cohort were on the LCP path with a male to female ratio of 10:1 (Moffitt, Caspi, Rutter et al., 2001).

Despite methodological difficulties, research examining the course of female delinquency in adolescence generally identifies a small subgroup of girls whose delinquency begins early and is notably more serious, frequent, and consistent than that of the average female offender (see Table 10.1). Soothill et al. (2003), for example, examined conviction records from a 1953 and 1978 birth cohort in England and Wales. In their sample, persistent offenders (both male and female) were defined as those who had a minimum of four separate convictions during an 8-year period between adolescence and early adulthood. While 4.7% of males exhibited persistent offending patterns, approximately 0.4% of the female population exhibited this pattern. Other studies also provide evidence of a persistent female offender group, although the percentage rates are always higher among males than among females (Danner, Blount, Silverman, & Vega, 1995; DeLisi, 2002; Steffensmeier & Allan, 1996; Warren & Rosenbaum, 1987). For example, a 6-year prospective study by Landsheer and van Dijkum (2005) of 270 Dutch adolescents (113 males and 157 females) aged 12 to 14 years at baseline identified a group of females (12.7% of the female sample) who were persistently delinquent throughout adolescence and into early adulthood (e.g., age 18 to 20). Notably, however, this group was smaller than its male equivalent (32.7% of the male sample falls into this group) but by a smaller factor than in Moffitt's research. Similarly, White and Piquero (2004) identified a group of early-onset LCP females (3.2%) from an African-American sample who exhibited criminal outcomes similar to those in their male early-onset counterparts (9.8%). Following this same sample into adulthood and examining both their juvenile and adult arrest records, Denno (1994) identified a

TABLE 10.1 Studies of Persistent Female Offenders

Study	Sample	Location	Method	Definition of Chronicity	Chronic Offender (%)
Aguilar et al., 2000	58 females 62 males Minnesota Longitudinal Study of Parents and Children High-risk urban sample (Kindergarden–16 years of age)	Minneapolis	12-year prospective longitudinal study; born 1975–1997, data collection began in kindergarten	Self-reported level of externalizing behavior (on CBCL) at six separate assessment points (kindergarden–16 years of age)	29.3 females 33.9 males
Ayers et al., 1999	269 females 297 males Seattle Social Development Project from high-crime neighborhoods (ages 12–15 years)	Washington State	2-year prospective longitudinal panel design (1988–1990)	Frequency and severity of self-reported delinquency consistently high at both time points	9.7 females 13.1 males
Baskin & Sommers, 1993	85 females (mean age 29 years)	United States	Retrospective (1990)	Descriptive: long histories of official and self-reported involvement in crime	NA (sample included only chronic offenders)
DeLisi, 2002	55 females 445 males adult sample of habitual offenders (ages 20–64 years for females; 18–74 years for males)	Western United States	Retrospective, data collection: 1995–2000	A minimum of 30 adult arrests based on criminal records qualified as habitual offender	NA (sample included only chronic offenders)
Denno, 1994	500 females 487 males Philadelphia Birth Cohort Study African-American (birth–22 years of age)	Philadelphia	22-year prospective longitudinal cohort design (born 1959)	Both official juvenile and adult arrest records	1.6 females 10.9 males

Study	Sample	Country	Design	Description	Rate
Elliott et al., 1989	672 females 740 males National Youth Survey (12–17 years of age)	United States	5-year prospective longitudinal (1976–1980)	Self-reported involvement in three or more of any violent FBI index offenses during a given year	0.3 females 3.1 males
Fergusson & Horwood, 2002	461 females 435 males Christchurch Health and Development Study (birth–21 years of age)	New Zealand	21-year prospective longitudinal design (born mid-1977)	Offending trajectories indicating consistently high levels of offending from adolescence to young adulthood (14–20 years) based on self-reported offenses	1.7 females 9.9 males
Kratzer & Hodgins, 1999	6,751 females 7,101 males (childhood–30 years of age)	Sweden	30-year prospective longitudinal cohort design (born 1953)	Evidence of official arrests over four time periods covering childhood (under 15), adolescence (15–18 years), young adulthood (18–21 years), and adulthood (21–30 years)	0.4 females 6.2 males
Lanctôt et al., 2004	97 high-risk adjudicated females (ages 15–23 years)	Canada	9-year prospective longitudinal study	High and stable violent offending trajectories from adolescence to early adulthood (15–23 years) based on self-reported violent offenses	14 females
Landsheer & van Dijkum, 2005	157 female 113 male Utrecht Study of Adolescent Development Dutch adolescents (ages 12–20 years)	Netherlands	6-year prospective longitudinal panel (three waves: 1991, 1994, 1997)	Offending trajectories representing involvement in delinquency across four stages of development: preadolescence (<10 years), early adolescence (12–14 years), middle adolescence (15–17 years), and late adolescence (18–20 years) based on self-reported offenses	12.7 females 32.7 males
Maughan et al., 2000	630 females 789 males Great Smoky Mountains Study of Youth (ages 9–16 years)	Western North Carolina	Accelerated cohort design of 9-, 11-, and 13-year olds, 4-year prospective longitudinal study (1992–1996)	Offending trajectories representing clinically significant conduct problems (frequent, severe) over 4 years based on parent- and self-reported conduct problems	2.3 females 11.7 males

(continued)

TABLE 10.1 Continued

Study	Sample	Method	Location	Definition of Chronicity	Chronic Offender (%)
Moffitt et al., 2001	498 females 539 males Dunedin Multidisciplinary Health and Development Study (ages 3–21 years)	21-year prospective longitudinal study (births 1972–1973)	Dunedin, New Zealand	Extreme childhood antisocial behavior stable across time (ages 5–11) and pervasive across situations (home, school); many antisocial acts during adolescence (ages 15 or 18 years)	1 females 10 males
Soothill et al., 2003	Sample sizes ranged from 636–2,532 females 3,456–10,489 males (ages 10–46 years)	Six different birth cohorts (1953, 1958, 1963, 1968, 1973, 1978) Longitudinal study that ends in 1999 (study period of 36 years)	England and Wales	A minimum of four separate convictions during an 8-year period between adolescence and early adulthood	0.4 females 4.7 males
Stattin & Magnusson, 1989	510 females 517 males Individual Development and Adjustment (ages 10–26 years)	16-year prospective longitudinal study (1965–1981)	Sweden	Teacher reports of aggression at age 13 and an official arrest record by age 26	10.2 females 35.8 males
Tracy & Kempf-Leonard, 1996	500 females 487 males Philadelphia Birth Cohort Study African-American (birth–26 years of age)	22-year prospective longitudinal cohort design (born 1959)	Philadelphia	Police contact before age 18 and an adult (18–26 years) offense (both based on official arrest records)	3.9 females 23.4 males
Warren & Rosenbaum, 1987	159 females (ages 9–37 years)	Retrospective longitudinal design of females committed to California Youth Authority (CYA) during the 1960s through 1981	California	Persistence of offending behavior through three career periods (first offense to CYA commitment, commitment to discharge, discharge to 1981) based on individual case files kept by the Youth Authority as well as adult records from CA Department of Justice	96 females males NA

Some of the studies report different percentages of chronic offenders from the same samples. This may reflect variation in the operationalization of chronicity.

considerably smaller group of persistent female offenders (1.6%) and a slightly larger group of persistent male offenders (10.88%). Still others have used this sample and found an even larger gender disparity in persistent offenders: 3.9% of females compared to 23.4% of males with juvenile arrests continued their criminal careers in adulthood (i.e., had an arrest between 18 and 26 years of age) (Tracy & Kempf-Leonard, 1996).

Clearly, approaches to defining persistence vary across studies. Some studies differentiate among chronic offenders by the frequency and/or diversity of their offenses whereas others do so by the severity of their offenses. Using trajectory analyses and a frequency approach to defining persistence, Maughan and colleagues (2000) identified stable low-level chronics—individuals who engage in conduct problems consistently but infrequently across time points (87.7% of females; 68.4% of males)—and a more extreme, smaller group of stable high-level chronics—individuals who engaged in consistently high rates of problem behaviors throughout their 4-year study (2.3% of females; 11.7% of males). In contrast, Ayers and associates (1999) used a severity approach and identified low- (1.8% of females; 1.7% of males), moderate- (8.9% of females; 15.2% of males), and high-level (9.7% of females; 13.1% of males) chronic groups. These findings are not just confined to the United States. Data from New Zealand also document a small group of early onset females who engage in delinquency at a consistently higher rate than other girls followed throughout adolescence (Fergusson & Horwood, 2002; Moffitt, Caspi, Rutter et al., 2001). Similarly, research by Kratzer and Hodgins (1999) as well as Stattin et al. (1989) found similar groups of female adolescent frequent offenders who persisted through adulthood in a Swedish sample.

Other data show quite a different pattern of chronicity. Using the criminal records of 500 adult offenders, DeLisi (2002) showed that female career offenders (defined as a minimum of 30 arrests) initiated their careers relatively late in life (compared to their male counterparts) and continued for nearly two decades throughout middle adulthood. These findings are unlike those from the aforementioned studies (that showed that female recidivists were younger than their male criminal peers and that chronic female offenders had relatively short criminal careers). Also challenging these patterns, Aguilar et al. (2000) are the only researchers to report similar percentages of early onset for chronic male and female offenders (33.9% and 29.3% respectively) among a fairly small (n = 120) high-risk sample from Minneapolis. However, it is important to note that this longitudinal study ends at age 16, when, according to Moffitt and colleagues (2001), males and females are most alike in their rates of antisocial behavior.

Despite variation in how they operationalize persistence, the aforementioned studies provide convergent evidence for the existence of an early onset, persistent female offender subtype. The bulk of these studies follow female offenders from adolescence into early adulthood and report rates of chronic offending ranging from 1% to 29.3%. In most cases, notably fewer girls compared to boys follow the early onset, chronic offending pathway. Furthermore, whether prospective or retrospective, with the exception of the DeLisi study, all the studies indicate roughly the same pattern for persistent female offenders. That is, delinquency begins early (and is notably more serious, frequent, and consistent than average female offending), progresses through adolescence, and then truncates more abruptly in adulthood than is the case for persistent male offenders.

Characteristics of the Persistent Female Offender

Some researchers suggest that we should expect to see an increase in female persistent offending in the future. Soothill et al. (2003) report that, of females who exhibited the earliest age of first arrest in each birth cohort (first arrested age 10–14 years), only 1 in 8 from the 1953 cohort exhibited long-term persistence. The rate of long-term persistence increased to 50% in the 1978 cohort. While this is still a relatively small group, the increase over time in persistence among those who enter the system early is notable. Given this shift, we might expect that more persistent female offenders will enter a justice system that does not understand them (e.g., programming is based on the needs of the more prevalent male offenders). Despite the justice system's lack of understanding of the female offender, researchers can shed light on the question: are persistent female offenders' defining characteristics comparable to their male counterparts?

In spite of the fact that the persistent female offender exists, there are few studies to represent and explain this group. Only recently have researchers been able to document female offending trajectories (Broidy, Nagin et al., 2003; D'Unger, land, & McCall, 2002; Lanctôt et al., 2004; Moffitt, Caspi, Rutter et al., 2001; White & Piquero, 2004). Furthermore, extant evidence on persistence among female offenders is difficult to evaluate. This may stem from inconsistencies among researchers in the conceptualization of persistent female offenders. In addition, much of the longitudinal data that documents female offending trajectories is abbreviated, ending in early adulthood (i.e., early 20s). As a result, most studies are purely descriptive in nature. Given these limitations, the next sections of this chapter will draw from the larger literature on female offending in general and then link these findings to persistent female offenders more specifically.

Age of Onset

Pathways to chronic adolescent delinquency do not appear to be the same for both genders. Some research suggests that males and females begin their antisocial behavior at roughly 15 years of age (within 6 months of each other) (Moffitt, Caspi, Rutter et al., 2001; Piper, 1985; Piquero & Chung, 2001; Piquero & White, 2003). Other research suggests that females begin their careers earlier than males. For example, Elliott et al. (1986) found that male hazard rates (i.e., the proportion of persons who initiate serious violence at a given age) for serious violent offending peaked at ages 16 through 18 (with prevalence rates ranging from 7% to 8%) and then declined to age 21 (with prevalence rates dropping to 3.1%), while female hazard rates for serious violent offending peaked earlier (ages 12–15 years) (2.9%–2.5% prevalence rate) and decreased considerably from ages 16 to 21 years (prevalence rates dropped from 2.2%–0.3%), suggesting an earlier onset age for females.

It is important to note, however, that these age gaps are particularly pronounced for serious aggressive types of delinquency, while less serious problem behavior such as drug- and alcohol-related offenses exhibit less of a gender differentiated progression (Moffitt, Caspi, Rutter et al., 2001). Thus, among females, peak age of initiation of serious violent offending appears to occur a few years earlier and their maturation out of serious violence tends to be both earlier and steeper than males. For instance, Lanctôt et al. (2004), using data from a sample of adjudicated females, provide evidence for this pattern. Their longitudinal analyses (from 15 to 23 years of age) indicate that violent behaviors are prevalent during mid-adolescence, but decrease considerably as these girls enter adulthood. More specifically, three subgroups of females were identified: those who engaged in less than one *type* of violent activity at each point of time (44%), those who engaged in a *wide variety* of violent offenses in mid-adolescence (17.5), which declined by the beginning of adulthood (42%), and those who engaged in the *greatest variety* of violent offenses in mid-adolescence, which also declined over time (14%).

Duration of Offending

Data chronicling the duration of persistent female offenders' "criminal career" supports the aforementioned, truncated pattern. Among a sample of persistent male and female offenders (born in 1958) followed through age 31, the average duration of offending was 4.9 years for females and 7.4 years of males (Tarling, 1993). Using the same sample as Tarling (1993) the British Home Office followed participants through age 40 and found that the average duration of female criminal careers (5.6 years) continued to be shorter than that of their male counterparts (9.7 years) (Home Office Statistical Bulletin, 1995). Another study by Farrington and colleagues (1998) examined the average duration of criminal careers among sisters and wives of LCP males and found that these women averaged 8 years compared to the males' average of 10 years.

Types of Offenses

Much theory and research supports the notion that males are more aggressive and commit more violent crime than females. A prime example comes from evolutionary psychology (EP) theory, which holds that an adaptive model of natural selection (e.g., gender-variant evolutionary pressures, intrasexual competition) may explain why men are more aggressive than women (Buss & Shackelford, 1997).[1] Similar support comes from official crime statistics showing that males outnumber females on both the property crime index (i.e., burglary, theft, auto theft, and arson) and the violent crime index (i.e., criminal homicide, sexual assault, robbery, and aggravated assault) (Office of Juvenile Justice and Delinquency Prevention [OJJDP], 2002). Some comprehensive, longitudinal data support these statistics. In a sample of males and females from Dunedin, tracked from age 3 to 21, males exhibited more physical aggression and violence than females over this time span (Moffitt, Caspi, Rutter et al., 2001). Broidy, Nagin et al. (2003) reported that, in addition to the Dunedin sample, a similar pattern of higher levels of physical aggression and violence among boys was evident as compared to girls throughout childhood and adolescence in five other samples. Official data show a similar pattern in that, compared to males, females are more likely to be arrested for less serious crimes such as status offenses or technical violations (e.g., violations of probation, parole, and valid court order) (OJJDP, 2002; Sickmund, 2004). In fact, nearly half of female inmates are nonviolent offenders (Bureau of Justice Statistics, 2005). Within the category of nonviolent offenses, some research shows that female offenders are disproportionately heavy drug abusers, (Danner et al., 1995) often charged with drug violations (Warren & Rosenbaum, 1987) and drug selling (Baskin & Sommers, 1993).

[1] Buss hypothesizes that the mechanisms underlying aggression—resource procurement, intrasexual competition, hierarchy negotiation, and mate retention—are more evolutionarily adaptive for males. Detractors of EP have criticized it as sexist, outdated, and biologically reductionistic.

While females tend to engage in proportionately less criminal behavior than males overall, it is important to note a 5% increase in person offenses (i.e., aggravated assault, criminal homicide, robbery, simple assault, violent sexual assault, and "other") among females in custody between 1997 and 1999 (Bureau of Justice Statistics, 2005). It also appears that female offenders have become a significant and increasing presence in the juvenile justice system. In fact, there has been a growing concern that while most juvenile arrests have been decreasing, the number of female juvenile arrests continues to rise at a greater rate than males and across more offense categories (Snyder, 2004). For example, compared to 2002 data, the number of males arrested in 2003 declined by 0.4% whereas the number of females arrested in 2003 increased by 1.9% (Federal Bureau of Investigation, 2003). Looking only at violent crime, we see the same pattern. The percentage of female juvenile violent crime arrests increased between 1980 and 2003, with the overall increase mainly in aggravated assault arrests (National Center for Juvenile Justice, 2006). More specifically, between 1993 and 2002, arrests for aggravated assault decreased by 29% for males and increased by 7% for females. Among females, the percentage of total juvenile assault arrests jumped from 21% to 32% between 1990 and 2003.

According to data from the John Jay Center on Terrorism and Public Safety, most female inflicted interpersonal violence (e.g., child and/or partner abuse) goes undetected by the criminal justice system (Ness, 2003). Hence, Ness (2003) holds that official crime rates for female-committed assaults, such as those reported by the U.S. Department of Juvenile Justice (e.g., 23% for aggravated assault; 18% for the total violence crime index) may actually be underestimates. Indeed, according to Ness' ethnographic study of African-American girls in inner city Philadelphia, most girls reported engaging in a serious fight in the past year (which is not only pervasive but an increase from the year prior). Additionally, mothers reported more fighting among girls nowadays and that the quality of the fighting has changed, with girls having become more likely to pull a weapon. In fact, in the "rough" neighborhoods surveyed, the willingness to fight was often construed as a form of self-protection.

This recent surge in female juvenile violence offenses has sparked some debate among researchers as to what is driving these arrest figures. Although lacking empirical evidence, some who hold a feminist theoretical perspective of criminality have proposed that the women's liberation movement and increased economic opportunities for women have allowed them to be as crime-prone as men (Adler, 1975; Simon, 1975). To date, however, this masculinization argument has not been supported by empirical data and as such, is widely criticized in the literature (Box & Hale, 1983; Hunnicutt & Broidy, 2004; Steffensmeier, Allan, & Streifel, 1989; Steffensmeier & Streifel, 1992). However, other feminist arguments focusing on the criminalization of girls' survival strategies (e.g., running away from a physically/sexually abusive home) do have empirical support (Chesney-Lind, 1989).

While the Ness ethnographic data suggest that there is a true increase in female juvenile violence, others disagree. Notably Steffensmeier and colleagues (Steffensmeier, Schwartz, Zhong, & Ackerman, 2005; Steffensmeier, Zhong, Ackerman, Schwartz, & Agha, 2006), argue that instead of the Uniform Crime Statistics reflecting a true increase in aggressive offending among females, the statistical shift described earlier may be an artifact of changes in criminal justice policy and practice. They note that, in contrast to arrest trends, self-report surveys such as monitoring the future do not suggest a rise in serious female offending, and, in fact, may imply recent declines in female juvenile offending. Contrary to feminist theory's chivalry thesis (that the criminal justice system treats women more leniently) recent evidence suggests that violent girls are now being treated more punitively by the juvenile justice system (Chesney-Lind, 1997; Steffensmeier et al., 2005). More aggressive policing of low-level crimes as well as the reclassification of simple assaults as aggravated assaults, indicate a broadening of the definition of what constitutes violent behavior (Steffensmeier et al., 2006). In fact, case files of girls charged with assault in four California counties in the late 1990s revealed that most of these charges were the result of nonserious mutual fights or struggles with parents (Acoca, 1999).

This may suggest that female violence is qualitatively distinct from male violence as research suggests that females are disproportionately more likely to engage in intrafamilial violence. Bloom and colleagues (2002) showed that girls fight with family members or siblings more frequently than do boys, who more often fight with friends or strangers. Additional research suggests that girls are three times as likely to assault a family member as boys (Franke, Huynh-Hohnbaum, & Chung, 2002). Interestingly further support for the inflation of violent offense rates comes from some parents who admit that they use juvenile detention as a time out from conflict for their daughters (Lederman & Brown, 2000). The relabeling of girls' arguments with parents from status offenses ("incorrigible" or "Persons In Need of Supervision" [PINS]) to assault is a form of "bootstrapping" or "up-criming" that has been particularly pronounced in official crime reports of delinquency of African-American girls (Bartollas, 1993). These changes are also reflected in school policy as many schools have implemented "zero tolerance" policies that classify threats as aggravated assaults (Holsinger & Latessa, 1999).

Sex-Specific Predictors and Developmental Discontinuity

Given the increase in violent offending among girls, whether representative of a true behavioral change or a shift in policy, it is important to consider the predictors and pathways that mark female offending trajectories. In a detailed investigation using data from six sites and three countries, Broidy, Nagin et al. (2003) examined the developmental course of physical aggression and other problem behaviors in childhood to predict violent and nonviolent offending outcomes in adolescence. The authors found that in childhood, though boys exhibited higher levels of physical aggression than girls, their trajectories of aggression look similar. However, as boys and girls enter adolescence, the trajectories of aggression diverged. The results indicated that, among boys, there is continuity in problem behavior from childhood to adolescence and that such continuity is especially acute when early problem behavior takes the form of physical aggression. Chronic physical aggression during the elementary school years specifically increased the risk for continued physical violence as well as other nonviolent forms of delinquency during adolescence.

Despite gender similarities in the developmental course of physical aggression in childhood, Broidy, Nagin et al. (2003) found no clear associations between childhood physical aggression and adolescent offending among females. It may be that such connections were difficult to document in multivariate models given the low base rates for the outcomes of interest among females. Subsequent research by Landsheer and van Dijkum (2005) also notes that female adolescent offending was much more difficult to predict than male adolescent offending. For example, whereas early aggression was a robust correlate of adolescent aggression among males, it is a much less sensitive predictor in multivariate models predicting adolescent female aggression (Bierman, Bruschi, Domitrovish, Fang, & Miller-Johnson, 2004; Piquero & Chung, 2001). Perhaps the pathway to and characteristics of persistence are distinct for females. More specifically, though ongoing aggression and offending are the hallmarks of male persistence, female persistence may be marked by a more heterotypic and less overtly criminal behavioral trajectory.

Research indicating gender differences in pathways to adolescent offending is consistent with arguments proposed by Silverthorn and Frick (1999). They argue that persistent delinquency among girls does not manifest itself until adolescence. More specifically, in their model, persistent delinquency for girls is linked to the same kinds of early biological, psychological, and social risk factors that shape the onset pathways of life-course-persistent males. Girls' delinquent onset, however, is delayed as a function of the more stringent informal social controls imposed on preadolescent girls compared to boys. Here adolescence is implicated in female onset only to the extent that it marks a period where the tight social controls imposed on girls are relaxed. However, the fundamental determinants of female onset, in this model, are biological, psychological, and social risks accumulated in childhood. Silverthorn et al. (2001) report evidence from a sample of 72 incarcerated youths that supports Silverthorn and Frick's contention that adolescent-onset females more closely resemble early-onset than adolescent-onset males in their early risk exposure. White and Piquero (2004) also find support for this model with late-onset females exhibiting constellations of risk similar to those of early-onset males. However, they also report evidence that some girls did, in fact, begin their onset in childhood. As such, there appears to be diverse pathways to persistent offending among females.

Risk Factors for Female Offending

Overall, males and females tend to share many of the same risk factors for offending (see Figure 10.1). Moreover, these risk factors tend to be highly cor-related, operating as clusters or constellations of risk factors. Though there

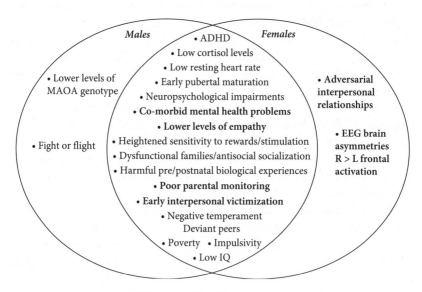

FIGURE 10.1   Gender-specific and gender-invariant risk factors. Items bolded in the center of the diagram, while relevant risk factors for both males and females, are particularly salient for females.

are scores of putative risk factors and many overlap, some are particularly salient or even unique to females. In the paragraphs that follow, it is these risk factors that we highlight (for a more general discussion of risk factors for offending see Loeber & Farrington, 1998b; Tremblay & LeMarquand, 2001; Wasserman, Keenan, Tremblay, Coie & Herrenkohl, 2003). It is important to note that research on risk factors does not necessarily distinguish between their influence on persistent offending and offending more generally. As such, we draw from literature on female offending in general and then link these findings, when possible, to persistent female offending.

Biological Risk Factors

While biological risk factors have primarily been invoked to explain higher rates of aggressive behavior among males, most research suggests that key biological factors are not sex specific. For example, exposure to high levels of testosterone in utero has been implicated in both male and female aggressive behavior in adolescence (Ellis, 1988). In addition, males and females with lower resting heart rate have also been found to engage in more delinquent behavior (Raine, 1993). However, more recent research has started to uncover some gender-specific risks at the level of basic brain biology. For example, electroencephalogram (EEG) research has shown a brain asymmetry of greater frontal activation on the right than on the left (R > L) side in the brains of antisocial females (Baving, Laucht, & Schmidt, 2000). These data also have indicated that antisocial boys exhibited no brain asymmetry, thereby reinforcing that this is a strictly female risk marker. In fact, this R > L pattern found in antisocial girls is identical to the asymmetry evident in healthy, nondelinquent boys. The authors hold that this (R > L) asymmetry suggests that antisocial girls have not developed the enhanced verbal abilities or emotion regulation associated with the left hemisphere and typical of (L > R) normative girls. In addition, Fishbein's (1992) review suggests that pre- or postnatal biological experiences (e.g., excessive androgen production, exposure to synthetic androgens, thyroid dysfunction, Cushing's disease, congential adrenal hyperplasia) combined with a socially disadvantageous environment predisposes certain women to antisocial behavior.

Psychological Risk Factors

Substantial literature shows that female offenders exhibit higher rates of comorbid mental health problems than male offenders (Antonishak, Reppucci, &

Mulford, 2004; Cauffman, 2004; Loeber & Keenan, 1994; Werner & Smith, 1992) and that this pattern holds well into adulthood (Acoca, 1998; Pajer, 1998; Teplin, Abram, McClelland, Dulcan, & Mericle, 2002). Some research indicates that depression is a sex-specific pathway to antisocial behaviors among girls in that it may serve to weaken social bonds while increasing females' indifference to their safety and their involvement in risky activities (Obeidallah & Earls, 1999). Moreover, research suggests that conduct problems among girls can make depressive symptoms more acute, putting these girls at risk for future behavior problems (Moffitt, Caspi, Rutter et al., 2001). Post-traumatic stress disorder (PTSD) in response to victimization and trauma was also found to be more prevalent among delinquent and incarcerated girls than boys (Cauffman, Feldman, & Steiner, 1998). PTSD has been associated not only with higher levels of distress but also lower levels of self-restraint (Cauffman et al., 1998). Previous research has shown that females are more likely than males to develop PTSD after exposure to trauma (Breslau, Davis, Andreski, & Peterson, 1991; Dembo, Williams, & Schmeidler, 1993; Horowitz, Weine, & Jekel, 1995).

Social Risk Factors

Victimization. Yet another risk factor that is common to both genders but is especially salient for females is childhood and adolescent victimization. Most female offenders have a history of abuse before their first offense (Girls Incorporated, 1996; Prescott, 1997; Schoen et al., 1997). According to a multidimensional study of girls in the California juvenile justice system, 92% reported that they had been subjected to some form of emotional, physical, and/or sexual abuse (OJJDP, 1998). Self-reported victimization rates for boys in the juvenile justice system, however, have been found to be considerably lower. For example, some studies describe the rates for males between 25% and 31% (Cocozza, 1992) while other studies report 10% for sexual abuse and 47% for physical abuse (Evans, Macari, & Mason, 1996). In addition, the traumas experienced by delinquent females have been found to be quite different than those experienced by delinquent males (Cauffman et al., 1998). Cauffman et al. (1998) found that males, for example, were more likely than females to report having witnessed a violent event (e.g., witnessing the killing of a friend or family member). Females, on the other hand, were more likely to mention being the victim of violence (e.g., being a victim of either sexual or physical abuse). The expression of conduct problems among girls is often precipitated by exposure to uncontrollable stressors and the incidence of these disorders appears to differ between the sexes (Nolen-Hoeksema, 1994; Tolin & Foa, 2006). It could be the case that dysfunctions among the stress systems of these girls may be a marker for the developmentally persistent form of antisocial behavior (Susman & Pajer, 2004). In other words, not only do persistent female offenders experience higher rates of childhood and adolescent victimization but they also exhibit limited abilities to cope with these stressors (Dornfeld & Kruttschnitt, 1992; Widom, 1991a).

Family. The general notion that "bad families" figure into delinquency has a long history (e.g., Glueck & Glueck, 1934; Thomas, 1923; Wattenberg & Saunders, 1954). In general, compromised family dynamics are implicated in both male and female antisocial behavior (Moffitt, Caspi, Rutter et al., 2001). However, the specific mechanisms linking family dynamics to behavioral outcomes are sometimes gender specific. For example, a greater number of parenting disruptions are more predictive of delinquency and drug abuse among girls of substance abusing parents than among boys (Keller, Catalano, Haggerty, & Fleming, 2002). Although a lack of family supervision has been associated with delinquent behavior for both boys and girls, conflict over supervision and control may provide a greater impetus for girls to engage in such behavior (Chesney-Lind, 1987). Additional evidence for a sex-specific link between poor family dynamics and offending comes from Heimer and DeCoster (1999) who found that poor emotional connections to the family were related to learning violent norms and values for girls but not for boys. In addition, some research indicates that families of female delinquents were especially chaotic (Leve & Chamberlain, 2005) and dysfunctional and exhibited more conflict and neuroticism than families of nondelinquent females (Henggeler et al., 1986). Family deficits, disruptions or stressors, may be especially detrimental to girls' well-being. Given these findings, it is not surprising that incarcerated females reported viewing their parents more negatively than did nonincarcerated females (Kroupa, 1988).

Interpersonal Relationships. As mentioned previously in this chapter, girls' violent offending is significantly more likely to occur within the context of the family than is the case for boys (Franke et al., 2002). For females, more so than males, adversarial interpersonal relationships are a particularly salient risk factor (Odgers & Moretti, 2002). Indeed, girls tend to be more sensitive to issues about social relationships (Maccoby, 1998). Some have theorized that girls' *perceptions of others' expectations of them* is related to emotional well-being, insecure attachment, and delinquency (Moretti, DaSilva, & Holland, 2004). Additional research has provided evidence for the importance of self-representation or self-interpretation to both direct and indirect forms of girls' aggression (Moretti, Holland, & MacKay, 2001). Accordingly, female delinquency is often directly associated with adversarial relationships with parents and/or, romantic partners (Moffitt et al., 2001). Within these interpersonal contexts, females may use aggression to coerce and control others and to ultimately sustain relationships. These may be failed attempts as research has shown that girls who bully are actually more likely to be rejected by their peers than their male counterparts (Pepler & Craig, 1995), putting them at further risk for chronic antisocial behavior (Coie, Terry, Lenox, & Lochman, 1995). Girls who engage in disruptive behaviors score lower on measures of empathy than girls without behavior problems. This empathy deficit is much more acute among female offenders than among male offenders (Broidy, Cauffman, Espelage, Mazerolle, & Piquero, 2003). It follows that female offenders who typically expressed lower levels of compassion and concern for others may have also had weaker affiliative ties. Given the disproportionate importance of affiliative ties (e.g., attachments and interpersonal relationships) for females compared to males (Maccoby, 1998; Moretti & Higgins, 1999), lower levels of empathy could pose a greater risk for these girls.

Despite these stand-out, sex-salient risk factors, the general consensus is that roughly the same risk factors predict antisocial behavior in both males and females (e.g., ADHD, negative temperament, impulsivity, compromised intelligence) (Giordano & Cernkovich, 1997; Moffitt, Caspi, Rutter et al., 2001; Odgers & Moretti, 2002; Zahn-Waxler, 1993). This has led some researchers to suggest that we stop searching for sex-specific risk factors and instead, search for the most parsimonious explanation (Moffitt, Caspi, Rutter et al., 2001). While we acknowledge that the most parsimonious explanation is certainly of value, it should not take precedence over a richer, more nuanced understanding of persistent female offending.

Protective Factors for Female Offending

In comparison to the vast risk factor literature, the work on protective factors is limited. As such, it is unclear as to whether there are any protective factors specific to females. However, given what we know about risk factors, we can speculate that some protective factors would also work in qualitatively distinct ways between males and females. In the section that follows, we will briefly detail some of the potential sex-salient protective factors for offending.

Biological

Males appear to have a distinct biological response to stress that places them at a greater risk for engaging in stress-related aggression. Whereas both sexes exhibit "fight or flight" responses, from a neuroendocrine standpoint, males engage in actual fight or flight behaviors more often than females. It appears that the female response to stress may be better characterized as a "tend and befriend" reflex (Klein & Corwin, 2002). This strategy involves the use of social interactions and supports to provide protection against stressful situations and/or their deleterious consequences. The same situation may spark an aggressive response in males while serving to further solidify female social networks.

Social

While school performance and attachment are protective for both males and females, they appear to work in qualitatively different ways. Some research has indicated that good school performance protects physically abused girls, but not boys, from delinquent involvement (Zingraff, Leiter, Johnsen, & Myers, 1994). Similarly, Anderson and colleagues (1999) found that attachment and bonding to school was a relevant protective factor for females but not for males. The process underlying girls' attachment to school may be due, in part, to the fact that girls consider life skills such as social awareness and obtaining, learning from, and utilizing information to be more important than do boys (Poole & Evans, 1989). Another empirically supported rationale comes from Cernkovich and Giordano's (1992) research that showed that girls enjoy stronger affective attachments to their teachers compared to boys.

Differential Outcomes in Adulthood

The behavioral trajectory that characterizes LCP males is marked by chronic criminality. However, the trajectories of persistent antisocial females are much more varied. For example, a review of adult outcomes for antisocial girls revealed a host of maladaptive consequences including poor educational achievement, high rates of service utilization, violent relationships, unstable work histories, early and poor parenting, and high mortality rates (Pajer, 1998). These harmful outcomes build on one another, affecting these women not only at the individual level but also across multiple contexts (e.g., social/familial, societal/structural). These diverse outcomes in adulthood are the focus of this section.

Individual Level Outcomes

Mental Health Problems. Compared to males, delinquent females exhibit a greater variety of psychiatric problems (mainly within the spectrum of somatic and depressive disorders) in adulthood (Moffitt, Caspi, Rutter et al., 2001). Research indicates that women with conduct disorder may also have a depressive or anxiety disorder by early adulthood (Serbin et al., 1998; Zoccolillo & Rogers, 1992). Perhaps even more problematic is that this major depression often grows more severe in adulthood and is linked to suicidal ideation (Moffitt, Caspi, Rutter et al., 2001). Still other forms of psychopathology, such as borderline personality disorder also occur at significantly higher rates among adult incarcerated women when compared with women in the community (Jordan, Schlenger, Fairbank, & Caddell, 1996). Antisocial behavior in females was also related to poorer *physical* health in adulthood, compared with that in males (Moffitt, Caspi, Rutter et al., 2001).

Substance Abuse Problems. For persistent female offenders, substance abuse often co-occurs with mental health problems. For instance, alcohol and drug abuse, along with other mental health problems and disorders (e.g., internalizing: emotional disturbance, depression) in adulthood, have been linked to girls' early, chronic problem behavior in childhood (Fergusson, Horwood, & Ridder, 2005) and adolescence (Pajer, 1998; Zoccolillo & Rogers, 1992). Similarly, Hawkins, Catalano, & Miller (1992) have shown a connection between female conduct disorder and adult substance abuse. Still other data have indicated that cocaine and poly-substance use common among adult antisocial women was linked with physical health problems (e.g., dental, female reproductive) as well as mental health problems (e.g., depression and anxiety) (Staton, Leukefeld, & Webster, 2003).

While both persistent male and female offenders evinced high rates of substance abuse (Mauer, Potler, & Wolf, 1999), some data suggested that persistent male offenders have significantly worse substance abuse outcomes at age 21 than persistent female offenders (e.g., having used a wider variety of drugs and having had more symptoms of alcohol dependence) (Moffitt, Caspi, Rutter et al., 2001). Conversely, other data have indicated that conduct disorder was found to increase the risk of substance use and abuse in adolescents regardless of gender (Disney, Elkins, McGue, & Iacono, 1999). These data also have suggested that girls with ADHD might be at a slightly higher risk than boys for later substance abuse (Disney et al., 1999).

It is unclear whether substance abuse problems are more serious among female or male persistent offenders. However, substance abuse problems (and their consequences) may be more *salient* for persistent female offenders than for males. For instance, some have suggested that adult antisocial substance abusing women were at greater risk for suicidal behavior than were their male counterparts (Pajer, 1998). Moreover, data have supported the argument that substance abuse treatment programs originally designed for men may be inappropriate for women (Langan & Pelissier, 2001), suggesting that the problem, even if equally common across males and females, manifests differently and may require distinct interventions.

Social/Familial Level Outcomes

Marriage. Both males and females with a history of antisocial behavior are more likely to marry individuals who are involved in crime and who exert an antisocial influence (Moffitt, Caspi, Rutter et al., 2001). Whereas, for males, entry into adult responsibilities (e.g., marriage, childrearing) can be related to desistance (Laub, Nagin, & Sampson, 1998; Sampson, Laub, & Wimer, 2006), this pattern is not as common among females (Moffitt, Caspi, Rutter et al., 2001). Particularly for females, the inverse is often the case, with marriage to an antisocial mate reinforcing and sustaining their offending behaviors throughout adulthood. Recent data implies that for some women, marriage was linked to increased drug use and crime (Brown, 2006). Additionally, these marital relationships are often fraught with conflict and marital instability (Pulkkinen & Pitkanen, 1993).

Moffitt, Caspi, Rutter et al. (2001) found that antisocial women transitioning from adolescence to young adulthood were more likely to face general relationship problems than their male counterparts. While it is often the case that these women's partners physically abused them, the reverse was also true. In fact, according to measures of self- and partner-reported violence, females matched or *exceeded* males' rates of inflicting partner violence (Archer, 2000; Capaldi, Kim, & Shortt, 2004; Moffitt, Caspi, Rutter et al., 2001). Furthermore, data suggest that antisocial women inflict abuse that is serious (e.g., injurious, treated, and/or adjudicated), elicits fear (Capaldi et al., 2004), and that cannot always be explained by self-defense (Giordano, Millhollin, Cernkovich, Pugh, & Rudolph, 1999; Moffitt, Caspi, Rutter et al., 2001). According to observational data from the Oregon Youth and Couples studies, females were consistently more likely to have *initiated* physical aggression than males (Capaldi et al., 2004).

Parenting. Antisocial women selectively reproduce at a younger age, often with an antisocial mate (Moffitt, Caspi, Rutter et al., 2001). Assortative mating and selective reproduction work together, placing both young mother and child with inadequate social, emotional, and financial support. Early parenthood presents its own set of problems for females with a history of early and chronic antisocial behavior. To begin, pregnancy complications are common among this group (Stack, Serbin, Schwartzman, & Ledingham, 2005). Add to this an elevated risk for socioeconomic disadvantage and relationship violence (Jaffee, Belsky, Harrington, Caspi, & Moffitt, 2006) and it is not surprising that parenting skills are often compromised among women with a history of childhood and adolescent aggression (Huh, Tristan, Wade, & Stice, 2006; Moffitt, Caspi, Rutter et al., 2001). Several studies have found a relationship between a history of maternal conduct disorder and unresponsive parenting (Cassidy, Zoccolillo, & Hughes, 1996; Serbin et al., 1998; Wakschlag & Hans, 1999). Especially troubling are more recent data that suggest that mothers with a history of aggression and/or conduct disorder pass on at least three major putative risk factors to their offspring: antisocial biological fathers via assortative mating, prenatal exposure to nicotine, and coercive (hostile) parenting style (Serbin et al., 2004; Zoccolillo, Paquette, Azar, Côté, & Tremblay, 2004; Zoccolillo, Paquette, & Tremblay, 2005).

Education. The risk of early parenthood was greatly increased by having dropped out of high school (Serbin et al., 1998). Data from the Ohio Serious Offender Study (Giordano, Cernkovich, & Lowery, 2004), indicated that incarcerated females specifically reported low rates of educational attainment, with only 16.8% graduating from high school. Similar findings from the Dunedin study provide support for antisocial behavior as a strong predictor of school drop out (Moffitt et al., 2001). More recent studies have also noted high rates of high school drop out, particularly among aggressive girls (Stack et al., 2005).

Work. Longitudinal data indicate that antisocial women have a higher lifetime probability of low occupational status, frequent job changes, and related welfare status (Pulkkinen & Pitkanen, 1993). According to an Ohio study, 54.8% of antisocial women earn less than $14,000 a year (1995–1996 dollars) (Giordano et al., 2004). Still other data from the Dunedin study revealed that antisocial women were already out of the labor force before age 21 (Moffitt, Caspi, Rutter et al., 2001). Moffitt and colleagues noted that one important factor that takes these young women out of the labor force is early childbirth. Data indicate that many of these women supplemented their incomes through drug sales and prostitution (Giordano et al., 2004).

Further, housing was also an issue for persistent female offenders (e.g., female persisters reported living in the basements of crack houses, battered women's shelters, and homeless shelters).

In sum, female offenders experience a variety of negative outcomes in adulthood that signal persistent behavioral and emotional problems. Moreover, these problems are broader than the problems of aggression and crime that mark the persistent pathway for males. The negative outcomes that females exhibit have serious implications for their own long-term emotional and physical health and, notably, those of the next generation. This has left some scientists to wonder: where do we go from here? What are we doing about it? And why do we care?

Interpersonal and Societal Costs

As the number of female offenders in all areas of correctional supervision increases at a dramatic rate, it is important for practitioners and policymakers to develop an understanding of the specific issues and concerns related to female offenders (National Council on Crime and Delinquency, U.S. Department of Justice, 1992).

Although the aformentioned quotation from the report "Female Offenders in the Community: An Analysis of Innovative Strategies and Programs" is over a decade old, little research has been conducted to explain why females are increasingly coming into the juvenile justice system or to examine strategic responses to this significant trend. As little is known about how juvenile females respond to interventions, many communities are unprepared to address the specific needs of the growing number of girls in the juvenile justice system. According to the OJJPD (2002) there is great demand for comprehensive needs assessments and gender-sensitive services and programs. While several states have tried or are trying to implement specific treatment programs for female juvenile offenders, as of yet no national standards are in place (National Criminal Justice Reference Service, 1992). Moreover, once female adolescents become involved in aggressive behavior, offending, and consequently incarceration, we know even less about how female offenders navigate transitions to adulthood and, ultimately how they adapt and make choices as they try to build their lives postincarceration.

Though less obvious than the long-term risks associated with male aggression (i.e., crime), the social costs associated with long-term outcomes for females who manifest early, chronic aggression are equally pronounced. A staggering two out of every three women in prison are mothers of young children (Bureau of Justice Statistics, 1994). Of these children, 6% are born to women who are pregnant when they enter prison (National Women's Law Center, 1995). While the majority of these children are under the care of other relatives, 10% of children with mothers in prison are sent to foster homes (OJJDP, Statistical Briefing Book, 2002). In addition to the cost of incarcerating these mothers, the annual cost of foster care for a prisoner's child is between $20,000 and $25,000 (George & LaLonde, 2002) and President Bush's 2007 budget calls for 40 million dollars toward the mentoring of children of prisoners (Lester, 2006).

Nevertheless, the impact is not simply financial as the children of incarcerated women suffer serious negative outcomes throughout their lives. Children of incarcerated parents differ from their peers in three critical ways: first, they experience inadequate quality of child care, mainly due to poverty; second, it follows that they grow up with a lack of family support; and third, these children are faced with enduring childhood trauma (Johnston, 1996). Hence it is not surprising that children with inmate mothers are six times more likely than their peers to end up behind bars (Johnston, 1996). Still other data show that when children were placed with caregivers during their mother's incarceration, 40% of the male adolescents had some involvement with the juvenile justice system; 60% of female adolescents were or had been pregnant, and one-third of these children experienced severe school-related problems (Myers, 1999).

In general, while mother–child separation is extremely difficult, the impact of having an incarcerated mother is so detrimental to the welfare of the child. Since states have a limited number of facilities devoted to housing women, female inmates are rarely housed close to home. As a result, half of the 250,000 children of incarcerated mothers never get to visit their mother while she is incarcerated (OJJDP, 2002). Moving women farther away from home and family, given the paramount nature of interpersonal relationships to females, makes future reintegration a challenge. Future research, policy, programs, and preventative efforts should facilitate the maintenance of family ties as well as enhancement of these women's parenting and life skills. Not only would these efforts benefit these women but they would also help the next generation of at-risk youth.

Conclusions

The lack of research on persistent (or chronic) female offending greatly limits our understanding of these offenders. Also, much of the longitudinal data that documents female offending trajectories is abbreviated, ending in early adulthood (i.e., early 20s). Indeed, given the small sample sizes employed in previous research (and an accompanying lack of statistical power), it is very difficult to identify predictors in general and sex-specific predictors in particular.

Nonetheless, in this chapter we addressed four key areas related to the persistent female offender. First, in regard to the existence and characteristics of the chronic female offender: limited but compelling evidence builds a cogent case for her existence. Most of the studies reviewed indicate roughly the same pattern for chronic female offenders. That is, delinquency begins *early* (and is notably more serious, frequent, and consistent than average female offending), progresses through adolescence, and is then *truncated more abruptly* in adulthood compared to persistent male offenders. While chronic female offenders tend to engage in more nonviolent (particularly drug) offenses, there is a substantial literature that depicts these women as increasingly violent.

Second, in regard to risk and protective factors for female persistent offending, we acknowledge that the vast majority of factors overlap across males and females. However, gendered nuances exist within those factors; while families matter for both males and females, for instance, they matter differently. For example, while a lack of a parental supervision leads to negative outcomes for both males and females, conflict over supervision provides a greater impetus for girls to engage in delinquent behavior and aggression. In addition, we highlighted a number of risk factors that are particularly salient for girls including brain asymmetry, comorbid mental health problems, early interpersonal victimization, and adversarial interpersonal relationships. Our review also examines the nature of adult outcomes for persistent female offenders and while quite disparate from males, these outcomes are certainly no less serious for females. Among the most troubling are violent relationships, early and poor parenting, and higher mortality rates. Finally, as some research suggests that female offending is on the rise, the interpersonal and societal costs of female persistence are too great to ignore.

As noted in the chapter, it is crucial that we amass more multi-informant, longitudinal data from varied birth cohorts of females. We call for more rigorous empirical work to shed light on whether the number of females who follow a persistent pathway is stable, rising, or falling over time and what accounts for these trends. Again, we stress that it is necessary that future research continue to identify sex-specific risk and protective factors. These advances are key to improving our understanding of the unique etiology, course, and treatment of the persistent female offender. Still, more work needs to be done toward the empirically based development and validation of gender-sensitive programming. In turn, these evidence-based programs can effect change at the policy level. Ultimately, it is critical that investigators understand the criminal life trajectories for girls, as well as the impact female criminality has on family members, the greater social ecological context, and the next generation.

CHAPTER 11

Foster Care Youth: Aging Out of Care to Criminal Activities

MARY ANN DAVIS

Approximately 20,000 youth complete the foster care system through reaching majority or "aging out" of foster care. Although those who age out of care are expected to function independently, their experience of multiple risk factors associated with placement in foster care, in addition to the effect of foster placement itself, put them at an elevated risk of persistent criminal behavior in adulthood. Researchers (Courtney & Herring, 2005; Foster & Gifford, 2005; Osgood, Foster, Flanagan, & Ruth, 2005) agree that since the state assumes responsibility for the foster care population, acting as guardians, it is imperative that they insure that foster children have the supports in place to attain successful outcomes. Instead, the adult outcome of many foster youth is persistence in criminal activity. Following is an exploration of the issues affecting the criminal persistence of this vulnerable population. This chapter will first describe foster care and the process of transition to independent living. Next, is a discussion of three models that predict persistence in criminal activities: the life-course model, the capital and attachment models, and the ecological model. Finally, summaries of current studies depicting the transition to independent living by foster care youth are discussed.

Foster Care Background

Foster Care in the United States is a federally funded entitlement program. According to the Child Welfare League of America (CWLA, 2005d) in 2005, 518,000 children were in the U.S. foster care system. Thirty percent were aged birth to 5; 20% were aged 6 to 10; 29% were aged 11 to 15; 18% were aged 16 to 18; and 2% were over age 18. Eighty-five percent of foster care youth are diagnosed with developmental, emotional, or behavioral problems. CWLA estimates that 30% to 40 % of youth in care are adolescents who will remain in care until emancipation. Of these, approximately 20,000 youth are emancipated to independent living each year: 23,121 in 2004.

The CWLA (2005c) notes that there is a definite social class bias in the decision to place children in foster care due in part to the three eligibility criteria of the Title IV-E Foster Care Program, the federal program that funds foster care, which stipulate that the child: (1) must have been a recipient of public assistance in the state when deprived of parental care, (2) must be placed in care for safety and welfare, and (3) reasonable efforts must have been made to resolve the family issues before removal of the child. Sciamanna (2006), codirector of CWLA Government Affairs, reports that funding for foster children, included in the Title IV-E funding program linked with Aid to Families with Dependent Children (AFDC), was severely limited beginning in 1996 when the foster care program was temporarily assumed to be under the administration of the new Temporary Assistance to Needy Families (TANF) program. While in 1998, 55% of foster care youth were eligible for federal funding, eligibility declined to 45% in 2004 so that, for example, in 25 states only children removed from families earning less than half of the federal poverty level (approximately $8000 for a family of three) were eligible for foster care (Sciamanna, 2006). Therefore, in spite of federal acts that address foster care and independent living foster care, youth who are not indigent are ineligible for Medicaid or Title IV-E funds. They rely on local or state funding, both of which are limited and are inconsistent with different programs offered across the states.

CWLA (2005c) further states that placement appears heavily influenced by race. Blacks represent 34% of the foster care population and only 15% of the U.S. population compared to Whites who comprise 40% of the foster care population and 61% of the general population. This minority overrepresentation may be due to nonracial factors such as poverty, family size, and related child abuse. In addition, minority families tend to live in neighborhoods with fewer community resources which may be protective of placement of abused children in foster care. Minorities are also more likely to live in areas with increased neighborhood violence (Hines, Lemon, Wyatt, & Merdinger, 2004).

Foster care youth are vulnerable, requiring placement as protection from their family/caretakers. Widom (1991b) cites five major reasons for placement in foster care: severe neglect or abuse (10%), mental illness of the mother (11%), emotional issues of the child (17%), physical illness or incapacity of the caregiver (29%), and general family problems (33%). There are four types of out-of-home placement. Basic foster care involves care in a foster home with general case management services available. Therapeutic foster care (TFC) is used for those youth who have a diagnosed medical or psychological condition. These consist of specialized medical foster homes to deal with medical issues, specially trained foster families, and supportive psychological services including counseling and psychotropic medications. The third type of placement is institutional care or residential treatment for emotionally disturbed individuals. This care involves a psychiatric component as well as restrictive residential setting. The fourth type of placement is psychiatric hospitalization which includes the possibility of using locked units as well as mechanical, physical, and chemical restraints for those with acute psychiatric and behavioral disturbances.

Although children may enter care at any age, foster care youth usually "age out" of care on their 18th birthday. Then they are expected to transition into financially independent adults, able to fully meet all of their living expenses, food, rent, insurance, transportation, and other requirements while the dependency of nonfoster care youth in the United States, those with family resource advantages, is often extended through college or trade school. The CWLA sponsored the Foster Care Independence Act of 1999 (HR 3443) to attempt to address this gap in resources. This act made provisions to help youth "aging out" of foster care, by funding education, vocational training, and an extension of Medicaid to emancipated ex-foster youth up to age 20 to have a safety net for launching into independent living. However, there continues to be a lag of time in the implementation of Independent Living federal initiatives services and the range of services offered. The CWLA (2005b) reported that in the year 2000, 90,152 youths over age 16 in foster care were eligible to receive Independent Living Services. A little over half, or 58,159, actually received these services in preparation for emancipation. There are significant difficulties in reaching and maintaining contact with this population. With about half of eligible young adults failing to receive emancipation services, and a percentage leaving care early by running away, it is difficult to know the needs of those lost to the system. Administrative data is neither accessible nor standardized and no consistent follow-up is required to determine the aftercare status of those who exit from foster care.

Three Models of Persistent Criminality among Foster Care Youth

Three models which are predictive of persistent antisocial behavior place former foster care youth at greater risk than those who grow up in their family of origin: the life-course model, the social capital model, and the ecological model.

The Life-Course Model

The life-course model addresses stages of development, normal developmental tasks, and the relationship of these to desistance or persistence in criminal activity. Sampson and Laub (2005b) argue that successful transitions to adult life are necessary for normal development. The normal process in most western industrialized countries is for youth to complete their education, obtain employment, get married, establish a home, and become parents (see also Chapter 18). If these transitional markers of education, employment, marriage, and other positive life outcomes are not met, there is a greater risk of criminal involvement. Obstacles are many; without education employment is limited; without employment there are no resources for meeting the normal trajectory including a married life with the security of a job, house, insurance and a partner's assets for financial stability (Sampson & Laub, 2005b).

Although Sampson and Laub (2005a) found that childhood antisocial behaviors were associated with adult criminality, they also found that criminal persistence is affected by turning points such as military careers and marriage. Foster care youth are more likely to experience adverse life-course transitions such as educational disruption. They are less likely to benefit from healthy transitions of marriage and employment because they are pushed abruptly into adult life with little family support that eases the transitions for normal youth. Another issue related to life-course criminology is the effect of incarceration itself. Pettit and Western (2004) note that once an individual is in the criminal justice system, his life course becomes significantly altered. Not only has he delayed entry into the normal transitional roles by an average of 30 to 40 months due to criminal justice intervention, but the stigma of imprisonment affects future wage earning and ex-prisoners are less likely to get married—all of which lead to a persistence in criminal behavior. Thus, if a youth is incarcerated during his or her transition to independent living this has a dramatic effect on later offending.

Another issue is education, usually attained sequentially by the young. Education has lifelong effects, as the pathway to employment and occupation, assuring a living wage necessary to purchase housing, food, and medical care. Each time a foster child moves, this disrupts his education. Since foster youth are able to be emancipated by age 17 or 18, multiple moves may prevent the youth from attaining a high school diploma or General Education Diploma (GED) by this time. Both high school diploma and GED are more difficult to attain after leaving care.

The Capital Model

The capital model addresses the links between the supports provided by family to the individual, which affect his or her future criminal involvement. The life-course and capital models intersect as they both address individual resources, such as education, social resources, such as spouses and family and friends, as well as biological aging. According to Coleman (1988), family includes three capital components: financial capital (intergenerational wealth), human capital (attained skills, genetic and psychological personality factors) and social capital (the relationships within the family). Financial capital provides additional advantages, which cross generations, allowing youth to attain tangible assets such as education, housing, jobs, and higher earnings. Although human capital is most frequently measured in terms of education and skills attained, a major subset of human capital is the psychological makeup of the individual, described in terms of attachment and personality. Examples of human capital related to successful foster care transition are intelligence, which allows the individual to attain higher educational levels, and pleasing personality traits, which allow the individual to make friends and find marital partners. Social capital is the basis for prosocial socialization. An example of social capital is the family interaction in the education of children through talking, supervising homework, and modeling the benefits of education. The family invests in the children through committed, trusting relationships. At the same time, parents actively steer children toward prosocial activities and away from criminal activities. These parent–child interactions are in effect a natural social exchange process, with parents giving to children and for these "gifts" children being obliged to respond by conforming to their parents' expectations.

Most researchers (Barth, 1990; Coleman, 1988; Hagan & McCarthy; 1997, Mech, 1994; Wright, Cullen, & Miller, 2001) agree that a financial support system is vital to successful transition to independent living. Conversely, if youth have no secure finances for expected and unexpected transition needs, the young adult may face numerous undesirable outcomes such as homelessness, which may lead down a path of street crimes and persistence in criminal activities. Moreover, Schwartz et al. (1994) suggest that being homeless targets these youth for arrest.

Most of the literature and policy development relies on financial capital issues to prevent a criminal trajectory for ex-foster youth. Two issues affecting foster youth are the age of emancipation compared to the general population and the lack of support through extended training or education programs which are becoming standard among American youth. Financial capital for the ex-foster youth is less than that for the general population. The ex-foster care youth is emancipated at age 18, with limited education and occupational resources, without financial capital of housing, health insurance, money, and personal possessions required to set up a residence (CWLA, 2005b). It can be argued that financial capital for the general population continues through college and beyond. Geary (2003) reported that in the general population over 60% of American college graduates, around aged 22 in 2003, were "boomerangs" returning home briefly for support until they found employment. It is likely that a far greater number receive other forms of capital from their families in the way of cash, health insurance, automobiles, furniture, and the security of a safety net available in the event of financial hardships.

The ex-foster youth thus is expected to become financially independent at a younger age, with fewer supports for the occasional hard times, often earning the minimum wage (which remains unchanged in spite of 10 years of inflation. Education is directly related to employment attainment as well as income and financial stability in adulthood. Education level affects income. Data from the U.S. census in 2000 suggest that in the general population those aged 25 to 34 with less than a high school education earned an average of $20,069 while those with a Bachelors degree earned an average of $37,233 and those with an advanced degree earned $44,065 (U.S. Census Bureau, Housing and Household Economics Division, 2007). Jonson-Reid (1998) argues that the educational capital model is not an adequate predictor of criminality, especially violent crimes. She explains that although low educational attainment is related to delinquency with one study showing that adding educational attainment to a predictive model improved prediction of delinquency by 23%, educational attainment did not predict serious delinquency and violence. Jonson-Reid noted a study which showed that although the minority dropout rate was 45%, only about 5% were arrested for violent crimes.

Financial capital is closely linked with social capital provided by the family. Hagan and McCarthy (1997) report that youth who grow up without parental control, supervision, and support have a greater risk for street crime.

Like Sampson and Laub (2005a), they found that social capital allowed a greater explanation for why some youth were able to leave the streets and enter the job market with a stable crime-free lifestyle while others remain on the streets, homeless, and persist in criminal activities (Hagan & McCarthy, 1997). Ex-foster youth have an increased risk of homelessness; Reilly (2003), studying ex-foster youth 6 months after emancipation, found that 36% of foster youth became homeless within the first 6 months after leaving care.

Attachment is thought to be an important component of family interactions. Here, I include attachment as a form of "capital," though it is sometimes seen as a model of its own. In the attachment model the path to normal behavior is through familial bonding. Family attachment is a protective mechanism, providing emotional stability which leads to increased mental health and decreased substance abuse so that the individual is less prone to a variety of pathologies including criminal behavior. Bowlby (1980) describes attachment as affectional bonding, beginning in infancy and lasting throughout the life cycle, initially between child and parent. This attachment process provides the child with the safety and sense of dependability necessary for developing trust in human relationships, the basis for secure social interactions with friends and intimate partners. As mentioned earlier, one of the significant strengths of family life is setting the stage for these healthy social relationships. The parent provides for the child, the child reciprocates by doing what the parent requests. The child trusts the parent and the parent trusts the child, setting the stage for positive social interactions based on trust for mutual benefit. Bowlby (1980) describes attachment as an instinctual process, as vital to human life as feeding behavior and sexual behaviors. Positive attachments early in life lead to better relationships in adult life and are protective against the development of antisocial personality disorder.

Attachment issues are part of the basis of the adolescent diagnosis of Conduct Disorder (American Psychiatric Association [APA], 2000) which also includes aggression, bullying, fighting, animal cruelty, fire setting, destroying property, running away, truancy, and lying or conning others. Obviously these are the behaviors which place one at risk for juvenile incarceration. By definition, adolescents with conduct disorder are at risk for maturing into the adult DSM-IV-TR diagnosis of antisocial personality disorder. Youth in foster care are vulnerable to attachment problems because they are often raised by parents unavailable for bonding due to their incarceration, mental health issues, or substance abuse, and they tend to be moved frequently in care and thus unable to bond with substitute caretakers. Thus, one would expect a positive relationship between a history of foster care placement or alternative living arrangement and conduct problems and psychopathic traits. In the general population, it is estimated that 20% or

13.7 million children have a diagnosed mental disorder, with only one-fifth of these receiving services. However, in a foster care population 85% have a developmental, emotional, or behavioral problem. If these youth receive specialized therapeutic services with psychiatric and psychological services, including medication, treatment, and counseling, these mental health conditions can be alleviated. Without treatment they are likely to worsen (APA, 2000). McWey (2004) found that children in foster care were 10 times more likely to have mental health problems than the other youth in California. Less than 4% of the population of youth in California was diagnosed with mental health problems but 41% of those in foster care were diagnosed with mental health issues. The primary diagnosis of foster care youth was conduct disorder, followed by attention-deficit/hyperactivity disorder, depression and anxiety, and behavior problems (McWey, 2004).

The assumption from a child welfare perspective is that attachment, either with the family or in a stable foster home, is necessary for normal psychological development. Thus, the first preference in the social service system is to reunite children with their natural families, assuming this provides a greater likelihood for attachment, and a better opportunity for normal emotional development leading to long-term mental health (Jonson-Reid & Barth, 2000a, 2000b). If the child must be removed from his/her biological family due to abuse or neglect, most agency policies mandate reunification (Redding, Fried, & Britner, 2000). It is hoped that the end result will be to allow the child the benefit of familial attachment, with the optimism that the violent and abusing families can be quickly and easily rehabilitated so that cycles of abuse are easily changed with short-term intervention.

However, it is not always in the best interest of the child to reunify him or her with the natural parents. The parents may not be available or accessible for attachment due to multiple issues such as family violence, substance abuse, antisocial personality, mental illness, and incarceration. Failing reunification, the next recommended practice is to seek termination of parental rights and place the child up for adoption. Unfortunately, this may entail a lengthy legal process; all the while the child is aging. As the child gets older, he or she has reduced chances of forming attachments, the most important of which are thought to develop in early life.

The overall goal based on the attachment model is to maintain stability in placement so that bonding may occur. Out-of-home placement is usually initiated in a crisis with the goal of family reunification within 6 months, though in some cases a long-term placement would have been the best option for attachment. Due to the aforementioned crisis intervention approach, which assumes that the best outcome is short-term intervention and family reunification, there is little tailoring of placement services to the age of the child. However, youth of different ages have different placement needs, ranging from the one-to-one parenting needs of an infant necessary for bonding, to adolescents who may have more difficulty accepting parenting from parent substitutes (Wulczn, Kogan, & Harden, 2003).

Attachment theory suggests that fewer foster placements will result in better outcomes. The minimization of moves is the preferred standard, and research is beginning to address the effect of multiple moves including the criminal trajectory. According to Jonson-Reid and Barth (2000b), two-thirds of the estimated 500,000 children in foster care are over age 6. Of these, the greatest likelihood for incarceration is among those placed between ages 12 and 15 that had experienced multiple moves.

Fahlberg (1994) has prescribed a way to minimize moves in placement. She suggests preparing both the child and the family for placement by involving both child and foster family in movement decisions, with extensive sharing of background and strategies for behavioral interventions, and having preplacement visits and lengthy transitions with social work support for transition issues as they occur. Although this is the ideal, the reality is that children are usually placed with limited preplanning. Quinton et al. (1998) studied the issue of preplacement planning with adoptive families. Preplacement planning with the older child happened in only 18 of the 32 families in their sample, and the social worker arranging the placement dealt primarily with the parent issues and to a lesser extent those of the siblings. We should keep in mind, however, that even with an imperfect system, children experience fewer moves in foster care than they do before child protective services (CPS) intervention, so placing a child in a foster home may actually limit his number of moves. Redding et al. (2000) evaluated services for adolescents who had multiple moves and found the mean number of moves before CPS intervention was 4.8 compared to 1.8 moves following CPS intervention.

A related attachment issue is the question of causality. It is possible that some foster children have genetic, neurodevelopmental, or personality problems which prevent strong attachments and bonding and cause behavior problems—and this may be one reason these children are in foster care. (See Chapter 8 for more on the dynamics of biology and environment). For such children, who are at an elevated risk of conduct disorder, multiple placements are common. The question is, does moving the child from placement to placement lead to attachment deficits that result in conduct disorder, or does the child's personality and behavior cause problems in the foster family that result in multiple placements? Researchers (Newton, Litrowik, & Landverk, 2000; Quinton et al., 1998; Quinton & Rutter, 1988) have studied the relationship between problem behaviors of the child and placement disruptions. The consensus is that youth who are aggressive are more likely to disrupt placements and have multiple placements. However, Newton et al. (2000) found that, controlling for aggression and conduct disorder, the number of placements was still predictive of aggressive and conduct disorders for those youth who entered placement without these behaviors, suggesting that the causal dynamic is in both directions. So foster children are at increased risk for attachment issues due to multiple factors: (1) the early bonding problems due to a lack of adequate parenting from a caretaker who may be unable to nurture when experiencing financial difficulties, mental health problems, substance abuse, or incarceration; (2) the foster care system itself generating multiple moves; and (3) the psychological or neurological factors that contribute to psychopathology.

The Ecological Model

The ecological model follows a historical tradition from the Chicago School suggesting that factors in the environment, such as neighborhood disorder, exposure to violence, a lack of community supports for education and employment, cause offending to persist. Recently, Hanson et al. (2006) used the National Survey of Adolescents to examine the relationship between environment and violence. They found a combination of risk factors such as exposure to domestic violence and substance abuse and living in households with incomes below the poverty level are associated with both abuse (neglect, physical, and sexual) and violence. As mentioned earlier, foster children are more likely to live in an environment with exposure to violence, poverty, and substance abuse so there is a strong relationship between community variables, such as poverty and minority status and foster care placement.

Jonson-Reid (1998, 2002) combines the ecological model with child development as an eco-developmental model. This model links child maltreatment, exposure to domestic violence and living in an environment of poverty and street violence, with future violence in youth. Thus, there is a pathway from living in a violent environment to becoming violent as an adult. According to Jonson-Reid (1998, 2002) even the most traumatic violence (murder) involves children. In the United States 2000 children, from birth to age 19, are killed per year with an additional 3.3 million youth witnessing domestic violence annually. She notes that between 20 and 40% of children have witnessed a violent crime, and that a large proportion of children live in poverty. Poverty is associated with child abuse, with estimated rates of abuse among the poor ranging from 40% in a study in Omaha to 60% to 75% in a Chicago study. Another study found that poverty, child care burden, population instability, and contiguousness to poverty were highly associated with violent crime (Jonson-Reid, 1998).

Jonson-Reid (1998) supports the concept of a dose–response effect or additive effect of environmental factors on criminality. She argues that youth exposed to multiple ecological factors, such as community violence, domestic violence, substance abuse in caretakers and financial instability, are at the greatest risk of violence. Thus, she proposes that violence is greatest when the systems of family violence and the ecosystems of media and societal violence are combined. She refers to reviews of 40 years of research that conclude that violence in the mass media contributes to aggressive behavior. These studies also indicate that low income and minority children and families have limited entertainment other than watching television so they watch more television and are exposed to more television violence. This supports the hypothesis that watching violent television together with witnessing family violence will escalate violence in youth.

Schwartz et al. (1994) reiterate the argument that child abuse is a leading cause of delinquency and youth crime. They state that since the 1960s with the publication of "The Battered-Child Syndrome" by Kempe et al. (1962), the dominant political impetus for child welfare funding has been the threat posed by the cycle of violence. There are multiple definitions of both delinquency and abuse with estimates of annual cases of child abuse and neglect in the United States ranging from 500,000 to 2.4 million (Schwartz et al., 1994). Schwartz et al. (1994) further note that the relationship between child maltreatment and crime has led to a political fatalism, the belief that these youth are somehow damaged for life, which has led to an increase in punitive sanctions against juveniles who commit crimes. One of these increased sanctions is making it easier to try juveniles in adult courts by lowering the age at which a youth is considered an adult. Second, there have been mandatory sentences for certain crimes, such as drug crimes and those committed with guns. Third, at least 14 major cities have curfews making it illegal for juveniles to be on the streets after a certain hour. All of these factors have led to an increase in arrests and an increase in the use of adult imprisonment for juveniles.

To summarize, the ecological model of persistence posits that those who are exposed to environments of poverty and violence, either as domestic violence or through living in an environment of violence, are more likely to persist in violence as adults. Foster youth are more likely to live in these high-risk environments of poverty and violence. They are more likely to be exposed to domestic violence and abuse and parental substance abuse (CWLA, 2005b). The issue of substance abuse and persistence is also an ecological issue in that those who are socialized in an environment accepting of substance abuse and illegal activities are more likely to persist in these activities as adults. Thus foster youth are exposed to what Jonson-Reid (1998) labels a higher dosage of ecological conditions which lead to a greater likelihood of persistence in crime.

Outcomes of Foster Youth Transitioning to Independent Living

There is limited research on the relationship between placement in out-of-home care and criminality despite a common acceptance that foster care youth are at risk for adult entry into the criminal justice system based on life-course, capital, and ecological models. In particular, there has been a scarcity of data and studies of the trajectory from foster care to independent living. This section will review findings from the existing studies.

It should be noted that one severe limitation of studies on this topic is a lack of longitudinal data necessary to address life-course issues of criminal persistence for foster care youth. Two multiwave studies from Chapin Hill at the University of Chicago have been conducted. Together, they demonstrate that ex-foster youth have high rates of adult serious criminality. First, Courtney et al. (2001) tracked 141 youth who left foster care in 42 counties of Wisconsin between 1995 and 1996, to test hypotheses related to life-course and capital models. The first wave included 141 individuals before their leaving care. The second wave included 113 (80%) who were interviewed when they had been out of care between 12 and 18 months. At Wave 2, 55% had completed high school, another 9% had entered college, with 37% not having either a high school diploma or GED. In the general U.S. census population, approximately 80% complete high school, 52% complete some college, and 19.6% do not have a high school or GED (Bauman & Graf, 2003). At Wave 2, 61% of the ex-foster care youth sample were employed and 18% had a history of arrests. Twenty-seven percent of the males and 10% of the females were incarcerated at least once after discharge.

The second study (Courtney et al., 2005) presents results from the Midwest Evaluation of the Adult Functioning of Former Foster Youth which is a longitudinal study of emancipated foster care youth in Iowa, Wisconsin and Illinois. Baseline interviews of 736 ex-foster care youth were conducted in 2002 and 2003 when the youth were aged 17 or 18. Follow-up interviews were conducted with 386 of these youth in 2004. At the 1-year follow-up interview 33.8% had been arrested, 29.6% had been incarcerated for a violent crime, with 19.7% and 28.2% incarcerated for property and other types of crime respectively.

The majority of studies address capital issues related to CWLA independent living standards and legislated in the Independence Living Act. These studies address capital issues of education, employment, housing, homelessness, financial support, medical issues, and support systems. Three of these studies further emphasize attachment issues which affect a criminal trajectory: the age at first placement, the number of out-of-home placements, and the psychological diagnoses or treatment needs that affect the likelihood of criminal or violent behavior.

Barth (1990) studied 55 adults emancipated from foster care over 1 year and under 10 years, using a convenience sample. He addressed capital issues and found that 55% left foster care without a high school education. Although the majority (75%) had employment, primarily full-time, more than 53% had serious financial problems such as inability to pay rent and 33% said that they had done an illegal act such as stealing, prostitution, or selling drugs, for money. Thirty-five percent had been arrested or incarcerated since leaving foster care.

Mech (1994) reviewed six studies addressing the adult functioning of youth who had been in foster care and used the aggregated data from these studies for a meta-analysis of the combined 1465 respondents. Five indicators were examined related to the capital model: education, employment, housing, support networks, and community expense. Unfortunately criminality (or incarceration) was not included as an outcome. Of the 1465 respondents, 847 or 58% completed high school compared to the 84% high school completion rate in the United States (based on census data for those in the 20–24 age range). More than 90% held a job at some point following leaving foster care, with 70% of the males and 55% of the females employed at the time of the study. However, mere employment does not equate to financial stability; most were working in low-paying service and part-time type jobs which "together with the changing nature of employment structure in the United States holds important implications for the world of work preparation of foster care graduates" (Mech, 1994, p. 605).

Haapasalo (2000) obtained the consent of 78 young Finnish offenders to analyze their child protective services, clinic and hospital records exploring issues of whether being in child welfare custody is associated with antisocial behavior and criminal behavior in adulthood. He found that although only 1% of Finnish youth are placed in foster care, 50% of the offenders had been in foster care. Looking at capital issues he found that maternal alcoholism, paternal alcoholism, and age of onset were all significantly related to offending. He also addressed attachment issues. Overall, foster care youth who had lived in four or more homes were four times more likely to be charged with a crime. A case could also be made for ecological issues. The results showed that the older the child at first placement, presumably experiencing longer exposure to the abusive or neglecting home or to neighborhood violence, and poverty, the greater the number of criminal arrests.

Farmer et al. (2003) analyzed a statewide sample in North Carolina 12 months before and following therapeutic foster care and examined whether treatment would help the foster care youth have an improved outcome. The purpose of this study was to show that even though those who received TFC entered care with more physical and psychiatric problems, they benefited from added psychiatric and psychological services received during TFC. Results showed that whereas 19.1% entered residential foster care from institutions, 4.2% from jails, 2.1% from hospitals and 12.8% from residential treatment, only 8.3% exited to institutions, and of these only 1.7% exited to jail. Those at greatest risk for institutional placement when they left foster care were those who were older at placement, supporting the ecological model as they would have lived longer in the abusive or neglectful environment.

Reilly (2003) studied 100 youth who had been out of foster care for at least 6 months. He addressed capital issues through data from Nevada's Child Welfare Action database, an administrative database used by Nevada's Division of Child and Family Services (DCFS) to track youth who exit from care. Notably, four of the subjects had died since leaving care. As a striking example of lack of financial capital, one of the four deceased was a diabetic who was discharged without health insurance necessary for necessary diabetes medication, without which he died. Education capital was similar to other studies. Only 50% had completed high school when they left care, 69% did so following care. Thirty six percent had been homeless at least once in the 6 months since they left care; 35% had moved five or more times since leaving care. Criminal justice involvement was high; 41% had been in jail and 7% were currently in a state prison.

Widom (1991b) studied the criminal records of 772 juveniles from the Midwest during 1967–1971. This study clearly showed the relationship between attachment, as measured by movement in care, and criminality. Widom found a positive relationship between the number of placements and arrests as a juvenile. Of the 123 subjects who had three or more placements, 53.9% were arrested as an adult. The length of time in first placement was also significant. Youth who spent more than 10 years in their first placement had the lowest overall arrest rates. The best outcomes were for those whose first placement was at the youngest ages, who remained in their first placement over 10 years, and who had fewer placements. This is consistent with the attachment model. Although earlier placement may be disruptive, the lengthier placement allowed for a greater attachment to the foster family and better outcomes. From an ecological viewpoint the earlier placement may also mean less exposure to the environment of abuse and neglect and possible criminality in the neighborhood (Widom, 1991b).

Campbell et al. (2004) provide a Canadian perspective in their retrospective study of 226 incarcerated adolescent offenders. They examine whether these offenders were more likely to have been foster children with attachment issues due to moves in placement. They found that 25.9% of the offenders had prior foster care placement and an additional 23.6% had a placement with a nonparent relative or friend. The average number of placements was 2.67. Their study supported the attachment hypothesis with a positive relationship between history of foster care placement or alternative living arrangement, multiple moves, and psychopathic traits.

Jonson-Reid and Barth (2003) studied foster children in California who entered care from 1988–1996 and tested whether ecological factors predicted incarceration before age 18 in the California Youth Authority (the state juvenile offender system). The results showed that slightly over 7 per 1000 school-aged children with at least one foster care placement entered the California Youth Authority. They found that the strongest predictors of incarceration were male sex, and placement between ages 12 and 14. Ethnic differences were strong with African-Americans and other minorities having the highest entry rates. Females with prior foster care were 10 times more likely to enter into the California Youth Authority than those in the general population. The authors postulated that the 12 to 14 year old youth had the greatest developmental stressors, such as puberty, plus weaker peer and teacher support in middle school as they are moved from class to class without the social support of ongoing high school activities. They found that children removed for sexual abuse were less likely to enter the California Youth Authority, hypothesizing that these youth were more likely to be placed in TFC and receive mental health services than foster children removed for physical abuse and neglect. The findings that those who received TFC and psychological services had better outcomes were similar to those reported earlier by Farmer et al. (2003). (See Chapter 16, for more on serious persistent criminality among juveniles in the California Youth Authority.)

Data Issues

The studies in this literature review reveal underlying weaknesses of data collection, which have limited research about the transition of foster care youth to adulthood. All of the studies report difficulties associated with contacting youth or young adults who were independent, so most studies were based on convenience samples. This population is difficult to reach on a one-time basis, with increased difficulties of maintaining contact over the several waves of data collection necessary to study life-course issues. Young adults with limited capital do not maintain the same address and there is no combined database of youth currently in the foster care or criminal justice systems or a systematic tracking of ex-foster youth.

Another problem is that foster care programs are administered by states with independent administrative systems that use individual standards, languages, and criteria for services. The Statewide Automated Child Welfare Information System (SACWIS) evolved in the 1990s due to the need for a coherent computerized data system to share data among all states. The current status of the implementation of SACWIS is that 5 states have full implementation, 20 states are in the process of implementation, an additional 23 states are in the planning phase of implementation and the remaining states are in the exploratory phase (U.S. Department of Health and Human Services, 2006). A wealth of data will be collected by the new system; however, the data are currently severely limited by the small number of states which have fully implemented data collection. Further, it will take years to follow the life paths of youth who enter care at infancy and exit at age 18 or 22.

Coordination of data between the child welfare and justice systems has similar issues. There is no federally mandated system combining data on criminal offenses with data on prior histories of abuse and neglect. The CWLA conducted a survey of juvenile justice agencies and found that nearly nine-tenths of the agencies did not have programs for juvenile offenders who were also abuse victims nor did they keep records identifying abuse victims' maltreatment (CWLA, 2007e). This documented failure to coordinate services between the two systems also means that it is difficult to research the trajectory between foster care and criminal incarceration. The data from the CWLA National Data Analysis System (NDAS) which utilizes information from SACWIS shows that of the 50 reporting states only 36 maintained computerized child welfare and juvenile justice statistical data which indicated whether a child was involved in both the Juvenile Justice and Child Welfare systems (CWLA, 2007f). Nine reporting states had data systems that allowed cross-referencing of cases in both the Juvenile Justice and Child Welfare Systems. Eight of the states report the number of children who exited the Child Welfare system and entered the Juvenile Justice system (CWLA, 2007f). Until these data are available, researchers are limited to expensive sample projects with the limitation of small populations and less generalizability.

Conclusion

This chapter explored the issue of youth exiting from foster care, and the likelihood of transitioning into persistent criminal activities. Although these youth represent only a small portion of the population, approximately 20,000 per year in the United States, their transition to criminal activity is significant because of their status as a vulnerable population (Osgood et al., 2005). This author agrees with researchers (e.g., Courtney & Herring, 2005; Foster & Gifford, 2005; Osgood et al., 2005) that since the state assumes responsibility for the foster care population, it is imperative that they ensure that foster children have the opportunity for successful outcomes. Unfortunately, all too often, these youth become persistent criminal offenders.

From the life-course perspective, foster youth are expected to transition to independence earlier than the normal population whose family support often extends through college, because services are stopped on the basis of age (18), not on behaviors, developmental level, or achievements. There remain unanswered questions about transitions from education to employment or entry into military, to marriage, a home, and parenthood. But data from initial waves of longitudinal studies show that foster youth face difficulties making some important transitions such as the completion of a high school education. From the life-course perspective if these transitional markers are not met, there is greater risk of criminal persistence. We do not know if foster youth, have the same opportunities for normalizing transitions such as joining the military or marriage as the normal population.

From the capital perspective, all studies agree that foster youth have capital deficits when compared to the normal population in terms of financial capital, human capital (with more genetic, psychological, and neurological challenges), attachment issues, and social capital (due to disrupted family relationships and limited social networks). Foster care youth are less likely to attain a high school degree or higher education at a time when the bar for educational attainment required by employment is rising. Most ex-foster youth work, but their employment consists of low-paying service and part-time type jobs. In today's economy, financial security means working in employment that has job security (Mech, 1994), and health insurance benefits and this is difficult to attain even for the college-educated without familial support.

Finally the ecological model emphasizes that foster youth are at increased risk of criminal persistence. The longer one lives in an abusive or neglectful environment, the greater the dosage of ecological factors which increase the risk of violence. Thus, the longer foster youth experience child abuse, exposure to domestic violence, often with drug abuse, and living in a violent environment of poverty and street violence the more likely they are to persist in criminal activities.

Although these three theoretical perspectives predict criminal persistence in foster care youth, few studies address the criminal trajectory and criminal persistence in this population. Part of the lack of research is due to the problems of accessing this vulnerable population, who are difficult to reach after discharge from care, frequently have no stable residence and may prefer to avoid contact agencies. The studies mentioned earlier have limitations such as small numbers of respondents, different definitions of terms, varying age at follow-up and a range of services provided by the foster care agencies which are funded by different state and private sources. In spite of these limitations there were some common findings.

First, although the studies are limited by different definitions of criminality ranging from arrest to jail to state imprisonment, and different follow-up times, from 6 months to a record review of 20 years, all of the studies noted ex-foster care youth had a significantly greater likelihood of incarceration than the general population.

Second, all agreed that the issue of the number of placements was a significant predictor of persistent behavior problems. Researchers show the benefits of maintaining long-term foster care and minimizing the number of moves while in care (Farmer et al., 2003; Haapasalo, 2000; Jonson-Reid & Barth, 2000b; Newton, et al., 2000; Quinton et al., 1998; Quinton & Rutter, 1988; Widom 1991b).

Third, educational attainment is a significant obstacle for foster children. Educational attainment is addressed in all studies with the consensus that youth leaving foster care do not have the same likelihood of high school graduation as the normal population.

Fourth, there were links among education, financial capital, housing, employment, and health care. Education level is a significant variable affecting capital; those with less than high school education earn lower wages. A lack of financial resources may lead to housing problems. High percentages of the young adults studied had periods of homelessness or instability in housing with frequent moves. The most critical issue addressed was homelessness, and the relationship of being homeless to criminal activity.

Although the CWLA-sponsored Foster Care Independence Act of 1999 (HR 3443) attempted to address gaps in resources for foster care youth, there continues to be problems with foster care youth receiving the mandated services. Plus, the economy is changing. When the foster care program was first developed it was possible to gain employment and self sufficiency with a high school education; however, in the current economy employment at a high school level is not sufficient to move out of poverty.

Suggestions for Future Research

Future research is needed into the criminal persistence of ex-foster youth. Fortunately, the availability of data for such research is imminent as the United States is on the cusp of having shared administrative computer data available from all 50 states through SACWIS, with the capacity of linkage between the juvenile justice and foster care systems. The SACWIS data will allow a more systematic study of life-course, capital, and ecological issues and their effect on criminal trajectories. For example, with common definitions of what constitutes a placement, one could determine how movements in care affect a criminal trajectory. Data related to the preparation for independence is included, so one will be able to determine what works and for whom. With combined data for comparison agencies we will have material for evaluative research geared to comparing practices with outcomes.

Using SACWIS data, we will also be able to examine questions of postcare, such as what is the actual trajectory of the total population of ex-foster youth. This would require some common definitions of what constitutes an arrest or an incarceration, so that one night in a jail for being homeless would not be coded the same as placement in a state prison for a violent crime.

An argument should also be made for a longitudinal research model. In other areas of criminology there is a focus on life-course issues and desistence from crime. At present, the "turning points" of ex-foster youth are unknown: who marries, who joins the military, enters a residential job core, college, or occupational program and the effects of these turning points on the high-risk population are also undocumented. While these studies are in process, qualitative studies of those who make successful transitions, targeting those who complete college and are employed, might fill some of the research gaps.

CHAPTER 12

Educational Achievement among Incarcerated Youth: Post-Release Schooling, Employment, and Crime Desistance

Thomas G. Blomberg, William D. Bales,
and Courtney A. Waid

Previous studies have documented a positive relationship between educational achievement and employment for the general adolescent population (e.g., Cernkovich & Giordano, 1992; Massey & Krohn, 1986; Stewart, 2003). In addition, graduation from high school has been found to significantly decrease involvement in serious crime for adolescent youth, in part, because of the greater likelihood of employment for high school graduates (e.g., Bernberg & Krohn, 2003; Thaxton & Agnew, 2004). Studies of incarcerated delinquent youth have reported that participation in educational programs that results in high school graduation or receipt of a General Education Diploma (GED) lowers post-release recidivism (Ambrose & Lester, 1988; Brier, 1994). Further, it has been found that employment training while incarcerated followed by post-release education has the greatest effect in reducing post-release recidivism (Harrison & Schehr, 2004). Overall, these prior research findings suggest the possibility of a positive and cumulative relationship between educational achievement among incarcerated delinquent youth and post-release schooling, employment, and crime desistance.

Beginning with Sampson and Laub (1993), a number of studies have focused upon particular life events occurring during young adulthood that may lead to crime desistance. For example, several studies have found that marriage or military experience can contribute to crime desistance for a number of young adults (Laub, Nagin, & Sampson, 1998; Laub & Sampson, 2003; Sampson & Laub, 1993; Warr, 1998). More recently, Laub and Sampson (2003), employing life history data, found that the reform school experience was especially important for some delinquents when combined with their subsequent post-release military or marriage experiences. While Laub and Sampson report remarkable employment stability among their life history cases, none of the study's subjects felt that work was a major contributor to their subsequent crime desistance. As a result, Laub and Sampson conclude that while work may not serve as a trigger to crime desistance in the same way as marriage or military experience, it may play an important role in sustaining the process of crime desistance. However, it is important to note that most delinquents released from incarceration are too young for either marriage, military, or full-time work. Rather, most released youth are age appropriate for returning to and continuing their schooling with the possibility of part-time employment.

Notably absent from the prior literature, however, have been studies that specifically address the potential for a positive and cumulative relationship between educational achievement while incarcerated and post-release schooling, employment and crime desistance for juvenile offenders. The present study is concerned with the potential for such a positive and cumulative relationship in its longitudinal assessment of educational achievement among incarcerated youth and post-release schooling, employment, and crime desistance. Considering the potential for the relationship between educational achievement while incarcerated and post-release schooling and crime desistance is particularly appropriate, given that less than 10% of the incarcerated youth population graduate from high school or receive a GED during the course of their incarceration, thereby making them unlikely prospects for immediately gaining and maintaining meaningful and longer term post-release employment until after high school graduation or further schooling.

Review of Relevant Research

Life-Course Criminology

In recent years, a continuous series of studies have contributed to a body of literature that has come to be known as life-course criminology. Among the themes of life-course criminology are developmental explanations of criminal behavior (Moffitt, 1993) and the beginning or onset of criminal careers (Paternoster & Brame, 1997; Piquero, 2000b). Two other prominent research themes are persistence and desistance in criminal behavior over the life course. A frequently reported finding has been stability in aggression from early childhood to adolescent delinquency and later adult criminal behavior. For example, a series of studies have reported that antisocial behavior can develop in early childhood as a trait that remains constant as one ages through adolescence and into adulthood (e.g., Huesmann, Eron, & Lefkowitz, 1984; Nagin & Paternoster, 1991; Paternoster, Dean, Piquero, Mazerolle, & Brame, 1997; West & Farrington, 1977; Wolfgang, Thornberry, & Figlio, 1987).

While studies of crime desistance have not been as numerous as studies of crime persistence in aggressive behavior, several studies have found the young adult life events of marriage, employment or military service can contribute to crime desistance (Laub et al., 1998; Laub & Sampson, 2003; Sampson & Laub, 1993; Sampson, Laub, & Wimer, 2006; Warr, 1998). While acknowledging that early antisocial traits are important, especially when considering persistence in career criminals, a number of life-course criminologists have come to embrace the concept of change in their respective studies of desistance from criminal careers. For example, Elder (1985) articulates several assumptions of life-course studies that explicitly or implicitly incorporate elements of change. These include (1) change as a continuous process, influenced by social situations and individual responses to these situations; (2) pathways in life as cumulative and reciprocal; (3) individual behavior as shaped by experienced social and historical contexts; and (4) individuals as being influenced by key events at particular points in life.

In conceptually integrating notions of life course and change, a number of studies have employed the concepts of life trajectories, transitions, and turning points. According to Sampson (2001), life trajectories are paths of development that become shaped over the life span and include such elements as education, employment, marriage, parenthood, criminal behavior, and incarceration. Sampson and Laub (2003) further specify that life trajectories are long-term and begin early in an individual's development and continue throughout one's life.

Another concept employed in life-course studies of change are "transitions," namely those life events that redirect and change life trajectories. Examples of life events that can redirect or lead to transitions in life trajectories include high school or college graduation, first employment, military experience, or marriage. Piquero and Mazerolle (2001) contend that transitions tend to be more abrupt and develop over much shorter periods of time as compared to longer term life trajectories. Like trajectories, however, the timing and sequencing of transitions can be crucial in the development of, persistence in or desistance from crime. Moreover, transitions can lead to continuity for the individual as one transition leads to another (Akers & Sellers, 2004; Benson, 2002).

There is considerable ambiguity in the literature regarding the precise definition of turning points. Sampson and Laub (1993) contend that turning points involve more gradual but significant changes that alter, reshape, and define one's subsequent life trajectory. Elder (1985) suggests, however, that turning points can involve more sharp and drastic changes that can occur suddenly. Benson (2002) claims that how individuals respond to particular life changes determines the actual occurrence of a turning point in life trajectories. For example, the life change of marriage for young adults can result in changes in prior criminal peer associations thereby resulting in the turning point of crime desistance (Warr, 1998).

Education, Employment, and Crime

Prior research has found that educational achievement and commitment decreases involvement in crime for many adolescents. To elaborate, surveys of adolescents from the general population find significantly less involvement in crime when adolescents are committed and attached to school, spend significant time studying, and make good grades (Cernkovich & Giordano, 1992; Massey & Krohn, 1986; Stewart, 2003; Thaxton & Agnew, 2004). In addition, longitudinal research has assessed whether adolescent experiences with education affect the likelihood of criminal involvement in adulthood. For example, Arum and Beattie (1999) report, from a national sample of young adults, that education-related factors such as total years of education, high school graduation, grade point average, and student–teacher ratio of one's high school significantly affect the likelihood of adult incarceration.

Wilson et al.'s (2000) meta-analysis of correctional programming included separate analyses for education and employment training programs. They found that participation in education programs during incarceration had an overall significant effect on reducing recidivism while participation in employment training programs had effects that were in the predicted direction but failed to be statistically significant. However, other studies have suggested that there may be a cumulative relationship between education and employment. For example, Bernberg and Krohn (2003) conclude that graduating from high school decreased crime in young adulthood because of high school graduation's positive role upon later employment. Further, Harrison and Schehr (2004) report that employment training while in prison had its greatest effect in reducing recidivism when it was followed by post-release education. It appears, then, that if the potential crime desistance role of educational achievement during incarceration is to be identified and understood, post-release schooling and associated employment experience should be addressed. Moreover, most youth released from incarceration are between the ages of 15 to 16 and therefore return to school, rather than entry into full-time employment, is the more age appropriate post-release activity for these youth.

Several studies have found that participation in education programming that results in high school graduation or the earning of a GED, lowers the rate of recidivism among incarcerated youths (Ambrose & Lester, 1988; Brier, 1994). However, most incarcerated youths do not graduate from high school or earn a GED while incarcerated, thereby reducing the likelihood of desistance after release (Foley, 2001; Haberman & Quinn, 1986; Leblanc & Pfannenstiel, 1991). To elaborate, using two cohorts that totaled over 10,000 youth released from all juvenile residential facilities in Florida for fiscal years 2000–2001 and 2001–2002, it was found that only 7% earned a GED or high school diploma before their release from incarceration (Juvenile Justice Educational Enhancement Program [JJEEP], 2005). Therefore, other measures beyond GED or high school graduation during incarceration are needed for more accurate assessments of the potential relationship between educational achievement among incarcerated youth and post-release crime desistance. Other potentially important factors that could be contributing to crime desistance include post-release schooling and subsequent employment.

Educational success or failure has enduring life consequences for both delinquent and nondelinquent youth. Unfortunately, the primary focus of education research has been on nondelinquent youth (Rothman, 2002). In terms of policy, incarcerated youth have traditionally been viewed as more suitable for vocational training rather than academic training because of their characteristic poor educational performance. Clausen (1986) points out, however, that it is the core educational areas of reading, mathematics, and writing that are most helpful in preparing noncollege-going youths for employment. Most delinquent youths entering incarceration are characterized by a series of disproportionate educational deficiencies compared to public school students in general. For example, Wang et al. (2005) found that incarcerated youth were significantly more likely to have lower grade point averages, lower school attendance rates, and greater numbers of school disciplinary actions than were a matched group of public school students. Further, it was reported that incarcerated youth were much less likely to be promoted to the next grade level as compared to public school students. Moreover, it was found that 43% of incarcerated youth suffered from various diagnosed learning and behavior disabilities, compared to only 15% of public school students (JJEEP, 2004). Clearly, incarcerated youth pose major educational challenges. Nonetheless, and while the prior research on education, employment and crime desistance is largely fragmented and inconclusive, there appears the possibility of a positive and cumulative relationship between educational achievement during incarceration and post-release schooling, employment, and crime desistance.

Data and Methods

In assessing the relationship between educational achievement among incarcerated youths and post-release schooling, employment, and crime desistance, the following research questions are addressed.

1. Do higher levels of educational achievement among incarcerated youth increase the likelihood of post-release return to school?
2. Do higher levels of post-release attendance in school reduce the likelihood of being rearrested within 12 and 24 months?
3. Does post-release return to school increase the likelihood of employment and the length of employment?
4. Does post-release employment reduce the likelihood of rearrest within 12 and 24 months?
5. Does the combination of post-release schooling and employment reduce the likelihood of rearrest within 12 and 24 months?

To answer these questions, the study employs a cohort of 4147 youths released from 115 juvenile justice institutions throughout Florida during fiscal year 2000–2001. The data employed were drawn from three different sources: the Florida Department of Education (DOE), the Florida Department of Law Enforcement (FDLE), and the Florida Education and Training Placement Information Program (FETPIP). Data from the DOE were used to identify youths released from residential commitment programs. The student data from DOE includes demographic characteristics, end of year school status, information on youths' disabilities, course types and high school credits earned while incarcerated, whether youths returned to school following release, and 2 years of data on attendance in school following release. The cohort was then matched to arrest information obtained from FDLE. FETPIP data were used to obtain information on post-release employment activity. Three years of data were used from each of the data sources that included the year of release (fiscal year 2000–2001) and two additional follow-up years (fiscal years 2001–2002 and 2002–2003).

Table 12.1 presents the variables employed in the analyses. Three outcomes were of interest. The first, return to school, was measured on the basis of whether youth were enrolled in a public school within the first full semester following release from incarceration in fiscal year 2000–2001. This outcome variable indicates whether continued participation in school occurs following incarceration. The second, rearrest, was measured by whether youth were arrested within two follow-up periods, 12 and 24 months. Only

TABLE 12.1 Descriptive Statistics of Outcome, Intervention, and Control Variables

Variables	Mean
Outcomes	
Returned to school after release (0 = No, 1 = Yes)	0.36
Rearrest within 12 months of release (0 = No, 1 = Yes)	0.48
Rearrest within 24 months of release (0 = No, 1 = Yes)	0.64
Employment within 12 months of release (number of quarters)	1.3
Employment within 24 months of release (number of quarters)	2.5
Interventions	
Above average educational achievement while incarcerated	0.39
Attendance in school within 12 months following release	52.0
Attendance in school within 24 months following release	80.9
Control Variables	
Age at release	16.8
Race—non-white (0 = No, 1 = Yes)	0.57
Sex—male (0 = No, 1 = Yes)	0.86
Low socioeconomic status (SES) (0 = No, 1 = Yes)	0.39
Length of incarceration	8.0
Severity of prior criminal record	136.9
Age at first arrest	14.1
Level of incarceration (1 = low, 2 = moderate, 3 = high, 4 = maximum)	2.2
Disability (0 = No, 1 = Yes)	0.38
Behind in school	0.53

crimes serious enough to warrant fingerprinting and submission of the arrest event to FDLE by a local law enforcement agency are considered in this measure. All youths in the cohort were observed for 12 and 24 months following their individual release from incarceration, using their release date as the beginning point for the follow-up period. The third, employment after release, was measured by the number of quarters youth were employed within 12 and 24 months post-release.

The two intervention variables used in the analyses are presented in Table 12.1. The first is an indicator of the level of educational achievement while youth were incarcerated. The measure was operationalized as follows. The numbers of academic, elective, and vocational credits earned while incarcerated were calculated. Based upon the prior literature (e.g., Clausen, 1986) it was decided to use only the number of academic credits earned as an indicator of educational achievement while incarcerated. The actual number of credits earned is largely contingent upon the length of time that youth are incarcerated as school attendance is mandatory for all incarcerated youth. In addition, there are differences between juvenile facilities in terms of the number of classes offered that are academic versus vocational or elective and not all of the facilities offer all four of the academic course areas of math, English, social studies, and science. Youth are required to take what the facility offers in terms of academic courses and they must complete the courses in order to earn academic credit. Most vocational and elective courses are not mandatory requirements for high school graduation, and therefore, are not ideal measures of educational achievement. For these reasons, we developed a measure of educational achievement that would include both the number of academic credits earned, including math, English, social studies, and science, and the extent to which youth concentrated their schooling on academic courses. Specifically, we multiplied the total number of academic credits earned by the proportion of total number of credits earned that were academic and standardized the scores across our cohort. The final step was to dichotomize the measure of educational achievement at the mean value for the cohort because of the nonlinear relationship found between this intervention variable and our outcome variables.[1]

---

[1] Additional methods were used for quantifying academic achievement beyond the dichotomized weighted measure just described. When using a simple count of academic credits while incarcerated, without considering nonacademic credits earned, stronger effects on returning to school were found. In addition, employing the measure of academic achievement used as a continuous variable rather than a dichotomous one resulted in the same directional effect on returning to school and was statistically significant.

The second intervention variable is the level of attendance in school following release within 12 and 24 months after incarceration, which is measured on a continuous scale using the number of days enrolled in school weighted by each youth's percentage of days actually present in school. Combining these two indicators acknowledges that while enrollment in school over some period of time could be indicative of some level of commitment to school, actual attendance in the classroom should be given more weight as a measure of actual attachment to school. Released youths who did not return to school were coded equal to zero and those who graduated from high school following release were assigned the maximum amount of time possible in school. An important reason for this delineation was that most youth released from incarceration that complete secondary education earn a GED and often do so in a relatively short period of time after release. Since these youth have completed school they were treated as having the maximum of education and were coded as attending school for the entire time period following release. To ensure the proper timing of events, youths' attendance in school after an arrest was not included in this measure; this allowed for the use of attendance in school as an intervention that occurred before rearrest.

Ten covariates were selected for the current analysis based on prior research and their availability in our dataset. The three demographic characteristics of age at release, race, and sex are standard control variables that previous studies have found to be related to post-release behavior. Specifically, older youths who are further behind in school are less likely to return to school following release and simultaneously tend to mature out of delinquency. Further, males have been found to have higher rates of rearrest compared to females (Dembo et al., 1998; Hoge, Andrews, & Leschied, 1996). Family socioeconomic status (SES) was measured using information on whether youth were receiving a free or reduced priced lunch in school before their incarceration.

The length of time incarcerated was included as a control variable for two reasons. First, because incarcerated juveniles are given an indeterminate sentence by the judge, who ultimately determines their length of stay. That decision is partially based on the youth's institutional behavior since youth who comply with institutional treatment requirements and behavioral rules are viewed favorably by the sentencing judge because they typically are less likely to recidivate after release. Second, because longer lengths of incarceration are related to greater educational deficiencies, the reduced likelihood of returning to school after release and associated employment difficulties, and the greater likelihood of rearrest.

Three measures of the breadth and severity of prior delinquency were used as control variables. The number and seriousness of prior offenses are important to control for because of their demonstrated importance in predicting post-release offending (Dean, Brame, & Piquero, 1996; Dembo et al., 1995; Tollet & Benda, 1999). Severity of prior criminal record occurring before incarceration was measured by applying a seriousness score to each offense for which youth in the sample had been arrested. These were then summed to derive an overall prior offense severity value, resulting in a range from 0 to 1364.[2]

Second, age at first arrest was used as an indicator of the onset of delinquency, since prior studies have found that the earlier youth experience their first arrest, the more likely they are to be rearrested (e.g., Cottle, Lee, & Heilbrun, 2001; Dembo et al., 1998; Hoge et al., 1996). In the small percentage of cases where no prior arrest record existed, age at the time of incarceration was used as a proxy for age at first arrest. What occurs in these rare instances of no prior arrest record is that youth are referred to the juvenile court for such reasons as running away from a foster home placement or are apprehended by law enforcement for multiple minor offenses and in either case the youth are not booked into local jails.

Third, the security level of the youth's institutional placement was used as a measure of the extent and seriousness of youths' prior delinquency and prior contacts with the juvenile justice system. Florida's juvenile institutions are categorized as low, moderate, high, or maximum risk by the Florida Department of Juvenile Justice. The security level of the institution in which youth are placed is determined by the juvenile court judge based on the severity and frequency of the youth's current and past offenses. Youths placed in low-security institutions have generally committed infrequent and nonviolent offenses including first- or second-degree misdemeanors and third-degree felonies. The majority of youths placed in moderately secure institutions have committed serious property offenses with more frequent and repeated prior arrests. High-security institutions are used for habitual offenders, sex offenders, and youths considered dangerous to themselves or others. Youths placed in maximum-risk institutions are largely chronic offenders who have been committed for violent or other serious felonies.

Two educational characteristics and performance measures were used as control variables. First, youths with learning, behavioral, and/or cognitive disabilities were identified based on assessments by the public school system prior to incarceration. Youths with disabilities are overrepresented in the

---

[2] Seriousness of offense was determined using Florida's Criminal Punishment Code. This law requires that sentencing points be assigned on the basis of the seriousness of the offense. Seriousness points are assigned to 52 different offenses (e.g., Burton et al., 2004).

delinquent population compared to youth in public schools, and the existence of a disability has been found to contribute to lower academic gains, delinquency, and recidivism (Archwamety & Katsiyannis, 1998; Wagner, D'Amico, Marder, Newman, & Blackorby, 1992). The number of years youth were behind in school was used to measure overall school performance before incarceration and to control for self-selection related to educational achievement. Prior research has demonstrated that one of the major correlates to dropping out of school is being overage for grade placement (Florida Department of Education, 2000). Further, Jimerson (1999) cites a number of studies that found grade retention to have a positive effect on the likelihood of youth dropping out of high school and increased behavioral problems. The number of years behind in school was determined by using the youth's age and grade in which he or she was enrolled at the time of release. Scores were coded (1) if youths were more than 1 year behind in school and (0) if they were at their appropriate age/grade level or were only 1 year behind in school. In our cohort, 53% of the youth were more than 1 year behind in school.

Findings

Table 12.2 addresses the first research question: Do higher levels of educational achievement among incarcerated youth increase the likelihood of post-release return to school? The findings indicate that youth with above average educational achievement while incarcerated were significantly more likely to return to school following their release from incarceration (Beta $= 0.525$, $p < .001$). Specifically, the odds of these youth returning to school were 69% higher than for those youth who were below average in their educational achievement while incarcerated, after controlling for prior school performance, age at first arrest, age at release, SES, race, gender, disability, severity of prior criminal record, length of incarceration, and level of incarceration.

Table 12.3 addresses Research Question 2: Do higher levels of post-release attendance in school reduce the likelihood of being rearrested within 12 and 24 months? The findings show that longer periods of attendance in school following release resulted in significant reductions in the likelihood of rearrest at both 12 and 24 months (12 months: Beta $= -0.006$, $p < .001$; 24 months: Beta $= -0.004$, $p < .001$). Given the many control variables included in the model that have been demonstrated to impact rearrest probabilities for youth released from incarceration, it is clear that returning to and staying in school following release from incarceration is positively related to crime desistance as measured by rearrest 12 and 24 months post release.

TABLE 12.2 Educational Achievement While Incarcerated
and the Likelihood of Returning to School Following Release:
Logistic Regression Model

Independent Variables	Returning to School		
	Beta[†]	SE	Odds Ratio
Educational achievement while incarcerated	.525***	.119	1.69
Behind in school	−.400**	.137	.67
Age at release	−.690***	.075	.50
Race (non-white)	−.121	.115	.89
Male	.732***	.171	2.08
Disability	.208	.117	1.23
Severity of prior criminal record	−.000	.000	1.00
Length of incarceration in months	−.054**	.018	.95
Level of incarceration	−.045	.058	.96
Age at first arrest	.068	.040	1.07
Low socioeconomic status	1.216***	.119	3.38
Constant	9.830		

SE, standard error.
Model Chi-square/df = 512.53/11***
*$p < .05$; ** $p < .01$; *** $p < .001$.
$N = 1918$.
[†]Beta—unstandardized coefficients.

Table 12.4 addresses the third research question: Does post-release return to school increase the likelihood of employment and the length of employment? During the first year following release, youth who returned to school were significantly more likely to be employed for some period of time (Beta = 0.416, $p < .001$). Youth who returned to school had a 52% greater likelihood of being employed as compared to youth who did not return to school. Moreover, the length of employment during the first 12 months following release was significantly increased among those youth who returned to school (Beta = 0.211, $p < .01$). These results demonstrate a positive and cumulative relationship between school and employment. Youth who were in school following release were more successful in both obtaining and sustaining employment following release.

Table 12.5 presents the findings for Research Question 4: Does post-release employment reduce the likelihood of rearrest within 12 and 24 months? The likelihood of rearrest declines significantly for youth who are employed for a longer period of time during the 12 months following release (Beta = −0.091, $p < .01$) and the second year (Beta = −0.042, p < .05). Specifically, within the

TABLE 12.3   Attendance in School Following Release and Rearrest Within 12 and 24 Months: Logistic Regression Models

Independent Variables	Rearrest Within 12 Months			Rearrest Within 24 Months		
	Beta†	SE	Odds Ratio	Beta†	SE	Odds Ratio
Attendance in school following release	−.006***	.001	.99	−.004***	.000	1.00
Behind in school	−.096	.084	.91	−.160	.089	.85
Age at release	.054	.037	1.06	.139***	.040	1.15
Race (non-white)	.325***	.072	1.38	.323***	.076	1.38
Male	.883***	.110	2.42	.938***	.109	2.55
Disability	.028	.075	1.03	.026	.081	1.03
Severity of prior criminal record	.005***	.000	1.01	.007***	.000	1.01
Level of incarceration	−.034	.036	.97	−.112**	.038	.89
Age at first arrest	−.135***	.025	.87	−.194***	.028	.82
Low socioeconomic status	.347***	.080	1.42	.379***	.086	1.46
Length of incarceration in months	−.002	.011	1.00	.007	.012	1.01
Constant	−.270			.018		
Model Chi-quare/df	699.66/11***			898.75/11***		

SE, standard error.
*p < .05; **p < .01; ***p < .001; 12 months.
N = 3880.
†Beta—unstandardized coefficients.

first year following release, each additional quarter of employment reduces the likelihood of rearrest by 8.7% and within the first 2 years, the likelihood of rearrest was reduced by 4.1% with each additional quarter of employment. These findings demonstrate that obtaining and sustaining post-release employment is positively related to crime desistance. These findings underscore what appears to be a positive and cumulative relationship between schooling, employment, and crime desistance for youth reentering their communities following incarceration.

Table 12.6 provides findings for Research Question 5: Does the combination of post-release schooling and employment reduce the likelihood of rearrest within 12 and 24 months? The table delineates the effects of employment on rearrest separately for those youth in school versus those youth not in school. The findings demonstrate that the combination of post-release schooling and employment results in greater levels of desistance from crime. Very importantly, the findings suggest that post-release schooling and employment

TABLE 12.4 Returning to School Following Release and Employment and Length of Employment: Regression Models

Independent Variables	Employment Within 12 Months (Logistic Regression Model)			Length of Employment Within 24 Months (Ordinary Least Squares Regression Model)	
	Beta[†]	SE	Odds Ratio	Beta[†]	SE
Returning to school following release	.416***	.102	1.52	.211**	.07
Behind in school	−.102	.096	.90	−.071	.06
Age at release	.447***	.060	1.56	.346***	.04
Race (non-white)	.454***	.087	.64	−.432***	.06
Male	.156	.129	1.17	.067	.09
Disability	−.432***	.089	.65	−.258***	.06
Severity of prior criminal record	−.001	.000	1.00	−.001*	.00
Level of incarceration	−.057	.042	.95	−.055	.03
Age at first arrest	.029	.029	1.03	.020	.01
Low socioeconomic status	−.086	.096	.92	−.119	.06
Length of incarceration in months	.002	.031	1.00	.003	.01
Constant	−7.331			−4.360	
Model Chi-square/df	151.00/11***				
Model F-value/df				20.69/11***	

SE, standard error.
*$p < .05$; **$p < .01$; ***$p < .001$.
N = 2527.
[†]Beta—unstandardized coefficients.

may interact in leading to crime desistance. Moreover, individuals who returned to school and got a job after release were significantly less likely to be rearrested as compared to those youth who got a job without returning to school. When examining the likelihood of rearrest within 1 year, those in school had a 17.0% reduction in the odds of reoffending with each additional quarter of employment that reduction was only 8.9% for those youth not in school. Extending the follow-up period to 2 years resulted in even greater differences in the combined effects of post-release schooling and employment. Specifically, those youth in school exhibited an 11.9% reduction in the odds of reoffending with each additional quarter of employment while those not in school were only 2.4% less likely to be rearrested as length of employment

TABLE 12.5 Employment Following Release and Rearrest Within 12 and 24 Months: Logistic Regression Models

Independent Variables	Rearrest Within 12 Months			Rearrest Within 24 Months		
	Beta†	SE	Odds Ratio	Beta†	SE	Odds Ratio
Length of employment	−.091**	.030	.91	−.042*	.018	.96
Behind in school	.089	.100	1.09	.069	.103	1.07
Age at release	.167**	.059	1.18	.135*	.065	1.15
Race (non-white)	.391***	.086	1.48	.426***	.094	1.53
Male	1.015***	.139	2.76	1.050***	.135	2.86
Disability	.061	.089	1.06	.049	.098	1.05
Severity of prior criminal record	.004***	.000	1.00	.006***	.001	1.01
Level of incarceration	−.017	.043	.98	−.102*	.046	.90
Age at first arrest	−.100***	.029	.91	−.172***	.033	.84
Low socioeconomic status	.128	.093	1.14	.159	.102	1.17
Length of incarceration in months	−.005	.013	1.00	−.006	.014	.99
Constant	−3.035	.918		−.277	.993	
Model Chi-square/df	389.4/11***			473.6/11***		

SE, standard error.
$*p < .05; **p < .01; ***p < .001.$
N = 2699.
†Beta—unstandardized coefficients.

TABLE 12.6 Effects of Employment Following Release on Rearrest for Youth Returning to School Versus Not Returning to School: Logistic Regression Models

Independent Variables	Youth Who Returned to School			Youth Who Did Not Return to School		
	Beta†	SE	Odds Ratio	Beta†	SE	Odds Ratio
Rearrest within 12 months	−.187**	.064	.83	−.093**	.036	.91
Rearrest within 24 months	−.127***	.038	.88	−.024	.022	.98

SE, standard error.
$*p < .05; **p < .01; ***p < .001.$
The full models from which the results for this table were derived are available upon request from the authors.
†Beta—unstandardized coefficients.

increased. Again, these results demonstrate the combined importance of post-release schooling and employment in crime desistance as measured by rearrest at 12 and 24 months following release from incarceration.

As mentioned earlier, Bernberg and Krohn (2003) concluded from their study that graduating from high school decreased crime during young adulthood largely because of high school graduation's role in increasing the likelihood of employment. Our findings suggest that the combination of school and employment are most likely to lead to desistance after release. In sum, the findings demonstrate that educational achievement during incarceration and post-release schooling reduce the likelihood of rearrest, thereby increasing the likelihood of crime desistance. Further, the findings show that youths in school post release are more likely to be employed and less likely to be rearrested thereby providing support for a positive and cumulative relationship between educational achievement during incarceration, post-release schooling, employment, and crime desistance. See Figure 12.1 for illustration.

Summary and Discussion

Our findings support the argument that higher levels of educational achievement among incarcerated youth results in a greater likelihood of post-release schooling, which, together with employment contributes to crime desistance. Applying life course criminology's crime desistance argument, it can be

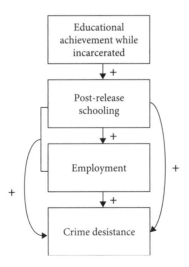

FIGURE 12.1   Summary of findings: Tables 12.2 through 12.6.

suggested that despite the disproportionate educational deficiencies and associated histories of poor school performance among incarcerated youth, those who experience higher levels of educational achievement during their incarceration seem to be positively bonding with and becoming more attached to school and other conventional life goals like employment. This apparent positive school and employment bond and attachment is subsequently demonstrated by the youths' post-release return to and continued attendance in school and their associated employment and crime desistance. Similar to young adulthood experiences with marriage, employment, or military service, there appears to be certain post-release educational and employment experiences among incarcerated youth that can lead to crime desistance. The combined role of education and employment appears to positively alter the post-release life trajectory of a number of incarcerated youth. It appears that a cumulative and positive effect occurs in the life trajectory of adolescent delinquents beginning with educational achievement while incarcerated and continuing with their post-release schooling, employment, and crime desistance experiences. It may be, given that the findings cover 24 months post release, that many of the youths in our cohort are indeed experiencing the beginning of a potential "turning point" from their prior delinquent life course trajectory toward a conventional and law-abiding life trajectory.

It is necessary to acknowledge several limitations of this study. We have tried to deal with these limitations in a responsible fashion. Because we were not able to carry out an experimental study, there may be some unmeasured factor(s) such as individual motivation that may have influenced some of our findings. However, it remains clear that educational achievement while incarcerated and post-release schooling and employment, independent of some other unmeasured factors, may be leading to crime desistance. Such selection effects and associated limitations are an endemic issue in criminological research given that true experimental designs are seldom feasible to carry out. Consequently, quasi-experimental designs with matched comparisons and relevant controls are what researchers must typically employ to advance our knowledge and understanding. Certainly, some of the educational achievement findings could be due to the individual youth's intelligence, prior scholastic ability or experiences, motivation, or other personality traits. Similarly, employment effects could also be due to characteristics of individual youths who went out and found jobs and maintained jobs. While there are controls for disability, SES, race, gender, and severity of prior criminal record—which likely account for many of these differences, there are no controls for intelligence or other personality traits that may have contributed to the youths' educational achievement during incarceration and post-release schooling and employment.

With regard to public policy, the findings presented here provide support for the argument that educational achievement during incarceration can play an important role in the successful community reintegration of delinquent youth. Further, these findings lend support for the current and controversial No Child Left Behind federal education reform act of 2002. The Act mandates that all incarcerated youth receive the same high quality education services and attain adequate annual educational gains as those youth in public schools and that they also be provided transition services that can assist them during their post-release return to school and employment. After more than a century of neglect in the education of incarcerated youth, we appear to be entering a new and more promising policy course. Moreover, there appears to be growing theoretical and empirical justification for this new policy.

Part IV

*Methodology for Understanding
the Criminal Career*

CHAPTER 13

Methodological Issues in the Study of Persistence in Offending

Alex R. Piquero

What does it mean to persist in something? Does it mean to be doing a lot of some thing over a long period of time? A lot of some thing in a short period of time? A little of some thing over a long period of time? Or a little of some thing over a short period of time? Definitionally, persistence tends to be conceived as the continuation or repetition of a particular behavior. The idea of persistence can be found in all aspects of life, and in particular music and sports.

For example, in the music world, Elvis Presley had the longest career span of hits on the charts, spanning 2527 weeks or 49 years from his first hit "Heartbreak Hotel" to the reissue of "A Little Less Conversation." Similarly, when the American Record Charts (ARC) calculated its Top Pop Artists between January 1980 and December 2004, Madonna was ranked at the top of the list, spending a total of 64 weeks at Number 1 with 24 Number 1 hits over that time period. Some may even say that bands like the Rolling Stones and Aerosmith, still touring after 40 years together, are persisters.

In the sports context, examples of persistence are profound. In tennis, only five players have been ranked Number 1 every week of a calendar year since tennis started its ranking system: Jimmy Connors in 1975, 1976, and 1978; Ivan Lendl in 1986 and 1987; Pete Sampras in 1994 and 1997; Lleyton Hewitt in 2002; and Roger Federer in 2005. Only four players have held the #1 spot for more than 100 consecutive weeks: Jimmy Connors (160, between 1974 and 1977); Ivan Lendl (157, between 1985 and 1988); Roger Federer (133, since February 2004); and Pete Sampras (102, between 1996 and 1998). In baseball, Cal Ripken's consecutive games-played streak and Ted Williams' consecutive game-hitting streak quickly come to mind. Turning away from individual players, teams also exhibit aspects of persistence in both winning and not winning. For example, of the four major professional sports in the United States, the Chicago Cubs baseball club has gone the longest (in years) between championships—97 years, while the Texas Rangers baseball club has never won a championship, going 45 years without doing so.[1]

The counter is also true; several professional sports franchises have had lengthy consecutive championship streaks. In the National Basketball Association (NBA), the Boston Celtics' reign was 8 years (1959–1966); in the National Hockey League (NHL), the Montreal Canadians had two separate 5-year stints (five in the pre-Stanley Cup era, 1895–1898 and five in the post era, 1956–1960); in the National Football League (NFL) eight teams are tied with two consecutive championships; and in Major League Baseball (MLB) the New York Yankees have multiple consecutive stints: 5 (1949–1953), 4 (1936–1939), 3 (1998–2000), and 2 (1977–1978).

Although the idea of persistence seems simple, it is much more difficult to provide an operational definition of persistence when it comes to criminal offending. Is persistence made up of offense frequency, chronicity, time-span or length of involvement, or some combination thereof? Laub and Sampson (2003) correctly note the difficult conceptual and methodological issues regarding the term persistence. For example, how many offenses should be included before one is considered a persistent offender? What is the difference between someone who commits seven crimes before age 18 and stops compared to someone who commits seven crimes over the course of 10 or 20 years? Who is the persistent offender, the former, the latter, either, or neither? How does frequency and timing factor into this conceptualization?

On this score, consider a recent analysis by Piquero, Moffitt, and Lawton (2005), who used data from the Second Philadelphia Birth Cohort (1958) to examine the distribution of arrests per individual, per year of observation. The data were comprised of the 6674 persons who experienced at least one arrest through age 27. For each arrest frequency, they subtracted the youngest arrest age in months from the oldest arrest age in months. This obviously produced missing values for individuals with an arrest frequency of one but

---

[1] Other championship droughts: NFL Phoenix (St. Louis) Cardinals 58 years, Minnesota Vikings 44 (never won), NBA Sacramento Kings 55, Denver Nuggets 39 (never won), NHL Chicago Blackhawks 46, Los Angeles Kings 40 (never won).

for all the others it produced a distribution of the amount of time, in months, that lapsed between the first and the last arrest. Their results showed that for those with two arrests, the mean time between the first and last arrest was 35 months, but this is a skewed distribution, so the median of 24 months is more representative. This compares to a mean and median of 104 months for those with seven or more arrests, implying that with increasing arrest frequency, the time between the first and last arrest is higher. Thus, among frequent offenders, arrests were more spread out than they were for relatively infrequent offenders, thereby suggesting that it is relatively unlikely that those who experienced many arrests were likely to commit them in a short time period.

This chapter seeks to examine the issues involved in defining, measuring, and studying persistence in offending. It first reviews conceptual and theoretical accounts of persistence, and follows with an overview of extant research. It then presents some ways of examining persistence using data from the Cambridge Study in Delinquent Development, a longitudinal study of 411 South London males followed from ages 10 to 40 (Piquero, Farrington, & Blumstein, 2007). The paper concludes by outlining an agenda for future research.

What is Persistence?

Criminologists do not currently employ a standard operational definition of persistence, thus leaving researchers to their own specific theoretical and operational definitions. For example, Wolfgang et al. (1987) defined persistence as offending at least once as a juvenile (<18) and at least once as an adult (≥18). Other researchers have used a similar conceptualization. The most recent, and arguably most precise, definition of persistence was articulated by Laub and Sampson (2003), in their recent follow-up of the Glueck delinquent males. According to these authors, persistence in offending can be defined as "being arrested at multiple phases of the life course" (p. 150), and is consistent with the "idea of persistent offending as enduring, repetitious, and tenacious." Still, even with this definition, as will be seen later there is likely to be a significant amount of heterogeneity within the group of persisters.

Theoretical Accounts of Persistence

The variation that exists across definitions of persistence has not precluded criminologists from developing theoretical accounts of persistence. Many classic and contemporary criminological theories, including labeling, social control, and strain, articulate causes for persistent offending. Due to space consideration, we focus on three current theoretical accounts of persistence, two of which emerge from developmental and life-course criminology (Farrington, 2003a). We begin with the developmental/life-course accounts.

According to Laub and Sampson's (2003) informal social control theory, persistence in offending is primarily due to a lack of human and social capital, as well as personal agency, the attraction and excitement of crime, and a long-standing resentment of authority. Further, persistent offenders exhibit a generally chaotic lifestyle in multiple dimensions, including residence, work, and family. Thus, instead of a single trait accounting for offending at all phases of the life course, the persistent offender is devoid of connective structures at each phase of the life course, especially involving relationships that can provide informal social control and social support. The persistent offenders interviewed in their long-term follow-up study of former delinquents experienced residential, marital, and job instability, failure in school and in the military, and many had relatively long periods of incarceration.

Moffitt's (1993) account of persistence in offending is different from the one advanced by Laub and Sampson. Moffitt articulates a two group offender model, where a very small number of individuals, life-course-persistent offenders, begin offending early in the life course, offend more while active, and are unlikely to follow traditional desistance curves. For these individuals, antisocial and criminal behavior emerges as a function of neuropsychological deficits combined with disadvantaged environments. A second, much larger group of offenders, adolescence-limited, offend primarily during adolescence as a function of a biological maturity gap that interacts with the aid and comfort of the peer social context. Unlike the serious/chronic/violent group of offenders, adolescence-limited offenders engage in offenses that resemble adult-oriented status (e.g., alcohol/drug use) and because of their generally prosocial orientation and personality structures, cease offending by early adulthood.

Importantly, Moffitt advances distinct reasons for persistence that vary across the typologies. For adolescence-limited offenders, persistence, while a rare phenomenon, can occur due to ensnaring events such as a pregnancy, a jail stint, or drug/alcohol addiction. A small subset of these transient offenders may fall into one of these traps and continue offending for a period of time. On the other hand, for life-course-persistent offenders, persistence is due not only to the putative root causes of life-course-persistent offending (trait-environmental interaction) but also the flawed choices (among a restricted set of choices) made by such offenders. Thus, the interaction between persons and their social environments promotes antisocial continuity across both time and life domains (Moffitt, 1993).

More to the point, life-course-persistent offenders fail to desist from delinquency as young adults and are quite impervious to intervention for two distinct reasons: (1) a restricted behavioral repertoire and (2) ensnarement by consequences of antisocial behavior. Regarding the former, it is the case that because the antisocial behavior of life-course-persistent offenders begins early in life, they miss out on opportunities to acquire and practice prosocial alternatives. Regarding the second, some life-course-persistent offenders may accumulate labels and snares that preclude options for conventional behavior. In short, because the theory of life-course-persistent behavior emphasizes the constant process of reciprocal interaction between traits and environmental reactions to them, an antisocial style develops, which penetrates all domains of behavior throughout the life course (Moffitt, 1993). This infiltration of anti-social disposition across life course domains diminishes the likelihood of change and opportunities for reform (Moffitt, 1993). Thus, in Moffitt's taxonomy, adolescence-limited offenders do not persist in crime because they are "exempt from the forces of (a) cumulative and (b) contemporary continuity" (Moffitt, 1993, p. 690). The lack of cognitive problems and personality disorder, along with the generally positive social and academic skills of adolescence-limiteds make them eligible for postsecondary education, good marriages, and desirable jobs, all of which, because of continuity, are unavailable to life-course-persistent offenders. In short, adolescence-limiteds have many options as adulthood nears and they are not caught in an antisocial path like their life-course-persistent counterparts.

Unlike the developmental/life-course accounts referenced earlier, Gottfredson and Hirschi (1990) also have particular views about persistence, except their account does not advocate the existence of distinct groups of offenders, different pathways to persistence and desistance, and/or allow for the influence of external sources of (informal) social control. To these theorists, persistence occurs naturally as a function of low self-control: those with the lowest self-control offend more while active and for longer durations of time. Once formed by the ages of 8 to 10, an individual's self-control remains relatively stable over his or her life course, and because self-control is the principal cause of crime at all ages, it is implicated in the continuation of an offender's career into adolescence and adulthood. At the same time, Gottfredson and Hirschi do anticipate that individuals will not persist over the entire life course, that is, the age effect. For them, desistance from crime occurs almost naturally as a result of the slowing down of individuals as they enter adulthood and not due to some sort of within-individual change (in self-control) or to some external informal social control mechanism (marriage, employment, etc.).

Empirical Research on Persistence

In one of the earliest reviews of the persistence literature, where persistence is conceptualized as offending before and after adolescence, Blumstein et al. (1986) provided consistent evidence that 30% to 60% of juvenile delinquents known to the police/juvenile courts persisted as adult offenders with at least one arrest or conviction as an adult for an index or felony offense (see also McCord, 1978; Wolfgang, Thornberry, & Figlio, 1987). For three Racine, Wisconsin birth cohorts, Shannon (1982) reported that 31 44, and 54% of males with police contacts for nontraffic offenses before age 20 were arrested again as adults at ages 21, 26, and 32.

The relationship between adult offending (prevalence) and the length of the juvenile career (measured as number of offenses as a juvenile) is strong. For example, in the Philadelphia Birth Cohort data, Wolfgang et al. find that among "chronic" offenders with five or more juvenile arrests, 78% became adult offenders. In the Racine data, the comparable estimate was between 85% and 98%. Data from the Cambridge Study in Delinquent Development show that among individuals with four juvenile convictions, 92% also offended as an adult. And finally, Tracy and Kempf-Leonard's (1996) analysis of the Second Philadelphia Birth Cohort (through age 26) revealed that as juvenile offending increased in number and/or severity, the probability of adult offender status also increased. Taken together, these findings underscore the observation that persistent offending does not appear to be limited to a small set of years and instead appears to be drawn out over an extended period of time and/or phases of the life course. Also, signs of persistence are evident in adolescence.

Before closing this brief review, it is important to highlight a recent study by Sampson and Laub, who tracked the offending careers of nearly 500 Boston area delinquent males between ages 7 and 70. In one interesting analysis, Sampson and Laub (2003) selected men who were arrested at least once at each decade of life to age 60, thus creating a very strict definition of persistence. Forty-six individuals were identified as persistent using these criteria, representing approximately 10% of the sample, and their lives were marked by dysfunctional relationships and employment patterns. Subsequent analysis showed that the frequency of crime among these highly persistent offenders evinced a similar decline with age as was true for most other offenders in the data. In short, even among the most active and persistent offenders, much like classic depictions of the age-crime curve, crime declines with time.

Methodological Issues

As noted earlier, a key concern in criminal careers research is the operational definition of persistence. Because of the wide array of operational definitions for persistence, even within the same study different individuals can be classified as persisters. Complicating matters is Moffitt's developmental taxonomy, which identifies a small, but distinct group of offenders termed life-course-persistent. This group of offenders is expected to offend at all phases of the life course, and at rates always higher than any other group of offenders (rank stability). Does Moffitt's taxonomy require that life-course-persistent offenders offend at stable and high rates constantly and consistently over the life course, as Sampson and Laub have interpreted? According to Sampson and Laub (2003) the term life-course-persistent offender is fraught with problems because as their research shows, the rate of offending declines with age even for high-rate and presumably chronic offenders. Further, when Sampson and Laub attempted to discriminate across distinct typologies of offenders using a constellation of childhood predictors of crime, they found that the childhood traits of the persistent offenders were much the same as those who desisted from crime. They see this as support for social control theories and contradictory to "trait" theories.

According to Moffitt (2006b; see also Piquero & Moffitt, 2005) however, Sampson and Laub have taken some liberties with the term life-course-persistent, and she criticizes their work on several grounds. First, she contends that the Glueck sample[2] was a somewhat biased one in the sense that "virtually all of the men studied would have been regarded as candidates for the life-course persistent subtype" (p. 587). This is so because all of the boys had been incarcerated as adolescents in reform schools. Second, Moffitt argues that Sampson and Laub misrepresented the taxonomy's prediction when they inferred that life-course-persistent offenders should commit crimes at the same high rate from adolescence through old age, right up until the

---

[2] The Glueck sample, which forms the basis of the Laub and Sampson study, is a longitudinal study comprised of nearly 500 Boston-area delinquents who were originally followed until age 32 by the Glueck researchers, and then subsequently to age 70 by Sampson and Laub.

age of their death. Moffitt's taxonomy never implied that this was the case, because it acknowledged the aging out process, thus not requiring that life-course-persistent offenders offend in old age. According to Moffitt, the taxonomy predicts that life-course-persistent offenders would continue offending well beyond the age when most young men have already desisted. Third, with regard to the finding that childhood risk factors were unable to distinguish offending trajectories, Moffitt argues that this failure is not surprising given that the childhood backgrounds of the Glueck males were almost uniformly high-risk.[3]

Moffitt's (2006b) defense of the taxonomy, and in particular the term life-course-persistent, in the wake of Sampson and Laub's empirical test could not be stronger

> Here we set the record straight. Life-course persistent delinquents
> do not have to be arrested for illegal crimes steadily up to age 70, but
> they do have to maintain a constellation of antisocial attitudes, values,
> and proclivities that affects their behavior toward others. Life-course
> persistent delinquents do not have to all live exactly the same crime
> trajectory as they age out of crime; it is interesting to learn how their
> lives diverge (p. 588).

This would seem to imply that to study persistence in offending, especially within the context of Moffitt's developmental taxonomy of life-course-persistent offenders, one needs to have been involved in crime at different phases of the life course and to maintain rank stability (even in the midst of declining crime) over other offenders: "...the taxonomy accepts that antisocial participation declines markedly in midlife, but nonetheless, it expects rank-order stability, particularly on age-relevant measures of antisocial activity" (Moffitt, 2006b, p. 587).

Aside from this definitional issue, the study of persistence is further complicated by the manner in which a researcher tackles the problem. Specifically, the use of self-report versus official records tends to identify different trajectories of crime (Piquero, 2008). The best example of this problem is from Nagin et al. (1995), who compared the self-report and official offending records of

---

[3] At the same time, because Sampson and Laub's trajectory analysis uncovered distinct offending trajectories, even within a highly select sample, it shows the variation that exists in crime careers—especially in mid life. Thus, it seems that concurrent life experiences may account for the divergence. According to Moffitt (2006b), this would constitute an interesting extension to the taxonomic theory: heterogeneity within life-course-persistent delinquents in the ways they age out of crime.

the Cambridge males through age 32. Their analysis showed that conviction records indicated desistance for many (chronic) offenders, but self reports continued to show evidence of offending. Laub and Sampson (2003) found similar results in the Glueck data.

Alternative Methods of Measuring Persistence in the Cambridge Study in Delinquent Development

The next section of the chapter presents several different operational definitions of persistence and applies them to official conviction records from the Cambridge Study in Delinquent Development, a longitudinal study of 411 South London males followed from ages 10 to 40. This exercise is designed to examine how changes in the measurement of persistence alter the manner in which offenders are categorized as persistent or not. More information on the Cambridge data may be found in Farrington (2003a) and Piquero, Farrington et al. (2007).

The first approach to measuring persistence, which was applied in response to the arbitrary designation of five or more police contacts as signifying a chronic offender (Wolfgang, Figlio, & Sellin, 1972), is to calculate persistence probabilities. This approach identifies the point at which the probability of persistence begins to plateau; that is, at some offense number, persisters will have the same rearrest probability. Blumstein and colleagues (1985) argued that the proportion of chronic offenders observed by Wolfgang et al. could have resulted from a homogenous population of persisters. Recently, Piquero, Farrington et al. (2007) applied this technique to the Cambridge conviction data from ages 10 to 40. A number of important findings emerged from their effort. First, the recidivism probabilities began at .399 (the prevalence of offending in the Cambridge Study in Delinquent Development [CSDD]), and increased quickly, because of the large proportion of one-time offenders who do not recidivate, to .682 for offenders with a second conviction. Between the second and third convictions, the recidivism probability remained in the 60% range, at which point it increased at the fourth conviction, after which the recidivism probability was .82. After the fourth conviction, the recidivism probabilities increased slowly and were quite stable. Because the recidivism probabilities were very close and based on a small number of individuals (n = 64), Piquero, Farrington et al. concluded that beginning at the fourth conviction, the recidivism probabilities reflected a homogenous group of persisters (with an average recidivism probability of 84.5%). This finding confirms the benefit of partitioning the persister population according to recidivism probabilities.

It is important to point out that the observed difference between a recidivism probability of .69 (at conviction #3) and .82 (at conviction #4) may appear small, but it can make an appreciable difference in the amount of subsequent offending. This effect is highlighted by a focus on the probability of nonrecidivism, which is reduced from .31 to .18. For the geometric distribution, the expected number of future convictions after any given conviction from the third conviction onward is $q/(1 - q)$, so that if q = .696, then each persister can expect to experience an additional 2.29 convictions; if the recidivism probability is .82 however, the expected number of future convictions is 4.55, which is 98% (4.55 − 2.29/2.29) larger.

This brief analysis of the recidivism probabilities in the Cambridge data indicates that there is a rapidly increasing probability of recidivism through the first few convictions, and a higher but stable recidivism rate for subsequent convictions, averaging 84.5% at and after the fourth conviction. The rise in the observed aggregate recidivism probability then reflects the changing composition of the offenders at each stage of involvement; the desisters stop relatively early and so leave a residue composed increasingly of the high-recidivism persisters (Blumstein, Farrington, & Moitra, 1985). From a policy perspective, these results suggest the possibility of early discrimination between the more and the less serious offenders, and also endorse

> the appropriateness of representing the typical observation of growth in recidivism probability with successive involvements with the criminal justice system as a process involving a changing mix of a high- and low-recidivism group that is increasingly composed of the high-recidivism group (Blumstein et al., 1985, p. 217).

In short, the calculation of recidivism probabilities presents the first way of operationalizing persistence proposed in this chapter.

Let us take a closer look at the offending careers of this group of 64 persisters, who accounted for 598 of the sample's 760 total convictions (or 78.7%). The age-crime curve for these individuals may be found in Figure 13.1. The average age at their first conviction was 14.9 years, while the average age at their fourth conviction was 20.7 years. The average time lapse between consecutive convictions for these persisters was relatively small: 1.93 years between the first and second conviction, and 2.15 years between the third and fourth convictions.

Parceling out the convictions of these persisters into different phases of the life course (ages 10–19, 20–29, and 30–40) indicates that 92% offended in the first part, 85% offended in the second part, and 55% offended in the third part. Further, 26 of these individuals (40.6%) offended at least once in all three

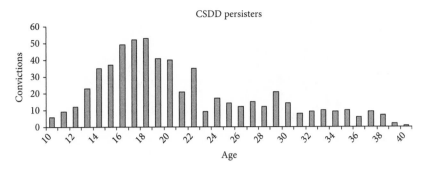

FIGURE 13.1   Age-crime curve of 64 persisters (4+ convictions).

parts of the life course. If we were to examine the offending patterns of these 26 individuals who were arrested at least four or more times and at three distinct phases of the life course even further we observe that they accounted for 299 total convictions, or 39.3% of the total sample's conviction history. There were a total of 121 convictions between ages 10 to 19, 112 convictions between ages 20 and 29, and 66 convictions between ages 30 and 40. Further, the average age of first conviction among these individuals was 15, while the average age of their last conviction was almost 35. Still, much as Sampson and Laub (2003) observed in the Glueck sample, the age-crime curve of these 26 individuals closely mirrors the aggregate age-crime curve: rising to a peak in late adolescence and dropping through the 20s and 30s (see Figure 13.2), but with a long tail.

So far we have focused on the use of recidivism probabilities and offending in different periods of the life course to study persistence in offending. A second way to operationalize persistence is to employ Nagin and Land's trajectory methodology. Briefly, this methodological technique assists researchers in ascertaining whether unique clusters or trajectories exist within a sample of individuals whose behavior has been measured repeatedly over time (Nagin, 1999, 2005). It does so by applying a semiparametric mixture model for modeling unobserved heterogeneity in a sample. The method, then, searches longitudinal data and asks whether one or more developmental trajectories exist (e.g., there may be a high-rate group of offenders, a medium-rate group of offenders, and a low-rate group of offenders). Because the method is agnostic with respect to the number of trajectory groups (i.e., it can detect one, two, three, four, or however many trajectories are distinct from one another), it can be quite free of investigator bias. The method is also able to compare the relative goodness of fit of competing models of different-numbered trajectories, and the best-fitting model is selected according to

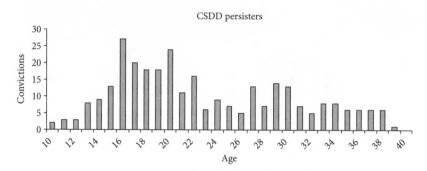

FIGURE 13.2   Age-crime curve of 26 persisters (4+ convictions and offending at all three different phases of the life course).

a number of empirical and graphical criteria. The method also has the desirable property in that it generates a listing about which individuals in the data set belong to which trajectory, which allows the researcher to compare trajectory group age-crime curves as well as theoretical correlates that can distinguish between trajectory classes. To date, this methodology has been used in over 80 studies to assess the longitudinal patterning of antisocial and criminal activity (see review in Piquero, 2007).

The trajectory methodology was applied to the Cambridge data by Piquero, Farrington et al. (2007), and their analysis and fit diagnostics (i.e., BIC) indicated that a five-trajectory model provided the best fit to the data (see Figure 13.3). The first group, labeled *nonoffenders*, represented 62.3% of the sample, and these individuals exhibited virtually zero expected convictions across all ages. The second group, *low adolescence peaked*, comprised 18.6% of the sample and exhibited an increase of expected conviction rates during the early to mid adolescence time period, only to be followed in late adolescence/early adulthood by a rapid decline toward zero expected convictions. By the early 20s and beyond, these individuals had virtually zero expected convictions. The third group, *very low rate chronics*, was represented by 11.3% of the sample and followed the same beginning and peak of expected conviction activity as did the *low adolescence peaked* group, but while the latter group's conviction activity dropped toward zero in the early 20s, the conviction activity of the *very low rate chronics* remained low but stable until the very late 30s. The fourth group, *high adolescence peaked*, included only 5.4% of the sample, but had the highest expected conviction rates throughout the first two decades of life. For this group, expected conviction rates peaked in the mid to late teenage years and then declined throughout the late 20s and early 30s. It was not until about the mid 30s that

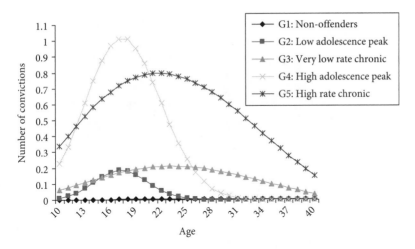

FIGURE 13.3   Trajectory estimates for predicted number of convictions from Cambridge Study in Delinquent Development (CSDD). (Adapted from Piquero et al. (2007); reprinted with permission from Cambridge University Press.)

their expected conviction rates approached zero. The fifth group, *high-rate chronics*, comprised approximately 2.5% of the sample, and this group displayed a trajectory whose overall shape and level was similar to the *high adolescence peaked* group, yet their expected conviction rates remained quite high in the 20s and through most of the 30s. Their offending remained high and stable throughout much of the observation period, which was censored at age 40. Because of the confluence of frequency and stability in convictions for these eight individuals, we examine in greater detail their persistent criminal activity.

Individually, these eight males were convicted of 152 of the sample's 760 total convictions (20%), averaging 19 convictions per person (range 16 to 22 convictions). The average age at first conviction for these eight males was 13.4, while the average age at last conviction was 35.25, with an average career length of 22 years. Additionally, because of their exceedingly high frequency of convictions, these individuals accumulated many convictions in short periods of time, but also did so over a relatively lengthy criminal career. For example, the average age at the second, third, fourth, and fifth conviction was 14.75, 15.62, 16.25, and 17.25. Thus, it is not surprising to learn that the difference in ages at convictions was very small over the course of these (and other) convictions. Recalling the three different life course phases constructed earlier (ages 10–19, 20–29, and 30–40), it is interesting to note that all eight males were convicted at each of the three life course phases. Thus, these eight males, identified via

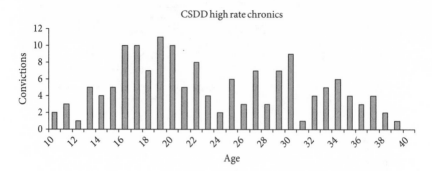

FIGURE 13.4   Age-crime curve of eight high-rate chronics identified via trajectory methodology.

the trajectory methodology, exhibited both high frequency and involvement in crime at multiple periods of the life course.[4]

It is also worth pointing out that the aggregate age-crime curve for these individuals does not necessarily mimic the age-crime curve shown earlier using different identifications of persistence (see Figure 13.4). For these eight males, there is the classic increase of offending in adolescence to a peak in the late teenage years, but the precipitous drop in early adulthood does not happen as was evident for the other operationalizations of persistence. In fact, for these eight individuals, there is a slight drop in convictions in the early 20s, followed by another uptick in offending in the late 20s, and then another drop in the late 30s. This uptick is not regularly observed in classic depictions of the age-crime curve.

In short, these different aspects of assessing persistence tend to show similarities and some differences. What is gained by the trajectory approach is not only an identification of a small, but very high-rate group of offenders, but also one that evinces an offending career that is marked by both frequency and length, the latter which is particularly evident from the trajectory estimation. In this case, the definition of persistence for the high-rate chronic group of offenders using the trajectory methodology nicely picks up the two aspects of persistence that seem to be critical for the understanding of this criminal career parameter: frequency of offending and involvement over multiple periods of the life course.

---

[4] Some readers may ask how such a small group of high-rate offenders is able to continue accumulating many convictions throughout the life course. Although many of their convictions were for minor offenses, they did also incur convictions for more serious crimes. Nevertheless, the use of incarceration was exceedingly rare in the United Kingdom during this time, and especially rare for the Cambridge males (see Piquero, Farrington et al., 2007).

Where To From Here?

The purpose of this chapter has been to review the issue of persistence within the criminal career framework, to outline the theoretical, conceptual, and measurement issues associated with persistence, and to compare findings when persistence is operationalized in different ways using longitudinal data from the Cambridge Study in Delinquent Development. To be sure, this chapter has merely highlighted the methodological issues associated with the persistence issue, and as a result a number of important directions for future research remain.

First, the field should come to some sort of working agreement as to what constitutes persistence. Granted, while this may ultimately fall under the purview of criminological theory, it seems important that empirical researchers be given some sort of instructions in order to stay within the lines. Having several different researchers operationalize the concept of persistence in a number of different ways will not allow the field to come to some sort of summary statement about the knowledge base. At the same time, the operational definition of persistence arrived at and employed by criminologists may not necessarily be the same definition that is arrived at and employed by a more practical audience in the criminal justice system, whose interests in detaining severe and persistent offenders is much more immediate. Although a resolution to these potentially competing definitions is beyond the scope of this chapter, the issue of prospective identification of persistent offenders remains at the fore (Gottfredson & Hirschi, 1990).

As a case in point, consider the similar problems associated with the issue of desistance (see Laub & Sampson, 2001; Bushway, Piquero, Broidy, Cauffman, & Mazerolle, 2001; Kazemian, in press). Because researchers have employed many different operationalizations of desistance, it has become difficult to pinpoint when desistance actually occurred—or was occurring. A similar set of issues obviously complicates the study of persistence, but it seems reasonable that both frequency and time are involved in any calculation. Depending on the restrictions of the data set, and recognizing that a longer stretch of data is always preferred to a shorter one, it seems that a useful starting point would be to conceptualize persistence as meeting some sort of threshold of offense frequency and a certain number of periods of the life course within which offenses were committed.[5] A sound operationalization

---

[5] While some of the other key concepts in developmental/life-course criminology may be approximated with fewer and shorter measurement periods (e.g., onset), persistence is one where several developmental stages need to be included.

of persistence must be one that relates well to matters of theory and policy. Consideration of the objectives outlined earlier will likely motivate stronger definitions of persistence and also allow for a paring down to definitions that are most appropriate.

It is worth noting here that the use of the age-crime curve as the beginnings of a benchmark for defining persistence may be useful. Researchers could consider persistent offenders simply as those whose careers have extended beyond the typically observed pattern of offending. Within the spirit of Moffitt's (2006b) response to Sampson and Laub's findings, a persister can be conceived as someone whose offending extends beyond what we normally observe in antisocial and criminal behavior. This may be a reasonable starting point for a persistence definition.

Second, taking into consideration the operational definition noted earlier, it is important that researchers carefully consider persistence across different measurement strategies (i.e., self reports and official records), while recognizing the difficulties and limitations associated with collection of criminal behavior data over time (Hindelang, Hirschi, & Weis, 1981; Thornberry & Krohn, 2003). Given the findings detected by Nagin et al., it will be important going forward to determine how best to consider persistence across measurement strategy. On this score, it would be particularly useful if researchers were able to calculate persistence using both methods and then perform an analysis where they can examine the extent to which someone is classified as persistent using both approaches, and the extent to which there is mismatch, and also explore the nature of the mismatch.

Third, there may be a need for a broader conceptual work on persistence. Recently, Houser-Marko and Sheldon (2006) examined the question of why some individuals persist in goal pursuit whereas others quickly give up their goals. Introducing a new motivational construct, the "self as," their analysis indicated that those who more strongly endorse doer statements regarding their goals showed greater behavioral persistence and attainment regarding such goals, even controlling for other relevant constructs such as expectancy, self-concordance, commitment, and neuroticism (p. 1037). Although not discussed within the context of persistence in criminal activity, their theoretical framework may be useful for criminologists to consider adopting. As their colorful and clever introduction reports about why a person runs on a regular basis, even when they do not want to "I am a runner—that's what I do." Thus, for the runner, "the question of *whether* she will run does not exist; instead the question is *when*" (Houser-Marko & Sheldon, 2006, p. 1037).

Lastly, theories and theorists need to better articulate their conceptualization and operationalization of persistence. Largely on the basis of Sampson and Laub's analysis of the offending careers of the Glueck delinquents through age 70, Moffitt has initiated this task, but clearly more work is needed. How long do offenders have to offend for them to be considered persistent? During how many periods of the life course must they have offended before they can be considered to be persistent? How many periods of the life course must be measured before we can be confident that we are truly studying persistence? From a policy perspective, how many false-positive identifications will be made when considering a particular offender a persister? These are difficult questions without ready answers, but before any further advances are made with regard to the knowledge base about persistence in criminal careers, some basic descriptive data must be provided. At the expense of closing this chapter as it began, I hope that some of the persistence definitions and operational-izations employed here serve as a springboard for theoretical and empirical research.

CHAPTER 14

Group-Based Trajectory Modeling of Externalizing Behavior Problems from Childhood through Adulthood: Exploring Discrepancies in the Empirical Findings

Manfred H. M. van Dulmen, Elizabeth A. Goncy,
Andrea Vest, and Daniel J. Flannery

A large body of research has investigated age-related changes in externalizing behavior problems during the first three decades of life. Research has increasingly focused on whether there is a taxonomy underlying the development of externalizing behavior problems, in other words, whether there are homogeneous subpopulations of individuals that are similar in terms of their rate of change in externalizing behavior problems across different developmental periods. The purpose of the current chapter is to integrate findings on trajectories of externalizing behavior problems and to investigate in a descriptive review whether there are systematic differences that may explain the discrepancies in these trajectory findings.

Much of the research on trajectories of antisocial behavior was stimulated by seminal work by Moffitt (1993). This 1993 paper has been cited in the literature over 1000[1] times. Moffitt proposes that there are homogeneous sub-groups of individuals who differ both on the course of externalizing behavior problems from childhood through young adulthood, and also differ in terms of their antecedents. Moffitt suggested that one group, life-course-persistent (or early/childhood onset) offenders, first gets involved in externalizing behavior problems during childhood and continues to have consistently high levels of externalizing behavior problems into adulthood whereas a second group, in the literature referred to as either the adolescence-limited or adolescent-onset group, engages in externalizing behavior problems primarily during adolescence. Empirical findings have provided support for Moffitt's theoretical framework and also suggest that these groups differ in terms of their risk and protective factors, with biological and neurological factors being more important in understanding life-course-persistent offending and contextual factors, such as deviant peer affiliation, as more important in understanding the course of adolescence-limited externalizing behavior problems (Moffitt, 2006b).

Much of the initial research supporting Moffitt's typology, however, is based on findings from studies assigning individuals to group membership based on their scores on various measures across time. For example, Aguilar and colleagues (2000) theorized four trajectories that spanned the first two decades of life. Within their 20-year longitudinal study, cutoffs determined a priori on the Achenbach scales established group membership in one of four groups: never antisocial, childhood-limited, adolescent-onset, and early-onset/persistent. Other studies have utilized these trajectories to reveal early adulthood outcomes in psychopathology, life stress and problem behavior based on assigned group membership. For example, using data from the same study (but extending the findings into adulthood), Roisman and colleagues (Roisman, Aguilar, & Egeland, 2004) categorized individuals into one of four groups (never antisocial in childhood and adolescence; antisocial in childhood, but not adolescence; not antisocial in childhood, but antisocial in adolescence; and antisocial in both childhood and adolescence) and compared young adulthood outcomes at age 23, assigning a category of either desistance, persistence, or ambiguous to the members of these four groups.

Research using a priori rules to assign group membership has received a considerable amount of critique. Nagin (2005) suggests that there are three disadvantages of using a priori rules for specifying group membership: (1) assuming homogeneous subpopulations exist without empirically verifying their existence, (2) incorrectly specifying the number of subpopulations, and (3) inability to specify the probability that an individual is a member of a certain subpopulation. In addition to the disadvantages noted by Nagin, a

---

[1] Results from Googlescholar.com search.

considerable amount of bias may be involved in a priori group membership assignment. For example, some studies have categorized continuous level behavioral measures by grouping individuals with scores one standard deviation above the mean as reflecting high levels of behavior problems (e.g., Moffitt, Caspi, Dickson, Silva, & Stanton, 1996) whereas other studies (e.g., Aguilar et al., 2000) have used a percentage cutoff (e.g., top 5%, 10%, or 15%). There is no procedure to investigate whether one particular cutoff rule is better than the next cutoff rule for assigning group membership. This makes it difficult to justify the decision for any specific cutoff rule. In addition, using different decision rules across studies makes it difficult to directly compare findings across studies.

In addition to the disadvantage of using different decision rules to assign individuals to low/high groups, dichotomizing continuous level variables is also problematic because interindividual differences are minimized by grouping individual scores on intraindividual change (MacCallum, Zhang, Preacher, & Rucker, 2002). In addition, magnitude of effect size and statistical power are diminished and researchers are at risk of finding spurious results (MacCallum et al., 2002). These disadvantages make it difficult to justify a priori assigning individuals to groups because one does not know to what degree the groups provide an accurate approximation of scores on a sampling distribution.

In light of the disadvantages of a priori assigning individuals to trajectory groups, several authors have advocated the use of statistical techniques to classify individuals (e.g., Nagin, 1999). Whereas statistical techniques for grouping longitudinal categorical data, such as latent class and latent transition analysis, have a long-standing tradition in the social and behavior sciences (e.g., McCutcheon, 1987), statistical techniques for group-based modeling using continuous level data were formally introduced to criminology scholars around the same time of the publication of Moffit's 1993 theoretical paper (e.g., Nagin, Farrington, & Moffitt, 1995; Nagin & Land, 1993). These statistical techniques (e.g., semi-parametric analysis, growth mixture modeling techniques) have enhanced the ability to accurately estimate group membership of individuals who follow a common trajectory across time. In addition to social and behavior scientists becoming familiar with these techniques, statistical software packages have become increasingly user-friendly, such as the Proc Traj module in SAS (Jones, Nagin, & Roeder, 2001) and the statistical software package Mplus (http://www.statmodel.com).

Increasingly, researchers use these statistical methodologies to identify developmental trajectories. This body of research has, however, not led to wider consensus regarding the "existence" of various developmental trajectories for externalizing behavior problems. Studies have identified anywhere from two to seven trajectories. Most studies find an abstainer and chronic offender group, with studies generally identifying a group of individuals engaging in externalizing behavior problems only during adolescence. Beyond that, it seems that studies have found a mixture of trajectories. So, despite the influx of studies on the topic of trajectories of externalizing behavior problems from childhood through young adulthood, there are large discrepancies in the findings (see also Osgood, 2005) and it is not completely clear as to what explains the variability in these findings.

The purpose of the current chapter is to investigate whether there are, based on a review of the extant literature, systematic factors that may help explain the large discrepancy in findings from group-based trajectory modeling. The preliminary step was to identify a number of confounding factors that potentially could clarify the incongruent findings. These confounding factors included measure of behavior problems, sample size, number of assessments, developmental periods studied, gender, and the use of single/multiple informant data.

Methodology

Studies were selected from searches of PsycINFO, SocIndex, Sociological Abstracts, Criminal Justice Abstracts, Criminal Justice Periodical Index, and the National Criminal Justice Reference Service (NCJRS) Abstracts Database, and papers listed in a recent review chapter by Moffitt in *The handbook of developmental psychopathology* (Moffitt, 2006b). We also conducted a Googlescholar search for all articles that cited the Moffitt 1993 paper. We selected studies that followed the participants at least beyond age 12 and started before age 18,[2] so that there was an opportunity to identify adolescent-onset externalizing behavior problems,[3] and limited our review to papers that had

---

[2] In one study (Piquero, Brame, Mazerolle, & Haapanen, 2002), the large majority of participants were included post age 18. Therefore, this study was not included in this review.

[3] Although the study by Land et al. (2001) met inclusion criteria, it was not considered for the current review. This study makes an important substantive contribution to statistical modeling of trajectories using discrete-time hazard models but only compares a two-class model with a one-class model and illustrates the use of discrete-time hazard models. Because the paper only compares a two-class model with a one-class model, it is not clear whether the two-class solution optimally represents the data (i.e., whether it is a better representation of the data than for example a three or four class solution).

been published since 1993 in peer-reviewed journals. The year 1993 was chosen as a cutoff because, as mentioned previously, the influx in empirical work in this area was strongly influenced by two papers published in that year (Moffitt, 1993; Nagin & Land, 1993).

We identified 59 empirical studies (see Table 14.1). Five studies (five data sets) identified two trajectories. Twenty studies (10 data sets) identified three trajectories. Twenty studies (12 data sets) identified four trajectories. Six studies (4 data sets) identified five trajectories. Seven studies (5 data sets) identified six trajectories and one study identified seven trajectories. If multiple articles reported information on a particular set of trajectories, we focused on the paper that originally identified the trajectories.

We only focused on studies that used a statistical technique to classify individuals in various trajectories. These techniques were limited to latent class analysis (McCutcheon, 1987) semi-parametric group-based modeling/ latent class growth curve analysis (Nagin, 1999), growth mixture modeling (Muthén & Muthén, 2000), and variations of the latter two techniques. The large majority of the studies in this review used semi-parametric group-based modeling. Papers that assigned individuals to trajectory membership based on a particular cutoff rule were not included in the analyses because these papers cannot be directly compared to the results from statistical identification of group membership. Statistical techniques that identify group membership work with probability estimates. Therefore, individual group membership is an approximation and not a true entity. Even if an individual is, based on her/his high probability, thought to be part of a group, there is still a nonzero chance that individual belongs in a different group. Techniques assigning individuals to a particular group a priori assume this probability of being part of a particular group is "1" (assigned) and the probability of being part of a different group is "0" (not assigned). Another way of phrasing this is that statistical techniques for group membership allow for the modeling of measurement error whereas a priori techniques assume measurement error is "0" (compare the analogy in variable-centered techniques path analysis versus structural equation modeling). Thus, because the statistical properties of trajectories based on a priori assigning of individuals to trajectories is different from the statistical properties of trajectories that are statistically identified, the two methods cannot be directly compared.

The studies selected for this review utilized a myriad of externalizing behavior problem outcomes. Externalizing behavior problems included outcomes that involved problematic behaviors within a finite category. These behavior problems incorporated delinquent and offending outcomes, antisocial behavior, conduct-disordered behaviors, opposition, and aggression. Studies were not included if the behavior focused on, or included, attention

TABLE 14.1 Overview of Studies Using Group-Based Trajectory Modeling to Identify Homogeneous Subgroups of Individuals Based on Course of Externalizing Behavior Problems (N = 59)

Study	Authors	Sample[1]	Assessments	Assessment Instruments[2,3]	Trajectories (% of sample)[4]	Analysis[5]
1	Barker et al. (2006)	N = 1037 B Montreal Study M (W1) = 13 Canada	W1–W5 (Annual—ages 13–17)	3-Proactive (PA) 3-Reactive (RA) Aggression items (S; Dodge & Coie, 1987)	AGGRESSION (1) Never observed (PA 58.7, RA 52.6) (2) Moderate desistors (PA 34.6, RA 40.8) (3) High peaking group (PA 6.7, RA 6.6)	SPGB
2	Blokland et al. (2005)	N = 4615 B/G CCLS M = 28.66 R = 12–72 Netherlands	Lifetime Criminal Record Review (ages 12–72)	Convicted offenses	OFFENDING (1) Sporadic offenders (70.9) (2) Moderate rate desisters (5.7) (3) Low-rate desisters (21.7) (4) High-rate persisters (1.6)	SPGB
3	Blokland & Nieuwbeerta (2005)	Same as 2	Same as 2	Same as 2	OFFENDING (1) Sporadic offenders (73.2) (2) Moderate rate offenders (10.3) (3) Low-rate offenders (12.8) (4) High-rate offenders (3.7)	SPGB
4	Blokland & Nieuwbeerta (2005)	N = 2951 B/G NCSR M = 33.38 R = 12–72 Netherlands	One-time interview	Lifetime offences based on interview (S)	EBP (1) Sporadic offenders (85.5) (2) Low-rate (14.5)	SPGB
5	Bongers et al. (2004)	N = 2076 B/G R = 4–18 Netherlands	Waves varied by cohort (Multiple birth cohort design)	CBCL Aggression subscale (P)	AGGRESSION (1) High decreasers (8) (2) Low decreasers (21) (3) Near zero (71)	SPGB

(continued)

TABLE 14.1 Continued

Study	Authors	Sample[1]	Assessments	Assessment Instruments[2,3]	Trajectories (% of sample)[4]	Analysis[5]
6	Bongers et al. (2004)	Same as 5	Same as 5	CBCL Property violation subscale (P)	EBP (1) Extremely high persisters (0.3) (2) High persisters (5) (3) Low decreasers (20) (4) Near zero (75)	SPGB
7	Bongers et al. (2004)	Same as 5	Same as 5	CBCL Status violations subscale (P)	EBP (1) High increasers (1) (2) Medium increasers (25) (3) Adolescent increasers (28) (4) Near zero (51)	SPGB
8	Bongers et al. (2004)	Same as 5	Same as 5	CBCL Opposition subscale (P)	OPPOSITION (1) High persisters (7) (2) High decreasers (24) (3) Medium decreasers (33) (4) Low decreasers (24) (5) Adolescent Increasers (6) (6) Near zero (7)	SPGB
9	Brame et al. (2005)[6]	N = 727 B RYDS M (W1) = 13.5 R (W1) = 12–15 United States	W1–W9 (Semiannual)	Self-reports of involvement in 8 violent and nonviolent offenses (S); official police contacts	EBP With OFFENDING[6] (1) Low-rate (52–86) (2) High-rate (14–48)	SPGB
10	Brame, Nagin et al. (2001)	N = 926 B M (W1) = 6 Canada	W1 (6), W2–5 (Annual, ages 10–13)	Fighting subscale of SBQ (T)	EBP (1) Low (51) (2) Medium (31) (3) High (18)	SPGB

	Study	Sample	Waves	Measure	Method / Groups	
11	Brame, Nagin et al. (2001)	Same as 10	W1–W5 (Annual, ages 13–17)	4-item self-reported physical aggression measure (S)	EBP (1) None (64) (2) Increasing (16) (3) Decreasing (15) (4) High (5)	SPGB
12	Brame, Mulvey et al. (2001) 1945 Cohort	N = 9945 B PBCS R = 10–18 United States	W1–W10 (Annual record reviews, ages 8–18)	Juvenile records of violent criminal acts (i.e., homicide, robbery, rape, assault)	OFFENDING (1) Low frequencies (81) (2) Moderate levels (16) (3) Relatively high (3)	SPGB
13	Brame, Mulvey et al. (2001) 1945 Cohort	Same as 12	Same as 12	Juvenile records of nonviolent criminal acts	OFFENDING (1) Low frequencies (81) (2) Moderate levels (16) (3) Relatively high (3)	SPGB
14	Brame, Mulvey et al. (2001) 1958 Cohort	N = 13,160 B PBCS R = 10–18 USA	Same as 12	Same as 12	OFFENDING (1) Low frequencies (83) (2) Moderate levels (15) (3) Relatively high (2)	SPGB
15	Brame, Mulvey et al. (2001) 1958 Cohort	Same as 14	Same as 12	Same as 13	OFFENDING (1) Low frequencies (83) (2) Moderate levels (15) (3) Relatively high (2)	SPGB
16	Broidy, Nagin et al. (2003)	N = 1037 B Montreal study M (W1) = 6 Canada	W1 (age 6), W2–W7 (Annual, ages 10–15)	Fighting subscale of SBQ (T)	EBP (1) Never (14) (2) Chronic (4) (3) Low desister (53) (4) High desister (28)	SPGB
17	Broidy, Nagin et al. (2003)	N = 635 B CHDS M (W1) = birth New Zealand	W9–W15 (Annual, ages 7–13)	3-items on Rutter et al. (1970) Child Scales (T)	EBP (1) Never (32) (2) Low (57) (3) Chronic (11)	SPGB

(continued)

TABLE 14.1 Continued

Study	Authors	Sample[1]	Assessments	Assessment Instruments[2,3]	Trajectories (% of sample)[4]	Analysis[5]
18	Broidy, Nagin et al. 2003)	N = 535 B Dunedin Sample M (W1) = 3 New Zealand	W3–W6 (Biennial, ages 7, 9, 11, 13)	2 items on Rutter et al. (1970) Child Scales (T)	AGGRESSION (1) Never (53) (2) Low (38) (3) Chronic (9)	SPGB
19	Broidy, Nagin et al. (2003)	N = 630 G CHDS M (W1) = birth New Zealand	Same as 17	Same as 17	EBP (1) Never (42) (2) Low (48) (3) Chronic (10)	SPGB
20	Broidy, Nagin et al. (2003)	N = 502 G Dunedin Sample M (W1) = 3 New Zealand	Same as 18	Same as 18	AGGRESSION (1) Stable-low (57) (2) Moderate decline (43)	SPGB
21	Bushway et al. (1999)[7]	N = 13,160 B PBCS (1958 cohort) R = 6–26 United States	W1–W19 (Annual record reviews, ages 6–26)	Records of official police contacts for criminal activity	OFFENDING[7] (1) (66.3) (2) (25.1) (3) (8.6)	SPGB
22	Bushway et al. (2003)	N = 846 B/G RYDS M (W1) = 13.5 R (W1) = 12–15 United States	W1–W9 (Biannual), W10–W12 (Annual) after 2.5 year gap	31-item delinquency inventory (S)	EBP (1) Very low-level (38.7) (2) Low-level (22.5) (3) Late starters (9.7) (4) Intermittent (8.6) (5) Bell-shaped desistors (8.5) (6) Slow-uptake chronic (7.9) (7) High-level chronic (4.2)	SPGB

#	Study	Sample	Measure	Waves	Groups	Method
23	Chung, Hawkins et al. (2002)	N = 423 B/G Low SES Subsample of SSDP M (W4) = 13 United States	16-item Offensive Seriousness Scale (S)	W4–W7 (Annual, ages 13–16) & W8 (age 18)	EBP (1) Nonoffenders (18.6) (2) Late onsetters (8.5) (3) Desisters (23.7) (4) Escalators (38.2) (5) Chronic (11.1)	SPGB
24	Chung, Hill et al. (2002)	N = 808 B/G SSDP M (W4) = 13 United States	Same as 23	W4–W7 (Annual, ages 13–16), W8 (age 18) & W9 (age 21)	EBP (1) Nonoffenders (24) (2) Late onsetters (14.4) (3) Desisters (35.3) (4) Escalator (19.3) (5) Chronic (7)	SPGB
25	Connell & Frye (2006)	N = 498 B/G ATP Study M (W1) = 12 United States	Survey from Oregon Research Institute (S); Review of Lifetime Arrest records	W1–W4 (Annual— ages 12–15) and W5 (age 17)	EBP WITH OFFENDING (1) Chronic-High (37.7) (2) Stable-low (62.3)	GMM
26	D'Unger et al. (2002)	N = 1000 B PBCS (1958 cohort) R = 8–26 United States	Records of official police contacts for criminal activity	(Annual record reviews, ages 8–26)	OFFENDING (1) Nonoffenders (60.8) (2) High-rate adolescent peak (1) (3) Low-rate adolescent peak (8.6) (4) Low-rate chronic (21.3) (5) High-rate chronic (8.3)	SPGB
27	D'Unger et al. (2002)	N = 3000 G PBCS (1958 cohort) R = 8–26 United States	Records of official police contacts for criminal activity	(Annual record reviews, ages 8–26)	OFFENDING (1) Nonoffenders (84.37) (2) High-rate adolescent peak (5.27) (3) Low-rate adolescent peak (10.37)	SPGB

(continued)

TABLE 14.1 Continued

Study	Authors	Sample[1]	Assessments	Assessment Instruments[2,3]	Trajectories (% of sample)[4]	Analysis[5]
28	Eggleston et al. (2004)	N = 500 B UJDA R = 7–24 United States	Lifetime Criminal Record Reviews (Annually)	Criminal records review	OFFENDING (1) Low-rate chronic (37.9) (2) Classic desister (24.4) (3) Moderate-rate desister (15.6) (4) Moderate-rate chronic (22.1)	SPGB
29	Eggleston et al. (2004)	N = 500 B UJDA R = 7–31 United States	Same as 28	Same as 28	OFFENDING (1) Low-rate chronic (27.3) (2) Classic desister (17.6) (3) Moderate-rate desister (17.8) (4) Moderate-rate chronic (29.2) (5) High-rate chronic (8)	SPGB
30	Eggleston et al. (2004)	N = 500 B UJDA R = 7–44 United States	Same as 28	Same as 28	OFFENDING (1) Low-rate chronic (27.2) (2) Classic desister (22) (3) Moderate-rate desister (24.8) (4) Moderate-rate chronic (23) (5) High-rate chronic (3.1)	SPGB
31	Eggleston et al. 2004)	N = 500 B UJDA R = 7–70 United States	Same as 28	Same as 28	OFFENDING (1) Low-rate chronic I (24.4) (2) Classic desister (19.9) (3) Moderate-rate desister (26.1) (4) Moderate-rate chronic (18.4) (5) High-rate chronic (3.2) (6) Low-rate chronic II (8.0)	SPGB

#	Study	Sample	Waves	Measures	Trajectory groups	Method
32	Fergusson & Horwood (2002)	N = 896 B/G CHDS M (W10) = 8 New Zealand	W10–W18 (Annual, ages 8–16), W19 (age 18), W20 (age 21)	Items from Rutter et al. (1970) & Conners (1969, 1970) Child Behavior Questionnaires (T, P), SRED (P, S), SRDI (S, O)	EBP (1) Low-risk (57) (2) Early onset adolescence-limited (18) (3) Intermediate onset adolescence-limited (7) (4) Late onset adolescence-limited (14) (5) Chronic (6)	LCA
33	Fergusson et al. (2000)	N = 1265 B/G CHDS M (W14) = 12 New Zealand	W14–18 (Annual, ages 12–16), W19 (age 18)	SRED (P, S), SRDI (S, O), Officially recorded police contacts (ages 12–18), Court appearances and convictions (ages 16–18)	EBP With OFFENDING (1) Nonoffenders (55.3) (2) Moderate (30.8) (3) Adolescent onset (7.6) (4) Chronic (6.3)	LCA
34	Fergusson et al. (1996)	N = 901 B/G CHDS M (W9) = 7 New Zealand	W9–W11 (Annual, ages 7–9), W16–W18 (Annual, ages 14–16)	Items from Rutter et al. (1970) and Conners (1969, 1970) Child Behavior Questionnaires (P, T); Revised Behavior Problem Checklist (P); SRED (S, P); DISC (S); Police contacts (S, P)	EBP With OFFENDING (1) Nonproblem (84.2) (2) Early onset/later remission (4.6) (3) Late onset (5.1) (4) Persistent (6.1)	LCA
35	Harachi et al. (2006)	N = 523 B RHCP M (W1) = 7.9 R (W1) = 7.0–9.2 United States	W1–W7 (Annual)	Two items from TOCA-R (T) and two items from CBCL (T)	EBP (1) None (19.5) (2) Low (41.7) (3) Moderate (27) (4) High (11.9)	SPGB
36	Harachi et al. (2006)	N = 461 G RHCP M (W1) = 7.9, R (W1) = 7.0–9.2 United States	Same as 35	Same as 35	EBP (1) None (44.3) (2) Low (31.9) (3) Moderate (13.4) (4) High (10.4)	SPGB

(continued)

TABLE 14.1 Continued

Study	Authors	Sample[1]	Assessments	Assessment Instruments[2,3]	Trajectories (% of sample)[4]	Analysis[5]
37	Herrenkohl et al. (2006)	N = 808 B/G SSDP M (W1) = 10.8 United States	Same as 24	Violent Offense Seriousness Scale (S)	EBP (1) Chronic (16.3) (2) Desister (14.8) (3) Late Increaser (8.8) (4) Non Offender (60)	SPGB
38	Lacourse et al. (2002)	N = 909 B Montreal study M (W2) = 11 Canada	W2–W8 (Annual ages 11–17)	7-item physical aggression scale over last 12 months (S)	EBP (1) High rising (4.8) (2) Medium decline (12) (3) Low rising (11.4) (4) Low decline (26.3) (5) Low 1 (29.9) (6) Low 2 (15.6)	SPGB
39	Lacourse et al. (2002)	Same as 38	Same as 38	6-item vandalism scale (S)	EBP (1) High rising (4.5) (2) Medium decline (5.9) (3) Low rising (6.9) (4) Low decline (11.1) (5) Low 1 (58) (6) Low 2 (13.6)	SPGB
40	Lacourse et al. (2002)	Same as 38	Same as 38	11-item theft scale (S)	EBP (1) High rising (5.9) (2) Medium decline (6.9) (3) Low rising (16.4) (4) Low decline (14.2) (5) Low 1 (32.3) (6) Low 2 (24.4)	SPGB

41	Land et al. (1996)	N = 1000 B PBCS (random subsample, 1958 cohort) R = 8–26 United States	W1–W19 (Annual record reviews, ages 8–26)	Records of official police contacts for criminal activity	OFFENDING (1) High (0.5) (2) Medium (6.2) (3) Low (47.4) (4) Nonoffenders (45.9)	SPGB
42	Laub et al. (1998)	N = 480 B Delinquent Subsample of Glueck & Glueck (1950, 1968) M (W1) = 14 United States	W1 (age 14) W2 (age 25) W3 (age 32)	Report of delinquent behavior (S, P, T); Dichotomous age of misbehavior onset (S); Official criminal history	EBP WITH OFFENDING (1) High rate through adult (2.8) (2) Chronic offenders (25.7) (3) Moderate high in adolescence, Low adult (slow decline) (42.5) (4) Moderate high in adolescence, Low adult (steep decline) (28.9)	**SPGB**
43	Maughan et al. (2000)	N = 1419 B/G GSMS R (W1) = 9, 11, 13 United States	W1–W4 (Annual) Accelerated Cohort Design	CAPA interview (S, P)—7 CD behaviors focusing on aggression	AGGRESSION (1) Stable-low (76.9) (2) Declining (15.5) (3) Stable-high (7.5)	SPGB
44	Maughan et al. (2000)	Same as 43	Same as 43	CAPA interview (S, P)—8 CD behaviors focusing on nonaggression	EBP (1) Stable-low (61.9) (2) Declining (35.1) (3) Stable-high (2.9)	SPGB
45	McDermott & Nagin (2001)	N = 835 B NYS R (W1) = 11–17 United States	W1–W6 (Annual)	5-item serious offenses scale (S)	EBP (1) Low-rate (89) (2) High rates early, declines (6) (3) Low rates early, rises until 18 (5)	SPGB

(continued)

TABLE 14.1 Continued

Study	Authors	Sample[1]	Assessments	Assessment Instruments[2,3]	Trajectories (% of sample)[4]	Analysis[5]
46	Nagin (1999)	N = 411 B CSDD M (W1) = 8 England	Criminal Record Review (ages 8–32)	Count of Criminal offense convictions for each 2 year period	OFFENDING (1) Never convicted (71) (2) Adolescence-limited (22) (3) Chronic (7)	SPGB
47	Nagin (1999)	N = 1037 B Montreal study M (W1) = 6 Canada	W1 (age 6) W2–W10 (Annual, ages 10–18)	Fighting (intensity) subscale of SBQ (T)	EBP (1) Never (15) (2) Low desister (50) (3) High desister (30) (4) Chronic (5)	SPGB
48	Nagin (1999)	Same as 47	Same as 47	Fighting (binary indicator) subscale of SBQ (T)	EBP (1) Never (20) (2) Desister (50) (3) Nondesister (30)	SPGB
49	Nagin & Land (1993)	N = 403 B CSDD M (W1) = 8 England	W1–W7 (Biannual, ages 8–32)	Criminal convictions	OFFENDING (1) High-rate chronic (13.4) (2) Adolescence-limited (12.7) (3) Low-rate chronic (10) (4) Nonoffending (64)	SPGB
50	Nagin & Tremblay (1999)	N = 1037 B Montreal Study M (W1) = 6 Canada	W1 (age 6), W2–W10 (Annual, ages 10–18)	Fighting subscale of SBQ (T)	EBP (1) Low (17%) (2) Moderate desister (52) (3) High desister (28) (4) Chronic (4)	SPGB
51	Nagin & Tremblay (1999)	Same as 50	Same as 50	Opposition subscale of SBQ (T)	OPPOSITION (1) Low (25) (2) Moderate desister (46) (3) High desister (25) (4) Chronic (5)	SPGB

#	Study	Sample	Waves	Measure	Classes	Method
52	Paternoster et al. (2001)	N = 403 B CSDD M (W1) = 8 England	W2–W5 (Biannual, ages 10–17)	Criminal convictions	OFFENDING (1) Low (72) (2) Medium (23) (3) High (5)	SPGB
53	Piquero et al. (2005)	N = 504 B Dunedin R = 13–26 New Zealand	W6–W19 (Annual, ages 13–26), trajectories separately for adolescence (13–16) and adulthood (17–26)	Criminal convictions	OFFENDING (1) Low (89.3) (2) Medium (9.5) (3) High (1.2)	SPGB
54	Piquero et al. (2005)	N = 481 G Dunedin R = 13–26 New Zealand	See 53	See 53	OFFENDING (1) Low (98.1) (2) Medium (1.9)	SPGB
55	Reinecke (2006)	N = 813 B/G JDMT M (W1) = 13 Germany	W1–W4 (Annual)	Self administered interviews	EBP (1) Nonoffenders (60 SPGB, 58 GMM) (2) Low-rate adolescents (32 SPGB, 33 GMM) (3) High-rate adolescents (8 SPGB, 9 GMM)	SPGB and GMM
56	White et al. (2001)	N = 698 B HHDP R (W1) = 12–18 United States	W1–W3 (Triennial), W4 (7 years after W3)	8-item delinquency scale over past 3 years (S)	EBP (1) Nondelinquents (47) (2) Adolescence-limited (33) (3) Persistent (7) (4) Escalating (13)	GMM
57	Wiesner & Capaldi (2003)	N = 204 B OYS M (W1) = 10.09 United States	W4–W15 (ages 12/13 to 23/24)	EDS (S)	EBP (1) Chronic high level (15.7) (2) Chronic low level (18.6) (3) Decreasing high level (27.9) (4) Decreasing low level (21.6) (5) Rare (11.3) (6) None (4.9)	GMM

(continued)

TABLE 14.1 Continued

Study	Authors	Sample[1]	Assessments	Assessment Instruments[2,3]	Trajectories (% of sample)[4]	Analysis[5]
58	Wiesner & Silbereisen (2003)	N = 318 B/G M (W1) = 11.45, R = 10–13 Germany	W1—W4 (Annual)	DBS (S)	EBP (1) High-level (14.2) (2) Medium level (13.2) (3) Low-level (20.1) (4) Rare (52.5)	GMM
59	Wiesner & Windle (2004)	N = 1218 B/G MAVS M (W1) = 15.5 United States	W1–W4 (Biannual)	7 delinquent behavior items (S)	EBP (1) Rare (50) (2) Moderate late peakers (19.6) (3) High late peakers (8.9) (4) Decreasers (5.2) (5) Moderate-level chronics (10) (6) High-level chronics (6.4)	GMM

[1] Sample: B = Boys; G = Girls; M = Mean Age; R = Age Range; W = Wave.

Studies: ATP = Adolescent Transitions Program Study; CCLS = Criminal Career and Life-Course Study; CHDS = Christchurch Health and Development Study; CSDD = Cambridge Study in Delinquency Development; GSMS = Great Smoky Mountains Study of Youth; HHDP = Rutgers Health and Human Development Project; JDMT = Juvenile Delinquency in Modern Towns Study; MAVS = Middle Adolescent Vulnerability Study; NCSR = Netherlands Institute for the Study of Crime and Law Enforcement Survey; NYS = National Youth Survey; OYS = Oregon Youth Study; PBCS = Philadelphia Birth Cohort Study; RHCP = Raising Healthy Children Project;

RYDS = Rochester Youth Development Study; SSDP = Seattle Social Development Project;

UJDA = Unraveling Juvenile Delinquency Archive

[2] O = Other individual; P = Parent; S = Self; T = Teacher

[3] CAPA = Child and Adolescent Psychiatric Assessment; CBCL = Child Behavior Checklist; DBS = German self-report delinquency questionnaire; DISC = Diagnostic Interview Schedule for Children; EDS = Elliot Delinquency Scale; SBQ = Social Behavior Questionnaire–Teacher form; SRED=Self-Report of Early Delinquency Scale; SRDI = Self-Report Delinquency Instrument; TOCA-R = Teacher Observation of Child Adaptation-Revised

[4] EBP = Externalizing Behavior Problems.

[5] Statistical Analysis:GMM = Growth Mixture Modeling; LCA = Latent Class Analysis; SPGB = Semi-parametric Group-Based Modeling

[6] The percentages of group membership in Study 9 (Brame, Bushway, Paternoster, & Thornberry, 2005) vary depending on official versus self-reported offending and violent versus nonviolent offending. Percentages in the high rate offending group are generally higher for self-reported offending (as compared to official records) and nonviolent offending (as compared to violent offending).

[7] The trajectories in Study 21 (Bushway, Brame, & Paternoster, 1999) were not named or described as they only were used as controls for heterogeneity (Bushway, Personal Communication, May 1st 2007).

problems or substance use. Within these studies, several specific topics were individually investigated, including offending, aggression, and opposition. All other studies were determined to mix a variety of externalizing behaviors that did not fit exclusively in one of the three specific topics mentioned above. Offending was defined as utilizing criminal records for an individual's criminal history. Studies that utilized self-report measures of delinquency were not included in this category, because they typically incorporated elements of broader externalizing behavior problems and aggression. When an outcome measure focused solely on an aggressive subscale (e.g., aggression subscale on the Child Behavior Checklist) or a selected set of aggressive items, the outcome measure was aggression. Aggressive items could include both physical aggression and indirect aggression and generally reflected intent to harm. Opposition was defined as disruptive behaviors that did not include problems with attention. These trajectories were identified using specific subscales, such as the opposition subscale of the Child Behavior Checklist. All other trajectory outcomes were therefore defined as externalizing behavior problems (EBP), broadly construed, with studies using both EBP-like measures and criminal records being defined as EBP with offending.

Results

Does the Conceptualization of Externalizing Behavior Affect Identification of Statistical Trajectories?

Table 14.1 lists the studies and summarizes their attributes. Because some studies report findings for separate analyses, they are given distinct study numbers and referred to separately in text and in the table. Only two studies focused on oppositional behavior. These two studies identified either four (Nagin & Tremblay, 1999, #51) or six (Bongers, Koot, van der Ende, & Verhulst, 2004, #8) trajectories. Studies focusing on aggression have generally found less variability in the number of trajectories than studies focusing more broadly on delinquency and/or EBP. Five studies analyzed aggression trajectories and all identified either two or three trajectories (Study # 1, 5, 18, 20 and 43).

Nineteen studies (Study #2, 3, 12, 13, 14, 15, 21, 26, 27, 28, 29, 30, 31, 41, 46, 49, 52, 53, and 54) focused on offending and found a range of three to five trajectories with two exceptions. Eggleston and colleagues (Eggleston, Laub & Sampson, 2004, #31) identified six trajectories of offending using only reviews of criminal record over a 63 year period. They reported four studies on offending. The first included a criminal record review from ages 7 to 24; the second included ages 7 to 30; the third included ages 7 to 44, and the fourth included ages 7 to 70. The trajectories identified by these studies increased as the life span increased (four, five, and six trajectories, respectively). One potential reason this study found a larger number of trajectories than any of the other studies is that the length of follow-up in this study was longer than any of the other studies. Piquero and colleagues (Piquero, Brame, & Moffitt, 2005, #54) identified two trajectories of offending using only criminal convictions in a female sample. This latter study focused on a relatively short time span (trajectories separately from age 13 to age 16 as well as age 17 to age 26) which may explain the small number of trajectories.

Twenty-eight studies examined EBP (Study # 4, 6, 7, 10, 11, 16, 17, 19, 22, 23, 24, 32, 35, 36, 37, 38, 39, 40, 44, 45, 47, 48, 50, 55, 56, 57, 58, and 59). The most variability in trajectories was found in this category, identifying a range of two to seven trajectories. Five studies (Study # 9, 25, 33, 34, and 42) that examined criminal convictions in conjunction with EBP do not appear to be much different than studies that examined EBP without considering criminal convictions. Two of these studies identified two trajectories and three of them identified four trajectories.

The findings suggest, in general, that the conceptualization of externalizing behavior problems affects the number of trajectories identified. More specifically, variability among research findings increased as the conceptualization of externalizing behavior problems became broader.

Does Sample Size Affect Statistical Identification of Trajectories?

Next, we considered whether sample size affects the number of trajectories identified. Studies were grouped into categories where samples were either less than 250, 251 to 500, 501 to 1000, or greater than 1000. Our findings suggest that sample size has no formal impact on the number of trajectories identified. However, only one study used a sample size fewer than 250 and identified six trajectories (Wiesner & Capaldi, 2003, #57). Thirteen studies used a sample size of 251 to 500 and found a range of two to six trajectories. Twenty-two studies used a sample size of 501 to 1000 and found a range of two to seven trajectories. Twenty-three studies used a sample greater than 1000 and found a range in trajectories from two to six.

Our results indicate that large heterogeneity in trajectories can still be found in samples fewer than 250. Wiesner and Capaldi (2003, #57) used a sample of 204 boys from the Oregon Youth Study and identified six trajectories. Their group of nonoffenders (N = 10) and rare offenders (N = 23) were relatively small. Given the small sample size for these two groups, it is diffi-cult to know how well these findings would replicate in other samples. On the other hand, little heterogeneity in trajectories can be found in samples greater than 1000. Blokland and Nieuwbeerta (2005, #4) used a sample of 2951 boys and girls from the Netherlands Institute for the Study of Crime and Law Enforcement and identified two trajectories. This study used one assessment point where participants were asked to recall offenses over a life-time. This study is the only study to use one time point for the identification of trajectories and it could be that this method compromised the ability to detect additional homogeneous developmental trajectories.

Does Number of Assessments Affect Statistical Identification of Trajectories?

Many studies examined offending by reviewing lifetime histories of official criminal records. The assessment points in these studies differed from those studies that administered questionnaires or interviews at several different time points. Thus, these studies were examined separately.

As stated previously, 19 studies used only criminal record reviews for the assessment of offending trajectories. There was less variability in the number of trajectories found in studies that used criminal record reviews (range of two to five) than studies that used questionnaires, interviews and other methods of assessment. Eggleston and colleagues (2004, #31), however, identified six trajectories of offending using criminal record reviews. As mentioned ear-lier, this study used a longer length of follow-up than any of the other studies mentioned in this review and one possible reason for the larger number of trajectories is the increased variability with age in offending trajectories.

Four studies (Studies #5, 6, 7, and 8) were excluded from this analysis because the number of assessments per participant could not be determined. On basis of the review of the remaining studies, it does not seem to be the case that the number of trajectories increases as a function of the number of assessment points. Rather, variability in the number of trajectories (two to seven) occurred in all studies ranging from 1 to 12 assessment points. The only exception occurred in five studies identifying EBP with offending tra-jectories, which consistently found either two or four trajectories (Studies #9, 25, 33, 34, and 42). Studies of only aggression trajectories (Studies #1, 18, 20, and 43), identified either two or three trajectories, regardless of num-ber of assessment points. This again suggests that a clear definition of the outcome behavior is necessary in identifying the appropriate number of trajectories.

Does Developmental Period Affect Statistical Identification of Trajectories?

We next explored whether the developmental period during which assessments were taken affects the number of trajectories. We separated developmental periods into early childhood (age 6 or below), middle childhood (7–12 years), adolescence (13–17 years), and adulthood (18 years and above).

Three studies focused on identifying trajectories during only adolescence and they identified three (aggression, Barker, Tremblay, Nagin, Vitaro, & Lacourse, 2006, #1), four (EBP, Brame, Nagin, & Tremblay, 2001, #11) and three (EBP, Reinecke, 2006, #55) trajectories, respectively. Twenty-seven studies analyzed data from two developmental periods. Fifteen (Studies # 17, 18, 19, 20, 25, 34, 35, 36, 38, 39, 40, 43, 44, 52, and 58) studies included middle childhood and adolescence, with ten identifying three or four trajectories. One study (Broidy, Nagin et al., 2003, #20) identified only two aggressive trajectories in a female-only sample. Another study (Connell & Frye, 2006, #25) identified only two externalizing behavior problem trajectories in conjunction with criminal conviction records. Three studies (Studies #38, 39, and 40) identified six EBP trajectories. However, these three studies (Lacourse et al., 2002), all from the same data set, analyzed self-reported offending-like outcomes, including physical aggression, vandalism and theft. Five studies (Studies #23, 24, 37, 42, and 59) integrated adolescence and adulthood, which identified a range of four to six EBP, with or without offending, trajectories. Two additional studies from the same data set (Studies #53 and 54) that integrated adolescence and adulthood identified a range of two and three offending trajectories respectively. These findings suggest that not necessarily the number of trajectories, but more so the variability in trajectory findings, increases from comparing studies that only focused on adolescence with studies that focused on adolescence and middle childhood or adolescence and adulthood.

Twenty-five studies focused on three developmental periods. Two of these 25 studies (Studies #10 and 16) analyzed samples with data from early childhood, middle childhood and adolescence. These two studies identified three and four trajectories, respectively. The greatest range of trajectories, from two to seven, occurred among 23 studies incorporating middle childhood, adolescence and adulthood (Studies #2, 3, 4, 9, 12, 13, 14, 15, 22, 26, 27, 28, 29, 30, 31, 32, 33, 41, 45, 46, 49, 56, and 57). These 23 studies identified trajectories based on EBP (range two to seven), offending (range three to six) outcomes or EBP with offending (range two to four).

Finally, nine studies (Studies #5, 6, 7, 8, 21, 47, 48, 50, and 51) examined trajectories based on early childhood, middle childhood, adolescence and adulthood. Generally, only three or four trajectories were identified in these studies. Only one study (Bongers et al., 2004, #8), which focused solely on opposition in a multiple birth cohort design, identified six trajectories.

In summary, the findings suggest that studies that only focused on adolescence generally found three or four trajectories. When studies included adolescence with one other developmental period (middle childhood or adulthood) there was a wide range in trajectory findings. However, when studies included assessments from early childhood through adulthood, the number of trajectories was more consistent across studies and generally limited to three or four trajectories.

Does Gender Affect the Statistical Identification of Trajectories?

Of all studies included in the review, 54 included males. Of these, 20 studies focused on males and females and 34 focused only on males. In papers with male-only samples (Studies #1, 9, 10, 11, 12, 13, 14, 15, 16, 17, 18, 21, 26, 28, 29, 30, 31, 35, 38, 39, 40, 41, 42, 45, 46, 47, 48, 49, 50, 51, 52, 53, 56, and 57), the number of trajectories ranged from two to six. However, only one study (Eggleston et al., 2004, #31) found six trajectories in the offending outcome category. As previously mentioned, this study followed participants for 63 years, which may explain the larger number of trajectories in this particular study.

Twenty studies included males and females (Studies #2, 3, 4, 5, 6, 7, 8, 22, 23, 24, 25, 32, 33, 34, 37, 43, 44, 55, 58, and 59) and identified two to seven trajectories. In two studies (Studies #5 and 43) focusing on aggression as the outcome behavior, only three trajectories were found. In two studies (Studies #2 and 3) focusing solely on offending as the outcome, four trajectories were found. The widest range, between two and seven trajectories, occurred when the behavioral outcome was EBP; however, only one paper (Blokland & Nieuwbeerta, 2005, #4) found two trajectories and only one paper (Bushway, Thornberry, & Krohn, 2003, #22) found seven trajectories. The Blokland paper, as mentioned earlier, used retrospective reports at one assessment for identifying trajectories, which may explain the limited number of trajectories in this paper. The Bushway et al. (2003) paper used a cubic form to estimate group trajectories, which is different from most of the other papers in our review. The cubic component enhances the ability to estimate desistance in antisocial behavior and identify groups of individuals that have intermittent periods of offending (see also the study by Blokland, Nagin, & Nieuwbeerta, 2005, #2).

Only three mixed-gender studies focused on EBP with offending behavior (Studies #25, 33 and 34). Two of these studies (Studies #33 and 34) identified four trajectories, similar to the males-only offending samples and the mixed-gender offending samples. The other mixed-gender study (Connell & Frye, 2006, #25) incorporating EBP and offending behavior identified only two trajectories. Five studies identified trajectories (Studies #19, 20, 27, 36, and 54) in female-only samples. Two studies (Studies #19 and 36) identified three and four trajectories respectively when analyzing an EBP outcome. One study (Broidy, Nagin et al., 2003, #20) focused solely on aggression as the outcome behavior, finding two trajectories. Only two studies (Studies #27 and 54) focused on offending and identified three and two trajectories respectively. Based on this review of the role of gender in the identification of trajectories of antisocial behavior, gender seems to affect the identification of the number of trajectories of antisocial behavior, as samples of females generally identified smaller number of trajectories than male-only or mixed-gender samples.

Does the Informant Affect Statistical Identification of Trajectories?

Thirty-two studies utilized a single informant, the youth, their parents or their teachers. Four studies used only information based on parental reports (Studies #5, 6, 7, and 8). Generally only three or four trajectories were identified. However, one study (Bongers et al., 2004, #8) strictly focusing on opposition and six trajectories were identified.

Twelve studies used only teacher reports and analyzed aggression, EBP, and oppositional behavior (Studies #10, 16, 17, 18, 19, 20, 35, 36, 47, 48, 50, and 51). All of the teacher-only studies, with the exception of one (Broidy, Nagin et al., 2003, #20), found three or four trajectories. Sixteen studies had youth-only data (Studies #1, 4, 11, 22, 23, 24, 37, 38, 39, 40, 45, 55, 56, 57, 58, and 59). These studies had the widest range of trajectories, ranging from two to seven. Fifteen of these studies focused on EBP outcomes, with one focusing on aggression (Barker et al., 2006, #1), which identified three trajectories.

Eight studies utilized multiple informants. In two studies incorporating youth and parent data (Studies #43 and 44), three aggression and EBP trajectories, respectively, were identified. Three studies (Studies #33, 34, and 42) incorporated data from three informants, plus criminal records, to identify four EBP with offending trajectories. Two studies incorporated data from youth self-reports and criminal records (Studies #9 and 25), which both identified two EBP with offending trajectories. One study (#32) utilized four informants, the youth, a parent, a teacher and another individual. In this study, five EBP trajectories were identified.

In summary, only a small group of studies had multiple informants. Studies that used more than two informants, however, seemed to identify a larger number of trajectories than studies that used a single or dual-informant.

Discussion

The purpose of this chapter was to review the literature on group-based modeling of externalizing behavior problems and to investigate whether there are systematic factors that explain the discrepancy in research findings. The conceptualization of externalizing behavior problems, the number of assessments, length of follow-up, gender, and whether or not studies employed multimethod/multiinformant designs, all affected the number of trajectories that studies identified. The majority of the studies identified three to five trajectories, with the biggest variations occurring when studies used broad operational definitions of externalizing behavior problems, more than five assessments, and integrated information from more than two informants.

With regard to the conceptualization of externalizing behavior problems, trajectory findings seem to be more reliable (as reflected by decreased variability in number of trajectories across studies) when scholars have a more specific conceptualization of externalizing behavior problems (e.g., focusing only on offending) as compared to using a broad definition of externalizing behavior problems (e.g., externalizing behavior problems across domains of offending, delinquency, and aggression). Tremblay (2000) has suggested that the problem in the field of research on externalizing behavior problems is one of definition. Clearly, it seems that this argument extends itself to research on developmental trajectories of externalizing behavior problems. Broad definitions of externalizing behavior problems make it difficult to compare the findings from different studies and may not be very useful in informing how many trajectories underlie the development of externalizing behavior problems.

Although the precise dynamics between the number of assessment points and trajectory findings are not completely clear here, the findings suggest that the greatest variability in trajectory findings occurs when comparing studies with at least four or five assessment points. The data also imply that the length of follow-up is important in capturing variability in trajectories (see also Eggleston et al., 2004). However, the results of our review do not indicate that greater variability is simply a function of length of follow-up. Studies that started in middle childhood and followed through adulthood seemed to find a greater range of trajectories than studies that started in early childhood and also followed through adulthood. This suggests that not only the length of follow-up but also the timing of the initial assessment (early childhood or later) is essential in understanding trajectory findings.

The study of externalizing behavior problems across different developmental periods does, however, pose the problem of how to handle nonequivalent measures for studying continuity and change in development. The items and informants that best capture behavior at one age may very well differ from the items and informants that best capture behavior at a different age. For example, indicators and informants of externalizing behavior problems at age five differ from indicators and informants of externalizing behavior problems at later ages. Teachers and parents may be good informants of children's behavior at young ages, whereas during adolescence most studies also incorporate reports from adolescents themselves. With regard to indicators, kicking may be a valid indicator of externalizing behavior problems during early childhood but not during adolescence, whereas painting graffiti may be a valid indicator during adolescence but not during early childhood. These differences in informants and indicators introduce the problem of nonequivalent measures across time (van Dulmen & Ong, 2006). In order to address these measurement issues, studies should use advanced analytic procedures (e.g., Confirmatory Factor Analysis, see Curran & Willoughby, 2003; Obradovic, van Dulmen, Yates, Carlson, & Egeland, 2006) to investigate, and account for, measurement equivalence across time.

Studies that used more than two informants identified a larger number of trajectories compared to studies using a single or dual-informant method. On the basis of this information it seems that the number of trajectories increased with the number of informants. However, in absence of a gold standard (i.e., how many trajectories there "truly" are), it could be that aggregating data from multiple informants simply muddies the water and introduces unreliability, leading to greater variability in trajectories. Individual differences research suggests that simply aggregating multiple informant data, as compared to considering the measurement error in the report of various informants, leads to a decrease of predictive validity (van Dulmen & Egeland, under review). It is important for future studies to investigate this methodological issue and to analyze data separately by informant and investigate whether type of informant (or integrating information from multiple informants) affects trajectory findings.

Studies that only focused on girls tended to find a smaller number of trajectories than studies that only focused on males or studies that included both females and males. Previous research and theoretical work has suggested that females follow a unique developmental trajectory (e.g., Silverthorn & Frick,

1999). The findings from this empirical review suggest that, rather than following a unique developmental trajectory, there may be less heterogeneity in trajectories of female externalizing behavior problems as compared to male externalizing behavior problems. It is notable, however, that few studies primarily focus on females, and most studies do not run the analyses separately for males versus females. Therefore, future studies should provide formal comparisons between males and females and investigate this issue.

The findings did not indicate that sample size systematically affected the trajectory findings. Almost all studies, however, included samples exceeding 250 participants. Previous simulation studies have suggested that samples over 250 (D'Unger, Land, McCall, & Nagin, 1998; Sampson, Laub, & Eggleston, 2004) provide reliable results with trajectory modeling.

Future Directions

The results of this review highlight the importance of analyzing trajectory data separately by subtype of externalizing behavior problems and using specificity when operationally defining externalizing behavior problems. In addition, the length of follow-up has a significant impact on trajectory findings with long-term assessments being better able to capture variability in trajectories (see also Eggleston et al., 2004), but our review also suggests that timing of initial assessments has important implications for trajectory findings. The findings from this review indicate that rather than asking whether a minimal number of assessments is necessary to reliably identify developmental trajectories, it is more important to consider whether these assessments span various developmental periods and thus capture age-related changes in behavior.

The various findings of different studies on trajectories further highlight the importance of conducting cross-validations and having multisite studies that enable us to replicate findings across different samples (similar to Broidy, Nagin et al., 2003). Formal statistical comparisons as to how, and why, certain factors may affect the identification of trajectories are dearly needed.

The statistical identification of trajectories of externalizing behavior problems, as well as their correlates and antecedents, has important implications for prevention and intervention efforts. As developmental scholars and criminologists become more familiar with these techniques, it is important quantitative scientists convey the challenges of applying these techniques. The development and application of group-based modeling techniques reflects a unique collaboration between quantitative scholars and developmentalists (Curran & Willoughby, 2003). Recent empirical findings suggest that psychometric and sample properties have important implications for the potential misidentification of trajectories (Bauer & Curran, 2003). In addition, there is some debate as to whether latent class growth modeling or growth mixture modeling provides a better approximation of group membership (see e.g., Muthén, 2004; Nagin, 2005). Latent class growth modeling assumes that there is no variability around the group mean whereas growth mixture modeling allows for variability around the group mean. In essence, this then boils down to a conceptual discussion about the definition of a group or trajectory (see Nagin, 2005). Because of these conceptual challenges that in all likelihood extend to a general understanding and conceptualization of continuity and change, advancing research on externalizing behavior problem trajectories benefits most from an ongoing collaboration between quantitative scholars and developmental scholars. These collaborations no doubt will enhance our ability to understand if, why, and how, children and adolescents are at risk for engaging in criminal activity.

CHAPTER 15

Sanction Threats and Desistance from Criminality

KiDeuk Kim

The term "developmental criminology" is rather novel, although its subject of interest is a long-lived research domain in social science. Traced back to earlier work on criminal careers, considerable efforts have been made to understand the onset of crime and the life course thereafter (see Farrington, 1986; Nagin, Farrington, & Moffitt, 1995; Sampson & Laub, 1993; Wolfgang, Figlio, & Sellin, 1972). There has been a significant amount of work by developmental criminologists, especially over the past decade, devoted to understanding the persistence of criminality. Abundant discussions elucidate issues surrounding the onset of crime and desistance from crime. In particular, numerous researchers draw from social control perspectives in explaining how an individual begins or continues a criminal lifestyle focusing on the lack of self-control or the lack of social bonding (Le Blanc & Kaspy, 1998; Thornberry, 1997).

There have also been discussions directed at understanding desistance from crime. One of the prevailing approaches involves a notion that social bonding would explain crime cessation. For instance, marriage and employment may be seen as strong social ties that offer reasons for offenders to stop offending (Laub & Sampson, 2001; Sampson & Laub, 1993). The discovery that such life events would contribute to the discontinuation of criminal behavior is certainly of great interest. Nonetheless, the fact that the restoration of social control yields an interruption in a criminal life adds relatively little to the current knowledge about the nature of desistance from crime because the lack of social control is often presumed to explain criminal behavior in the first place.

The actual mechanism by which an active offender might stop committing crime has not received a great deal of attention in developmental studies of crime. There are numerous discussions of desistance, but they tend to emphasize how one defines and measures desistance, rather than reasons for desistance (see Bushway, Thornberry & Krohn 2003; Uggen & Piliavin, 1998). That being said, the current essay begins with the recognition that theoretical accounts of desistance from crime should receive more attention than they have yet been given. In comparison to the research on the onset of crime, relatively few studies have been directed at explaining why active offenders would desist from crime.

This essay aims to enrich scholarship and research in the area of the criminal life course by exploring another potential explanation for the desistance from crime: that is, deterrence. Punishment has long been seen as a social institution that is first and foremost a matter of morality and social solidarity (Garland, 1990, p. 28). It appears to be a reasonable proposition that offenders with punishment experiences would be less willing than unpunished offenders to continue criminal behavior. It is of primary interest in this essay to delineate how sanction threats are related to offending behavior. Given that desistance is equal in theoretical significance to onset (Gottfredson & Hirschi, 1990), it also seems important to do so (see Chapter 16, for their conclusions regarding the effectiveness of incarceration for serious juvenile offenders).

In what follows, the existing studies of deterrence are examined to review some of the basic premises underlying criminal behavior and sanction threats. Second, the significance of studying the effect of sanction threats on *change* in criminal behavior is discussed. Third, an analytic framework for examining the effect of sanction threats on change in criminal behavior is proposed. This section illustrates a set of conceptual models to parameterize the effect of legal sanctions on criminal behavior over time. Lastly, the essay concludes by addressing some of the limitations and implications for later studies on the relationship between sanction threats and criminality.

Basic Premises of Deterrence

Despite the complexity involved in the literature, deterrence doctrines are quite simple; first, human beings are presumed to be rational actors and potential offenders engage in rational calculations, which take into account the anticipated benefits and costs associated with the criminal enterprise (Piquero & Rengert, 1999). Sanction threats are therefore expected to deter potential offenders from committing a crime by increasing the perceived costs of criminal behavior. Similarly, actual punishment is also presumed to adjust sanction risk perceptions upward.[1]

Second, specific deterrence refers to the impact of punishment on offenders (who learn from their mistakes and wish to avoid more punishment in the future), whereas general deterrence pertains to the impact of threatened punishment on potential offenders in the population (Zimring & Hawkins, 1973, p. 224). Sanction threats are therefore more suitable for general deterrence and actual punishment is applicable to specific deterrence. From the perspective of developmental criminology, desistance from crime is only relevant for those who have, at least once, been an offender. Therefore, research might focus on the extent to which offenders are deterred from committing a crime due to actual punishment imposed on them. Past research on deterrence has, in fact, focused heavily on whether actual punishment yields a deterrent effect (Ehrlich, 1975; Lynch, 1999; Stolzenberg & D'Alessio, 2004). There is no reason to believe, however, that an offender population is completely immune from legal threats in general. Otherwise stated, offenders are subject to both specific deterrence and general deterrence. Hence, it seems reasonable not to constrain the scope of deterrence to specific deterrence in the current essay.

To examine whether punishment deters crime, researchers have traditionally chosen either an aggregate-level analysis of crime statistics or an individual-level analysis of survey data on offending and punishment experiences.[2] Among numerous approaches, the work of a cadre of scholars that has long focused on how an individual-level assessment of sanction risk perceptions changes in response to self-reported offending/punishment experiences seems particularly relevant to the current discussion (e.g., Grasmick, Jacobs, & McCollom, 1983; Paternoster, Saltzman, Waldo, & Chiricos, 1983). How do offending/punishment experiences in the past

[1] The distinction between actual punishment and sanction risk perceptions has been critical in the research on deterrence, partly because the causal modeling of punishment was often applied in a cross-sectional research design in which risk perceptions were parameterized to reflect a present effect on future behavior. The distinction between actual punishment and perceived sanction threat is therefore relatively less important from the developmental perspective.

[2] This is not to suggest, by any means, that a research design combining macro-level and individual-level processes of deterrence is infeasible or undesirable (see Kleck, Sever, Li, & Gertz, 2005).

explain current perceptions of sanction risk and how do current sanction risk perceptions correlate with offending behavior in the future are two frequently asked questions. The underlying tenet of this approach is that those who expect to be punished would not engage in criminal behavior in the future. Since it is difficult to conduct the type of study required to address these future-tense questions, researchers often undertake a retrospective approach, asking subjects about offending behavior and punishment experience in the past and risk perceptions in the present (Paternoster & Piquero, 1995). Sometimes, deterrence researchers resort to an indirect measure for future offending: offending propensity. Survey respondents are asked to estimate how likely it is that they will engage in a criminal act on the basis of the current knowledge of sanction risk and its consequences. Since the reliability between intended offending and actual future offending is usually unknown, one might prefer testing a relationship between self-reported past behavior and current risk perceptions rather than a relationship between current risk perceptions and projected offending behavior (Grasmick et al., 1983). More recent research does suggest that projected offending is generally correlated with prior offending, future offending, and other criminogenic traits (Pogarsky, 2004).

The literature also shows that the relationship between past offending/punishment experience and perceived sanction risk is likely to be low. Saltzman et al. (1982) argue that most criminal activities are not likely to be punished, and offenders soon recognize that their chances of being apprehended or punished are low relative to their criminal activities (see also Paternoster et al., 1983).[3]

Acknowledging the significance of a causal sequence in the research on perceptual deterrence, a series of related studies has drawn attention to a temporal change in sanction risk perceptions (see Piliavin, Gartner, Thornton, & Matsueda, 1986). One of the fundamental research questions that has emerged is how risk perceptions at a time point A differ from risk perceptions at a time point B with respect to what happened during the interval. While controlling for offending experiences during the interval (experiential effect), researchers predict a positive association between risk perceptions in a later time point and punishment experiences that occurred during the interval (deterrence effect).

---

[3] The negative correlation between offending behavior in the past and risk perceptions in the present may not necessarily reflect the deterrent effect of legal threats, but the "experiential effect" of offending behavior. The distinction between the experiential effect and deterrence effect has since been further discussed (Nagin & Pogarsky, 2003; Pogarsky, 2004; Scheider, 2001).

Some authors have found empirical support for this prediction over several decades. Paternoster et al. (1985) investigated how the perceptions of arrest risk change over time in response to offending and punishment experiences. In their two-wave panel study, formal sanctions were found to elevate the perceived risk of punishment. Similarly, Horney and Marshall (1992) found that individuals who had higher arrest ratios reported high sanction risk perceptions. Lochner (2007) also provided buttressing evidence that prior arrest would raise the estimated chance of arrest and that prior offending behavior would negatively affect the estimated chance of arrest. Wright et al. (2004) also found that perceived risk of getting caught is significantly related to the frequency of self-reported offending.

Much evidence reported in the literature seems largely consistent with the notion that punishment would raise the perceived risk of formal sanctions and thereby lower the offending propensity. However, there have been several other studies reporting an equivocal or null effect of formal sanctions on perceived risk of sanctions or offending. Piliavin et al. (1986) found that the number of prior arrests affected sanction risk perceptions significantly for the youth sample but not for the other samples in their study. Spohn and Holleran (2002) examined the effect of imprisonment on recidivism rate among felony offenders and concluded that there was no support for the deterrent effect of punishment. Pogarsky et al. (2005) also reported that the presence of a prior arrest history yielded a null effect on risk perceptions. Scheider (2001) found that personal experience with crime had no effect on the perceived certainty of formal sanctions. One should not consider such studies as contradicting the principle of deterrence theory, but as complementing the provision of bounded rationality (Simon, 1957); that is, the rational choice framework operates for potential offenders within constraints. The deterrent effect of punishment can therefore be found in empirical studies as conditional on, for example, the characteristics of survey respondents, the design of survey questions, or the adequacy of model specifications.

Saltzman et al. (1982) reported that the effect of offending behavior on risk perceptions was strongest for those who had limited offending experience. Nagin and Paternoster (1993) argued that individuals who are neither strongly committed to crime nor unwaveringly conformist would be most subject to the threat of punishment. Pogarsky (2002) elaborated on the idea of deterrability and characterized three offending profiles—acute conformist, deterrable, and incorrigible—to which the influence of legal sanctions can be differently applied. Likewise, Klepper and Nagin (1989) claimed that the assessment of risk perceptions in panel studies can be unstable and therefore subject to mixed findings concerning the deterrent effect of punishment and offending propensity. The mixed or inconclusive evidence can also be ascribed to the adequacy of model specifications. Nagin and Pogarsky (2003), for example, indicate that because deterrence research may embed (a) ambiguous causality between risk perceptions and punishment experiences and/or (b) equivocal modeling with confounded variables, it has become common to employ certain controls and covariates in the model. The effect of punishment has been estimated in several studies after accounting for extra-legal constraints on crime or other covariates of offending. It seems plausible to assume that there may not be much variation left in the dependent variable to be explained by punishment after removing the shared variance with other controls and covariates of offending. Extra-legal factors such as social support, conventional norms, or personality traits would reportedly yield a strong effect on both individual perceptions and offending behavior (Meier & Johnson, 1977; Nagin & Pogarsky, 2003). Controlling for such factors may effectively "control out" some of the effects of deterrence. The effect of legal sanctions can be moderated by extra-legal sanctions or vice versa. The complexity involved in the model can certainly make it demanding to detect the negative effect of punishment on offending.

To summarize, the deterrence doctrine posits that punished offenders should adjust their sanction risk perceptions in a way that discounts the rewards of criminal enterprise. Desistance from crime should therefore follow punishment or serious threat of punishment. One of the enduring approaches undertaken to test such a theoretical account involves examining the change in sanction risk perceptions between two time points and its association with offending and punishment experiences. However, the dynamics of offending and punishment or perceptions of risk of sanctions and future offending have been scarcely appreciated in a longitudinal framework. It thus appears that several improvements forwarded in developmental criminology to study the continuity and discontinuity of offending behavior might be useful for the research on deterrence.

Modeling Change in Sanction Risk Perceptions

The current chapter is most concerned with sanction risk perceptions and desistance from criminality. This section evaluates the study of change in sanction risk perceptions over time in response to offending/punishment experiences. Let us begin by formulating an analytic framework that tackles the temporal linkage between perceptual and behavioral change toward legal threats.

I begin with the conventional approach. Ideally, using longitudinal data from a panel design, researchers can examine sanction risk perceptions at two sequential time points. Offending/punishment experiences between those two time points can be measured, and any change in sanction risk perceptions from Time 1 to Time 2 may then be examined in relation to those offending/ punishment experiences. The underlying idea involved in this approach is that criminal behavior and its consequences modify and update sanction risk perceptions. Using these data, it is possible to examine the relationship between punishment and risk perceptions at a later time point, while controlling for risk perceptions at an earlier time point. This is one of the conventional approaches to studying the effect of punishment.

Along similar lines, Paternoster et al. (1985) were among the first to examine changes in sanction threats by calculating so-called residual change scores (RCS). Simply put, RCSs are the difference between an observed perceptual measure at Time 2, and its predicted score, using least squares procedures, based on the observed perceptual measure at Time 1. This residualization procedure can be denoted as follows. First, estimate the coefficients:

$$Y = a + bX + \mu \qquad \text{Equation 15.1}$$

where Y is the observed risk perception at Time 2, X is the observed risk perception at Time 1, and μ is an error term. Using the parameter estimates from Equation 15.1, one can simply obtain the predicted score of Y at Time 2 as shown subsequently.

$$\hat{Y} = a + bX \qquad \text{Equation 15.2}$$

where $\hat{Y}$ is the predicted value of Y (perceived risk at Time 2). To obtain residual change scores, Y_{rcs}, one can simply subtract $\hat{Y}$ from Y. That is,

$$Y_{rcs} = Y - \hat{Y} \qquad \text{Equation 15.3}$$

The RCSs are interpreted to reflect the change in the risk perceptions between Time 1 and Time 2 that is not attributable to the initial level of risk perception at Time 1, but to other factors (Pogarsky et al., 2005). Explained differently, Y_{rcs} reflects change, if any, in risk perceptions while controlling for the initial risk perception at Time 1.

Since the earliest discussion of RCSs (Bohrnstedt, 1969), this approach has often been used by criminologists (Bursik & Grasmik, 1992; Bursik & Webb, 1982; Paternoster, Saltzman, Waldo, & Chiricos, 1985; Pogarsky et al., 2005) and researchers in other disciplines (Gordon, 1970; Musick 1996). Yet there seem to be some minor shortcomings embedded in residual change scores. First, as clearly seen in Equation 15.1, the variation in Y is attributable to both X and μ. The residual scores do not exclusively represent perceptual change from Time 1 to Time 2, but are a joint function of perceptual change and the disturbance term, μ. Because the disturbance term captures the effect of all omitted variables in Equation 15.1, the inclusion of the disturbance term interferes with the interpretation of the parameter estimates for the effect of offending or punishment experiences on risk perceptions. Hence, the model specification in Equation 15.1, can have a significant influence on later analyses using residual change scores.

The second shortcoming is rather conceptual and generic to developmental studies. If two observations in different time points are not in a stable metric, it would be misleading to compare pre- and postmeasures. This is not to say that sanction probability estimates should be static over time, but the way survey respondents interpret a questionnaire concerning sanction threats should be stable between earlier and later time points. Put differently, if survey respondents treat the same survey question differently over time, the use of change scores derived from the prediction of the postmeasure can be problematic. This observation challenges deterrence research in that the stability of measurement is least likely to emerge among those whom deterrence researchers want to learn about the most. First, during late childhood, adolescence, and early adulthood, cognitive abilities related to thinking about the future, estimating probabilities, or judgments about severity of punishment are likely to change due to the normal developmental process. Second, going through extreme life events such as starting a criminal career or being sent to a prison can demand from the individual some major change in attitudes and personality (Brim & Kagan, 1980; Connell & Furman, 1984). Perhaps it is not entirely misleading to presume that the cognitive interpretation of sanctions may differ before and after the occurrence of such transitional events. The RCS framework thus requires particular caution in its use even though deterrence research using the RCS framework is rather a significant improvement over cross-sectional research because deterrence is seen as a process, not as an event.

Another motivation for enhancing the RCS framework would be its limitation to examine change of risk perceptions from one time point to the next. The existing studies on perceptual/behavioral change have captured the extent or presence of change, not necessarily the progression of change. Through an examination of the difference between two measurements in different time periods, it is difficult to fully understand how risk perceptions have been developed over time. One should not overlook how would-be offenders engage in criminal activities, get punished or unpunished, and accordingly adjust risk perceptions gradually over time. Given some of the research evidence favoring a causal claim for sanction risk perceptions and other covariates, it seems desirable for deterrence studies to explore the change of behavioral and perceptual measures in a more dynamic framework. The next section introduces models that reflect the progression of change in risk perceptions. A suggested framework for analyzing the dynamics of offending and punishment using longitudinal data will be presented.

Modeling the Effect of Legal Threats over Time

In modeling change with longitudinal data from a panel design, a few approaches have proliferated in recent decades. Two such examples are group-based trajectory modeling (Nagin 1999, 2005) and growth curve modeling (Muthén, 1997; Singer & Willett, 2003). A structured discussion about the pros and cons of both approaches is beyond the scope of the current discussion. Yet the current section focuses on the deterrent effect of punishment (or legal threats) in the framework of growth curve modeling because it has the advantage of retaining individual variations in the dependent variable unlike group-based modeling techniques, which summarize individual properties into trajectory groups (Nagin 1999, 2005; also see Chapter 14).

Basic Growth Models

Change in offending behavior or risk perceptions over time can be modeled as the temporal dependence of individual status on time. In other words, a repeated measure of offending (or offending propensity) or punishment (or punishment threats) can be examined as a function of time. For the current purpose of illustration, modeling perceptual measures (i.e., perceived risk of sanctions or projected offending) seems largely equivalent to modeling actual events (i.e., the number of crimes committed or sentences received). Although the distinction between both approaches will be made clear in a later section, all the models described hereafter will focus on the change in offending behavior in the interest of simplicity. Applications or extensions to more complex models are also easily achievable, but not crucial to understand the main proposition of this essay. First, we can specify a basic model as follows:

$$\text{OFFENDING}_{ij} = p_{oj} + p_{1j}T_{ij} + e_{ij}, \qquad \text{Equation 15.4a}$$

where OFFENDING $_{ij}$ represents the offending measure for individual j at time i, p_{oj} is the intercept of the offending growth (or trajectory) for individual j, p_{ij} is the slope of that growth for individual j, T_{ij} is the time corresponding to each measurement for individual j, and e_{ij} represents a random component for individual j at time i.

This is a pure within-subject design because no other explanatory variables are included except for the measurement occasions (T_{ij}). The model examines the within-subject variation in offending behavior over time. The intercept and slope of the individual growth of offending behavior can be relaxed on each measurement occasion by including random components:

$$p_{oj} = \text{\ss}_{oo} + \mu_{oj} \qquad\qquad\qquad \text{Equation 15.4b}$$

$$p_{ij} = \text{\ss}_{10} + \mu_{1ij}, \qquad\qquad\qquad \text{Equation 15.4c}$$

where $\text{\ss}_{oo}$ and $\text{\ss}_{10}$ reflect the initial status and the rate of the growth, respectively; and μ_{oi} and μ_{1i} are random components for the growth parameters. By substitution, we obtain the single equation:

$$\text{OFFENDING}_{ij} = (\text{\ss}_{oo} + \mu_{oj}) + (\text{\ss}_{10} + \mu_{1ij})\, T_{ij} + e_{ij} \qquad \text{Equation 15.5}$$

This model simply draws a straight line that best summarizes the population relationship between individual growth parameters, $\text{\ss}_{oo}$ and $\text{\ss}_{10}$, which are the intercept and slope of that straight line respectively. Both random components (μ_{oj} and μ_{1ij}) attached to the growth parameters allow them to vary across individuals. Suppose, for example, that we intend to model the growth pattern of drug use among adolescents and our dependent variable was measured by the number of times one used illegal drugs last year. The value of $\text{\ss}_{oo}$ will indicate how much drug use was prevalent among the adolescents when first measured. The value of $\text{\ss}_{10}$ will then show how rapidly or slowly drug use increases or decreases among adolescents over time.

Since the straight-line model has limited flexibility in capturing individual growth, one might well consider a nonlinear approach, which allows a versatile growth rate relative to time. Shown subsequently is one such example.

$$\text{OFFENDING}_{ij} = p_{oj} + p_{1j}T_{ij} + p_{2j}T^2_{ij} + e_{ij} \qquad \text{Equation 15.6}$$

The aforementioned quadratic model is identical to Equation 15.4a except for the inclusion of $p_{2j}T^2_{ij}$, which permits the accelerating or decelerating growth rate of offending behavior. All other coefficients should be interpreted in much the same way as before and as any other regression models. It is straightforward to construct a higher polynomial trend or even more versatile nonlinear pattern. Although no further elaboration of the basic growth model seems necessary for the current discussion, it should be noted that choosing the lowest-order polynomial is often preferable not only because it is parsimonious, but also because it allows more precision in estimating effects of interest (Raudenbush, 2004).

Covariate Adjustment and Change Score Models

In examining change in longitudinal data, it is fairly common to use prior observations as covariates in models for current observations (Diggle, Liang, & Zeger, 1996). The inclusion of prior observations can serve as a baseline for estimation. For example, offending behavior at Time 0 can be included in the model predicting offending behavior at Time 1 and control for the earlier status of offending behavior. From Equation 15.4a the inclusion of a prior offending measure can be denoted as follows:

$$\text{OFFENDING}_{ij} = p_{oj} + p_{1j} T_{ij}$$
$$+ p_{2j} \text{OFFENDING}_{(i-1)j} + e_{ij}, \qquad \text{Equation 15.7}$$

where $\text{OFFENDING}_{(i-1)j}$ is offending behavior measured at Time i-1 for individual j. This model controls for "trait" or typical continuity; that is, those with high levels of criminal involvement in the past would be more likely than their counterparts to show high levels of criminal involvement in the present. Again, one can expand Equation 15.7 by including random components for the growth parameters or by introducing nonlinear terms in the model.

There are a few empirical restrictions involved in the model. This model carries the assumption that residual error terms are independent across multiple measurement points. Also, the correlation across multiple measurement points is assumed to be explained by the inclusion of the prior offending measure in the model. Such a constraint can become more restrictive as other covariates are inserted in the model. For instance, let us consider an indicator of whether one has ever been a victim of child abuse. Using the earlier example of drug use among adolescents, one can theorize that having been a victim of child abuse (VICTIM) would cause poor attachment formation, poor physical development, or antisocial behavior such as illegal drug use. The relationship between VICTIM and drug use can then be expressed as follows:

$$\text{OFFENDING}_{ij} = p_{oj} + p_{1j} T_{ij} + p_{2j} \text{OFFENDING}_{(i-1)j}$$
$$+ p_{3j} \text{VICTIM}_j + e_{ij}, \qquad \text{Equation 15.8}$$

where the dichotomous indicator VICTIM represents whether individual j has even been a victim of child abuse. In the aforementioned example, both OFFENDING$_{ij}$ and OFFENDING$_{(i-1)j}$ can be a function of VICTIM, and its effect on offending behavior is theorized to persist over time. Depending on measurement intervals and/or the nature of covariates to be adjusted, assuming such an enduring effect could be a demanding challenge for researchers.

As an alternative approach to examining the individual growth of offending behavior while adjusting for the "trait," it is also feasible to use first differences of the offending measure. That is,

$$\Delta(\text{OFFENDING})_{ij} = p_{oj} + p_{1j}T_{ij} + p_{2j}\text{VICTIM}_j + e_{ij}, \quad \text{Equation 15.9}$$

where $\Delta(\text{OFFENDING})_{ij}$ is a change score, OFFENDING$_{ij}$ – OFFENDING$_{(i-1)j}$. Change score models bear a restrictive assumption about residual terms. No correlation is assumed across time in the residual error terms for an individual change in offending behavior (McCaffrey, Lockwood, Koretz, Louis, & Hamilton, 2004, pp. 78–80). Another noteworthy drawback in using change scores is that a valid observation is required for two time points to extract a difference score. If the measured score of offending behavior at either one of the time points is not missing at random, the model might suffer a selection bias (Little & Rubin, 1987). Nonetheless, there are some grounds on which to prefer change score models over covariate adjustment models. The efficiency in model estimation and the transparency in result interpretations would be two most conspicuous advantages. Because change scores simply represent how much a subject of interest changed over time, the interpretation of estimates should be straightforward.

Parameterizing a Punishment Effect

Let us now focus on how to parameterize the deterrent effect of punishment. A simplistic form of growth models is considered subsequently.

$$\text{Level-1: OFFENDING}_{ij} = p_{oj} + p_{1j}T_{ij} + e_{ij} \qquad \text{Equation 15.10a}$$

$$\text{Level-2: } p_{oi} = \beta_{oo} + \beta_{o1}(\text{SANCTION}_j) \qquad \text{Equation 15.10b}$$

$$\text{Level-2: } p_{1i} = \beta_{10} + \beta_{11}(\text{SANCTION}_j), \qquad \text{Equation 15.10c}$$

where the dichotomous indicator SANCTION indicates whether individual j had been punished in a given time period. The growth of offending is characterized at Level-1 by two parameters, p_{oj} and p_{1j}, and sanction was inserted at Level-2 to have an effect on both parameters. By substitution, we obtain the following:

$$\text{OFFENDING}_{ij} = \text{\ss}_{oo} + \text{\ss}_{o1}(\text{SANCTION}_{j}) + \text{\ss}_{1o}T_{ij}$$
$$+ \text{\ss}_{11}(\text{SANCTION}_{j}){\cdot}T_{ij} + e_{ij} \qquad \text{Equation 15.11}$$

There are two parameters estimating the effect of punishment. The coefficient, $\text{\ss}_{o1}$, assesses the main effect of punishment on offending, and the coefficient, $\text{\ss}_{11}$, captures the interaction between punishment and time. This equation, as depicted in Figure 15.1, represents a piecewise linear growth model with differential slopes.

The slopes reflect growth rates of offending behavior before and after punishment. The main effect of punishment, $\text{\ss}_{o1}$, is shown as a break between two slopes. The interaction term of sanction and time allows the slopes of offending to vary before and after punishment. The value of $\text{\ss}_{1o}$ reflects the growth rate of offending before punishment and the value of $(\text{\ss}_{1o} + \text{\ss}_{11})$ indicates the growth rate of offending after punishment. To avoid complexity, Figure 15.1 and Equation 15.11 do not consider any nonlinear growth patterns or multiple punishment occasions resulting in more than two differential slopes.

There are many ways of modeling the effect of punishment. This model, however, is particularly useful for detecting an abrupt discontinuity in individual growth. Since it is reasonable to think that the deterrent effect is largest immediately upon the infliction of punishment, testing a sudden change in offending trajectories before and after punishment is an appropriate test of sanction effects on criminal behavior. Further, it is notable to acknowledge

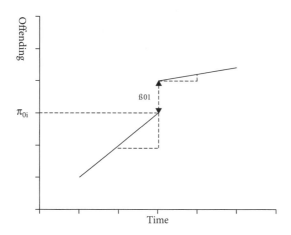

FIGURE 15.1   Modeling the effect of punishment.

that the model truly examines the progression of change in that the effect of punishment measured on multiple occasions can now be fully explored.

There also emerges an interesting facet of modeling the effect of punishment from a longitudinal perspective; that is, the deterrent effect of punishment can be conceived as both within-subject and between-subject processes. On the one hand, deterrence researchers have long examined if those who have been punished show significantly lower levels of criminal involvement (or equivalently higher levels of sanction threat perceptions) than those who have not. Punishment experience may differ between individuals, and therefore the deterrent effect of punishment can be modeled as a between-subject effect. On the other hand, when an individual has received a legal sanction on multiple occasions, he or she could have been punished more often or more severely in one time period than another. The effect of punishment can thus vary within a subject.

Among others, one theoretical motivation for researching the within-subject effect of punishment deserves particular attention because it bears on an intriguing question that has long been proposed: would offenders be influenced by punishment more at a younger age than at an older age or, analogously, would the deterrent effect of punishment vary relative to where offenders are situated on their offending trajectory yet to unfold? Deterrence researchers have long suggested that acute offenders are less sensitive than naïve offenders to legal threats (Block & Gerety, 1995; Bridges & Stone, 1986; Pogarsky 2002). Although the sensitivity to punishment has only been discussed as a between-subject effect, it seems reasonable to explore how an offender modifies cognitive or behavioral reaction to legal sanctions during the progression of his own criminal career or with age.

As far as parameterizing this effect is concerned, one of the simplest approaches to building a model would be through the use of time-variant effects and random components. Using the same equations discussed earlier, we can express the full model with random effects as follows:

$$\text{Level-1: OFFENDING}_{ij} = p_{oj} + p_{1j}T_{ij}$$
$$+ p_{2j}\text{SANCTION}'_{ij} + e_{ij} \qquad \text{Equation 15.12a}$$

$$\text{Level-2: } p_{oi} = \text{\ss}_{oo} + \mu_{oj} \qquad\qquad\qquad \text{Equation 15.12b}$$

$$\text{Level-2: } p_{1i} = \text{\ss}_{10} + \mu_{1j}, \qquad\qquad\qquad \text{Equation 15.12c}$$

$$\text{Level-2: } p_{2i} = \text{\ss}_{20} + \mu_{2j},$$

where SANCTION' is a repeated measure of punishment for individual j at time i (e.g., how often, how severely, or whether an individual has been punished since the last measurement occasion), and $\{\mu_{oj}...\mu_{3j}\}$ are the error variance of the estimates. By substitution, the combined single model can be expressed as follows:

$$\text{OFFENDING}_{ij} = [\text{ß}_{00} + \text{ß}_{10}T_{ij} + \text{ß}_{20}\text{SANCTION}'_{ij}] + [\mu_{0j} + \mu_{1j}T_{ij} + \mu_{2j}\text{SANCTION}'_{ij} + e_{ij}], \qquad \text{Equation 15.13}$$

where structural and random elements of the equation were separately bracketed. This model has two major alterations from the earlier model wherein punishment was considered as a time-invariant effect. First, a repeated measure of punishment is employed as a time-variant effect at Level-1. Of particular interest in this model is to examine a within-subject difference in the effect of punishment (ß_{20}). Therefore, a measure of punishment or sanction threats assessed on multiple measurement occasions is required for this model. Second, a compound symmetry model is assumed in a hierarchical approach to analyzing longitudinal data. That is, all population variances of the repeated measures are equal and all population covariances of the repeated measures are equal (Hox, 2002; Snijders & Bosker, 1999). This model relaxes the assumption of uniformity across measurement occasions by allowing all the structural coefficients, the slope and intercept, to have random effects. The random components, μ_{0j}, μ_{1j}, and μ_{2j}, thus represent a between-subject residual variance in the initial status of offending behavior, the growth rate of offending, and the deterrent effect of punishment, respectively. In other words, the model implies that the rate of growth or trend across measurement occasions is not the same for all individuals.

To summarize, the effect of punishment has been structured into an analytic framework involving longitudinal data from a panel design. The models and examples demonstrated earlier are based on analytic techniques already in use and are offered to stimulate research and analysis on an underdeveloped question in deterrence research: that is, how legal threats or sanctions can longitudinally affect the development of criminality. It is important to recognize that such an attempt to learn about deterrence can be more hampered by theory or data than by the ability to parameterize models.

Considerations for Future Research

Essential in the purpose of this chapter is to explore how individuals are restrained from crime as a consequence of legal threats. Individual trajectories of offending behavior and risk perceptions were particularly considered from empirical and theoretical perspectives. There are a few implications and considerations for future research that seem noteworthy.

Benefits of Longitudinal Approach

Decades of research has investigated how punishment affects criminal behavior by modifying sanction risk perceptions. Most approaches adopted a cross-sectional research design in which behavioral measures and perceptual measures of punishment and offending were tested for causality. Findings have often been challenged and contested over the adequacy of causal modeling (see Paternoster et al., 1983). Thus, a longitudinal approach to modeling the effect of punishment has long been sought. An analytic framework based on longitudinal data may alleviate difficulties involved in establishing the causal relationship between offending behavior and punishment. Without resorting to controversial causality or measures (i.e., projected offending), it is feasible to directly test deterrence by examining change in offending behavior over time in relation to punishment experiences. One can also examine change in sanction risk perceptions over time if a cognitive process of deterrence is of major interest. In all, the longitudinal approach to modeling behavioral or perceptual change can improve conceptual clarity in testing deterrence.

How Should Punishment Work?

The effect of punishment has been tested in numerous studies, most of which adhered to the doctrine of deterrence research and did not add much to the notion that punishment should deter a would-be offender. However, a few approaches extended the scope of deterrence research by recounting the specific conditions or processes by which punishment exerts a deterrent effect. Particularly, one thread of discussion regarding the longevity of deterrence seems highly relevant to and useful for the present chapter. Often conceived as deterrence decay in studies examining the effect of consolidated police activities on crime (Millie, 2005; Sherman, 1990) or as a short-term/long-term effect of deterrence in studies modeling time-series of crime and punishment (Chamlin, Grasmick, Bursik, & Cochran, 1992; Stolzenberg & D'Alessio, 2004), it has been of interest to learn how long the deterrent effect of punishment would last. Yet little effort has been forwarded to theorize the duration for which the deterrent effect of punishment persists or the process by which punishment exerts its deterrent effect.

In the context of growth modeling, examining such features of punishment seems quite viable at an individual level. On the basis of the models discussed in the present chapter, one can develop an analytic framework to explore several aspects of deterrence that have not been much researched. Is the effect of punishment time-dependent? Does the effect of punishment persist over time or is it transitory? Is the deterrent effect of punishment instantaneous or delayed? There emerge several time-related questions on the deterrent effect of punishment, which can feasibly be studied in the growth modeling framework by specifying a linear or nonlinear growth pattern (or the combination of both) of offending behavior or sanction risk perceptions. Much research is needed to advance our understanding on the duration, timing, or longevity of deterrence and circumstances under which punishment exerts the most instantaneous and persistent effect on would-be offenders.

Punishment Sensitivity and Its Implications

Another observation worth emphasizing in the present chapter is that the effect of punishment is sensitive to levels of criminality or criminal history of the offender. An experienced criminal can develop a calloused indifference to legal sanction threats whereas an acute conformist can easily be intimidated by such threats. Thus, a nonoffender or individual with few offending experiences would perceive legal sanctions to be more certain than others (Pogarsky, 2002). The effect of punishment can differ across individuals with varying levels of sensitivity to punishment.

It is largely unknown, however, whether the effect of punishment would vary within the same individual. One might speculate that the effect of punishment may vary depending on where the offender is located on the age-crime curve. One might also hypothesize that the offender would be more impervious to sanction threats at the peak of a criminal career than at the onset of a criminal career. In the present chapter, several models were presented to demonstrate how to design such an analysis examining the within-subject effect of punishment on offending trajectory. It seems highly promising to learn about how an offender would change responsiveness to sanction threats relative to time in his or her life.

One caveat against modeling the within-subject effect of punishment is, however, that finding data with sufficient within-subject variation in punishment experiences can be difficult. It would take extensive time and effort to capture the full spectrum of variation in probation and imprisonment, for example. To obtain sufficient variation in such experiences, one might therefore consider focusing on (or oversampling) high-risk offenders, which adds another dimension to the complexity of data. Because offenders cannot be (or at least are not fully) at risk for offending while serving a jail or prison term, the calculation of the actual time at risk or exposure time would be necessary to yield unbiased estimates (and especially so when high-risk offenders are oversampled in the study). Without accounting for the actual time at risk, one would be likely to underestimate the effect of covariates for those who have been incarcerated for a long period. Moreover, data attrition would be expected for those who are most subject to repeated sanctioning processes. As would-be offenders experience through the criminal justice system and engage in criminal activities over time, it would be more difficult to maintain contact with them and obtain cooperation from them in the second or subsequent waves of a panel study.

In modeling the within-subject effect of punishment, it thus seems reasonable to relax the scope of punishment. Punishment can refer to a variety of forcible controls over wrongdoers. State-imposed sentences are not the only mechanism to deter would-be offenders. Administrative restrictions or supervisory orders can also serve as a punitive threat to would-be offenders. For example, school punishment can be an intimidating or, at least, an unpleasant experience for adolescents. Being stopped or searched by the police can also be an unnerving experience for likely criminals. Feeney et al. (1983) found evidence that arrests that did not result in convictions may be punitive, probably through informal social processes. In all, a flexible approach to conceptualizing and operationalizing punishment should be encouraged to explore the within-subject effect of punishment.

Part V

Conceptualizing the Persistent Offender

CHAPTER 16

Serious Juvenile Offenders and Persistent Criminality

RUDY HAAPANEN, LEE BRITTON, TIM CROISDALE,
AND BRANKO COEBERGH

Youth entering state-level institutions at the California Youth Authority[1] (CYA) are, with few exceptions, already persistent offenders. Typically, these young offenders have a combination of serious and violent behavior and a history of repeated failure to respond to earlier interventions.[2] They average around 10 prior arrest charges, typically have several prior local confinements, and tend to be well-known to the youth-serving and social service agencies in their communities (Richardson, 2001). In early adulthood they will commit

[1] In July 2005, the CYA was merged with the California Department of Corrections to form the California Department of Corrections and Rehabilitation. The CYA became the Juvenile Justice Division of this new Department. For clarity, this chapter will use the former name, which was used when the wards upon whom this chapter is based were housed there.

[2] The California Juvenile Justice System is decentralized, with 99% of all juvenile arrests handled at the county level. State-level commitment to secure California Youth Authority (CYA) facilities, while available as an option, is reserved for the most serious and persistent offenders—those for whom county-level options, such as probation, group homes, short-term stays in juvenile hall, or camp placements are considered inappropriate.

more offenses than they did as juveniles (considering an equal number of years) and, if followed long enough, virtually all (over 90%) will continue to be arrested as adults (Croisdale, 2007). Thus, these youth fit almost any definition of "persistent offender," both as juveniles and as adults. As juveniles, they have reached the end of the line—the last stop in the California juvenile justice system, largely based on their persistence in criminal behavior. As adults, they are starting down a road that, for most, will include additional arrests and incarcerations, although at a rate that decreases with age.

Not surprisingly, these youths have attracted considerable interest from researchers. As the largest population of very serious youthful offenders in secure, relatively long-term confinement (averaging over 2 years), the youths committed to the California Youth Authority have been the subject of a great deal of research over the years. Some of the more notable research has included studies of institutional treatment programs and approaches (Bottcher & Ezell, 2005; Jesness, 1971, 1975; Palmer, 2002), parole programs (Haapanen & Britton, 2002; Palmer 1974), classification systems for delinquents (Jesness, 1988), gender differences (Bottcher, 1986, 2001), mental health and substance abuse issues (Cauffman, Feldman, Waterman, & Steiner, 1998; Haapanen & Steiner, 2003; Steiner & Humphreys, 2001; Wilson, Rojas, Haapanen, Duxbury, & Steiner, 2001), personality (Steiner, Cauffman, & Duxbury, 1999) and long-term trends, and predictability of criminal careers (Croisdale, 2007; Ezell & Cohen, 2005; Haapanen, 1990; Haapanen & Jesness, 1982; Piquero, Brame, Mazerolle, & Haapanen, 2002; Skonovd & Haapanen, 1998).

Taken together, these studies, supplemented by recent analysis of admission trends and arrest follow-up data for youth released from California Youth Authority facilities over the past fifteen years, paint an interesting picture of persistent juvenile offending and its relation to adult offending patterns. We will summarize these findings, and then discuss their implications for understanding serious, persistent criminality.

As noted earlier, these young offenders tend to be very active in crime before admission to the CYA, averaging about ten arrest charges prior to commitment. Over 60% of youth entering the CYA are committed for violent offenses, and of those committed for other offenses, six in ten have a violent or sex offense included as part of their referral package. In all, 85% have a violent or sex offense in their histories along with a number of other types of offenses.

These young men (and women) also have multiple, major social deficits. Many have already dropped out of school and most have few, if any, employment skills. Average reading levels are below the sixth grade. The vast majority (over 70%) are substance abusers. Not counting conduct and substance-related disorders, 30% of the males and 60% of the females entering the CYA have serious mental health problems (Steiner & Humphreys, 2001). Many have parents or siblings in the criminal justice system and most (over 80%) are involved with gangs. Thus, in addition to their substantial criminality, these youth also have serious obstacles to developing normal, prosocial lifestyles. There is considerable variation among these offenders; however, in such characteristics as self-restraint, anger, or personality characteristics that might be thought important to serious delinquency.

Despite their heavy involvement in serious delinquency before commitment, arrests in the years following release average about one arrest per year or less, and one in three have no arrests at all during the first 3 years after release. Moreover, the arrest rate continues to decline overall each year following release. This massive, sudden drop in arrests for those committed to the CYA goes beyond what might be expected simply from maturation, and suggests a rather strong overall effect of this intervention, as we shall see subsequently.

Within this general pattern, there is a great deal of variation among individuals. Arrest charges within 5 years of release range from zero to over forty. Over 10 years, the number of charges ranges from zero to over fifty. These kinds of individual differences seem to suggest variability in criminal "propensity," or "risk of recidivism" (Andrews & Bonta, 2006) that might reasonably be related to (even "caused by") the kinds of social deficits and individual characteristics, also known as criminogenic needs, noted previously. Such presumed causal factors are the targets of interventions aimed at reducing the criminal behavior of these, most active, offenders. Prediction studies have focused on numbers of arrests (Ezell & Cohen, 2005; Haapanen & Jesness, 1982; Lattimore, McDonald, Piquero, Linster, & Visher, 2004; Lattimore, Visher, & Linster, 1995), on the "seriousness" of the arrests (Haapanen & Jesness, 1982), the "timing" of arrests (Visher, Lattimore, & Linster, 1991), specialization (Lattimore, Visher, & Linster, 1994), and the "trajectories" of arrest patterns over time (Ezell, 2007b; Haapanen, Britton, & Croisdale, 2007; Piquero, Brame et al., 2002). The results for CYA youth have paralleled those for other populations of offenders, finding, for the most part, that prediction of differences in future criminal behavior within populations of persistent offenders is extremely difficult (Cernkovich & Giordano, 2001; Gottfredson & Gottfredson, 1986, 1994).

The best predictors of future arrests among all serious criminal populations are indicators of prior criminality, for instance, the age of first arrest and the number of prior arrests (Gottfredson & Hirschi, 1990; Laub & Sampson, 2003; Moffit, 1993). The additional predictive power provided by prior noncrime characteristics (substance abuse, parental supervision, mental health, gang involvement as a measure of criminal associates, etc.) tends to be fairly low. Once prior arrests are taken into account, there is little additional contribution of these social variables to explaining relative levels of post-release arrest among persistent offenders. Despite advances in statistical analysis techniques and computerized modeling methods, the goal of identifying the characteristics that make some young, persistent offenders more active in crime as adults than others has been elusive.

Further complicating this effort is the fact that adult criminal behavior patterns vary substantially over time for individual offenders. Not only do persistent offenders commit a wide variety of crimes, but their arrests tend not to be spaced evenly throughout their "careers" (DeLisi, 2005; Haapanen, 1990; Haapanen et al., 2007). Relative to one another, the highest rate offenders during particular periods (of as much as 4 years) tend not to be the highest rate offenders in subsequent periods (Haapanen, 1990). While Croisdale (2007) suggests that persistent offenders may simply offend in cyclical patterns, we will suggest below that these up-and-down changes over time reflect natural instability in the criminal behavior of persistent offenders and the effects of prison terms or other criminal justice interventions that are applied to these offenders. Offenders tend to be incarcerated following a period of accelerating arrests and then show, again, a major drop-off in arrests following release. This before–after decline is considerably larger than the natural decline by age over similar periods observed for offenders who avoid incarceration (Haapanen et al., 2007).

Coupled with this instability of criminal behavior is a similar instability in lifestyles. Offenders released from CYA institutions, like other populations of serious, chronic offenders, tend to have unstable (and marginal) employment, unstable marriages, and unstable living arrangements (DeLisi, 2005; Gottfredson & Hirschi, 1990; Haapanen, 1990; Robins, 1966; Sampson & Laub, 1993, 2003, 2005a). It appears that criminality (as measured by arrests) is highest during periods of unemployment, drug use, and single living, but the ameliorative effects of jobs, marriage, and abstinence tend to be small and short-lived (Blumstein, Cohen, Roth, & Visher, 1986; Haapanen, 1990; Robins, 1966; Sampson & Laub, 2005a). Qualitative studies have shown that among serious youthful offenders, few, if any, escape the criminal life altogether (Hagedorn, 1994) and may even find a lifestyle free from jobs, marriages, and other social entanglements to be to their liking (Allerton, 1972; Jacobs & Wright, 1999).

Overall, the picture that emerges from these studies of former CYA wards and other populations of very persistent offenders is that persistence is not a matter of becoming more criminal or of becoming a busier and better offender. Rather, persistence appears to be more a matter of failure to do anything else, an unwillingness or inability to meet the expectations and constraints that characterize more legitimate lifestyles. If the substantial variation in arrests among these persistent offenders as adults were due to individual differences in criminal propensity, we would expect to be able to predict those differences, but their predictability is very low (Sampson & Laub, 2003). We might also expect those propensity differences to manifest themselves in stable differences in criminality (arrests) over time, as offenders settle into patterns of crime and hone their criminal skills, but this kind of stability has not been found. We might expect that arrest differences would be paralleled by differences in lifestyle characteristics, such as marriage, employment, or drug use, but these relationships are modest, at best, and these characteristics are themselves very unstable (Haapanen, 1990; Robins, 1966; Sampson & Laub, 2003). We might expect persistent criminals to be committed to crime as a way of life, but first-hand accounts tend to show a greater devotion to "getting by," making a "fast buck," and avoiding the day-to-day grind of steady work than to crime itself (Allerton, 1972; Hagedorn, 1994; Jacobs & Wright, 1999). As a common characteristic, persistent criminals appear to be as much (or more) anticonventional-lifestyle than procriminal-lifestyle.

Persistence and Resistance to Social Control

Elsewhere, we presented the idea that these kinds of findings can be understood from a perspective that links persistent offending to "resistance to social control" (Haapanen et al., 2007). In this view, persistent criminality is not so much about crime as it is about the failure to establish a viable alternative to it. The persistent offender resists the demands and expectations of family, friends, employers, spouses, and authorities. This resistance is evidenced most clearly in relation to criminal justice sanctions, in that the persistent offender continues to get arrested despite repeated, and increasingly severe, sanctions. Through their natural processes, the juvenile and criminal justice systems identify offenders who are resistant to formal efforts; each new arrest indicates resistance to all sanctions to that point. Offenders with many arrests, then, are by definition, resistant to formal social control. But this resistance also extends to other forms of social control, as well—most notably those associated with jobs and marriages. Resistance is the external aspect of what Gottfredson and Hirschi (1990) describe as self-control. It manifests both as an aversion to long-term social entanglements such as marriages or steady jobs, that bring with them demands and expectations (i.e., social control) and as a reduced amenability to attempts at external control through punitive and/or rehabilitative efforts.

As an explanation of crime continuance, the significance of this resistance perspective is that it places the emphasis on persistence, rather than on criminality. It suggests that for those who resist social control, an extraordinarily high level of motivation toward criminal behavior is not required in order to sustain crime. In addition to a basic willingness to break the law, all that is needed for sustained criminal behavior is that offenders fail to pursue other avenues. For resistant offenders, crime is an option requiring little effort, and offending may therefore be little more than what is left after more legitimate pursuits have been rejected. As such, this perspective suggests that the resultant crime will have little character of its own. It is not driven by particular motivation or patterned by social structures in the offender's life. Resistance to social control, in fact, implies little motivation and the absence of stabilizing social structures. The resultant crime would be influenced primarily by immediate, situational circumstances and opportunities, and would be relatively unstable and unpredictable. As such, we expect persistent offenders to be more versatile than specific in offending and commit any number of different crime types.

As suggested earlier, this perspective is most closely linked to the concept of "low self-control" (Gottfredson & Hirschi, 1990). This concept includes both a lack of internal self-restraint, making pleasure-seeking, hedonistic, selfish, and risky behaviors more likely, as well as lower responsiveness to external controls against those behaviors. The two are often regarded as two sides of the same coin; after all, acting out in hedonistic and impulsive ways presupposes that external controls have failed as well. However, the two aspects can be separated, at least conceptually. It is possible, for example, that a person with a low drive for excitement or adventure could find it easy to control those impulses and yet still find the demands of school or work to be too taxing. This person would have high internal control (relative to his own impulses) and be resistant to external controls. Conversely, an individual with little internal self-control may still respond to the demands and expectations of others simply to avoid the consequences of not doing so. The graduated sanctions embedded in the juvenile and criminal justice systems, indeed, are predicated on the idea that those with low internal control may still be kept in check by applying appropriate consequences for misbehavior. It would be safe to say, however, that the two sources of control tend to go together, for the most part, because those with higher self-restraint will find it easier to respond to the expectations of those around them. It is the contribution and consequences of this reduced response to formal authority and its general foundation in resistance to social control more generally that are the focus of this discussion.

It is very important to note that this resistance does not have to be "active," in the sense of deliberate defiance. It is not necessarily "antisocial," in the common sense of the term, but simply anti-social-control. A resistant offender may be openly antagonistic to the boss or may also just walk off the job or fail to show up because he's tired of the boss telling him what to do. Offenders may not be aware of their resistance. Resistance to social control does not necessarily suggest a conscious strategy of these offenders, but rather simply describes the outcome of their interactions with the forces of control in their lives. An offender may have chronic car trouble or hangovers, or other personal problems that prevent him from getting to work on time, resulting in job loss, and yet never attribute the consequences to anything besides bad luck or an over-controlling boss.

People seem to differ along a dimension of resistance, with some individuals finding it easier than others to meet the demands and expectations of conventional life and some being more compliant by nature. Some individuals may want to succeed but simply find themselves unable to do so. Others may chafe at the demands of normal social life, choosing to resist despite having the ability and opportunity to succeed. These resistant individuals, moreover, may have a variety of ways of interpreting and understanding their own situations and their own motivations. Some may see themselves as failures, while others may experience the lifestyle more as positive self-actualization, as independence, and as freedom from the day-to-day grind of the workaday world (Allerton, 1972; Jacobs & Wright, 1999). Being context-specific, differences in resistance may be difficult to observe if demands are low, and the same individual may find certain social settings more difficult to manage than others.

It is also important to note that this kind of general resistance to social control does not necessarily lead to crime, but its chronic, extreme form does lead to conditions that increase the salience of crime as a way of life. Many people long for freedom from entanglements at particular points in their lives. Students, for example, may take a year off to travel or play. Other individuals may opt for lifestyles that minimize demands and long-term expectations. Individuals who strongly resist social control are unlikely to achieve a great deal of success at legitimate pursuits, but they may still manage to get by on handouts, social welfare, odd jobs, or the generosity of family. These noncriminal sources of "income" generally are minimal and short-lived, and they also often bring with them well-meaning concern, pressure, stigma, disapproval, and/or demands for change—that is, attempts at social control. Moreover, sources of livelihood, which require more than a minimum of skill, knowledge, and experience, get farther and farther out of reach for those who chronically resist social control, cutting them off from all but the most menial jobs.

Such individuals may avoid major involvement with the criminal justice system, but options for legitimate lifestyles become fewer and fewer, and these require greater and greater effort. The longer one resists, the harder it is to get back on track. For those who do choose to offend, resistance to social control puts alternatives to crime farther and farther out of reach, and may make persistent criminality more likely. In her discussion of mechanisms that create continuity of antisocial behavior from early childhood through adolescence, Moffit (1993) refers to this process as "cumulative consequences" (p. 683).

Arrests and Juvenile Commitment as Indicators of Resistance

Resistance to social control can, of course, be seen as part of the basic definition of persistent offending: continuing to commit crimes despite criminal (and juvenile) justice attention. Arrests are not simply counts of actual or suspected crimes, they are indicators of interventions. Repeated arrests, moreover, indicate repeated, and typically escalating, interventions. As a general rule, juvenile offenders who get arrested many times experience increasingly severe sanctions and/or intensive efforts to change their behavior. Each new crime is taken as evidence that earlier interventions failed and that more harsh, intensive, and/or restrictive sanctions are needed.

While the tendency for sanctions to increase in severity with repeated crimes is found both at the adult and juvenile levels, this pattern is clearest at the juvenile level, where persistent offending typically has its origins. Interventions at the juvenile level are supposed to be crafted to meet the particular needs of the youth and his/her family. Rather than meting out particular punishments for particular crimes, as in the adult justice system, the juvenile justice system uses crime as an indicator that the juvenile's family needs help in keeping the youth on track. Dispositions are supposed to be tailored to the youth's circumstances, and are therefore influenced by the sex of the offender, the philosophy of the particular court, the seriousness of the offense, the juvenile's prior record, and his or her response to earlier efforts (Cohen & Kluegel, 1979). This system is intended to be benign—to minimize punishment and encourage rehabilitative interventions—but there is a clear tendency to ratchet up the negative aspects of the intervention in response to continuing criminal or delinquent behavior. These punitive efforts and threats of even more punitive efforts down the road are intended to demonstrate that crime has costs and also to support the efforts of family, schools, and other social agencies to motivate the youth to stay in school, learn job-related skills or otherwise prepare for adulthood. Given this position, it follows then that numerous arrests indicate that a youth has resisted increasingly severe efforts at formal social control and, presumably, has also resisted less formal efforts as well.

Studies of juvenile arrest patterns show the interplay between resistance and numbers of arrests under a general *graduated sanctions* approach. Large-scale birth cohort studies have shown that the probability of getting arrested again is less than 50% after the first arrest, but goes up substantially with each successive arrest (Carrington, Matarazzo, & deSouza, 2005; Shannon, 1991; Shannon, McKim, Curry, & Haffner, 1988; Wolfgang, Figlio, & Sellin, 1972). Most youth respond to the consequences associated with the first arrest, avoiding a second arrest. A smaller proportion respond to the (increased) sanction associated with a second arrest, and a smaller proportion still respond to the sanction associated with the third. Despite increasing levels of formal intervention, fewer and fewer youth seem to respond at each level. The few who get arrested more than a few times account for the majority of all arrests.[3] These offenders, termed *chronic offenders* by Wolfgang et al. (1972), are very likely to keep getting arrested despite relatively severe consequences. From this perspective, the juvenile justice system can be seen to act as a filter, gradually identifying youth who are most resistant to formal social control.

Formal social control, as we have argued, is only part of the picture. Serious juvenile (persistent) offenders, like those committed to the CYA have not only resisted formal sanctions, but have typically experienced and resisted a variety of increasingly serious interventions by parents, schools, and social service agencies as well (Richardson, 2001). While few were openly defiant in their communities, they continued to avoid school, to use drugs, and hang around with other delinquents despite much pressure to change. State-level institution programs are theoretically designed to address these issues by placing youth in secure residential settings that require education and/or employment training, separate youth from their current community-based criminal associates, and prevent them from using drugs or engaging in delinquent behavior for some period. Success at these endeavors varies, partly because of differences in resources, resolve, and commitment to standards of care, but also because these young people resist treatment efforts. Studies of very high risk youths have found them difficult to treat effectively

[3] Similar results were found in a study in Orange County, California, where 8% of the youth who were referred to probation accounted for most of the arrests in their cohort and garnered substantial probation department resources (Schumacher & Kurz, 2000). These findings led to projects intended to identify and respond to these youth more intensively at earlier stages of intervention.

(Loeber & Farrington, 1998a; McCord & McCord, 1959; Moffit, 1993). Not only do they fail to respond to rehabilitative opportunities provided to them but they also find ways to actually sabotage treatment efforts that require commitment, discipline, and hard work (Ahlstrom & Havighurst, 1971; Bonta, 1995; Preston, 2000). They have even been shown to support one another in these efforts at sabotage through a process termed *deviancy training* (Dishion, McCord, & Poulin, 1999; Gifford-Smith, Dodge, Dishion, & McCord, 2005; Poulin, Dishion, & Haas, 1999). Intervention at this level becomes an issue of trying to overcome the youths' resistance to social control and providing opportunities for them to overcome the deficits they already have.

In general, then, the process that selects youths for commitment to secure state-level juvenile institutions like the CYA identifies youth who are resistant both to the sanctions and interventions of the juvenile justice system and to the demands and expectations associated with the development of more legitimate lifestyles. These youth would not be committed to juvenile institutions if they were not committing crimes, but crime is generally only part of the picture. Youth committed to the CYA not only have rather long criminal histories but have also failed to meet other social demands, such as applying themselves in school, developing job skills, or meeting conditions of probation. All of these problems become the focus of programs and services, under the presumption that they are causes of the delinquent behavior. From our perspective, however, these risk factors can also be seen, at least in part, as additional manifestations of an underlying resistance to social control, as these youth find it difficult to put up with the demands of school, jobs, and correctional programs. These youth also find it more difficult to resist the lure of drug abuse and gang membership because the costs, in terms of lost opportunities, are lower. They may find these activities more attractive than do other youth, but the point here is that they are also less reluctant to get involved. The argument that substance use and gang membership are impediments to developing prosocial lifestyles would not be very persuasive to a youth that resists the demands of solid citizenship already. The result is a self-perpetuating lifestyle predicated, in large part, on resistance to the kind of hard work, discipline, and commitment required of more legitimate pursuits.

Implications

This emphasis on resistance to social control offers a number of advantages for understanding persistent offending and has important implications both for studying this phenomenon and for treating persistent offenders. It can help us understand the development of persistent criminality by suggesting that the causes of criminality in general may be different from the causes of persistent criminal behavior. Resistance complicates the study of crime among persistent offenders by suggesting that the critical characteristic of persistence is the chronic absence of stabilizing factors in the lives of these individuals, making predictability low and random instability high. This perspective also suggests that interventions, whether punitive or rehabilitative, will not have huge impacts, but that they may help to keep criminal behavior minimized and enhance the overall tendency for crime to decline with age.

This is not to say that some persistent offenders are not strongly drawn to the criminal lifestyle, finding it very rewarding, and that these rewards are simply large enough to outweigh the perceived costs. For these offenders, even doing time might be an acceptable consequence of their continuation of a lifestyle that they find extremely rewarding—social approval and standing, protection from threats (gang affiliation), the materialistic gains of crime, drug use, the heightened arousal and risk taking associated with many forms of crime, or the romanticizing of the criminal lifestyle. Similarly, their apparent resistance to the demands of conventional lifestyles may simply be a by-product of their pursuit of criminal activity. They neglect incompatible obligations and avoid those activities, such as education, jobs, and family that stand in the way of their crime-related pursuits. For most persistent offenders, however, we would argue that such extreme motivation is not the case—that they are not more attracted to criminal lifestyles than are other offenders but rather are less attracted to conventional ones.

Implications for Understanding Persistent Offending

Many of the commonly-recognized risk factors for delinquency can be seen as indicators of resistance to social control and/or its consequences, such as poor attitudes toward school, low achievement, or lack of involvement in prosocial activities. Concomitant behaviors, such as drug use and gang membership,[4] may be seen as ways of obtaining immediate gratification with little demand for work, discipline, or commitment (Gottfredson & Hirschi, 1990; Klein, 1971, 1995; Yablonski, 1959). The more of these risk factors, or resistance indicators, there are, the more they would appear to suggest a general

---

[4] Klein summarizes the psychological factors related to gang membership by saying that "the gang is seen as an aggregate of individuals held together more by their own shared incapacities than by mutual goals. Primarily, group identification is important as it serves individual needs; it leads to delinquent group activity only secondarily and only in the absence of prosocial alternatives" (Klein, 1995, p. 201).

and strong resistance to social control and the more likely a youth is to have a criminal record and to have repeated arrests (Farrington, 2003b). Evidence of early criminal tendencies (aggressiveness and antisocial behavior) contributes to prediction, as demonstrated by the longitudinal studies carried out in New Zealand (Caspi, Moffit, Silva, Stouthamer-Loeber, Krueger, & Schmutte, 1994; Moffit, 1993; Moffitt, Caspi, Harrington, & Milne, 2002).

The combination of aggressiveness and "impersistence" at an early age led to rebelliousness at age 18. These indicators of resistance to social control were closely related to delinquency.

> In particular, we found that children who were "undercontrolled" at age 3 had elevated scores at age 18 on MPQ Negative Emotionality and very low scores on MPQ Constraint.... At age 3, undercontrolled children were described by the examiners as irritable, impulsive, and impersistent; they had difficulty sitting still, were rough and uncontrolled in their behavior, and were labile in their emotional responses. At age 18, the same children described themselves as reckless and careless; they enjoyed dangerous and exciting activities, and preferred rebelliousness to conformity. They also enjoyed causing discomfort to others; yet they felt mistreated, deceived, and betrayed by others. This is the very personality configuration that we have linked to delinquency in the present study. (Caspi et al., 1994, pp. 188–189).

In this sense, our perspective is consistent with Moffitt's (1993) characterization of life-course-persistent offending, differing only in where the resistance comes from. Moffitt's characterization focuses on the continuity of aggressive and antisocial behavior and suggests that the kind of resistance to social control of interest here is simply the by-product of this behavioral tendency. Early aggressive or antisocial behavior is seen to come from "difficult temperament," and children who are "difficult to manage." These difficult children resist their parents' efforts to socialize them, and the resultant interactional patterns exacerbate the children's problems. Continued antisocial behavior results in exclusion from opportunities to engage in legitimate lifestyles ("contemporary consequences") and over time create "cumulative consequences" as the antisocial child fails to learn prosocial skills and behaviors ("restricted behavioral repertoire") and becomes "ensnared by the consequences of antisocial behavior." Especially in disadvantaged environments,

> ... difficult behavior is gradually elaborated into conduct problems and a dearth of prosocial skills. Thus, over the years, an antisocial personality is slowly and insidiously constructed. Likewise, deficits in language and

reasoning are incrementally elaborated into academic failure and a dearth of job skills. Over time, accumulating consequences of the youngster's personality problems and academic problems prune away the options for change… Through this process, relatively subtle childhood variations in neuropsychological health can be transformed into an antisocial style that pervades all domains of adolescent and adult behavior. It is this infiltration of the antisocial disposition into the multiple domains of a life that diminishes the likelihood of change. (Moffitt, 1993, p. 684)

Whether these differences arise through these specific developmental paths, we would argue that tolerance for meeting the demands of others or its flip side, resistance to social control, is a dimension along which everyone finds a comfort level. Meeting the demands of conventional life may be more difficult for some than others. Lower IQ, aggressive tendencies, hyperactivity, poor attention span, mental health problems, abusive parenting, and other factors that have been associated with delinquency (Farrington, 2003b) make it difficult for some youth to succeed at school and other prosocial tasks. Alongside this dimension of ability, however, is the dimension of willingness. It would be safe to say that for everyone there are limits as to how much they are willing to put up with in order to succeed within any particular social arena. That tolerance level may be conditioned by past experiences, the likelihood of success, the rewards for success, certain personality traits, and so on, and could differ for different situations. Overall, however, and across a variety of dimensions, people seem to differ in this regard. Some people seem more compliant, *socializable*[5] or, in athletic terms, *coachable*. Less socializable individuals may be viewed as disinterested, strong-willed, or lacking in drive, ambition, or commitment, but they are nevertheless easily diverted from tasks that require commitment to long-term, goal-oriented activity and acceptance of demands and expectations.

Rational choice theory presents the view that individuals act on free will and seek pleasure over pain, suggesting a cost–benefit component to rational decision making (Felson & Clarke, 1998). As part of the decision making process, individuals weigh the benefit of engaging in the crime against a perceived cost of doing the crime. Such a decision process includes individual perception, interpretation, and preferences (McCarthy, 2002). Under our resistance perspective, an individual's level of resistance may be best

---

[5] Gottfredson and Hirschi (1990) use this term to describe differences in peoples' abilities to accept the kind of parental teaching that leads to self-control. They suggest that this factor may explain delinquency differences between girls and boys, for example.

understood as a preference that affects general choices for engaging in *life-styles* that include or exclude crime. A low tolerance for social control (high level of resistance) would reduce the satisfactions (and increase the non-monetary costs) associated with, say, legitimate employment opportunities and increase the value of quick, easy, direct methods of gaining goods and services—that is, crime. Crime is consistent with lifestyles that favor fast and easy solutions to immediate problems and is inconsistent with lifestyles that favor long-term commitment to legitimate goals and acceptance of social control.

Resistance to social control can produce the same interactional down-ward spiral described by Moffit without aggressive or particularly antiso-cial tendencies early in life. The adventurous, thrill-seeking, reckless, and hedonistic aspect of low self-control, described by Gottfredson and Hirschi (1990), when coupled with low tolerance to social control, could also lead to behaviors that evoke responses that, in turn, trigger resistance. The bored, rest-less student becomes the chronic truant who falls behind in school and finds it increasingly difficult to get back on track, leading to the kinds of cumulative consequences described by Moffit (1993). The lure of gangs, drugs, and crime could easily overshadow the perceived benefits of going back to school sev-eral grade levels behind and with the prospect of considerable hard work to do for many, many years. Lack of effort leads to closer supervision and greater demands for evidence of devotion. Thus, more is demanded of those who fall behind, and even higher tolerance (less resistance) is required for success. The road gets steeper, and for those with the least traction, climbing the hill to suc-cess is increasingly difficult even without aggressiveness. Early and persistent aggressiveness and antisocial tendencies may lead to this state, but are not required.

This kind of downward spiral can help to explain the instability and mar-ginality of the adult lifestyles of former serious juvenile offenders. As noted previously, persistent offenders play an active, albeit not conscious or delib-erate, role in sustaining the very conditions that are conducive to crime. The lure of jobs, sobriety, and marriage would be minimal for those who have an aversion to social control, and it is no surprise that these aspects of their lives are unstable and unproductive. If acceptance of social control is fundamental to success at prosocial lifestyles, those who resist social control are seriously unsuited to conventional lives. Persistent offenders avoid social commitments, and have difficulty managing those they make. They would not only be unwill-ing to work hard at maintaining jobs or marriages, they would be seriously unattractive as employees or mates.

The data on adult lifestyles of persistent offenders supports this perspec-tive. Adult persistent offenders have been described as having major problems (and failures) in many areas of their lives (DeLisi, 2005). Our own follow-up studies of young offenders released from the CYA paint a similar picture (Haapanen, 1990). On average, the youths who left the CYA and went on to prison or probation spent less than 15% of the follow-up period married; the inclusion of "common-law" relationships increased this percentage, but it was still less than 30%. The average amount of time per year spent in any employment was less than 20%. Several studies have shown that persistent offenders tend to get arrested less during periods of marriage or employment but that these periods tend to be short (Bonta, Lipinski, & Martin, 1992; Haapanen, 1990; Sampson & Laub, 2005a). It appears that whatever causes persistence in offending also causes instability and lack of success in other aspects of life as well. Resistance to social control, especially in the extreme, certainly has that potential.

Moving forward, it will be important to better differentiate resistance to social control from characteristics typically associated with it, such as impulsiveness, recklessness, aggressiveness, or crime. We have argued that the continued expression of these characteristics requires resistance to social control efforts aimed at curbing them, but have suggested that the resistance can exist without these behavioral tendencies. Indeed, it may be that only in its extreme form does resistance pose a problem. After all, resistance to social control also suggests independence and autonomy, and can bring with it a sense of freedom and personal empowerment. Much of the American culture and economy is predicated on this kind of freedom and individual initiative. Creativity presupposes resistance to social control. However, in its extreme variety, resistance reduces an individual's ability to navigate the social environment very effectively, increasing employment problems and exacerbating social problems like drug use and crime. It will be important to gain a better understanding of the point at which resistance becomes a problem for people with various penchants for antisocial behavior.

It will also be important to attempt to operationalize the concept of resistance to social control, both to better differentiate it from crime and to set the stage for studying its etiology and development. Throughout our discussions, we have posited the existence of resistance to social control as a way of helping to account for chronic failure across multiple life domains. We have tried to emphasize that such resistance is not necessarily deliberate or even conscious. We have also suggested that resistance leads to "cumulative consequences," which may be founded on early antisocial tendencies and/ or simple differences in responsiveness to others. These consequences create hurdles that are more and more difficult to overcome, creating an ongoing correlation between higher resistance and bigger obstacles to success. The challenge, then, is to measure this concept independent of these consequences and recognizing that it may not be at the level of conscious awareness. If such measurement is possible, the relationship of resistance to crime could be studied as both develop through adolescence.

Implications for Studying Crime among Persistent Offenders

The concept of resistance to social control as a defining characteristic of serious persistent offenders helps make sense of low predictability and high instability of arrests or other indicators of criminal behavior. When numbers of offenses, measured as numbers of arrests, is used as the criterion for prediction studies, our logic would suggest that the focus of the prediction is not on criminal propensity but on resistance. Arrests are a direct measure of the extent to which offenders resist efforts at social control. We have argued that extreme resistance to social control leads to the chronic absence of stabilizing factors in the lives of persistent offenders, and thereby opens them to the influence of momentary and fleeting impulses, opportunities to offend, and chance encounters. The number of times that an offender is arrested therefore comes also to represent the degree to which his behavior is free from stabilizing influences, and is instead influenced by the randomness and unpredictability of interacting in different situations, different events, and with different individuals within their environment. Further, because individuals tend both to seek and to create environments that fit with their personal proclivities (Gottfredson & Hirschi, 1990; McCarthy, 2002; Moffit, 1993), we would expect that the randomness and unpredictability of the environmental interactions themselves are greater for these offenders.

This inherent randomness and unpredictability not only reduces the ability to meaningfully differentiate among persistent offenders, but it also reduces the stability of behavior patterns over time, thereby complicating the study of criminal "careers" or trajectories and the meaningful evaluation of programs that attempt to reduce recidivism. A longitudinal follow-up study of youth released from CYA institutions found that, relative to one another, the highest rate offenders during particular periods (of as much as 4 years) tended not to be the highest rate offenders in subsequent periods (Haapanen, 1990). A more recent analysis of adult arrests among nearly 30,000 former CYA releases (Haapanen et al., 2007) found that random samples of 100 or even 250 offenders showed a great deal of variation in age-crime trajectories. This random variation suggests that samples as large as 250 persistent offenders may not provide accurate pictures of criminal career patterns by age. Our analysis found substantial random differences both in terms of magnitude at any particular age and in terms of the shape of the overall age-crime curve. Generalizations to the wider persistent offender population based on any sample could be very far off. As noted also by Sampson and Laub (2005a), those differences that are found would be unpredictable because they are based largely on chance variations; consequently, the observed differences in trajectories within samples of persistent offenders may not be very meaningful.

The continuation of criminal behavior well into adulthood for serious juvenile offenders has been well-documented (Blokland, 2005; Croisdale, 2007; Haapanen, 1990; Haapanen & Jesness, 1982; Nagin & Farrington, 1992b; Nagin & Paternoster, 1991; Piquero et al., 2002; Sampson & Laub, 1993, 2005a). On the basis of resistance to social control alone, we might expect that these persistent offenders would continue to commit crimes at high rates throughout their lives. However, equally well-documented is the tendency for these offenders to show declines in arrests with age, although these rates continue to be higher than those found for the general population at any age (Gottfredson & Hirschi, 1990; Haapanen, 1990; Haapanen et al., 2007). Further, some of these offenders appear to slow down faster than others and may desist completely at earlier ages, suggesting to many criminologists the potential fruitfulness of research into the factors that speed desistance in this population (Brame, Bushway, & Paternoster, 2003; Bushway, Piquero, Broidy, Cauffman, & Mazerolle, 2001; Farrington, 2003a; Laub & Sampson, 1993; Nagin & Farrington, 1992a; Piquero, Brame et al., 2002).

Our own earlier studies suggested that this downward trend may be influenced considerably by criminal justice sanctions, such as juvenile incarceration or adult prison (Haapanen, et al., 2007). In one analysis, pre-prison arrest rates were compared to post-prison arrest rates, controlling for age. Rates of arrest by age were calculated separately for the period before offenders went to adult prison and after they were released. Rates of arrest before prison were much higher at each age than rates of arrest after release. It would appear from these results that the prison experience had a profound crime-reduction effect for these persistent offenders. Further, the post-prison arrest rates continued to decrease with age, approaching the rate for those with no prison terms. Therefore, as more and more of the sample moved from pre-prison to post-prison rates, they drove the overall age-crime line downward.

To further illustrate both the crime-reduction effects of incarceration for these offenders and the complications introduced by the instability of their criminal behavior, we calculated rates of arrest for the 5 years before and 10 years following incarceration in the CYA and, for those who went

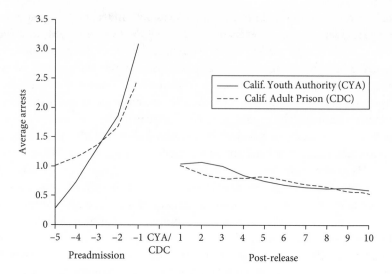

FIGURE 16.1   Average arrests for any offense pre-CYA or CDC and post-release.

on to prison, the California Department of Corrections[6] (CDC). Figure 16.1 shows the overall patterns observed around these two points of state-level incarceration. In both instances, these sanctions seemed to follow a period of increasing arrest and were followed by a marked reduction in arrests. On average, the reductions were to levels found several years before the incarceration. In part, the rise in arrests before incarceration reflects the selection process inherent in these incarceration decisions—at least one major arrest is required—but the increases shown here were far above the one arrest required to trigger such a sanction.[7] The similarities in arrest rates following these types of incarceration are striking. In the year after release, both groups averaged about one arrest each, and this rate gradually declined from there. Thus, these "interventions" appear to interrupt escalating behavior patterns and lead to permanent reductions—they literally seem to bring

---

[6] The CYA does not routinely gather data on all prior arrests for youth committed to its care. However, special studies have been conducted where prior record information was gathered. The data used in this chart came from a study of drug testing among parolees (Haapanen & Britton, 2002).

[7] More arrests preceded the admission to the CYA, and this is consistent with the efforts of the juvenile justice system to use incarceration as a last resort for youth. Commitment to state-level juvenile corrections typically occurs when youth continue to accumulate arrests despite less serious sanctions.

these offenders back "in line" with the general age-related reduction in arrests found for this population as a whole.

It is important, however, to keep in mind that these effects operate on a general level. Indeed, the instability of these offenders' behavior makes detailed analysis of the effects of interventions very difficult. While it might be tempting to look for subgroups or interventions that stop criminal behavior altogether, this goal is complicated by this instability. The following graphs illustrate this point. Figure 16.2 shows the results of an analysis again focusing on rates of arrest in the 5 years before and 10 years following incarceration in the CYA. The two lines represent groups differing on whether they experienced any arrests during the first 2 years following release from CYA facilities—a period that is often used to measure recidivism. Figure 16.3 shows the same information for periods before and after the first prison term for youth leaving the CYA and subsequently serving a term in adult prison. Again, both graphs show the characteristic rise in arrests before incarceration and the sharp reduction in arrests following release. However, both graphs show that offenders who did not recidivate during the first 2 years after release were not that different from recidivists in years 3 through 10. These 24-month "non-recidivists," if followed longer, would have been much more similar to recidivists than is implied by their "success" during the first 2 years out.

Thus, a hiatus in arrests for several years often does not indicate permanent substantial changes in behavior. In some cases, criminal activity continues

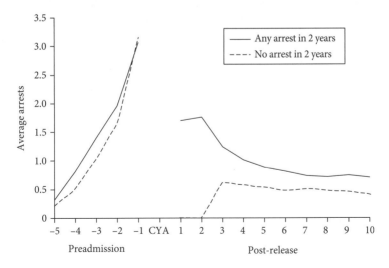

FIGURE 16.2   Average arrests for any offense pre-CYA and post-release by any arrest in the first 2 years following release.

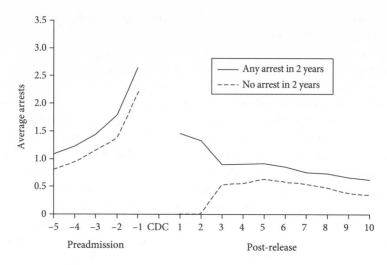

FIGURE 16.3   Average arrests for any offense pre-prison (CDC) and post-release by any arrest in the first 2 years following release.

undetected. In other cases, offenders may make genuine attempts to desist. The point is that these periods do not last—that the offenders' lives are unstable and so are their criminal behavior patterns.

Thus, while there appears to be a clear incarceration effect for these offenders, observed differences over specific time periods may not be very informative in terms of longer range, or permanent, changes in criminal behavior. The instability of the behavior, which we have argued is a by-product of resistance to social control, hinders not only the examination of differences in long-term criminal careers or trajectories, but also hinders the evaluation of programs or alternative sanctions. Standard measures of recidivism, such as percentages of groups arrested within 1 or 2 years of release, appear questionable in their ability to indicate long-term differences between groups. Only by using large samples and long-term follow-up studies could the relative merits of various treatment options in terms of true desistance for persistent offenders be determined.

Using approaches described earlier and in our earlier work (Haapanen et al., 2007), it may be possible to study the effects (if any) of other life events, such as full-time employment or marriage. It might also be possible to investigate the timing of these events (and incarceration) to better understand their impact within offenders' lives (Croisdale, 2007). For example, it might be that due to the crime-reduction effect of prison, an early prison sentence could mean fewer crimes overall during the lifespan than a later prison term. It might also be that marriage has a short-term suppression effect but little effect over the life course or, alternatively, that it marks a permanent shift in resistance and a lower rate of arrest from then on.

Along these lines, it would be interesting to determine whether resistance to social control can be measured independent of the consequences. We have suggested, for example, that continued crime indicates resistance, almost by definition, but that resistance does not necessarily lead to crime. An offender could reduce his criminal behavior in response to criminal justice sanctions and not become less resistant to demands and expectations embedded in legitimate lifestyles. Such individuals would lead unstable, unproductive lives, but may be disinclined to commit crimes for fear of the consequences. It is not clear, then, that even permanent reductions in criminal behavior indicate changes in resistance. Better indicators of reduced resistance might be voluntary, prolonged participation in social institutions like jobs or marriages that require acceptance of, or acquiescence to, social control. Unstable marriages or employment would not serve this purpose, and may only indicate a failed attempt to "go straight" or "pull a life together." Such studies would require, of course, periodic measurement of lifestyle details that are expensive to obtain for offenders who may be difficult to locate and uncooperative (Sampson & Laub, 2003).

Implications for Treatment

Overall, the picture that emerges for these very persistent offenders is that continued criminal involvement leads to frequent brushes with the law, leading (for most) eventually to a term in jail or prison (Haapanen, 1990). These sanctions seem to lead to a reduction in arrests to a level found several years before the incarceration, and the level continues to decline slowly from there. Some offenders stay arrest-free for years following such a sanction, but as shown in the figures previously, that hiatus does not necessarily mean that criminal behavior has stopped altogether. In this context, periods of relatively high-rate arrests or zero arrests are not very meaningful because they tend to be followed by rather typical patterns of arrest. The high-rate periods trigger interventions that bring the offenders back into line, and the low-rate periods appear difficult for these offenders to maintain.

These findings suggest a different perspective on the role of incarceration in the lives of persistent offenders. Serious criminal justice sanctions might best be understood as part of the general landscape for persistent offenders, moderating their behavior but not controlling it. Given that most of these offenders get arrested again following prison terms, it is tempting to assume that these sanctions are completely ineffective for these particular offenders.

Going farther, proponents of life-course theories argue that incarceration is likely to be detrimental because it separates offenders from their communities and hinders the establishment or maintenance of attachments to family, friends, and jobs (Sampson & Laub, 2005a). More important, however, is the message that continued criminal behavior will have undesirable consequences. The continued threat of prison, made more salient by having actually served a prison term, may permanently alter these offenders' perception of the costs of crime and thus their future decisions about criminal behavior (McCarthy, 2002). This alteration in the cost–benefit calculation may help to keep criminal behavior minimized (if not eliminated) and contribute to the overall tendency for crime to decline with age. Criminal justice sanctions may simply "wear down" these offenders, especially as they age. Fewer and fewer may wish to spend a proportion of their remaining years locked up for some relatively small-gain crime.

It may also be that these sanctions motivate offenders either to put up with a level of demands and expectations that they would not accept earlier or to attempt to draw on the combination of support and control that are inherent in marriages (and some jobs). In this latter sense, getting married may be approached, at some level, like joining Alcoholics Anonymous—as a conscious or unconscious attempt at self-help. It is unclear, of course, how resistance to social control itself might change over the life course. We have argued that resistance is not necessarily a conscious struggle, but rather simply the fact that there is a struggle. While some people seem to be more resistant by nature, there is no reason to believe that they will continue to struggle so hard. Having been worn down by the criminal justice system, the offender may simply find it easier at some point to go along and get along. They may find a way to eke out a living doing work that is relatively undemanding. They may find mates and friends who are equally undemanding. While it is possible, it is unlikely that many will forge normal, legitimate lifestyles (Hagedorn, 1994; Sampson & Laub, 2003). Eventually, the "easy way out" may be to stay within the law.

It is probably true that the particular treatment programs or services offered to these offenders during their incarceration or supervision is not extremely important in this regard. Rehabilitative services offered in prison may not have an appreciable impact on common short-term measurements of recidivism, but they may have a long-term value in reducing levels of resistance. Persistent offenders resist rehabilitation in the same ways and for the same reasons that they resist legitimate social roles in the first place. However, to the extent that these offenders are persuaded by recurring sanctions to reduce their criminal behavior, it is important that they master skills to enable them to participate in society as a noncriminal. Without job skills, the alternative to crime may be severe poverty, homelessness, or other lifestyles that have social costs as well. Having employment and social skills makes holding a decent job easier and thereby changes the general cost–benefit calculation of crime versus noncrime. Although these offenders may still resist social control, that resistance may be easier to keep from becoming overt if the demands of others are easier to meet.

On this note then, we caution that expectations of the success of rehabilitative services, as measured through recidivism, need to be tempered. The current literature on offender risk and needs in correctional settings argues that treatment should be targeted toward those offenders with the highest risk and highest need, that is, persistent offenders. Yet these offenders are most resistant to treatment efforts or, in modern parlance, have the greatest internal "responsivity barriers" (Andrews & Bonta, 2006). Further, we have suggested that recidivism measured over 2 years may not provide an accurate indication of future criminal behavior. Thus, although correctional agencies are often admonished, in the name of "evidence-based policy," to limit their resources only to those programs that have been proven to reduce short-term recidivism rates, such reductions are likely to be difficult to find, and ambiguous in their meaning. If put to a rigorous test, few programs and services are likely to have substantial recidivism-reduction effects with these offenders. The value of prison-based programs and services may be far in the future. Perhaps long-term follow-up studies focusing on the value of these rehabilitative efforts can determine their impact. In the meantime, research and discussions concerning rehabilitation are well advised to temper expectations and to not *expect* short-term differences in recidivism for persistent offenders based on programs and services in prison settings.

Under the resistance perspective, rehabilitative efforts are not viewed as only those services offered or provided in correctional environments. As mentioned earlier, rehabilitative efforts may have a positive effect in making it easier to engage in noncriminal lifestyle even if general resistance levels do not change much over time. Naturally, then, rehabilitative efforts provided in nonincarceration settings should also serve this function. There is no reason to assume that beneficial employability services, substance abuse treatment, or anger management training could not be provided in the community, as long as the offender recognizes the consequences of the conduct that led to this intervention and is persuaded to see it through. Indeed, given a particular crime and a particular readiness (based on previous experiences with the criminal justice system), probation or other community sanctions may be the most effective and appropriate, even for persistent offenders. The point is that they "get the message" and maybe learn something useful in the process.

Along these lines, it might appear to some that the resistance perspective would lead to the conclusion that longer periods of incarceration are called for with persistent offenders—that incapacitating them may be the only way to reduce their adverse impact on society. However, data presented earlier show that arrest rates following CYA or prison were about one arrest per year per offender. Similar rates were found for periods following shorter jail terms (Haapanen, 1990). All three types of incarceration followed on an escalating rate of arrest for several years. While the circumstances that resulted in terms in CYA, jail, or prison differed and the length of time incarcerated differed, the outcomes were about the same. Thus, although it might seem effective to extend the prison sentences of offenders who were very persistent juvenile offenders, the overall crime-reduction benefit would be small (one arrest per additional offender-year). For example, during the years 1998 to 2002, there were approximately 5000 offenders released from prison after an earlier release from CYA facilities. By our calculations, those offenders would have been responsible for about 5000 arrests during the first year out of prison. Keeping them in prison an extra year would have prevented, then, about 5000 arrests. During those 5 years, there were over seven million arrests in California (California Attorney General, 2007). Incapacitating these offenders would have resulted in a reduction in arrests of less than one-tenth of one percent. Similar calculations for felony-level arrests suggest their incapacitation would have reduced felony arrests by just over one-tenth of 1%. In fact, even if this high figure of one-arrest-per-year were applied to all 50,000 first-time parolees from California prison in 2002 (California Department of Corrections and Rehabilitation, 2003), an extra year in prison would have prevented less than 4% of arrests that year. It would appear, then, that simply lengthening prison terms, even for very persistent offenders, would not have a huge impact on crime.

In addition to the policy considerations of incarceration and rehabilitative services is the area of crime prevention. The resistance perspective, based on criminal career research including analyses we have conducted both jointly and separately, assigns much of the responsibility for reducing the crime caused by persistent offenders on crime prevention efforts aimed at reducing or eliminating opportunities to offend. As such, this strategy is aligned with the tenets of environmental criminology and more specifically, situational crime prevention in which targets are hardened and opportunities blocked (Brantingham & Brantingham, 1991). Further work could be conducted to examine the plausibility and effectiveness of a crime prevention strategy focused specifically on persistent offenders and specific crime types.

Summary

Throughout this chapter, we have argued that persistent offenders are different from other offenders. They are not, however, necessarily any more *driven* to antisocial or criminal behavior than any other offender group. Rather, they seem to differ from other offenders primarily in their unwillingness or inability to conform to the demands and expectations of others. This resistance to social control manifests itself in failure to engage in long-term, goal-oriented efforts, in serious instability of jobs, marriages and other relationships, and in lower responsiveness to formal sanctions. Consciously or unconsciously, persistent offenders seem to avoid situations that would provide leverage against misbehavior and are therefore both *free* to commit crimes if it suits them and ill-adapted to any alternative. Certain behavioral tendencies, such as aggressiveness, impulsiveness, or being easily frustrated, may exacerbate this condition, but are not required. With this freedom, however, comes relative instability and unpredictability of both criminal and noncriminal activities. Compared to other people persistent offenders have little to lose except their freedom, and even "doing time" may not be too difficult to endure because little work is required.

Our characterization of resistance is consistent with Gottfredson and Hirschi's (1990) *A General Theory of Crime* in that we posit a general difference between people that is very basic and that will differentiate people throughout life. This characteristic seems to manifest itself very early in life, making budding persistent offenders difficult to manage and difficult to motivate both as very young children and as adolescents. It is thereby consistent also with the adolescence-limited versus life-course-persistent differentiation of Moffit (1993) and others. Rather than pointing to neurological deficits and aggressiveness, however, the current perspective suggests a more general and benign difference among people in their resistance to social control— their willingness and ability to meet the day-to-day demands of other people. Extreme resistance to social control does not lead to crime necessarily, but when criminal behavior is present, resistance sustains crime by first, reducing the efficacy of formal and informal efforts to curb criminal behavior and second, by preventing the establishment and maintenance of social connections and commitments that are inconsistent with crime.

We have illustrated these points by describing the adult arrest patterns of offenders released from California Youth Authority institutions over the last 15 years. By the time these persistent juvenile offenders were committed to the CYA, they had accumulated an average of ten or more arrests in the few years prior to commitment. To have withstood the pressure behind that many interventions, these young offenders must have been keenly able to resist social control. These individuals can be seen as *extreme resisters* (Croisdale, 2007) who are likely to continue resisting and to offend well into adulthood. It is not surprising, therefore, that we found them to have long and extensive criminal careers following release from the CYA. Under these circumstances, we should not expect the next criminal justice experience to have a profound effect either. We have suggested that interventions such as jail, probation, or prison are more apt to slowly wear these offenders down, reducing their criminal behavior without totally overcoming their resistance.

The resistance perspective has a number of implications regarding current issues within the persistence and criminal career areas of research. As a perspective suggesting an explanation as to why individuals continue to offend, resistance elicits a new way of thinking about topics within the criminal career literature regarding continuance of offending such as the age-crime curve, career length, desistance and the specialization/versatility debate. While further examination of these topics would not be changed methodologically, the resistance perspective provides a plausible explanation of why offenders included in those analyses are so unpredictable and unstable and a direction to look for sources of variation among offenders. Moving forward, it would be helpful to better understand the concept of resistance to social control, independent of criminal behavior itself, and to examine its variations among individuals (criminal and noncriminal) and over time. It would also be important to better understand how, and how much this characteristic can change. Such understanding could help greatly in developing intervention strategies aimed at helping these offenders become better citizens.

CHAPTER 17

Reconsidering Gottfredson and Hirschi's General Theory of Crime: Linking the Micro- and Macro-Level Sources of Self-Control and Criminal Behavior over the Life Course

Travis C. Pratt

Since its arrival on the criminological scene, an impressive roster of studies has emerged supporting Gottfredson and Hirschi's (1990) core theoretical proposition—that criminal behavior is caused by individuals' deficiencies in levels of self-control (Pratt & Cullen, 2000; see also Chapple, 2005; Hay, 2001; Schoepfer & Piquero, 2006; Vazsonyi & Crosswhite, 2004). To be sure, self-control has been linked empirically to a wide variety of criminal and deviant behaviors within samples drawn from juvenile, adult, and even offender populations (DeLisi, Hochstetler, & Murphy, 2003; Nagin & Pogarsky, 2001; Perrone, Sullivan, Pratt, & Margaryan, 2004; Piquero, Gomez-Smith, & Langton, 2004; Pratt & Cullen, 2000). Self-control has also been found to be significantly related to a host of other negative social outcomes such as joblessness and marital instability (Evans, Cullen, Burton, Dunaway, & Benson,

1997). Recent research has even shown that those with low self-control are less likely to be deterred by the threat of punishment for their misdeeds (Piquero & Tibbetts, 1996; Pogarsky, 2002; Pratt, Cullen, Blevins, Daigle, & Madensen, 2006). It is clear, therefore, that self-control plays a major role in persistent criminal behavior over the life course.

While the link between self-control and crime/deviance has been consistently demonstrated empirically, what is less clear at this point is how self-control is established within individuals. The primary explanation regarding the genesis of self-control in the criminological literature is Gottfredson and Hirschi's (1990) parenting thesis. In short, Gottfredson and Hirschi contend that self-control will develop in children through effective parenting, where parents who monitor their kids' behavior, recognize deviant behavior when it happens, and punish such behavior consistently will produce in their children the internal control mechanisms necessary for resisting the temptations that criminal and deviant behavior provide. Support for this proposition is certainly present (see, e.g., Cochran, Wood, Sellers, Wilkerson, & Chamlin, 1998; McGloin, Pratt, & Maahs, 2004; Unnever, Cullen, & Pratt, 2003). Nevertheless, empirical evidence has emerged indicating that the processes that establish individuals' levels of self-control are more complex than those specified by Gottfredson and Hirschi.

This chapter addresses this issue by presenting an explanatory model of the development of self-control that pulls together micro- (e.g., biological, neuropsychological, family context) and macro-level (e.g., community and institutional contexts) criminogenic influences. The purpose of this revised model is to demonstrate how self-control can be integrated into a more comprehensive—and empirically robust—theoretical framework for explaining between-individual variation in offending, within-individual variation in criminal behavior over the life course, and the spatial distribution of crime.

The Sources of Low Self-Control

Gottfredson and Hirschi (1990) argued that individuals will develop self-control at an early age and that once the level of self-control is "set" within a given child (roughly between the ages of 8 and 10), his inability to consistently control his impulses will endure well into adulthood (see also Hirschi & Gottfredson, 1995; cf. Laub & Sampson, 2003; Moffitt, 1993; Sampson & Laub, 1993). Thus, gaining an understanding of the development of—or causes of—self-control becomes a key link in Gottfredson and Hirschi's theory.

Highlighting the relative absence of criminological knowledge about the subject, Gottfredson and Hirschi (1990) even conceded that they "know better what deficiencies in self-control lead to than where they come from" (p. 94); and, they confessed that "the sources of self-control are complex" (p. 96). Nevertheless, as stated earlier they do settle on a parenting explanation for the origin of self-control. In particular, children who develop low self-control do so as the result of ineffective parenting, which entails the failure of parents to effectively monitor their children's behavior, to recognize deviant behavior when it occurs, and to punish children for misbehaving. Put simply, crime could be prevented if parents would do a better job of raising their kids.

Parenting and Low Self-Control

Only in the last decade or so have researchers directed their attention toward the issue of parenting in the genesis of self-control. Polakowski's (1994) analysis of data from the Cambridge Youth Study, Feldman and Weinberger's (1994) assessment of 81 sixth-grade boys, the student samples analyzed by Cochran et al. (1998) and by Gibbs et al. (1998), and Hay's (2001) survey of 197 urban high school youth have all explored the dynamics of parenting and self-control. Others have followed suit as well (see, e.g., Blackwell & Piquero, 2005; Brannigan, Gemmel, Pevalin, & Wade, 2002; Lynskey, Winfree, Esbensen, & Clason, 2000; McGloin et al., 2004; Pratt, Turner, & Piquero, 2004; Turner, Piquero, & Pratt, 2005; Unnever et al., 2003), with the recent analysis by Perrone et al. (2004) of the data from the first wave of the National Longitudinal Survey of Adolescent Health (a nationally representative sample of over 13,000 youths) providing some of the most convincing evidence. Indeed, with the exception of the study by Cochran et al. (1998) on self-control and academic dishonesty, the research conducted thus far generally lends credence to the notion that, net of statistical controls, parental efficacy is important to the process of developing self-control in children.

Biological and Neuropsychological Sources of Low Self-Control

Notably, Gottfredson and Hirschi (1990) clearly downplay the possibility that low self-control has a genetic/biological component. For example, following their analysis of adoption studies, they argued that the research provides "strong evidence that the inheritance of criminality is *minimal*.... we conclude that the 'genetic effect'...is near zero" (p. 60, emphasis in the original). They also observed that, "obviously, we do not suggest that people are born criminals, inherit a gene for criminality, or anything of that sort. In fact, we explicitly deny such notions...." (p. 96). Gottfredson and Hirschi, however, raised the *possibility* that "individual differences may have an impact on the prospects for effective socialization (or adequate control)" (p. 96).

Yet in contrast to other criminologists who have systematically incorporated individual differences into their theoretical models (e.g., Moffitt, 1993; Sampson & Laub, 1995; Wilson & Herrnstein, 1985), Gottfredson and Hirschi failed to develop further the interplay between individual differences and self-control. In fact, they went on to assert that, "effective socialization is...always possible whatever the configuration of individual traits" (p. 96). Further, in a more recent statement of their theory (Hirschi & Gottfredson, 2001), they refrained from mentioning the idea that individual traits—such as genetic/biological predispositions—could underlie self-control. Instead, they suggested that at the inception of life, criminal propensity is virtually universal, and that "all of us...are born with the ability to use force and fraud in the pursuit of our private goals" (p. 90).

A number of criminologists, however, fundamentally disagree with this position and have instead adopted a more interdisciplinary (as opposed to strictly sociological) view of the sources of self-control—one that recognizes the intellectual contributions of psychology and biology to the understanding of human behavior (see, e.g., Pratt, Cullen, Blevins, Daigle, & Unnever, 2002; Pratt, McGloin, & Fearn, 2006). Accordingly, despite the evidence of a parenting-self-control link, these scholars have noted a potential model misspecification problem with this line of research. In particular, they emphasize that much of this work has failed to consider potential biological/neuropsychological sources of self-control independent of (and in conjunction with) parental sources.

To that end, research has begun to emerge, which examines these alternative sources of low self-control (see, e.g., Binder, Dixon, & Ghezzi, 2000; Brannigan, Gemmel, Pevalin, & Wade, 2002; Dixon, Horner, & Guercio, 2003; Kalff et al., 2003; Neef, Bicard, & Endo, 2001; Strayhorn, 2002; Unnever & Cornell, 2003). Two primary conclusions can be reached from this body of work. First, indicators of biological predisposition (e.g., attention-deficit/hyperactivity disorder (ADHD), indicators of neuropsychological deficits such as low birth weight and low cognitive ability) are significantly related to levels of self-control independent of measures of effective parenting (McGloin et al., 2004; McGloin, Pratt, & Piquero, 2006; Unnever et al., 2003). Second, controls for such biological/neuropsychological factors tend to partially mediate—and in some cases fully mediate—the effect of parenting on the development of self-control (see, e.g., Wright & Beaver, 2005). Taken together, this research indicates that certain biological and neuropsychological risk factors need to be considered in the formation of self-control.

Community Influences on Low Self-Control

Turning back to a more traditional social-psychological framework, collective socialization theories are typically based on the psychological literature on parenting, supervision, and role models, as well as the sociological literature on monitoring and isolation (see also Chase-Lansdale, Gordon, Brooks-Gunn, & Klebanov, 1997). Neighborhoods experiencing high levels of social isolation, economic deprivation, and adverse familial circumstances are oftentimes referred to as "socially disorganized" (Sampson & Groves, 1989). In such neighborhoods, social isolation is believed to result in family practices that may be less conducive to the development of skills associated with school and work life—factors which may be associated with the positive development of self-control.

In socially cohesive neighborhoods, however, parental efficacy is high, and an emphasis is placed on school, work skills, future orientation, and the general development of self-control. Neighbors in these community contexts are more likely to encourage higher-quality parenting techniques and to help supervise neighborhood children (Chase-Lansdale et al., 1997; Garbarino & Sherman, 1980; Klebanov, Brooks-Gunn, Chase-Lansdale, & Gordon, 1997). This conceptual link with the self-control framework is particularly important since, according to Furstenberg (1993), "[t]he connectedness or embeddedness of the family in its immediate context shapes the strategies of parenting" (p. 255). Furstenberg (1993) went on to note that "where parents live affects how parents manage their children—their means of shielding their children from dangers and exposing them to opportunities" (p. 254) (see also the discussions of family factors and crime/delinquency by Hirschi, 1995; Loeber & Farrington, 1998c; Loeber & Stouthamer-Loeber, 1986).

Bursik and Grasmick's (1993) systemic model of neighborhood control also indicates that neighborhoods characterized by social disorganization are the least likely to provide the setting for the types of child-rearing practices that Gottfredson and Hirschi believe are the most suitable for the development of effective self-control. Specifically, research has shown informal social control processes and/or collective efficacy to be related to various forms of criminal behavior (Bellair, 1997, 2000; Morenoff, Sampson, & Raudenbush, 2001; Sampson, Raudenbush, & Earls, 1997). To the extent that communities act "as a complex system of friendship and kinship networks and formal and informal associational ties rooted in family life and ongoing socialization processes" (Kasarda & Janowitz, 1974, p. 329), it seems particularly important to focus on how different types of neighborhoods influence parenting behavior and, in turn, the development of self-control in children.

Accordingly, research has begun to do just that. The first study in this tradition was the analysis by Pratt et al. (2004), using data drawn from the National Longitudinal Survey of Youth (NLSY), which found that conditions of neighborhood deprivation significantly influenced measures of parental monitoring and socialization. Furthermore, such neighborhood conditions directly affected the development of self-control in children independent of the measures of parental efficacy. A subsequent study by Hay et al. (2006) went a step further and found a significant interaction term between neighborhood conditions and parental efficacy on the development of self-control. As such, this work clearly indicates that community context is yet another factor that must be seriously considered by scholars with regard to the development of self-control in children.

Institutional Influences on Low Self-Control

While the family is arguably most important in the early formative years for children, Gottfredson and Hirschi (1990) also noted that it is not the only institution responsible for socializing individuals. For example, Gottfredson and Hirschi (1990) pointed out that

> We do not restrict the meaning of "familial institution" to the traditional family unit composed of a natural father and mother. The socialization function does not, in our view, require such an institution. It does, however, require responsible adults committed to the training and welfare of the child (p. 273).

This statement therefore implies that social institutions other than the family have the ability to contribute to the development of self-control (Gottfredson, 2001; Gottfredson & Hirschi, 1990, pp. 105–107). The school context may be one such institution.

To be sure, children typically enter formal education between the ages of 5 and 6—an age when self-control is largely malleable and its development is underway. Children therefore experience the structure and imposition of restraints offered by the school early in the life course. This argument is not necessarily novel. Gottfredson and Hirschi (1990) recognized the school as

a potentially important institution and noted its role as a socializing institution, "socializing institutions impose restraints; they do not allow unfet-
tered pursuit of self-interest; they require accomplishment" (p. 107). In short,
schools, and in particular teachers, possess the ability to effectively socialize
individuals and influence self-control.

Although attributing the main sources of self-control to parental socialization, Gottfredson and Hirschi (1990) also acknowledged that the school
has certain advantages for socializing children. First, schools, and teachers in
particular, have the ability to monitor several students at one time. Second,
because of their interest in maintaining a healthy educational environment,
teachers are in a good position to recognize antisocial behavior. Third, many
schools and teachers are given the authority to maintain order and to implement effective discipline. As such, Gottfredson and Hirschi (1990) suggested
that "like the family, the school in theory has the authority and the means to
punish lapses in self-control" (p. 105). And as Denise Gottfredson (2001) also
observed, "schools have the potential to teach self-control and to engage informal social controls to hold youthful behavior in check" (p. 48).

Indeed, the evidence surrounding the effectiveness of schools to teach
self-control has been supportive. In fact, in her review of several experimental
and nonexperimental intervention programs aimed at teaching self-control
within schools, Gottfredson (2001) concluded that, "programs that focus on
teaching self-control and social competency skills are most effective" (p. 227).
For example, in the Montreal Longitudinal Experimental Study, which examined disruptive second grade boys, Tremblay and his colleagues used a two-
pronged intervention that focused on teaching parents to monitor behavior,
to reinforce positive behavior, and to punish negative behavior, and on teaching prosocial skills and self-control within the schools (Tremblay et al., 1991;
Tremblay et al., 1992). Analyses using a 2-year follow-up period suggested that
those in the treatment group were less likely to have engaged in a variety of
deviant behaviors, including fighting. Although the measurement of self-
control was not taken directly, the reduction of disruptive behaviors in the
experimental group compared to the control group is persuasive evidence that
levels of self-control increased. In short, there appears to be evidence to suggest that programs designed to teach self-control within schools possess positive benefits for individuals (see Gottfredson, 2001 for an extensive review of
these programs).

In developing this argument, it is important to remain sensitive to the fact
that families and schools are embedded within the larger community context
(Gottfredson, 2001). Specifically, it should be recognized that child-rearing
and socialization efforts, whether occurring within the household or the

school, do not occur irrespective of their neighborhood environment (Chase-Lansdale et al., 1997; Klebanov et al., 1997). This should come as no surprise since the research noted earlier has suggested that neighbors in socially cohesive neighborhoods encourage and contribute to higher-quality parenting techniques (Garbarino & Sherman, 1980). Again, parents in these neighborhoods exchange strategies to deal with difficult children, share supervision responsibilities, and encourage prosocial activities (Chase-Lansdale et al., 1997). Moreover, as Denise Gottfredson (2001) points out, "the key socializing institutions, such as families, schools, and churches, are less effective in disorganized areas" (p. 65). This suggests that the effects of parental and school socialization could potentially vary in accordance with the type of neighborhood (e.g., whether it is socially organized vs. disorganized) where one resides.

Empirical work that has tested these various propositions has recently emerged (see, e.g., Bennett, Elliott, & Peters, 2005; Sartory, Bauske, & Lunenburg, 2000). The analysis by Turner et al. (2005), of the NLSY data revealed two conclusions along these lines. First, indicators of "school socialization" (which closely resembled typical parenting measures associated with the monitoring and supervision of children) were significantly related to the development of self-control independent of parental efficacy. Second, the effects of school socialization on youths' levels of self-control varied according to (i.e., interacted with) levels of parental efficacy, as well as conditions of neighborhood deprivation. In particular, the effect of school socialization on children's development of self-control was strongest when parental efficacy was low and when neighborhood conditions were criminogenic. These results therefore highlight the ability of social institutions—in this case the school—to "pick up the slack" for instilling self-control in children when other mechanisms, such as parents and the community, break down.

A Revised Model of the Sources of Self-Control

Based on the body of empirical research presented earlier, it is clear that the causes of how and why self-control develops within individuals are far more complex than the simple parenting thesis offered by Gottfredson and Hirschi (1990). To be sure, multiple individual-level and macro-level factors have both direct and indirect effects—along with significant interaction effects—on the formation of self-control within individuals. In an effort to pull this body of literature together systematically, Figure 17.1 presents a revised model of the sources of self-control. Accordingly, on the basis of this

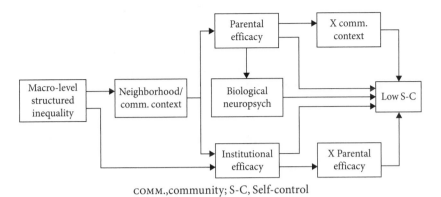

COMM.,community; S-C, Self-control

FIGURE 17.1   Sources of low self-control.

revised model, five empirical propositions regarding the sources of self-control are specified and discussed below.

1. *Parental efficacy has a direct effect on a child's level of self-control.* Gottfredson and Hirschi's (1990) original statement that self-control in children is the result of effective parenting certainly has empirical support. Indeed, multiple studies support the claim that parents who do a more effective job at monitoring and supervising their children's behavior, and correcting misbehavior when it happens, are more likely to instill a high level of self-control in their kids. These results are a clear challenge to Harris's (1998) assertion that when it comes to delinquent involvement, parents really do not matter. It is also important to note, however, that empirical research has not supported Gottfredson and Hirschi's claim that indicators of effective parenting should fully mediate the effects of other potential sources of self-control.

2. *Parental efficacy has an indirect effect on a child's level of self-control through its influence on neuropsychological deficits.* Given the growing influence of biological perspectives in criminology in recent years (McCartan, 2007), it is not surprising that researchers have begun to tackle the issue of self-control from theoretical traditions other than sociology. For example, Moffitt (1993) argued that prenatal risk factors indirectly impact crime and delinquency by increasing the likelihood that children will develop neuropsychological deficits. According to Lynam et al. (1993), "deficits in the neuropsychological abilities referred to as 'executive functions' interfere with a person's ability to monitor and control his or her own behavior" (p. 188).

The problem in this context is that certain prenatal risk factors, which may be empirically related to neuropsychological deficits in children, may be voluntary. Indeed, unlike exposure to lead, poor nutrition, and birth-related injuries, a number of behaviors demonstrated by mothers-to-be, such as cigarette smoking, excessive drinking, and drug use during pregnancy, are arguably *voluntary* prenatal risk factors. As noted by McGloin et al. (2006), a mother who engages in such voluntary prenatal risk behaviors that are known to carry developmental risks for the fetus may be illustrating hedonistic tendencies by putting her desires and needs before those of the child. It is, of course, possible that such tendencies toward hedonism—which may also be an indicator of low self-control—may be passed from parent to child through biological mechanisms (Pratt et al., 2002; Unnever et al., 2003; Wright & Beaver, 2005). Yet it is equally plausible that mothers who engage in such risky behaviors during pregnancy may also be foreshadowing the inability to be an effective parent. The body of work in this area clearly indicates that many neuropsychological deficits have roots in parental practices such as maternal smoking, drinking, or taking drugs during pregnancy. It is not completely evident whether the relationship between those behaviors and later child outcomes is due to neurobiological effects on the child or simply due to ongoing irresponsibility in the parent.

3. *Parental efficacy and self-control are influenced by community context.* Also along the lines of the dynamics associated with effective parenting, it is critical to note that parenting strategies—particularly those that are related to the development of self-control in children—are shaped to a significant degree by community context. This influence plays out empirically as both a direct effect of community context (particularly conditions of harsh economic conditions) on parental efficacy, as well as an interaction between parenting and community context in their effects on the development of self-control in children. In short, good parenting, the kind that leads to high levels of self-control in children, becomes more challenging in socially disorganized neighborhoods.

4. *Institutional efficacy is important in the development of self-control in children.* In addition to community context, research has indicated that certain social institutions (such as schools) directly influence levels of self-control in children. Furthermore, the effect of such institutions is most important when parents have failed in their mission to instill self-control in their children. It is also important to note that institutional efficacy is intertwined with community context, where economically deprived communities are less likely to be able to produce

and maintain the kind of social institutions (like quality schools) that
are capable of positively influencing youths' levels of self-control.

5. *Structural factors explain the spatial distribution of self-control and
   crime.* One of the challenges facing Gottfredson and Hirschi's (1990)
   theory is that it is focused exclusively on the individual level of analysis.
   Indeed, they are consistent in their argument that the structural factors
   favored by macrosocial scholars (e.g., poverty, inequality, and so on) are
   substantively irrelevant to the explanation of criminal behavior once
   self-control is taken into account.

   Nevertheless, Gottfredson and Hirschi (1990) did argue that the
   spatial distribution of crime—where certain macro-level units (e.g.,
   neighborhoods, cities, and beyond) experience more crime than others—
   can be explained fully by differences in the levels of self-control of each
   community's residents. Although this discussion was not central to their
   argument, it becomes relevant here, in that many of the processes that
   are responsible for the development of self-control (e.g., parental efficacy,
   community context, and institutional efficacy) are themselves a consequence of the broader social environment. In particular, macro-level factors such as structured inequality, which are strongly related to crime rates
   across virtually all levels of aggregation (Pratt & Cullen, 2005), essentially
   "set the table" for both community-level problems such as social disorganization and institutional problems such as poorly performing schools.

   Indeed, the importance of the effect of structural inequality on crime
   was highlighted by Blau and Blau (1982), particularly when such inequalities are concentrated within particular racial/ethnic groups (see, e.g.,
   Pratt & Cullen, 2005). This kind of racial inequality is important in this
   discussion for a number of reasons, not the least of which is that it results
   in the concentration of economic deprivation within certain communities and, by extension, within schools (Pratt, 2008; see also Wilson,
   1987). Thus, despite its status as a rather "distal" cause of both individual
   levels of self-control and criminal behavior, understanding the nature
   of either still requires an appreciation of the consequences of structural
   inequality.

Directions for Future Research

Along with the anomie/strain and social learning traditions, Gottfredson
and Hirschi's self-control theory has emerged in the last couple of decades
as one of the major criminological paradigms in the field. While a virtual

empirical consensus has been reached with regard to the *consequences* of low self-control (i.e., its effect on criminal and analogous behaviors), there is considerably less agreement among criminologists concerning the *causes* of low self-control. Accordingly, the revised model presented here was intended to pull together the body of research examining the sources of self-control—much of which comes out of fields other than "traditional" criminology—and to set forth a series of propositions that may be subjected to further testing under varying conditions in an effort to assess their robustness. Three directions for future research on the nature of self-control are thus identified.

First, future empirical work should continue to focus on the complex relationships surrounding parenting and the development of self-control in children. In particular, the literature examining the influence of structural/community characteristics on parental efficacy, while certainly important, is still in its infancy. In addition, there is still a need to systematically assess the causal mechanisms underlying the relationship between ineffective parenting and self-control in children. Specifically, some scholars have highlighted the potential for "child effects" on parenting, where children with early temperament and behavioral problems may be more likely to elicit problematic responses from parents (e.g., overly lenient or inconsistently harsh parenting practices, see Moffitt, 1993; Unnever et al., 2003). Nevertheless, it is still unclear whether these effects exist independent of parents' levels of self-control. That is, is it that difficult children elicit bad parenting or simply that parents of such children may lack self-control themselves, and therefore the capacity to exert vigilant and consistent control over their children? Either way, the problem is that the comparative validity of these two explanations for the parenting–self-control relationship has yet to be assessed.

Second, it would be particularly useful for future studies to continue to assess systematically the interaction effects surrounding parenting, biological and neuropsychological deficits, and community and institutional efficacy on self-control. As such, three questions are immediately salient: (1) Is the effect of neuropsychological deficit on self-control more pronounced for children with low parental efficacy? (2) Is the effect of neuropsychological deficit on self-control more pronounced for children in environments with low community or institutional efficacy? (3) Are "child effects" on parental efficacy more pronounced for parents with low self-control? Answering each of these questions would help to flesh out the complexity of the causes of self-control in critically important ways.

Finally, future studies should continue the recent work of Baumeister and colleagues regarding self-control depletion (see, e.g., Baumeister, 2002; Muraven & Baumeister, 2000; see also Muraven, Pogarsky, & Shmueli, 2006). In essence, this perspective focuses on the consequences to individuals when they exercise self-control; namely, since self-control may be a limited resource within any given person, using it in one situation may partially consume it so that it may less available in future situations. This prospect may be particularly important for individuals with relatively high levels of self-control who reside in neighborhoods plagued by multiple criminogenic risk factors (e.g., limited opportunities for legitimate participation in the labor market; constantly having to resist cultural pressures to engage in "code of the street" behavior, see Anderson, 1999). Indeed, since such individuals will inevitably be forced to exercise their self-control on a regular basis should they want to resist the criminal opportunities and temptations surrounding them, they are most likely to be susceptible to self-control depletion. Furthermore, since replenishing one's reserves of self-control takes time and distance away from the kinds of social pressures that cause depletion in the first place, those residing in harsh neighborhood conditions will find it more difficult to restock their levels of self-control. If so, it may be that variations in the degree to which individuals' self-control becomes depleted—not merely variations in the distribution of individuals' levels of self-control—may help explain the spatial distribution of crime across communities.

Given this line of work, two critical questions have yet to be addressed, the first of which is whether indicators of self-control depletion mediate the effects of other individual and structural characteristics on self-control and analogous behaviors in the same way as an individual's level of self-control? Second, are the precursors to self-control depletion similar to those for one's level of self-control (i.e., the sources of self-control identified in this chapter)? In the end, this last line of work may be most important since it indicates that the self-control perspective in general may need to be revised. In particular, these recent empirical developments highlight how an individual's self-control contains both static (i.e., one's overall level of self-control) and dynamic components (i.e., one's vulnerability to self-control depletion), both of which may exert independent influences on criminal and deviant behavior. Accordingly, examining both the consequences (e.g., for criminal and analogous behaviors) and causes of these components may represent the next generation of self-control research in criminology.

CHAPTER 18

A Dynamic Developmental Systems Approach to Understanding Offending in Early Adulthood

DEBORAH M. CAPALDI AND MARGIT WIESNER

One of the oldest and most widely accepted assumptions in criminology is that criminal involvement diminishes with age (Steffensmeier & Allan, 2000). Recent longitudinal findings regarding crime involvement indicate that even subgroups that seem to offend the most frequently, and follow the most chronic career paths, show decreases in criminal activity as they enter early adulthood (D'Unger, Land, McCall, & Nagin, 1998; Thornberry, 2005; Wiesner, Capaldi, & Kim, 2007), however, reasons for the normative decrease are not well understood. Explaining persistence in crime, despite the overall strong tendency to desist, is therefore an intriguing task. But even further, persistence and desistance are not the only questions of interest with regard to crime in early adulthood. Recent studies have indicated that more individuals without prior criminal records are arrested in early adulthood than had generally been hypothesized. Moffitt et al. (2002) identified a group of men who had not been very delinquent as adolescents, but who emerged as low-level chronic offenders at age 26. Looking retrospectively from adulthood, Farrington et al. (1998) found that almost one-half of the offenders in the Cambridge Study were either late adolescent—young adult or adult onset offenders. Knowledge of adult onset of crime, in addition to persistence and desistance, is therefore of critical importance to understanding crime in adulthood as a whole.

This chapter introduces a dynamic developmental systems approach to understanding criminal activity during the early adult years that we have begun testing in our recent work with the Oregon Youth Study (OYS). The framework is grounded in life-span developmental and also ecological theory and largely applies to male criminal behavior, although we would expect that the fundamental principles would also apply to women's behavior. The chapter begins with a brief review of, first, conceptual models regarding the development of delinquency and, second, dual taxonomy theories of delinquency, as these relate to expectations regarding early adult persistence and desistance. Next, an early adult model detailing processes hypothesized to account for persistence in criminal behavior during the early adult years is delineated. In the final sections, recent findings from the OYS, including crime trajectories and outcomes, are examined and a further model test is described briefly.

Conceptual Approaches to Understanding the Development of Delinquency

In order to create the theoretical backdrop for the consideration of crime in adulthood, conceptual models regarding the development of delinquency are first considered briefly, as they point to processes that may also be associated with persistence. This is particularly important because prior offending is predictive of persistence in crime in early adulthood (Laub & Sampson, 1988). The life-span developmental approach emphasizes the transactions between an individual's prior developmental history and current social environments, within a framework sensitive to the individual's developmental stage (Cairns & Cairns, 1995; Capaldi, Shortt, & Kim, 2005; Caspi & Elder, 1988; Hetherington & Baltes, 1988; Magnusson & Torestad, 1993; Rutter, 1989). This general approach has emerged as the predominant model for preventive interventions for antisocial behavior (e.g., Tolan, Guerra, & Kendall, 1995). Bronfenbrenner's (1986) ecological model, which posits a hierarchy of four nested systems involving intrapersonal factors (e.g., temperament) microsystems of face-to-face interactions, behavioral settings (e.g., neighborhood), and macrocontextual factors involving cultural and community practices, has been similarly valuable in conceptualizing the etiology of antisocial behavior.

At the heart of life-span and ecological approaches are individual transactions with the social environment.

Our general conceptual approach is based on an integrative theoretical framework that helps to clarify the role of the different domains of risk factors in the emergence and continuance of antisocial and related behaviors, namely the dynamic developmental systems model. It is an extension of the general life-span approach and the ecological model, which encompasses biological influences and further articulates both developmental and social influence processes. Because of the very strong evidence that biological systems are related to aggression and associated behaviors, it is critical, to move forward in our understanding of aggressive and antisocial behaviors across the early life span, including crime, that theoretical models are developed that can encompass biological systems within broader frameworks, including psychological systems as well as social and physical environmental systems (e.g., the chemical environment). For example, Simonoff (2001) reviewed molecular genetic influences on conduct disorder, and there have been a number of studies on genetic bases of risk factors, including sensation seeking, impulsivity, and physical aggression. Genetic loading may be associated particularly with dimensions of temperament that relate to brain activity and, thus, to neural pathways (Hill, 2002). There are promising findings of associations of several candidate genes and implicated brain metabolic pathways.

Figure 18.1 (Capaldi & Eddy, 2005) summarizes the developmental model across childhood and adolescence that relates to the development of delinquency that may persist into adulthood. The focus of the model is on the interaction of the individual characteristics of the developing child, such as temperament risk including irritability and impulsivity (Caspi & Bem, 1990), with his or her immediate social environment. For simplicity, only parent and peer domains are illustrated. These transactions occur within and are affected by larger contextual factors affecting the family (e.g., income, parental divorce). In sum, the process of development, including the development of delinquency, may be conceptualized as the functioning of, and transactions across and within, biological, psychological, and social systems, with constant feedback and interaction over time. Thus, the processes are conceptualized as those of dynamic developmental systems (Capaldi et al., 2005).

Delinquency Typologies and Persistence and Desistance

Predictions regarding characteristics of juvenile offenders who will persist or desist from crime in adulthood are made by the dual taxonomy theories of

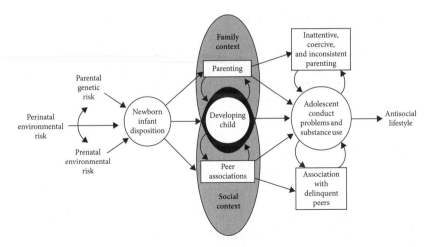

FIGURE 18.1   Dynamic developmental systems model: Development of antisocial behavior. (Reprinted from *The handbook of adolescent behavioral problems: Evidence-based approaches to prevention and treatment*, 2005, *Oppositional defiant disorder and conduct disorder*, by Capaldi & Eddy. By permission of Springer Science and Business Media.)

juvenile delinquency that have been predominant in the field for the past decade (e.g., Moffitt, 1993, 1997; Patterson & Yoerger, 1993, 1997). It is well established that several aspects of juvenile offending have been found to be significant predictors for adult offending (Blumstein, Farrington, & Moitra, 1985). In particular, both age at first arrest and chronicity of juvenile offending are significant predictors of adult arrest (Laub & Sampson, 1988). Several investigators have posited that chronic versus transitory juvenile offending may have fundamentally different features (Farrington & Hawkins, 1991; Moffitt, 1993; Patterson & Yoerger, 1997; Pulkkinen, 1990; Simons, Wu, Conger, & Lorenz, 1994; Stattin & Magnusson, 1991). Notably, early or childhood onset of antisocial behavior and offending predicts chronic offending and is expected to predict persistence in adulthood (see Chapter 9). Later onset of delinquency, in adolescence, has been hypothesized to be associated with better overall adjustment and more transitory engagement in delinquent peer groups and delinquency, and it is expected to predict desistance in adulthood. The life-course-persistent group is hypothesized by Moffitt (1993, 1997) to be a much smaller group than the adolescence-limited group.

We posit that persistence and desistance from crime across adulthood cannot be fully explained by individual differences and experiences in early childhood and age of onset of delinquent behavior, and thus by the dual taxonomy models. Persistence and desistance are expected also to be influenced by experiences and transitions undergone from the early 20s to the early 30s. Processes that relate to selection into social contexts, interactions within those social contexts that relate to cumulative or contemporaneous continuity in behavior (Caspi & Herbener, 1990), and processes that may influence change are addressed below.

Early Adult Pathways to Persistence in Criminal and Antisocial Behavior

Figure 18.2 extends the model of the development of antisocial behavior shown in Figure 18.1 to illustrate mechanisms hypothesized to account for persistence of criminal behavior from adolescence through ages 31 to 32 years among young adult men. These factors, when present for individual men,

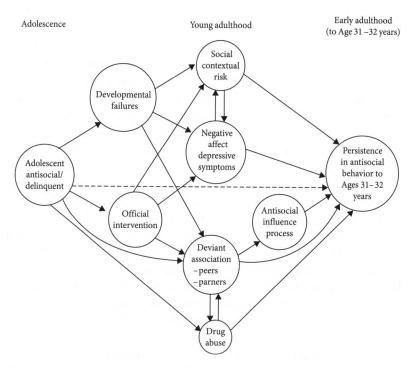

FIGURE 18.2   Dynamic developmental systems model: Persistence of antisocial behavior.

are thought to hinder the developmentally normative movement toward desistance that is seen overall across the age period from late adolescence to around ages 31 to 32 years. Intraindividual changes in biological processes over time, particularly associated with maturation, relate to overall levels of antisocial behavior in the population at different ages. In particular, the effects of brain maturation may account, at least in part, for the overall decrease in criminal activity that occurs from late adolescence through early adulthood. Major brain development, including myelinization, reaches a mature stage by early adulthood (Casey, Tottenham, Liston, & Durston, 2005; Giedd et al., 1999) and relates to the maturity of inhibitory control systems (Welsh, Pennington, & Groisser, 1991). Brain maturity and associated improved inhibitory control is posited to be a major developmental factor related to desistance in crime across early adulthood. Thus, a compelling task is to explain why some prior offenders persist in crime, rather than following the more usual developmental pathway of desistance.

The starting point of the model illustrated in Figure 18.2 is the stability of antisocial or delinquent behavior across time (in terms of rank ordering of individuals, though not necessarily mean levels); thus, prior delinquency is a risk factor for persistence in the early adult years, with risk being higher for those men with earlier onset and more severe histories (Blumstein et al., 1985). Prior antisocial behavior also places the young men at risk for (a) developmental failures in key areas of adjustment, including school achievement, work, intimate relationships, fathering, and subsequently increased depressive symptoms; (b) substance use, especially more severe drug use; (c) official intervention, including arrests and incarceration; (d) continued associations with deviant peers; (e) a romantic partner with higher levels of antisocial behavior.

Individual–Environment Transactions in the Early Adult Period

Aspects of individual–environment transactions that are particularly pertinent to continuity and change in offending behavior in the early adult period include selection into differing social environments. Individual characteristics and behaviors may expand or contract the range of future environmental options (e.g., a young man who did not graduate from high school has limited employment and further education options; a young man who smokes or uses drugs may be not considered as a romantic partner by a young woman who dislikes these behaviors). *Restriction of environmental options* is an unintended but powerful consequence of antisocial behaviors and juvenile offending. Remaining in or entering higher risk and antisocial environments is more likely when prior developmental failures, which are associated with conduct disorder (e.g., substance use, failure to graduate from high school, arrest, and incarceration), have occurred (Capaldi & Stoolmiller, 1999). Similarly, Moffitt (1997) has characterized the effect that past problems have on future offending behavior as "snares" that trap the individual and hinder improvement.

A further influential factor regarding selection into social environments involves the *active* selection of environments that suit the individual's dispositions and goals (Patterson, Reid, & Dishion, 1992; Scarr & McCartney, 1983). Thus, active selection of antisocial peers and romantic partners (involving assortative partnering or mating in the latter case) is considered to be a major contributor to continuance of antisocial behavior (Capaldi, Shortt, & Crosby, 2003; Dishion, Andrews, & Crosby, 1995; Elliott, Huizinga, & Ageton, 1985; Krueger, Moffitt, Caspi, Bleske, & Silva, 1998). Conversely, a continuing association with a prosocial partner may be predictive of stability in nonaggressive behavior. However, this association between prior antisocial behavior and selection of higher-risk social environments is not fully determinative. A young man may have enough attractive characteristics that he finds a socially skilled partner, or at least a partner who is considerably less antisocial than himself. This is posited to relate to decrease or even desistance from criminal behaviors.

Official interventions are hypothesized to increase contextual risk involving engagement in a more deleterious social environment through such factors as increased association with deviant and drug using peers and partners (due again to rejection by prosocial partners and to increased engagement with deviant peers while incarcerated). Official interventions are also expected to predict increased negative affect, including irritability, anger, and depressive symptoms more generally, due partially to stress and disruption in close social relationships.

Drug abuse, negative affect and depressive symptoms, and contextual risk are each hypothesized to increase the probability of antisocial acts via direct and indirect mechanisms. Depressive symptoms are related to ongoing developmental failures (Capaldi & Stoolmiller, 1999), lower social support, and reduced energy and motivation for the effortful process of improvement, such as employment training, establishing more productive work patterns, and establishing new social relationships. Depressive symptoms have been found to predict offending in men (Ostrowsky & Messner, 2005), although their role in persistence has not been strongly established and is posited to be less strong than differential association (e.g., association with deviant peers and partners). Drug abuse and contextual risk each contribute to reduced prosocial and employment opportunities, relationship problems, and continued deviant associations and motivate antisocial behavior (e.g., obtaining money for drugs). In addition, substance use is associated with antisocial behavior during the transition to adulthood and tends to hinder desistance in offending behavior (Hussong, Curran, Moffitt, Caspi, & Carrig, 2004; Roisman, Masten, Coatsworth, & Tellegen, 2004). For example, examining predictors of crime persistence for a predominantly African-American sample with extensive arrest histories, Uggen and Kruttschnitt (1998) found that, for men, recidivists tended to have more extensive histories of crime and drug use.

There is consistent evidence indicating the importance of partner's influence on the individual's subsequent psychopathology, including antisocial behavior and substance use (e.g., Leonard & Mudar, 2003; Moffitt, Caspi, Rutter, & Silva, 2001). Further, Kim and Capaldi (2004) found that the antisocial behavior of both men and women predicted partner violence, and both were associated with arrests of either or both partners for domestic violence (Capaldi et al., 2007), suggesting a dynamic of mutual influence. Given that antisocial behavior, depressive symptoms, and substance use tend to be associated in adolescence and adulthood, it is important to examine the role that these individual dimensions of men's and women's risk characteristics play in explaining offending in early adulthood. It also may be that these co-occurring factors account for any association of women's antisocial behavior and men's persistence in crime. Associations with deviant peers and partners are hypothesized to contribute to persistence in antisocial behavior, both directly, due to increased criminal opportunity (e.g., a friend suggests committing a burglary), and indirectly, via the antisocial influence process whereby the interactions with peers (and partners) may be supportive of antisocial behaviors. Deviant associations and antisocial influence process are very closely associated ongoing processes.

Thus far, the majority of our work has focused on examining heterogeneity in crime patterns including (a) chronic crime trajectories as identified by self-reports (Wiesner, Kim, & Capaldi, 2005), along with young adult outcomes (e.g., substance use), and (b) heterogeneity in arrest trajectories and persistence patterns in relation both to trajectories of self-reported offending and dual taxonomy models (Wiesner et al., 2007), rather than predictors of persistence and desistance. A further study is underway to examine social influence processes from romantic partners on young men's persistence in crime as well as adult onset of arrests (Capaldi, Kim, & Owen, in press).

Findings Regarding Adult Crime in the Oregon Youth Study

In the following section , we will describe some of our recent empirical work on pathways of criminal behavior, beginning with a brief characterization of the OYS sample and the levels of criminal activity displayed by the study participants.

The OYS Sample

The first wave of the OYS was conducted in 1984 with a sample of 206 at-risk boys who were ages 9 to 10 years. The study was conducted in a medium-sized metropolitan area and the sample was drawn from neighborhoods with a high incidence of delinquency; all families with a fourth-grade boy living in these neighborhoods were invited to participate, and 74% agreed to do so. The original goal was to provide an intensive analysis of the family and peer social interactional processes associated with the development of anti-social behavior in childhood and adolescence. The sample was surveyed every year, and data collection is ongoing. The sample is predominantly White and lower or working class. We have studied the OYS boys and young men in multiple settings using natural raters for those settings (e.g., parents for behavior at home, teachers for behavior at school), as well as observational data (e.g., observed family problem-solving interactions), and now have close to 22 yearly waves of multimethod, multiagent data (some major and some minor waves) collected and available for analysis. The retention rates are 95% of living subjects at ages 28 to 29 years.

Over one half of the participating boys had at least one arrest in the juvenile period, and 49 cases (24%) had six or more arrests through ages approximately 23 to 25 years, indicating that the sample contains a substantial proportion of young men with high levels of antisocial behavior. Only 52% graduated from high school, indicating that they are predominantly working and lower class, which is relatively rare for a Euro-American community sample.

Prevalence of Adult Crime in the OYS Sample

By their late 20s, 59 OYS men (29%) had never been arrested, 33 (16%) had been arrested as juveniles only (i.e., before age 18 years), 79 (38%) were persistent offenders by the definition that they were arrested in both the juvenile and adult periods, and 35 (17%) were arrested only in adulthood. These findings indicate several interesting points. First, the prevalence of arrest was relatively high in the OYS sample, despite the fact that it was an at-risk, rather than a high-risk, sample (which would have involved selection of conduct problem boys or by a similarly strong risk factor). Second, the prevalence of men experiencing arrests only in the juvenile years was considerably lower (less than one-half) than the number who persisted by the criterion of being arrested both as juveniles *and* as adults. According to the Moffitt dual taxonomy theory, life-course-persistent offenders are a relatively small group of offenders. By comparison, adolescence-limited offenders are posited to be a relatively much larger group of youth (Moffitt, 1993, 1997). Findings from the OYS are inconsistent with this prediction, though this could be, in part, due to sampling from neighborhoods with higher crime rates.

Adult onset of offending (after age 18 years) occurred for 17% of the sample. This finding, although not predicted by the predominant dual taxonomy models, is consistent with prior studies showing that a sizable portion of adult offenders do not have records of juvenile police contacts. As reviewed by Blumstein et al. (1986), findings of a number of long-term studies of criminal careers indicated that a prevalence for adult onset of arrest of around 17% appeared modal.

There are a number of factors that may relate to the relatively high arrest rates found in the current study. First, improvements in record keeping due to improved computer software and usage may have resulted in more accurate updating of arrest files in recent years compared to earlier studies. Second, a very intensive record search procedure was used in the current study, with regular searches of juvenile and adult files and searches of all areas where each study participant had lived. Finally, the study experienced both high recruitment and high retention rates and, thus, may have retained more of the highly delinquent participants than is usual for a community sample.

Self-Reported Versus Official Records of Offending

Self-report and official records measures of offending behavior each have specific strengths and weaknesses. Official records may include more of the worst offenses and are an objective measure with accurate recording of age at offense; however, they capture only a small fraction of the true number of offenses committed. Many crimes go undetected by the police, some offenders do not get caught, and some crimes are not accurately recorded by the authorities. On the other hand, self-report measures are affected by a variety of biases, including memory and concealment problems, but capture a larger fraction of the true number of offenses committed (Farrington et al., 2003; Farrington, Loeber, Stouthamer-Loeber, van Kammen, & Schmidt, 1996; Huizinga & Elliott, 1986; Lauritsen, 1998; Maxfield, Weiler, & Widom, 2000). The ratio of police contacts to self-reported offenses has been estimated at around 3 to 10:100 (Elliott & Voss, 1974; Gold, 1966). Therefore, self-report measures and official records provide two alternative views on offending behavior (Farrington et al., 2003), which will be related to different empirical findings.

Trajectories of Offending Across Adolescence and Early Adulthood

In a series of studies, Wiesner and colleagues have focused on mapping out distinctive developmental pathways of offending from early adolescent to young adult years, using both self-reported data and official records. For self-report data, six trajectories of offending were identified for the OYS using growth mixture modeling (Wiesner & Capaldi, 2003). In addition to rare and nonoffenders, two chronic groups (chronic high-level, chronic low-level) and two decreasing groups (decreasing high-level, decreasing low-level) were found. Typical of much empirical trajectory work (Piquero, 2005), the identified developmental pathways were more complex than predicted by developmental taxonomies (e.g., Moffitt, 1993; Patterson & Yoerger, 1993, 1997). In a further study examining early adult outcomes related to differential histories of self-reported offending, findings supported the contention that varying developmental courses of offending may have plausible causal effects on key hypothesized outcomes (alcohol use, drug use, depressive symptoms) beyond the effects of an underlying propensity for crime (Wiesner et al., 2005).

In a third study (Wiesner et al., in press), trajectories of officially recorded arrests were modeled and compared to self-reported offending. The extent to which trajectory groupings identified through self-reports may relate to groupings identified by official records is not well understood. Further, the extent to which key features of arrest trajectories identified by mixture modeling techniques will relate to the dual taxonomies of offending is also relatively understudied. Because official arrest rates reflect the "tip of the iceberg" and provide a rather conservative estimate of the actual amount of criminal activity, it is unlikely that mixture modeling of arrests will result in as many pathway groups as is the case with self-report data (Piquero, 2005). Consequently, we expected that a minimum of three but less than six trajectory groups would be identified for officially recorded offending behavior for the OYS sample.

A second goal of the study was to examine key aspects of the identified arrest trajectory groups and to relate them to expectations derived from early taxonomy theories, particularly pertaining to ages of onset and to associations with severity of offending. We hypothesized that any high-level chronic arrest trajectory group would contain a relatively high proportion of young men with both an early onset (first arrest before age 14 years) and a history of more severe offending behavior (as indexed by the lifetime frequencies of arrests and on being arrested for one or more violent crimes). However, based on prior evidence from self-report data (Wiesner & Capaldi, 2003), we expected that the highest level and chronic arrest trajectory would show some decrease in offending in early adulthood and that the less severe offenders would also show some decrease, but that their offending behavior would continue and not be strictly limited to adolescence.

Using semi-parametric group-based modeling (Nagin, 1999) and controlling for dormancy periods and exposure time, three trajectories of officially recorded offending behavior were identified: rare offenders (69%), low-level chronic offenders (22%), and high-level chronic offenders (9%). As expected, the majority of the young men belonged to the rare-offender group. The three groups were quite distinctive from each other and well separated. As expected, fewer groups were identified by arrest data than by self-report data (Wiesner & Capaldi, 2003). However, there were significant associations between the two sets of groupings. For example, almost 58% of the high-level chronic arrest trajectory members were also members of the self-report chronic high-level trajectory, and none of them belonged to the three low-level offending self-report trajectories (i.e., decreasing low-level, rare, and nonoffenders).

The groups showed some substantive divergence from predictions from dual taxonomy theories. Notably, both the high- and low-level chronic groupings contained relatively equal numbers of early onset youth, whereas both dual taxonomy models hypothesize that the less severe group starts later. Further differences included the fact that the arrests of the low-level chronic group, which was most analogous to the adolescence-limited group in being less severe, were not limited to adolescence but continued into the twenties. The high-level chronic group showed the adolescent peak followed by decline hypothesized for the adolescence-limited group, although with an unexpected upsurge in the mid twenties. Laub and Sampson (2003) also found a pattern of peak offending at around age 16 years followed by a steep decline for a sample of serious delinquents. Thus, the substantial decline in arrests in the later teens and early 20s found for the high-level chronic group in the OYS sample is in keeping with the Laub and Sampson (2003) findings for a much earlier cohort. Of those adult onset men, a substantial proportion (almost one-third) were in the high-level chronic group and, therefore, had five or more arrests across the adult period. Thus, it was not the case that the adult onset men all showed relatively trivial crime careers. Overall, the findings suggest the need for modification of existing developmental taxonomies of life-span criminal behavior.

Romantic Partner Influence on Men's Arrests in Adulthood in the OYS Sample

One of the most notable features of the early adult period is the establishment of stable romantic relationships, and social control theorists have emphasized the role of such conventional social bonds in crime desistance. Thus, it has been theorized that marriage is a turning point in the life course of criminally involved men (Sampson & Laub, 1990). Marriage has been found to have a main effect on crime, and in one study it was associated with a 35% average reduction in the probability of crime (Sampson & Laub, 2005b). Sampson and Laub (1990) posit that attachment or bonding to a partner is the key social control mechanism of marriage (Sampson & Laub, 1990, 2005b). In a study of the Glueck and Glueck (1968) sample of delinquent boys committed to juvenile detention and a control sample of nondelinquent boys, Sampson and Laub (1990) found that men who showed higher attachment to their spouse were less likely to be arrested across ages 17 to 32 years, controlling for prior levels of criminal involvement. In recent work, Sampson and Laub (200b5) have tested more dynamic models that can help account for time-varying processes across adulthood. Intraindividual analyses over time indicated that the same man commits less crime when married than when not married. Laub et al. (1998) concluded that childhood and juvenile characteristics were insufficient for predicting patterns of future offending and that early marriages characterized by social cohesiveness led to a growing preventive effect. Overall, the degree to which relationship stability and attachment are protective against persistence of crime has been tested in very few longitudinal samples, and thus further evidence of their role is needed.

Notwithstanding broad recognition of the importance of social learning mechanisms in the development of antisocial behavior (Dishion & Patterson, 2006), including the central role of association with deviant peers (Matsueda & Anderson, 1998), relatively few studies have examined the direct social influence of romantic partners' deviant or criminal behavior on men's persistence in crime (e.g., Farrington & West, 1995; Haynie, Giordano, Manning, & Longmore, 2005; Woodward, Fergusson, & Horwood; 2002). Overall, a consensus has not been reached in part because of varying research designs and statistical models and limited measurement of women's antisocial behavior. The dynamic developmental systems approach conceptualizes behavior in the romantic dyad as mutually influential and as responsive to developmental characteristics of each of the partners, as well as to both broader and more proximal contextual factors (Capaldi et al., 2005). In this approach, partner's behavior is viewed as a strong social environmental influence, because the intimate partner represents arguably the individual's most proximal and influential social relationship in early adulthood (Capaldi et al., 2005). We view partner's social influence related to their own behavior as a more important predictor of men's criminal engagement in adulthood than men's attachment to partner, as assessed by relationship satisfaction. However, social control factors are viewed as influential, mainly via relationship stability, which is likely related to more engagement in normative adult roles, including work and parenthood.

In recent work, hypotheses based in both social learning and social control perspectives regarding female romantic partner influence on official crime occurrence for the OYS men were tested across a 12-year period in early adulthood (from ages 17–18 to 28–29 years) in a comprehensive dynamic prediction model (Capaldi et al., in press). This study focused on specifying the influence of romantic partners on men's likelihood of arrest in adulthood within the context of a dynamic model including other expected predictors (e.g., deviant peer association) based in social learning theory, and integrating predictors based in social control theory. It was hypothesized that both partner antisocial behavior and relationship stability would relate, positively and negatively respectively, to men's criminal engagement and that men's attachment to partner would not be predictive in multivariate models accounting for each of these factors and the control factors (e.g., prior criminal behavior). Models were examined for both the persistence and onset of crime in early adulthood (from ages 17–18 to 28–29 years) for men, and were tested using Zero-Inflated Poisson (ZIP) modeling, with predictions to arrest class (interpretable as any arrest versus no arrest) for both onset and persistence of crime, and also to arrest count for the group showing persistent crime in adulthood.

Overall, findings confirmed the hypotheses that predictors based in social learning (and differential association) theory, namely both deviant peer association and romantic partner's antisocial behavior, are associated with men's involvement in crime in adulthood. Also as predicted, relationship stability was the key social control factor related to desistance, whereas, attachment to partner was not predictive in the full multivariate models. Findings indicated partner and peer influences on men's persistence in crime over prior propensity and thus, in contrast to the general theory of crime (Gottfredson & Hirschi, 1990) that posits that prior propensity explains criminal behavior, deviant social influences were found to have an effect even in early adulthood.

Conclusions and Future Directions

In this chapter, we have introduced a dynamic developmental systems approach to understanding criminal activity of young men during the early adult years. This conceptual framework permits a considerably more detailed assessment of the complex individual-environment transactions that may affect young adult men's criminal behavior compared to much prior research based on a general theory of crime and on social control theory.

Several studies have been conducted with the OYS sample examining trajectories of persistence and desistance from crime across adolescence and early adulthood (Wiesner & Capaldi, 2003; Wiesner et al., in press; Wiesner et al., 2005). Findings from these studies using empirically-based approaches to identify heterogeneity in crime trajectories indicated that, as expected, greater heterogeneity in pathways can be identified from self-reported rather than official crime. In both cases, some notable divergence from influential dual taxonomy theories of crime were seen in long-term growth patterns for the differing trajectories. Findings, along with those of other recent growth mixture modeling studies, indicate that aspects of those theories need considerable revision. Further, the issue of adult onset of crime in men is little understood and needs further examination. Now that recent studies have made substantial progress both in identifying the biological underpinnings of the overall developmental trend toward crime desistance in adulthood and in identifying longer-term crime patterns, future studies need to focus particularly on factors in adulthood that account for variation in persistence and onset of crime over and above childhood and adolescence propensity (Capaldi et al., in press).

CHAPTER 19

What Drives Persistent Offending?
The Neglected and Unexplored Role
of the Social Environment

Per-Olof H. Wikström and Kyle Treiber

One of the most intriguing, yet challenging, questions that continue to confront criminologists is *why* some offenders embark upon a sustained "career" of criminal involvement. The answer is important not only for our understanding of crime causation, but also for the development of effective crime policy and prevention practices.

This chapter will approach the topic by addressing the question of what drives stability and change in people's crime involvement, illuminating some of the life-course characteristics and patterns which may perpetuate offending. Most current theory and research that attempts to explain "chronic offending" focuses on the individual and factors such as dispositions and propensities that increase the likelihood of offending but neglect the role of the wider social environment and its impact on how individuals *develop* (e.g., the processes of socialization and habituation which they experience) and *act* (via their differential exposure to criminogenic inducements and constraints).

This chapter will present two key arguments: (1) stability and change in crime involvement are driven by stability and change in the *interplay* between an individual's propensity to offend (based on his or her morality and ability to exercise self-control) and his or her exposure to criminogenic settings (criminogenic moral contexts); and (2) the role that the *social environment* undoubtedly plays in promoting (or, alternatively, subduing) persistent offending has been, for the most part, neglected (theoretically) and unexplored (empirically). We reason that to address the question of why some individuals chronically offend, we need to develop less constricted theories regarding the factors which drive stability and change in crime involvement, taking into consideration external factors that affect the expression of propensity, and we need to devise and employ better methods for studying how the social environment influences development and change in propensity, and how individuals are differentially exposed to criminogenic settings.

We will begin by addressing the problematic concept of "chronic offenders." We will then review several prominent contemporary criminological developmental and life-course theories and consider how effectively they can explain sustained (chronic, persistent) offending. These include Gottfredson and Hirschi's general theory of crime (self-control theory), Moffitt's dual developmental taxonomy and Sampson and Laub's age-graded theory of informal social control. Finally, we will discuss how the recently developed *situational action theory* (Wikström, 2004, 2005, 2006, 2007a, 2007b, 2007c; Wikström & Treiber, 2007) surmounts some of the shortcomings discernible in these (and other) theories that seek to explain (and study) "chronic" offending, particularly as regards the role of agency and the role of the social environment in stability and change in crime involvement.

The Problematic Concept of "Chronic Offenders"

The popular notion of "chronic offenders" rose to the forefront of criminological attention following the seminal study by Wolfgang et al. (Wolfgang, Figlio, & Sellin, 1972), which identified a small group of offenders responsible for a disproportionately large percentage of recorded acts of crime, a finding which has since been replicated in other longitudinal studies (e.g., Farrington, 2003b; Moffitt, Caspi, Rutter, & Silva, 2001; Pulkkinen, 1988; Wikström, 1985, 1990). However, the term "chronic offender" refers, in principle, to a *persistent* offender, one who has committed repeated acts of crime over a longer period of time, not simply a *frequent* offender, one who has committed a particular number of offenses. Frequent offending may be considered one of the defining characteristics of a chronic (or persistent) offender, but the duration of offending is fundamental to the concept of "chronic." Yet it is unclear *how* frequent offending must be over *how* long a stretch of time to qualify as chronic (or persistent). Many criminologists use frequency as a criterion for defining a "chronic" offender, following Wolfgang et al.'s lead, and classify chronic offenders as those who have committed five or more recorded crimes (or experienced five or more convictions). This is an arbitrary definition which Piquero et al. (2007) show does not isolate a qualitatively distinct group of offenders. They point out that it is abundantly clear from the available chronic offending literature that expedient "theoretical and empirical definitions of chronicity have yet to be established" (Piquero, Farrington, & Blumstein , 2007, p. 18).

An important question that arises from this inquiry is how useful is it to the explanation of crime to identify groups of offenders by the frequency of their offending and *then* ask questions about the causal backgrounds for their different levels of crime involvement. Does the fact that individuals vary in the frequency of their offending inevitably imply that their crime involvement stems from different causes? We would reason it does not. The fact that some offend infrequently, others very frequently, and others not at all (within a given time period) does not necessarily signify that their offending has different causes. It is more likely, in our opinion, that what differs between offenders, leading to differences in their level of offending, is whether and to what degree they present individual causal characteristics (e.g., weak moral values and/or difficulties in exhibiting self-control) and are exposed to environmental causal characteristics (e.g., opportunities to offend and/or low levels of monitoring).

Another crucial question is whether the causal factors that influence crime involvement exhibit stability or are malleable and have the potential to change. It seems improbable that causally relevant individual and environmental characteristics could become completely intractable over the entire life course (or the remainder of the life course after a certain age). Yet, to argue that some offenders exhibit the same stable pattern of offending across the life course, one has to assume (implausibly) that the causal factors which influence those individuals' actions (e.g., acts of crime) will remain the same indefinitely. Such an argument cannot allow for individual or environmental change in factors that are important to an individual's level of crime involvement. If correct, this argument imparts a grim message to crime prevention, because without the possibility for change in the individual or environmental factors affecting individuals' crime involvement, the only avenue open for crime prevention will be incapacitation.[1]

We do not, of course, deny the great heuristic value of descriptions of individual differences in crime involvement, and of patterns of individual changes in crime involvement over time. However, we do believe that acts of

---

[1] Which is, in fact, an environmental change!

crime should be thought of and treated as an outcome of causal processes and that theories of crime causation should focus on causal factors (and their changes) when explaining those outcomes. Similarly, to understand persistent offending (outcome) we need to understand what causal factors drive stability and change (causal processes) in individuals' crime involvement. The focus, consequently, should be placed on explaining chronic (or persistent) *offending* rather than chronic (or persistent) *offenders*.

Explaining Chronic Offending—Prominent Approaches

Contemporary theories that seek to explain change and stability in patterns of offending have typically taken one of two approaches: the typological (or taxonomical) approach, which focuses primarily upon sources of stability (generally presumed to be established during childhood); or the life-course approach, which focuses primarily upon sources of change (especially during adulthood). *Typological theories* suggest there are distinct kinds of offenders who may be identified by unique characteristics and/or patterns of offending. A chronic offender typology assumes that some individuals exhibit (stable) characteristics (traits, propensities, deficiencies, etc.) that increase their propensity to offend across settings and situations and, consequently, promote stability in their offending. *Life-course theories*, alternatively, argue that patterns of offending are more tractable and shaped by later as well as early life events and circumstances. Chronic offending, thus, results from stability in life circumstances conducive to offending, or stability in the conduciveness of changing life circumstances to offending.

Whether of the typological or life-course variety, many current theories of chronic offending suffer key shortcomings in their explanation of the sources of stability and change that perpetuate or terminate criminal careers. Namely, they frequently fail to adequately address individual and environmental levels of explanation, and particularly the interaction of individual and environmental factors in crime causation, and to clearly depict the causal mechanisms which link purported causes to acts of crime (Wikström, 2004, 2006, 2007b, 2007c).

Some of the most popular contemporary theories of crime are in fact theories of *criminality*, in that what they explain is what causes the *propensity* to commit acts of crime but not what causes acts of crime themselves (see Gottfredson, 2005, for more on this distinction). This makes them more theories of predilection than theories of action, which is arguably not as viable an approach to the explanation of crime.

There are two key differences between a theory of propensity and a theory of action. A theory of action requires a context in which that action takes place, whereas propensity exerts its influence independent of the setting. A theory of action introduces the notion of agency, through which the individual is able to respond to a setting, whereas propensity presumes some degree of predisposition entailing at least the probability that an individual will act in a predetermined manner. From an action theory perspective it is not sufficient to explain only individual-level mechanisms of crime causation (i.e., what links individual characteristics to acts of crime); one must also explain environmental-level mechanisms of crime causation (what links environmental characteristics to acts of crime) and, ideally, how the two interact, to adequately explain why certain individuals in certain settings *perceive* an act of crime as an action alternative and *choose to* carry out that act.

Another intrinsic weakness of propensity theories is that they rely on inflated assumptions about behavior. Two important behavioral dimensions that these theories consistently misrepresent are motivation and constraint. Many rely on principles of control and rational choice, which imply that all individuals perceive and value actions and potential outcomes the same way but differ in how they perceive and value possible consequences. By this logic all individuals will be similarly motivated to commit a certain action, but differentially restrained. Consequently, restraint becomes the variable of interest in explaining individual differences in offending.

Motivation is a complex topic which cannot be explained solely from the individual level. Arguably, motivation represents the combination of an individual's desire for (or commitment to) a particular outcome and the belief that *in a given setting* he or she may acquire that outcome through a certain course of action (Wikström, 2005, 2006). In other words, motivation is a situational concept. Without taking into consideration the motivational role of the characteristics of a given setting, and how an individual interacts with and perceives those characteristics, it is impossible to adequately explain what about that setting leads an individual to believe a desired outcome is possible and that a given action represents a potential means of acquiring that outcome, that is, what it is that motivates that individual to act in that way. Presuming that all individuals will be equally motivated to commit a certain act in all settings provides a false simplification of behavior that undermines the explanation of what causes individuals to commit acts of crime (and persist in their offending).

These key limitations are demonstrated (in some cases glaringly) even by some of the most prominent criminological theories to date. We consider three such theories: Gottfredson and Hirschi's general theory of crime (1990), Moffitt's dual developmental taxonomy (1993) and Sampson and Laub's age-graded theory of informal social control (1993). These theories have all contributed markedly to the present state of knowledge regarding the sources of stability and change that perpetuate or terminate patterns of chronic offending. However, they leave several important topics underdeveloped or even unaddressed.

We discuss these omissions and suggest how we may advance theory and research into chronic offending by building on the strengths, and addressing the weaknesses, of existing approaches.

Gottfredson and Hirschi's General Theory of Crime

First posited in 1990, the general theory remains one of the most popular, if controversial, criminological theories today (Goode, 2008). Historically, it has played a key role in focusing criminological interest on the role of individual differences in crime involvement. It is a descriptive and probabilistic theory of crime (raising some concerns about its explanatory value) that has brought the concept of *propensity* to the forefront of criminological inquiry. Propensity is an individual's inclination to behave in a particular manner. Because Gottfredson and Hirschi's theory focuses on explaining the propensity to offend and its role in determining between-individual differences in offending, it is arguably more a general theory of criminality than of crime (indeed, Gottfredson and Hirschi use the term "criminality" almost interchangeably with "self-control") (Gottfredson & Hirschi, 1990). The theory adopts a semitypological approach by arguing for different kinds of people who exhibit different patterns of offending. Rather than conceiving discrete groups, however, it places individuals along a continuum, positing that some are *more likely to offend* in any given situation than others. Those who are more likely to offend have low self-control.

Self-control represents a (relatively) stable individual trait determined by an individual's general impulsivity, insensitivity to consequences, preference for physical rather than mental activities, penchant for risk-taking and short-sightedness in regards to actions and outcomes (Gottfredson & Hirschi, 1990). Individuals who exhibit these traits have *low* self-control. Having low self-control means they are less likely to consider the consequences of their actions and therefore more likely to be susceptible to immediate temptations that may have delayed negative outcomes. As a control theory, the general theory considers these temptations to include acts of crime (because such acts provide large rewards for little effort). Thus, by default, having low self-control increases the probability that an individual will offend in any situation at any time.

The juxtaposition of a trait (low self-control) with a propensity is problematic as it argues both for a discrete and a continuous typology. Gottfredson and Hirschi give no clear indication of *how* impulsive, insensitive, physical, risk-taking, and short-sighted an individual has to be to qualify as having low self-control (i.e., whether there is a qualitatively distinct cutoff between individuals with enough self-control to avoid a life of crime and those with low self-control who probably will not). This has implications for theory and research as it blurs the definition of low self-control and obscures the target group. The notion of propensity generally suggests a continuum, while a typology argues for greater degrees of separation. Both describe behavior from an individual-level perspective and are not necessarily mutually exclusive, but it is important for theories that use these classifications to explain precisely where their concepts lie.

According to Gottfredson and Hirschi (1990), self-control is acquired through socialization, a social learning process by which individuals learn to repeat controlled behaviors through reinforcement and the monitoring and censure of uncontrolled behaviors. Socialization is especially critical during childhood and relies primarily upon effective parenting, although other social institutions (such as schools) may play a supplementary role. By early adolescence, relative levels of self-control stabilize, although socialization continues through adulthood via social interactions, meaning that self-control continues to increase with age for all individuals. Thus those with higher self-control in adolescence will continue to display greater self-control than those with lower self-control in adolescence, although self-control will continue to increase for both groups. This helps to explain both the negative slope on the latter face of the age-crime curve and within-individual differences, while still providing for between-individual stability.

According to Gottfredson and Hirschi, this propensity to take into consideration the consequences of one's actions "is the only enduring personal characteristic productive of criminal (and related) behaviour" (1990, p. 111). Although initially noting that situational factors like opportunity could impact the expression of low self-control, the authors later assert that the relationship between self-control and acts of crime can be studied "without undue concern for differences in opportunities to commit criminal, deviant, or reckless acts" (Gottfredson & Hirschi, 2003, p. 18). This suggests that really only individual-level factors are important for explaining acts of crime, and only self-control affects individuals' propensity to offend. The variability of self-control must therefore explain both stability and change in patterns of offending.

Although sources of stability lie at the core of their theory, Gottfredson and Hirschi have struggled to adequately address sources of change. The notion of relative stability over time touches upon the issue of gradual, age-related change, while the notion of heterogeneous continuity through "analogous" acts makes evidence of change more consistent with their explanation; however, it is clear that the theory is more interested in and provides a better argument for stability.

If, according to Gottfredson and Hirschi, self-control alone explains offending, it should also explain chronic offending. The general theory predicts that individuals will chronically offend if their self-control is low enough to ensure they offend regularly, and continue to offend despite subsequent socialization. As all offending is explained by the same mechanism, chronic offending requires no special consideration or differential treatment.

Although a classic explanation of crime, the general theory exemplifies the theoretical shortcomings previously described: it fails to integrate levels of explanation, being a purely individual-level theory of crime, and its commentary on causal mechanisms is underdeveloped, as it relies on several gross assumptions which are arguably no longer tenable, including notions of rational choice and the outdated pleasure/pain principle (Wikström & Treiber, 2007). It is clearly a theory of propensity (criminality) rather than action (crime), and avoids the issue of environmental-level explanations of crime by ultimately disregarding the role of environmental factors in the expression of propensity (Gottfredson & Hirschi, 2003). Similarly, although it recognizes the importance of decision making, the theory also says very little about human agency.

The latter is primarily a consequence of its theoretical heritage. By relying on the pleasure/pain principle, it presumes that behavior is motivated by immediacy and self-interest. As a theory of rational choice, it presumes that all individuals utilize a similarly rational process to evaluate the costs and benefits of any given action. As a theory of social control, it also presumes that certain kinds of actions convey qualities which universally motivate individuals to pursue them. In other words, individuals' action choices are not differentiated by their potential benefits, as these are uniformly perceived by all individuals, or the decision-making process, which follows the same rational method for all individuals, but rather their potential costs, which individuals are more or less likely to take into consideration. Thus, according to the general theory of crime, although "there will be little variability among people in their ability to see the pleasures of crime, there will be considerable variability in their ability to calculate potential pains" (Gottfredson & Hirschi, 1990, p. 95).

This, of course, ignores differential motivation and the fact that external as well as internal factors can affect motivation amongst different individuals and in different settings. At the same time it ignores the fact that the human decision-making process is not truly *rational*; emotions, for instance, play a large (but here unconsidered) role in general and immediate preferences for action. It also ignores the fact that human action may be driven by habitual, unconscious mechanisms as well as (and probably more frequently than) deliberate mechanisms (Wikström & Treiber, 2007). Because it relies on these flawed and overly simplistic assumptions about human behavior, the general theory cannot effectively explain action or propensity. It might have benefited from a less obstinate rejection of biological facts, which could have helped clarify these aspects of human behavior, providing a more valid basis for explaining crime.

The general theory has been critiqued at length in other publications (see, e.g., Akers, 1991; Geis, 2000, 2008; Marcus, 2004; Simpson & Geis, 2008; Wikström & Treiber, 2007). Despite its shortcomings, the theory has made substantial contributions to the explanation of crime, generating a vast amount of empirical research into individual-level explanations of crime and serving as a catalyst for more comprehensive approaches, including those detailed below. It should without a doubt be esteemed for these contributions. However, researchers should also recognize its limitations, especially when designing future, and interpreting past, research.

Moffitt's Dual Developmental Taxonomy

Building on the foundation of individual-level explanation laid by Gottfredson and Hirschi, Moffitt (1993, 1997) developed an alternative propensity theory that addresses more interactive processes between individuals and the social environment. Despite drawing attention to the importance of this interaction, Moffitt's theory continues to approach the explanation of crime from a decidedly individual-level perspective, focusing on propensity rather than action. At the same time, while paying tribute to the role of social environmental variables in the acquisition of the propensity to offend and in the motivation of offending, Moffitt does not fully develop the role of situational variables in crime causation, leaving the topic open for further expansion.

Unlike many propensity theories, Moffitt's dual developmental taxonomy argues for two types of offenders whose offending requires different causal explanations: *adolescence-limited offenders*, who, as the name implies, offend only during adolescence when they are denied legitimate access to desired adult resources (e.g., recognition and autonomy, but also drugs, sex, etc.); and *life-course-persistent offenders*, who exhibit continuity in offending from childhood throughout adulthood (Moffitt, 1993). Both categories remain contentious. Little evidence supports the concept of "normative" adolescent offending, as Moffitt (2003) herself points out in a research review. There is also evidence ruling out the existence of "life-course-persistent offenders" (Sampson & Laub, 2003). However, evidence does support certain aspects of the theory associated with persistent (but not *life-course*-persistent) offending.

According to Moffitt (1993), life-course-persistent offenders (equivalent to chronic offenders) account for approximately 4% to 9% of the male population and are identified by "a continuous lifelong antisocial course" (p. 674). This "course" manifests in diverse antisocial behaviors, including but not limited to criminal offending, and demonstrates *heterotypic continuity* as well as *cross-situational consistency* across different settings (Moffitt, 1993, p. 679). Individuals acquire this propensity through the interaction of early neurological deficits (arising from genetic vulnerability, developmental delay, or adverse life events such as birth complications or head injury) with early disadvantages (such as poor parenting and deprivation). These neurological deficits typically manifest as autonomic and/or motor impairments, such as inattentiveness, poor affect regulation, awkwardness, and poor communication, which may provoke negative responses from parents and other carers, as well as from colleagues and peers in later life. Such adverse person-environment interactions can transform "subtle childhood variations in neuropsychological health... into an antisocial style that pervades all domains of adolescent and adult behaviour" (Moffitt, 1993, p. 684).

Moffitt argues that individuals who suffer neurological deficits are more likely to be born into life circumstances in which they experience adverse person-environment interactions, as they are more likely to be born to teenage, single or mentally ill parents and/or to parents who carry a genetic predisposition for such deficits; as a result, they are also more likely to experience neglect, harsh or inconsistent discipline, family conflict, and low socioeconomic status (Moffitt, 1993). These early disadvantages exacerbate antisocial personality traits (fostering psychopathy, for example), self-regulatory deficiencies such as impulsivity and hyperactivity (leading to early conduct disorders), and cognitive deficits (especially in verbal intelligence and memory). Once this constellation of life-course-persistent traits becomes "fixed" (generally before the age of 18), it alone can predict behavioral outcomes (Moffitt, 1993, p. 684). These antisocial outcomes are perpetuated by three kinds of person-environment interaction: *evocative interactions*, in which individuals evoke responses which exacerbate their antisocial behaviors; *reactive interactions*, in which individuals respond to their environments in a manner consistent with their antisocial propensities; and *proactive interactions*, in which individuals seek out (or create) environments which support their antisocial propensities (Moffitt, 1993, p. 683).

Like Gottfredson and Hirschi's theory, Moffitt's focuses on sources of behavioral continuity, but pays less attention to sources of change. It even suggests that chronic offenders may actively perpetuate their offending by transforming "opportunities for change... into opportunities for continuity" (Moffitt, 1993, p. 684). Because they lack the appropriate social skills and behavioral flexibility to take advantage of prosocial experiences, life-course-persistent offenders may still respond antisocially to, or provoke antisocial responses from, potentially reformative situations. The role of agency in this process remains unexplored and apparently overshadowed by propensity.

The concept of agency is generally underdeveloped in Moffitt's theory. Although the development and expression of propensity is determined by individual factors and experience, Moffitt leaves little room for the discussion of perception and choice during person-environment interactions. Although she discusses reactive and proactive interactions, which imply willfulness, the outcome of these interactions are determined by the individual's propensity, regardless of the setting, suggesting the individual has little actual control (Moffitt, 1993).

The theory's main contribution to the explanation of chronic offending is the attention it pays to person-environment interactions. However, the theory is more interested in explaining how characteristics of the social environment reinforce the propensity to offend than how more concrete environmental factors may influence offending directly. It limits the role of social environmental factors to the development and expression of the propensity to offend; once that propensity stabilizes it dictates behavior regardless of the (social) setting. Prior to socialization, characteristics of the social environment may exacerbate antisocial tendencies, compel (heterogeneous) continuity, and promote the acquisition of "new behavioural components" (Moffitt, 1993, p. 684). However, when an individual enters a setting, it is his or her propensity which determines whether his or her behavior will be antisocial; characteristics of the setting merely determine how, not if, that propensity is expressed. Thus it is the individual's propensity which causes (and perpetuates) offending.

Moffitt's theory is reasonably clear about the indirect causal processes that link individual characteristics to offending (e.g., the processes which explain the propensity to offend); the combination of neurological deficits and early disadvantage hampers the acquisition of prosocial skills, constricting an individual's behavioral repertoire to more antisocial behaviors. The theory is less clear about the direct causal processes which link propensity to offending, for example, what situational factors cause life-course-persistent offenders to express their propensity and evoke a negative person-environment interaction. The theory is also unclear about the direct causal processes which link environmental characteristics to offending, for example, those which reactively prompt, or proactively support, antisocial behavioral styles. Moffitt does, however, discuss indirect processes that link environmental factors to propensity: *negative feedback* from disadvantaged environments exacerbates antisocial tendencies and prosocial deficiencies, "slowly and insidiously" constructing an antisocial personality (Moffitt, 1993, p. 684).

This "feedback" is arguably confounded by the fact it is generated by the individual and the environment and is therefore a situational, not a solely environmental, characteristic. This makes it doubly unclear as to what role the environment plays in the link between the propensity to offend and offending itself, and begs the question of what environmental factors might influence environmental feedback, and how. Clearly, greater elaboration is required to clarify the role of environmental factors in, and the causal processes which link them to, propensity and/or offending, including how they interact with individual factors.

Research evidence supports the supposition that the small percentage of offenders who are responsible for a disproportionate amount of crime also disproportionately exhibit neurological abnormalities and have experienced early disadvantages (Donker, Smeenk, van der Laan, & Verhulst, 2003; see Moffitt, 1993, pp. 676–678, for a review; Moffitt, 2003; Moffitt, Caspi, Harrington, & Milne, 2002; Moffitt et al., 2001; Piquero, Daigle, Gibson, Piquero, & Tibbetts, 2007). However, studies have also posited a number of other offending trajectories, including one characterizing lower frequency chronic offenders (Nagin, Farrington, & Moffitt, 1995; Nagin & Land, 1993). These low-level chronic offenders also exhibit a disproportionate number of neurological deficits, generally in the form of internalizing disorders such as anxiety and depression, rather than externalizing disorders such as conduct and attention deficits, which are traditionally associated with life-course-persistent offending (Moffitt, 2003; Moffitt et al., 2002; Nagin et al., 1995). This suggests that similar but not identical mechanisms may explain high-level or low-level chronic propensity, a finding which requires further explanation.

At the same time, little evidence supports the notion that these offenders may be termed *"life-course-persistent."* Sampson and Laub discredit this claim using one of the few datasets available that covers most of the life span: their extension of Eleanor and Sheldon Glueck's (1950) *Unraveling Juvenile Delinquency* study (Laub & Sampson, 2003; Sampson & Laub, 2003, 2005b). They found that regardless of early life propensity, all offenders demonstrated marked patterns of desistance in later life. Moffitt, however, suggests that while official offending may indeed decline over the life course, antisocial behavior does not. Rather, it becomes expressed "in a form that is simply not yet well measured by epidemiological surveys of official crime" (Moffitt, 1993, p. 680). A lack of appropriate longitudinal data makes it difficult to disprove this assertion, but the topic certainly warrants further consideration. Unfortunately,

Moffitt has done little to adapt her original theory to reflect these and other unexpected findings.

Despite Moffitt's failure to explore these opportunities for advancing the original theory, her dual developmental taxonomy has played a pivotal role in advancing interest in the interaction between individual traits and experiences and its role in the etiology of offending. The theory has laid the groundwork for many of the most progressive approaches to criminological research, some of which have been pioneered by Moffitt herself (e.g., gene-environment interactions). It has advocated the importance of neurological factors in individual differences in cognition and behavior and the role of the environment in how these factors develop and are expressed. Later theories have drawn upon these advances, elaborating on aspects of offending which Moffitt's theory has not addressed, but which further advance our understanding of chronic offending.

Sampson and Laub's Age-Graded Theory of Informal Social Control

At first glance, Sampson and Laub's age-graded theory of informal social control presents a very different explanation of crime than the theories previously described. For one thing, it takes a life-course approach to explain offending, focusing on sources of change rather than stability. For another, it focuses on external rather than internal constraints on behavior (informal social controls vs. self-control or antisocial personality traits).

Sampson and Laub showed that even chronic offending tapers into desistance over time, leading them to reject the concept of *life-course-persistent* offenders (Glueck & Glueck, 1950; Laub & Sampson, 2003; Sampson & Laub, 1993, 2003, 2005b). Instead, they argue that stability in life circumstances conducive to offending, and the expression of human agency in continued offending, can explain continuity (Laub & Sampson, 2003; Sampson & Laub, 2005b). This continuity, however, is susceptible to changing life circumstances and events which affect individuals' choices to offend. These circumstances determine the constraints on behavior and consequently explain individuals' offending (Laub & Sampson, 2003; Sampson & Laub, 1993).

The central premise of Sampson and Laub's theory is that individuals offend when their bonds to society are weak or broken (Laub & Sampson, 2003; Sampson & Laub, 1993). Without these social bonds, individuals' behavior is unconstrained by the threat of losing "social capital" (the utility of social ties) and therefore they are free to commit crime. As a control theory, Sampson and Laub's theory (like Gottfredson and Hirschi's) assumes that without constraints (in this case social bonds) individuals may act upon natural motivations to commit acts of crime (because crimes are easily undertaken and provide immediate, relatively large rewards). Individuals who experience weaker social control during childhood and adolescence tend to develop an antisocial personality which shapes their behavior into adulthood (Laub & Sampson, 2003; Sampson & Laub, 1993). Their offending is then perpetuated by heterotypic continuity in their behavior, cumulative continuity via the accumulation of consequences from their earlier behaviors ("cumulative disadvantage"), and interactional continuity via adverse responses to the adverse responses of others (equivalent to Moffitt's evocative interactions) (Sampson & Laub, 1993). Patterns of offending change when social bonds change, altering short and long-term inducements to offend. When individuals acquire new social bonds and, often as a consequence, experience greater structure in their routine activities, informal social constraints on their behavior increase, as does their commitment to additional social capital (Laub & Sampson, 2003; Sampson & Laub, 1993, 2005b).

More recently, Sampson and Laub have emphasized the role of agency in these patterns of stability and change (Laub & Sampson, 2003; Sampson & Laub, 2005b). Agency moderates the influence of new social bonds on established patterns of behavior. Consequently,

> persistence in crime is explained by a lack of social controls, few structured routine activities, and purposeful human agency. Simultaneously, desistance from crime is explained by a confluence of social controls, structured routine activities, and purposeful human agency... the fundamental causes of offending are thus the same for all persons (Laub & Sampson, 2003, p. 37).

By introducing agency to their explanation of offending, Sampson and Laub recognize that an act of crime represents an instance of action the expression and outcomes of which are determined by a unique constellation of factors that includes not only dispositional factors which affect an individual's propensity to offend, but also environmental factors that affect an individual's opportunities and motivation to offend. As Sampson and Laub point out, "it is important to ground crime and social control in their situational context" (Laub & Sampson, 2003, p. 55). As we have argued earlier, this fact is too often overlooked in criminological theory and research.

Although they introduce important concepts such as agency and situational context in their explanation of offending, Sampson and Laub do not fully develop either line of inquiry. While giving a nod to agency, they do not discuss how it plays a role in the process of choice that leads to persistence or desistance in offending. At the same time, their discussion of situational context is limited to the concept of "lifestyle" and involvement in social institutions (e.g., marriage, the military), which routinize behavior. Involvement in these institutions represents a change in social bonds (and social capital), making it difficult to disentangle the unique contribution of Sampson and Laub's "situated context" to their explanation of offending. Their theory, like Gottfredson and Hirschi's, relies on notions of control which neglect differences in individuals' motivation, focusing instead on differences in constraints (in this case, informal social controls). This may lead them to overlook the causal mechanisms that link situational factors such as marriage, employment, or the use of alcohol to offending, as these factors may actually exert their influence upon the initial motivation to offend, rather than ex post facto deterrence. By presuming, as Gottfredson and Hirschi do, that motivation is unproblematic, Sampson and Laub, like other control theorists, oversimplify the causal mechanisms which drive, and subsequently help explain, offending.

One contextual factor which potentially has substantial implications for Sampson and Laub's theory but which they fail to address is *collective efficacy*. This is particularly surprising because Sampson originally developed collective efficacy theory (e.g., Sampson, Raudenbush, & Earls, 1997). Collective efficacy refers to the degree to which communities monitor and maintain common rules in public places. When individuals' routine activities take place in settings which have strong collective efficacy, individuals are more likely to conform to common rules. For example, an individual who joins the military will routinely act in a military environment in which common rules are strictly monitored and enforced. Thus, the relationship between changes in an individual's routine activities and changes in his or her offending may be linked to changes in the collective efficacy of the settings in which he or she takes part. Other contextual factors, undoubtedly, also link changes in routine activities to changes in offending, but Sampson and Laub do not develop their discussion of such factors and therefore leave their argument underdeveloped.

Although on the surface, Sampson and Laub's theory differs substantially from Gottfredson and Hirschi's and Moffitt's, at the core theirs is ultimately also a theory of propensity, albeit of a more pliable variety which acknowledges the importance (if not the specifics) of environmental influences and agency. Individual differences in internalized social constraints (informal social controls arising from social bonds and commitment to social institutions) explain offending because individuals with weaker constraints have less (social capital) to lose, and therefore perceive, and experience, fewer consequences for their actions. This is the same causal mechanism purported by Gottfredson and Hirschi simply working through a different medium (informal social, rather than self, control). To fully explain acts of crime, however, one needs to look beyond these individual-level variables and consider how the propensities they cultivate become expressed in action, and what role environmental-level variables may play in that expression. While Sampson and Laub discuss the notion of agency, they do not develop their argument as to why "persistent offenders knowingly engage in [criminal] activities at the expense of a future self," that is, how agency exerts its influence and why some individuals choose or choose not to continue offending (Sampson & Laub, 2005b, p. 37). Similarly, although they discuss the notion of situated action (and agency), they do not develop their argument as to how immediate situational factors specifically influence the choice to offend. They recognize, however, the importance of these variables to the explanation of crime, conceding that they complicate the issue, making prediction even more problematic (Sampson & Laub, 2005b, p. 40).

Ultimately, the age-graded theory of informal social control has provided an alternative route for thinking about sources of change and stability in offending from other prominent approaches (such as Gottfredson and Hirschi's and Moffitt's), presenting complementary, and not always contradictory, explanations. The expansion of theoretical thinking into the realms of human agency and situational context (see also Wikström & Sampson, 2003) inspire exploration of these important behavioral dimensions and enhance our knowledge of the link between some external events and individual differences related to offending. However, Sampson and Laub have left many questions unanswered about agency and context in crime causation and their role in stability and change in individuals' crime involvement.

Shortcomings of Major Developmental Theories of Chronic Offending

The theories detailed above exemplify current criminological thinking regarding the sources of stability and change in offending. All three theories suggest that chronic offending is ultimately driven by individual-level factors, whether low self-control, antisocial personality traits, or weak social bonds. The causal mechanisms which link these factors to offending are similar, if not the same–each affects whether an individual is likely to, can, or has consequences to take into consideration that may influence his or her decision to offend. At the same time, all three theories fail to adequately consider what *external* factors might motivate offending, necessitating an action decision, or provide additional deterrence (or deterrence cues). They also say little about the *interaction* between individuals and their environments, including how individuals perceive and evaluate deterrents, or how differential exposure to external factors may impact immediate offending (as well as the propensity to offend), or what role human agency may play in any of these processes. Clearly, dramatic change in exposure to criminogenic environments (e.g., incarceration) can dramatically affect the continuity of offending, and it is reasonable to assume that even minor variations may have similar, if smaller, effects. To date, few theories have tackled this side of the argument, and few empirical studies have gathered adequate data to test burgeoning hypotheses.

Because behavior is driven by the interaction of individuals and their environments, offending may arise from two sources—the individual and/or the environment. Subsequently, there are three potential sources of change (1) change in the individual, (2) change in the environment, and (3) change in the individual's exposure to certain environments (i.e., change in an individual's activity field).

Gottfredson and Hirschi and Moffitt demonstrate more interest in stability than change in offending, and perceive the individual, once developed, as static and relatively unmalleable. Sampson and Laub, alternatively, posit external sources for individual change (e.g., life events). All three theories, however, fail to fully address the effect of change in the characteristics of the environments that individuals encounter, or the effect of change in those individuals' exposure to those environments, on their offending. They do not discuss which specific characteristics of an environment might influence offending, and how. All imply that an individual-level factor (low self-control, antisocial personality traits, or social bonds) motivates, perpetuates and explicates offending.

We submit that the recently developed *situational action theory* may help overcome some of the identified shortcomings, particularly those associated with the neglected role of agency and that of the wider social environment, and help advance the study of the sources of stability and change in individuals' crime involvement which support, or terminate, chronic patterns of offending.

Wikström's Situational Action Theory

To understand why some people embark on sustained careers of crime involvement, we first need to understand why people engage in acts of crime. The situational action theory (SAT) (Wikström, 2004, 2005, 2006, 2007b, 2007c; Wikström & Treiber, 2007) is a general theory of crime (and more broadly of

moral action) that seeks to explain acts of crime by explaining the key processes which lead to offending, and the individual and environmental factors which directly (and indirectly) influence those processes. Specifically,
it seeks to explain *moral rule-breaking*, arguing that what all crimes (in all
places, at all times) have in common is that they break moral rules (rules about
what it is right or wrong to do in a given setting). The law is a set of moral rules
and an act of *crime* is a breach of a moral rule defined in law. Acts of crime may
be regarded as a subcategory of general moral rule-breaking, and theories of
crime causation may be considered as a subcategory of theories of moral rule-
breaking (or more generally, moral action). What a theory of crime causation
should, therefore, explain is why individuals follow and breach moral rules
(defined in law).

Many criminological theories fail to clearly define what it is they propose
to explain. We reason that by being explicit about the outcome variable of
interest, the situational action theory clearly depicts the kinds of causes and
causal processes that are relevant to the explanation of crime, and thus also
helps to distinguish which correlates of crime involvement are likely causes
and which are merely correlates. When crime is perceived as moral action
(action guided by rules about what it is right or wrong to do) attention is
focused on the importance of individuals' moral values (and associated emotions) and the moral contexts in which they operate. This will, of course, be
important for understanding chronic offending, for example, how individual
differences in moral values and exposure to moral contexts lead some individuals
to persistently break moral rules.

Individuals as Rule-Guided Actors

Most criminological theories, if they make any explicit assumptions about
human nature, assume that humans are self-interested (egoistic), rational (util-
itarian) actors and that these two qualities can satisfactorily explain human
action. While the situational action theory accepts that rationality and self-
interest (at times) play a role in guiding human actions, it reasons that, on a
more fundamental level, human behavior is guided by *rules* which simplify
and economize the process of choice. These rules are moral rules[2] (rules about
what it is right or wrong to do), which are linked to a *moral context* (the setting to which certain moral rules apply and in which it is right or wrong to

[2] Another major group of rules are *conventions* (how things should be done) but
since these are of less relevance to the explanation of crime we will not elaborate on
their role in shaping human action.

perform certain actions). Humans are therefore essentially *rule-guided actors*, and human action should be explained in reference to moral rules and moral contexts. This we submit is a novel approach to the explanation of action by criminological theories and may provide a better foundation for understanding the forces which guide action (e.g., acts of crime), and how their influence may persist or vary over time.

The Concept of Agency

The concept of *agency* and its role in the explanation of crime is not generally well dealt with in criminological theory. Voluntaristic approaches to the explanation of behavior suggest that individuals are able to deliberately choose their actions, exhibiting free will, while deterministic approaches suggest that individuals' actions are predetermined (e.g., by biological, psychological, and/or social forces). Most criminological theories appear to accept the implicitly deterministic approach linked to the notion of propensity—a predetermined inclination to act in a certain manner, often regardless of setting. When the concept of agency is touched upon in criminological theory, it is rarely developed; many theories happily accept that individuals make choices (commonly, rational choices) without developing the concept of choice or integrating it into explanations that are basically deterministic in nature.

The situational action theory recognizes that human behavior exhibits elements of free will and predictability and incorporates voluntaristic and deterministic processes into its explanation of crime. The theory suggests that human choices (including the choice to abide by or break a moral rule defined in law) may be *habitual* (preset) or *deliberate* (chosen wilfully), depending on the circumstances in which the individual acts (see further Wikström, 2006).

Individuals exhibit *agency* (the power to make things happen intentionally) through both habitual and deliberate choices. Through habitual choices, they "allow" the setting to determine their actions (by triggering associative mechanisms developed through repeated exposure to particular circumstances), while through deliberate choices they choose their actions themselves (by assessing pros and cons). In both cases the resulting action is *intentional* (expresses agency). We reason that much of human action (including acts of crime) is habitual in nature and thus habituation may be an important driving force behind offending, particularly persistent offending. However, the extent to which acts of crime may be committed out of habit and the role of habit in persistent offending has been highly underdeveloped in criminological theory, as most theories focus on explaining why individuals deliberately choose to offend. *Habituation* may be particularly relevant to the explanation of chronic offending, as it suggests stability in the interactions between individuals and the settings they encounter, leading to enduring patterns of behavior, which could include persistent offending. Incidentally, this also suggests that breaking habits may be a key factor in the process of desistance.

Integrating Individual and Environmental Influences on Action

Most criminological theories focus *either* on the role of the individual or the role of the environment in the explanation of crime (see Wikström, 2004, 2005). Although some authors allude to the importance of the interaction between individuals and environments (and even misleadingly label their theories "interactional"), few adequately detail *how* (via what mechanisms) this interaction ultimately produces acts of crime. This omission arguably debilitates the development of comprehensive theories about crime causation and, consequently, about the forces which drive chronic (persistent) offending. As we have documented earlier, most leading developmental and life-course theories focus on the individual and neglect the role of stability and change in the wider social environment, and its interaction with the individual, in stability and change in individuals' crime involvement.

The situational action theory was developed to overcome the common (but in our opinion unfruitful) divide between individual and environmental explanations of crime and to provide an explanation of *how* individual and environmental factors interact to cause acts of crime. It achieves this by proposing a *situational mechanism* (a process of perception and choice) that links individuals (their experiences and characteristics) and environments (their inducements and constraints) to actions. Crucially, the theory argues that the immediate process which moves an individual to break a moral rule is fundamentally the same regardless of the rule which is being broken or the action required to break it (e.g., cheating on a test, shoplifting, or corporate fraud).

The Situational Mechanism

The central argument of the situational action theory is that acts of crime are the outcome of a process by which an individual *perceives alternatives for action* and *chooses* (habitually or deliberately) which alternative to pursue. This process is moderated by the *interplay* between an individual's *propensity* to offend and the criminogenic features of the moral context to which he or she is *exposed*. This process of perception and choice is the *situational mechanism* that links individuals' characteristics and experiences and the features of the settings in which they take part to their actions.

The situational action theory suggests that the perception of alternatives is more fundamental to the explanation of action and therefore more important than the process of choice because individuals who do not perceive an action as an alternative (e.g., an act of crime) will not need to choose between that and other alternatives (see further Wikström, 2006). Thus the process of choice will only play a role in the explanation of crime when an individual perceives that crime is a viable alternative for action; he or she may then (but only then) choose whether to commit that crime. This may have particular implications for the explanation of chronic offending as it places the emphasis first on explaining why individuals repeatedly perceive crime as an action alternative and then on why they repeatedly choose to commit acts of crime. Most theories of crime involvement (if they even consider what moves people to action) focus solely on the latter process of choice, ignoring why individuals perceive crime (or a specific crime) as an alternative in the first place. We argue that this is a crucial omission that limits our understanding of the process which moves individuals to action (and the reasons behind stability and changes in their behavior).

The Causes of Acts of Crime

Since crime represents moral action, it stands to reason that individuals' moral values and the moral contexts in which they operate will be key factors which influence what alternatives they perceive and, in turn, choose to carry out. Individuals' *moral values* refer to the moral rules that they acknowledge and the strength with which they adhere to those rules. The strength of an individual's moral values is determined by the *moral emotions* (such as shame and guilt) that he or she attaches to breaking particular moral rules, in general and in specific moral contexts. The extent to which an individual's moral values correspond with the moral rules defined by law will influence the likelihood that he or she will commit an act of crime (i.e., violate a moral rule defined by law); the greater the correspondence, the lower the likelihood of offending, particularly if the individual has strong moral values (i.e., values associated with high levels of shame and guilt). This *principle of moral correspondence* is a cornerstone of the situational action theory. More generally, it states that the higher the correspondence between an individual's moral values and the moral rules of the settings in which he or she takes part, the more likely it is that he or she will act in accordance with the moral rules of those settings (e.g., not offend).[3]

This suggests that changes in the correspondence between an individual's moral values and the moral contexts in which he or she operates, resulting either from a change in his or her values or the contexts he or she encounters, may lead to changes in moral behavior, including crime involvement. This potential source of stability and change in offending is not acknowledged or discussed by theories which do not recognize the importance of moral rules in human action.

Hence *morality* may be considered the most important individual factor and the *moral context* of the settings in which an individual operates (the setting's moral rules and their enforcement and sanctioning) the most important environmental factor in crime causation, because their interaction largely determines what action alternatives an individual perceives and whether any of those alternatives represent acts of crime. However, these are not the only important causal factors which the situational action theory identifies.

An individual's *ability to exercise self-control* (i.e., to act in accordance with his or her morality in the face of temptations and provocations[4]) can also significantly affect his or her crime involvement. We reason that an individual's ability to exercise self-control is influenced both by relatively stable individual characteristics (executive capabilities) and momentary influences, such as high levels of stress and intoxication (see further Wikström & Treiber, 2007). The ability to exercise self-control is *only* important, however, when an individual perceives crime (or moral rule-breaking) as an alternative, because self-control exerts its effects through the process of choice. When an individual deliberates over whether to commit an act of crime, his or her ability to exercise self-control influences the process of choice and plays a causal role in his or her decision to offend (or not offend). Consequently, the *propensity* to offend can be explained (primarily) by the *combination* of an individual's moral values (and emotions) and his or her ability to exercise self-control.

Individuals do not, however, act within a vacuum and whether that propensity is expressed through action (e.g., offending) depends on the moral

[3] The situational action theory makes no specific assumptions or assessment about whether the moral rules defined in law are justified from a specific moral perspective.

[4] Please note that this is a very different conception of self-control from that advocated by Gottfredson and Hirschi (1990).

context of the settings to which the individual is exposed. The interplay between an individual's propensity and a moral context will influence what action alternatives he or she perceives and what choices he or she makes for action. Theories which focus on the individual often overlook the important motivational role which the social context plays in triggering the expression of propensity, causing individuals to respond differently to different settings despite their general predispositions. This means that chronic offending cannot be explained solely by propensity driving the individual to offend across all settings but must take into account the individual's exposure to settings that excite expression of that propensity and the characteristics of those settings that play a key role in that excitation.

Habitual and Deliberate Action

The situational action theory proposes that the process of perception and choice in a given setting (circumstance) can be either *habitual* or *deliberate*, depending on the actor's familiarity with the setting (environment). The more familiar the setting and its circumstances, the more likely that the individual's process of perception and choice will be predominantly habitual (automated) in nature. The more unfamiliar the setting and its circumstances, the more likely that the individual's process of perception and choice will involve active deliberation. An individual exhibits free will only when his or her process of perception and choice is deliberate (i.e., the individual consciously considers his or her alternatives for action), and only then does his or her ability to exercise self-control and sensitivity to the presence of deterrence cues play an active role in his or her actions (e.g., acts of crime) (see further Wikström, 2007a). According to the situational action theory, acts of crime may thus be committed out of habit (predetermined) or as a result of deliberation (voluntaristic). To date, the extent to which acts of crime may be committed out of habit and the role of habit in persistent offending are highly understudied, as most criminological theories, if they have any explicit theory of action, tend to explain crime with reference to deliberate (rational) choice only.

The notion of habitual choice may in fact be particularly relevant to the explanation of chronic offending, as habituation suggests stability in the interactions between individuals and the settings they encounter, leading to enduring patterns of behavior, which could arguably include persistent offending. We suspect that there may be strong habitual elements in what drives much of persistent offenders' criminality.

The Importance of Distant Factors (the Causes of the Causes)

The fact that the situational action theory emphasizes morality and the ability to exercise self-control (individual characteristics) and the moral contexts in which individuals operate (environmental characteristics) as the most important factors directly influencing an individual's perception of alternatives and process of choice, and therefore his or her actions (including acts of crime), does not mean that other more distant (indirect) factors are unimportant (see Wikström & Sampson, 2003). On the contrary, we need to better understand what role broad social factors like *social integration* and *disadvantage* play for (1) individual moral development and change; (2) individual development and change in the ability to exercise self-control; (3) the emergence of particular moral contexts; and (4) individuals' exposure to different moral contexts.

These other (more distant) factors should be thought of, and analysed, as *the causes of the causes*, and their relevance should be judged by the extent to which they can be analytically and empirically shown to influence the development of morality and the ability to exercise self-control and the emergence of criminogenic moral contexts, as well as individuals' exposure to those moral contexts. All too often, analyses of crime causation (theoretical and empirical) fail to distinguish between causes and causes of the causes and their role in crime causation, encumbering the advancement of knowledge about crime causation.

The Causes of Stability and Change in Crime Involvement

If, as we have argued, individuals' morality and ability to exercise self-control and the moral context in which they operate are the most important factors directly influencing moral actions (including acts of crime), stability and change in individuals' crime involvement is ultimately caused by stability and change in these individual factors (morality and self-control) and environmental factors (the moral context).

Stability in these factors will promote stability in the action alternatives an individual perceives and the choices he or she makes, while change in these factors may cause changes in the perception of alternatives and the process of choice (see further Wikström, 2005). *Onset, duration,* and *desistance* from crime are thus ultimately explained by the situational action theory as the outcome of change (onset and desistance) or stability (duration[5]) in the proposed factors that affect whether and to what degree individuals perceive crime as an action alternative, and the process of choice when an individual does see crime as an alternative.

Thus the simple answer to the question of what factors drive persistent offending is (1) stability in an individual's *propensity* to offend (which depends upon stability in his or her morality and ability to exercise self-control) and (2) stability in an individual's *exposure* to moral contexts (settings) that promote the violation of moral rules defined by law (e.g., by presenting conflicting moral rules or weakly enforcing rule-abidance or sanctioning rule-breaking), as illustrated in this basic model:

Propensity and Exposure = Crime Involvement

Consequently, *changes* in an individual's crime involvement (e.g., de-escalation or desistance) may be caused by changes in his or her propensity to offend and/or his or her exposure to criminogenic moral contexts:

(*Change*) Propensity and/or (*Change*) Exposure = (*Change*) Crime Involvement

The situational action theory does not propose a simple additive model of propensity and exposure but that propensity and exposure *interact* to determine individual crime involvement (cross-sectionally) and the shape of individual trajectories of crime involvement (longitudinally). Specific combinations of propensity and exposure are likely to produce specific outcomes in terms of an individual's level of crime involvement. For example, the relative importance of an individual's exposure to criminogenic moral contexts may vary depending on his or her current propensity to offend. Moreover, changes in exposure to criminogenic moral contexts may (in the long run) affect an individual's propensity to offend. At the same time, changes in an individual's propensity to offend may change how often he or she takes part in criminogenic moral contexts. Specific combinations of change in an individual's propensity and exposure are likely to produce specific changes in his or her level of crime involvement (see further Wikström, 2005). A key challenge for developmental and life-course criminology will be to better understand (and study) the dynamics of this interaction between propensity and exposure over the life course (and its causes) and how it

[5] Please note that duration may refer to persistence in crime involvement or in law-abiding behavior.

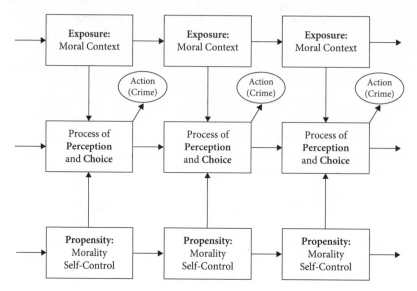

FIGURE 19.1 Simple model of key drivers of stability and change in crime involvement.

impacts upon patterns of stability and change in individuals' crime involvement (see Figure 19.1).

Advancing the Study of the Role of the Social Environment in Crime Causation

One likely reason why the role of the social environment (and changes in the social environment) in determining criminal career patterns has been regularly disregarded in longitudinal research is simply that most longitudinal studies lack adequate data about their subjects' exposure to different social environments (i.e., their activity fields). Most longitudinal studies include data about characteristics and individuals' experience of social institutions like the family and schools, but few incorporate data about individuals' *exposure* to different social settings, and the environmental characteristics of those settings which individuals encounter in their daily life.

Some longitudinal studies include data on *neighborhoods* as a measure of social environments. This is problematic because subjects tend to spend a lot of their time outside their neighborhoods (especially as they age) during which they are exposed to other kinds of environments. The neighborhood units used are often very large (units which on average encompass more than 5000 inhabitants are not uncommon) and generally heterogeneous in the behavior settings they represent, therefore subjects residing in the same neighborhood may still be differentially exposed to different behavior settings depending on the location of their residence and the related typical spatial patterns of use of their neighborhood (for a detailed discussion of these problems, see Oberwittler & Wikström, 2009).

According to the situational action theory, individuals are only influenced by the environment through the behavior settings in which they take part (see Wikström, 2006). A *behavior setting* represents the social and physical environment (objects, persons, and events) which the individual, at a particular moment in time, can access with his or her senses (e.g., what he or she can see, hear, and feel) including any media. To adequately study the role of exposure to such settings in crime involvement, empirical research will need to develop a method for gathering data on approximate behavior settings, their relevant features, and subjects' exposure.

The *Peterborough Adolescent and Young Adult Development Study* (PADS+) has risen to this challenge by developing methods to collect data about subjects' exposure to behavior settings, and about their moral contexts (and other characteristics). To achieve this, the study combines two key methods. These include a community survey targeting a random sample of inhabitants living in small scale area units (which approximate behavior settings). Using *ecometrics* (see Raudenbush & Sampson, 1999), we have developed a range of measures to tap into these social environments (e.g., we have used collective efficacy as a key measure of an area's moral context).

We have also developed a *space-time budget* technique to collect further data about behavior settings and subjects' exposure to those behavior settings. The technique involves interviewing each subject regarding his or her hourly activities over a specific period of time (in our case, 4 days), and gathers detailed data about the subject's main activity (e.g., socialising, studying, watching television), companions (e.g., peers, parents, teachers), the kind of setting he or she was in (e.g., park, schoolyard, friend's house), and the geographical location, which was located on a map and coded into the same small area units used by the community survey. This made it possible to combine the datasets and create measures representing subjects' exposure to specific behavior settings (e.g., the number of hours spent (awake) with peers in areas of poor collective efficacy), which could be used as indicators of individual levels of exposure to criminogenic moral contexts. As far as we are aware, this is the first longitudinal criminological study to seriously address the measurement of behavior settings and individuals' *exposure* to different social environments and criminogenic contexts (including those located in the wider local community outside the subjects' neighborhood).

Analyses of these data for the adolescent period are currently under way and will help advance knowledge about the role which exposure to social environments (particularly those with criminogenic moral contexts), and its interaction with individual characteristics (morality and the ability to exercise self-control), plays in shaping individuals' crime involvement, and subsequently further our knowledge about what drives persistent offending.

Conclusion

Our key intention in this chapter has been to argue that the importance of the social environment for stability and change in individuals' crime involvement has been highly undervalued by the majority of criminology's developmental and life-course theories, and that this reduces their ability to comprehensively explain what drives persistent offending.

We supported this argument by first reviewing three prominent developmental and life-course theories to illustrate how criminological thinking about the role of the social environment in offending has developed (especially in relation to *persistent* offending) and identify topics which merit further development.

We began with Gottfredson and Hirschi's general theory of crime, which has established a strong foundation for studying the role of stability and change (although mostly stability) in *individual-level* factors (e.g., propensity) in crime involvement. *Environmental-level* factors, on the other hand, play only an indirect role in their explanation of crime, via the process of socialization, which determines individual propensity. We discussed how the theory relies upon large assumptions about human nature to downplay the direct role of the social environment in crime causation, and how these assumptions may limit the theory's ability to explain all acts of crime.

We then turned to Moffitt's dual developmental taxonomy, which also explains crime via individual propensity. Moffitt's theory also suggests that the role of the environment in crime involvement is indirect, exerting its influence on stability and change (again, mostly stability) through the development of propensity, but recognizes and begins to explore how individuals and environments interact to determine propensity, and the expression of propensity. We discussed the importance of this advancement, but also how the theory fails to detail how environmental factors determine the expression of propensity (which drives chronic offending), which environmental factors may be important, or through what situational processes those factors interact with individual propensity to cause acts of crime (or perpetuate offending).

Finally, we considered Sampson and Laub's age-graded theory of informal social control, which also ultimately relies on propensity (arising through weak social bonds) to explain crime involvement, but also incorporates notions of agency and context, two important contributions to the explanation of crime. However, although it recognizes that agency and context play important roles in individuals' choices for action, the theory does not detail the mechanisms by which individuals express agency, or acquire agency in the first place, nor does it discuss what characteristics of a context may perpetuate crime involvement, or galvanize agency, limiting its discussion of how particular changes in context (such as those which result from life events) lead to changes in crime involvement.

Having thus presented the strengths and shortcomings of prominent developmental and life-course theories, we then introduced the situational action theory, a developmental ecological theory of crime involvement, and discussed how it has addressed these (and other) theoretical deficiencies. We forwarded three key arguments for why it may provide a better foundation for furthering our understanding of the causes of persistent offending (and patterns of offending more generally), especially those causes which relate to the social environment: (1) it provides a clearer conception of crime by defining it as *moral action*; (2) it conceives of human behavior (including acts of crime) as *rule-guided action* characterized by the expression of agency, rather than rational behavior driven by self-interest and utility; and (3) it explains acts of crime, and change and stability in crime involvement, through an *explicit situational mechanism* that encompasses the interaction of direct (but also indirect) individual and environmental factors.

The situational action theory's clear definition of offending as the breaking of moral rules defined by law clearly delineates what is meant by stability and change in offending (i.e., stability and change in individuals' adherence to or breaking of moral rules defined by law). This, of course, is determined both by their moral values *and the moral contexts they encounter.*

The situational action theory conceives of human behavior as (moral) *rule-guided action*, an assertion which is supported by neurocognitive research (for a review, see Bunge, 2004). Moral values represent individual differences in adherence to those rules, while moral contexts represent environmental differences in the behavioral significance of those rules. This approach to human behavior can advance our thinking about the role of *social order* from that of constraining to supporting natural human tendencies, and how social order may influence the development of individuals' moral values and/or the moral contexts they encounter. By discussing crime as moral action, the theory can also link criminal behavior to broader social processes such as *social integration*, which may be perceived as a process by which individuals transition from one set of moral rules and moral contexts to another, and *social cohesion*, which can be seen as emerging from a process by which individuals adapt their moral values to match the moral rules of the settings in which they operate. As the *principle of moral correspondence* stipulates, successful transitioning and adaptation will reduce the likelihood that individuals will break moral rules when they change environments, while unsuccessful transitioning or maladaption may lead to the escalation, or continuation, of offending. Social integration and social cohesion may also be understood as characteristics of behavior settings which represent the general correspondence between a population's moral values and the moral rules associated with those settings; the more uniform the population's moral values, and the more they correspond to the moral rules under which that population generally operates, the less likely members of that population will be to break those moral rules, and the lower the aggregate crime rate.

The situational action theory also develops the concept of agency by detailing how it is expressed through deliberate (voluntary) individual choices, *but crucially also through habitual (predetermined) choices which are triggered by familiar environments*. This has particular implications for explaining the role of the social environment in persistent offending, as habitual choices are driven by factors of the setting that perpetuate particular behavioral responses (behaviors that are learned through repeated exposure to those settings). Habituation may therefore be particularly important in the explanation of persistent offending because it is often linked to continuous exposure to specific environmental factors. Some prime examples of kinds of offending which are likely to have particularly strong elements of habituation are persistent *domestic violence*, which typically occurs in the same family setting; *group delinquency*, which occurs in settings which include specific peers, often in a limited set of locations to which all peers have access (and which lack effective monitoring); and *gang violence*, which often occurs in settings which not only include specific peers (or specific rivals) but also are limited to specific geographical territories. If habit is an important element in persistent offending, changes in habits are likely to be a prime factor in any *process of desistance*.

The central argument of the situational action theory is that a situational mechanism (a process of perception and choice) can explain all acts of crime as the outcome of an *interaction* between individual *and environmental* factors. This mechanism remains the same regardless of stability and change in the individual (and his or her offending); what changes is the *input into* that process (the individual and environmental factors present to interact and influence perception and the process of choice). Propensity theories, conversely, assume that the *input* into the equation is always the same, perpetuating the output. This may be attributed to their tendency to focus on a constricted time span, especially when that time span is limited to childhood and adolescence. Individual change is generally very gradual, occurring over an extended period of time and often requiring continuous inducements to change, therefore individual-level factors often appear stable.

This is especially true once the individual has physically matured. During physical maturation, individual-level factors are most susceptible to external influence (i.e., they exhibit greater plasticity). This means that the behavior (and crime involvement) of individuals who are studied before they reach adulthood may exaggerate the *indirect* role of the social environment, advocating individual-level factors as the direct causes of crime. For individuals who are studied after they reach adulthood, the *indirect* role of the social environment may be even less apparent. In either case, a constricted time scale will limit the ability of research to observe individual-level change.

Environmental-level factors, on the other hand, may change very quickly (e.g., in times of war) or more gradually. The *indirect* impact of environmental change on propensity will be gradual regardless. This means that immediate changes in behavior must represent the *direct* influence of environmental factors, rather than changes in propensity (via the *indirect* influence of environmental factors), which occur much later. This fact is often overlooked in criminological research, for several reasons: (1) to date most developmental studies have focused on individual-level change, neglecting environmental-level change; (2) there are far fewer effective methodologies for measuring environmental-level characteristics and change than individual-level characteristics and change; and (3) many current theories fail to distinguish direct and indirect environmental influences on crime involvement. To effectively explain stability and change in crime involvement and, consequently, persistent offending, it is important to delineate direct and indirect individual *and* environmental influences on crime involvement. This, of course, is one of the central aims of the situational action theory.

The situational action theory recognizes that propensity alone cannot drive behavior and must be expressed to influence action *and that the moral context ultimately triggers that expression*. It discusses the consequent importance of *exposure to settings and moral contexts which trigger the expression of propensity* to behavioral stability and change. Thus stability and change in propensity, and also in exposure to certain (criminogenic) moral contexts, will influence crime involvement and the persistence of offending. Finally, the theory differentiates between the causes of crime and the causes of the causes, providing a clearer framework for understanding the causal processes and the role of direct and indirect individual *and environmental* factors in the explanation of crime, including that of persistent offending.

We also offered preliminary insights into how we can advance the study of the role of the social environment and its changes through longitudinal research into criminal career patterns by briefly describing the new methodologies used by PADS+ (e.g., the combination of a small area community survey and the space-time budget technique), which collect, and link together, detailed data on environments and individuals' exposure to those environments.

We posit that a truly ecological approach to explaining stability and change in crime involvement across the life course will be crucial for comprehensively identifying both direct and indirect causal factors, whether individual or environmental, and effectively conceptualizing the causal mechanisms which link those factors to action. Such an approach would require a clear understanding of the nature of human action, a clear conceptualisation of how individuals and environments interact to determine that action, strong methodologies to measure both individual and environmental factors, advanced analytical techniques to model their interaction, and a robust theoretical framework to inform research designs and interpret findings. We submit that the situational action theory may provide one of the staunchest theoretical designs for studying, and explaining, the role of individual and environmental factors in crime causation, and that PADS+ presents an important research opportunity for testing that design and identifying casual mechanisms and the key individual and environmental factors that influence stability and change in crime involvement and therefore play a critical role in persistence, or desistance, in offending.

Part VI

Conclusions

CHAPTER 20

What We Have Learned? Directions for Future Research and Policy

JOANNE SAVAGE

The contributors to this book have added to our knowledge of the development of persistent criminality and its investigation in a variety of ways and I wish to highlight a few important areas here. I shall also discuss what is yet to be learned on this topic and recommend directions for future research.

Understanding Key Risk Factors

Depth

In this book, we have learned that key risk areas such as biology (Chapters 7 and 9), poverty (Chapter 3), emotional strain (Chapter 5) and family (Chapters 2 and 6) are associated with persistent offending. It is important to note that we have a long way to go. First, it is clear that a deeper understanding of the meaning and breadth of association is needed. There are several areas where depth in our understanding should be expanded.

The link between persistent/chronic and serious/violent offending is not perfectly understood. While theory and some research indicate that the correlates of persistent/chronic offending may be the same as those for serious violent offending, it is unlikely that the causes of the two phenomena are identical. Some studies find that persistent offenders do tend to be the most likely to commit violent acts, but this is not true in all cases (e.g., Lutz & Baughman, 1988). A notable exception is a recent, large-scale study by Blokland (2005), which characterizes persistent offenders as drug addicts who steal to obtain money for drugs. Looking at trajectories of specific crime types may be helpful in determining the extent to which persistent and chronic offending are aligned with serious violent offending. However, due to the serious nature of violent offenses it is not likely that a person can persist in serious violence for very long before the criminal justice system will intervene, making it difficult to capture persistently violent offending in empirical studies. Distinguishing between individuals who persistently commit minor offenses and those who commit serious ones is very important for the planning of interventions, treatment, or deterrence measures.

It is also important for us to seek greater depth in our understanding of the meaning and timing of risk factors. Risk factors such as family size are so easily measured, that we frequently fail to establish what they mean. What is it about larger families that results in greater delinquency among children? Lack of supervision? Delinquent elder siblings? Is there a floor effect (e.g., does an enhanced risk require at least four children in the family)? The more we know, the better chance we have to target intervention efforts.

Though distinguishing between risk factors for adolescence-limited and persistent offenders has been useful in tests of Moffitt's typology, the real-life distinction between a person who commits numerous serious crimes in adolescence and then desists, and a person who commits those same crimes from adolescence into adulthood is not particularly useful for public safety or for crime victims. In some studies, we currently find and compare, for example, high-rate chronics to high-rate adolescence-peaked offenders. As Haapanen et al. point out in Chapter 16, many of these adolescent offenders are already offending in a serious and persistent manner. So distinguishing between these groups may not have the practical utility of comparing, for example, a group of minor adolescent offenders who desist from criminality to a group of chronic offenders or to those who ultimately commit violent offenses.

Understanding more about the transition period between adolescence and adulthood is likely to have significant applied potential because of the normative desistance processes that take place for both minor and many serious adolescent offenders during this time. Capaldi and Wiesner explore the roles of and dynamics between prior antisocial behavior, school achievement, work, drug use, association with deviant peers, and antisocial romantic partners in perpetuating antisocial behavior into adulthood. Davis explores a commonly ignored area, the cessation of programming for foster care children when they turn 18. Juvenile offenders who end up in the criminal justice system are at a significant risk for "missing" the developmental milestones necessary for making a transition to a prosocial adult life because of disruptions in school, family, prosocial friendships, and employment opportunities. Overcontrol of adolescent offenders, then, is likely to cause persistent criminality in some offenders who would likely desist.

Early Onset

Developmental level and type of behavior should be more clearly delineated in discussions of cutoff ages for measuring early onset. We read that age 14 should be the cutoff in one study, age 16 in another—age 11 in yet another. Because the authors used different behaviors to mark early onset, this is not necessarily a contradiction. For example, any arrest prior to age 15 might be a good marker for early onset, but only arrests for some of the more serious offenses (adult offenses) may be a marker of "early onset" among 15-year-olds. Taking illegal drugs, a minor type of offense for a 16-year-old, could be seen as a major sign of early onset if an 11-year-old is taking them. School suspensions, oppositional behavior and the like would be markers of early onset for younger children.

Further, a better understanding of what "early onset" means, exactly, is required for any kind of intervention planning. Moffitt would likely argue that early onset is a sign of neuropsychological abnormalities–nervous system irregularity or damage—that, in conjunction with social adversity, will lead to aggressive behavior patterns. Authors in this book have discussed relationships between early onset and factors such as maternal smoking during pregnancy and early psychomotor test scores (e.g., Chapters 8 and 9), supporting that view. But if early onset is indicative of neuropsychological injury, we still do not know what these myriad neuropsychological injuries do to create antisocial conduct. Do they act to create greater emotional volatility, reduced response to ordinary informal social control, sensation-seeking, reduced central nervous system response to punishment, or something else? More detailed understanding of the exact processes is required here.

It could be the case, simply, that early onset is an indicator of a behavioral dynamic. To take this argument to its extreme, suppose that an initial aggressive act is almost random (a child trying out a new behavior). If the consequences for that act are positive, the child is likely to commit that act, and others like it, again. Those who start misbehaving, in a serious way, at a younger age have more time to develop antisocial habits at a young age and time to accrue many criminal offenses before the normal time when other youths commit their adolescence-limited offending. In these cases, perhaps the development of aggressive habits also overshadows normative development of prosocial behaviors. The correlation between early onset and biological markers could thus reflect only an increased likelihood that children with neurological impairments will "try out" aggressive behavior at inappropriate ages—and the link between biology and chronic offending could end there. Of course, this is an extreme example. Really, biological and social factors and the consequences of behavior are likely to work in combination to facilitate early onset and chronic offending; understanding the correlations between neuropsychological deficits, early behavior disorders, later delinquent behavior and ongoing criminality would be a major contribution to our field.

Biology

Despite the bewilderment expressed about the meaning of the association between biology and early onset expressed above, conclusions from neurophysiological studies of antisociality are beginning to converge. Sylvers et al. emphasize the role of prenatal stress, maternal smoking, drug and alcohol use during pregnancy, and genetics. The authors conclude that the evidence strongly favors a model where persistent offenders are chronically physiologically underaroused which causes sensation seeking and a reduced likelihood of learning from punishment. Tibbetts's review in this book concurs with this major conclusion—physiological factors associated with low levels of arousal are also associated with early onset. These include slower brain wave patterns as measured by electroencephalogram (EEG) studies and lower heart rate (which has received very consistent support). Tibbetts concludes that brain trauma is another "likely candidate"; this often occurs prenatally, perinatally, or sometimes through child abuse. The amygdala, orbitofrontal, and ventrolateral frontal cortex are implicated in both psychopathy and in the development of early-onset conduct disorder. From this, one can begin to visualize a model of persistence that begins early in life, with genetic predispositions or pre- or perinatal complications resulting in any of a variety of neurophysiological conditions that are marked by underarousal. A later pattern of behavior marked by a weak response to punishment results in disturbed child–parent relations (abuse, attachment problems), school problems, and the increased likelihood of the child persisting in early childhood aggression beyond the period during which it is normative. The child is more likely to "try out" aggressive behaviors at inappropriate times. If parents and other socializing agents are inconsistent, ineffective, or too harsh, the child may find aggressive behavior rewarding—at least compared to his alternatives which may be limited—and develop aggressive and antisocial habits. This dynamic would be compounded by emotional problems due to maltreatment or peer rejection. Testing this model should be a major focus of research in this area.

Family Factors

I earlier expressed doubt about the ability of mild family factors such as family structure, family size, and maternal age to contribute significantly to the development of serious pathological behavior patterns unless they are part of a cumulative set of risk factors (see Chapter 1). Even in this case, it seems unlikely that they would overcome the impact of profound overarching cultural norms that dictate behavior for young adults and reward conformity so richly. Pagani reviewed the evidence in detail; however, and reports many factors that are related to persistent behavior problems. She discusses both discrete factors (including family size, family adversity and poverty, maternal education, early parenthood, family structure, antisocial parents and siblings, maternal depression, and parental substance use) and process factors (family dysfunction, parenting, supervision, corporal punishment, and parent–child relations) which are linked to conduct disorders. The nature of these relationships should be explored in more depth in future research. *How* do family factors foster the development of persistent patterns of antisocial conduct? Is it through lack of supervision or real changes in personality? It is likely that other factors interact with these "mild" family factors to enhance risk of adverse outcomes.

Child Maltreatment. Abuse is likely to be related to the interruption of very important and fundamental developmental processes, such as attachment and the acquisition of empathy and morality. It can result in a wide array of emotional and behavioral disorders, which sometimes include antisocial personality disorder, oppositional defiant disorder, and aggression. Many studies have found a longitudinal relationship between childhood physical abuse and later violent behavior (e.g., Cohen, Kasen, Smailes, & Fagan, 2002; Malinosky-Rummell & Hansen, 1993; Rivera & Widom, 1990). Ireland and Widom (1994) found that child maltreatment was a significant predictor of adult, not juvenile, arrests for alcohol and drug offenses. Cicchetti and Valentino (2006) explore, in detail, the reasons why child abuse disrupts development and the many ways its harmfulness is manifested in psychological and behavioral symptomatology. In this volume, Pagani suggests an association between corporal punishment and aggression and Millar found that corporal punishment and even yelling at children are associated with persistent aggressive behavior problems.

Although developmental psychologists tend to find that "resilience is rare among maltreated children" (Luthar, 2006, p. 755) some research on child abuse disputes it as a major cause of future violence (e.g., Schwartz, Rendon, & Hsieh, 1994). It is likely that such studies are not focusing on traumatic child abuse which may be an important predictor of long-term patterns of antisocial behavior (see Chapter 1). It is possible that the relationship between abuse and persistent offending is mediated by other factors such as parenting styles, socioeconomic status (SES), school attachment, intelligence, and so on. Some findings suggest that only when child abuse results in emotional, personality, or cognitive disorders will it cause future antisocial behavior. Green (1985) suggests that a "child-abuse syndrome" mediates this relationship; Dodge (2003) concludes that distorted social information processing is the link. Findings by Weiler and Widom (1996) suggest that the relationship between child victimization (abuse or neglect) and later violence is mediated by the development of psychopathy. Future research should address such interactions and indirect effects and attend closely to the type and severity of abuse.

Situational Factors

How much power does the situation have to cause persistent criminality? Are persistent criminals who are "situational" offenders easier to rehabilitate? To what extent can situations affect enduring personality or behavioral "traits"? These are important questions which are yet unanswered. Some situational factors are likely candidates for setting the stage for the development of persistent antisocial conduct.

Poverty. Because poverty is quite a bit more common than persistent offending, it is clear that it cannot be a "sturdy" predictor. Hay (Chapter 3) cites comparisons of individuals in the criminal justice system to the general population, which show that the former are marked by significant socioeconomic disadvantage. He found that persistent poverty is a significant predictor of chronic behavior problems in late childhood but little is yet known about the association between poverty and persistent *offending*. Theoretically, there are several reasons why we might believe that living in poverty could have long-term effects on behavioral development. Bernard (1990) discusses "angry aggression" among the urban poor and the dynamics of life in disadvantaged neighborhoods where high stress levels spur the development of violent cultures, which could cause long-term behavior change among individuals living in those neighborhoods. Hay reviews several other theories on this matter. Chiricos et al. (2007) found that living in a neighborhood of concentrated disadvantage was associated with recidivism in their sample of Florida felons. Stouthamer-Loeber et al. (2002) found that while the same factors were promotive (i.e., fostering resilience) in low-SES neighborhoods as higher-SES neighborhoods, subjects living in low-SES neighborhoods were more likely to become serious persistent delinquents given the same combination of other risks and promotive effects, showing that neighborhood SES is likely to have an independent effect on the development of serious persistent delinquency.

Neighborhoods and Community. It may be inadequate to focus on the developmental issue—the person—if we have millions of people living in neighborhoods that instigate and sustain antisocial behavior. In addition to poverty discussed previously, neighborhoods may be characterized by violence. In this book, Wikström emphasizes the "moral context" in which individual actors make their decisions to commit crimes and argues that communities can have an effect on the development of individual behavior patterns. Ng-Mak et al. (2002) discuss the "normalization of violence" among many inner-city youth. We can imagine that the development of criminal tendencies may be caused by these environments even in the absence of the individual risk factors we have been discussing. As many as 97% of urban youth in community surveys report witnessing some sort of violence (Scarpa, 2001) and witnessing violence is associated with higher levels of violent behavior. In a recent survey of Washington D.C. students, it was reported that 80% of youths in the city are "highly exposed" to gun violence (Williams, 2008). Behaving in a violent way in such environments may be *adaptive*. Thus, future research on persistence should account for neighborhood context and the possibility that committing crime may be unassociated with individual traits or propensities in these situations.

Beyond violent culture, it is also possible that neighborhood disorder and weak informal social control fail to set expected limits on behavior and "free up" individuals to behave deviantly. In this case we must assume that individuals are either naturally inclined to be deviant (*per Durkheim*), or that something is causing them to want to commit criminal acts. The importance of weak informal social control in affecting moral decision making is certainly implied by Wikström's situational action theory. It is also likely that neighborhood disadvantage is highly correlated with this weakness, thus compounding the criminogenic effects in neighborhoods that suffer from both problems.

Some authors have proposed that neighborhood factors are likely to interact with personal or family factors in the etiology of offending. Lynam et al. (2000) found that nonimpulsive boys in poor neighborhoods were no more delinquent than nonimpulsive boys in better-off neighborhoods, suggesting that impulsivity was more likely to foster delinquency only in neighborhoods which exert weak social control.

Peers. Although it is difficult to imagine that deviant peers alone could cause an individual to become a persistent, serious offender, evidence does suggest that persistent offenders tend to associate with antisocial peers. Capaldi and Wiesner emphasize the importance of antisocial ties during the transition to adulthood in the etiology of young adult criminality. Deviant peers may reinforce and sustain behavioral tendencies, prevent normative desistance, and encourage continuity in offending (Chapter 18; Fergusson & Horwood, 1996). It is clear, however, that the effects of peers may be limited—or may be mediated or mitigated by other factors. For example, Mears et al. (1998) found that moral values tempered the effects of deviant peers. Several studies have shown that the effects of deviant peers are weaker for girls than for boys and Vitaro et al. (2000) found that boys who were attached to their parents were resistant to peer influence. Vitaro et al. (2000) also found that the influence of deviant peers was limited by characteristics such as low disruptiveness in adolescence, and unfavorable attitudes toward delinquency. More research on these interactive factors would help us better understand how to combat persistent criminality that is related to peer associations.

Interactions, Indirect Effects, and Reciprocal Causation

In several areas of research related to persistent criminality there is a growing consensus that interactions, indirect effects and reciprocal relationships are important. This is fertile territory for future research and while it is beyond the scope of this chapter to review these completely, I will highlight several areas where these types of effects are likely to be important.

Interaction Effects. Many authors have discussed the importance of interaction effects in analyses of persistent behavior. The most studied seem to be the interactions between biological (e.g., birth complications, infant temperament, etc.) and social risk factors (e.g., maternal depression, parental substance abuse, etc.). Tibbetts (Chapter 9) reports that significant interaction effects have been found in the etiology of early onset criminality: low birth weight and disadvantaged social environment; family adversity and low verbal IQ; gender and low birth weight; SES and low birth weight; family instability and minor physical anomalies (MPAs); obstetrical complications and family adversity; hyperactivity and deviant peers; and antisocial temperament and maternal negativity. In this book, Ellis and Savage found evidence that social support mediates the effects of strain on later offending.

Other areas that might be fruitful include interactions between exposure to deviant peers and other factors (see above), temperament and parenting (e.g., Lahey, Waldman, & McBurnett, 1999), parental monitoring and various child risk factors (Graber, Nichols, Lynn, Brooks-Gunn, & Botvin, 2006), neighborhood factors and individual factors, individual factors such as attention deficit problems and parenting and school factors, cognitive deficits and parenting, cognitive deficits and school factors, and finally, individual risk factors and family factors (such as family size and SES). In addition, effects of various factors on the development of persistent criminality may be different for males and females, for children of different ages, or for different racial groups, so these interactions should be tested as well.

Indirect Effects. Given the conventional wisdom about the cumulative effects of risk factors (see Chapter 1), it is surprising to find that few studies explore indirect effects on persistent offending. For example, in the area of neurobiological risk, we expect that most of the total effect sequence is indirect, but few authors actually test these dynamics in their studies. We see fewer structural equations models that test indirect effects in this literature than we would expect, given the theoretical consensus on this topic.

There are a number of areas where indirect effects are likely. For example, problems with attachment relationships are likely to have strong indirect effects on antisocial behavior as are maternal age and education. The effects of child abuse on delinquency may be partially direct, through violent socialization, for example, but it is likely that child abuse has indirect effects as well. In the first chapter, I discussed how child abuse is thought to be associated with major disruptions in developmental processes associated with attachment relationships, regulation of emotions, social awareness, cognitive abilities, neurobiological processes, and social information processing.

Links within the chain that would help us understand persistent offending include empathy deficits, psychopathy, and cognitive impairments (especially verbal). Factors that cause these may be important "ultimate" causes of persistent offending. Additionally, certain protective factors are also links in the chain—attachment to school, school achievement—and understanding their precursors can help us achieve a fuller understanding of this complex developmental process.

Some authors have reported indirect effects. Feldman and Weinberger (1994) found that family functioning operates on boys' self-restraint, which then affects delinquency (consistent with Gottfredson & Hirschi, 1990). Sampson and Laub argue that structural factors influence offending via their effects on parenting. Patterson et al. (2000) suggest that hyperactivity leads to problems with disciplinary practices and this may lead to antisocial behavior. Blomberg et al. (Chapter 12) found that educational achievement while incarcerated increased the likelihood of going back to school post-release, which was associated with employment and desistance.

Reciprocal Causation. Sometimes criminality or behavior problems bring about their own continuity by increasing the level or likelihood of other criminogenic factors. One such reciprocal system is that of prior antisocial behavior and its ongoing effects on itself. While stability in offending may be due to an antisocial "trait," numerous authors including Capaldi and Wiesner (Chapter 18) have emphasized how delinquency can have adverse effects on prosocial ties with school and parents, and lead to school failure, and problems finding employment. Prior antisocial behavior can steer people into criminogenic environments with increased exposure to things that foster criminality, such as antisocial peers and drugs and alcohol. We are coming to understand this system fairly well. There is still debate regarding the overall effect of criminal justice intervention, for example, which some believe leads to a greater likelihood of persistence, while others dispute this (see Chapter 16). It is clear that we need to develop criminal justice interventions that can deter criminal acts without adversely affecting educational and employment opportunities.

A second reciprocal system is the dynamic between child behavior and parenting. This issue remains controversial and it was alluded to in several chapters in this book (Chapters 2, 6, 8, and 17). It is possible that infants with poor temperaments, young children with behavior problems, and delinquent adolescents *elicit* poor parenting which serves, then, to sustain antisocial behavior. Reiss (2003) argues that genetic differences in children influence "almost all dimensions of parent-child relationships" (p. 7) especially parental warmth, support, conflict, and negativity. He concludes that "...a substantial portion of genetic variation in antisocial behavior in later adolescence is associated with a *lack of endearing, heritable qualities* in the child rather [than] with the *presence of objectionable heritable qualities*" (p. 15). Rowe (1994) makes many of these same arguments. While Millar (Chapter 6) argues against the idea that aggressive children *elicit* severe discipline by parents, further research on this matter may help elucidate exactly what child risks are associated with this phenomenon, and may help inform interventions to support those with children who are difficult to parent.

Resilience

An important fact about the development of antisociality, one that affords us a ray of optimism, is that while the vast majority of serious persistent offenders have experienced significant abuse and adversity during childhood and adolescence, most children who experience abuse and adversity do not go on to become chronic offenders. Felsman and Vaillant (1987) emotionally describe the "...human strength and resiliency that sometimes emerge amidst stark, relentless, and seemingly unforgiving social conditions" (p. 289). Smith et al. (1995) found that two-thirds of the youth in their high-risk category were resilient to negative outcomes. Factors associated with "resilience," positive adaptation despite experiences of significant adversity or trauma (Luthar, 2006), are of keen interest because they may help us make better predictions and design appropriate interventions.

Werner (1987) summarizes predictors of resiliency from the Kauai *Overcoming the Odds* study. These include positive characteristics such as an active affectionate and good-natured temperament, high self-esteem, and internal locus of control. Among delinquents, they found that those with parents or guardians who were very involved with them during the criminal justice process were less likely to persist in offending later on. But the authors also found that having some characteristics at levels that were simply normative or better (in other words, not deficient) was protective: having fewer serious illnesses in childhood, having adequate academic skills and verbal skills, achieving appropriate developmental levels on various measures, being from a family with four children or less, and having at least a 2-year spacing before the next sibling (also see Taylor et al., 2005). Other authors have concluded that the following factors are associated with resilience: family factors such as positive attachments, nurturance and social support (Chapter 4; Luthar, 2006; Morrison, 2000; Simons et al., 2006; Thompson, Flood, & Goodvin, 2006), discipline and monitoring (Luthar, 2006; Smith et al., 1995), empathy (Broidy, Cauffman, Espelage, Mazerolle, & Piquero, 2003), positive school experiences and enrollment (Rutter, 1978; Rutter & Quinton, 1984; Smith et al., 1995; Stouthamer-Loeber, Wei, Loeber, & Masten, 2004), positive relationship with a nondeviant spouse (Rutter & Quinton, 1984), prosocial behavior (Tremblay & LeMarquand, 2001), low physical punishment (Stouthamer-Loeber et al., 2004), employment (Stouthamer-Loeber et al., 2004), social cognitive skills (Bennett, Farrington, & Huesmann, 2005), maternal competence (McCord, 1990), temperament (Rutter, 1978), warm relationships and attachment to parents (Rutter, 1978; Smith et al., 1995), change in family circumstances that removes discord (Rutter, 1978), and other resources such as self-esteem (Smith et al., 1995).

One might speculate that there are many factors that have largely gone unexplored—having an interested grandmother, or a special talent for art or sports—that could help a child navigate his way through a high-risk environment. Unfortunately, as Rutter (1985) points out, a protective factor "may not constitute a pleasurable happening" (Rutter, 1985, p. 600). Some unpleasant or hazardous events "may toughen an individual—what has come to be termed the 'steeling' effect of stressors" (p. 600).

Stouthamer-Loeber et al. (2002) also found that protective factors have cumulative effects similar to those seen for risk factors. In their study, a cumulative score of promotive effects was associated with a reduced chance of becoming a persistent serious delinquent. They also found that combining risk and promotive scores improved their predictions of serious persistent delinquency. This lends credence to the notion that complex interactions are occurring that that future research must account for them.

Applicability of Criminological Theory to the Problem of Persistent Offending

In this book, several chapters discussed the ability of current criminological theories to tackle the problem of persistence. Pratt argues that the sources of self-control are more complex than originally proposed by Gottfredson and Hirschi (1990). He proposes that constructs such as neuropsychological deficits, community context, institutional efficacy, and structural inequality be integrated into a more complete theory of self-control. Hay and Forrest find that using long-term poverty, versus a static measure of poverty, can better predict persistent conduct problems in older children. This is consistent with theories by Cohen (1955), Moffitt (1993), and Wilson (1987). Ellis and Savage tested whether strain theory could predict persistent offending based on the idea that the effects of strain are cumulative (Agnew, 1992). They found that strain in early adolescence did not have a strong direct effect on young adult offending, but in the absence of social support, early adolescent strain does appear to be related to both violent and nonviolent young adult criminality. Ireland et al. tested a similar hypothesis using dynamic measures of trajectories of stressful life events and found that membership in high strain trajectories was a significant predictor of certain serious trajectories of offending. They write that this is consistent with general strain theory and Agnew's (1992) call for more dynamic measures of causal factors, expecting that the timing and duration of strains matters in the etiology of delinquency.

It is interesting to note, with all the emphasis on theory testing in the field of criminology generally, how few studies examine the question of whether a particular theory can predict chronic, persistent, or violent offending. This area is wide open and theory tests that focus on the ability of our theories to distinguish the most problematic offenders would have applied relevance that many prior studies lack. Future research testing these theories would benefit from looking at more serious outcomes. It is likely that many of our theories will need to be expanded to meet this challenge.

Conceptualizing Reasons for Persistence

Rising to the occasion, several of our authors proposed new ways of thinking about the causal dynamics of persistent criminality. Pratt provides a modified view of the etiology of low self-control, which integrates both micro- (neurobiological, parenting), macro- (institutions, neighborhoods), and structural factors (inequality). Wright and Beaver emphasize the importance of considering why individuals may respond to the same environment in different ways. They explain gene-environment interactions (such as the possible enhanced sensitivity to maltreatment by individuals with low activity MAOA alleles) and reciprocal causation (the environment influences the individual; the individual influences his own environment) and how these should be accounted for in models of serious persistent offending.

Capaldi and Wiesner's conceptualization includes a nuanced view of early adult development. According to their view, there are normative developmental milestones in key areas of adjustment such as school achievement, work, drug use, association with deviant peers, and antisocial romantic partners. Prior antisocial behavior affects this normative development and leads to adult offending rather than age-normative desistance from offending. Wikström and Treiber (Chapter 19) shift the focus to the criminal act, the moral beliefs about that act, the moral context, and the beliefs associated with the motivation to commit the act. They ask why some individuals repeatedly see criminal acts as action alternatives and how moral environments are conducive to this mindset.

One theory of criminal offending that might help frame the connection between developmental psychology and criminology is Vila's (1994) evolutionary-ecological paradigm, which bridges the ultimate causes of behavior, and individual-level and macro-level theories. Vila, like other human ecologists, characterizes humans as behavior strategists. In contrast with the view that prosocial behavior is necessarily healthy behavior, this view emphasizes the adaptability of human beings to their environment. Individuals begin life with whatever their genes and biological make-up provide for them in the way of differential personality characteristics, intellectual resources, and other abilities. Their response to their environment is limited by these resources, and the environment will respond to them differentially based on these resources. For example, the social environment will be more positive for a lively, warm, physically attractive child. The developmental stage of the individual (age) will sometimes play a role in determining whether a particular experience matters much (Savage & Vila, 2003) (e.g., it could be the case that early physical abuse will have more profound emotional effects than abuse that occurs only in adolescence). The individual will develop various behavioral habits over time on the basis of the reinforcements and adverse consequences he experiences in association with these behaviors (and his response to those consequences). Thus, this theory suggests that persistent offending results when individuals develop a propensity to use behavioral strategies such as force, fraud, or stealth in a variety of situations.

The general evolutionary-ecological paradigm also integrates the influence of situational factors in the etiology of offending. Motivation plays a role (even people low in criminal propensity may end up committing crime under certain circumstances) and criminal opportunity can provide temptation. Based on the principles of routine activities theory, even a motivated, habitually criminal individual cannot commit a crime unless there is a suitable target and the absence of capable guardianship (Cohen & Felson, 1979).

Finally, ecological theory tells us that within a given ecological system, the likelihood of using a particular strategy (e.g., drug dealing) is influenced by the number of others using that strategy (Cohen & Machalek, 1988). When few individuals use a particular strategy, the pay-offs may be high, but in the human world the attention of the criminal justice system may also be more intense (see Kleiman, 1998). When greater numbers of individuals use a particular criminal strategy, the risks of punishment decline, but so do the pay-offs. Thus the cost to benefit ratio changes based on the behavior of others in the system, and individual behavior is likely to bend in response to modifications in the reward structure.

From this point of view, humans, like other species, develop behavioral habits that work for them and continue to use these behaviors across a variety of situations, provided that opportunities are afforded. Habits develop early and early intervention is recommended for crime prevention (Savage & Vila, 2003). The evolutionary-ecological paradigm thus provides the theoretical complexity needed to produce specific hypotheses about individuals who commit many crimes, and also about places where a great deal of crime occurs.

But the conceptualization of causes of persistent offending is not as far advanced as the realm of general theories of crime. More discussion and theorizing on this topic may help spur research that focuses on this issue.

Linking Criminology with Developmental Psychology

Research and theory from the field of developmental psychology are likely to be an important resource for understanding persistent offending. Authors in this area can provide us with conceptual models of why, for example, early experiences are thought to affect long-term behavior at all (O'Connor, 2006)—the kind of depth often missing in criminological work.

There are several observations from the field of child development that I would like to highlight here due to their relevance for understanding persistent criminal behavior. First, developmental psychology can provide information about normative development. Criminological studies are often poorly informed on this point. Early aggression, for example hitting and pushing, is very common among toddlers but is usually absent from children by the age of 4. Developmental psychologists look at our criminological "age-crime" curve and point out that a life course age-crime curve would include a large spike in early childhood as well (Chapter 9). Normal adolescents will challenge their parents—which might be considered a sign of opposition at a younger age. Rutter (1994) points out that we should expect continuity or stability in certain characteristics at some ages but at some points in development, change or discontinuity is normative (e.g., at puberty). Over the course of development we expect cognitive skills to increase, fears to decrease, and depression to increase, for example, as part of a normative process. A better understanding of what is normal can help us understand the departures from the norm that might lead to persistent offending.

Authors in this area tend to find a developmental sequence of antisocial acts which become more serious over time. However, Patterson (1992) points out that three kinds of changes associated with development are masked by our observation of stability over time. First, the relationships between delinquency and other variables is probably not stationary over time; the effects of parental monitoring in his sample appeared to be stronger for 8th grade subjects than for 4th grade subjects, for example. The form and intensity of antisocial acts also changes over time; new types of antisocial behavior are being added and old ones deleted. There is also a shift in the setting in which antisocial acts occur (e.g., in the company of deviant peers instead of at school).

Another little-acknowledged fact, understood in other fields, is that normal development may sometimes be *dependent* on environmental input. Rutter (1994) provides great depth about these complexities:

> ... somatic growth processes are much influenced by, indeed some are dependent upon environmental input. For example, there is a mass of evidence that the growth of the visual system of the brain is crucially dependent upon visual experiences (p. 2).

Normal sexual behavior in adult male primates may require prior rough and tumble play among same-sex peers. We might guess that normal social development requires early attachment relationships and, certainly, social contact. The learning of empathy may require exposure to suffering during some stage of cognitive development or to role modeling of empathic behavior. Alternatively, the learning of the tough, fearless style characteristic of violent offenders, for example, may only occur given particular environmental exposure, during a particular developmental stage.

Finally, our concept of development should encompass the process of individuation as well as normative progression. For example, we need to understand how cognitive skills increase with age and why different people have different levels of cognitive functioning. Rutter (1994) explains how all children acquire moral values for the first time toward the end of the second year because the relevant cognitive skills are acquired at that age, but the particular moral standards acquired are due to specific experiences. Thus an integrated view of the normal course of antisocial behavior, the natural history if you will, together with a grasp of the features that differentiate among individuals would provide us a developmentallyinformed understanding of our topic.

Methodology

We have struggled with the appropriate methods for studying the life course of criminal behavior for many years (e.g., Clarke & Clarke, 1984; Farrington, Loeber, Yin, & Anderson, 2002). There are still several methodological debates that bear attention. First, there is an ongoing debate about the use of self-report or official data for tracing criminal careers (Brame, Fagan, Piquero, Schubert, & Steinberg, 2004; Cernkovich, Giordano, & Pugh, 1985; Jang, 1999; Kirk, 2006; Lauritsen, 1998, 1999). Other methodological issues include length of follow-up, inclusion of exposure time (incarceration) (Piquero, Blumstein, Brame, Haapanen, Mulvey, & Nagin, 2001), involuntary desistance through death in assessing criminal careers (Eggleston, Laub, & Sampson, 2004; Nagin, 2004) and the ongoing discussion about the use of typologies in research and policy (Sampson, Laub, & Eggleston, 2004). Recently, Bushway has been comparing methodological techniques such as random effects, fixed effects, and growth mixture models for looking at stability and change in offending (Bushway, 2007; Bushway, Brame, & Paternoster, 1999).

In this book, Piquero reviewed the methodologies that have been used to study the issue of persistence. First, he discussed the importance of understanding our construct and the difficulties and inconsistencies of measuring it. If we are really interested in persistence, we may miss chronicity; if we focus on persistent and chronic, we may miss seriousness. This is still an important issue. Piquero notes that recidivism probabilities vary as offenders commit more offenses. He also discusses the debate about operationally defining a chronic offender.

Recently, there has been a growing use of residual change scores in research (e.g., Pogarsky, Piquero, & Paternoster, 2004). In this book, Kim proposes a method for examining the effects of punishment longitudinally, modifying the traditional residual change score approach.

Both Hay and Forrest and Ireland et al. raised the issue of using dynamic measures of key risk factors to predict trajectories of offending or persistence. Hay and Forrest found that a long-term measure of poverty led to a larger odds ratio in predicting persistent late-childhood conduct problems compared to a static measure taken at one point in time. Similarly, Ireland et al. found that certain trajectories of stressful life events were significantly associated with trajectories of persistent offending, while early static predictors were not. The measurement of ongoing exposure to criminogenic factors may be a key ingredient in predicting ongoing or serious offending. This may be accomplished with trajectory modeling when the data allow it, but creative ways of measuring duration and intensity of risk factors could be developed.

Piquero (2004) points out that criminal careers are characterized more by intermittency of offending, rather than actual desistance. He argues that researchers have not fully developed operationalizations of intermittency and that understanding *temporary* stoppages in offending might help us intervene.

The development of methods for studying careers is receiving a great deal of attention and it will be interesting to see which techniques and practices will gain ascendancy, so we can train students to use them to carry out this research.

Policy Implications

Interventions

It is clear that we need to know more about the prospects for interventions for persistent and serious offenders. Schumacher and Kurz (2000) suggest that early identification is possible:

> Our research shows that the kids who become the 8% Problem are dramatically different from those youth who are arrested once and do not return to juvenile court. These differences are evident at the first arrest and referral to juvenile court (p. 5).

Further, some authors argue that we miss opportunities to help. Stouthamer-Loeber and Loeber (2002) note that while major problems among many serious persistent juvenile offenders are evident very early, fewer than half of them receive any help from school or mental health personnel.

Blomberg et al. and Davis (Chapters 11 and 12) both address very important policy matters. Davis points out that high-risk foster children are shunted into adult responsibilities suddenly and with little help, thus increasing the chances that these already troubled children will commit adult crimes. Blomberg et al. find that educational programs offered to incarcerated juveniles can have a pronounced effect on future life chances and offending after release.

Preventing early onset or intervening once early onset problem behavior is identified, could have a pronounced effect on the development of persistent offending (Chapter 9). So far, however, the most prominent predictors of early onset in the literature are a wide array of biological factors. In order to apply the information, we need a very systematic review that results in a list of risk factors with the highest magnitude of effects. Those effects should include indirect effects. Wright and Beaver suggest that pharmacological treatments should be considered, and also suggest exploring enriched preschools, multisystemic therapy (MST), and functional family therapy (FFT) for high-risk children. The implication of Tibbetts's review is that prenatal care, including fostering healthy pregnancy behavior, may help reduce early onset. Additionally, for children who incur neuropsychological risks, interventions that address parenting and schooling may help these high-risk children avoid chronic behavior problems.

Developmental Prevention. There are many studies that suggest that developmental interventions can reduce the risk of delinquent behavior (e.g., Webster-Stratton, 2003). Olds et al. (1997) find very long-term effects of an intervention that began with high-risk pregnant women on a variety of outcomes among their children. The intervention appears to operate by disrupting potential chains of events such as parent stress $\rightarrow$ child abuse $\rightarrow$ head injury $\rightarrow$ delinquency, or parent lack of education $\rightarrow$ rapid subsequent pregnancy $\rightarrow$ low supervision of older child $\rightarrow$ delinquency.

While many authors have reported that "trait" characteristics are likely to be associated with the development of persistent conduct problems (e.g., Nagin & Farrington, 1992a; Moffitt, 2003), many believe that these constitutional characteristics interact with the environment and thus, prevention efforts that target the family, school, and community could forestall the development of serious offending patterns. Calls for "developmental prevention" are currently widespread in the aftermath of decades of "get tough" rhetoric. Cohen (1998) estimated that the potential monetary value of saving a high-risk youth is between $1.7 and $2.3 million, so the potential benefit of effective pre-vention strategies is staggering. Numerous very promising programs, such as the Seattle Social Development Project (Hawkins, Catalano, Morrison et al., 1992), the Elmira PEIP nurse home visit program (Olds et al., 1998), the Montreal Longitudinal-Experimental program (Haapasalo & Tremblay, 1994), and the Perry Preschool (Schweinhart & Weikart, 1997), have been under-way for a long time and cost-benefit analyses suggest that the benefits of these programs compare favorably to their costs (Greenwood et al., 2001; Welsh & Farrington, 2001). Aos et al. (2001) compared the costs and benefits of several developmental programs with other crime prevention programs and these estimates suggest that the benefits of the Perry Preschool program and nurse home visit program exceeded some popular programs such as drug courts and inmate job programs (though targeted multisystemic therapies for juve-nile offenders and treatment foster care programs targeted at offending juve-niles had even higher returns on their investment).

Interventions for children and adolescents already involved in delin-quent activity are also widespread and afford promise (e.g., Tarolla, Wagner, Rabinowitz, & Tubman, 2002), but little is known about their ability to treat those on a path to serious and chronic delinquent patterns. Schumacher and Kurz (2000) report some success targeting a family-focused intervention to the chronic "8%" of juvenile offenders in their sample; the program reduced the likelihood of multiple subsequent juvenile court petitions filed 6 months and 12 months after the program.

To implement interventions with this subgroup of children and adoles-cents, we have to recognize the coexistence of a variety of problems among these individuals such as emotional and behavioral disorders and substance use (Ellickson, Saner & McGuigan, 1996). Another problem is the possibility that interventions won't work for everyone. For example, Pagani et al. (1998) found that the preschool program they were evaluating may have had an iatro-genic effect on some of their subjects.

Criminal Justice Intervention. In recent decades in the United States, we have increasingly turned to criminal justice interventions to address the problem of delinquency and persistent offending. Some researchers have con-cluded that these measures work (e.g., Haapanen, Britton, & Croisdale, 2007) but many authors reason that incarceration is ultimately criminogenic (e.g., Chung, Little, & Steinberg, 2005). Chung et al. (2005) argue that placement can cause deterioration in already strained relationships with parents, can interrupt prosocial friendships, and is likely to cause disruption in education and problems finding employment. In addition, youth may be exposed to haz-ardous conditions in placement—overcrowding, use of restraints and isolation for managing misbehavior, physical punishment, humiliation, fights, and acts of violence, including rape. Uggen and Wakefield (2005) reiterate the extensive problems with school and work experienced by juvenile offenders. Stewart et al. (2002) also point out that contact with the police may harm relationships between youth and their parents. Others emphasize the enormous obstacles offenders face when they reenter the community after release from prison (Maruna, Immarigeon, & LeBel, 2004). Many studies find significant adverse effects of criminal justice intervention on recidivism for juveniles.

But some have argued against giving up on punishment, pointing out that our current system was not designed for the reckless and "irrationally present-oriented" (p. 6) persistent offender (Kleiman, 1998). Kleiman (1998) suggests implementing methods systematically designed to influence this group, such as increasing the certainty of nontrivial punishment for nontrivial offenses and using graduated sanctions. In keeping with this logic, Schumacher and Kurz (2000) call for exacting "a swift and a sure punishment for each offense" (p. 14) committed by young offenders to try to prevent them from becoming chronic offenders. It is reasonable to assume that because persistent offenders have more experience actually committing offenses than the general public does, they understand better than we do the *un*likelihood that they will get caught (crime clearance rates tend to be quite low). Their behavior may be more "rational" than ours if fear of punishment (alone) is supposed to deter us from crime. Findings regarding the effects of deterrence on offending among highly impulsive or criminal individuals are mixed, but Wright et al. (2004) report that individuals high in criminality are deterred when they believe they will get caught—even more so than high self-control, low criminality individuals. If criminal justice interventions are to be used to address the problem of chronic offending, the best prospects for using them is probably to increase the certainty of punishment, but not necessarily the use of severe punishment. In this book, Haapanen et al. remark that incarceration by the California Youth Authority resulted in a decline in offending after release for most offenders (they speculate that this was due to altering the cost-benefit calculation of offending). However, they also stress that it is important to encourage persistent juvenile offenders to master skills so that they can participate in society as noncriminals by finding suitable employment, or they are likely to reoffend or experience severe poverty and homelessness.

Informal Social Control. We always seem to forget *informal* social control. Most everyday behavior is not shaped by the fear of being punished by the criminal justice system, but instead is influenced merely by concerns about social relationships, what others think, reputation, and so on. Savage and Kanazawa (2002, 2004) have argued that humans are innately sociable, that sociability is an integral part of our nervous systems, and therefore, social relationships are likely to be a very powerful ultimate motivator of behavior. This is consistent with control theories of crime (e.g., Hirschi, 1969). It is also consistent with more recent theoretical discussions about the power of social bonds such as marriage, employment, and military service to change a trajectory of criminality (e.g., Sampson & Laub, 1993). Can informal social control affect the development of persistent offending? Haapanen et al. have here posited that persistent offenders may be *resistant* to the influences of social control. Ellis and Savage (Chapter 4) found strong effects of social support on the development of a persistent pattern of offending. Wyatt and Carlo (2002) found that adolescents' behavior is influenced by what they think their parents think about what they do. Many studies have found that moral beliefs are related to delinquency (e.g., Mears et al., 1998; Regnerus, 2003; Schoepfer & Piquero, 2006).

Unfortunately, it may also be the case that part of the maintenance of persistent patterns of criminality is associated with informal social control exerted by deviant and delinquent neighbors, family, and peers. The desire to be "cool" or "tough" or a "gangsta" is part of some subcultures (e.g., Bernard, 1990; Canada, 1996) and works directly against the ideals of mainstream society. More attention to the causative role of informal social control in the etiology of persistence as well as the possible mitigating role it might play could be very useful for intervention planning.

Re-entry

Due to the large numbers of individuals released from prison in the United States (Petersilia [2003] estimates 1600 per *day*), Maruna et al. (2004) encourage a desistance-oriented approach to policy. Ex-convicts are at high risk for developing and sustaining persistent criminal behavior, and they are an easily identifiable subgroup that could be targeted for intervention. Ex-offenders tell stories "of being delivered from a prison to an inner-city bus station in the middle of the night, with $40 in gate money, nowhere to go and no one except drug dealers waiting for them in the station" (Maruna et al., 2004, p. 5). Hundreds of thousands of individuals are released from prison each year (lately) and many will not receive any preparation for release or re-entry services. Those that do enter work release may even incur enormous debts almost immediately due to charges for food and lodging and even their legal fees (Richards & Jones, 2004).

The convict point of view is one of a "perpetual incarceration machine" (Richards & Jones, 2004, p. 201) wherein incarcerated offenders are first, inadequately prepared for release, then ejected into the world with very little financial or social support. Many have experienced significant losses due to their incarceration; marriages, homes, cars, and even furniture and clothing are often missing when they return from prison. On the basis of what we have learned in this book, it is clear that all of this conspires to create an unstructured environment in which ex-convicts are almost compelled to reoffend. This has got to change.

Uggen et al. (2004) argue that although many offenders use their time in prison as a time of reflection and recommitment to rebuilding broken families, our policies do not capitalize on this by providing the training and socialization necessary for offenders to achieve their goals. In particular, it is very difficult for young prisoners to make the normal role transitions that other young adults are making (finishing school, finding employment, getting married) and to establish a prosocial identity given their lack of experience and the stigma of a felony conviction.

Petersilia (2003) argues that increasingly punitive crime policies are due to a change in values, not a change in crime rates. She asks whether we, in the United States, will "embrace the noble idea that we have a responsibility to help offenders make new lives for themselves" (p. 244). Whether we decide to be noble or not, the fact remains that serious practical problems are likely to arise with increasing urgency in the coming years if we do not accept that responsibility. It is clear that addressing the reentry problem in the United States is one of the first steps that should be taken to address the problem of persistent criminality.

Closing Comments

As Osgood and colleagues point out, "the period from the end of high school through the twenties is enormously eventful and consequential" (Osgood, Foster, Flanagan, & Ruth, 2005, p. 1). In our society, individuals are expected to complete their educations, begin full-time employment, enter long-term romantic relationships, and, in many cases, begin having children during this time. But there are many "vulnerable" teenagers who are disadvantaged with regard to making the transition to becoming a psychologically healthy, happy, and contributing member of adult society. As Davis (Chapter 11) has discussed, children who have been living in foster care are very vulnerable, as are children who have been incarcerated (Chung et al., 2005; Uggen & Wakefield, 2005), homeless (Hagan & McCarthy, 2005), those who have had educational problems, or psychological or behavioral problems.

Not only do we want to identify persistent offenders from among the throng of offenders entering our criminal justice system, but we also want to predict which children will become persistent offenders in order to prevent the harms that these offenders cause. Incapacitating persistent offenders can prevent the crimes that would have been committed had they been free, but preventing the development of the persistent offending pattern has the potential of preventing many more. And not only would we protect victims, but we would protect the offenders themselves, whose lives are otherwise characterized by serious problems, discord, victimization, and even early death. Developmental psychologists have made very significant inroads to understanding the development of problem behavior in children. It is now time to differentiate between those behavior-disordered children who will outgrow their problems and those who will persist, to specify those problem behaviors which will evolve into delinquency, and identify those delinquent adolescents who will commit serious crimes and persist in criminal activity.

Wolfgang (1995) reports that 22% of juvenile chronic offenders in his sample *did not* get arrested as adults. Understanding those individuals and raising the number in that category should be a major goal of the field of criminology in the coming years.

REFERENCES

Aber, J. L., Brown, J. L., & Jones, S. M. (2003). Developmental trajectories toward violence in middle childhood: Course, demographic differences, and response to school-based intervention. *Developmental Psychology, 39*(2), 324–348.

Accornero, V. H., Anthony, J. C., Morrow, C. E., Xue, L., & Bandstra, E. S. (2006). Prenatal cocaine exposure: An examination of childhood externalizing and internalizing behavior problems at age 7 years. *Epidemiologia e Psichiatria Sociale, 15*(1), 20–29.

Acoca, L. (1998). Outside/inside: The violation of American females at home, on the streets, and in the juvenile justice system. *Crime and Delinquency, 44,* 561–589.

Acoca, L. (1999). Characteristics of girls at risk of entering or involved with the juvenile justice system. *Juvenile Justice, 6,* 3–13.

Addis A., Moretti M. E., Ahmed, S. F., Einarson, T. R., & Koren G. (2001). Fetal effects of cocaine: An updated meta-analysis. *Reproductive Toxicology, 15*(4), 341–369.

Adler, F. (1975). *Sisters in crime: The rise of the new female criminal.* New York: McGraw-Hill.

Agnew, R. (1992). Foundation for a general strain theory of crime and delinquency. *Criminology, 30,* 47–87.

Agnew, R. (1997). Stability and change in crime over the life course: A strain theory explanation. In T. P. Thornberry (Ed.), *Developmental theories of crime and delinquency* (pp. 101–132). New Brunswick, NJ: Transaction Publishers.

Agnew, R. (2001). Building on the foundation of general strain theory: Specifying the types of strain most likely to lead to crime and delinquency. *Journal of Research in Crime and Delinquency, 38,* 319–361.

Agnew, R. & Huguley, S. (1989). Adolescent violence toward parents. *Journal of Marriage and the Family, 51,* 699–711.

Agnew, R. & White, H. R. (1992). An empirical test of general strain theory. *Criminology, 30*(4), 475–498.

Aguilar, B., Sroufe, A., Egeland, B., & Carlson, E. (2000). Distinguishing the early-onset/persistent and adolescence-onset antisocial behavior types: From birth to 16 years. *Development and Psychopathology, 12,* 109–132.

Ahlstrom, W. & Havighurst, R. (1971). *400 losers.* San Francisco, CA: Jossey-Bass Inc.

Akers, R. (1991). Self-control as a general theory of crime. *Journal of Quantitative Criminology, 7*(2), 201–211.

Akers, R. L. (1998). *Social learning and social structure: A general theory of crime and deviance.* Boston, MA: Northeastern University Press.

Akers, R. L. & Sellers, C. S. (2004). *Criminological theories: Introduction, evaluation, and application.* Los Angeles, CA: Roxbury.

Allen, J. P., Marsh, P., McFarland, C., McElhaney, K. B., Land, D. J., Jodl, K. M., et al. (2002). Attachment and autonomy as predictors of the development of social skills and delinquency during midadolescence. *Journal of Consulting and Clinical Psychology, 70*(1), 56–66.

Allerton, R. (1972). Some comments on being a criminal. In D. Petersen & M. Truzzi (Eds.), *Criminal life: Views from the inside* (pp. 25–34). Englewood Cliffs, NJ: Prentice-Hall.

Ambert, A-M. (2000). Children's role in the parent-child relationship: An interactive perspective on socialization. In N. Mandell & A. Duffy (Eds.), *Canadian families: Diversity, conflict, change* (pp. 48–77). Scarborough, ON: Nelson Thomson Learning.

Ambrose, D. M. & Lester, D. (1988). Recidivism in juvenile offenders: Effects of education and length of stay. *Psychological Reports, 63,* 778.

American Psychiatric Association. (2000). *Diagnostic and statistical manual of mental disorders* (4th ed.). Washington, DC: Author.

Ananth, C. V., Demissie, K., Smulian, J. C., & Vintzileos, A. M. (2001). Relationship among placenta previa, fetal growth restriction, and preterm delivery: A population-based study. *Obstetrics and Gynecology, 98*(2), 299–306.

Andershed, H., Kerr, M., Stattin, H., & Levander, S. (2002). Psychopathic traits in non-referred youths: A new assessment tool. In E. Blaauw & L. Sheridan (Eds.), *Psychopaths: Current international perspectives* (pp. 131–158). The Hague: Elsevier.

Anderson, B. J., Holmes, M., & Ostresh, E. (1999). Male and female delinquents' attachments and effects of attachments on severity of self-reported delinquency. *Criminal Justice and Behavior, 26,* 435–452.

Anderson, E. (1994). Code of the streets. *Atlantic Monthly, 273,* 80–94.

Anderson, E. (1999). *Code of the street: Decency, violence, and the moral life of the inner city.* New York: W.W. Norton.

Andrews, D. & Bonta, J. (2006) *The psychology of criminal conduct* (4th ed.). Cincinnati, OH: Anderson.

Antonishak, J., Reppucci, N. D., & Mulford, C. F. (2004). Girls in the justice system: Treatment and intervention. In M. M. Moretti, C. L. Odgers, & M. A. Jackson (Eds.),

Girls and aggression: Contributing factors and intervention principles (pp. 165–180). New York: Kluwer Academic/Plenum Publishers.

Aos, S., Phipps, P., Barnoski, R., & Lieb, R. (2001). The comparative costs and benefits of programs to reduce crime: A review of research findings with implications for Washington state. In B. C. Welsh, D. P. Farrington, & L. W. Sherman (Eds.), *Costs and benefits of preventing crime* (pp. 149–178). Boulder, CO: Westview Press.

Appleyard, K., Egeland, B., van Dulmen, M. H. M., & Sroufe, L. A. (2005). When more is not better: The role of multiple risks in child behavior outcomes. *Journal of Child Psychology and Psychiatry, 46*(3), 235–245.

Archer, J. (2000). Sex differences in aggression between heterosexual partners: A meta-analytic review. *Psychological Bulletin, 126,* 651–680.

Archwamety, T. & Katsiyannis, A. (1998). Factors related to recidivism among delinquent females at a state correctional facility. *Journal of Child and Family Studies, 7,* 59–67.

Arendt, R., Angelopoulos, J., Salvator, A., & Singer, L. (1999). Motor development of cocaine-exposed children at age two years. *Pediatrics, 130*(1), 86–92.

Arendt, R. E., Short, E. J., Singer, L. T., Minnes, S., Hewitt, J., Flynn, S., et al. (2004). Children prenatally exposed to cocaine: Developmental outcomes and environmental risks at seven years of age. *Journal of Developmental & Behavioral Pediatrics, 25*(2), 83–90.

Arseneault, L., Moffitt, T. E., Caspi, A., Taylor, A., Rijsdijk, F. V., Jaffee, S. R., et al. (2003). Strong genetic effects on cross-situational antisocial behaviour among 5-year-old children according to mothers, teachers, examiner-observers, and twins' self-reports. *Journal of Child Psychology and Psychiatry, and Allied Disciplines, 44*(6), 832–848.

Arseneault, L., Tremblay, R. E., Boulerice, B., Seguin, J. F. & Saucier, J. F. (2000). Minor physical anomalies and family adversity as risk factors for violent delinquency in adolescence. *American Journal of Psychiatry, 157,* 917–923.

Arseneault, L., Tremblay, R. E., Boulerice, B., & Saucier, M. (2002). Obstetrical complications and violent delinquency: Testing two developmental pathways. *Child Development, 73*(2), 496–508.

Arum, R. & Beattie, I. (1999). High school experience and the risk of adult incarceration. *Criminology, 37,* 515–540.

Asbury, K., Dunn, J. F., Pike, A., & Plomin, R. (2003). Nonshared environmental influences on individual differences in early behavioral development: A monozygotic twin differences study. *Child Development, 74,* 933–943.

Aseltine, R. H., Gore, S., & Gordon, J. (2000). Life stress, anger and anxiety, and delinquency: An empirical test of general strain theory. *Journal of Health and Social Behavior, 41,* 256–275.

Athens, L. (1997). *Violent acts and actors revisited.* Urbana, IL: University of Illinois Press.

Atlas, R. S. & Pepler, D. J. (1998). Observations of bullying in the classroom. *Journal of Educational Research, 92*, 86–99.

Ayers, C. D., Williams, J. H., Hawkins, J. D., Peterson, P. L., Catalano, R. F., & Abbott, R. D. (1999). Assessing correlates of onset, escalation, deescalation, and desistance of delinquent behavior. *Journal of Quantitative Criminology, 15*(3), 277–306.

Azuma, S. & Chasnoff, I. (1993). Outcome of children prenatally exposed to cocaine and other drugs: A path analysis of three-year data. *Pediatrics, 92*, 396–402.

Bagley, C. (1992). Maternal smoking and deviant behaviour in 16-year-olds: A personality hypothesis. *Personality and Individual Differences, 13*, 377–378.

Baker, L. A., Jacobson, K. C., Raine, A., Lozano, D. I., & Bezdjian (2007). Genetic and environmental bases of childhood antisocial behavior: A multi-informant twin study. *Journal of Abnormal Behavior, 116*(2), 219–235.

Bandstra, E. S., Morrow, C. E., Anthony, J. C., Churchill, S. S., Chitwood, D. C., Steele, B. W., et al. (2001). Intrauterine growth of full-term infants: Impact of prenatal cocaine exposure. *Pediatrics, 108*(6), 1309–1319.

Bandstra, E. S., Morrow, C. E., Vogel, A. L., Fifer, R. C., Ofir, A. Y., Dausa, A. T., et al. (2002). Longitudinal influence of prenatal cocaine exposure on child language functioning. *Neurotoxicology and Teratology, 24*(3), 297–308.

Bank, L., Burraston, B., & Snyder, J. (2004). Sibling conflict and ineffective parenting as predictors of adolescent boy's antisocial behavior and peer difficulties: Additive and interactional effects. *Journal of Research on Adolescence, 14*, 99–125.

Bank, L., Patterson, G. R., & Reid, J. B. (1996). Negative sibling interaction patterns as predictors of later adjustment problems in young male adolescents. In G. H. Brody (Ed.), *Sibling relationships: Their causes and consequences* (pp. 197–229). Norwood, NJ: Ablex.

Barber, B. K. (1996). Parental psychological control: Revisiting a neglected construct. *Child Development, 67*, 3296–3319.

Barker, E. D., Tremblay, R. E., Nagin, D. S., Vitaro, F., & Lacourse, E. (2006). Development of male proactive and reactive physical aggression during adolescence. *Journal of Child Psychology and Psychiatry, 47*, 783–790.

Barrera, M. E. & Maurer, D. (1981). Recognition of mother's photographed face by the three-month-old infant. *Child Development, 52*(2), 714–716.

Barth, R. (1990).On their own: The experiences of youth after foster care. *Child and Adolescent Social Work, 7*, 219–240.

Bartollas, C. (1993). Little girls grown up: The perils of institutionalization. In C. Culliver (Ed.), *Female criminality: The state of the art*. New York: Garland Press.

Bartusch, D. R. J., Lynam, D. R., Moffitt, T. E., & Silva. (1997). Is age important? Testing a general versus a developmental theory of anti-behavior. *Criminology, 35*(1), 13–48.

Baskin, D. & Sommers, I. (1993). Females' initiation into violent street crime. *Justice Quarterly, 10*, 559–583.

Bateman, D. A. & Chiriboga, C. A. (2000). Dose-response effect of cocaine on newborn head circumference. *Pediatrics, 106*(3), E33.

Bauer, D. J. & Curran, P. J. (2003). Distributional assumptions of growth mixture models: Implications for overextraction of latent trajectory classes. *Psychological Methods, 8,* 338–363.

Bauman, K. & Graf, N. (2003). *Census 2000 brief: Educational attainment 2000.* Retrieved September 8, 2006, from http://www.census.gov/prod/2003pubs/c2kbr-24.pdf

Baumeister, R. F. (2002). Ego depletion and self-control failure: An energy model of the self's regulatory function. *Self Identity, 1,* 129–136.

Baumrind, D. (1993). The average expectable environment is not good enough: A response to Scarr. *Child Development, 64,* 1299–1317.

Baving, L., Laucht, M., & Schmidt, M. H. (2000). Oppositional children differ from healthy children in frontal brain activation. *Journal of Abnormal Child Psychology, 28,* 267–275.

Beauchaine, T. P. (2001). Vagal tone, development, and Gray's motivational theory: Toward an integrated model of autonomic nervous system functioning in psychopathology. *Development and Psychopathology, 13,* 183–214.

Beauchaine, T. P., Katkin, E. S., Strassberg, Z., & Snarr, J. (2001). Disinhibitory psychopathology in male adolescents: Discriminating conduct disorder from attention-deficit/hyperactivity disorder through concurrent assessment of multiple autonomic states. *Journal of Abnormal Psychology, 110,* 610–624.

Beaver, K. M. & Wright, J. P. (2005). Evaluating the effects of birth complications on low self-control in a sample of twins. *International Journal of Offender Therapy and Comparative Criminology, 49,* 450–471.

Beeghly, M., Martin, B., Rose-Jacobs, R., Cabral, H., Heeren, T., Augustyn, M., et al. (2006). Prenatal cocaine exposure and children's language functioning at 6 and 9.5 years: Moderating effects of child age, birthweight, and gender. *Journal of Pediatric Psychology, 31*(1), 98–115.

Behnke, M., Eyler, F. D., Garvan, C. W., Wobie, K., & Hou, W. (2002). Cocaine exposure and developmental outcome from birth to 6 months. *Neurotoxicology and Teratology, 24*(3), 283–295.

Belfrage H., Lidberg L., & Oreland L. (1992). Platelet monoamine oxidase activity in mentally disordered violent offenders. *Acta Psychiatrica Scandinavica, 85*(3), 218–21.

Bellair, P. E. (1997). Social interaction and community crime: Explaining the importance of neighbor networks. *Criminology, 35,* 677–703.

Bellair, P. E. (2000). Informal surveillance and street crime: A complex relationship. *Criminology, 38,* 137–170.

Belsky, J. (2005). Attachment theory and research in ecological perspective: Insights from the Pennsylvania Infant and Family Development Project and the NICHD Study of Early Child Care. In K. E. Grossmann, K. Grossmann, & E. Waters (Eds.),

Attachment from infancy to adulthood: The major longitudinal studies (pp. 71–97). New York: Guilford.

Benda, B. B., Corwyn, R. F., & Toombs, N. J. (2001). Recidivism among adolescent serious offenders: Prediction of entry into the correctional system for adults. *Criminal Justice and Behavior, 28*(5), 588–613.

Bennett, P., Elliott, M., & Peters, D. (2005). Classroom and family effects on children's social and behavioral problems. *The Elementary School Journal, 105,* 461–482.

Bennett, S., Farrington, D. P., & Huesmann, L. R. l. (2005). Explaining gender differences in crime and violence: The importance of social cognitive skills. *Aggression and Violent Behavior, 10,* 263–288.

Benson, M. (2002). *Crime and the life course.* Los Angeles, CA: Roxbury.

Berg, M. T. & Delisi, M. (2005). Do career criminals exist in rural America? *Journal of Criminal Justice, 33*(4), 317–325.

Bernard, T. J. (1990). Angry aggression among the "truly disadvantaged." *Criminology, 28*(1), 73–96.

Bernburg, J. G. & Krohn, M. D. (2003). Labeling, life chances, and adult crime: The direct and indirect effects of official intervention in adolescence on crime in early adulthood. *Criminology, 41,* 1287–1318.

Bierman, K. L., Bruschi, C., Domitrovich, C., Fang, G. Y., & Miller-Johnson, S. (2004). Early disruptive behaviors associated with emerging antisocial behavior among girls. In M. Putallaz & K. L. Bierman (Eds.), *Aggression, antisocial behavior, and violence among girls: A developmental perspective* (pp. 137–161). New York: Guilford Publications.

Binder, L. M., Dixon, M. R., & Ghezzi, P. M. (2000). A procedure to teach self-control to children with attention deficit hyperactivity disorder. *Journal of Applied Behavior Analysis, 33,* 233–237.

Bjerk, D. (2007). Measuring the relationship between youth criminal participation and household economic resources. *Journal of Quantitative Criminology, 23,* 23–39.

Blackwell, B. S. & Piquero, A. R. (2005). On the relationships between gender, power control, self-control, and crime. *Journal of Criminal Justice, 33,* 1–17.

Blair, R. J. R. (2001). Neurocognitive models of aggression, the antisocial personality disorders, and psychopathy. *Journal of Neurology, Neurosurgery, and Psychiatry, 71,* 727–731.

Blair, R. J. R., Peschardt, S., Budhani, S., Mitchell, D. G., & Pine, D. S. (2006). The development of psychopathy. *Journal of Child Psychology and Psychiatry, 47*(3–4), 262–276.

Blau, P. M. & Blau, J. R. (1982). The cost of inequality: Metropolitan structure and violent crime. *American Sociological Review, 47,* 114–129.

Block, J. (1995). On the relation between IQ, impulsivity, and delinquency: Remarks on the Lynam, Moffitt, and Stouthamer-Loeber (1993) interpretation. *Journal of Abnormal Psychology, 104,* 395–398.

Block, M. & Gerety, V. (1995). Some experimental evidence on differences between student and prisoner reactions to monetary penalties and risk. *Journal of Legal Studies, 24,* 123–138.

Blokland, A. (2005). *Crime over the lifespan: Trajectories of criminal behavior in Dutch offenders.* Leiden, Netherlands: Institute for the Study of Crime and Law Enforcement.

Blokland, A. A. J., Nagin, D., & Nieuwbeerta, P. (2005). Life span offending trajectories of a Dutch conviction cohort. *Criminology, 43,* 919–954.

Blokland, A. A. J. & Nieuwbeerta, P. (2005). The effects of life circumstances on longitudinal trajectories of offending. *Criminology, 43,* 1203–1240.

Blonigen, D. M., Carlson, S. R., Krueger, R. F., & Patrick, C. J. (2003). A twin study of self reported psychopathic personality traits. *Personality and Individual Differences, 35,* 179–197.

Bloom, B., Owen, B., Deschenes, E. P., & Rosenbaum, J. (2002). Moving toward justice for female juvenile offenders in the new millennium: Modeling gender-specific policies and programs. *Journal of Contemporary Criminal Justice, 18,* 37–56.

Blumstein, A., Cohen, J., & Farrington, D. (1988a). Criminal career research: Its value for criminology. *Criminology, 26,* 1–36.

Blumstein, A., Cohen, J., & Farrington, D. (1988b). Longitudinal and criminal career research: Further clarifications. *Criminology, 26,* 57–74.

Blumstein, A., Cohen, J., Roth J. A., & Visher, C. A. (Eds.). (1986). *Criminal careers and "career criminals": Vols. 1–2.* Washington DC: National Academy Press.

Blumstein, A., Farrington, D. P., & Moitra, S. (1985). Delinquency careers: Innocents, desisters, and persisters. In M. Tonry & N. Morris (Eds.), *Crime and justice: An annual review of research: Vol. 6* (pp. 187–219). Chicago, IL: University of Chicago Press.

Bohrnstedt, G. W. (1969). Observations on the measurement of change. *Sociological Methodology, 1,* 113–133.

Bongers, I., Koot, H., van der Ende, J., & Verhulst, F. (2004). Developmental trajectories of externalizing behaviors in childhood and adolescence. *Child Development, 75,* 1523–1537.

Bonta, J. (1995). The responsivity principle and offender rehabilitation. *Forum on Corrections Research, 7*(3), 34–37.

Bonta, J., Lipinski, S., & Martin, M. (1992). *Characteristics of federal inmates who recidivate.* Ottawa: Statistics Canada.

Book, A. S., Starzyk, K. B., & Quinsey, V. L. (2001). The relationship between testosterone and aggression: A meta-analysis. *Aggression and Violent Behavior, 6,* 579–599.

Booth, A., Johnson, D. R., Granger, D. A., Crouter, A. C., & Mchale, S. (2003). Testosterone and child and adolescent adjustment: The moderating role of parent-child relationships. *Developmental Psychology, 39,* 85–98.

Boswell, G. (1996). *Young and dangerous: The backgrounds and careers of Section 53 offenders*. Aldershot, England: Avebury.

Botha, M. P. & Mels, G. (1990). Stability of aggression among adolescents over time: A South African study. *Aggressive Behavior, 16*, 361–380.

Bottcher, J. (1986). Risky lives: Female versions of common delinquent life patterns. Sacramento, CA: California Youth Authority.

Bottcher, J. (2001). Social practices of gender: How gender relates to delinquency in the everyday lives of high-risk youths. *Criminology, 39*, 893–931.

Bottcher, J. & Ezell, M. (2005). The effectiveness of boot camps: A randomized experiment with a long-term follow-up. *Journal of Research in Crime and Delinquency, 42*, 309–332.

Bouffard, L. A. & Laub, J. H. (2004). Jail or the army: Does military service facilitate desistance? In S. Maruna & R. Immarigeon (Eds.), *After crime and punishment: Ex-offender reintegration and desistance from crime* (pp. 129–151). London: Willan Publications.

Bourdieu, P. (2000). *Pascalian meditations* (R. Nice, Trans.). Stanford, CA: Stanford University Press and Polity Press.

Bowen, G. L. & Chapman, M. V. (1996). Poverty, neighborhood danger, social support, and the individual adaptation among "at risk" youth in urban areas. *Journal of Family Issues, 17*, 641–666.

Bowlby, J. (1980). *Attachment and loss: Vol. 3. Loss, sadness and depression*. New York: Basic Books Inc.

Box, S. & Hale, C. (1983). Liberation and female criminality in England and Wales. *British Journal of Criminology, 23*, 35–49.

Braithwaite, J. (1981). The myth of social class and crime reconsidered. *American Sociological Review, 46*, 36–47.

Brame, R., Bushway, S., & Paternoster, R. (2003). Examining the prevalence of criminal desistance. *Criminology, 41*(2), 423–448.

Brame, R., Bushway, S. D., Paternoster, R., & Thornberry, T. P. (2005). Temporal linkages in violent and nonviolent criminal activity. *Journal of Quantitative Criminology, 21*, 149–174.

Brame, R., Fagan, J., Piquero, A. R., Schubert, C. A., & Steinberg, L. (2004). Criminal careers of serious delinquents in two cities. *Youth Violence and Juvenile Justice, 2*(3), 256–272.

Brame, R., Mulvey, E. P., & Piquero, A. R. (2001). On the development of different kinds of criminal activity. *Sociological Methods & Research, 29*, 319–341.

Brame, R., Nagin, D. S., & Tremblay, R. E. (2001). Developmental trajectories of physical aggression from school entry to late adolescence. *Journal of Child Psychology and Psychiatry, 42*, 503–512.

Brannigan, A., Gemmel, W., Pevalin, D. J., & Wade, T. J. (2002). Self-control and social control in childhood misconduct and aggression: The role of family structure, hyperactivity, and hostile parenting. *Canadian Journal of Criminology, 44*, 119–143.

Brantingham, P. J. & Brantingham, P. L. (Eds.). (1991). *Environmental criminology.* Prospect Heights, IL: Waveland Press.

Brennan, P. A., Grekin, E. R., & Mednick, S. A. (1999). Maternal smoking during pregnancy and adult male criminal outcomes. *Archives of General Psychiatry, 56,* 215–219.

Brennan, P. A., Grekin, E. R., & Mednick, S. A. (2003). Prenatal and perinatal influences on conduct disorder and serious delinquency. In B. B. Lahey, T. E. Moffitt, & A. Caspi (Eds.), *Causes of conduct disorder and juvenile delinquency* (pp. 319–341). New York: Guilford Press.

Brennan, P. A., Hall, J., Bor, W., Najman, J. M., & Williams, G. (2003). Integrating biological and social processes in relation to early-onset persistent aggression in boys and girls. *Developmental Psychology, 39*(2), 309–323.

Brennan, P. A., Mednick, S., & Kandel, E. (1993). Congenital determinants of violent and property offending. In D. J. Pepler & K. H. Rubin (Eds.), *The development and treatment of childhood aggression* (pp. 81–92). Hillsdale, NJ: Erlbaum.

Brennan, P. A., Mednick, B. R., & Mednick, S. A. (1993). Parental psychopathology, congenital factors and violence. In S. Hodgins (Ed.), *Mental disorder and crime* (pp. 244–261). Newbury Park, CA: Sage.

Brennan, P. A. & Raine, A. (1997). Biosocial bases of antisocial behavior: Psychological, neurological, and cognitive factors. *Clinical Psychology Review, 17*(6), 589–604.

Breslau, N., Davis, G., Andreski, P., & Peterson, E. (1991). Traumatic events and post-traumatic stress disorder in an urban population of young adults. *Archives of General Psychiatry, 48,* 216–222.

Brezina, T. (1998). Adolescent maltreatment and delinquency: The question of intervening processes. *Journal of Research in Crime and Delinquency, 35,* 71–99.

Bridges, G. S. & Stone, J. A. (1986). Effects of criminal punishment on perceived threat of punishment: Toward an understanding of specific deterrence. *Journal of Research in Crime and Delinquency, 23,* 207–239.

Brier, N. (1994). Targeted treatment for adjudicated youth with learning disabilities: Effects on recidivism. *Journal of Learning Disabilities, 27,* 215–222.

Brim, O. G. Jr., & Kagan, J. (1980). *Constancy and change in human development.* Cambridge, MA: Harvard University Press.

Brizendine, L. (2006). *The female brain.* New York: Morgan Road Books.

Brody, G., Ge, X., Conger, R., Gibbons, F. X., Murry, V. M., Gerrard, M., et al. (2001). The influence of neighborhood disadvantage, collective socialization, and parenting on African American children's affiliation with deviant peers. *Child Development, 72,* 1231–1246.

Broidy, L. (2001). A test of general strain theory. *Criminology, 39,* 9–35.

Broidy, L., Cauffman, E., Espelage, D. L, Mazerolle, P., & Piquero, A. (2003). Sex differences in empathy and its relation to juvenile offending. *Violence and Victims, 18*(5), 503–516.

Broidy, L., Nagin, D. S., Tremblay, R., Bates, J., Brame, B., Dodge, K., et al. (2003). Developmental trajectories of childhood disruptive behaviors and adolescent delinquency: A six-site, cross-national study. *Developmental Psychology, 39,* 222–245.

Bronfenbrenner, U. (1979). *The ecology of human development: Experiments by nature and design.* Cambridge, MA: Harvard University Press.

Bronfenbrenner, U. (1986). Ecology of family as a context for human development: Research perspectives. *Developmental Psychology, 22,* 723–742.

Brown, M. (2006). Gender, ethnicity, and offending over the life course: Women's pathways to prison in the Aloha state. *Critical Criminology, 14,* 137–158.

Brown, S. E. (1984). Social class, child maltreatment, and delinquent behavior. *Criminology, 22,* 259–278.

Brownfield, D. (1986). Social class and violent behavior. *Criminology, 24,* 421–438.

Bunge, S. (2004). How we use rules to select actions: A review of evidence from cognitive neuroscience. *Cognitive, Affective and Behavioral Neuroscience, 4*(4), 564–579.

Bureau of Justice Statistics (1994). *Crime characteristics.* Washington, DC: U.S. Department of Justice.

Bureau of Justice Statistics (2005). *Crime characteristics.* Washington, DC: U.S. Department of Justice.

Bureau of Labor Statistics. (2007). Average annual unemployment rate. Retrieved December 26, 2007, from http://www.bls.gov/cps/prev_yrs.htm

Burke, J. D., Loeber, R., Mutchka, J. S., & Lahey, B. B. (2002). A question for DSM-V: Which better predicts persistent conduct disorder–delinquent acts or conduct symptoms? *Criminal Behavior and Mental Health, 12*(1), 37–52.

Bursik, R. J. Jr. & Grasmick, H. G. (1992). Longitudinal neighborhood profiles in delinquency: The decomposition of change. *Journal of Quantitative Criminology, 8,* 247–263.

Bursik, R. J. Jr. & Grasmick, H. G. (1993). *Neighborhoods and crime: The dimensions of effective community control.* New York: Lexington Books.

Bursik, R. J. Jr. & Webb, J. (1982). Community change and patterns of delinquency. *American Journal of Sociology, 88,* 24–42.

Burton, S. E., Finn, M., Livingston, D., Scully, K., Bales, W. D., & Padgett, K. (2004). Applying a crime seriousness scale to measure changes in the severity of offenses by individuals arrested in Florida. *Justice Research and Policy, 6,* 1–18.

Bushnell, I. W. R., Sai, F., & Mullin, J. T. (1989). Neonatal recognition of the mother's face. *British Journal of Developmental Psychology, 7*(1), 3–15.

Bushway, S. (2007). Estimating (and understanding) individual trajectories of offending. Paper presented at the meeting of the American Society of Criminology, Atlanta, GA.

Bushway, S., Brame, R., & Paternoster, R. (1999). Assessing stability and change in criminal offending: A comparison of random effects, semiparametric, and fixed effects modeling strategies. *Journal of Quantitative Criminology, 15*(1), 23–61.

Bushway, S., Piquero, A., Broidy, L., Cauffman, E., & Mazerolle, P. (2001). An empirical framework for studying desistance as a process. *Criminology, 39*(2), 491–515.

Bushway, S. D., Thornberry, T. P., & Krohn, M. D. (2003). Desistance as a developmental process: A comparison of static and dynamic approaches. *Journal of Quantitative Criminology, 19,* 129–153.

Buss, D. M. & Shackelford, T. K. (1997). Human aggression in evolutionary psycho-logical perspective. *Clinical Psychology Review, 17,* 605–619.

Byng-Hall, J. (1999). Family and couple therapy: Toward greater security. In J. Cassidy & P. R. Shaver (Eds.), *Handbook of attachment: Theory, research, and clinical applica-tions* (pp. 625–645). New York: Guilford Press.

Cadoret, R. J., Yates, W. R., Troughton, E., Woodworth, G., & Stewart, M. A. (1995). Genetic-environmental interaction in the genesis of aggressivity and conduct disor-ders. *Archives of General Psychiatry, 52*(11), 916–924.

Cairns, R. B. & Cairns, B. D. (1995). Social ecology over time and space. In P. Moen, G. H. Elder, Jr., & K. Luscher (Eds.), *Examining lives in context* (pp. 397–421). Washington, DC: American Psychological Association.

California Attorney General, Criminal Justice Statistics Center. (2007). Crime in California by city and county. Retrieved March 1. from http://ag.ca.gov/cjsc/datatabs.php

California Department of Corrections and Rehabilitation. *California prison-ers and parolees* 2003. Retrieved March 1, 2007 from http://www.cdcr.ca.gov/ReportsResearch/OffenderInfoServices/Annual/CalPris/CALPRISd2003.pdf

Campbell, M. A., Porter, S., & Santor D. (2004). Psychopathic traits in adolescent offenders: An evaluation of criminal history, clinical and psychosocial correlates. *Behavioral Sciences and the Law, 22,* 23–47.

Campbell, S. B., Shaw, D. S., & Gilliom, M. (2000). Early externalizing behavior problems: Toddlers and preschoolers at risk for later maladjustment. *Development and Psychopathology, 12,* 467–488.

Canada, G. (1996). *Fist stick knife gun: A personal history of violence in America.* Boston, MA: Beacon Press.

Cantor, J. M., Blanchard, R., Robichaud, L. K., & Christensen, B. K. (2005). Quantitative reanalysis of aggregate data on IQ in sexual offenders. *Psychological Bulletin, 131,* 555–568.

Capaldi, D. M. & Eddy, J. M. (2005). Oppositional defiant disorder and conduct disor-der. In T. P. Gullotta & G. R. Adams (Eds.), *The handbook of adolescent behavioral problems: Evidence-based approaches to prevention and treatment* (pp. 283–308). New York: Springer.

Capaldi, D. M., Kim, H. K., & Owen, L. D. (2008).. Romantic partners' influence on men's likelihood of arrest in early adulthood. *Criminology, 46*(2), 267–299.

Capaldi, D. M., Kim, H. K., & Shortt, J. W. (2004). Women's involvement in aggres-sion in young adult romantic relationships: A developmental systems model. In M. Putallez & K. L. Bierman (Eds.), *Aggression, antisocial behavior, and violence among girls: A developmental perspective* (pp. 223–241). New York: Guilford Press.

Capaldi, D. M. & Patterson, G. R. (1996). Can violent offenders be distinguished from frequent offenders: Prediction from childhood to adolescence. *Journal of Research in Crime and Delinquency, 33,* 206–231.

Capaldi, D. M., Pears, K. C., Patterson, G. R., & Owen, L. D. (2003). Continuity of parenting practices across generations in an at-risk sample: A prospective comparison of direct and mediated associations. *Journal of Abnormal Child Psychology, 31,* 127–142.

Capaldi, D. M. & Stoolmiller, M. (1999). Co-occurrence of conduct problems and depressive symptoms in early adolescent boys: III. Prediction to young-adult adjustment. *Development and Psychopathology, 11,* 59–84.

Capaldi, D. M., Shortt, J. W., & Crosby, L. (2003). Physical and psychological aggression in at-risk young couples: Stability and change in young adulthood. *Merrill-Palmer Quarterly, 49,* 1–27.

Capaldi, D. M., Shortt, J. W., & Kim, H. K. (2005). A life span developmental systems perspective on aggression toward a partner. In W. M. Pinsof & J. Lebow (Eds.), *Family psychology: The art of the science* (pp. 141–167). New York: Oxford University Press.

Capaldi, D. M., Shortt, J. W., Kim, H. K., Wilson, J., Crosby, L., & Tucci, S. (2007). Official incidents of domestic violence: Violence used, injury, and associations with nonofficial couple aggression. Manuscript submitted.

Carr, M. B. & Vandiver, T. A. (2001). Risk and protective factors among youth offenders. *Adolescence, 36*(143), 409–426.

Carrington, P., Matarazzo, A., & deSouza, P. (2005). *Court careers of a Canadian birth cohort.* Ottawa: Statistics Canada.

Carroll, A., Hemingway, F., Bower, J., Ashman, A., Hougton, S., & Durkin, K. (2006). Impulsivity in juvenile delinquency: Differences among early-onset, late-onset, and non-offenders. *Journal of Youth and Adolescence, 35*(4), 519–529.

Cases, O., Seif, I., & Grimsby, J. (1995). Aggressive behavior and altered amounts of brain serotonin and norepinephrine in mice lacking MAOA. *Science, 268*(5218), 1763–1766.

Casey, B. J., Tottenham, N., Liston, C., & Durston, S. (2005). Imaging the developing brain: What have we learned about cognitive development? *Trends in Cognitive Sciences, 9,* 104–110.

Caspi, A. (2000). The child is the father of the man: Personality continuities from childhood to adulthood. *Journal of Personality and Social Psychology, 78*(1), 158–172.

Caspi, A. & Bem, D. J. (1990). Personality continuity and change across the life course. In L. A. Pervin (Ed.), *Handbook of personality: Theory and research* (pp. 549–575). New York: Guilford Press.

Caspi, A. & Elder, G. H. (1988). Childhood precursors of the life course: Early personality and life disorganization. In E. M. Hetherington, R. M. Lerner, & M. Perlmutter (Eds.), *Child development in life-span perspective* (pp. 115–142). Hillsdale, NJ: Lawrence Erlbaum Associates.

Caspi, A., Harrington, H., Milne, B., Amell, J. W., Theodore, R. F., & Moffitt, T. E. (2003). Children's behavioral styles at age 3 are linked to their adult personality traits at age 26. *Journal of Personality, 71,* 851–854.

Caspi, A. & Herbener, E. S. (1990). Continuity and change: Assortative marriage and the consistency of personality in adulthood. *Journal of Personality and Social Psychology, 58*, 250–258.

Caspi, A., Lynam, D., Moffitt, T. E., & Silva, P. A. (1993). Unraveling girls' delinquency: Biological, dispositional, and contextual contribution to adolescent misbehavior. *Developmental Psychology, 29*(1), 19–30.

Caspi, A., McClay, J., Moffitt, T. E., Mill, J., Martin, J., Craig, I.W., et al. (2002). Role of genotype in the cycle of violence in maltreated children. *Science, 297,* 851–854.

Caspi, A. & Moffitt, T. E. (1995). The continuity of maladaptive behavior: From description to understanding in the study of antisocial behavior. In D. Cicchetti, & D. Cohen (Eds.), *Manual of developmental psychopathology* (pp. 472–511). New York: Wiley.

Caspi, A., Moffitt, T., Morgan, J., Rutter, M., Taylor, A., Arseneault, L., et al. (2004). Maternal expressed emotion predicts children's antisocial behavior problems: Using monozygotic-twin differences to identify environmental effects on behavioral development, *Developmental Psychology, 40*(2), 149–161.

Caspi, A., Moffitt, T., Silva, P., Stouthamer-Loeber, M., Krueger, R., & Schmutte, P. (1994). Are some people crime-prone? Replications of the personality-crime relationship across countries, genders, races, and methods. *Criminology, 32*(2), 163–195.

Caspi, A. & Roberts, B. W. (2001). Personality development across the life course: The argument for change and continuity. *Psychological Inquiry, 12*(2), 49–66.

Cassidy, B., Zoccolillo, M., & Hughes, S. (1996). Psychopathology in adolescent mothers and its effects on mother-infant interactions: A pilot study. *Canadian Journal of Psychiatry, 41,* 379–384.

Cauffman, E. (2004). A statewide screening of mental health symptoms among juvenile offenders in detention. *Journal of the American Academy of Child & Adolescent Psychiatry, 43,* 430–439.

Cauffman, E., Feldman, S., Waterman, J., & Steiner, H. (1998). Posttraumatic stress disorder among incarcerated females. *Journal of the American Academy of Child and Adolescent Psychiatry, 37*(11), 1209–1216.

Cernkovich, S. A. & Giordano, P. C. (1992). School bonding, race, and delinquency. *Criminology, 30,* 261–291.

Cernkovich, S. & Giordano, P. (2001). Stability and change in antisocial behavior: The transition from adolescence to early adulthood. *Criminology, 39*(2), 371–410.

Cernkovich, S. A., Giordano, P. C., & Pugh, M. D. (1985). Chronic offenders: The missing cases in self-report delinquency research. *Journal of Criminal Law and Criminology, 76,* 705–32.

Chamlin, M., Grasmick, H. G., Bursik, R. J., & Cochran, J. K. (1992). Time aggregation and time lag in macro-level deterrence research. *Criminology, 30,* 377–395.

Chapple, C. L. (2005). Self-control, peer relations, and delinquency. *Justice Quarterly, 22,* 89–106.

Chase-Lansdale, P. L., Gordon, R. A., Brooks-Gunn, J., & Klebanov, P. K. (1997). Neighborhood and family influences on the intellectual and behavioral competence of preschool and early school-aged children. In J. Brooks-Gunn, G. J. Duncan, & J. L. Aber (Eds.), *Neighborhood poverty: Vol 1. Context and consequences for children* (pp. 79–118). New York: Russell Sage Foundation.

Chase-Landsdale, P. L., Mott, F. L., Brooks-Gunn, J. & Phillips, D. A. (1991). Children of the NLSY: A unique research opportunity. *Developmental Psychology, 27*, 918–931.

Chesney-Lind, M. (1987). Girls and violence: An exploration of the gender gap in serious delinquent behavior. In D. H. Crowell & I. M. Evans (Eds.), *Childhood aggression and violence: Sources of influence, prevention, and control* (pp. 207–229). New York: Plenum Press.

Chesney-Lind, M. (1989). Girls' crime and woman's place: Toward a feminist model of female delinquency. *Crime and Delinquency, 35*, 5–29.

Chesney-Lind, M. (1997). *The female offender: Girls, women, and crime.* Thousand Oaks, CA: Sage.

Child Welfare League of America. (2006a). *Advocacy: Independent living testimony.* Retrieved February 1, 2006, from http://www.cwla.org/advocacy/indlivtest991013.htm

Child Welfare League of America. (2005b). *Child Welfare League of America and the children's village release results of first long-term study on the effect of aftercare on foster care youth.* Retrieved February 1, 2005, from http://www.cwla.org/newsevents/news001108ac.htm

Child Welfare League of America. (2005c). *Children of color in the child welfare system.* Retrieved December 21, 2006, from http://ndas.cwla.org/Include/text/Children%20of%20Color05.pdf

Child Welfare League of America. (2005d). *Quick facts about foster care.* Retrieved July 14, 2005, from http://www.cwla.org/programs/fostercare/factsheet.htm

Child Welfare League of America. (2007e). Raising the level of awareness between child maltreatment and juvenile delinquency: Results of an on-line survey. Retrieved March 28, 2007, from http://www.cwla.org/programs/juvenilejustice/jjdsurvey.htm

Child Welfare League of America. (2007f). Relationship between juvenile justice data and child welfare data, 2004: National data analysis system 2004. Retrieved March 28, 2007 from http://ndas.cwla.org/data_stats/access/predefined/Report.asp?ReportID=546

Chiriboga, C. A. (1998). Neurological correlates of fetal cocaine exposure. *Annals of the New York Academy of Sciences, 846*, 109–125.

Chiriboga, C. A., Brust, J. C. M., Bateman, D., & Hauser, W. A. (1999). Dose-response effect of fetal cocaine exposure on newborn neurologic function. *Pediatrics, 103*(1), 79–85.

Chiricos, T., Barrick, K., Bales, W., & Bontrager, S. (2007). The labeling of convicted felons and its consequences for recidivism. *Criminology, 45*(3), 547–582.

Chorpita, B. F. & Barlow, D. H. (1998). The development of anxiety: The role of control in the early environment. *Psychological Bulletin, 124*, 3–21.

Chung, H. L., Little, M., & Steinberg, L. (2005). The transition to adulthood for adolescents in the juvenile justice system: A developmental perspective. In D. W. Osgood, E. M. Foster, C. Flanagan, & R. G. Ruth (Eds.), *On your own without a net: The transition to adulthood for vulnerable populations* (pp. 27–67). Chicago, IL: University of Chicago Press.

Chung, H. L. & Steinberg, L. (2006). Relations between neighborhood factors, parenting behaviors, peer deviance, and delinquency among serious juvenile offenders. *Developmental Psychology, 42*, 319–331.

Chung, I-J, Hawkins, J. D., Gilchrist, L. D., Hill, K. G., & Nagin, D. S. (2002). Identifying and predicting offending trajectories among poor children. *Social Service Review, 76*, 663–685.

Chung, I-J, Hill, K. G., Hawkins, J. D., Gilchrist, L. D., & Nagin, D. S. (2002). Childhood predictors of offense trajectories. *Journal of Research in Crime and Delinquency, 39*(1), 60–90.

Cicchetti, D. (1993). Developmental psychopathology: Reactions, reflections, projections. *Developmental Review, 13*, 471–502.

Cicchetti, D. & Cohen, D. J. (Eds.). (1995). *Developmental psychopathology: Vol. 3. Risk, disorder, and adaptation.* Hoboken, NJ: Wiley.

Cicchetti, D. & Valentino, K. (2006). An ecological-transactional perspective on child maltreatment: Failure of the average expectable environment and its influence on child development. In D. Cicchetti & D. J. Cohen (Eds.), *Developmental psychopathology: Vol. 3. Risk, disorder and adaptation* (2nd ed., pp. 129–201). Hoboken, NJ: John Wiley.

Clarke, A. D. & Clarke, A. M. (1984). Constancy and change in the growth of human characteristics. *Journal of Child Psychology and Psychiatry, 25*, 191–210.

Clausen, J. (1986). *The life course: A sociological perspective.* Englewood Cliffs, NJ: Prentice Hall.

Cleveland, H. H., Wiebe, R. P., & Rowe, D. C. (2005). Sources of exposure to smoking and drinking friends among adolescents: A behavioral-genetic evaluation. *The Journal of Genetic Psychology, 166*(2), 153–169.

Cline, H. F. (1980). Criminal behavior over the life span. In O. Brim & J. Kagan (Eds.), *Constancy and change in human development* (pp. 641–674). Cambridge, MA: Harvard University Press.

Cloward, R. A. & Ohlin, L. E (1960). *Delinquency and opportunity: A theory of delinquent gangs.* New York: Free Press.

Cnattingius S. & Lambe M. (2002). Trends in smoking and overweight during pregnancy: Prevalence, risks of pregnancy complications, and adverse pregnancy outcomes. *Seminars in Perinatology, 26*(4), 286–295.

Cochran, J. K., Wood, P. B., Sellers, C. S., Wilkerson, W., & Chamlin, M. B. (1998). Academic dishonesty and low self-control: An empirical test of a general theory of crime. *Deviant Behavior, 19*, 227–255.

Cocozza, J. J. (Ed.). (1992). *Responding to the mental health needs of youth in the juvenile justice system.* Seattle, WA: National Coalition for the Mentally Ill in the Criminal Justice System.

Cohen, A. K. (1955). *Delinquent boys: The culture of the gang.* Glencoe, IL: Free Press.

Cohen, L. & Felson, M. (1979). Social change and crime rate trends: A routine activity approach. *American Sociological Review, 44*, 588–608.

Cohen, L. & Kluegel, J. (1979). Selecting delinquents for adjudication. *Journal of Research in Crime and Delinquency, 16*(1), 143–163.

Cohen, L. & Machalek, R. (1988). A general theory of expropriative crime: An evolutionary ecological approach. *American Journal of Sociology, 94*(3), 465–501.

Cohen, L. J., Nikiforov, K., Gans, S., Poznansky, O., McGeoch, P., Weaver, C., et al. (2002). Heterosexual male perpetrators of childhood sexual abuse: A preliminary neuropsychiatric model. *Psychiatric Quarterly, 73*, 313–335.

Cohen, M. A. (1998). The monetary value of saving a high-risk youth. *Journal of Quantitative Criminology, 14*(1), 5–33.

Cohen, M. A. (2001). The crime victim's perspective in cost-benefit analysis: The importance of monetizing tangible and intangible crime costs. In B. C. Welsh, D. P. Farrington, & L. W. Sherman (Eds.), *Costs and benefits of preventing crime* (pp. 23–50). Boulder, CO: Westview Press.

Cohen, M. A., Miller, T. R., & S. B. Rossman. (1994). The costs and consequences of violent behavior in the United States. In A. J. Reiss, Jr. & J. A. Roth (Eds.), *Understanding and preventing violence: Vol 4. Consequences and control* (pp. 67–166). Washington, DC: National Academy Press.

Cohen, P., Kasen, S., Smailes, E., & Fagan, J. (2002). Childhood antecedents of adolescent and adult crime and violence, final Report (Grant Number 1999-IJ-CX-0029). Washington, DC: National Institute of Justice.

Cohen, S., Kaplan, J. R., & Manuck, S. B. (1994). Social support and heart disease: Underlying psychological and biological mechanisms. In S. Shumaker & S. M. Czajkowski (Eds.), *Social support and cardiovascular disease* (pp. 195–221). New York: Plenum.

Cohen, S., Underwood, L. G., & Gottlieb, B. H. (2000). *Social support measurement and intervention: A guide for health and social sciences.* Oxford: Oxford University Press.

Cohen, S. E. (1974). Developmental differences in infants' attentional responses to face-voice incongruity of mother and stranger. *Child Development, 45*(4), 1155–1158.

Coie, J., Terry, R., Lenox, K., & Lochman, J. (1995). Childhood peer rejection and aggression as predictors of stable patterns of adolescent disorder. *Development and Psychopathology, 7*, 697–713.

Coleman, J. S. (1988). Social capital in the creation of human capital. *The American Journal of Sociology, 94*, S95–S120.

Collins, J. J. (1986). The relationship of problem drinking to individual offending sequences. In A. Blumstein, J. Cohen, J. A. Roth, & C. A. Visher (Eds.), *Criminal careers and "career criminals": Vol. 2* (pp. 89–120). Washington, DC: National Academy Press.

Colvin, M., Cullen F. T., & Vander Ven, T. (2002). Coercion, social support, and crime: An emerging theoretical consensus. *Criminology, 40*(1), 19–42.

Comings, D. E., Muhleman, D., Johnson, J. P., & MacMurray, J. P. (2002). Biobehavioral development, perception, and action parent-daughter transmission of the androgen receptor gene as an explanation of the effect of father absence on age of menarche. *Child Development, 73*(4), 1302–1321.

Conger, R. D., Patterson, G. R., & Ge, X. (1995). It takes two to replicate: A mediational model for the implication of parents' stress on adolescent adjustment. *Child Development, 66,* 80–97.

Connell, A. M. & Frye, A. A. (2006). Growth mixture modeling in developmental psychology: Overview and demonstration of heterogeneity in developmental trajectories of adolescent antisocial behavior. *Infant and Child Development, 15,* 609–621.

Connell, J. P. & Furman, W. (1984). The study of transitions: Conceptual and methodological issues. In R. N. Emde & R. J. Harmon (Eds.), *Continuities and discontinuities in development* (pp. 153–173). New York: Plenum.

Conners, C. K. (1969). A teacher rating scale for use in drug studies with children. *American Journal of Psychiatry, 126,* 884–888.

Conners, C. K. (1970). Symptom patterns in hyperkinetic, neurotic and normal children. *Child Development, 41,* 667–682.

Connor, D. F., Steingard, R. G., Anderson, J. J., & Melloni, R. H. (2003). Gender differences in reactive and proactive aggression. *Child Psychiatry & Human Development, 33,* 279–294.

Conseur, A., Rivara, F. P., Barnoski, R., & Emanuel, I. (1997). Maternal and perinatal risk factors for later delinquency. *Pediatrics, 99*(6), 785–790.

Converse, J. M. & Presser, S. (1986). *Survey questions: Handcrafting the standardized questionnaire.* Thousand Oaks, CA: Sage Publications.

Coolidge, F. L., DenBoer, J. W., & Segal, D. L. (2004). Personality and neuropsychological correlates of bullying behavior. *Personality and Individual Differences, 36,* 1559–1569.

Coolidge, F. L., Reilman, B. J., Becker, L. A., Cass, V. J., Coolidge, R. L., & Stocker, R. (1992). Emotional problems and neuropsychological symptoms in juvenile nonviolent offenders. *Journal of Personality and Clinical Studies, 8,* 7–13.

Cornell, D. G. & Wilson, L. A. (1992). The PIQ > VIQ discrepancy in violent and nonviolent delinquents. *Journal of Clinical Psychology, 48*(2), 256–261.

Cottle, C. C., Lee, R. J., & Heilbrun, K. (2001). The prediction of criminal recidivism in juveniles: A meta-analysis. *Criminal Justice and Behavior, 28*(3), 367–394.

Courtney, M. E., Dworsky, A., Ruth, G., Keller, T., Havlicek, J., & Bost, N. (2005). *Midwest evaluation of the adult functioning of former foster youth: Outcomes at age 19.* Chapin Hall Center for Children at the University of Chicago. Retrieved March 26, 2007, from http://www.rikidscount.org/matriarch/documents/ Midwest%20Evaluation%20of%20the%20Adult%20functioning%20of%20 former%20foster%20youth%281%29.pdf

Courtney, M. E. & Herring, D. H. (2005). The transition to adulthood for youth "aging out" of the foster care system. In D. W. Osgood, E. M. Foster, C. Flanagan, & G. R. Ruth (Eds.), *On your own without a net: The transition to adulthood for vulnerable populations* (pp. 27–67). Chicago, IL: University of Chicago Press.

Courtney, M. E., Pilavin, I., Grogan-Kaylor, A., & Nesmith, A. (2001). Foster youth transitions to adulthood: A longitudinal view of youth leaving care. *Child Welfare, 80*, 685–718.

Cox, M. J. & Paley, B. (1997). Families as systems. *Annual Review of Psychology, 48*, 243–267.

Crandall, J. (2002). Poll: Most approve of spanking kids, *ABC News* (Vol. 2007): ABC News.

Crick, N. R. & Dodge, K. A. (1996). Social information-processing mechanisms in reactive and instrumental aggression. *Child Development, 67*, 993–1002.

Croisdale, T. (2007). *The persistent offender: A longitudinal analysis.* Unpublished doctoral dissertation, Simon Fraser University, Burnaby, British Columbia, Canada.

Cullen, F. T. (1994). Social support as an organizing concept for criminology: Presidential address to the Academy of Criminal Justice Sciences. *Justice Quarterly, 11*(4), 527–559.

Cullen, F. T. & Wright, J. P. (1997). Liberating the anomie-strain paradigm: Implications from social support theory. In N. Passas, & R. Agnew (Eds.), *The future of anomie theory* (pp. 187–206). Boston, MA: Northeastern University Press.

Curran, P. J. & Willoughby, M. T. (2003). Implications of latent trajectory models for the study of developmental psychopathology. *Development and Psychopathology, 15*, 581–612.

Damasio, A. R. (1994). *Descartes' error: Emotion, rationality and the human brain.* New York: Putnam (Grosset Books).

Danner, T., Blount, W., Silverman, I., & Vega, M. (1995). The female chronic offender: Exploring life contingency and offense history dimensions for incarcerated female offenders. *Women and Criminal Justice, 6*, 45–65.

Davies, P. T. & Cicchetti, D. (2004). Toward an integration of family systems and developmental psychopathology approaches. *Development and Psychopathology, 16*, 477–481.

Davies, P. T., Cummings, E. M., & Winter, M. A. (2004). Pathways between profiles of family functioning, child security in the interparental subsystem, and child psychological problems. *Development and Psychopathology, 16*, 525–550.

Davis-Keane, P. E. (2005). The influence of parent education and family income on child achievement: The indirect role of parental expectations and the home environment. *Journal of Family Psychology, 19*(2), 294–304.

Davis-Keane, P. E. (2006). The influence of parents' educational attainment on child development. Manuscript submitted for publication.

Davis-Keane, P. E., Sexton, H. R., & Magnuson, K. (2006). How does parents' educational level influence parenting and children's achievement. Manuscript submitted for publication.

Dawson, G., Ashman, S. B., & Carver, L. J. (2000). The role of early experience in shaping behavioral and brain development and its implications for social policy. *Development and Psychopathology, 1294*, 695–712.

Day, N. L., Richardson, G. A., Goldschmidt, L., & Cornelius, M. D. (2000). Effects of prenatal tobacco exposure on preschoolers' behavior. *Developmental and Behavioral Pediatrics, 21*(3), 180–188.

Dean, C. W., Brame, R., & Piquero, A. (1996). Criminal propensities, discrete groups of offenders, and persistence in crime. *Criminology, 34*, 547–574.

DeCasper, A. J. & Fifer, W. P. (1980). Of human bonding: Newborns prefer their mothers' voices. *Science, 208*(4448), 1174–1176.

DeKloet, E. R., Korte, S. M., Rots, N. Y., & Kruk, M. R. (1996). Stress hormones, genotype, and brain organization: Implications for aggression. In C. F. Ferris & T. Grisso (Eds.), *Understanding aggressive behavior in children* (pp. 179–191). New York: New York Academy of Sciences.

DeLisi, M. (2002). Not just a boy's club: An empirical assessment of female career criminals. *Women and Criminal Justice, 13*, 27–45.

DeLisi, M. (2005). *Career criminals in society.* Thousand Oaks, CA: Sage.

DeLisi, M. (2006). Zeroing in on early arrest onset: Results from a population of extreme career criminals. *Journal of Criminal Justice, 34*(1), 17–26.

DeLisi, M., Hochstetler, A., & Murphy, D. S. (2003). Self-control behind bars: A validation study of the Grasmick et al. scale. *Justice Quarterly, 20*, 241–263.

Dembo, R., Schmeidler, J., Nin-Gough, B., Sue, C. C., Borden, P., & Manning, D. (1995). Predictors of recidivism to a juvenile assessment center. *International Journal of Addictions, 30*, 1425–1452.

Dembo, R., Schmeidler, J., Nini-Gough, B., Sue, C. C., Borden, P., & Manning, D. (1998). Predictors of recidivism to a juvenile assessment center: A three-year study. *Journal of Child and Adolescent Substance Abuse, 7*, 57–77.

Dembo, R., Williams, L., & Schmeidler, J. (1993). Gender differences in mental health service needs. *Journal of Prison and Jail Health, 12*, 73–101.

Dennis, T., Bendersky, M., Ramsay, D., & Lewis, M. (2006). Reactivity and regulation in children prenatally exposed to cocaine. *Developmental Psychology, 42*(4), 688–697.

Denno, D. W. (1990). *Biology and violence: From birth to adulthood.* Cambridge: Cambridge University Press.

Denno, D. W. (1994). Gender, crime, and the criminal law defenses. *The Journal of Criminal Law and Criminology, 85*, 80–180.

Dewberry, B. O. Q. (2007, February 15). Spanking wins parental backing. *The Republican.*

DeWolfe, A. S. & Ryan, J. J. (1984). Wechsler performance IQ>Verbal IQ index in a forensic sample: A reconsideration. *Journal of Clinical Psychology, 40*, 291–294.

DeYoung, C. G., Peterson, J. B., Seguin, J. R., Mejia, J. M., Pihl, R. O., Beitchman, J. H., et al. (2006). The dopamine D4 receptor gene and moderation of the association between externalizing behavior and IQ. *Archives of General Psychiatry, 63*, 1410–1416.

Dick, D. M., Li T. K., Edenberg H. J., Hesselbrock V., Kramer J., Kuperman S., et al. (2004). A genome-wide screen for genes influencing conduct disorder. *Molecular Psychiatry, 9*(1), 81–86.

Diggle, P. J., Liang, K. Y., & Zeger, S. L. (1996). *Analysis of longitudinal data*. New York: Oxford University Press.

DiLalla, L. F. & Gottesman, I. I. (1989). Heterogeneity of causes for delinquency and criminality: Lifespan perspectives. *Development and Psychopathology, 1*(4), 339–349.

Dishion, T. J., Andrews, D. W., & Crosby, L. (1995). Antisocial boys and their friends in adolescence: Relationship characteristics, quality, and interactional processes. *Child Development, 66*, 139–151.

Dishion, T. J., McCord, J., & Poulin, F. (1999). When interventions harm: Peer groups and problem behavior. *American Psychologist, 54*, 755–764.

Dishion, T. J., Owen, L. D., & Bullock, B. M. (2004). Like father, like son: Toward a developmental model for the transmission of male deviance across generations. *European Journal of Developmental Psychology, 1*, 105–126.

Dishion, T. J. & Patterson, G. R. (2006). The development and ecology of antisocial behavior in children and adolescents. In D. Cicchetti & D. J. Cohen (Eds.), *Developmental psychopathology: Vol. 3. Risk, disorder, and adaptation* (pp. 503–541). New York: Wiley.

Disney, E. R., Elkins, I. J., McGue, M., & Iacono, W. G. (1999). Effects of ADHD, conduct disorder, and gender on substance use and abuse in adolescence. *American Journal of Psychiatry, 156*, 1515–1521.

Dix, T. (1991). The affective organization of parenting: Adaptive and maladaptive processes. *Psychological Bulletin, 110*, 3–25.

Dixon, M. R., Horner, M. J., & Guercio, J. (2003). Self-control and the preference for delayed reinforcement: An example in brain injury. *Journal of Applied Behavior, 36*, 371–374.

Dodge, K. A. (1991). The structure and function of reactive and proactive aggression. In Pepler, D. J. & Rubin, K. H. (Eds.), *The development and treatment of childhood aggression* (pp. 201–219). Hillsdale, NJ: Lawrence Erlbaum.

Dodge, K. A. (2003). Do social information-processing patterns mediate aggressive behavior? In B. B. Lahey, T. E. Moffitt, & A. Caspi (Eds.), *Causes of conduct disorder and juvenile delinquency* (pp. 254–276). New York: Guilford.

Dodge, K. A., Bates, J. E., & Pettit, G. S. (1990). Mechanisms in the cycle of violence. *Science, 250*, 1678–1683.

Dodge, K. A. & Coie, J. D. (1987). Social information processing factors in reactive and proactive aggression in children's peer groups. *Journal of Personality and Social Psychology, 53*, 1146–1158.

Dodge, K. A., Coie, J. D., Pettit, G. S., & Price, J. M. (1990). Peer status and aggression in boys' groups: Developmental and contextual analyses. *Child Development, 61*, 1289–1309.

Dodge, K. A. & Pettit, G. S. (2003). A biopsychosocial model of the development of chronic conduct problems in adolescence. *Developmental Psychology, 39*(2), 349–371.

Donker, A., Smeenk, W., van der Laan, P., & Verhulst, F. (2003). Individual stability of antisocial behavior from childhood to adulthood: Testing the stability postulate of Moffitt's developmental theory. *Criminology, 41*(3), 593–610.

Donnellan, M. B., Ge, X., & Wenk, E. (2000). Cognitive abilities in adolescent-limited and life-course persistent criminal offenders. *Journal of Abnormal Psychology, 109*(3), 396–402.

Dornfeld, M. & Kruttschnitt, C. (1992). Do the stereotypes fit? Mapping gender specific outcomes and risk factors. *Criminology, 30*, 397–419.

Dowrick, C., Lehtinen, V., Vazquez-Barquero, J., Casey, P., Wilkinson, G., Ayuso-Mateos, J. L., et al. (2006). Negative life events, social support and gender difference in depression. *Social Psychiatry and Psychiatric Epidemiology, 41*(6), 444–451.

Doyle, A. E., McGue, M., & Iacono, W. G. (1998). Genetic and environmental influences on antisocial behavior in child and adolescent twins. Unpublished manuscript, University of Minnesota.

Duncan, G. J. & Brooks-Gunn, J. (1997). Income effects across the life-span: Integration and interpretation. In G. J. Duncan & J. Brooks-Gunn (Eds.), *Consequences of growing up poor* (pp. 596–610). New York: Russell Sage Foundation.

Duncan, G. J. & Rodgers, W. (1988). Longitudinal aspects of childhood poverty. *Journal of Marriage and the Family, 50*, 1007–1021.

Dunford, F. W. & Elliott, D. S. (1984). Identifying career offenders using self-reported data. *Journal of Research in Crime and Delinquency, 21*, 57–86.

D'Unger, A. V., Land, K. C., & McCall, P. L. (2002). Sex differences in age patterns of delinquent/criminal careers: Results from Poisson latent class analyses of the Philadelphia cohort study. *Journal of Quantitative Criminology, 18*, 349–375.

D'Unger, A. V., Land, K. C., McCall, P. L., & Nagin, D. S. (1998). How many latent classes of delinquent/criminal careers? Results from mixed poisson regression analyses. *American Journal of Sociology, 103*, 1593–1630.

Dunkel-Schetter, C. (1998). Maternal stress and preterm delivery. *Prenatal and Neonatal Medicine, 3*, 39–42.

Eggleston, E. P., Laub, J. H., & Sampson, R. J. (2004). Methodological sensitivities to latent class analysis of long-term criminal trajectories. *Journal of Quantitative Criminology, 20*(1), 1–26.

Ehrlich, I. (1975). The deterrent effect of capital punishment: A question of life and death. *American Economic Review, 65*, 397–417.

Eisenberg, N., Guthrie, I. K., Murphy, B. C., Shepard, S. A., Cumberland, A., & Gustavo, C. (1999). Consistency and development of prosocial dispositions: A longitudinal study. *Child Development, 70*, 1360–1372.

Eisner, M. (2001). Modernization, self-control and lethal violence: The long-term dynamics of European homicide rates in theoretical perspective. *British Journal of Criminology, 41*(4), 618–638.

Eitle, D., Gunkel, S., & Van Gundy, K. (2004). Cumulative exposure to stressful life events and male gang membership. *Journal of Criminal Justice, 32*, 95–111.

Elder, G. H., Jr. (1985). Perspectives on the life course. In G. H. Elder Jr. (Ed.), *Life course dynamics: Trajectories and transitions, 1968–1980* (pp. 23–49). Ithaca, NY: Cornell University Press.

Elder, G. H., Jr. (1993). Time, human agency, and social change: Perspectives on the life course. *Social Psychology Quarterly, 57*(1), 4–15.

Elder, G. H. (1995). The life course paradigm: Social change and individual development. In P. Moen, G. H. Elder, & K. Luscher (Eds.), *Examining lives in context: Perspectives on the ecology of human development* (pp. 101–135). Washington, DC: American Psychological Association.

Elder, G. H. (1996). Human lives in changing societies: Life course and developmental insights. In R. B. Cairns & G. H. Elder, Jr. (Eds), *Developmental science* (pp. 31–62). New York: Cambridge University Press.

Eley, T. C. (1997). General genes: A new theme in developmental psychopathology. *Current Directions in Psychological Science, 6*(4), 90–95.

Elias, N. (2000). *The civilizing process* (Rev. ed.). Malden, MA: Blackwell.

Ellickson, P. & McGuigan, K. A. (2000). Early predictors of adolescent violence. *American Journal of Public Health, 90*(4), 566–572.

Ellickson, P., Saner, H., & McGuigan, K. A. (1996). Profiles of violent youth, substance use, and other concurrent problems. *American Journal of Public Health, 87*(6), 985–991.

Elliott, D. S. (1994). 1993 Presidential address—serious violent offenders: Onset, developmental course, and termination. *Criminology, 32*(1), 1–22.

Elliott, D. S. & Ageton, S. S. (1980). Reconciling race and class differences in self-reported and official estimates of delinquency. *American Sociological Review, 45*, 95–110.

Elliott, D. S., Huizinga, D., & Ageton, S. S. (1985). *Explaining delinquency and drug use.* Beverly Hills, CA: Sage.

Elliott, D. S., Huizinga, D., & Menard, S. (1989). *Multiple problem youth: Delinquency, substance use, and mental health problems.* New York: Springer-Verlag.

Elliott, D. S., Huizinga, D., & Morse, B. (1986). Self-reported violent offending: A descriptive analysis of juvenile violent offenders and their offending careers. *Journal of Interpersonal Violence, 1*, 472–514.

Elliott, D. S. & Voss, H. L. (1974). *Delinquency and dropout.* Lexington, MA: Lexington Books.

Ellis, L. (1988). Neurohormonal bases of varying tendencies to learn delinquent and criminal behavior. In E. Morris & C. Braukmann (Eds.), *Behavioral approaches to crime and delinquency* (pp. 499–520). New York: Plenum Press.

Ellis, S. (2006). Dynamics of strain and social support in the develoment of persistent offending (Doctoral dissertation, American University, 2006). *Dissertation Abstracts International, 67* (05). (UMI No.3218575).

Emery, R. E. (1999). *Marriage, divorce, and children's adjustment* (2nd ed.). New York: Sage.

Emery, R. E. (2001). Interparental conflict and social policy. In J. H. Grych & F. D. Fincham (Eds.), *Interparental conflict and child development: Theory, research, and applications* (pp. 417–439). London: Cambridge University Press.

Eron, L. D. & Huesmann, L. R. (1990). The stability of aggressive behavior—even into the third generation. In M. Lewis & S. M. Miller (Eds.), Handbook of developmental psychopathology (pp. 147–156). New York: Plenum.

Evans, M., Hastings, N., & Peacock, B. (2000). *Statistical distributions* (3rd ed.). New York: John Wiley & Sons.

Evans, T. D., Cullen, F. T., Burton, V. S., Dunaway, R. G., & Benson, M. L. (1997). The social consequences of self-control: Testing the general theory of crime. *Criminology, 35,* 475–501.

Evans, W., Albers, E., Macari, D., & Mason, A. (1996). Suicide ideation, attempts, and abuse among incarcerated gang and nongang delinquents. *Child and Adolescent Social Work Journal, 13,* 115–126.

Ezell, M. E. (2007a). The effect of criminal history variables on the process of desistance in adulthood among serious youthful offenders. *Journal of Contemporary Criminal Justice, 23*(1), 28–49.

Ezell, M. (2007b). Examining the overall and offense-specific criminal career lengths of a sample of serious offenders. *Crime and Delinquency, 53*(1), 3–37.

Ezell, M. & Cohen, L. (2005). *Desisting from crime: Continuity and change in long-term crime patterns of serious chronic offenders.* Oxford, UK: Oxford University Press.

Fagan, A. A. (2005). The relationship between adolescent physical abuse and criminal offending: Support for an enduring and generalized cycle of violence. *Journal of Family Violence, 20*(5), 279–290.

Fahlberg, V. (1994). *A child's journey through placement.* London: British Agencies for Adoption and Fostering.

Farmer, E. M. Z., Wagner, H., R., Burns, B., J., & Richards, J. T. (2003). Treatment foster care in a system of care: Sequences and correlates of residential placements. *Journal of Child and Family Studies, 12,* 11–25.

Farnworth, M., Thornberry, T. P., Krohn, M. D., & Lizotte, A. J. (1994). Measurement in the study of class and delinquency: Integrating theory and research. *Journal of Research in Crime and Delinquency, 31,* 32–61.

Farrington, D. P. (1978). The family backgrounds of aggressive youths. In L. A. Hersov, M. Berger, & D. Shaffer (Eds.), *Aggression and antisocial behavior in childhood and adolescence* (pp. 73–93). New York: Pergamon.

Farrington, D. P. (1986). Age and crime. In M. Tonry & N. Morris (Eds.), *Crime and justice: A review of research: Vol. 7* (pp. 189–249). Chicago, IL: University of Chicago Press.

Farrington, D. P. (1987). Predicting individual crime rates. In M. Tonry & N. Morris (Eds.), *Crime an justice: A review of research: Vol. 9. Prediction and classification: Criminal justice decision making* (pp. 53–101). Chicago: University of Chicago Press.

Farrington, D. P. (1993). Childhood origins of teenage antisocial behaviour and adult social dysfunction. *Journal of the Royal Society of Medicine, 86*, 3–17. (Reprinted in *Developmental psychology—A reader*, pp. 338–346, by D. Messer & J. Dockrell, Eds., 1998, London: Arnold).

Farrington, D. P. (1995). The development of offending and anti-social behaviour from childhood: Key findings from the Cambridge Study in Delinquent Development. *Journal of Child Psychology and Psychiatry, 36*(6), 929–64.

Farrington, D. P. (1997). A critical analysis of research on the development of antisocial behavior from birth to adulthood. In D. M. Stoff, J. Breiling, & J. D. Maser (Eds.), *Handbook of antisocial behavior* (pp. 234–242). New York: Wiley.

Farrington, D. P. (2000). Psychosocial predictors of adult antisocial personality disorder and adult convictions. *Behavioral Sciences and the Law, 18*(5), 605–622.

Farrington, D. P. (2001). Predicting adult official and self-reported violence. In G-F. Pinard & L. Pagani (Eds.), *Clinical assessment of dangerousness: Empirical contributions* (pp. 66–88). Cambridge, UK: Cambridge University Press.

Farrington, D. P. (2003a). Developmental and life-course criminology: Key theoretical and empirical issues—the 2002 Sutherland Award Address. *Criminology, 41*(2), 221–256.

Farrington, D. P. (2003b). Key results from the first forty years of the Cambridge Study in delinquent development. In T. P. Thornberry & P. Krohn (Eds.), *Taking stock of delinquency: An overview of findings from contemporary longitudinal studies* (pp. 137–184). New York: Kluwer.

Farrington, D. P. (2003c). *What has been learned from self-reports about criminal careers and the causes of offending?* London: UK Home Office.

Farrington, D. P. & Coid, J. (2003). *Early prevention of adult antisocial behavior.* Cambridge, UK: Cambridge University Press.

Farrington, D. P., Gallagher, B., Morley, L., St. Ledger, R. J., & West, D. J. (1988). A 24-year follow-up of men from vulnerable backgrounds. In R. L. Jenkins & W. K. Brown (Eds.), *The abandonment of delinquent behavior: Promoting the turnaround* (pp. 155–176). New York: Praeger.

Farrington, D. P. & Hawkins, J. D. (1991). Predicting participation, early onset, and later persistence in officially recorded offending. *Criminal Behavior and Mental Health, 1*, 1–33.

Farrington, D. P., Jolliffe, D., Loeber, R., Stouthamer-Loeber, M., & Kalb, L. M. (2001). The concentration of offenders in families, and family criminality in the prediction of boys' delinquency. *Journal of Adolescence, 24*(5), 579–596.

Farrington, D. P., Lambert, S., & West, D. J. (1998). Criminal careers of two generations of family members in the Cambridge Study in Delinquent Development. *Studies on Crime and Crime Prevention, 7*, 85–106.

Farrington, D.P. & Loeber, R. (1999). Transatlantic replicability of risk factors in the development of delinquency. In P. Cohen, C. Slomkowski, & L. Robins (Eds.),

Historical and geographical influences on psychopathology (pp. 299–329). Mahwah, NJ: Erlbaum.

Farrington, D. P., Loeber, R., Elliott, D. S., Hawkins, J. D., Kandel, D., Klein, M., et al. (1990). Advancing knowledge about the onset of delinquency and crime. In B. B. Lahey & A. E. Kazdin (Eds.), *Advances in clinical and child psychology: Vol. 13* (pp. 283–342). New York: Plenum.

Farrington, D. P., Loeber, R., & van Kammen, W. B. (1990). Long-term criminal outcomes of hyperactivity-impulsivity-attention deficit and conduct problems in childhood. In L. N. Robins & M. Rutter (Eds.), *Straight and devious pathways from childhood to adulthood* (pp. 62–81). Cambridge, England: Cambridge University Press.

Farrington, D. P., Loeber, R., Stouthamer-Loeber, M., van Kammen, W. B., & Schmidt, L. (1996). Self-reported delinquency and a combined delinquency seriousness scale based on boys, mothers, and teachers: Concurrent and predictive validity for African-Americans and Caucasians. *Criminology, 34*(4), 493–517.

Farrington, D. P., Loeber, R., Yin, Y., & Anderson, S. J. (2002). Are within-individual causes of delinquency the same as between-individual causes? *Criminal Behavior and Mental Health, 12*(1), 53–69.

Farrington, D. P. & Welsh, B. (2007). *Saving children from a life of crime: Early risk factors and effective interventions.* New York: Oxford University Press.

Farrington, D. P. & West, D. J. (1993). Criminal, penal and life histories of chronic offenders: Risk and protective factors and early identification. *Criminal Behaviour and Mental Health, 3,* 492–523.

Farrington, D. P. & West, D. J. (1995). Effects of marriage, separation and children on offending by adult males. In Z. S. Blau & J. Hagan (Eds.), *Current perspectives on aging and the life cycle: Vol. 4. Delinquency and disrepute in the life course* (pp. 249–281). Greenwich, CT: JAI Press.

Federal Bureau of Investigation. (2003). *Uniform Crime Report.* Washington, DC: Department of Justice.

Feeney, F., Dill, F., & Weir, A. W. (1983). *Arrests without conviction: How often they occur and why.* Washington, DC: U.S. Dept. of Justice, National Institute of Justice.

Feldman, S. S. & Weinberger, D. A. (1994). Self-restraint as a mediator of family influences on boys' delinquent behavior: A longitudinal study. *Child Development, 65,* 195–211.

Felsman, J. K. & Vaillant, G. E. (1987). Resilient children as adults: A 40 year study. In E. J. Anthony & B. J. Cohler (Eds.), *The invulnerable child* (pp. 289–314). New York: Guilford.

Felson, M. & Clarke, R. (1998). *Opportunity makes the thief: Practical theory for crime prevention.* London: Home Office.

Fergusson, D. M. & Horwood, L. J. (1996). The role of adolescent peer affiliations in the continuity between childhood behavioral adjustment and juvenile offending. *Journal of Abnormal Child Psychology, 24,* 205–221.

Fergusson, D. M. & Horwood, L. J. (2002). Male and female offending trajectories. *Development and Psychopathology, 14*, 159–177.

Fergusson, D. M., Horwood, L. J., & Lynskey, M. T. (1992). Family change, parental discord and early offending. *Journal of Child Psychology and Psychiatry, 33*(6), 1059–1075.

Fergusson, D. M., Horwood, L. J., & Nagin, D. S. (2000). Offending trajectories in a New Zealand birth cohort. *Criminology, 38*(2), 525–552.

Fergusson, D. M., Horwood, L. J., & Ridder. (2005). Show me the child at seven: The consequences of conduct problems in childhood for psychosocial functioning in adulthood. *Journal of Child Psychology and Psychiatry, 46*, 837–849.

Fetters, L. & Tronick, E. Z. (1996). Neuromotor development of cocaine-exposed and control infants from birth through 15 months: Poor and poorer performance. *Pediatrics, 98*(5), 938–943.

Fincham, F., Grych, J. H., & Osborne, L. N. (1994). Does marital conflict cause child maladjustment? Directions and challenges for longitudinal research. *Journal of Family Psychology, 8*, 128–140.

Fishbein, D. (2001). *Biobehavioral perspective in criminology.* Belmont, CA: Wadsworth.

Fishbein, D. H. (1992). The psychobiology of female aggression. *Criminal Justice and Behavior, 19*, 99–126.

Flannery, D. J., Singer, M. I., & Wester, K. L. (2003). Violence, coping, and mental health in a community sample of adolescence. *Violence and Victims, 18*(4), 403–418.

Florida Department of Education. (2000). Developing effective educational programs in Department of Juvenile Justice programs: 1999 report. Tallahassee, FL: Florida Department of State.

Foley, D. L., Eaves, L. J., Wormley, B., Silberg, J. L., Maes, H. H., Kuhn, J., et al. (2004). Childhood adversity, monoamine oxidase A genotype, and risk for conduct disorder. *Archives of General Psychiatry, 61*, 738–744.

Foley, R. M. (2001). Academic characteristics of incarcerated youths and correctional education programs: A literature review. *Journal of Emotional and Behavior Disorders, 9*, 248–260.

Foster, E. M. & Gifford, E. J. (2005). The transition to adulthood for youth leaving, public systems: Challenges to policies and research. In R. A. Settersten Jr., F. R. Furstenberg, & A. G. Rumbant (Eds.), *On the frontier of adulthood: Theory, research and public policy* (pp. 501–533). Chicago, IL: University of Chicago Press.

Foster, E. M., Jones, D. E., & the Conduct Problems Prevention Research Group. (2005). The High costs of aggression: Public expenditures resulting from conduct disorder. *American Journal of Public Health, 95*, 1767–1772.

Fowles, D. C. (1988). Psychophysiology and psychopathology: A motivational approach. *Psychophysiology, 25*(4), 373–391.

Frank, D. A., Augustyn, M., Knight, W. G., Pell, T., & Zuckerman, B. (2001) Growth, development, and behavior in early childhood following prenatal cocaine exposure: A systematic review. *Journal of the American Medical Association, 285,* 1613–1625.

Frank, D. A., McCarten, K. M., Robson, C. D., Mirochnick, M., Cabral, H., Park, H., et al. (1999). Level of in utero cocaine exposure and neonatal ultrasound findings. *Pediatrics, 104*(5), 1101–1105.

Franke, T. M., Huynh-Hohnbaum, A. T., & Chung, Y. (2002). Adolescent violence: With whom they fight and where. *Journal of Ethnic and Cultural Diversity in Social Work, 11,* 133–158.

Frazzetto, G., Di Lorenzo, G., Carola, V., Proietti, L., Sokolowska, E., Siracusano, A., et al. (2007). Early trauma and increased risk for physical aggression during adulthood: The moderating role of MAOA genotype. *PLoS ONE, 2*(5): e486.

Furstenberg, F. F. (1993). How families manage risk and opportunity in dangerous neighborhoods. In W. J. Wilson (Ed.), *Sociology and the public agenda* (pp. 231–258). Newbury Park, CA: Sage.

Garbarino, J. & Sherman, D. (1980). High-risk neighborhoods and high-risk families: The human ecology of child maltreatment. *Child Development, 51,* 188–98.

Garland, D. (1990). *Punishment and modern society: A study in social theory.* Chicago, IL: University of Chicago Press.

Gaultney, J. F., Gingras, J. L., Martin, M., & DeBrule, D. (2005) Prenatal cocaine exposure and infants' preference for novelty and distractibility. *Journal of Genetic Psychology, 166*(4), 385–406.

Ge, X., Conger, R., Cadoret, R., Neiderhiser, J. M., Yates, W., Troughton, E., et al. (1996). The developmental interface between nature and nurture: A mutual influence model of child antisocial behavior and parent behaviors. *Developmental Psychology, 32*(4), 574–589.

Ge, X., Donnellan, M. B., & Wenk, E. (2001). The development of persistent criminal offending in males. *Criminal Justice and Behavior, 28*(6), 731–755.

Ge, X., Lorenz, F. O., Conger, R. D., Elder, G. H., Jr., & Simons, R. L. (1994). Trajectories of stressful life events and depressive symptoms during adolescence. *Developmental Psychology, 30,* 467–483.

Geary, L. H. (2003, June 4). $100k on a degree—now what? With jobs scarce, more than half of this year's college graduates will head home to Mom and Dad. *CNN/ Money. Retrieved on September 13, 2006, from* http://money.cnn.com/2003/06/02/pf/ college/q_gradhome/index.htm

Geis, G. (2000). On the absence of self-control as the basis for a general theory of crime. *Theoretical Criminology, 4*(1), 35–53.

Geis, G. (2008). Self-control: A hypercritical assessment. In E. Goode (Ed.), *Out of control: Assessing the general theory of crime* (pp. 203–216). Stanford: Stanford University Press.

Geer, J. H., Estupinan, L. A., & Manguno-Mire, G. M. (2000). Empathy, social skills, and other relevant cognitive processes in rapists and child molesters. *Aggression and Violent Behavior, 5*(1), 99–126.

George, S. & LaLonde, R. (2002). Incarcerated mothers in Illinois state prisons: An analysis of administrative data. The Chicago project on female prisoners and their children. Initial Report, Irving B. Harris Graduate School of Public Policy Studies.

Gershoff, E. T. (2002). Corporal punishment by parents and associated child behaviors and experiences: A meta-analytic and theoretical review. *Psychological Bulletin, 128*(4), 539–579.

Ghiglieri, M. P. (1999). *The dark side of man: Tracing the origins of male violence.* Cambridge, MA: Perseus Books.

Giancola, P. R. & Zeichner, A. (1994). Intellectual ability and aggressive behavior in nonclinical-nonforensic males. *Journal of Psychopathology and Behavioral Assessment, 16*, 121–130.

Gibbs, J. J., Giever, D., & Martin, J. S. (1998). Parental management and self-control: An empirical test of Gottfredson and Hirschi's general theory of crime. *Journal of Research in Crime and Delinquency, 35*, 40–70.

Gibson, C. L., Piquero, A., & Tibbetts, S. G. (2000). Assessing the relationship between maternal cigarette smoking during pregnancy and age at first police contact: A research note. *Justice Quarterly, 17*(3), 519–542.

Gibson, C. L., Piquero, A. R., & Tibbetts, S. G. (2001). The contribution of family adversity and verbal IQ to criminal behavior. *International Journal of Offender Therapy and Comparative Criminology, 45*(5), 574–592.

Gibson, C. L. & Tibbetts, S. G. (1998). Interaction between maternal cigarette smoking and Apgar scores in predicting offending behavior. *Psychological Reports, 83*(2), 579–86.

Gibson, C. L. & Tibbetts, S. G. (2000). A biosocial interaction in predicting early onset of offending. *Psychological Reports, 86*(4), 509–518.

Gibson, H. B. & West, D. J. (1970). Social and intellectual handicaps as precursors of early delinquency. *British Journal of Criminology, 10*(1), 21–32.

Gibson, M. & Rafter, N. (2006). *Cesare Lombroso—criminal man.* Durham, NC: Duke University Press.

Giedd, J. N., Blumenthal, J., Jeffries, N. O., Castellanos, F. X., Liu, H., Zijdenbos, A., et al. (1999). Brain development during childhood and adolescence: A longitudinal MRI study. *Nature Neuroscience, 2*, 861–863.

Gifford-Smith, M., Dodge, K., Dishion, T., & McCord, J. (2005). Peer influence in children and adolescents: Crossing the bridge from developmental to intervention science. *Journal of Abnormal Child Psychology, 3*, 255–265.

Gilbert, T. (2005). The effect of family size on the development of delinquency. Unpublished master's thesis, California State University, San Bernardino.

Gingras, J. L. & O'Donnell, K. J. (1998). State control in the substance-exposed fetus. I. The fetal neurobehavioral profile: an assessment of fetal state, arousal, and regulation competency. *Annals of the New York Academy of Sciences, 846*, 262–276.

Giordano, P. C. & Cernkovich, S. A. (1997). Gender and antisocial behavior. In D. M. Stoff, J. Breiling, & J. D. Maser (Eds.), *Handbook of antisocial behavior* (pp. 496–510). New York: Wiley.

Giordano, P. C., Cernkovich, S. A., & Lowery, A. R. (Eds.). (2004). A long-term follow-up of serious adolescent female offenders. In M. Putallaz & K. L. Bierman (Eds.), *Aggression, antisocial behavior, and violence among girls: A developmental perspective* (pp. 186–202). New York: Guilford Publications.

Giordano, P. C., Millhollin, T. J., Cernkovich, S. A., Pugh, M. D., & Rudolph, J. L. (1999). Delinquency, identity, and women's involvement in relationship violence. *Criminology, 37,* 17–40.

Girls Incorporated (1996). *Prevention and parity: Girls in juvenile justice.* Indianapolis, IN: Girls Incorporated National Resource Center.

Gjerde, P. F., Block, J., & Block, J. H. (1988). Depressive symptoms and personality during late adolescence: Gender differences in the externalization-internalization of symptom expression. *Journal of Abnormal Psychology, 97,* 475–486.

Glover, D., Gough, G., Johnson, M., & Cartwright, N. (2000). Bullying in 25 secondary schools: Incidence, impact, and intervention. *Educational Research, 42,* 141–156.

Glueck, S. & Glueck, E. (1934). *One thousand juvenile delinquents: Their treatment by court and clinic.* Cambridge, MA: Harvard University Press.

Glueck, S. & Glueck, E. (1940). *Juvenile delinquents grown up.* Oxford, UK: Commonwealth Fund.

Glueck, S. & Glueck, E. (1950). *Unraveling juvenile delinquency.* New York: Commonwealth Fund.

Glueck, S. & Glueck, E. (1968). *Delinquents and nondelinquents in perspective.* Cambridge, MA: Harvard University Press.

Gold, M. (1966). Undetected delinquent behavior. *Journal of Research in Crime and Delinquency, 3,* 27–46.

Goode, E. (Ed.). (2008). *Out of control? Evaluating the general theory of crime.* Stanford, CA: Stanford University Press.

Goodman, S. H. & Gotlib, I. H. (1999). Risk for psychopathology in the children of depressed mothers: A developmental model for understanding mechanisms of transmission. *Psychological Review, 106,* 458–490.

Gordon, D. N. (1970). Immigrants and municipal voting turnout: Implications for the changing ethnic impact on urban politics. *American Sociological Review, 35,* 665–681.

Gorman-Smith, D., Tolan, P. H., Loeber, R., & Henry, D. B. (1998). Relation of family problems to patterns of delinquent involvement among urban youth. *Journal of Abnormal Child Psychology, 26*(5), 319–333.

Gottesman, I. I. & Hanson, D. R. (2005). Human development: Biological and genetic processes. *Annual Review of Psychology, 56*(1), 263–286.

Gottfredson, D. C. (2001). *Schools and delinquency.* New York: Cambridge University Press.

Gottfredson, M. (2005). Offender classifications and treatment effects in developmental criminology: A propensity/event consideration. *Annals of the American Academy of Political and Social Science, 602*, 46–56.

Gottfredson, M. & Hirschi, T. (1987). The methodological adequacy of longitudinal research on crime. *Criminology, 25*, 581–614.

Gottfredson, M. & Hirschi, T. (1988). Science, public policy, and the career paradigm. *Criminology, 26*, 37–55.

Gottfredson, M. & Hirschi, T. (1990). *A general theory of crime.* Stanford, CA: Stanford University Press.

Gottfredson, M. & Hirschi, T. (2003). Self-control and opportunity. In C. Britt & M. Gottfredson (Eds.), *Control theories of crime and delinquency* (pp. 5–19). New Brunswick: Transaction Publishers.

Gottfredson, S. & Gottfredson, D. (1986). Accuracy of prediction models. In A. Blumstein, J. Cohen, J. A. Roth, & C. A. Visher (Eds.), *Criminal careers and 'career criminals': Vol. 2.* Washington DC: National Academy Press.

Gottfredson, S. & Gottfredson, D. (1994). Behavioral prediction and the problem of incapacitation. *Criminology, 32*, 441–474.

Gove, W. R. (1985). The effect of age and gender on deviant behavior: A biopsychological perspective. In A. S. Rossi (Ed.), *Gender and the life course* (pp. 115–144). New York: Aldine de Gruyter.

Graber, J. A., Nichols, T., Lynne, S. D., Brooks-Gunn, J., & Botvin, G. J. (2006). A longitudinal examination of family, friend, and media influences on competent versus problem behaviors among urban minority youth. *Applied Developmental Science, 10*(2), 75–85.

Grasmick, H. G., Jacobs, D., & McCollom, C. B. (1983). Social class and social control: An implication of deterrence research. *Social Forces, 62*, 359–374.

Gray, J.A. (1982). *The neuropsychology of anxiety: An enquiry into the functions of the septo-hippocampal system.* New York: Oxford University Press.

Gray, J.A. (1994). Framework for a taxonomy of psychiatric disorder. In S. van Goozen, N. Van de Poll, & J. Sergeant (Eds.), *Emotions: Essays on emotion theory* (pp. 29–59). Hillsdale, NJ: Lawrence Erlbaum.

Green, A. H. (1985). Children traumatized by physical abuse. In S. Eth, & R. S. Pynoos (Eds.), *Post-traumatic stress disorder in children* (pp. 135–154). Washington, DC: American Psychiatric Press.

Greenwood, P. W., Karoly, L. A., Everingham, S. S., Hoube, J., Kilburn, M. R., Rydell, C. P., et al. (2001). Estimating the costs and benefits of early childhood interventions: Nurse home visits and the Perry Preschool. In B. W. Welsh, D. P. Farrington, & L. W. Sherman (Eds.), *Costs and benefits of preventing crime* (pp. 123–148). Boulder, CO: Westview Press.

Griffith, D. R., Chasnoff, I. J., & Azuma, S. (1994). Three-year outcome of children exposed prenatally to drugs. *Journal of the American Academy of Child & Adolescent Psychiatry, 33*, 20–27.

Grigsby, J. & Stevens, D. (2000). *The neurodynamics of personality.* New York: Guilford.

Grusec, J. E. (2002). Parenting and the socialization of values. In M. Bornstein (Ed.), *Handbook of parenting* (pp. 143–168). Mahwah NJ: Erlbaum.

Grusec, J. E., Davidov, M., & Lundell, L. (2002). Prosocial and helping behavior. In P. Smith & C. Hart (Eds.), *Handbook of children's social development* (pp. 457–474). New York: Blackwell.

Grych, J. H., Fincham, F. D., Jouriles, E. N., & McDonald, R. (2001). Interparental conflict and child adjustment: Testing the mediational role of appraisals in the cognitive contextual framework. *Child Development, 71,* 1648–1661.

Grych, J. H., Harold, G. T., & Miles, C. J. (2003). A prospective investigation of appraisals as mediators of the link between interparental conflict and child adjustment. *Child Development, 74,* 1176–1193.

Guerra, V. S., Asher, S. R., & DeRosier, M. E. (2004). Effect of children's perceived rejection on physical aggression. *Journal of Abnormal Child Psychology, 32*(5), 551–563.

Haapanen, R. (1990). *Selective incapacitation and the serious offender: A longitudinal study of criminal career patterns.* New York: Springer-Verlag.

Haapanen, R. & Britton, R. (2002). Drug testing for youthful offenders on parole: An experimental study. *Criminology and Public Policy, 1*(2), 217–244.

Haapanen, R., Britton, L., & Croisdale, T. (2007). Persistent criminality and career length. *Crime and Delinquency, 53*(1), 133–155.

Haapanen, R. & Jesness, C. (1982). *Early identification of the chronic offender.* Sacramento, CA: California Youth Authority.

Haapanen, R. & Steiner, H. (2003). *Identifying mental health treatment needs among serious institutionalized delinquents using paper-and-pencil screening instruments: Final report to the National Institute of Justice.* Sacramento, CA: California Youth Authority.

Haapasalo, J. (2000). Young offenders' experiences of child protection services. *Journal of Youth and Adolescence, 29,* 355–371.

Haapasalo, J. & Tremblay, R. E. (1994). Physically aggressive boys from ages 6 to 12: Family background, parenting behavior, and prediction of delinquency. *Journal of Consulting and Clinical Psychology, 62,* 1044–1052.

Haberman, M. & Quinn, L. M. (1986). The high school re-entry myth: A follow-up study of juveniles released from two correctional high schools in Wisconsin. *Journal of Correctional Education, 37,* 114–117.

Hagan, J. (1992). The poverty of a classless criminology—The American Society of Criminology. 1991 Presidential address. *Criminology, 30,* 1–18.

Hagan, J. & McCarthy, B. (1997). *Mean streets: Youth crime and homelessness.* Cambridge, United Kingdom: Cambridge University Press.

Hagan, J. & McCarthy, B. (2005). Homeless youth and the perilous passage to adulthood. In D. W. Osgood, E. M. Foster, C. Flanagan, & R. G. Ruth (Eds.), *On your own without a net: The transition to adulthood for vulnerable populations* (pp. 178–201). Chicago, IL: University of Chicago Press.

Hagedorn, J. (1994). Homeboys, dope fiends, legits, and new jacks. *Criminology, 32(2)*, 197–219.

Hamermesh, D. (1999). The timing of work time over time. *Economic Journal, 109*, 37–66.

Hamparian, D. M., Schuster, R., Dinitz, S., & Conrad, J. P. (1978). *The violent few—A study of dangerous juvenile offenders*. New York: Lexington Books.

Hanson, R. F., Self-Brown, S., Fricker-Elhai, A. E., Kilpatrick, D. G., Saunders, B. E., & Resnick, H. S. (2006). The relations between family environment and violence exposure among youth: Findings from the national survey of adolescents. *Child Maltreatment, 11*, 3–15.

Harachi, T. W., Fleming, C. B., White, H. R., Ensminger, M. E., Abbott, R. D., Catalano, R. F., et al. (2006). Aggressive behavior among girls and boys during middle childhood: Predictors and sequelae of trajectory group membership. *Aggressive Behavior, 32(4)*, 279–293.

Harbin, H. T. & Madden, D. J. (1979). Battered parents: A new syndrome. *American Journal of Psychiatry, 136*, 1288–1291.

Hare, R. D. (1978). Psychopathy and electrodermal responses to nonsignal stimulation. *Biological Psychology, 6*, 237–246.

Harlow, C. W. (1998). Profile of jail inmates 1996. (Special Report Bureau of Justice Statistics). Washington, DC: U.S. Department of Justice.

Harlow, C. W. (2003). Education and Correctional Populations. (Special Report Bureau of Justice Statistics). Washington, DC: U.S. Department of Justice.

Harris, J. R. (1998). *The nurture assumption: Why children turn out the way they do.* New York: The Free Press.

Harrison, B. & Schehr, R. C. (2004). Offenders and post-release jobs: Variable influencing success and failure. *Journal of Offender Rehabilitation, 39*, 35–59.

Hawkins, J. D., Catalano, R. F., & Miller, J. Y. (1992). Risk and protective factors for alcohol and other drug problems in adolescence and early adulthood: Implications for substance abuse prevention. *Psychological Bulletin, 112*, 64–105.

Hawkins, J. D., Catalano, R. F., Morrison, D. M., O'Donnell, J., Abbott, R. D., & Day, L. E. (1992). The Seattle Social Development Project: Effects of the first four years on protective factors and problem behaviours. In J. McCord & R. E. Tremblay (Eds.), *Preventing antisocial behaviour* (pp. 139–161). New York: Guilford.

Hawkins, J. D., Herrenkohl, T., Farrington, D. P., Brewer, D, Catalano, R. F., & Harachi, T. W. (1998). A review of predictors of youth violence. In R. Loeber & D. P. Farrington (Eds.) *Serious and violent juvenile offenders: Risk factors and successful interventions* (pp. 106–146). Thousand Oaks, CA: Sage.

Hay, C. (2001). Parenting, self-control, and delinquency: A test of self-control theory. *Criminology, 39*, 707–736.

Hay, C., Fortson, E. N., Hollist, D. R., Altheimer, I., & Schaible, L. A. (2006). The impact of community disadvantage on the relationship between the family and juvenile crime. *Journal of Research in Crime and Delinquency, 43*, 326–356.

Hay, C., Fortson, E. N., Hollist, D. R., Altheimer, I., & Schaible, L. M. (2007). Compounded risk: The implications for delinquency of coming from a poor family that lives in a poor community. *Journal of Youth and Adolescence, 36,* 593–605.

Hayden, L.C., Schiller, M., Dickstein, S., Seifer, R., Sameroff, A. J., Miller, I., et al. (1998). Levels of family assessment 1: Family, marital, and parent-child interaction. *Journal of Family Psychology, 12,* 7–22.

Haynie, D. L., Giordano, P. C., Manning, W. D., & Longmore, M. A. (2005). Adolescent romantic relationships and delinquency involvement. *Criminology, 43,* 177–210.

Hechtman, L., Weiss, G., Perlman, T., & Amsel, R. (1984). Hyperactives as young adults: Initial predictors of adult outcome. *Journal of the American Academy of Child Psychiatry, 23,* 250–260.

Heimer, K. & DeCoster, S. (1999). The gendering of violent delinquency. *Criminology, 37,* 277–317.

Hemphill, J. F., Hare, R. D., & Wong, S. (1998). Psychopathy and recidivism: A review. *Legal and Criminological Psychology, 3,* 141–172.

Henggeler, S. W., Rodick, J. D., Borduin, C. M., Hanson, C. L., Watson, S. M., & Urey, J. R. (1986). Multisystemic treatment of juvenile offenders: Effects on adolescent behavior and family interaction. *Developmental Psychology, 22,* 132–141.

Henry, B., Caspi, A., Moffitt, T. E., & Silva, P. A. (1996). Temperamental and familial predictors of violent and nonviolent criminal convictions: Age 3 to age 18. *Developmental Psychology, 32,* 614–23.

Henry, B. & Moffitt, T. E. (1997). Neuropsychological and neuroimaging studies of juvenile delinquency and adult criminal behavior. In D. M. Stoff, J. Breiling, & J. D. Maser (Eds.), *Handbook of antisocial behavior* (pp. 280–288). New York: John Wiley and Sons.

Herrenkohl, T. I., Hill, K. G., Hawkins, J. D., Chung, I-J, & Nagin, D. S. (2006). Developmental trajectories of family management and risk for violent behaviors in adolescence. *Journal of Adolescent Health, 39,* 206–213.

Herrenkohl, T. I., Huang, B., Kosterman, R., Hawkins, J. D., Catalano, R. F., & Smith, B. H. (2001). Comparison of social development processes leading to violent behavior in late adolescence for childhood initiators and adolescent initiators of violence. *Journal of Research in Crime and Delinquency, 38*(1), 45–63.

Herrera, V. M. & McCloskey, L. A. (2001). Gender differences in the risk for delinquency among youth exposed to family violence. *Child Abuse and Neglect, 25*(8), 1037–1051.

Hesselbrock, V., Higuchi, S., & Soyka, M. (2005). Recent developments in the genetics of alcohol-related phenotypes. *Alcoholism: Clinical & Experimental Research, 29*(7), 1321–1324.

Hetherington, E. M. & Baltes, P. B. (1988). Child psychology and life-span development. In E. M. Hetherington & R. M. Lerner (Eds.), *Child development in life-span perspective* (pp. 1–19). Hillsdale, NJ: Lawrence Erlbaum Associates.

Hill, J. (2002). Biological, psychological, and social processes in the conduct disorders. *Journal of Child Psychology and Psychiatry, 43*, 133–164.

Hill, S. Y., Lowers, L., Locke-Wellman, J., & Shen, S. (2000). Maternal smoking and drinking during pregnancy and the risk of child and adolescent psychiatric disorders. *Journal of Studies on Alcohol, 61*(5), 661–668.

Hindelang, M. J., Hirschi, T., & Weis, J.G. (1979). Correlates of delinquency: The illusion of discrepancy between self-report and official measures. *American Sociological Review, 44*, 995–1014.

Hindelang, M., Hirschi, T., & Weis, J. (1981). *Measuring delinquency.* Beverly Hills, CA: Sage.

Hines, A. M., Lemon, K., Wyatt, P., & Merdinger, J. (2004) Factors related to the disproportionate involvement of children of color in the child welfare system: A review and emerging themes. *Children and Youth Services Review, 26*(6), 507–527.

Hirschi, T. (1969). *Causes of delinquency.* Berkeley, CA: University of California Press.

Hirschi, T. (1995). The family. In J. Q. Wilson & J. Petersilia (Eds.), *Crime* (pp. 121–140). San Francisco, CA: ICS Press.

Hirschi, T. & Gottfredson, M. R. (1983). Age and the explanation of crime. *American Journal of Sociology, 89*, 552–584.

Hirschi, T. & Gottfredson, M. (1995). Control theory and the life-course perspective. *Studies on Crime and Crime Prevention: Annual Review, 4*, 131–142.

Hirschi, T. & Gottfredson, M. (2001). Self-control theory. In R. Paternoster & R. Bachman (Eds.), *Explaining criminals and crime: Essays in contemporary criminological theory* (pp. 81–96). Los Angeles: Roxbury.

Hobel C. J., Dunkel-Schetter C., Roesch S. C., Castro L. C., & Arora, C. P. (1999). Maternal plasma corticotropin-releasing hormone associated with stress at 20 weeks' gestation in pregnancies ending in preterm delivery. *American Journal of Obstetrics & Gynecology. 180*, S257–S263.

Hodgins, S. (1994). Status at age 30 of children with conduct problems. *Studies on Crime and Crime Prevention, 3*, 41–62.

Hoeve, M., Smeenk, W., Loeber, R., Stouthamer-Loeber, M., van der Laan, P. H., Gerris, J. R. M., et al. (2007). Long-term effects of parenting and family characteristics on delinquency of male young adults. *European Journal of Criminology, 4*(2), 161–194.

Hoffmann, J. P. (2004). *Generalized linear models: An applied approach.* Boston: Pearson Education.

Hoffmann, J. P. & Cerbone, F. G. (1999). Stressful life events and delinquency escalation in early adolescence. *Criminology, 37*, 343–374.

Hoffmann, J. P. & Ireland, T. O. (2004). Strain and opportunity structures. *Journal of Quantitative Criminology, 20*, 263–292.

Hoffmann, J. P. & Miller, A. S. (1998). A latent variable analysis of general strain theory. *Journal of Quantitative Criminology, 14*, 83–110.

Hoffmann, J. P. & Su, S. (1997). Conditional effects of stress on delinquency and drug use: A strain theory assessment of sex differences. *Journal of Research in Crime and Delinquency, 34*(1), 46–78.

Hoge, R. D., Andrews, D. A., & Leschied, A. W. (1996). An investigation of risk and protective factors in a sample of youth offenders. *Child Psychology and Psychiatry, 37*, 419–424.

Hollander, H. E. & Turner, F. D. (1985). Characteristics of incarcerated delinquents: Relationship between developmental disorders, environmental and family factors, and patterns of offense and recidivism. *Journal of the American Academy of Child Psychiatry, 24*(2), 221–226.

Hollingshead, A. B. (1975). *Four factor index of social status.* New Haven, CT: Yale University Department of Sociology.

Hollingshead, A. B. & Redlich, F. C. (1958). *Social class and mental illness.* New York: John Wiley and Sons.

Holsinger, A. M. & Latessa, E. J. (1999). An empirical evaluation of a sanction continuum: Pathways through the juvenile justice system. *Journal of Criminal Justice, 27*, 155–172.

Home Office Statistical Bulletin. (1995). *Criminal careers of those born between 1953 and 1973.* London: Home Office.

Horney, J. & Marshall, I. (1992). Risk perceptions among serious offenders: The role of crime and punishment. *Criminology, 30*, 575–594.

Horney, J., Osgood, D. W., & Marshall, I. H. (1995). Criminal careers in the short-term: Intra-individual variability in crime and its relation to local life circumstances. *American Sociological Review, 60*, 655–673.

Horowitz, K., Weine, S., & Jekel, J. (1995). PTSD symptoms in urban adolescent girls: Compounded community trauma. *Journal of the American Academy of Child and Adolescent Psychiatry, 34*, 1353–1361.

House, J. (2002). Understanding social factors and inequalities in health: 20th century progress and 21st century prospects. *Journal of Health and Social Behavior, 43*(2), 125–142.

Houser-Marko, L. & Sheldon, K. M. (2006). Motivating behavioral persistence: The self-as-doer construct. *Personality and Social Psychology Bulletin, 32*, 1037–1049.

Hox, J. (2002). *Multilevel analysis: Techniques and applications.* Mahwah, NJ: Lawrence Erlbaum Associates.

Hubbard, J. A., Smithmyer, C. M., Ramsden, S. R., Parker, E. H., Flanagan, K. D., Dearing, K.F., et al. (2002). Observational, physiological, and self-report measures of children's anger: Relations to reactive versus proactive aggression. *Child Development, 73*, 1101–1118.

Huebner, B. M. (2005). The effect of incarceration on marriage and work over the life course. *Justice Quarterly, 22*(3), 281–303.

Huesmann, L. R., Eron, L. D., & Lefkowitz, M. M. (1984). Stability of aggression over time and generations. *Developmental Psychology, 20*, 1120–1134.

Huesmann, L. R., Eron, L. D., & Yarmel, P. W. (1987). Intellectual functioning and aggression. *Journal of Personality and Social Psychology, 52,* 232–240.

Huh, D., Tristan, J., Wade, E., & Stice, E. (2006). Does problem behavior elicit poor parenting? A prospective study of adolescent girls. *Journal of Adolescent Research, 21,* 185–204.

Huizinga, D. & Elliott, D. S. (1986). Reassessing the reliability and validity of self-report delinquency measures. *Journal of Quantitative Criminology, 2,* 293–327.

Huizinga, D., Loeber, R., Thornberry, T. P., & Cothern, L. (2000). Co-occurrence of delinquency and other problem behaviors. *Juvenile Justice Bulletin,* November. Washington, DC: Office of Justice Programs, Office of Juvenile Justice and Delinquency Prevention.

Huizink, A. C., Robles de Medina, P. G., Mulder, E. J. H., Visser, G. H. A., & Buitelaar, J. K. (2002). Psychological measures of prenatal stress as predictors of infant temperament. *Journal of the American Academy of Child and Adolescent Psychiatry, 41*(9), 1078–1085.

Hunnicutt, G. & Broidy, L. M. (2004). Liberation and economic marginalization: A reformation and test of (formerly?) competing models. *Journal of Research in Crime and Delinquency, 41,* 130–155.

Hurt, H., Malmud, E., Betancourt, L. M., Brodsky, N. L., & Giannetta, J. M. (2001). A prospective comparison of developmental outcome of children with in utero cocaine exposure and controls using the Battelle Developmental Inventory. *Journal of Developmental & Behavioral Pediatrics, 22*(1), 27–34.

Hussong, A. M., Curran, P. J., Moffitt, T. E., Caspi, A., & Carrig, M. M. (2004). Substance abuse hinders desistance in young adult's antisocial behavior. *Development and Psychopathology, 16,* 1029–1046.

Huttunen , M. O. & Niskanen, P. (1978). Prenatal loss of father and psychiatric disorders. *Archives of General Psychiatry, 35*(4), 429–431.

Ireland, T. O., Thornberry, T. P., & Smith, C. A. (2002). Development issues in the impact of child maltreatment on later delinquency and drug use. *Criminology, 40,* 359–399.

Ireland, T. & Widom, C. S. (1994). Childhood victimization and risk for alcohol and drug arrests. *The International Journal of the Addictions, 29*(2), 235–274.

Ishikawa, S. S. & Raine, A. (2002). The frontal lobe hypothesis of antisocial behavior. In Lahey, B., Moffitt, T. E., & Caspi, A. (Eds.), *The causes of conduct disorder and serious juvenile delinquency* (pp. 51–65). New York: Guilford Press.

Ishikawa, S. S. & Raine, A. (2003). Prefrontal deficits and antisocial behavior: A causal model. In B. B. Lahey, T. E. Moffitt, & A. Caspi (Eds.), *Causes of conduct disorder and juvenile delinquency* (pp. 277–304). New York: Guilford.

Jacobs, B. & Wright, R. (1999). Stick-up, street culture, and offender motivation. *Criminology, 37*(1), 149–173.

Jacobson, S. W., Jacobson, J. L., Sokol, R. J., Martier, S. S., & Chiodo, L. M. (1996). New evidence for neurobehavioral effects of in utero cocaine exposure. *Journal of Pediatrics, 129*(4), 581–590.

Jaffee, S. R., Belsky, J., Harrington, H., Caspi, A., & Moffitt, T. E. (2006). When parents have a history of conduct disorder: How is the caregiving environment affected? *Journal of Abnormal Psychology, 115,* 309–319.

Jaffee, S. R., Caspi, A., Moffitt, T. E., Dodge, K. A., Rutter, M., Taylor, A., & Tully, L. A. (2005). Nature X nurture: Genetic vulnerabilities interact with physical maltreatment to promote conduct problems. *Development and Psychopathology, 17*(1), 67–84.

Jaffee, S. R., Caspi, A., Moffitt, T. E., Taylor, A., & Dickson, N. (2001). Predicting early fatherhood and whether young fathers live with their children: Prospective findings and policy reconsiderations. *Journal of Child Psychology and Psychiatry, 42,* 803–815.

Jaffee, S. R., Moffitt, T. E., Caspi, A., & Taylor, A. (2003). Life with (or without) father: The benefits of living with two biological parents depend on the father's antisocial behavior. *Child Development, 74*(1), 109–126.

Jaffee, S. R. & Poulton, R. (2006). Reciprocal effects of mothers' depression and children's problem behaviors from middle childhood to early adolescence. In A. Huston & M. N. Ripke (Eds.), *Developmental contexts in middle childhood: Bridges to adolescence and adulthood* (pp. 107–129). New York: Cambridge University Press.

Jang, S. J. (1999). Age-varying effects of family, school, and peers on delinquency: A multilevel modeling test of interactional theory. *Criminology, 37*(3), 643–686.

Jang, S. J. & Johnson, B. R. (2003). Strain, negative emotions, and deviant coping among African-Americans: A test of general strain theory. *Journal of Quantitative Criminology, 19*(1), 79–105.

Janson, C-G. & Wikström, P-O. H. (1995). Growing up in a welfare state: The social class-offending relationship. In Z. S. Blau & J. Hagan (Eds.), *Current perspectives on aging and the life cycle: Vol. 4. Delinquency and disrepute in the life course* (pp. 191–215). Greenwich, CT: JAI Press.

Japel, C., Pagani, L. S., McDuff, P., Mousseau, M., & Tremblay, R. E. Increments in mothers' education during their children's preschool years and their association with indicators of school readiness. *Merrill Palmer Quarterly.* (In press).

Jargowsky, P. A. (1997). *Poverty and place: Ghettos, barrios, and the American city.* New York: Russell Sage Foundation.

Jarjoura, G. R., Triplett, R. A., & Brinker, G. P. (2002). Growing up poor: Examining the link between persistent childhood poverty and delinquency. *Journal of Quantitative Criminology, 18,* 159–187.

Jesness, C. (1971). The Preston Typology Study: An experiment with differential treatment in an institution. *Journal of Research in Crime and Delinquency, 8,* 38–52.

Jesness, C. (1975). Comparative effectiveness of behavior modification and transactional analysis programs for delinquents. *Journal of Consulting and Clinical Psychology, 43,* 758–779.

Jesness, C. (1988). The Jesness Inventory classification system. *Criminal Justice and Behavior, 15*(1), 78–91.

Jessor, R., Donovan, J. E., & Costa, F. M. (1991). *Beyond adolescence: Problem behavior and young adult development.* Cambridge: Cambridge University Press.

Jimerson, S. R. (1999). On the failure of failure: Examining the association between early grade retention and education and employment outcomes during late adolescence. *Journal of School Psychology, 37,* 243–272.

John, V., Dai, H., Talati, A., Charnigo, R. J., Neuman, M., & Bada H. S. (2007). Autonomic alterations in cocaine-exposed neonates following orthostatic stress. *Pediatric Research, 61*(2), 251–256.

Johnson, J. G., Cohen, P., Kasen, S., Smailes, E., & Brook, J. S. (2001). Association of maladaptive parental behavior with psychiatric disorder among parents and their offspring. *Archives of General Psychiatry, 58,* 453–460.

Johnson, J. G., Smailes, E., Cohen, P., Kasen, S., & Brook, J. S. (2004). Anti-social parental behaviour, problematic parenting and aggressive offspring behaviour during adulthood: A 25-year longitudinal investigation. *British Journal of Criminology, 44*(6), 915–930.

Johnston, D. (1996). Interventions. In K. Gabel & E. Johnston (Eds.), *Children of incarcerated parents* (pp. 199–236). New York: Lexington Books.

Jones, B. L., Nagin, D. S., & Roeder, K. (2001). A SAS procedure based on mixture models for estimating developmental trajectories. *Sociological Methods and Research, 29,* 374–393.

Jonson-Reid, M. (1998). Youth violence and exposure to violence in childhood: An ecological review. *Aggression and Violent Behavior, 3,* 159–179.

Jonson-Reid, M. (2002). Exploring the relationship between child welfare intervention and juvenile corrections involvement. *American Journal of Orthopsychiatry, 22*(4), 559–576.

Jonson-Reid, M. & Barth, R. P. (2000a). From maltreatment report to juvenile incarceration: The role of child welfare. *Child Abuse and Neglect, 24,* 505–520.

Jonson-Reid, M. & Barth, R. P. (2000b). From placement to prison: The path to adolescent incarceration from child welfare supervised foster of group care. *Child and Youth Services Review, 22,* 493–516.

Jonson-Reid, M. & Barth, R. P. (2003). Probation foster care as an outcome for children exiting child welfare foster care. *Social Work, 48,* 348–361.

Jordan, B. K., Schlenger, W. E., Fairbank, J. A., & Caddell, J. M. (1996). Prevalence of psychiatric disorders among incarcerated women. II. Convicted felons entering prison. *Archives of General Psychiatry, 53,* 513–519.

Juby, H. & Farrington, D. P. (2001). Disentangling the link between disrupted families and delinquency. *British Journal of Criminology, 41*(1), 22–40.

Juon, H., Doherty, E. E., & Ensminger, M. E. (2006). Childhood behavior and adult criminality: Cluster analysis in a prospective study of African Americans. *Journal of Quantitative Criminology, 22*(3), 193–214.

Juvenile Justice Educational Enhancement Program. (2004). *2003 annual report to the Florida Department of Education.* Tallahassee, FL: Florida Department of Education.

Juvenile Justice Educational Enhancement Program. (2005). *2004 annual report to the Florida Department of Education.* Tallahassee, FL: Florida Department of Education.

Kalff, A. C., de Sonneville, L. M. J., Hurks, P. P., Hendricksen, J. G. M., & Kroes, M., Feron, F. et al. (2003). Low- and high-level controlled processing in executive motor control tasks in 5- and 6-year old children at risk of ADHD. *Journal of Child Psychology, Psychiatry and Allied Disciplines, 44,* 1049–1065.

Kandel, D. B. (1990). Parenting styles, drug use, and children's adjustment in families of young adults. *Journal of Marriage and the Family, 52,* 183–196.

Kandel, D. B. (1996). The parental and peer contexts of adolescent deviance: Algebra of interpersonal influences. Empirical validity of theories of drug abuse. *Journal of Drug Issues, 26,* 289–315.

Kandel, D. B. & Wu, P. (1995). Disentangling mother-child effects in the development of antisocial behaviour. In L. McCord (Ed.), *Coercion and punishment in long term perspective* (pp. 106–123). New York: Cambridge University Press.

Kandel, D. B., Wu, P., & Davies, M. (1994). Maternal smoking during pregnancy and smoking by adolescent daughters. *American Journal of Public Health, 84,* 1407–1413.

Kandel, E. & Freed, D. (1989). Frontal-lobe dysfunction and antisocial behavior: A review. *Journal of Clinical Psychology, 45,* 404–413.

Kandel, E., Brennan, P., Mednick, S. A., & Michelson, N. M. (1989). Minor physical anomalies and recidivistic adult violent criminal behavior. *Acta Psychiatra Scandinavia, 79,* 103–107.

Kandel, E. & Mednick, S. A., (1991). Perinatal complications predict violent offending. *Criminology, 29,* 519–529.

Kasarda, J. D. & Janowitz, M. (1974). Community attachment in mass society. *American Sociological Review, 39,* 328–339.

Kaslow, M. H., Deering, C. G., & Racusia, G. R. (1994). Depressed children and their families. *Clinical Psychological Review, 14,* 39–59.

Kazemian, L. Taking stock of some unresolved issues in desistance research. *Journal of Contemporary Criminal Justice* (in press).

Keenan, K. (2001). Uncovering preschool precursors to problem behavior. In D. P. Farrington & R. Loeber (Eds.), *Child delinquents: Development, interventions, and service needs* (pp. 117–134). Thousand Oaks, CA: Sage.

Keller, T. E., Catalano, R. F., Haggerty, K. P., & Fleming, C. B. (2002). Parent figure transitions and delinquency and drug use among early adolescent children of substance abusers. *American Journal of Drug and Alcohol Abuse, 28,* 399–427.

Kelly, T., Richardson, G., Hunter, R., & Knapp, M. (2002). Attention and executive function deficits in adolescent sex offenders. *Child Neuropsychology, 8,* 138–143.

Kempe, C. H., Silverman, F. N., Steele, B. F. Droegemueller, W., & Silver, H. K. (1962). The battered-child syndrome. *Journal of the American Medical Association. 181,* 7–24.

Kempf, K. L. (1990). Career criminals in the 1958 Philadelphia birth cohort: A follow-up of the early adult years. *Criminal Justice Review, 15,* 151–172.

Kendler, K. S., Kuo, P. H., Todd, W. B., Kalsi, G., Neale, M. C., Sullivan, P. F., et al. (2006). A joint genomewide linkage analysis of symptoms of alcohol dependence and conduct disorder. *Alcoholism: Clinical and Experimental Research, 30*(12), 1972–1977.

Kerr, M. (2000). What parents know, how they know it, and several forms of adolescent adjustment: Further support for a reinterpretation of monitoring. *Developmental Psychology, 36*, 366–380.

Kessler, R. C. (2000). Gender differences in major depression: Epidemiological findings. In E. Frank (Ed.), *Gender and its effects on psychopathology* (pp. 61–84). Washington DC: American Psychiatric Press.

Kim, H. K. & Capaldi, D. M. (2004). The association of antisocial behavior and depressive symptoms between partners and risk for aggression in romantic relationships. *Journal of Family Psychology, 18*, 82–96.

Kim, K. J., Conger, R. D., Elder, G. H., Jr., & Lorenz, F. O. (2003). Reciprocal influences between stressful life events and adolescent internalizing and externalizing problems. *Child Development, 74*, 127–143.

Kim-Cohen, J., Caspi, A., Moffitt, T. E., Harrington, H., Milne, B. J., & Poulton, R. (2003). Prior juvenile diagnoses in adults with mental disorder: Developmental follow-back of a prospective-longitudinal cohort. *Archives of General Psychiatry, 60*, 709–717.

Kim-Cohen, J., Caspi, A., Taylor, A., Williams, B., Newcombe, R., Craig, I.W., et al. (2006). MAOA, maltreatment, and gene–environment interaction predicting children's mental health: new evidence and a meta-analysis. *Molecular Psychiatry, 11*(10), 903–913.

Kirk, D. S. (2006). Examining the divergence across self-report and official data sources on inferences about the adolescent life-course of crime. *Journal of Quantitative Criminology, 22*(2), 107–129.

Klebanov, P. K., Brooks-Gunn, J., Chase-Lansdale, P. L., & Gordon, R. A. (1997). Are neighborhood effects on young children mediated by features of home environment?" In J. Brooks-Gunn, G. J. Duncan, & J. L. Aber (Eds.), *Neighborhood poverty: Vol. 1. Context and consequences for children* (pp. 119–145). New York: Russell Sage Foundation.

Kleck, G. (1982). Comment: On the use of self-report data to determine the class distribution of criminal and delinquent behavior. *American Sociological Review, 47*, 427–433.

Kleck, G., Sever, B., Li, S., & Gertz, M. (2005). The missing link in general deterrence research. *Criminology, 43*, 623–629.

Kleiman, M. A. R. (1998). *Getting deterrence right: Applying tipping models and behavioral economics to the problems of crime control.* Perspectives on Crime and Justice: 1998–1999 Lecture Series. Washington, DC: National Institute of Justice.

Klein, L. C. & Corwin, E. J. (2002). Seeing the unexpected: How sex differences in stress responses may provide a new perspective on the manifestation of psychiatric disorders. *Current Psychiatry Reports, 4*, 441–448.

Klein, M. (1971). *Street gangs and street workers*. Englewood Cliffs, NJ: Prentice-Hall.

Klein, M. (1995). *The American street gang: Its nature, prevalence and control*. New York: Oxford University Press Inc.

Klepper, S. & Nagin, D. (1989). The deterrent effect of perceived certainty and severity of punishment revisited. *Criminology, 27*, 721–746.

Klevens, J., Restrepo, O., Roca, J., & Martinez, A. (2000). Comparison of offenders with early- and late-starting antisocial behavior in Colombia. *International Journal of Offender Therapy and Comparative Criminology, 44*(2), 194–203.

Kratzer, L. & Hodgins, S. (1999). A typology of offenders: A test of Moffitt's theory among males and females from childhood to age 30. *Criminal Behaviour and Mental Health, 9*(1), 57–73.

Krisberg, B. (1992). Youth crime and its prevention: A research agenda. In I. M. Schwarz (Ed.), *Juvenile justice and public policy* (pp. 1–19). New York: Lexington Books.

Krohn, M., Thornberry, T., Rivera, C., & Le Blanc, M. (2001). Later delinquency careers. In R. Loeber & D. P. Farrington (Eds.), *Child delinquents: Development, intervention, and service needs* (pp. 67–93). Thousand Oaks, CA: Sage.

Kroupa, S. (1988). Perceived parental acceptance and female juvenile delinquency. *Adolescence, 23*, 171–185.

Krueger, R. F., Moffitt, T. E., Caspi, A., Bleske, A., & Silva, P. A. (1998). Assortative mating for antisocial behavior: Developmental and methodological implications. *Behavior Genetics, 28*, 173–186.

Kruttschnitt, C., Uggen, C., & Shelton, K. (2000). Predictors of desistance among sex offenders: the interaction of formal and informal social controls. *Justice Quarterly, 17*(1), 61–88.

Kubany, E. S., Richard, D. C., Bauer, G. B., & Muraoka, M. Y. (1992). Verbalized anger and accusatory 'you' messages as cues for anger and antagonism among adolescents. *Adolescence, 27*, 505–516.

Kyvsgaard, B. (2002). *The criminal career: The Danish longitudinal study*. New York: Cambridge University Press.

Lacourse, E., Côté, S., Nagin, D., Vitaro, F., Brendgen, M., & Tremblay, R. (2002). A longitudinal-experimental approach to testing theories of antisocial behavior development. *Development and Psychopathology, 14*, 909–924.

Lacourse, E., Nagin, D.S., Vitaro, F., Côté, S., Arsenault, L., & Tremblay, R.E. (2006). Prediction of early-onset deviant peer group affiliation: A 12-year longitudinal study. *Archives of General Psychiatry, 63*, 562–568.

Lahey, B. B. & Loeber, R. (1997). Attention-deficit/hyperactivity disorder, oppositional defiant disorder, conduct disorder, and adult antisocial behavior: A life span perspective. In D. M. Stoff, J. Breiling, & J. D. Maser (Eds.), *Handbook of antisocial behavior* (pp. 51–59), New York: John Wiley.

Lahey, B. B., Waldman, I. D., & McBurnett, K. (1999). Annotation: The development of antisocial behavior: An integrative causal model. *Journal of Child Psychology and Psychiatry, 40*, 669–682.

Lally, J. R., Mangione, P. L., Honig, A. S., & Wittner, D. S. (1988). More pride, less delinquency: Findings from the ten-year follow-up study of the Syracuse University Family Development Research Program. *Zero to Three, 8*(4), 13–18.

Lanctôt, N., Cernkovich, S. A., & Giordano, P. C. (2007). Delinquent behavior, official delinquency, and gender: Consequences for adulthood functioning and well-being. *Criminology, 45*(1), 131–158.

Lanctôt, N., Emond, C., & Le Blanc, M. (2004). Adjudicated females' participation in violence from adolescence to adulthood: Results from a longitudinal study. In M. M. Moretti, C. L. Odgers, & M. A. Jackson (Eds.), *Girls and aggression: Contributing factors and intervention principles* (pp. 75–84). New York: Kluwer Academic/ Plenum Publishers.

Land, K. C., McCall, P. L., & Nagin, D. S. (1996). A comparison of poisson, negative binomial, and semiparametric mixed poisson regression models. *Sociological Methods and Research, 24*, 387–442.

Land, K. C. & Nagin, D. S. (1996). Micro-models of criminal careers: A synthesis of the criminal careers and life course approaches via semiparametric mixed poisson regression models, with empirical applications. *Journal of Quantitative Criminology, 12*(2), 163–191.

Land, K. C., Nagin, D. S., & McCall, P. L. (2001). Discrete-time hazard regression models with hidden heterogeneity: The semiparametric mixed poisson regression approach. *Sociological Methods and Research, 29*, 342–373.

Landry, S. H. & Whitney, J. A. (1996). The impact of prenatal cocaine exposure: Studies of the developing infant. *Seminars in Perinatology, 20*(2), 99–106.

Landsheer, J. A. & van Dijkum, C. V. (2005). Male and female delinquency trajectories from pre through middle adolescence and their continuation in late adolescence. *Adolescence, 40*(160), 729–748.

Langan, N. P. & Pelissier, B. M. (2001). Gender differences among prisoners in drug treatment. *Journal of Substance Abuse, 13*, 291–301.

Larsson, H., Tuvblad, C., Rijsdijk, F. V., Andershed, H., Grann, M., & Lichtenstein, P. (2007). A common genetic factor explains the association between psychopathic personality and antisocial behavior. *Psychological Medicine, 37*, 15–26.

Larzelere, R. E. & Patterson, G. R. (1990). Parental management: Mediator of the effect of socio-economic status on early delinquency. *Criminology, 28*, 301–323.

Lattimore, P., McDonald, J., Piquero, A., Linster, R., & Visher, C. (2004). Studying the characteristics of arrest frequency among paroled youthful offenders. *Journal of Research in Crime and Delinquency, 41*(1), 37–57.

Lattimore, P., Visher, C., & Linster, R. (1994). Specialization in juvenile careers: Markov results for a California cohort. *Journal of Quantitative Criminology, 10*(4), 291–316.

Lattimore, P., Visher, C., & Linster, R. (1995). Predicting re-arrest for violence among serious youthful offenders. *Journal of Research in Crime and Delinquency, 32*(1), 54–83.

Laub, J. H., Nagin, D. S., & Sampson, R. J. (1998). Trajectories of change in criminal offending: Good marriages and the desistance process. *American Sociological Review, 63*, 225–238.

Laub, J. H. & Sampson, R. J. (1988). Unraveling families and delinquency: A reanalysis of the Gluecks' data. *Criminology, 26*, 355–380.

Laub, J. & Sampson, R. (1993). Turning points in the life course: Why change matters to the study of crime. *Criminology, 31*(3), 301–326.

Laub, J. H. & Sampson, R. J. (1995). Crime and context in the lives of 1000 Boston men, circa 1925–1955. In Z. S. Blau & J. Hagan (Eds.), *Current perspectives on aging and the life cycle, Vol. 4. Delinquency and disrepute in the life course: Contextual and dynamic analyses* (pp. 119–140). Greenwich, CT: JAI Press.

Laub, J. H. & Sampson, R. J. (2001). Understanding desistance from crime. In Tonry, M. (Ed.), *Crime and justice: A review of research: Vol. 28* (pp. 1–69). Chicago, IL: University of Chicago Press.

Laub, J. & Sampson, R. (2003). *Shared beginnings, divergent lives: Delinquent boys to age 70.* Cambridge, MA: Harvard University Press.

Laub, J. H., Sampson, R. J., & Sweeten, G. A. (2006). Assessing Sampson and Laub's life-course theory of crime. In F. T. Cullen, J. P. Wright, & K. Belvins (Eds.) *Advances in criminological theory: Vol. 15. Taking stock: The status of criminological theory* (pp. 313–333). New Brunswick, NJ: Transaction Publishers.

Lauritsen, J. L. (1998). The age-crime debate: Assessing the limits of longitudinal self-report data. *Social Forces, 77*(1), 127–155.

Lauritsen, J. L. (1999). Limitations in the use of longitudinal self-report data: A comment. *Criminology, 37*(3), 687–694.

Lay, B., Ihle, W., Esser, G. R, & Schmidt, M. H. (2005). Juvenile-episodic, continued, or adult-onset delinquency? Risk conditions analysed in a cohort of children followed up to the age of 25 years. *European Journal of Criminology, 2*(1), 39–66.

Le Blanc, M. (1990). Two processes of the development of persistent offending: Activation and escalation. In L. N. Robins, & M. Rutter (Eds.), *Straight and devious pathways from childhood to adulthood* (pp. 82–100). Cambridge, UK: Cambridge University Press.

Le Blanc, M. & Kaspy, N. (1998). Trajectories of delinquency and problem behavior: Comparison of social and personal control characteristics of adjudicated boys on synchronous and nonsynchronous paths. *Journal of Quantitative Criminology, 14*(2), 181–214.

Le Blanc, M. & Loeber, R. (1998). Developmental criminology updated. In M. Tonry & M. H. Moore (Eds.), *Crime and justice: A review of research: Vol. 23* (pp. 115–198). Chicago, IL: University of Chicago Press.

Leblanc, L. A. & Pfannenstiel, J. C. (1991). *Unlocking learning: Chapter 1 in correctional facilities.* Rockville, MD: Westat, Inc.

Lederman, C. S. & Brown, E. N. (2000). Entangled in the shadows: Girls in the juvenile justice system. *Buffalo Law Review, 48*, 909–925.

LeMarquand, D. G., Pihl, R. O., Young, S. N., Tremblay, R. E., Seguin, J. R., Palmour, R. M., et al. (1998). Tryptophan depletion, executive functions, and disinhibition in aggressive, adolescent males. *Neuropsychopharmacology, 19*, 333–341.

Leonard, K. E. & Mudar, P. (2003). Peer and partner drinking and the transition to marriage: A longitudinal examination of selection and influence processes. *Psychology of Addictive Behaviors, 17*, 115–125.

Lester, B. M., LaGasse, L., Seifer, R., Tronick, E. Z., Bauer, C. R., Shankaran, S., et al. (2003). The Maternal Lifestyle Study (MLS): Effects of prenatal cocaine and/or opiate exposure on auditory brain response at one month. *Journal of Pediatrics, 142*(3), 279–285.

Lester, P. (2006). *The Bush Administration's FY 2007 budget.* Washington, DC: United Way of America.

Leve, L. D. & Chamberlain, P. (2004). Female juvenile offenders: Defining an early-onset pathway for delinquency. *Journal of Child and Family Studies, 13*(4), 439–452.

Leve, L. D. & Chamberlain, P. (2005). Girls in the juvenile justice system: Risk factors and clinical implications. In D. Pepler, K. Madsen, C. Webster, & K. Levine (Eds.), *Development and treatment of girlhood aggression* (pp. 191–215). Mahwah, NJ: Erlbaum.

Lewis, O. (1961). *The children of Sanchez.* New York: Random House.

Lewis, O. (1968). *La vida: A Puerto Rican family in the culture of poverty—San Juan and New York.* New York: Vintage.

Little, R. J. A. & Rubin, D. B. (1987) *Statistical analysis with missing data.* New York: Wiley.

Lochner, L. (2007). Individual perceptions of the criminal justice system. *American Economic Review, 97*, 444–460.

Loeber, R. (1982). The stability of antisocial and delinquent child behavior: A review. *Child Development, 53*(6), 1431–1446.

Loeber, R. (1988). Natural histories of conduct problems, delinquency, and associated substance use: Evidence for developmental progressions. In B. B. Lahey & A. E. Kazdin (Eds.), *Advances in clinical child psychopathology: Vol. 11* (pp. 73–124). New York: Plenum.

Loeber, R. & Farrington, D. (1998a). Never too early, never too late: Risk factors and successful interventions for serious and violent juvenile offenders. *Studies on Crime and Crime Prevention, 7*, 7–30.

Loeber, R. & Farrington, D. (Eds.). (1998b). *Never too early, never too late: Risk factors and successful interventions for serious violent and juvenile offenders.* Thousand Oaks, CA: Sage.

Loeber, R. & Farrington, D. P. (1998c). *Serious and violent juvenile offenders.* Thousand Oaks, CA: Sage.

Loeber, R. & Hay, D. (1997). Key issues in the development of aggression and violence from childhood to early adulthood. *Annual Review of Psychology, 48*, 371–410.

Loeber, R. & Keenan, K. (1994). Interaction between conduct disorder and its comorbid conditions: Effects of age and gender. *Clinical Psychology Review, 14*, 497–523.

Loeber, R. & Le Blanc, M. (1990). Towards a developmental criminology. In M. Tonry & N. Morris (Eds.), *Crime and justice: A review of research: Vol. 12* (pp. 375–473). Chicago: University of Chicago Press.

Loeber, R. & Stouthamer-Loeber, M. (1986). Family factors as correlates and predictors of juvenile conduct problems and delinquency. In M. Tonry & N. Morris (Eds.), *Crime and justice: A review of research: Vol. 7* (pp 29–149). Chicago: University of Chicago Press.

Loeber, R., Stouthamer-Loeber, M., Farrington, D. P., Lahey, B. B., Keenan, K., & White, H. R. (2002). Editorial introduction: Three longitudinal studies of children's development in Pittsburgh: The Developmental Trends study, the Pittsburgh Youth Study, and the Pittsburgh Girls Study. *Criminal Behavior and Mental Health, 12*(1), 1–23.

Loeber, R., Wei, E., Stouthamer-Loeber, M., Huizinga, D., & Thornberry, T. P. (1999). Behavior antecedents to serious and violent offending. Joint analyses from the Denver Youth Survey, Pittsburgh Youth Study and the Rochester Youth Development Study. *Studies on Crime and Crime Prevention, 8*, 245–263.

Loney, B. R., Butler, M. A., Lima, E. N., Counts, C. A., & Eckel, L. A. (2006). The relation between salivary cortisol, callous-unemotional traits, and conduct problems in an adolescent non-referred sample. *Journal of Child Psychology and Psychiatry, 47*(1), 30–36.

Loney, B. R., Taylor, J., Butler, M., & Iacono, W. G. (2002). The Minnesota Temperament Inventory: A psychometric study of adolescent self-reported psychopathy. Unpublished manuscript.

Lorber, M. F. (2004). Psychophysiology of aggression, psychopathy, and conduct problems: A meta-analysis. *Psychological Bulletin, 130*(4), 531–552.

Ludwig, J., Duncan, G. J., & Hirschfield, P. (2001). Urban poverty and juvenile crime: Evidence from a randomized housing-mobility experiment. *Quarterly Journal of Economics, 116*, 655–680.

Luthar, S. S. (2006). Resilience in development: A synthesis of research across five decades. In D. Cicchetti & D. Cohen (Eds.), *Developmental psychopathology: Vol. 3. Risk, disorder and adaptation* (2nd ed., pp. 739–795). New York: Wiley.

Lutz, G. M. & Baughman, K.(1988). Serious delinquents who do not become adult criminals. In R. L. Jenkins & W. K. Brown (Eds.), *The abandonment of delinquent behavior: Promoting the turnaround* (pp. 137–154). New York: Praeger.

Lykken, D. T. (1995). *The antisocial personalities.* Hillsdale, NJ: Erlbaum.

Lynam, D. R. (1998). Early identification of the fledgling psychopath: Locating the psychopathic child in the current nomenclature. *Journal of Abnormal Psychology, 107*, 566–575.

Lynam, D. R., Caspi, A., Moffitt, T. E., Wikström, P.-O., Loeber, R., & Novak, S. P. (2000). The interaction between impulsivity and neighborhood context on offending: The effects of impulsivity are stronger in poorer neighborhoods. *Journal of Abnormal Psychology, 109,* 563–574.

Lynam, D. R., Moffitt, T. E., & Stouthamer-Loeber, M. (1993). Explaining the relationship between IQ and delinquency: Class, race, test motivation, school failure or self-control? *Journal of Abnormal Psychology, 102,* 187–196.

Lynch, A. K. Rasmussen, D. W. (2001). Measuring the impact of crime on house prices. *Applied Economics, 33,* 1981–1989.

Lynch, M. J. (1999). Beating a dead horse: Is there any basic empirical evidence for the deterrent effect of imprisonment? *Crime, Law, and Social Change, 31,* 347–362.

Lynn, L. E., Jr. & McGeary, M. G. H. (1990). *Inner-city poverty in the United States.* Washington, DC: National Academy Press.

Lynskey, D. P., Winfree, T. L., Esbensen, F. A., & Clason, D. L. (2000).Linking gender, minority group status and family matter to self-control theory: A multivariate analysis of key self-control concepts in a youth-gang context. *Juvenile and Family Court Journal, 51,* 1–19.

MacCallum, R. C., Zhang, S., Preacher, K. J., & Rucker, D. D. (2002). On the practice of dichotomization of quantitative variables. *Psychological Methods, 7,* 19–40.

Maccoby, E. (1998). *The two sexes: Growing up apart, coming together.* Cambridge MA: Belknap/Harvard University Press.

MacMillan, H. L., Boyle, M. H., Wong, M. Y.-Y., Kuku, E. K., Fleming, J. E., & Walsh, C. A. (1999). Slapping and spanking in childhood and its association with lifetime prevalence of psychiatric disorders in a general population sample. *Canadian Medical Association Journal, 161,* 805–809.

Macmillan, R. (2000). Adolescent victimization and income deficits in adulthood: Rethinking the costs of criminal violence from a life-course perspective. *Criminology, 38*(2), 553–588.

Magnuson, K. A. (2006). The effect of mothers' returns to schooling on their children's academic achievement: Evidence of the ECLS-K. Paper presented at the *19th Biennial Meeting of the International Society for the Study of Behavioral Development (ISSBD).* New York, NY.

Magnusson, D. & Torestad, B. (1993). A holistic view of personality: A model revisited. *Annual Review of Psychology, 44,* 427–452.

Malinosky-Rummell, R. & Hansen, D. J. (1993). Long-term consequences of childhood physical abuse. *Psychological Bulletin, 114,* 68–79.

Marcus, B. (2004). Self-control in the general theory of crime: Theoretical implications of a measurement problem. *Theoretical Criminology, 8*(1), 33–55.

Maruna, S., Immarigeon, R., & LeBel, T. P. (2004). Ex-offender reintegration: Theory and practice. In S. Maruna & R. Immarigeon (Eds.), After crime and punishment: Pathways to offender reintegration (pp. 3–26). Portland, OR: Willan Publishing.

Maschi, T. (2006). Unraveling the link between trauma and male delinquency: The cumulative versus differential risk perspectives. *Social Work, 51,* 59–70.

Mason, D. A. & Frick, P. J. (1994). The heritability of antisocial behavior: A meta-analysis of twin and adoption studies. *Journal of Psychopathology and Behavioral Assessment, 16*(4), 301–323.

Massey, J. L. & Krohn, M. D. (1986). A longitudinal examination of an integrated social process model of deviant behavior. *Social Forces, 63*, 106–134.

Matsueda, R. L. & Anderson, K. (1998). The dynamics of delinquent peers and delinquent behavior. *Criminology, 36*, 269–308.

Mauer, M., Potler, C., & Wolf, R. (1999). *Gender and justice: Women, drugs, and sentencing policy.* Washington, DC: The Sentencing Project.

Maughan, B., Pickles, A., Rowe, R., Costello, E. J., & Angold, A. (2000). Developmental trajectories of aggressive and non-aggressive conduct problems. *Journal of Quantitative Criminology, 16*, 199–221.

Maume, M. O., Ousey, G. C., & Beaver, K. (2005). Cutting the grass: A reexamination of the link between marital attachment, delinquent peers, and desistance from marijuana use. *Journal of Quantitative Criminology, 21*, 27–53.

Maxfield, M. G., Weiler, B. L., & Widom, C. S. (2000). Comparing self-reports and official records of arrest. *Journal of Quantitative Criminology, 16*, 87–110.

Mayes, L. C., Cicchetti, D., Acharyya, S., & Zhang, H. (2003). Developmental trajectories of cocaine-and-other-drug-exposed and non-cocaine-exposed children. *Journal of Developmental & Behavioral Pediatrics, 24*(5), 323–335.

Mazerolle, P. (2000). Strain, anger, and delinquent adaptations specifying general strain theory. *Journal of Criminal Justice, 28*(2), 89–101.

Mazerolle, P., Brame, R., Paternoster, R., Piquero, A., & Dean, C. (2000). Onset age, persistence, and offending versatility: Comparisons across gender. *Criminology, 38*(4), 1143–1172.

Mazerolle, P. & Maahs, J. (2000). General strain and delinquency: An alternative examination of conditioning influences. *Justice Quarterly, 17*(4), 753–777.

Mazerolle, P. & Piquero, A. (1998). Linking exposure to strain with anger: An investigation of deviant adaptations. *Journal of Criminal Justice, 26*(3), 195–211.

Mazerolle, P. & Piquero, A. (Eds.). (2001). *Life-course criminology.* Belmont, CA: Wadsworth/Thompson Learning.

McAra, L. & McVie, S. (2007). Youth justice? The impact of system contact on patterns of desistance from offending. *European Journal of Criminology, 4*(3), 315–345.

McBurnett, K., Lahey, B. B., & Frick, P. J. (1991). Anxiety, inhibition and conduct disorder in children: II relation to salivary cortisol. *Journal of the American Academy of Child & Adolescent Psychiatry, 30*(2), 192–196.

McBurnett, K., Lahey, B. B., Rathouz, P. J., & Loeber, R. (2000). Low salivary cortisol and persistent aggression in boys referred for disruptive behavior. *Archives of General Psychiatry, 57*, 38–43.

McCaffrey, D. F., Lockwood, J. R., Koretz, D., Louis, T. A., & Hamilton, L. (2004). Models for value-added modeling of teacher effects, *Journal of Educational and Behavioral Statistics, 29*, 67–101.

McCartan, L. M. (2007). Inevitable, influential, or unnecessary? Exploring the utility of genetic explanation for delinquent behavior. *Journal of Criminal Justice, 35,* 219–233.

McCarthy, W. (2002). New economics of sociological criminology. *Annual Review of Sociology, 28,* 417–442.

McCord, J. (1978). A thirty-year follow-up of treatment effects. *American Psychologist, 33,* 284–289.

McCord, J. (1979). Some child-rearing antecedents of criminal behavior in adult men. *Journal of Personality and Social Psychology, 37,* 1477–1486.

McCord, J. (1990). Long-term perspectives on parental absence. In L. N. Robins & M. Rutter (Eds.), *Straight and devious pathways from childhood to adulthood* (pp. 116–134). New York: Cambridge University Press.

McCord, W. & McCord, J. (1959). *Origins of crime: A new evaluation of the Cambridge-Somerville Youth Study.* New York: Columbia University Press.

McCutcheon, A. L. (1987). *Latent class analysis (Series: quantitative applications in the social sciences No. 64).* Newbury Park, CA: Sage Publications.

McDermott, S. & Nagin, D. S. (2001). Same or different? Comparing offender groups and covariates over time. *Sociological Methods and Research, 29,* 282–318.

McGloin, J. M. & Pratt, T. C. (2003). Cognitive ability and delinquent behavior among inner-city youth: A life-course analysis of main, mediating and interaction effects. *International Journal of Offender Therapy and Comparative Criminology, 47*(3), 253–271.

McGloin, J. M., Pratt, T. C., & Maahs, J. (2004). Re-thinking the IQ-delinquency relationship: A longitudinal analysis of multiple theoretical models. *Justice Quarterly, 21,* 601–631.

McGloin, J. M., Pratt, T. C., & Piquero, A. (2006). A life-course analysis of the criminogenic effects of maternal cigarette smoking during pregnancy: A research note on the mediating impact of neuropsychological deficit. *Journal of Research in Crime and Delinquency, 43*(4), 412–426.

McWey, L. M. (2004). Predictors of attachment styles of children in foster care: An attachment theory model for working with families. *Journal of Marital and Family Therapy, 30,* 439–452.

McWilliams, E. (1994). The association of perceived support with birthweights and obstetric complications. *Journal of Reproductive and Infant Psychology, 12,* 115–122.

Meadows, S. O., Brown, J. S., & Elder, G. H., Jr. (2006). Depressive symptoms, stress, and support: Gendered trajectories from adolescence to young adulthood. *Journal of Youth and Adolescence, 35,* 93–103.

Mears, D. P., Ploeger, M., & Warr, M. (1998). Explaining the gender gap in delinquency: Peer influence and moral evaluations of behavior. *Journal of Research in Crime and Delinquency, 35*(3), 251–266.

Mech, E. V. (1994). Foster youth in transition: Research perspectives on preparation for independent living. *Child Welfare, 73,* 603–624.

Mednick, S. A., Gabrielli, W. F., & Hutchings, B. (1984). Genetic influences in criminal convictions: Evidence from an adoption cohort. *Science, 224*(4651), 891–894.

Mednick, S. A. & Kandel, E. S. (1988). Congenital determinants of violence. *Bulletin of the American Academy of Psychiatry and the Law, 16*(2), 101–109.

Meier, R. & Johnson, W. (1977). Deterrence as social control: The legal and extralegal production of conformity. *American Journal of Sociological Review, 42*, 292–304.

Merton, R. K. (1938). Social structure and anomie. *American Sociological Review, 3*, 672–682.

Messinger, D. S., Bauer, C. R., Das, A., Seifer, R., Lester, B. M., Lagasse, L. L., et al. (2004). The Maternal Lifestyle Study: Cognitive, motor, and behavioral outcomes of cocaine-exposed and opiate-exposed infants through three years of age. *Pediatrics, 113*(6), 1677–1685.

Meyer-Lindenberg, A., Buckhoitz, J. W., Kolachana, B., Haririt, A. R., Pezawas, L., Blasi, G., et al. (2006). Neural mechanisms of genetic risk for impulsivity and violence in humans. *Proceedings of the National Academy of Sciences of the United States of America, 103*(1), 6269–6274.

Michalides, R., Griekspoor, A., Balkenende, A., Verwoerd, D., Janssen, L., Jalink, K., et al. (2004). Tamoxifen resistance by a conformational arrest of the estrogen receptor alpha after PKA activation in breast cancer. *Cancer Cell, 5*(6), 597–605.

Miller, J. D. & Lynam, D. (2001). Structural models of personality and their relation to antisocial behavior: Analytic review. *Criminology, 39*(4), 765–798.

Miller, T. R., Cohen, M. A., & Wiersema, B. (1996). *Victim costs and consequences: A new look*. Washington, DC: National Institute of Justice.

Miller, W. B. (1958). Lower class culture as a generating milieu of gang delinquency. *Journal of Social Issues, 14*, 5–19.

Millie, A. (2005). Reducing burglary by crackdown and consolidation. *Policing, 28*, 174–188.

Mills, S. & Raine, A. (1994). Neuroimaging and aggression. *Journal of Offender Rehabilitation, 21*, 145–158.

Minuchin, P. (1985). Families and individual development: Provocations from the field of family therapy. *Child Development, 56*, 289–302.

Moffitt, T. E. (1990a). Juvenile delinquency and attention deficit disorder: Boys' developmental trajectories from age 3 to age 15. *Child Development, 61*, 893–910.

Moffitt, T. E. (1990b). The neuropsychology of delinquency: A critical review of theory and research. In N. Morris & M. Tonry (Eds.), *Crime and justice: An annual review of the research: Vol. 12* (pp. 99–169). Chicago, IL: University of Chicago Press.

Moffitt, T. (1993). Adolescence-limited and life-course-persistent antisocial behavior: A developmental taxonomy. *Psychological Review, 100*(4), 674–701.

Moffitt, T. E. (1997). Adolescence-limited and life-course-persistent offending: A complementary pair of developmental theories. In T. P. Thornberry (Ed.), *Advances in criminological theory: Vol. 7. Developmental theories of crime and delinquency.* (pp. 11–54). New Brunswick, NJ: Transaction Publishers.

Moffitt, T. E. (2003). Life-course-persistent and adolescence-limited antisocial behavior: A 10-year research review and a research agenda. In B. B. Lahey, T. E. Moffitt, & A. Caspi (Eds.), *Causes of conduct disorder and juvenile delinquency* (pp. 49–75). New York: Guilford.

Moffitt, T. E. (2006a). A review of research on the taxonomy of life-course persistent versus adolescence-limited antisocial behavior. In F. T. Cullen, J. P. Wright, & K. Belvins (Eds.) *Advances in criminological theory. Vol. 15. Taking stock: The status of criminological theory* (pp. 277–311). New Brunswick, NJ: Transaction Publishers.

Moffitt, T. E. (2006b). Life-course persistent versus adolescence-limited antisocial behavior. In D. Cicchetti & D. Cohen (Eds.), *Developmental psychopathology: Vol. 3. Risk, disorder and adaptation* (2nd ed., pp. 570–598). New York: Wiley.

Moffitt, T. E. & Caspi, A. (2001). Childhood predictors differentiate life-course persistent and adolescence limited pathways, among males and females. *Development and Psychopathology, 13,* 355–375.

Moffitt, T. E., Caspi, A., Dickson, N., Silva, P., & Stanton, W. (1996). Childhood-onset versus adolescent-onset antisocial conduct problems in males: Natural history from ages 3 to 18 years. *Development and Psychopathology, 8,* 399–424.

Moffitt, T. E., Caspi, A., Harrington, H., & Milne, B. J. (2002). Males on the life-course persistence and adolescence-limited antisocial pathways: Follow-up at age 26. *Development and Psychopathology, 14,* 179–207.

Moffitt, T. E., Caspi, A., Rutter, M., & Silva, P. A. (2001). *Sex differences in antisocial behaviour.* Cambridge, United Kingdom: Cambridge University Press.

Moffitt, T. E., Caspi, A., Silva, P. A., & Stouthamer-Loeber, M. (1995). Individual differences in personality and intelligence are linked to crime: Cross-context evidence from nations, neighborhoods, genders, races, and age-cohorts. In Z. S. Blau & J. Hagan (Eds.), *Current perspectives on aging and the life cycle: Vol. 4. Delinquency and disrepute in the life course* (pp. 1–34). Greenwich, CT: JAI Press.

Moffitt, T. E., Lynam, D. R, & Silva, P. A. (1994). Neuropsychological tests predicting persistent male delinquency. *Criminology, 32*(2), 277–300.

Moffitt, T. E. & Silva, P. A. (1988). IQ and delinquency: A direct test of the differential detection hypothesis. *Journal of Abnormal Psychology, 97,* 330–333.

Morash, M. & Rucker, L. (1989). An exploratory study of the connection of mother's age at childbearing to her children's delinquency in four data sets. *Crime and Delinquency, 35,* 45–93.

Morenoff, J. D., Sampson, R. J., & Raudenbush, S. W. (2001). Neighborhood inequality, collective efficacy, and the spatial dynamics of urban violence. *Criminology, 39,* 517–559.

Moretti, M. M., DaSilva, K., & Holland, R. (2004). Aggression and violence from an attachment perspective: Gender issues and therapeutic implications. In M. Moretti, C. Odgers, & M. Jackson (Eds.), *Girls and aggression: Contributing factors and intervention principles* (pp. 41–56). New York: Kluwer Academic Press.

Moretti, M. M. & Higgins, E. T. (1999). Own versus other standpoints in self-regulation: Developmental antecedents and functional consequences. *Review of General Psychology, 3,* 188–223.

Moretti, M. M., Holland, R., & McKay, S. (2001). Self-other representations and relational and overt aggression in adolescent girls and boys. *Behavioral Sciences and the Law, 19,* 109–126.

Morgan, A. B. & Lilienfeld, S. O. (2000). A meta-analytic review of the relation between antisocial behavior and neuropsychological measures of executive function. *Clinical Psychology Review, 20,* 113–156.

Morizot, J. & Le Blanc, M. (2003). Continuity and change in personality traits from adolescence to midlife: A 25-year longitudinal study comparing representative and adjudicated men. *Journal of Personality, 71,* 705–755.

Morizot, J. & Le Blanc, M. (2007). Behavioral, self, and social control predictors of desistance from crime: A test of launch and contemporaneous effect models. *Journal of Contemporary Criminal Justice, 23*(1), 50–71.

Morrison, G. M., Robertson, L., Laurie B., & Kelly, J. (2002). Protective factors related to antisocial behavior tendencies. *Journal of Clinical Psychology, 58*(3), 277–290.

Morrison, J. A. (2000). Protective factors associated with children's emotional responses to chronic community violence exposure. *Trauma, Violence and Abuse, 1*(4), 299–320.

Morrow, C. E., Vogel, A. L., Anthony, J. C., Ofir, A. Y., Dausa, A. T., & Bandstra, E. S. (2004). Expressive and receptive language functioning in preschool children with prenatal cocaine exposure. *Journal of Pediatric Psychology, 29*(7), 543–554.

Moss, H. B., Mezzich, A., Yao, J. K., Gavaler, J., & Martin, C. S. (1995) Aggressivity among sons of substance-abusing fathers: Association with psychiatric disorder in the father and son, paternal personality, pubertal development, and socioeconomic status. *American Journal of Drug and Alcohol Abuse, 21,* 195–208.

Mullis, R. L., Mullis, A. K., Cornille, T. A., Kershaw, M. A., Beckerman, A., & Perkins, D. (2005). Young chronic offenders: A case study of contextual and intervention characteristics. *Youth Violence and Juvenile Justice, 3*(2), 133–150.

Mulvey, E. P. & Aber, M. (1988).Growing out of delinquency: Development and desistance. In R. L. Jenkins & W. K. Brown (Eds.), *The abandonment of delinquent behavior: Promoting the turnaround* (pp. 99–116). New York: Praeger.

Muraven M. & Baumeister, R. F. (2000). Self-regulation and depletion of limited resources: Does self-control resemble a muscle? *Psychological Bulletin, 126,* 247–259.

Muraven, M., Pogarsky, G., & Shmueli, D. (2006). Self-control depletion and the general theory of crime. *Journal of Quantitative Criminology, 22,* 263–277.

Musick, M. A. (1996). Religion and subjective health among black and white elders. *Journal of Health and Social Behavior, 37,* 221–237.

Muthén, B. (1997). Latent variable modeling of longitudinal and multilevel data. *Sociological Methodology, 27,* 453–480.

Muthén, B. (2004). Latent variable analysis: Growth mixture modeling and related techniques for longitudinal data. In D. Kaplan (Ed.), *Handbook of quantitative methodology for the social sciences* (pp. 345–368). Thousand Oaks, CA: Sage Publications.

Muthén, B. & Muthén, L. K. (2000). Integrating person-centered and variable-centered analyses: Growth mixture modeling with latent trajectory classes. *Alcoholism: Clinical and Experimental Research, 24*(6), 882–891.

Myers, B. J. (1999). Children of incarcerated mothers. *Journal of Child and Family Studies, 8,* 1062–1024.

Nagin, D. S. (1999). Analyzing developmental trajectories: A semi-parametric, group-based approach. *Psychological Methods, 4,* 139–157.

Nagin, D. S. (2000). Population heterogeneity and state dependence: State of the evidence and directions for future research. *Journal of Quantitative Criminology, 16*(2), 117–144.

Nagin, D. S. (2004). Response to "Methodological sensitivities to latent class analysis of long-term criminal trajectories". *Journal of Quantitative Criminology, 20,* 27–35.

Nagin, D. S. (2005). *Group-based modeling of development.* Cambridge, MA: Harvard University Press.

Nagin, D. S. & Farrington, D. (1992a). The onset and persistence of offending. *Criminology, 30*(4), 501–523.

Nagin, D. S. & Farrington, D. (1992b). The stability of criminal potential from childhood to adulthood. *Criminology, 30*(2), 235–260.

Nagin, D. S., Farrington, D. P., & Moffitt, T. E. (1995). Life-course trajectories of different types of offenders. *Criminology, 33,* 111–139.

Nagin, D. S. & Land K. C. (1993). Age, criminal careers, and population heterogeneity: Specification and estimation of a nonparametric, mixed poisson model. *Criminology, 31*(3), 327–362.

Nagin, D. S. & Paternoster, R. (1991). On the relationship of past and future participation in delinquency. *Criminology, 29*(4), 163–190.

Nagin, D. S. & Paternoster, R. (1993). Enduring individual differences and rational choice theories of crime. *Law and Society Review, 27,* 467–496.

Nagin, D. S. & Pogarsky, G. (2001). Integrating celerity, impulsivitry, and extralegal sanction threats into a model of general deterrence: Theory and evidence. *Criminology, 39,* 865–891.

Nagin, D. S. & Pogarsky, G. (2003). An experimental investigation of deterrence: Cheating, self-serving bias, and impulsivity. *Criminology, 41,* 167–193.

Nagin, D. S. & Tremblay, R. E. (1999). Trajectories of boys' physical aggression, opposition, and hyperactivity on the path to physically violent and nonviolent juvenile delinquency. *Child Development, 70*(5), 1181–1196.

Nagin, D. S. & Tremblay, R. E. (2001a). Analyzing developmental trajectories of distinct but related behaviors: A group-based method. *Psychological Methods, 6,* 18–34.

Nagin, D. S. & Tremblay, R. E. (2001b). Parental and early childhood predictors of persistent physical aggression in boys from kindergarten to high school. *Archives of General Psychiatry, 58*, 389–394.

Nagin, D. S. & Tremblay, R. E. (2005). Developmental trajectory groups: Fact or a useful statistical fiction? *Criminology, 43*(4), 873–904.

National Center for Juvenile Justice. (2006). *Statistical briefing book*. Washington, DC: US Department in Justice.

National Council on Crime and Delinquency, U.S. Department of Justice. (1992). Female offenders in the community: An analysis of innovative strategies and programs. San Francisco, CA: Austin, J., Bloom, B., & Donahue, T.

National Criminal Justice Reference Service. (1992). *Women and girls in the criminal justice system*. Washington, DC: U.S. Department of Justice.

National Women's Law Center. (1995). *Women in prison fact sheet*. Washington, DC: The Center.

Neef, N. A., Bicard, D. F., & Endo, S. (2001). Assessment of impulsivity and the development of self-control in students with attention deficit hyperactivity disorder. *Journal of Applied Behavior Analysis, 34*, 397–408.

Nelson, G. E. & Lewak, R. W. (1988). Delinquency and attachment. In R. L. Jenkins & W. K. Brown (Eds.), *The abandonment of delinquent behavior: Promoting the turnaround* (pp. 85–98). New York: Praeger.

Ness, C. D. (2003). Why girls fight: Female youth violence in the inner city. *Annals of the American Academy of Political and Social Science, 595*, 32–48.

Neugebauer, R., Hoek, H. W., & Susser, E. (1999). Prenatal exposure to wartime famine and development of antisocial early adulthood. *Journal of the American Medical Association, 282*(3), 455–462.

Newcomb, M. & Loeb, T. B. (1999). Poor parenting as an adult problem behavior: General deviance, deviant attitudes, inadequate family support and bonding, or just bad parents? *Journal of Family Psychology, 13*, 175–193.

Newton, R. R., Litrowik, A. J., & Landverk, J. A. (2000). Children and youth in foster care: Disentangling the relationship between problem behaviors and number of placements. *Child Abuse and Neglect, 24*, 1363–1374.

Ng-Mak, D. S., Salzinger, S., Feldman, R., & Stueve, A. (2002). Normalization of violence among inner-city youth: A formulation for research. *American Journal of Orthopsychiatry, 72*(1), 92–101.

Nigg, J. T. & Huang-Pollock, C. L. (2003). An early-onset model of the role of executive functions and intelligence in conduct disorder/delinquency. In B. B. Lahey, T. E. Moffitt, & A. Caspi (Eds.), *Causes of conduct disorder and juvenile delinquency* (pp. 227–253). New York: Guilford.

Nolen-Hoeksema, S. (1994). An interactive model for the emergence of gender differences in depression in adolescence. *Journal of Research on Adolescence, 4*, 519–534.

Nolen-Hoeksema, S., Wolfson, A., Mumme, D., & Guskin, K. (1995). Helplessness in children of depressed and nondepressed mothers. *Developmental Psychology, 31,* 377–387.

Nott, K. H. & Power, M. J. (1995). The role of social support in HIV infection. *Psychological Medicine, 25,* 971–983.

Nulman, I., Rovet, J., Greenbaum, R., Loebstein, M., Wolpin, J., Pace-Asciak, P., et al. (2001). Neurodevelopment of adopted children exposed in utero to cocaine: The Toronto Adoption Study. *Clinical and Investigative Medicine - Medecine Clinique et Experimentale, 24*(3), 129–137.

Nye, F. I. (1958). *Family relationships and delinquent behavior.* New York: Wiley.

O'Callaghan, M. J., Williams, G. M., Anderson, M. J., Bor, W., & Najman, J. M. (1997). Obstetric and perinatal factors as predictors of child behaviour at five years. *Journal of Pediatrics and Child Health, 33*(6), 497–503.

O'Connor, T. G. (2006). The persisting effects of early experiences on psychological development. In D. Cicchetti & D. J. Cohen (Eds.), *Developmental psychopathology: Vol. 3. Risk, disorder and adaptation* (2nd ed., pp. 202–234). Hoboken, NJ: John Wiley.

O'Connor, T. G., Deater-Deckard, K., Fulker, D., Rutter, M., & Plomin, R. (1998). Genotype-environment correlations in late childhood and early adolescence: Antisocial behavior problems and coercive parenting. *Developmental Psychology, 34,* 970–981.

Obeidallah, D. A. & Earls, F. J. (1999). *Adolescent girls: The role of depression in the development of delinquency.* National Institute of Justice Research Preview. Washington, DC: National Institute of Justice.

Oberwittler, D. & Wikström, P-O. H. (2009). Why small is better: Advancing the study of the role of behavioural contexts in crime causation. In D. Weisburd, W. Bernasco, & G. Bruinsma (Eds.), *Putting crime in its place: Units of analysis in geographic criminology.* New York: Springer.

Obradovic, J., van Dulmen, M. H. M., Yates, T. M., Carlson, E. A., & Egeland, B. (2006). Developmental assessment of competence from early childhood through middle adolescence. *Journal of Adolescence, 29,* 857–889.

Odgers, C. L. & Moretti, M. M. (2002). Aggressive and antisocial girls: Research update and challenges. *International Journal of Forensic Mental Health, 1,* 103–119.

Office of Juvenile Justice and Delinquency Prevention. (1998). *National Council on Crime and Delinquency.* Washington, DC: US Department of Justice.

Office of Juvenile Justice and Delinquency Prevention. (2002). *Statistical briefing book.* Washington, DC: US Department of Justice.

Olds, D., Eckenrode, J., Henderson, C. R., Kitzman, H., Powers, J., Cole, R., et al. (1997). Long-term effects of home visitation on maternal life course and child abuse and neglect: Fifteen year follow-up of a randomized trial. *Journal of the American Medical Association, 278*(8), 637–643.

Olds, D., Henderson, C. R., Cole, R., Eckenrode, J., Kitzman, H., Luckey, D., et al. (1998). Long-term effects of nurse home visitation on children's criminal and antisocial behavior. *Journal of the American Medical Association, 280*(14), 1238–1244.

Olson, H. C., Streissguth, A. P., Sampson, P. D., Barr, H. M., Bookstein, F. L., & Thiede, K. (1997). Association of prenatal alcohol exposure with behavioral and learning problems in early adolescence. *Child and Adolescent Psychiatry, 36*(9), 1187–1194.

Olweus, D. (1986). Aggression and hormones: Behavioral relationship with testosterone and adrenaline. In D. Olweus, J. Block, & M. Radke-Yarrow (Eds.), *Development of antisocial and prosocial behavior* (pp. 51–72). Orlando, FL: Academic Press.

Orlebeke, J. F., Knol, D. L., & Verhulst, F. C. (1999). Child behavior problems increased by maternal smoking during pregnancy. *Archives of Environmental Health, 45*(1), 15–19.

Osgood, D. W. (2005). Making sense of crime and the life course. *Annals of the American Academy of Political and Social Science, 602,* 196–211.

Osgood, D. W., Foster E. M., Flanagan, C., & Ruth, G. R. (2005) Introduction: Why focus on the transition to adulthood for vulnerable populations? In D.W. Osgood, E. M. Foster, C. Flanagan, & G. R. Ruth (Eds.), *On your own without a net: The transition to adulthood for vulnerable populations* (pp. 1–26). Chicago, IL: University of Chicago Press.

Ostrowsky, M. K. & Messner, S. F. (2005). Explaining crime for a young adult population: An application of general strain theory. *Journal of Criminal Justice, 33,* 463–476.

Paaver, M., Eensoo, D., Pulver, A., & Harro, J. (2006). Adaptive and maladaptive impulsivity, platelet monoamine oxidase (MAO) activity and risk-admitting in different types of risky drivers. *Psychopharmacology, 186*(1), 32–40.

Pagani, L. S., Boulerice, B., & Tremblay, R. E. (1997). The influence of poverty on children's classroom placement and behavior problems during elementary school: A change model approach. In G. Duncan & J. Brooks-Gunn (Eds.), *Consequences of growing up poor* (pp. 311–339). New York: Russell Sage Foundation.

Pagani, L. S., Boulerice, B., Tremblay, R. E., & Vitaro, F. (1999). Effects of poverty on academic failure and delinquency in boys: A change and process model approach. *Journal of Child Psychology and Psychiatry, 40*(8), 1209–1219.

Pagani, L. S., Japel, C., Girard, A., Farhat, A., Côté, S., & Tremblay, R. E. (2006). Middle childhood life-course trajectories: Links between family dysfunctionand children's behavioral development. In A. Huston & M. N. Ripke (Eds.), *Developmental contexts in middle childhood. Bridges to adolescence and adulthood* (pp. 130–149). New York: Cambridge University Press.

Pagani, L. S., Tremblay, R. E., Vitaro, F., & Parent, S. (1998). Does preschool help prevent delinquency in boys with a history of perinatal complications? *Criminology, 36*(2), 245–267.

Pagani, L. S., Tremblay, R. E., Vitaro, F., Kerr, M. A., & McDuff, P. (1998). The impact of family transition on the development of delinquency in adolescent boys: A 9-year longitudinal study. *Journal of Child Psychology and Psychiatry, 39*(4), 489–499.

Pajer, K. A. (1998). What happens to "bad" girls? A review of the adult outcomes of antisocial adolescent girls. *American Journal of Psychiatry, 155,* 862–870.

Palmer, T. (1974). The youth authority's community treatment project. *Federal Probation, 38*(1), 3–13.

Palmer, T. (2002). *Individualized intervention with young multiple offenders.* New York: Routledge.

Parker, R. N. & Auerhahn, K. (1998). Alcohol, drugs, and violence. *Annual Review of Sociology, 24,* 291–311.

Paternoster, R. & Brame, R. (1997). Multiple routes to delinquency? A test of developmental and general theories of crime. *Criminology, 35,* 49–84.

Paternoster, R., Brame, R., & Farrington, D. (2001). On the relationship between adolescent and adult conviction frequencies. *Journal of Quantitative Criminology, 17,* 201–225.

Paternoster, R., Dean, C. W., Piquero, A., Mazerolle, P., & Brame, R. (1997). Generality, continuity, and change in offending. *Journal of Quantitative Criminology, 13,* 231–266.

Paternoster, R. & Mazerolle, P. (1994). General strain theory and delinquency: A replication and extension. *Journal of Research in Crime and Delinquency, 31*(3), 235–263.

Paternoster, R. & Piquero, A. (1995). Reconceptualizing deterrence: An empirical test of personal and vicarious experiences. *Journal of Research in Crime and Delinquency. 32,* 251–286.

Paternoster, R., Saltzman, L. E., Waldo, G. P., & Chiricos, T. G. (1983). Perceived risk and social control: Do sanctions really deter? *Law and Society Review, 17,* 457–479.

Paternoster, R., Saltzman, L. E., Waldo, G. P., & Chiricos, T. G. (1985). Assessment of risk and behavioral experience: An exploratory study of change. *Criminology, 23,* 417–433.

Patterson, G. L., Crosby, L., & Vuchinich S. (1992). Predicting risk for early police arrest. *Journal of Quantitative Criminology, 8*(4), 335–355.

Patterson, G. R. (1992). Developmental changes in antisocial behavior. In R. D. Peters, R. J. McMahon, & V. L. Quinsey (Eds.), *Aggression and violence throughout the life span* (pp. 52–82). Newbury Park, CA: Sage.

Patterson, G. R. (1995). Coercion - a basis for early age of onset for arrest. In J. McCord (Ed.), *Coercion and punishment in long-term perspective* (pp. 81–124). New York: Cambridge University Press.

Patterson, G. R. (2002). The early development of coercive family process. In J. B. Reid & G. R. Patterson (Eds.), *Antisocial behavior in children and adolescents: A developmental analysis and model for intervention* (pp. 25–44). Washington, DC: American Psychological Association.

Patterson, G. R., Capaldi, D., & Bank, L. (1991). An early starter model for predicting delinquency. In D. J. Pepler & K. H. Rubin (Eds.), *The development and treatment of childhood aggression* (pp. 139–168). Hillsdale, NJ: Lawrence Erlbaum.

Patterson, G. R., DeBaryshe, B. D., & Ramsey, E. (1989). A developmental perspective on anti-social behavior. *American Psychologist, 44*, 329–335.

Patterson, G. R., DeGarmo, D. S., & Knutson, N. (2000). Hyperactive and antisocial behaviors: Comorbid or two points in the same process? *Development and Psychopathology, 12*, 91–106.

Patterson, G. R., Reid, J. B., & Dishion, T. J. (1992). *A social learning approach: Vol. 4. antisocial boys.* Eugene, OR: Castalia.

Patterson, G. R. & Yoerger, K. (1993). Developmental models for delinquent behavior. In S. Hodgins (Ed.), *Crime and mental disorders* (pp. 140–172). Newbury Park, CA: Sage.

Patterson, G. R. & Yoerger, K. (1997). A developmental model for late-onset delinquency. In D. W. Osgood (Ed.), *Motivation and delinquency: Vol.44 of the Nebraska Symposium on Motivation.* Lincoln, NE: University of Nebraska Press.

Penninx, B. W. J. H., Van Tilburg, T., Deeg, D. J. H., & Kriegsman, D. M. W. (1997). Direct and buffer effects of social support and personal coping resources in individuals with arthritis. *Social Science and Medicine, 44*, 393–402.

Pepler, D. J. & Craig, W. M. (1995). A peek behind the fence: Naturalistic observations of aggressive children with remote audiovisual recording. *Developmental Psychology, 31*, 548–553.

Perrone, D., Sullivan, C., Pratt, T. C., & Margaryan, S. (2004). Parental efficacy, self-control, and delinquent behavior: A test of a general theory of crime on a nationally-representative sample. *International Journal of Offender Therapy and Comparative Criminology, 48*, 298–312.

Petee, T. A. & Walsh, A. (1987). Violent delinquency, race, and the Wechsler performance-verbal discrepancy. *Journal of Social Psychology, 127*, 353–354.

Peter, T., LaGrange, T. C., & Silverman, R. A. (2003). Investigating the interdependence of strain and self-control. *Canadian Journal of Criminology and Criminal Justice, 45*(4), 431–464.

Petersilia, J. (1980). Criminal career research: A review of recent evidence. In N. Morris & M. Tonry (Eds.), *Crime and justice: A review of research* (pp. 321–379). Chicago, IL: University of Chicago Press.

Petersilia, J. (2003). *When prisoners come home: Parole and prisoner reentry.* New York: Oxford University Press.

Pettit, B. & Western, B. (2004). Mass imprisonment and the life course: Race and class inequality in U S incarceration. *American Sociological Review, 69*, 151–169.

Pihl, R. O. & Ervin, F. (1990). Lead and cadmium levels in violent criminals. *Psychological Reports, 66*, 839–844.

Piliavin, I., Gartner, R., Thornton, C., & Matsueda, R. L. (1986). Crime deterrence, and rational choice. *American Sociological Review, 51*, 101–119.

Pine, D., Schonfeld, I. S., Davies, M., & Shaffer, D. (1997). Minor physical anomalies: Modifiers of environmental risk for psychopathology. *Journal of the American Academy of Child and Adolescent Psychiatry, 36,* 395–403.

Pine, D. S., Wasserman, G. A., Miller, L., Coplan, J. D., Bagiella, E., Kovelenku, P., et al. (1998). Heart period variability and psychopathology in urban boys at risk for delinquency. *Psychophysiology, 35,* 521–529.

Pinker, S. (2002). *The blank slate: The modern denial of human nature.* New York: Viking.

Piper, E. S. (1985). Violent recidivism and chronicity in the 1958 Philadelphia cohort. *Journal of Quantitative Criminology, 1,* 319–344.

Piquero, A. R. (2000a). Assessing the relationships between gender, chronicity, seriousness, and offense skewness in criminal offending. *Journal of Criminal Justice, 28,* 103–115.

Piquero, A. R. (2000b). Frequency, violence and specialization in offending careers. *Journal of Research in Crime and Delinquency, 37,* 392–418.

Piquero, A. R. (2001). Testing Moffitt's neuropsychological variation hypothesis for the prediction of life-course persistent offending. *Psychology, Crime and Law, 7*(3), 193–215.

Piquero, A. R. (2004). Somewhere between persistence and dseistance: The intermittency of criminal careers. In S. Maruna & R. Immarigeon (Eds.), *After crime and punishment: Pathways to offender reintegration* (pp. 102–128). Portland, OR: Willan Publishing.

Piquero, A. R. (2005). *Taking stock of developmental trajectories of criminal activity over the life course.* Paper presented at the National Institute of Justice, Washington, DC.

Piquero, A. R. (2008). Taking stock of developmental trajectories of criminal activity over the life course. In A. M. Liberman (Ed.), *The long view of crime: A synthesis of longitudinal research.* New York: Springer.

Piquero, A. R., Blumstein, A., Brame, R., Haapanen, R., Mulvey, E. P., & Nagin, D. S. (2001). Assessing the impact of exposure time and incapacitation on longitudinal trajectories of criminal offending. *Journal of Adolescent Research, 16*(1), 54–74.

Piquero, A. R., Brame, R., & Lynam, D. (2004). Studying criminal career length through early adulthood among serious offenders. *Crime and Delinquency, 50*(3), 412–435.

Piquero, A. R., Brame, R., Mazerolle, P., & Haapanen, R. (2002). Crime in emerging adulthood. *Criminology, 40*(1), 137–169.

Piquero, A. R., Brame, R., & Moffitt, T. E. (2005). Extending the study of continuity and change: Gender differences in the linkage between adolescent and adult offending. *Journal of Quantitative Criminology, 21*(2), 219–243.

Piquero, A. R. & Chung, H. L. (2001). On the relationship between gender, early onset, and the seriousness of offending. *Journal of Criminal Justice, 29,* 189–206.

Piquero, A. R., Daigle, L., Gibson, C., Piquero, N., & Tibbetts, S. (2007). Are life-course-persistent offenders at risk for adverse health outcomes? *Journal of Research in Crime and Delinquency, 44*(2), 185–207.

Piquero, A. R., Farrington, D. P., & Blumstein, A. (2003a). The criminal career paradigm: Background and recent developments. In M. Tonry (Ed.), *Crime and justice: A review of research: Vol. 30* (pp. 137–83). Chicago, IL: University of Chicago Press.

Piquero, A. R., Farrington, D. P., & Blumstein, A. (2003b). Criminal career paradigm: Background, recent developments, and the way forward. *International Annals of Criminology, 41*, 243–269.

Piquero, A. R., Farrington, D. P., & Blumstein, A. (2007). *Key issues in criminal career research: New analyses of the Cambridge Study in Delinquent Development.* Cambridge: Cambridge University Press.

Piquero, A. R., Gibson, C. L., Tibbetts, S. G., Turner, M. G., & Katz, S. H. (2002). Maternal cigarette smoking during pregnancy and life-course-persistent offending. *International Journal of Offender Therapy & Comparative Criminology, 46*(2), 231.

Piquero, A. R., Gomez-Smith, Z, & Langton, L. (2004). Discerning unfairness where others may not: Low self-control and unfair sanction perceptions. *Criminology, 42,* 699–733.

Piquero, A. R. & Mazerolle, P. (2001). Introduction. In A. Piquero & P. Mazerolle (Eds.), *Life-course criminology* (pp. vii–xx). Belmont, CA: Wadsworth/Thomson Learning.

Piquero, A. R. & Moffitt, T. E. (2005). Explaining the facts of crime: How the developmental taxonomy replies to Farrington's invitation. In D.P. Farrington (Ed.), *Advances in criminological theory: Vol. 14. Integrated developmental and life-course theories of offending* (pp. 51–72). New Brunswick, NJ: Transaction.

Piquero, A. R., Moffitt, T. E., & Lawton, B. (2005). Race and crime: The contribution of individual, familial, and neighborhood level risk factors to life-course-persistent offending. In D. Hawkins & K. Kempf-Leonard (Eds.), *Our children, their children: Race, crime, and the juvenile justice system* (pp. 202–245). Chicago, IL: University of Chicago Press.

Piquero, A. R. & Rengert, G. F. (1999). Studying deterrence with active residential burglars. *Justice Quarterly, 16*, 451–471.

Piquero, A. R. & Tibbetts, S. (1996). Specifying the direct and indirect effects of low self -control and situational offenders' decision making, *Justice Quarterly, 13*(3), 481–510.

Piquero, A. R. & Tibbetts, S. (1999). The impact of pre/perinatal disturbances and disadvantaged familial environment in predicting criminal offending. *Studies on Crime and Crime Prevention, 8*(1), 52–70.

Piquero, A. R. & White, N. A. (2003). On the relationship between cognitive abilities and life-course-persistent offending among a sample of African Americans: A longitudinal test of Moffitt's hypothesis. *Journal of Criminal Justice, 31*, 399–409.

Plomin, R. & Asbury, K. (2002). Nature and nurture in the family. *Marriage and Family Review, 33*, 275–283.

Pogarsky, G. (2002). Identifying "deterrable" offenders: Implications for research on deterrence. *Justice Quarterly, 19*, 431–542.

Pogarsky, G. (2004). Projected offending and contemporaneous rule-violation: Implications for heterotypic continuity. *Criminology, 42*, 111–136.

Pogarsky, G., Kim, K. D., & Paternoster, R. (2005). Perceptual change in the National Youth Survey: Lessons for deterrence theory and offender decision-making. *Justice Quarterly, 22*, 1–29.

Pogarsky, G., Piquero, A. R., & Paternoster, R. (2004). Modeling change in perceptions about sanction threats: The neglected linkage in deterrence theory. *Journal of Quantitative Criminology, 20*, 343–369.

Polakowski, M. (1994). Linking self- and social control with deviance: Illuminating the structure underlying a general theory of crime and its relation to deviant identity. *Journal of Quantitative Criminology, 10*, 41–78.

Poole, M. E. & Evans, G. T. (1989). Adolescents' self-perceptions of competence in life skill areas. *Journal of Youth and Adolescence, 18*, 147–173.

Porges, S. W. (1995). Orienting in a defensive world: Mammalian modifications of our evolutionary heritage. A polyvagal theory. *Psychophysiology, 32*, 301–318.

Poulin, F., Dishion, T., & Haas, E. (1999). The peer influence paradox: Friendship quality and deviancy training within male adolescent friendships. *Merrill-Palmer Quarterly, 45*, 42–61.

Pratt, T. C. (2008). *Addicted to incarceration: Corrections policy and the politics of misinformation in the United States.* Thousand Oaks, CA: Sage.

Pratt, T. C. & Cullen, F. T. (2000) The empirical status of Gottfredson and Hirschi's General theory of crime: Analysis. *Criminology, 38*(3), 931–964.

Pratt, T. C. & Cullen, F. T. (2005). Assessing macro-level predictors and theories of crime: A meta-analysis. In M. Tonry (Ed.), *Crime and justice: A review of research: Vol. 32* (pp. 373–450). Chicago: University of Chicago Press.

Pratt, T. C., Cullen, F. T., Blevins, K. R., Daigle, L. E., & Madensen, T. D. (2006). The empirical status of deterrence theory: A meta-analysis. In F. T. Cullen, J. P. Wright, & K. R. Blevins (Eds.), *Advances in criminological theory: Vol. 15. Taking stock: The status of criminological theory* (pp. 367–395). New Brunswick, NJ: Transaction.

Pratt, T. C., Cullen, F. T., Blevins, K. R., Daigle, L., & Unnever, J. D. (2002). The relationship of Attention Deficit Hyperactivity Disorder to crime and delinquency: A meta-analysis. *International Journal of Police Science and Management, 4*, 344–360.

Pratt, T. C., McGloin, J. M., & Fearn, N. E. (2006). Maternal cigarette smoking during pregnancy and criminal/deviant behavior: A meta-analysis. *International Journal of Offender Therapy and Comparative Criminology, 50*, 672–690.

Pratt, T. C., Turner, M. G., & Piquero, A. R. (2004). Parental socialization and community context: A longitudinal analysis of the structural sources of low self-control. *Journal of Research in Crime and Delinquency, 41*, 219–243.

Prescott, L. (1997). *Adolescent girls with co-occurring disorders in the juvenile justice system.* Delmar, NY: The National GAINS Center for People with Co-occurring Disorders in the Justice System.

Preston, D. (2000). Treatment resistance in corrections. *Forum on Corrections Research, 12*(2), 24–28.

Preston, S. D. & de Waal, F. B. M. (2002). Empathy: Its ultimate and proximate bases. *Behavioral and Brain Sciences, 25*, 1–72.

Prior, P. (1999). *Gender and mental health.* New York: New York University Press.

Pritchard, D.A. (1979). Stable predictors of recidivism: A summary. *Criminology, 17*, 15–21.

Pulkkinen, L. (1988). Delinquent development: Theoretical and empirical considerations. In M. Rutter (Ed.), *The power of longitudinal data: Studies of risk and protective factors for psychosocial disorders* (pp. 184–199). Cambridge: Cambridge University Press.

Pulkkinen, L. (1990). Adult life-styles and their precursors in the social behaviour of children and adolescent. *European Journal of Personality, 4*, 237–251.

Pulkkinen, L. & Pitkanen, T. (1993). Continuities in aggressive behavior from childhood to adulthood. *Aggressive Behavior, 19*, 249–263.

Quay, H. C. (1993). The psychobiology of undersocialized aggressive conduct disorder: A theoretical perspective. *Development and Psychopathology, 5*, 165–180.

Quinton, D. & Rutter, M. (1988). *Parental breakdown: The making and breaking of inter-generational links.* Aldershot, UK: Avebury/Gower Publishing Company.

Quinton, D., Rushton, A., Dance, C., & Mayes D. (1998). *Joining new families: A study of adoption and fostering in middle childhood* .Chichester, UK: John Wiley and Sons.

Raine, A. (1993). *The psychopathology of crime: Criminal behavior as a clinical disorder.* San Diego, CA: Academic Press.

Raine, A. (2002). Biosocial studies of antisocial and violent behavior in children and adults: A review. *Journal of Abnormal Child Psychology, 30*, 1773–2835.

Raine, A., Brennan, P., & Mednick, S. A. (1994). Birth complications combined with early maternal rejection at age 1 predispose to violent crime at age 18 years. *Archives of General Psychiatry, 51*, 984–988.

Raine, A., Brennan, P., & Mednick, S. A. (1997). Interaction between birth complications and early maternal rejection in predisposing individuals to adult violence: Specificity to serious, early-onset violence. *American Journal of Psychiatry, 154*(9), 1265–1271.

Raine, A., Brennan, P., Mednick, B., & Mednick, S. A. (1996). High rates of violence, crime, academic problems and behavioral problems in males with both early neuromotor deficits and unstable family environments. *Archives of General Psychiatry, 53*, 544–549.

Raine, A., Buchsbaum, M. S., Stanley, J., Lottenberg, S., Abel, L., & Stoddard, J. (1994). Selective reductions in prefrontal glucose metabolism in murderers. *Biological Psychiatry, 36*, 365–373.

Raine, A., Moffitt, T. E., Caspi, A., Loeber, R., Stouthamer-Loeber, M., & Lynam, D. (2005). Neurocognitive impairment in boys on the life-course persistent antisocial path. *Journal of Abnormal Psychology, 114*(14), 38–49.

Raine, A., Venables, P. H., & Mednick, S. A. (1997). Low resting heart rate at age 3 years predisposes to aggression at age 11 years: Evidence from the Mauritius ChildHealth Project. *Journal of the American Academy of Child & Adolescent Psychiatry, 36*(10), 1457–1464.

Raine, A., Venables, P. H., & Williams, M. (1990). Relationships between central and autonomic measures of arousal at age 15 years and criminality at age 24 years. *Archives of General Psychiatry, 47*(11), 1003–1007.

Räsänen, P., Hakko, H., Isohanni, M., Hodgins, S., Järvalin, M-R., & Tiihonen, J. (1999). Maternal smoking during pregnancy and risk of criminal behavior among adult male offspring in the Northern Finland 1966 Birth Cohort. *American Journal of Psychiatry, 156*(6), 857–862.

Raudenbush, S. W. (2004). What are value-added models estimating and what does this imply for statistical practice? *Journal of Educational and Behavioral Statistics, 29*, 121–129.

Raudenbush, S. & Sampson, R. (1999). Ecometrics: Toward a science of assessing ecological settings, with application to the systematic social observation of neighborhoods. *Sociological Methodology, 29*(1), 1–41.

Raz, S., Shah, F., & Sander, C. J. (1996). Differential effects of perinatal hypoxic risk on early developmental outcome: A twin study. *Neuropsychology, 10*(3), 429–436.

Redding, R. E., Fried, C., & Britner, P. A. (2000) Predictors of placement outcomes in treatment foster care: Implications for foster parent selection and service delivery. *Journal of Child and Family Studies, 9*, 425–447.

Regnerus, M. D. (2003). Linked lives, faith, and behavior: Intergenerational religious influence on adolescent delinquency. *Journal for the Scientific Study of Religion, 42*(2), 189–203.

Reilly, T. (2003). Transition from care: Status and outcomes of youth who age out of foster care. *Child Welfare, 82*, 727–746.

Reinecke, J. (2006). Longitudinal analysis of adolescents' deviant and delinquent behavior: Applications of latent class growth curves and growth mixture models. *Methodology: European Journal of Research Methods for the Behavioral and Social Sciences, 2*, 100–112.

Reiss, A. J. Jr. (1986). Co-offender influences on criminal careers. In A. Blumstein, J. Cohen, J. A. Roth, & C. A. Visher (Eds.), *Criminal careers and "career criminals": Vol. 2* (pp. 121–160). Washington, DC: National Academy Press.

Reiss, D. (2003). Child effects on family systems: Behavioral genetic strategies. In A. C. Crouter & A. Booth (Eds.), *Children's influence on family dynamics: The neglected side of family relationships* (pp. 3–25). Mahwah, NJ: Lawrence Erlbaum.

Repetti, R. L., Taylor, S. E., & Seeman, T. E. (2002). Risky families: Family social environments and the mental and physical health of offspring. *Psychological Bulletin, 128*, 330–366.

Rhee, S. H. & Waldman, I. D. (2002). Genetic an environmental influences on antisocial behavior: A meta-analysis of twin and adoption studies. *Psychological Bulletin, 128*(3), 490–529.

Richards, S. C. & Jones, R. S. (2004). Beating the perpetual incarceration machine: Overcoming structural impediments to re-entry. In S. Maruna & R. Immarigeon (Eds.), *After crime and punishment: Pathways to offender reintegration* (pp. 201–232). Portland, OR: Willan Publishing.

Richardson, G. A., Conroy, M. L., & Day, N. L. (1996). Prenatal cocaine exposure: Effects on the development of school-age children. *Neurotoxicology & Teratology, 18*(6), 627–634.

Richardson, G. A., Hamel, S. C., Goldschmidt, L., & Day, N. L. (1999). Growth of Infants Prenatally Exposed to Cocaine/Crack: Comparison of a Prenatal Care and a No Prenatal Care Sample. *Pediatrics, 104*(2), 18e–18.

Richardson, N. (2001). *Out of sight, out of mind: Central San Joaquin valley delinquents and the California Youth Authority.* Sacramento, CA: California Youth Authority.

Richerson, P. J. & Boyd, R. (2005). *Not by genes alone: How culture transformed human evolution.* Chicago: University of Chicago Press.

Richters, J. E. (1997). The Hubble hypothesis and the developmentalist's dilemma. *Development and Psychopathology, 9,* 193–229.

Rivera, B. & Widom, C. S. (1990). Childhood victimization and violent offending. *Violence and Victims, 5,* 19–34.

Robbers, M. L. P. (2004). Revisiting the moderating effect of social support on strain: A gendered test. *Sociological Inquiry, 74*(4), 546–569.

Robin, A. L. & Foster, S. L. (2002). *Negotiating parent-adolescent conflict: A biobehavioral-family systems approach.* New York: Guilford.

Robins, L. (1966). *Deviant children grown up: A sociological and psychiatric study of sociopathic personality.* Baltimore, MD: Williams and Wilkins.

Robins, L. (1978). Sturdy childhood predictors of adult antisocial behavior: Replications from longitudinal studies. *Psychological Medicine, 8,* 611–622.

Robins, L. (1993). Childhood conduct problems, adult psychopathology, and crime. In S. Hodgins (Ed.), *Mental disorder and crime* (pp. 173–193). Newbury Park, CA: Sage.

Robins, L. & Ratcliff, K. (1980). Childhood conduct disorders and later arrest. In L. Robins, P. J. Clayton, & J. K. Wing (Eds.), *The social consequences of psychiatric illness* (pp. 248–263). New York: Brunner/Mazel.

Roisman, G. I., Aguilar, B., & Egeland, B. (2004). Antisocial behavior in the transition to adulthood: The independent and interactive roles of developmental history and emerging developmental tasks. *Development and Psychopathology, 16,* 857–871.

Roisman, G. I., Masten, A. S., Coatsworth, J. D., & Tellegen, A. (2004). Salient and emerging developmental tasks in the transition to adulthood. *Child Development, 75,* 123–133.

Rothbaum, F., Rosen, K., Ujiie, T., & Uchida, N. (2002). Family systems theory, attachment theory and culture. *Family Process, 41*(3), 328–350.

Rothbaum, F. & Weisz, J. R. (1994). Parental caregiving and child externalizing behavior in nonclinical samples: A meta-analysis. *Psychological Bulletin, 116,* 55–74.

Rothman, D. J. (2002). *Conscience and convenience: The asylum and its alternatives in progressive America.* New York: Aldine de Gruyter.

Rowe, D. C. (1994). *The limits of family influence: Genes, experience, and behavior.* New York: Guilford.

Rowe, D. C., Almeida, D. M., & Jacobson, K. C. (1999). School context and genetic influences on aggression in adolescence. *Psychological Science, 10*(3), 277–280.

Rowe, D. & Farrington, D. P. (1997). The familial transmission of criminal convictions. *Criminology, 35,* 177–201.

Rowe, R., Maughan, B., Worthman, C. M., Costello, E. J., & Angold, A. (2004). Testosterone, antisocial behavior, and social dominance in boys: Pubertal development and biosocial interaction. *Biological Psychiatry, 55,* 546–552.

Rubin, K. H., Burgess, K. B., Dwyer, K. M., & Hastings, P. D. (2003). Predicting preschoolers' externalizing behaviors from toddler temperament, conflict, and maternal negativity. *Developmental Psychology, 39,* 164–176.

Rudy, D. (1986). *Becoming alcoholic: Alcoholics anonymous and the reality of alcoholism.* Carbondale, IL: Southern Illinois University Press.

Ruff, H. A. & Rothbart, M. K. (1996). *Attention in early development: Themes and variations.* New York: Oxford University Press.

Rutter, M. (1978). Family, area and school influences in the genesis of conduct disorders. In L. A. Hersov, M. Berger, & D. Shaffer (Eds.), *Aggression and anti-social behaviour in childhood and adolescence* (pp. 95–113). New York: Pergamon.

Rutter, M. (1979). Protective factors in children's responses to stress and disadvantage. In M. W. Kent & J. E. Rolf (Eds.), *Primary prevention of psychopathology. III. Social competence in children* (pp. 49–74). Hanover, NH: University Press of New England.

Rutter, M. (1985). Resilience in the face of adversity: Protective factors and resistance to psychiatric disorder. *British Journal of Psychiatry, 147,* 598–611.

Rutter, M. (1989). Pathways from childhood to adult life. *Journal of Child Psychology and Psychiatry and Allied Disciplines, 30,* 23–51.

Rutter, M. (1994). Continuities, transitions and turning points in development. In M. Rutter & D. F. Hay (Eds.), *Development through life: A handbook for clinicians* (pp. 1–25). London: Blackwell Scientific Publications.

Rutter, M. (2002). Nature, nurture, and development: From evangelism through science toward policy and practice. *Child Development, 73,* 1–21.

Rutter, M. (2003). Poverty and child mental health: Natural experiments and social causation. *Journal of the American Medical Association, 290*(15), 2063–2064.

Rutter, M. (2006). *Genes and behavior: Nature-nurture interplay explained*. Malden, MA: Blackwell.

Rutter, M. (2007). Gene-environment interdependence. *Developmental Science, 10*(1), 12–18.

Rutter M., Champion, L., Quinton, D., Maughan, B., & Pickles, A. (1995). Understanding individual differences in environmental risk exposure. In P. Moen, G. H. Elder, & K. Luscher (Eds.), *Examining lives in context: Perspectives on the ecology of human development* (pp. 61–93). Washington, DC: American Psychological Association.

Rutter M., Pickles A., Murray R., & Eaves L. (2001). Testing hypotheses on specific environmental causal effects on behavior. *Psychological Bulletin, 127*(3), 291–324.

Rutter, M. & Quinton, D. (1984). Long-term follow-up of women institutionalized in childhood: Factors promoting good functioning in adult life. *British Journal of Developmental Psychology, 18*, 225–234.

Rutter M. & Rutter, M. (1993). *Developing minds: Challenge and continuity across the life span*. New York: Basic books.

Rutter, M., Tizard, J., & Whitmore, K. (1970). *Education health and behaviour*. London: Longmans.

Sabol, S. Z., Hu, S., & Hamer, D. (1998). A functional polymorphism in the mono-amine oxidase: A gene promoter. *Human Genetics, 103*(3), 273–279. Saddle River, NJ: Prentice Hall.

Sakai, J. T., Young, S. E., Stallings, M. C., Timberlake, D., Smolen, A., Stetler, G. L., et al. (2006). Case-control and within-family tests for and association between conduct disorder and 5HTTLPR. *American Journal of Medical Genetics, 141B*, 825–832.

Saltzman, L. E., Paternoster, R., Waldo, G. P., & Chiricos, T. G. (1982). Deterrent and experiential effects: The problem of causal order in perceptual deterrence research. *Journal of Research in Crime and Delinquency, 19*, 172–189.

Sameroff, A. J. (1998). Environmental risk factors in infancy. *Pediatrics, 102*, 1287–1292.

Sameroff, A. J., Bartko, W. T., Baldwin, A., Baldwin, C., & Seifer, R. (1998). Family and social influence on the development of child competence. In M. Lewis & C. Feiring (Eds.), *Families, risk, and competence* (pp. 161–185). Mahwah, NJ: Lawrence Erlbaum Associates.

Sameroff, A. J., Peck, S. C., & Eccles, J. S. (2004). Changing ecological determinants of conduct problems from early adolescence to early adulthood. *Development and Psychopathology, 16*, 873–896.

Sampson, R. J. & Groves, W. B. (1989). Community structure and crime: Testing social-disorganization theory. *American Journal of Sociology, 94*, 774–802.

Sampson, R. J. & Laub, J. H. (1990). Crime and deviance over the life course: The salience of adult social bonds. *American Sociological Review, 55*, 609–627.

Sampson, R. & Laub, J. (1992). Crime and deviance in the life course. *Annual Review of Sociology, 18*, 63–84.

Sampson, R. & Laub, J. (1993). *Crime in the making: Pathways and turning points through life*. Cambridge, MA: Harvard University Press.

Sampson, R. J. & Laub, J. H. (1995). Understanding variability in lives through time: Contributions of life-course criminology. *Studies on Crime and Crime Prevention, 4*, 143–158.

Sampson, R. J. & Laub, J. H. (1996). Socioeconomic achievement in the life course of disadvantaged men: Military service as a turning point, circa 1940–1965. *American Sociological Review, 61*(3), 347–367.

Sampson, R. J. & Laub, J. H. (1997). A life-course theory of cumulative disadvantage and the stability of delinquency. In. T. P. Thornberry (Ed.), *Advances in criminological theory: Vol. 7.* (pp. 133–161). *Developmental theories of crime and delinquency*. New Brunswick, NJ: Transaction Publishers.

Sampson, R. J. (2001). Foreword. In A. Piquero & P. Mazerolle (Eds.), *Life-course criminology* (pp. v–vii). Belmont, CA: Wadsworth/Thomson Learning.

Sampson, R. & Laub, J. (2003). Life-course desisters? Trajectories of crime among delinquent boys followed to age 70. *Criminology, 41*(3), 555–592.

Sampson, R. & Laub, J. (2005a). A general age-graded theory of crime: Lessons learned and the future of life-course criminology. In D. P. Farrington (Ed.), *Integrated developmental and life-course theories of offending: Vol. 14. Advances in criminological theory* (pp. 165–182). New Brunswick, NJ: Transaction Publishers.

Sampson, R. J. & Laub, J. H. (2005b) A life-course view of the development of crime. *Annals of the American Academy of Political and Social Science, 602*, 12–45.

Sampson, R. J., Laub, J. H., & Eggleston, E. P. (2004). On the robustness and validity of groups. *Journal of Quantitative Criminology, 20*, 37–42.

Sampson, R. J., Laub, J. H., & Wimer, C. (2006). Does marriage reduce crime? A counterfactual approach to within-individual causal effects. *Criminology, 44*, 465–508.

Sampson, R. J., Raudenbush, S., & Earls, F. (1997). Neighborhoods and violent crime: A multilevel study of collective efficacy. *Science, 277*, 918–924.

Sampson, R. J. & Wilson, W. J. (1995). Toward a theory of race, crime, and urban inequality. In J. Hagan & R. Peterson (Eds.), *Crime and inequality* (pp. 37–54). Stanford, CA: Stanford University Press.

Sartory, M. A., Bauske, T., & Lunenburg, F. C. (2000). Pupil control behavior, classroom robustness, and self-control: Public and military secondary schools. *American Secondary Education, 29*, 10–19.

Satterfield, J. H., Hoppe, C. M., & Schell, A. M. (1982). A prospective study of delinquency in 110 adolescent boys with attention deficit disorder and 88 normal adolescent boys. *American Journal of Psychiatry, 139*, 795–798.

Sattler, J. M. (1992). *Assessment of children* (3rd ed.). San Diego, CA: Author.

Savage, J. (2006). Interpreting "percent Black": An analysis of race and violent crime in Washington, D.C. *Journal of Ethnicity in Criminal Justice, 4*(1/2), 29–64.

Savage, J. & Kanazawa, S. (2002). Social capital, crime, and human nature. *Journal of Contemporary Criminal Justice, 18*(2), 188–211.

Savage, J. & Kanazawa, S. (2004). Social capital and the human psyche: Why is social life 'capital'? *Sociological Theory, 22*(3), 504–524.

Savage, J. & Vila, B. J. (2003). Human ecology, crime, and crime control: Linking individual behavior and aggregate crime. *Social Biology, 50*(1–2), 77–101.

Scafidi, F. A., Field, T. M., Wheeden, A., Schanberg, S., Kuhn, C., Symanski, R., et al. (1996). Cocaine-exposed preterm neonates show behavioral and hormonal differences. *Pediatrics, 97*(6), 851–855.

Scarpa, A. (2001). Community violence exposure in a young adult sample: Lifetime prevalence and socioemotional effects. *Journal of Interpersonal Violence, 16*(1), 36–53.

Scarpa, A. & Raine, A. (1997). Psychophysiology of anger and violent behavior. *Psychiatric Clinics of North America, 20*(2), 375–394.

Scarr, S. (1992). Developmental theories for the 1990s: Development and individual differences. *Child Development, 63*, 1–19.

Scarr, S. & McCartney, K. (1983). How people make their own environments: A theory of genotype → environment effects. *Child Development, 54*, 424–435.

Scheider, M. (2001). Deterrence and the base rate fallacy: An examination of perceived certainty. *Justice Quarterly, 18*, 63–86.

Schoen, C., Davis, K., Collins, K., Greenberg, L., Des Roches, C., & Abrams, M. (1997). *The Commonwealth Fund survey of the health of adolescent girls*. New York: Commonwealth Fund.

Schoepfer, A. & Piquero, A. R. (2006). Self-control, moral beliefs, and criminal activity. *Deviant Behavior, 27*, 51–71.

Scholte, E. M. (1999). Factors predicting continued violence into young adulthood. *Journal of Adolescence, 22*, 3–20.

Schuetze, P. & Eiden, R. D. (2006). The association between maternal cocaine use during pregnancy and physiological regulation in 4- to 8-week-old infants: An examination of possible mediators and moderators. *Journal of Pediatric Psychology, 31*(1), 15–26.

Schuetze, P., Eiden, R. D., & Coles, C. D. (2007). Prenatal cocaine and other substance exposure: Effects on infant autonomic regulation at 7 months of age. *Developmental Psychobiology, 49*(3), 276–289.

Schumacher, M. & Kurz, G. A. (2000). *The 8% solution: Preventing serious, repeat juvenile crime*. Thousand Oaks, CA: Sage.

Schwartz, I. M., Rendon, J. A., & Hsieh, C-M. (1994). Is child maltreatment a leading cause of delinquency? *Child Welfare, 73*, 639–655.

Schweinhart, L. L. & Weikart, D. P. (1997). *Lasting differences: The High/Scope Preschool Curriculum Comparison Study through age 23*. Ypsilanti, MI: High-Scope Press.

Sciamanna, J. (2006). Ten years of leaving foster children behind: A long decline in federal support for children in foster care. Retrieved on December 1, 2005, from http://www.cwla.org/advocacy/childreninfostercarereport.pdf

Scott, S., Knapp, M., Henderson, J., & Maughan, B. (2001). Financial cost of social exclusion: Follow-up study of antisocial children into adulthood. *British Medical Journal, 323*, 1–6.

Seguin, J. R., Boulerice, B., Harden, P. W., Tremblay, R. E., & Pihl, R. O. (1999). Executive functions and physical aggression after controlling for attention deficit hyperactivity disorder, general memory and IQ. *Journal of Child Psychology and Psychiatry, 40*, 1197–1208.

Seguin, J. R., Nagin, D., Assaad, J., & Tremblay, R. E. (2004). Cognitive-neuropsychological function in chronic physical aggression and hyperactivity. *Abnormal Psychology, 113*, 603–613.

Seguin, J. R., Pihl, R. O., Harden, P. W., Tremblay, R. E., & Boulerice, B. (1995). Cognitive and neuropsychological characteristics of physically aggressive boys. *Journal of Abnormal Psychology, 104*, 614–624.

Sellin, T. E. (1938). *Culture conflict and crime.* New York: Social Science Research Council.

Serbin, L. A., Cooperman, J. M., Peters, P. L., Lehoux, P. M., Stack, D. M., & Schwartzman, A. E. (1998). Intergenerational transfer of psychosocial risk in women with childhood histories of aggression, withdrawal, or aggression and withdrawal. *Developmental Psychology, 34*, 1246–1262.

Serbin, L. A., Stack, D. M., De Genna, N., Grunzeweig, N., Temcheff, C. E., & Schwartzman, A. E. (2004). When aggressive girls become mothers: Problems in parenting, health, and development across two generations. In M. Putallaz & K. L. Bierman (Eds.), *Aggression, antisocial behavior, and violence among girls: A developmental perspective* (pp. 262–285). New York: Guilford Publications.

Sergeant, J. A. Geurts, H., & Oosterlaan, J. (2002). How specific is a deficit of executive functioning for attention-deficit/hyperactivity disorder? *Behavioural Brain Research, 130*(1–2), 3–28.

Seydlitz, R. & Jenkins, P. (1998). The influence of families, friends, schools, and communityon delinquent behavior. In T. P. Gullotta, G. R. Adams, & R. Montemayor (Eds.) *Delinquent violent youth: Theory and interventions* (pp. 53–97). Thousand Oaks, CA: Sage.

Shankaran, S., Das, A., Bauer, C. R., Bada, H. S., Lester, B., Wright, L. L., et al. (2004). Association between patterns of maternal substance use and infant birth weight, length, and head circumference. *Pediatrics, 114*(2), e226–e234.

Shannon, L. (1978). A longitudinal study of delinquency and crime. In C. F. Wellford (Ed.), *Papers Presented at the 1977 Meetings of the American Society of Criminology.* Beverly Hills, CA: Sage Publications.

Shannon, L. (1982). *Assessing the relationship of adult criminal careers to juvenile careers.* Office of Juvenile Justice and Delinquency Prevention. Washington, DC: U.S. Department of Justice.

Shannon, L. (1991). *Changing patterns of delinquency and crime: A longitudinal study in Racine.* Boulder, CO: Westview press.

Shannon, L., McKim, J., Curry, J., & Haffner, L. (1988). *Criminal career continuity: Its social context.* New York: Human Sciences Press.

Shaw, D. S. & Bell, R. Q. (1993). Developmental theories of parental contributors to antisocial behavior. *Journal of Abnormal Child Psychology, 21*, 493–518.

Shaw, C. & McKay, H. (1942). *Juvenile delinquency and urban areas*. Chicago: University of Chicago Press.

Shaw, D. S. (2003). Advancing our understanding of intergenerational continuity in antisocial behavior. *Journal of Abnormal Child Psychology, 31*, 193–199.

Shaw, D. S. Gilliom, M., Ingoldsby, E. M., & Nagin, D. S. (2003). Trajectories leading to school-age conduct problems. *Developmental Psychology, 39*, 189–200.

Sherman, L. (1990). Police crackdown: Initial and residual deterrence. In M. Tonry & N. Morris (Eds.), *Crime and justice: A review of research: Vol. 12*. Chicago, IL: University of Chicago Press.

Sherwood, A., Allen, M. T., Obrist, P. A., & Langer, A. W. (1986). Evaluation of beta-adrenergic influences on cardiovascular and metabolic adjustments to physical and psychological stress. *Psychophysiology, 23*, 89–104.

Sickmund, M. (2004). *Juveniles in corrections*. Washington, DC: Office of Juvenile Justice and Delinquency Prevention.

Silverthorn, P. & Frick, P. (1999). Developmental pathways to antisocial behavior: The delayed-onset pathway in girls. *Development and Psychopathology, 11*, 101–126.

Silverthorn, P., Frick, P. J., & Reynolds, R. (2001). Timing of onset and correlates of severe conduct problems in adjudicated girls and boys. *Journal of Psychopathology and Behavioral Assessment, 23*, 171–181.

Simon, H. A. (1957). *Models of man: Social and rational*. New York: Wiley.

Simon, R. J. (1975). *Women and crime*. Lexington, MA: D.C. Heath.

Simonoff, E. (2001). Genetic influences on conduct disorder. In J. Hill & B. Maughan (Eds.), *Conduct disorders in childhood and adolescence* (pp. 202–234). New York: Cambridge University Press.

Simons, R. L., Johnson, C., Conger, R. D., & Elder, G. Jr. (1998). A test of latent trait versus life-course perspectives on the stability of adolescent antisocial behavior. *Criminology, 36*(2), 217–244.

Simons, R. L., Simons, L. G., Burt, C. H., Drummond, H., Stewart, E., Brody, G. H., et al. (2006). Supportive parenting moderates the effect of discrimination upon anger, hostile view of relationships, and violence among African American boys. *Journal of Health and Social Behavior, 47*, 373–389.

Simons, R. L., Wu, C-I., Conger, R., & Lorenz, F. O. (1994). Two routes to delinquency: Differences between early and late starters in the impact of parenting and deviant peers. *Criminology, 32*, 247–275.

Simpson, S. & Geis, G. (2008). The undeveloped concept of opportunity. In E. Goode (Ed.), *Out of control: Assessing the general theory of crime* (pp. 49–60). Stanford: Stanford University Press.

Singer, J. D. & Willett, J. B. (2003). *Applied longitudinal data analysis: Modeling change and event occurrence*. New York: Oxford Press.

Singer, L. T., Salvator, A., Arendt, R., Minnes, S., Farkas, K., & Kliegman, R. (2002). Effects of cocaine/polydrug exposure and maternal psychological distress on infant birth outcomes. *Neurotoxicology & Teratology, 24*(2),127–135.

Sjoberg, R. L., Ducci, F., Barr, C. S., Newman, T. K., Dell'osso, L., Virkkunen, M., et al. (2008). A non-additive interaction of a functional MAO-A VNTR and testosterone predicts antisocial behavior. *Neuropsychopharmacology, 33,* 425–430.

Skonovd, N. & Haapanen, R. (1998). *Predicting parole performance in the era of crack cocaine.* Washington, DC: United States Department of Justice, National Institute of Justice.

Slomkowski, C., Rende, R., Conger, K. J., Simons, R. L., & Conger, R. D. (2001). Sisters, brothers, and delinquency: Evaluating social influence during early and middle adolescence. *Child Development, 72*(1), 271–283.

Smith, C. A. & Farrington, D. P. (2004). Continuities in antisocial behavior and parenting across three generations. *Journal of Child Psychology and Psychiatry, 45,* 230–247.

Smith, C. A., Krohn, M. D., Lizotte, A. J., McCluskey, C. P., Stouthamer-Loeber, M., & Weiher, A. W. (2000). The effect of early delinquency and substance use on precocious transitions to adulthood among adolescent males. In G. L. Fox & M. L. Benson (Eds.), Families, crime and criminal justice: Charting the linkages: Vol. 2. Contemporary perspectives in family research (pp. 233–256). Amsterdam: JAI Press.

Smith, C., Lizotte, A. J., Thornberry, T. P., & Krohn, M. D. (1995). Resilient youth: Identifying factors that prevent high-risk youth from engaging in delinquency and drug use. In Z. S. Blau, & J. Hagan (Eds.), *Current perspectives on aging and the life cycle: Vol. 4. Delinquency and disrepute in the life course* (pp. 217–247). Greenwich, CT: JAI Press.

Smith, C. & Thornberry, T. P. (1995). The relationship between childhood maltreatment and adolescent involvement in delinquency. *Criminology, 33,* 451–477.

Smith, R. (1999). The timing of birth. *Scientific American, 280*(3), 68–75.

Snijders, T. A. B. & Bosker R. J. (1999). *Multilevel analysis: An introduction to basic and advanced multilevel modeling.* Thousand Oaks, CA: Sage Publications.

Snyder, H. (2004). *Juvenile arrests 2002.* Washington, DC: Office of Juvenile Justice and Delinquency Prevention.

Snyder, J., Bank, L., & Burraston, B. (2005). The consequences of antisocial behavior in older male siblings for younger brothers and sisters. *Journal of Family Psychology, 19,* 643–653.

Snyder, J. & Patterson, G. R. (1995). Individual differences in social aggression: A test of a reinforcement model of socialization in the natural environment. *Behavior Therapy, 26,* 371–391.

Soothill, K., Ackerley, E., & Francis, B. (2003). The persistent offenders debate: A focus on temporal changes. *Criminal Justice, 3,* 389–412.

Spohn, C. & Holleran. D. (2002). The effect of imprisonment on recidivism rates of felony offenders: A focus on drug offenders. *Criminology, 40,* 329–357.

Sroufe, L. A., Egeland, B., Carlson, E. H, & Collins, W. A. (2005). Placing early attachment experiences in developmental context: The Minnesota Longitudinal Study. In K. E. Grossmann, K. Grossmann, & E. Waters (Eds.), *Attachment from infancy to adulthood: The major longitudinal studies* (pp. 48–70). New York: Guilford.

Sroufe, L. A. & Rutter, M. (1984). The domain of developmental psychopathology. *Child Development, 56*, 316–325.

Stack, D. M., Serbin, L. A., Schwartzman, A. E., & Ledingham, J. (2005). *Girls' aggression across the life course: Long-term outcomes and intergenerational risk.* Mahwah, NJ: Lawrence Erlbaum Associates.

Stallings, M. C., Corley R. P., Dennehey, B., Hewitt, J. K., Krauter, K. S., Lessem, J. M., et al. (2005). A genome-wide search for quantitative trait Loci that influence anti-social drug dependence in adolescence. *Archives of General Psychiatry, 62*(9), 1042–1051.

Statistics Canada. (2003). *National Longitudinal Survey of Children and Youth: Cycle 4 survey instruments 2000–2001.* Ottawa, Canada: Statistics Canada.

Statistics Canada. (2005). *Family violence in Canada: A statistical profile 2005* (85-224-XIE). Ottawa: Canadian Centre for Justice Statistics.

Staton, M., Leukefeld, C., & Webster, J. M. (2003). Substance use, health, and mental health: Problems and service utilization among incarcerated women. *International Journal of Offender Therapy and Comparative Criminology, 47*, 224–239.

Stattin, H. & Magnusson, D. (1984). *The role of early aggressive behavior for the frequency the seriousness, and the types of later criminal offences.* Stockholm: University of Stockholm.

Stattin, H. & Magnusson, D. (1989). The role of early aggressive behavior in the frequency, seriousness, and types of later crime. *Journal of Consulting and Clinical Psychology, 57*, 710–718.

Stattin, H. & Magnusson, D. (1991). Stability and change in criminal behaviour up to age 30. *The British Journal of Criminology, 31*, 327–346.

Stattin, H., Magnusson, D., & Reichel, H. (1989). Criminal activity at different ages: A study based on a Swedish longitudinal research population. *British Journal of Criminology, 29*, 368–385.

Steffensmeier, D. & Allan, E. (1996). Gender and crime: Toward a gendered theory of female offending. *Annual Review of Sociology, 22*, 459–487.

Steffensmeier, D. & Allan, E. (2000). Looking for patterns: Gender, age, and crime. In J. Sheley (Ed.), *Criminology: The contemporary handbook* (pp. 85–127). Belmont, CA: Wadsworth.

Steffensmeier, D. E., Allan, E., & Streifel, C. (1989). Development and female crime: A cross-national test of alternative explanations. *Social Forces, 68*, 262–283.

Steffensmeier, D. & Streifel, C. (1992). Time-series analysis of the female percentage of arrests for property crimes, 1960–1985: A test of alternative explanations. *Justice Quarterly, 9*, 77–103.

Steffensmeier, D., Schwartz, J., Zhong, H., & Ackerman, J. (2005). An assessment of recent trends in girls' violence using diverse longitudinal sources: Is the gender gap closing? *Criminology, 43*, 355–406.

Steffensmeier, D., Zhong, H., Ackerman, J., Schwartz, J., & Agha, S. (2006). Gender gap trends for violent crimes, 1980 to 2003: A UCR-NCVS comparison. *Feminist Criminology, 1*, 72–98.

Steinberg, L., Lambron, S.D., Darling, N., Mounts, N. S., & Dornbusch, S. M. (1994). Over-time changes in adjustment and competence among adolescents from authoritative, authoritarian, indulgent, and neglectful families. *Child Development, 65,* 754–770.

Steiner, H., Cauffman, E., & Duxbury, E. (1999). Personality traits in juvenile delinquents: Relation to criminal behavior and recidivism. *Journal of the American Academy of Child and Adolescent Psychiatry, 38*(3), 256–262.

Steiner, H. & Humphreys, K. (2001). The assessment of the mental health system of the California Youth Authority. Sacramento CA: California Youth Authority. Retrieved March 3, 2007, from http://www.cdcr.ca.gov/ReportsResearch/docs/Stanford%20 Mental%20

Steissguth, A. P., Aase, J. M., Clarren, S. K., Randels, S. P., LaDue, R. A., & Smith, D. F. (1991). Fetal alcohol syndrome in adolescents and adults. *Journal of the American Medical Association, 265*(15), 1961–1967.

Stewart, E. A. (2003). School social bonds, school climate, and school misbehavior: A multilevel analysis. *Justice Quarterly, 20,* 575–604.

Stewart, E. A., Simons, R. L., Conger, R. D. & Scaramella, L. V. (2002). Beyond the interactional relationship between delinquency and parenting practices: The contribution of legal sanctions. *Journal of Research in Crime and Delinquency, 39*(1), 36–59.

Stewart, S. (2007, January 25). Poll: God, readers voice approval of spanking children. *The Decatur Daily.*

Stolzenberg, L. & D'Alessio, S. (2004). Capital punishment, execution publicity and murder in Houston, Texas. *Journal of Criminal Law and Criminology, 94,* 351–379.

Stouthamer-Loeber, M. & Loeber, R. (2002). Lost opportunities for intervention: Undetected markers for the development of serious juvenile delinquency. *Criminal Behavior and Mental Health, 12*(1), 69–82.

Stouthhamer-Loeber, M., Loeber, R., Wei, E., Farrington, D. P., & Wikström, P-O. (2002). Risk and promotive effects in the explanation of persistent serious delinquency in boys. *Journal of Consulting and Clinical Psychology, 70,* 111–123.

Stouthamer-Loeber, M., Wei, E., Loeber, R., & Masten, A. S. (2004). Desistance from persistent serious delinquency in the transition to adulthood. *Development and Psychopathology, 16,* 897–918.

Straus, M. (1991). Discipline and deviance: Physical punishment of children and violence and other crimes in adulthood. *Social Problems, 38,* 133–154.

Straus, M. A. (2001a). *Beating the devil out of them* (2nd ed.). New Brunswick, NJ: Transaction.

Straus, M. A. (2001b). New evidence for the benefits of never spanking. *Society, 38*(6), 52–60.

Straus, M. A. & Donnelly, D. A. (1993). Corporal punishment of adolescents by American parents. *Youth & Society, 24*(4), 419–422.

Strayhorn, J. M. (2002). Self-control: Towards systematic training programs. *Journal of the American Academy of Children and Adolescent Psychiatry, 41,* 17–27.

Sullivan, M. L. (1998). Integrating qualitative and quantitative methods in the study of developmental psychopathology in context. *Development and Psychopathology, 10*, 377–393.

Suomi, S. (1997). Early determinants of behavior: Evidence from primate studies. *British Medical Bulletin, 53*, 170–184.

Susman, E. J., Nottelmann, E. D., Dorn, L. D., Inoff-Germain, G., & Chrousos, G. P. (1988). Physiological and behavioral aspects of stress in adolescents. In G. P. Chrousos, D. L. Loriaux, & P.W. Gold, (Eds.), *Mechanisms of physical and emotional stress* (pp. 341–352). New York: Plenum Press

Susman, E. J. & Pajer, K. (2004). Biology-behavior integration and antisocial behavior in girls. In M. Putallaz & K. Bierman (Eds.), *Aggression, antisocial behavior, and violence among girls: A developmental perspective* (pp. 34–36). New York: Guilford Publications, Inc.

Sutherland, E. & Cressey, D. R. (1974). *Criminology* (9th ed.). Toronto, Canada: J.B. Lippincott.

Tabachnick, B. G. & Fidell, L. S. (2007). *Using multivariate statistics* (5th ed.). Boston: Allyn & Bacon.

Tarling, R. (1993). *Analyzing offending: Data, models and interpretations.* London: Her Majesty's Stationery Office.

Tarolla, S. M., Wagner, E. F., Rabinowitz, J., & Tubman, J. G. (2002). Understanding and treating juvenile offenders: A review of current knowledge and future directions. *Aggression and Violent Behavior, 7*(2), 125–143.

Tarter, R., Vanyukov, M., Giancola, P., Dawes, M., Blackson, T., Mezzich, A., et al. (1999). Etiology of early age onset substance use disorder: A maturational perspective. *Development and Psychopathology, 11*(4), 657–683.

Taylor, C. S., Smith, P. R., Taylor, V. A., von Eye, A., Lerner, R. M., Balsano, A. B., et al. (2005). Individual and ecological assets and thriving among African American adolescent male gang and community-based organization members: A report from wave 3 of the "Overcoming the Odds" Study. *Journal of Early Adolescence, 25*(1), 72–93.

Taylor, J., Iacono, W. G., & McGue, M. (2000). Evidence for a genetic etiology of early-onset delinquency. *Journal of Abnormal Psychology, 109*(4), 634–643.

Taylor, J., Loney, B. R., Bobadillo, L., Iacono, W. G., & McGue, M. (2003). Genetic and environmental influences on psychopathy trait dimensions in a community sample of male twins. *Journal of Abnormal Child Psychology, 31*(6), 633–645.

Teicher, M. H. (March, 2002). The scars that won't heal: The neurobiology of child abuse. *Scientific American*, 68–75.

Tennes, K. & Kreye, M. (1985). Children's adrenocortical responses to classroom activities and tests in elementary school. *Psychosomatic Medicine, 47*(5), 451–460.

Teplin, L., Abram, K., McClelland, G., Dulcan, M., & Mericle, A. (2002) Psychiatric disorders in youth in juvenile detention. *Archives of General Psychiatry, 59*, 1133–43.

Thapar, A., Langley, K., & Fowler, T. (2005). Catechol O-methyltransferase gene variant and birth weight predict early-onset antisocial behavior in children with attention-deficit/hyperactivity disorder. *Archives of General Psychiatry, 62*(11), 1275–1278.

Thaxton, S. & Agnew, R. (2004). The nonlinear effects of parental and teacher attachment on delinquency: Disentangling strain from social control explanations. *Justice Quarterly, 21*, 763–791.

Thomas, W. (1923). *The unadjusted girl.* Boston, MA: Little, Brown.

Thompson, R. A., Flood, M. F., & Goodvin, R. (2006). Social support and developmental psychopathology. In D. Cicchetti & D. J. Cohen (Eds.), *Developmental psychopathology: Vol. 3. Risk, disorder and adaptation* (2nd ed., pp. 1–37). Hoboken, NJ: John Wiley.

Thompson G. E. (2002). Corporal punishment by parents and associated child behaviors and experiences: A meta-analytic and theoretical review, *Psychological Bulletin, 128*, 539–579.

Thornberry T. P. (1987). Toward an interactional theory of delinquency. *Criminology, 25*, 863–891.

Thornberry, T. P. (1997). *Developmental theories of crime and delinquency.* New Brunswick, NJ: Transaction.

Thornberry, T. P. (2005). Explaining multiple patterns of offending across the life course and across generations. *The Annals of the American Academy of Political and Social Science, 602*, 156–195.

Thornberry, T. P., Freeman-Gallant, A., Lizotte, A. J., Krohn, M. D., & Smith, C. A. (2003). Linked lives: The intergenerational transmission of antisocial behavior. *Journal of Abnormal Child Psychology, 31*, 171–184.

Thornberry, T. P., Huizinga, D., & Loeber, R. (1995). The prevention of serious delinquency and violence: Implications from the program of research on the causes and correlates of delinquency. In J. C. Howell, B. Krisberg, J. D. Hawkins, & J. J. Wilson (Eds.), *Serious, violent, and chronic juvenile offenders: A sourcebook* (pp 213–237). Thousand Oaks, CA: Sage.

Thornberry, T. P., Ireland, T. O., & Smith, C. A. (2001). The importance of timing: The varying impact of childhood and adolescent maltreatment on multiple problem outcomes. *Developmental Psychopathology, 13*, 957–979.

Thornberry, T. P. & Krohn, M. D. (2003). Comparison of self-report and official data for measuring crime. In J. Pepper & C. Petrie (Eds.), *Measurement problems in criminal justice research: Workshop summary* (pp. 43–94). Washington, DC: National Academies Press.

Tibbetts, S. G. (2003). Selfishness, social control, and emotions: An integrated perspective on criminality. In A. Walsh & L. Ellis (Eds.), *Biosocial criminology: Challenging environmentalism's supremacy* (pp. 83–101). New York: Nova Science.

Tibbetts, S. G. & Piquero, A. R. (1999). The influence of gender, low birth weight, and disadvantaged environment in predicting early onset of offending: A test of Moffitt's interactional hypotheses. *Criminology, 37*(4), 843–877.

Tittle, C. R., Villemez, W. J., & Smith, D. A. (1978). The myth of social class and criminality: An empirical assessment of the empirical evidence. *American Sociological Review, 43,* 643–656.

Tolan, P. H. (1987). Implications of age of onset for delinquency risk. *Journal of Abnormal Child Psychology, 15*(1), 47–65.

Tolan, P. H. & Gorman-Smith, D. (1998). Development of serious and violent offending careers. In R. Loeber & D. P. Farrington (Eds.), *Serious and violent juvenile offenders: Risk factors and successful interventions* (pp. 68–85). Thousand Oaks, CA: Sage Publications, Inc.

Tolan, P. H., Guerra, N. G., & Kendall, P. C. (1995). A developmental-ecological perspective on antisocial behavior in children and adolescents: Toward a unified risk and intervention framework. *Journal of Consulting and Clinical Psychology, 63,* 57–584.

Tolan, P. H. & Thomas, P. (1995). The implications of age of onset for delinquency risk II: Longitudinal data. *Journal of Abnormal Child Psychology, 23*(2), 157–199.

Tolan, P. H., Gorman-Smith, D., & Henry, D. B. (2003). The developmental ecology of urban males' youth violence. *Developmental Psychology, 39,* 274–291.

Tolin, D. F. & Foa, E. B. (2006). Sex differences in trauma and posttraumatic stress disorder: A quantitative review of 25 years of research. *Psychological Bulletin, 132,* 959–992.

Tollet, C. L. & Benda, B. B. (1999). Predicting 'survival' in the community among persistent and serious juvenile offenders: A 12-month follow-up study. *Journal of Offender Rehabilitation, 28,* 49–76.

Tomz, M., Wittenberg, J., & King, G. (2001). CLARIFY: Software for interpreting and presenting statistical results (Version 2.0) [Computer software]. Cambridge, MA: Harvard University.

Tracy, P. E. & Kempf-Leonard, K. (1996). *Continuity and discontinuity in criminal careers.* New York: Plenum.

Tracy, P. E., Wolfgang, M. E., & Figlio, R. M. (1985). *Delinquency in two birth cohorts: Executive summary.* U.S. Dept. of Justice, Office of Juvenile Justice and Delinquency Prevention.

Tracy, P. E., Wolfgang, M. E., & Figlio, R. M. (1990). *Delinquency careers in two birth cohorts.* New York: Plenum Press.

Tremblay, R. E. (2000). The development of aggressive behaviour during childhood: What have we learned in the past century? *International Journal of Behavioural Development, 24,* 129–143.

Tremblay, R. (2004). The development of human physical aggression: How important is early childhood? In L. A. Leavitt & D. M. B. Hall (Eds.), *Social and moral development: Emerging evidence on the toddler years* (pp. 221–238). New Brunswick, NJ: Johnson and Johnson Pediatric Institute.

Tremblay, R. E. (2006). Tracking the origins of criminal behavior: Back to the future. *The Criminologist, 31*(1), 1, 3–7.

Tremblay, R. E. & LeMarquand, D. (2001). Individual risk and protective factors. In D. P. Farrington & R. Loeber (Eds.), *Child delinquents: Development, interventions, and service needs* (pp. 137–164). Thousand Oaks, CA: Sage.

Tremblay, R. E., McCord, J., Boileau, H., Charlebois, P., Gagnon, C., Le Blanc, M., et al. (1991). Can disruptive boys be helped to become competent? *Psychiatry, 54,* 148–161.

Tremblay, R. E., Nagin D. S., & Seguin, J. R. (2004). Physical aggression during early childhood: Trajectories and predictions. *Pediatrics, 114*(1), 43–50.

Tremblay, R. E., Nagin, D. S., Sequin, J. R., Zoccolillo, M., Zelazo, P. D., Boivin, M., et al. (2004). Physical aggression during early childhood: Trajectories and predictors. *Pediatrics, 114,* e43–e50.

Tremblay, R. E., Pihl, R. O., Vitaro, F., & Dobkin, P. L. (1994). Predicting early onset of male antisocial behavior from preschool behavior. *Archives of General Psychiatry, 51,* 732–739.

Tremblay, G., Tremblay, R. E., & Saucier, J. (2004). The development of parent-child relationship perceptions in boys from childhood to adolescence: A comparison between disruptive and non-disruptive boys. *Child and Adolescent Social Work Journal, 21,* 407–426.

Tremblay, R. E., Vitaro, F., Bertrand, L., Le Blanc, M., Beauchesne, H., Boileau, H., et al. (1992). Parent and child training to prevent early onset of delinquency: The Montreal longitudinal experimental study. In J. McCord & R. E. Tremblay (Eds.), *Preventing antisocial behavior: Interventions from birth to adolescence* (pp. 117–138). New York: Guilford Press.

Tremblay, R. E., Vitaro, F., Nagin, D., Pagani, L., & Séguin, J. R. (2003). The Montreal longitudinal and experimental study: Rediscovering the power of descriptions. In T. Thornberry & M. D. Krohn (Eds.), *Taking stock of delinquency: An overview of findings from contemporary longitudinal studies* (pp. 205–254). New York: Kluwer Academic/Plenum.

Tronick, E. Z., Frank, D. A., Cabral, H., Mirochnick, M. M. D., & Zuckerman, B. (1996). Late dose-response effects of prenatal cocaine exposure on newborn neurobehavioral performance. *Pediatrics, 98*(1), 76–83.

Trouton, A., Spinath, F. M., & Plomin, R. (2002). Twins Early Development Study (TEDS): A Multivariate, Longitudinal Genetic Investigation of Language, Cognition and Behavior Problems in Childhood. *Twin Research, 5*(5), 444–448.

Trulson, C. R., Marquart, J. W., Mullings, J. L., & Caeti, T. J. (2005). In between adolescence and adulthood: Recidivism outcomes of a cohort of state delinquents. *Youth Violence and Juvenile Justice, 3*(4), 355–387.

Trzesniewski, K. H., Moffitt, T. E., Caspi, A., Taylor, A., & Maughan, B. (2006). Revisiting the association between reading achievement and antisocial behavior: New evidence of an environmental explanation from a twin study. *Child Development, 77*(1) 72–88.

Turner, M. G., Piquero, A. R., & Pratt, T. C. (2005). The school context as a source of self-control. *Journal of Criminal Justice, 33,* 327–339.

Ulman, A. & Straus, M. A. (2003). Violence by children against mothers in relation to violence between parents and corporal punishment by parents. *Journal of Comparative Family Studies, 34,* 41–60.

U.S. Census Bureau, Housing and Household Economics Division. (2007). Earnings by occupation and education (Table). Retrieved August 7, 2007 from http://www.census.gov/hhes/www/income/earnings/call1usboth.html

U.S. Department of Health and Human Services. (2006) *Statewide automated child welfare information system (SACWIS) Status,* Retrieved August 31, 2006, from http://www.acf.hhs.gov/programs/cb/systems/sacwis/about.htm

Uggen, C. & Kruttschnitt, C. (1998). Crime in the breaking: Gender differences in desistance. *Law and Society Review, 32,* 339–366.

Uggen, C., Manza, J., & Behrens, A. (2004). 'Less than the average citizen': Stigma, role transition and the civic reintegration of convicted felons. In S. Maruna & R. Immarigeon (Eds.), *After crime and punishment: Pathways to offender reintegration* (pp. 261–293). Portland, OR: Willan Publishing.

Uggen, C. & Piliavin, I. (1998). Asymmetrical causation and criminal desistance. *Journal of Criminal Law and Criminology, 88,* 1399–1422.

Uggen, C. & Wakefield, S. (2005). Young adults reentering the community from the criminal justice system: The challenge of becoming an adult. In D. W. Osgood, E. M. Foster, C. Flanagan, & R. G. Ruth (Eds.), *On your own without a net: The transition to adulthood for vulnerable populations* (pp. 114–144). Chicago, IL: University of Chicago Press.

Unnever, J. D. & Cornell, D. G. (2003). Bullying, self-control and ADHD. *Journal of Interpersonal Violence, 18,* 129–148.

Unnever, J. D., Cullen, F. T., & Pratt, T. C. (2003). Parental management, ADHD, and delinquent involvement: Reassessing Gottfredson and Hirschi's general theory. *Justice Quarterly, 20,* 471–500.

Vaillant, G. E. & Milofsky, E. S. (1982). The etiology of alcoholism: A prospective viewpoint. *American Psychologist, 37,* 494–503.

Van Dulmen, M. H. M. & Egeland, B. (under review). *Aggregating multiple informant data on child behavior problems: Predictive validity and comparison of four empirical approaches.*

Van Dulmen, M. H. M. & Ong, A. (2006). New methodological directions in the study of adolescent competence and adaptation. *Journal of Adolescence, 29,* 851–856.

Van Goozen, S. H. M., Matthys, W., & Cohen-Kettenis, P. T. (1998). Salivary cortisol and cardiovascular activity during stress in oppositional-defiant disorder boys and normal controls. *Biological Psychiatry, 43*(7), 531–539.

van Kammen, W. B. & Loeber, R. (1994). Are fluctuations in delinquent activities related to the onset and offset in juvenile illegal drug usage. *Journal of Drug Issues, 42,* 184–201.

Van Lier, P. A., Wanner, B., & Vitaro, F. (2007). Onset of antisocial behavior, affiliation with deviant friends, and childhood maladjustment: A test of the childhood and adolescent-onset models. *Development and Psychopathology, 19*(1), 167–185.

Vazsonyi, A. T. & Crosswhite, J. M. (2004). A test of Gottfredson and Hirschi's general theory of crime in African-American adolescents. *Journal of Research in Crime and Delinquency, 41,* 407–432.

Veneziano, C., Veneziano, L., LeGrand, S., & Richards, L. (2004). Neuropsychological executive functions of adolescent sex offenders and nonsex offenders. *Perceptual and Motor Skills, 98,* 661–674.

Viding, E., Blair, R. J. R., Moffitt, T. E., & Plomin, R. (2005). Evidence for substantial genetic risk for psychopathy in 7 year-olds. *Journal of Child Psychology and Psychiatry, 46*(6), 592–597.

Vila, B. J. (1994). A general paradigm for understanding criminal behavior: Extending evolutionary ecological theory. *Criminology, 32*(3), 311–359.

Visher, C., Lattimore, P., & Linster, R. (1991). Predicting the recidivism of serious youthful offenders using survival models. *Criminology, 29*(3), 329–366.

Vitaro, F., Brendgen, M., & Tremblay, R. E. (2000). Influence of deviant friends on delinquency: Searching for moderator variables. *Journal of Abnormal Child Psychology, 28*(4), 313–325.

Vitaro, F., Brendgen, M., & Tremblay, R.E. (2001). Preventive intervention: Assessing its effects on the trajectories of delinquency and testing for meditational processes. *Applied Developmental Science, 5*(4), 201–213.

Vitaro, F. & Tremblay, R. E. (1994). Impact of a prevention program on aggressive children's friendships and social adjustment. *Journal of Abnormal Child Psychology, 22*(4), 457–475.

Vitaro, F., Tremblay, R. E., Kerr, M. A., Pagani, L., & Bukowski, W. M. (1997). Disruptiveness, friends' characteristics, and delinquency in early adolescence: A test of two competing models of development. *Child Development, 68*(4), 676–689.

Vuchinich, S. (1986). On attenuation in verbal family conflict. *Social Psychology Quarterly, 49,* 281–293.

Wachs, T. D. (2000). *Necessary but not sufficient: The respective roles of single and multiple influences on individual development.* Washington, DC: American Psychological Association.

Wade, N. (2006). *Before the dawn: Recovering the lost history of our ancestors.* New York: Penguin Press.

Wadhwa, P. D., Porto, M., Garite, T. J., Chicz-DeMet, A., & Sandman, C. A. (1998). Maternal corticotrophin-releasing hormone levels in the early third trimester predict length of gestation in human pregnancy. *American Journal of Obstetrics and Gynecology, 179*(4), 1079–1085.

Wagner, B. M. (1997). Family risk factors for child and adolescent suicidal behavior. *Psychological Bulletin, 121,* 246–298.

Wagner, M., D'Amico, R., Marder, C. L., Newman, L., & Blackorby, J. (1992). *What happens next? Trends in post-school outcomes of youth with disabilities: The second comprehensive report from the National Longitudinal Transition Study of Special*

Education Students, U.S. Department of Education S-2. Menlo Park, CA: SRI International.

Wakschlag, L. & Hans, S. (1999). Relation of maternal responsiveness during infancy to the development of behavior problems in high risk youths. *Developmental Psychology, 37,* 569–579.

Wakschlag, L. S., Lahey, B. B., Loeber, R., Green, S. M., Gordon, R. A., & Leventhal, B. L. (1997). Maternal smoking during pregnancy and the risk of conduct disorder in boys. *Archives of General Psychiatry, 54,* 670–676.

Wakschlag, L. S., Pickett, K. E., Cook, E., Benowitz, N. L., & Leventhal, B. (2002). Maternal smoking during pregnancy and severe antisocial behavior in offspring: A review. *American Journal of Public Health, 92*(6), 966–974.

Wallander, J. L. (1988). The relationship between attention problems in childhood and antisocial behavior eight years later. *Journal of Child Psychology and Psychiatry, 29,* 53–61.

Walsh, A., Petee, T. A., & Beyer, J. A. (1987). Intellectual imbalance and delinquency: Comparing high verbal and high performance IQ delinquency. *Criminal Justice and Behavior, 14,* 370–379.

Walters, G. D. (2000). Disposed to aggress?: In search of the violence-prone personality. *Aggression and Violent Behavior, 5*(2), 177–190.

Wang, X., Blomberg, T., & Li, S. (2005). Comparison of the educational deficiencies of delinquent and nondelinquent students. *Evaluation Review, 29,* 291–312.

Warner, T. D., Behnke, M., Hou, W., Garvan, C. W., Wobie, K., & Eyler, F. D. (2006). Predicting caregiver-reported behavior problems in cocaine-exposed children at 3 years. *Journal of Developmental & Behavioral Pediatrics, 27*(2), 83–92.

Warr, M. (1998). Life course transitions and desistance from crime. *Criminology, 36,* 183–216.

Warr, M. (2002). *Companions in crime: The social aspects of criminal conduct.* New York: Cambridge University Press.

Warr, M. & Stafford, M. (1991). The influence of delinquent peers: What they think or what they do? *Criminology, 29,* 851–866.

Warren, M. & Rosenbaum, J. (1987). Criminal careers of female offenders. *Criminal Justice and Behavior, 13,* 393–418.

Wass, T. S., Persutte, W. H., & Hobbins J. C. (2001). The impact of prenatal alcohol exposure on frontal cortex development in utero. *American Journal of Obstetrics & Gynecology, 185*(3), 737–742.

Wasserman, G., Keenan, K., Tremblay, R. E., Coie, J. D., & Herrenkohl, T. I. (2003). *Risk and protective factors of child delinquency.* Washington, DC: U.S. Department of Justice, Office of Justice Programs, Office of Juvenile Justice and Delinquency Prevention.

Wattenberg, N. & Saunders, F. (1954). Sex differences among juvenile offenders. *Sociology, 39,* 24–31.

Webster-Stratton, C. (2003). Aggression in young children perspective: Services proven to be effective in reducing aggression. In R. E. Tremblay, R. G. Barr, R. D. Peters (Eds.), *Encyclopaedia on early childhood development* [online]. Montreal, Quebec: Centre of Excellence for Early Childhood Development. Available at http://www.excellence-earlychildhood.ca/documents/PeplerANGxp.pdf.

Weichold, K. (2004). Evaluation of an antiaggressiveness training with antisocial youth. *Gruppendynamik, 35*(1), 83–105.

Weiler, B. L. & Widom, C. S. (1996). Psychopathy and violent behavior in abused an neglected young adults. *Criminal Behavior and Mental Health, 6*, 253–271.

Weissman, M. M., Warner, V., Wickramaratne, P. J., & Kandel, D. B. (1999). Maternal smoking during pregnancy and psychopathology in offspring followed in adulthood. *Child and Adolescent Psychiatry, 38*(7), 892–899.

Welsh, B. C. & Farrington, D. P. (2001). Assessing the economic costs and benefits of crime prevention. In B. C. Welsh, D. P. Farrington, & L. W. Sherman (Eds.), *Costs and benefits of preventing crime* (pp. 3–22). Boulder, CO: Westview Press.

Welsh, M. C., Pennington, B. F., & Groisser, D. B. (1991). A normative-developmental study of executive function: A window on the prefrontal function in children. *Developmental Neuropsychology, 7*, 131–149.

Werner, E. E. (1987). Vulnerability and resiliency in children at risk for delinquency: A longitudinal study from birth to young adulthood. In J. D. Burchard & S. N. Burchard (Eds.), *Primary prevention of psychopathology* (pp. 16–43). Newbury Park, CA: Sage.

Werner, E. E. & Smith, R. S. (1992). *Overcoming the odds: High risk children from birth to adulthood.* Ithaca, NY: Cornell University Press.

West, D. J. & Farrington, D. P. (1977). *Delinquent way of life: Third report from the Cambridge Study in Delinquent Development.* London, England: Heinemann.

White, H. R., Bates, M. E., & Buyske, S. (2001). Adolescence-limited versus persistent delinquency: Extending Moffitt's hypothesis into adulthood. *Journal of Abnormal Psychology, 110*, 600–609.

White, N. (2002). *Individual and conflict in Greek ethics.* Oxford: Oxford University Press.

White, N. A. & Piquero, A. R. (2004). A preliminary empirical test of Silverthorne and Frick's delayed-onset pathway in girls using an urban, African-American, U.S.-based sample. *Criminal Behavior and Mental Health, 14*, 291–309.

Whitney, I. & Smith, P. K. (1993). A survey of the nature and extent of bullying in junior/middle and secondary schools. *Educational Research, 35*, 3–25.

Widom, C. S. (1989a). Child abuse, neglect, and violent criminal behavior. *Criminology, 27*(2), 251–271.

Widom, C. S. (1989b). The cycle of violence. *Science, 244*, 160–164.

Widom, C. S. (1989c). The intergenerational transmission of violence. In N. A. Weiner & M. E. Wolfgang (Eds.), *Pathways to criminal violence* (pp. 137–201). Newbury Park, CA: Sage.

Widom, C. S. (1991a). Childhood victimization: Risk factor for delinquency. In M. E. Colten, & S. Gore (Eds.), *Adolescent stress: Causes and consequences. Social institutions and social change* (pp. 201–221). Hawthorne, NY: Aldine de Gruyter.

Widom, C. S. (1991b). The role of placement experiences in mediating the criminal consequences of early childhood victimization. *American Journal of Orthopsychiatry, 61*, 195–209.

Widom, C. S. & Maxfield, M. G. (2001). *An update on the "cycle of violence."* Research in Brief. (NCJ 184894) U.S. Department of Justice, Office of Justice Programs, National Institute of Justice. Washington, DC. Retrieved September 6, 2007, from http://www.ojp.usdoj.gov/nij

Wiesner, M. & Capaldi, D. M. (2003). Relations of childhood and adolescent factor to offending trajectories of young men. *Journal of Research in Crime and Delinquency, 40*(3), 231–262.

Wiesner, M., Capaldi, D. M., & Kim, H. K. (2007). Arrest trajectories across a 17-year span for young men: Relation to dual taxonomies and self-reported offense trajectories. *Criminology, 45*, 835–863.

Wiesner, M., Capaldi, D. M., & Patterson, G. R. (2003). Development of antisocial behavior and crime across the life-span from a social interactional perspective: The coercion model. In R. L. Akers & G. F. Jensen (Eds.), *Advances in criminological theory: Vol. 11. Social learning theory and the explanation of crime: A guide for the new century* (pp. 317–337). Piscataway, NJ: Transaction.

Wiesner, M., Kim, H. K., & Capaldi, D. M. (2005). Developmental trajectories of offending: Validation and prediction to young adult alcohol use, drug use, and depressive symptoms. *Development and Psychopathology, 17*, 251–270.

Wiesner, M. & Silbereisen, R. K. (2003). Trajectories of delinquent behaviour in adolescence and their covariates: Relations with initial and time-averaged factors. *Journal of Adolescence, 26*, 753–771.

Wiesner, M. & Windle, M. (2004). Assessing covariates of adolescent delinquency trajectories: A latent growth mixture modeling approach. *Journal of Youth and Adolescence, 33*(5), 431–442.

Wikström, P-O. H. (1985). *Everyday violence in contemporary Sweden: Situational and ecological aspects.* Stockholm: Liber förlag.

Wikström, P-O. H. (1990). Age and crime in a Stockholm cohort. *Journal of Quantitative Criminology, 6*, 61–83.

Wikström, P-O. H. (2004). Crime as alternative: Towards a cross-level situational action theory of crime causation. In J. McCord (Ed.), *Advances in criminological theory: Vol. 13. Beyond empiricism: Institutions and intentions in the study of crime.* (pp. 1–37). New Brunswick: Transaction.

Wikström, P-O. H. (2005). The social origins of pathways in crime: Towards a developmental ecological action theory of crime involvement and its changes. In D. Farrington (Ed.), *Integrated developmental and life course theories of offending. Advances in criminological theory: Vol. 14.* New Brunswick: Transaction.

Wikström, P-O. H. (2006). Individuals, settings, and acts of crime: Situational mechanisms and the explanation of crime. In P-O. H. Wikström & R. Sampson (Eds.), *The explanation of crime: Context, mechanisms and development* (pp. 61–107). Cambridge: Cambridge University Press.

Wikström, P-O. H. (2007a). Deterrence and deterrence experiences: Preventing crime through the threat of punishment. In S. Shoham, O. Beck, & M. Kett (Eds.), *International handbook of penology and criminal justice* (pp. 345–378). London: CRC Press: Taylor & Francis Group.

Wikström, P-O. H. (2007b). In search of causes and explanations of crime. In R. King & E. Wincup (Eds.), *Doing research on crime and justice* (2nd ed., pp. 117–140). Oxford: Oxford University Press.

Wikström, P-O. H. (2007c). The social ecology of crime: The role of the environment in crime causation. In H. Schneider (Ed.), *Internationales handbuch der kriminologie* (pp. 333–358). Berlin: de Gruyter.

Wikström, P-O. H. & Loeber, R. (2000). Do disadvantaged neighborhoods cause well-adjusted children to become adolescent delinquents? A study of male juvenile serious offending, individual risk and protective factors, and neighborhood context. *Criminology, 38*(4), 1109–1142.

Wikström, P-O. H. & Sampson, R. (2003). Social mechanisms of community: Influences on crime and pathways in criminality. In B. Lahey, T. Moffitt & A. Caspi (Eds.), *The causes of conduct disorder and serious juvenile delinquency* (pp. 118–148). New York: Guilford Press.

Wikström, P-O. H. & Treiber, K. (2007). The role of self-control in crime causation: Beyond Gottfredson and Hirschi's general theory of crime. *European Journal of Criminology, 4*(2), 237–264.

Wilkinson, L., Blank, G., & Gruber, C. (1996). *Desktop data analysis with SYSTAT.* Upper Saddle River, NJ: Prentice Hall.

Williams, C. (2008, February 11). Tackling gun violence and the scars it leaves. *The Washington Post*, p. B1, B8.

Williams, G. M., O'Callaghan, M., Najman, J. M., Bor, W., Richards, D., & Chinlyn, U. (1998). Maternal cigarette smoking and child psychiatric morbidity: A longitudinal study. *Pediatrics, 102*(1), e11.

Williams, J. R. & Gold, M. (1972). From delinquent behavior to official delinquency. *Social Problems, 20*, 209–229.

Wilson, D. B., Gallagher, C. A., & Mackenzie, D. L. (2000). A meta-analysis of corrections-based education, vocation, and work programs for adult offenders. *Journal of Research in Crime and Delinquency, 37*, 347–368.

Wilson, J., Rojas, N., Haapanen, R., Duxbury, E., & Steiner, H. (2001). Substance abuse and criminal recidivism: A prospective study of adolescents. *Child Psychiatry and Human Development, 31*(4), 297–312.

Wilson, J. Q. & Herrnstein, R. J. (1985). *Crime and human nature.* New York: Simon and Schuster.

Wilson, W. J. (1987). *The truly disadvantaged: The inner city, the underclass and public policy*. Chicago: University of Chicago Press.

Winner, L., Lanza-Kaduce, L., Bishop, D. M., & Frazier, C. E. (1997). The transfer of juveniles to criminal court: Reexamining recidivism over the long term. *Crime and Delinquency, 43*(4), 548–563.

Wish, E. D. & Johnson, B. D. (1986). The impact of substance abuse on criminal careers. In A. Blumstein, J. Cohen, J. A. Roth, & C. A. Visher (Eds.), *Criminal careers and "career criminals": Vol. 2* (pp. 52–88). Washington, DC: National Academy Press.

Wolfe, D. A. (1999). *Child abuse: Implications for child development and psychopathology* (2nd ed.). Newbury Park, CA: Sage.

Wolfgang, M. E. (1995). Transitions of crime in the aging process. In Z. S. Blau, & J. Hagan (Eds.), *Current perspectives on aging and the life cycle: Vol. 4. Delinquency and disrepute in the life course* (pp. 141–153). Greenwich, CT: JAI Press.

Wolfgang, M. E. & Ferracuti, F. (1967). *The subculture of violence*. London: Social Science Paperbacks.

Wolfgang, M. E., Figlio, R., & Sellin, T. (1972). *Delinquency in a birth cohort*. Chicago, IL: University of Chicago Press.

Wolfgang, M. E., Thornberry, T., & Figlio, R. M. (1987). *From boy to man, from delinquency to crime*. Chicago, IL: University of Chicago Press.

Wong, S. (1985). Criminal and institutional behaviors of psychopaths. Ottawa, Ontario: Programs Branch Users Report, Ministry of the Solicitor General of Canada.

Wong, W. & Cornell, D. G. (1999). PIQ>VIQ discrepancy as a correlate of social problem solving and aggression in delinquent adolescent males. *Journal of Psychoeducational Assessment, 17*, 104–112.

Woodward, L. J., Fergusson, D. M., & Horwood, J. (2002). Deviant partner involvement and offending risk in early adulthood. *Journal of Child Psychology and Psychiatry, 43*, 177–190.

Wright, B. R. E., Caspi, A., Moffitt, T. E., & Paternoster, R. (2004). Does the perceived risk of punishment deter criminally prone individuals? Rational choice, self-control, and crime. *Journal of Research in Crime and Delinquency, 41*(2), 180–213.

Wright, B. R. E., Caspi, A., Moffitt, T. E., & Silva, P. A. (2001). The effects of social ties on crime vary by criminal propensity: A life-course model of interdependence. *Criminology, 39*(2), 321–351.

Wright, B. R. E., Caspi, A., Moffitt, T. E., Miech, R. A., & Silva, P. A. (1999). Reconsidering the relationship between SES and delinquency: Causation but not correlation. *Criminology, 37*, 175–194.

Wright, J. P. & Beaver, K. M. (2005). Do parents matter in creating self-control in their children? A genetically informed test of Gottfredson and Hirschi's theory of low self-control. *Criminology, 43*, 1169–1202.

Wright, J. P., Cullen, F. T., & Miller, J. T. (2001). Family social capital and delinquent involvement. *Journal of Criminal Justice, 29*, 1–9.

Wulczn, F., Kogan, J., & Harden, B. J. (2003). Placement stability and movement trajectories. *Social Service Review, 77,* 212–237.

Wyatt, J. M. & Carlo, G. (2002). What will my parents think? Relations among adolescents' expected parental reactions, prosocial moral reasoning, and prosocial and antisocial behaviors. *Journal of Adolescent Research, 17*(6), 646–666.

Yablonski, L. (1959). The delinquent gang as a near-group. *Social Problems, 7*(2), 108–117.

Yeudall, L. T., Fromm-Auch, D., & Davies, P. (1982). Neuropsychological impairment of persistent delinquents. *Journal of Nervous and Mental Disease, 170,* 257–265.

Yolton, K., Dietrich, K., Auinger, P., Lanphear, B. P., & Hornung, R. (2005). Exposure to environmental tobacco smoke and cognitive abilities among U.S. children and adolescents. *Environmental Health Perspectives, 113*(1), 98–103.

Yoshikawa, H. (1994). Prevention as cumulative protection: Effects of early family support and education on chronic delinquency and its risks. *Psychological Bulletin, 115,* 28–54.

Young, S. E., Smolen, A., Hewitt, J. K., Haberstick, B. C., Stallings, M. C., Corley, R. P., et al. (2006). Interaction between MAO-A genotype and maltreatment in the risk for conduct disorder: Failure to confirm in adolescent patients. *The American Journal of Psychiatry, 163*(6), 1019–1025.

Zahn-Waxler, C. (1993). Warriors and worriers: Gender and psychopathology. *Development and Psychopathology, 5,* 79–89.

Zahn-Waxler, C., Kochanska, G., Krupnick, J., & McKnew, D. (1990). Patterns of guilt in children of depressed and well mothers. *Developmental Psychology, 26*(1), 51–59.

Zimring, F. E. & Hawkins, G. J. (1973). *Deterrence: The legal threat in crime control.* Chicago, IL: University of Chicago Press.

Zingraff, M. T., Leiter, J., Johnsen, M. C., & Myers, K. A. (1994). The mediating effect of good school performance on the maltreatment delinquency relationship. *Journal of Research in Crime and Delinquency, 31,* 62–91.

Zoccolillo, M., Paquette, D., Azar, R., Côté, S., & Tremblay, R. (2004). Parenting as an important outcome of conduct disorder in girls. In M. Putallaz & K. L. Bierman (Eds.), *Aggression, antisocial behavior, and violence among girls: A developmental perspective* (pp. 242–261). New York: Guilford Publications.

Zoccolillo, M., Paquette, D., & Tremblay, R. (2005). Maternal conduct disorder and the risk for the next generation. In D. J. Pepler, K. C. Madsen, C. Weber, & K. S. Levene (Eds.), *The development and treatment of girlhood aggression* (pp. 225–250). Mahwah, NJ: Lawrence Erlbaum Associates Publishers.

Zoccolillo, M. & Rogers, K. (1992). Characteristics and outcome of hospitalized adolescent girls with conduct disorder: Erratum. *Journal of the American Academy of Child and Adolescent Psychiatry, 31,* 561.

AUTHOR INDEX

SUBJECT INDEX

Academic attainment. *See* Education
Active rGE. *See* Gene X environment
    correlation
Addiction, 169
Additive effects, 146, 241, 251, 434
Adolescence-limited offending, 17, 18, 92,
    184, 206, 274, 275, 289, 383, 397
Adolescent delinquency, 31, 96, 266
Age-crime curve, 72, 180, 181, 280–284, 331
Age-graded theory of informal social
    control. *See* Sampson and Laub's
    age-graded theory of informal
    social control
Agency, 393, 399, 402, 404, 407–408, 418
Aggression, 123
    by age and sex, 130–131
    and conduct disorder, 240
    in early childhood, 93–94, 113, 200
    marginal direct effects on, 133
    and property offenses, 132
    risk factors for, 5–16
    and testosterone, relationship between,
       153–154
Aid to Families with Dependent Children
    (AFDC), 232. *See also* Temporary
    Assistance to Needy Families
Alcohol abuse. *See* Substance abuse
Amygdala, 143, 157, 177, 189, 426
Angry aggression, 117, 428
Antisocial behavior, 37, 165, 173, 181, 224, 225
    behavioral genetics, 49–50
    extrafamilial predictors of, 41–42
    family predictors, 42–46

    parenting, 47–49, 50–51
    persistence, 378–381
       individual–environment
       transactions, 379–381
    stability of, 5–9
Antisocial parents, 44
Antisocial personality disorder (APD),
    190, 237
Anxiety, 124, 189–190
Aristotle, 37
Arousal and early onset, 188, 189–190
Attachment, 10, 26, 38, 237–240, 244–245
Attachment to school. *See* School factors:
    school bonding
Attention deficit disorder (ADD), 8, 24
Attention-deficit/hyperactivity disorder
    (ADHD), 8, 153, 188, 190
Autonomic nervous system (ANS), 153, 189
Aversive stimuli. *See* Strain

Bayesian information criterion (BIC), 104
Behavior settings, 415–416
Behavioral activation system (BAS), 144
Behavioral genetics, 49–50, 52, 150, 168, 188
Behavioral inhibition system (BIS), 144
Bernard's angry aggression. *See* Angry
    aggression
Biological factors, 8–9, 239, 426–427
    and bullying behavior and proactive
       aggression, 157–160
    and conduct disorder, 144–154
    and early onset, 188–192
    and female offending, 219